Managerial Excellence Through Diversity

Managerial Excellence Through Diversity

Text & Cases

Mary C. Gentile

Harvard Business School

WAVELAND

PRESS, INC.

Prospect Heights, Illinois

For information about this book, write or call:
    Waveland Press, Inc.
    P.O. Box 400
    Prospect Heights, Illinois 60070
    847/634-0081

Case material of the Harvard Graduate School of Business Administration is made possible by the cooperation of business firms and other organizations which may wish to remain anonymous by having names, quantities, and other identifying details disguised while maintaining basic relationships. Cases are prepared as the basis for class discussion rather than to illustrate either effective or ineffective handling of an administrative situation.

First published by Richard D. Irwin, a Times Mirror Higher Education Group, Inc. company, 1996.

Copyright © 1996 by Mary C. Gentile
1998 reissued by Waveland Press, Inc.

ISBN 1-57766-016-1

Printed in the United States of America

7 6 5 4 3 2 1

To the Students of Differences That Work: Managerial Effectiveness through Diversity, *Harvard Business School, Spring 1995.*

Preface

At a time when management practitioners and scholars alike expound about the accelerating pace of change both within and around our business organizations, most will agree that the ability to recognize and respond to diversity of all kinds is a critical skill for success today and into the future. We are talking here about diversity in the workforce and in the customer base, and we are talking about diversity along all dimensions: race, gender, ethnicity, nationality, religion, age, physical ability, sexual orientation, economic and educational background, learning and communication styles, functional expertise, and so on.

Once we acknowledge this reality, the challenge becomes not *whether* to address and adapt to diversity, but *how* individuals and organizations can do so effectively, efficiently, and productively. The focus of this book is just this challenge. Here diversity is framed as an opportunity to learn—for the experience of differences brings us up against the limits of our prior understanding and our previous ways of doing things.

Although no text can raise and address every potential manifestation of diversity, this casebook is an attempt to look clearly and without flinching at the ways we encounter differences, the ways we prevent ourselves from recognizing and learning from them, and the ways we can learn to change these "anti-learning" behaviors. The habits of critical thought and respectful openness we can learn from these readings and cases will prove useful—even critical—for success, not only in an increasingly diverse business environment but also in an increasingly complex and diverse world.

Acknowledgments

Many people deserve gratitude and recognition for their contributions to the development of this book. First, I wish to thank James I. Cash, Professor and Chairman of the MBA Program at the Harvard Business School, for his vision, his guidance, and his unfailing support. Without him, I would never have had the opportunity and the resources to develop the course on which this book is based.

Throughout my work on this material, several colleagues have given unfailingly of their time, their knowledge and insights, their materials, and their personal and institutional support. Among them are: Lynda M. Applegate, Joseph L. Badaracco, Louis B. Barnes, Gregory J. Dees, Anne Donnellon, Robin Ely, Willis Emmons, Raymond A. Friedman, John J. Gabarro, Stephen A. Greyser, Linda A. Hill, Herminia Ibarra, Rosabeth Moss Kanter, Gary W. Loveman, Michele S. Marram, Deborah N. Mauger, Lynn S. Paine, V. Kasturi Rangan, Jeffrey F. Rayport, Stephen Robbins, Robert J. Robinson, Philip M. Rosenzweig, Jonathan Rotenberg, Leonard A. Schlesinger, Roy D. Shapiro, Richard S. Tedlow, David A. Thomas, and Maureen M. Walker. Thanks also to Taylor Cox, Jr., William B. Johnston, and Stella Nkomo for permission to reprint their work.

I wish to thank the Division of Research of the Harvard Business School, and in particular, Richard S. Tedlow, Ann Walter, and F. Warren McFarlan for providing the resources necessary for the course development project. Thanks go also to Roy D. Shapiro for his dedication in chairing the Harvard Business School Diversity Task Force. Thanks go as well to Benson P. Shapiro for his leadership on this subject and his personal support to me.

I am deeply grateful to my research associates, Pamela Maus and Sarah Gant, for their creativity, their initiative, their research and writing skills, and their colleagueship. In particular, Sarah Gant's contribution to this project is incalculable and her friendship has been an added and much appreciated bonus.

My assistant, Hilary Gallagher, went well beyond my expectations in her support for this project and for me. I can hardly begin to thank her for her professionalism and her talents, and her generous spirit in applying them to this work.

None of this work could have been accomplished without the support, in the broadest sense, of the Harvard Business School under the leadership of Dean John H. McArthur.

Finally I thank my partner, Mary H. Jacobsen, for her intelligence, her loving support, and, most of all, her belief in me.

Contents

Introduction: Overview of Book

This text is entitled *Managerial Excellence through Diversity* because it begins from the premise that "diversity" is not a problem to be managed away, but rather an opportunity to develop greater personal and organizational effectiveness.

The reality is that we all confront and respond, more or less well, to various forms of diversity every day. Even in a so-called homogeneous group, we make distinctions among ourselves; some individuals "fit in" more or less easily. The more pronounced the differences and the less powerful and/or numerous the individuals manifesting those differences are perceived to be, the more easily we tend to create hierarchies, stereotypes, and categories for exclusion or oppression.

There is, however, another reality that tells us it is precisely through our interactions and confrontations with *difference*—of perspective, of prior experience, of style, of identity—that we come to recognize the limits of our own perspectives, experiences, and styles. It is our ability to remain open to new points of view, to respect new input even when it is expressed in ways that are difficult for us to understand or accept, that enables us to learn, grow, and adapt to our ever-changing world.

Similarly, it is an organization's ability to accommodate new ideas and different kinds of employees that allows it to foresee necessary changes and to embody the "continuous learning" that management gurus tell us is required for survival in a rapidly evolving business environment.

This text will provide a tool kit of perspectives and critical thinking skills that can enable us to develop the individual and organizational abilities needed to reap the benefits of diversity. It will also provide a series of case examples wherein we can begin to practice the application of these perspectives and skills. Finally, it offers an approach to self-assessment regarding our own individual leadership motivations and readiness around the topic of diversity.

WAYS OF THINKING

The five essays in Part I of this text introduce us to different ways of thinking about difference: different lenses for viewing the challenges and opportunities that diversity brings to our interpersonal interactions and our organizational experiences.

The first piece, "Ways of Thinking About and Across Difference," provides a descriptive critique of the reasoning pitfalls to which we often fall prey when we encounter differences of all kinds, but particularly differences of identity such as race, gender, and ethnicity. Reading this essay requires a self-reflection and self-awareness that is the first step toward understanding the ways our own thinking patterns restrict our ability to respond effectively to, and learn from, those who are different from us. We become conscious of the ways we limit our understanding of diversity by forcing our thinking into dichotomous patterns of either/or, right/wrong, yes/no, you/me.

After examining nine common reasoning models, each of which is based to some extent upon dichotomous thinking, the essay suggests an alternate approach for confronting differences—based on an acceptance of our own multiple identities and multiple perspectives. By learning to recognize, understand, and learn from the diversity within ourselves, we can begin to do the same with the diversity around us. The essay provides a new framework for problem-solving and thinking about diversity, and concludes with an example of how we might apply this framework to the questions of diversity we encounter in the workplace.

While the first essay in Part I encourages us to look at our own reasoning tendencies around diversity, the second essay, "Gender Differences in Managerial Behavior: The Ongoing Debate," takes a look at two of the most important, and often conflicting, perspectives on difference—in particular, gender difference—that derive from research studies. The authors, Herminia Ibarra and Kristin Daly, summarize these two views, the psychological and the situational: "Psychological theories emphasize the different outlook, attitudes, and values inculcated in men and women during their development and socialization. In contrast, situational theories argue that gender differences are few, and largely an artifact of differences in opportunity, power, and lack of representation in business and organizational settings."[1] Ibarra and Daly explain that the research that has been done on these questions is often contradictory. Where some work suggests real, measurable differences in the ways men and women act and interact, other studies suggest these differences are rooted in the organizational contexts where the men and women work. Obviously, as the authors note, these two ways of viewing gender differences in the workplace have different implications for the actions we might take to address inequities. The problem-solving framework introduced in the earlier essay, "Ways of Thinking About and Across Difference," suggests possible methods for resolving this seeming contradiction.

In "Race and Ethnicity," Taylor Cox, Jr., and Stella Nkomo extend the discussion raised in Daly and Ibarra's essay from gender to race and ethnicity. Cox and Nkomo do a detailed review of the research literature on racioethnic effects in five areas: job satisfaction/attitudes, performance appraisal, leadership, motivation, and careers (entry and upward mobility). Where Daly and Ibarra raise the broad question of whether psychological perspectives or situational perspectives most adequately explain gender differences, Cox and Nkomo take a more detailed look at just exactly what these different research perspectives have revealed when applied to race and

---

1. Herminia Ibarra and Kristin Daly, "Gender Differences in Managerial Behavior: The Ongoing Debate," in this volume.

ethnicity. They contribute to our growing tool kit for thinking about diversity by offering tangible examples of the ways differences can impact workplace experience. They also introduce the broad conceptual questions of race and ethnicity as cultural phenomena (as well as biological realities); the use of intergroup theory to enrich our understanding of racial and ethnic diversity;[2] the implications of the intersection of racioethnicity and gender; and the theory of "everyday racism" as a means of exploring the ways in which values, beliefs, and prejudices about race and ethnicity are embedded—invisibly—in the codes of our everyday language and experiences.

In "National Culture and Management," Philip M. Rosenzweig looks at the differences that we encounter between countries and how those differences can affect interactions between and within business organizations. As Ibarra and Cox and Nkomo reviewed some of the leading research on gender, race, and ethnicity, Rosenzweig introduces us to the theories of anthropologist Edward T. Hall and management scholar Geert Hofstede on national cultures. As noted above, none of this research can serve as the definitive guide to any individual's or group of individuals' behavior. Each of us has multiple identities: gender, race, ethnicity, and national culture, among others. And none of us is entirely ruled by the tendencies of any of these identities. The anthropologist Hall points us toward five areas of cultural importance (the "languages" of time, space, material goods, friendship, and agreements), as a sort of guide for exploration and learning. Hofstede offers a set of four continua (individualism/collectivism, power/distance, uncertainty/avoidance, and masculinity/femininity[3]) for similar purposes. But no single categorization captures a culture. Rather, Hall's "languages" and Hofstede's spectrums provide us with useful questions to ask as we try to understand others.

Finally, in his *Harvard Business Review* article, "Global Work Force 2000: The New World Labor Market," William B. Johnston illustrates yet another way of thinking about diversity—through demographics. Although much of the rhetoric and common wisdom concerning diversity in the workplace will point to shifting labor market demographics as a motivation for attending to this issue, Johnston's article puts this idea into a global and more complex context. As we will discuss later in this volume,[4] demographic projections have sometimes been used in simplistic and misleading ways in the discussion of diversity; and although they are very important, they must be seen in the context of interlocking and interdependent variables—immigration patterns, educational patterns, cultural realities around gender and racial equity, age representation, availability of health and retirement benefits, and so forth—both within and between countries.

Each of the essays in Part I of this text provides additional information and points of view for addressing diversity in the workplace: Ibarra and Daly help us structure

2. Intergroup theory provides the foundation for the concept of "multiple identities" introduced in "Ways of Thinking About and Across Difference" in this volume.

3. As Rosenzweig notes in his essay, this dichotomy of "masculinity/femininity" in itself is based on unclear and unexamined assumptions about gender, and is problematic in its theoretical underpinnings as well as in its application.

4. See "Managerial Effectiveness and Diversity; Organizational Choices" in Part III of this volume.

our insights and the insights of researchers into two causal perspectives, the psychological and the situational; Cox and Nkomo flesh out those perspectives by reporting on studies that focus on key aspects of the managerial experience; Rosenzweig introduces us to useful categories for exploration into cultural difference; and Johnston illustrates the interdependencies and wide influence of global demographic trends. Taken together, these four essays provide specific insights into four types of diversity: gender, race, ethnicity, and national culture. Although these do not cover the universe of differences that we encounter in the workplace (for example, there are age, physical ability, sexual orientation, and religion, to name just a few of the others) and although this text focuses primarily (but not exclusively) on the United States experience, these essays suggest some of the specific ways in which the general reasoning framework introduced in "Ways of Thinking About and Across Difference" might be fleshed out and applied.

INDIVIDUAL CHOICES

In Part II of this text, we will take a look at the kinds of challenges and opportunities we encounter as individual managers interacting with superiors, peers, and subordinates who are different from ourselves. The case studies in this section will provide illustrations of the **Individual Choices** we will face in responding to diversity in the workplace, and they will provide the opportunity for us to apply the reasoning and problem-solving skills introduced in Part I.

The introductory essay, "Managerial Effectiveness and Diversity: Individual Choices," explains the organization of this section of the book around three topics—entry into the organization or work group, performance development, and conflict—which capture many of the most common and critical diversity-related questions faced by individual managers. This essay proceeds to identify many of the key questions triggered by these interactions and to identify some of the reasoning frameworks, research, and theory most relevant for responding.

Two cases, "Anne Livingston and Power Max Systems" and "Thurgood Marshall High School," raise many issues salient to a discussion of entry into the organization or work group. In the first of these, a series of five case installments detail the decision of Anne Livingston, an African-American woman, to join a new-product development group in a high technology firm dominated by white males and an insular culture, as well as the challenges and decisions she faces in her first year in the position. The case allows for a discussion of group norms, intergroup dynamics, stereotypes, and self-fulfilling prophecies, as well as the rationale for diversity in team formation and the costs of pursuing it.

In "Thurgood Marshall High School," we experience the dilemmas encountered by David Kane, an African-American man and the new principal at an institution devoted to innovative approaches to inner-city education, including an intentionally balanced student body with equal numbers of Hispanics, Caucasians, and African-Americans. He walks into a situation fraught with faculty and student tension as well as academic performance issues. The case provides the opportunity to understand the interaction of issues of racial and ethnic diversity with issues of individual leadership and organizational conflict.

Questions related to diversity and performance development are illustrated in the next cluster of case studies. "Jensen Shoes: "Lyndon Twitchell's Story" and "Jensen Shoes: Jane Kravitz's Story" provide the opportunity to identify with and analyze the experiences of a white female marketing manager and an African-American male professional working on her team. We view the story of their first three months working together first from the perspective of one and then from that of the other, allowing for a richer understanding of the ways individual expectations and past experiences (related to gender and race, as well as company culture) can affect a working relationship.

In "Karen Leary," we can examine the impact of cultural differences and organizational practices and goals on the developmental relationship between Merrill Lynch manager, Karen Leary, and the Taiwan-born financial consultant, Ted Chung, who reports to her. Leary hired Chung precisely because they hoped he would provide access to the affluent Taiwanese community in the firm's area, but she was taken aback by some of his expectations and demands, and clearly encountered some communication barriers with him.

"Steve Findley" allows us to identify not with the performance manager but with a junior-level employee in a New York investment bank as he confronts a career-enhancing opportunity that may have come his way precisely because he is a member of a minority group in the firm. How does he think about this kind of issue? What is best for his career? for his self-esteem? for his sense of ethics?

Whereas Steve Findley wrestles with an opportunity he is not sure he has earned, Laura Wollen (in "Laura Wollen and ARPCO, Inc.") faces a decision of whether to deny her only African-American employee a career-making international assignment precisely because she fears racial bias in the overseas office.

And finally, "A Case of AIDS" provides an opportunity to consider questions of fairness and reasonable accommodation to differences in physical ability as a team supervisor must respond to a manager who is HIV Positive. The manager and his supervisor proceed from a hiring decision through a performance question to the promotion choice. The three vignettes are followed by commentary from managers and experts in this field.

The last cluster of case studies in Part II examine the choices individuals face in response to workplace conflicts triggered or complicated by diversity. The vignettes and commentary included in the first piece, "Managing Conflict in a Diverse Workplace," illustrate seven types and/or aspects of conflict:

1. *Intent versus Perception:* How do we understand and handle conflicts where the affected party's perception of the behavior in question does not match the actor's intention?
2. *Power and Access:* How do we recognize, understand, and respond to conflict that is triggered by conscious (or unconscious) attempts to preserve or acquire power, and to preserve and/or restrict access to opportunity?
3. *Is Equal Fair?* Is equality of treatment actually equality of opportunity when the

affected individuals are diverse and may achieve the same or comparable ends through different means?

4. *Creative Conflict:* When and how can one reap the creative and productive rewards of workforce diversity?

5. *Bystanders and Third Parties:* What are the roles, obligations, and opportunities (the costs and benefits) for witnesses to conflict rooted in inadequate responses to diversity?

6. *Freedom of Expression:* Where is the line between freedom of expression and irresponsible or hurtful speech and behavior?

7. *The Implications of Involvement:* What are the costs of taking a stand in diversity-related conflicts? What are the rewards? What are the consequences of not doing so?

The "Tom Reese" case provides a compellingly personal perspective on one gay man's struggle to balance career effectiveness with personal dignity and self-respect. This piece provides an effective vehicle for inquiry into the impact of workplace diversity conflicts on personal identity, and vice versa.

In "Star Distributors, Inc.," we witness the way that unexamined, unnamed, and unaddressed racial conflict between the co-owners and managers of a bottling distributorship affects both the interpersonal and organizational dynamics of the entire operation, as well as its business viability.

Finally, "Ann Hopkins" presents a detailed depiction of Hopkins's failed candidacy for partner at Price Waterhouse and her subsequent decision to file a sex discrimination lawsuit. We have the opportunity to examine how the decision to exclude occurs and how identity difference affects receptivity and openness in colleagues.

Taken together, the cases in Part II of this text encourage us to identify with individuals of many identities and in various organizational positions as they negotiate interpersonal relationships complicated and enriched by difference. We have the opportunity to practice empathy, analysis, decision-framing ability, and communication skills. In particular, the application of the insights and critical thinking skills introduced in Part I of this text should widen the set of constructive actions available to us in responding to these case studies.

ORGANIZATIONAL CHOICES

Part III of this text provides a set of case studies that illustrate many of the organizational opportunities and challenges raised by an increasingly diverse workforce and customer base. The introductory essay, "Managerial Effectiveness and Diversity: Organizational Choices," conceives of diversity in a broad and inclusive fashion, encouraging organizations to see the scope and ubiquity of diversity's impact on their operations and effectiveness, and its potential for transferable learnings. Additionally, this essay presents a descriptive framework for considering the impact of diversity on organizations and the ways they respond to it. This framework details a set of *motivators* that trigger organizational responses to diversity; a description of varied *mindsets* that characterize organizations' expectations, implicit goals, and probable results in addressing diversity; a catalogue and discussion of the most common *methods* that organizations utilize to address diversity; and the *measures* they can and sometimes do use to monitor and evaluate their methods' impact.

Many of the cases in this section of the book are illustrative of the different *motivators* detailed in this introductory essay: legal and regulatory pressures; labor market demographics; globalization of business; diversifying customer base; external pressures from community, religious, and/or political groups; internal employee pressures; personal commitment.

For example, in "Accountants and Business Advisors, Inc.: City Office," the office managing partner in the city office of a major public accounting firm is faced with the impact of *changing demographics* in the labor pool from which the firm can hire new accountants. As the number of women in this pool grows, the traditional practices and expectations within the firm become the subject of critical inquiry, especially with regard to the balance between work and the rest of an employee's life. The attrition rates for women are higher than those for men, and the firm is becoming concerned about the cost of this turnover.

In "Kurt Landgraf and Du Pont Merck Pharmaceutical Company," the new CEO and president is faced with *internal employee pressures* when African-American scientists in his R&D division threaten a class-action suit if changes are not made with regard to their representation and career opportunity in the firm. Although Landgraf is committed to equal opportunity and has a track record of success in increasing representation and opportunity for women and minorities in his prior position leading pharmaceutical marketing, he now faces new challenges. A previously fast-growing industry with ample margins is facing new regulatory and competitive pressures, not to mention the fact that the hiring pool for minority candidates in marketing (college graduates) is much larger than the pool for research scientists. How does Landgraf's firm respond to the employee's concerns in a time of down-sizing?

The "Balanced Workforce at Xerox Corporation" continues this discussion of appropriate representation goals, as well as fair and effective means for achieving them. What does a "balanced" workforce look like, and what steps are needed to achieve it in a time of slow or no growth?

While the previous cases look at the organization's goals and role in achieving fairness and balance in the workforce, "Black Caucus Groups at Xerox Corporation" examines the role of self-help caucus groups and networks, as well as the attitudes and roles organizations can adopt toward them.

Bridging the two *motivators*—internal employee pressures and *legal/regulatory pressures*[5]—"Sexual Harassment, Free Speech Or . . . ?" and "A Note on the Law of

---

5. Legal and regulatory guidelines related to diversity continue to evolve and change as new questions are litigated, and as social reality and pressures shift. In addition to the legal note on sexual harassment mentioned above, there is a brief discussion of these realities in the essay, "Managerial Effectiveness and Diversity: Organizational Choices" in this volume. For a more detailed discussion of relevant United States law and regulation, see *Primer on Equal Employment Opportunity*, Nancy J. Sedmak and Chrissie Vidas, 6th ed., 1994, Bureau of National Affairs, Washington, D.C.

Sexual Harassment" provide the opportunity to consider the obligations and the liability of the organization (as opposed to the individual focus in Part II) with regard to complaints of sexual harassment. Additionally, although this case text is focused primarily on the United States experience, the legal note includes a brief discussion of harassment law outside the United States.

While several of the previous cases have raised internal pressures related to employee dissatisfaction, "Mod IV Product Development Team" introduces the questions of functional diversity in teams and ways in which diversity can enhance and/ or challenge efficiency and productivity.

In "Lotus Development Corporation: Spousal Equivalents," employee initiative coupled with corporate leadership surface the question of potential benefits policy revisions that would send a signal of acceptance and welcome to current and potential gay and lesbian employees. This case dramatizes the questions of organizational fairness, efforts to be—and remain—an employer of choice to all qualified employees, as well as the need to be fiscally responsible in times of competitive pressure.

Finally, "Quantum Semiconductor, Inc.," raises another issue that bridges labor demographics, internal employee concerns, and legal pressures—this time a question of employee safety is balanced against concerns about sexual discrimination where a semiconductor producer must wrestle with potential reproductive risks associated with working in so-called "clean room" fabrication processes.

Moving from demographic shifts, internal employee pressures, and legal/regulatory pressures to the demands of a *diversifying customer base,* "The Miami Herald Publishing Company" describes the interaction of newspaper industry changes with a large and growing Hispanic population in the Miami area. The case raises questions concerning the appropriate role and mission of a major metropolitan newspaper—both fiscal and social—particularly in an extremely diverse and often divided market/community.

In the next case, "BayBank Boston," a diverse customer base triggers questions not only of new or untapped sources of business, but of reported discrimination in the provision of services—in this instance, mortgage loans.

Bridging the topics of a diverse customer base with the *external pressures from community, religious, and/or political groups,* the "G. Heileman Brewing Company: Power Failure at PowerMaster" case describes the experience of a brewing company which attempted to market a higher alcohol version of its malt liquor beer product. The effort drew criticism from many quarters (government, health, religious, etc.) both for marketing the product on its "power" (i.e., higher alcohol content) and for planning a product launch in inner-city Black neighborhoods.

The final two case studies in Part III discuss efforts to enhance opportunities for minority and/or women-owned businesses. In "The FCC and License Auctions for Emerging Technologies," we learn about the efforts of the Federal Communications Commission, at the direction of Congress, to create real opportunities for minority and women-owned businesses, as well as small businesses, to get in on the ground floor in telecommunications industries developing to serve the much heralded "information superhighway." In "Peak Electronics: Vendor Relationship with the Ford Motor Company," we learn of the efforts of an individual corporation to encourage the growth and development of minority-owned vendors. Each case raises questions of ends and means, theory and implementation, and intended and unintended consequences.

All of the cases in Part III, taken together, provide us with a rich and varied view of the different challenges and opportunities inherent in a diversifying labor force, customer base, and business environment. Once again they provide us with the chance to practice the critical thinking and decision-framing skills introduced in the first section of this text. And although unnoted above, many of these cases provide examples of the personal commitment and leadership of individual managers around issues of diversity, bringing us to the subject of Part IV.

REDEFINING LEADERSHIP

Part IV, the final section of this text, includes an introductory essay, "Redefining Leadership through Diversity," and one case study. The introductory essay provides a kind of personal assessment model for recognizing, understanding, and developing the motivations and skills necessary to take a leadership position around issues of diversity—both individually and organizationally. The risks and the rewards of such positions are discussed, as well as a set of competencies necessary for effective action in this realm.

The last case study of the text, "Monitor Company: Personal Leadership on Diversity," presents the voices of several individuals at this consulting firm, ranging from relatively junior consultants to directors and a founding partner, discussing the organization and its efforts to build and nurture a more diverse work environment there. The speakers represent a mix of identities—of gender, of racial and ethnic diversity, of sexual orientation, or of age—and they each comment on the personal experiences that helped them to become leaders around issues of diversity. The case provides an opportunity to consider the many, and sometimes conflicting, definitions of diversity we encounter in organizations, and to explore the varied sources of personal motivation for taking leadership positions on it.

This final section encourages us to think about our own diversity commitments and competencies, and the ways in which they have been affected by studying the materials in this text. It asks us to think about our own roles in the organizations where we work and study and to consider the kind of leadership we can take to maximize the opportunities, productivity, and learning for all of us. After all, maximizing these opportunities and learnings *through diversity* is the theme of this book.

PART I

Ways of Thinking

WAYS OF THINKING ABOUT AND ACROSS DIFFERENCE

This note begins with the hypothesis that many of us genuinely feel "stuck" when we engage in reflection and discussion about issues of "diversity."* At the level of explicit content, we generate limitless examples of seemingly insoluble dilemmas and untenable trade-offs: how do we respect another's point of view without devaluing our own, how can we be sensitive to the experiences and feelings of others without curtailing our own experience of fundamental personal liberty, and how can we address societal inequity toward some without imposing it upon others. At the level of implicit content and interpersonal reactions, we face another set of obstacles: a whole range of learned but unconscious assumptions about those who are different from us, as well as feelings of anxiety, fear, anger, guilt, mistrust, and hopelessness that block communication and learning.

Most of us want to see ourselves as (and, in actuality, to be) fair, open-minded, intellectually honest, self-aware, and even empathetic. In fact, most of us *do* see ourselves as all these things. But nevertheless, most of us would acknowledge the great and painful conflicts and inequities that wrack our personal relationships, businesses, governments, countries, and our world—conflicts and inequities that often break down along lines of group differences (racial, ethnic, religious, gender, etc.).

So somewhere between all our individual good intentions on the one hand, and our interpersonal and group behaviors or impacts on the other, the equation breaks down. It seems that the way we think and talk about our interactions with difference limits the responses we can generate.

Psychologists tell us that when we are considering change, we can target three levels: our beliefs, our feelings, and our actions. They will further explain that the most difficult target is the first, and that the most feasible approach to change is through actions (or behavior), where changes will in turn affect our feelings and finally our beliefs. Therefore, in this note we have targeted reasoning behaviors, our cognitive strategies—not the thoughts and beliefs themselves but rather the way we put them together. By changing our thinking habits (and consequently the conclusions we act upon), we can begin to have an impact on feelings and beliefs.

The purpose of this note is to examine some of the habitual ways of thinking that are applied to so-called diversity questions, to reveal the commonalities and limitations of these models—the ways they can reinforce unexamined assumptions and destructive emotional reactions, and to suggest an alternative way of framing such questions that opens up the possibility for creativity and new learning.

Diversity Questions

Before we look at some of our mental models and ways of reasoning about diversity questions, let's define just what these questions are. The term *diversity* has come to refer to any number of issues and concerns, and although you or I

---

* Over the last decade or so in the United States, the term *diversity* has become a kind of code word for issues triggered by the impacts of race and gender, and increasingly other types of difference—ethnicity, religion, national origin, sexual orientation, class, etc.—in businesses, schools, government, and other contexts. This note is written out of, and refers to, experience in the United States, but the reasoning model can be applied in other contexts as well.

This note was prepared by Mary C. Gentile.

Harvard Business School note 395-117 (Rev. June 1, 1995).

may be thinking of very different things, we will often talk about diversity as if we mean the same thing. In fact, one of the barriers to fresh and unbiased thinking about diversity that we will discuss below is our tendency to present equivocal concepts as if they are clear, solid, and single in their meaning.[1]

To avoid this pitfall and to facilitate our discussion here, it may be useful to identify several of the *types* of questions that are often subsumed under this rubric of diversity:

* How and why we, as individuals, perceive, feel about, and behave toward other individuals whom we characterize as "different" from ourselves. We may attribute these differences to individual traits or to membership in a particular "group."
* How and why we, as individuals, perceive, feel about, and behave toward groups to which we do not belong.
* How and why institutions (families, businesses, schools, churches, governments) reflect, operationalize, and perpetuate these perceptions, feelings, and behaviors by rendering them invisible and/or "undiscussable."
* How and why these perceptions, feelings, and behaviors might be changed.

These are questions of efficiency, productivity, equity, social harmony, group and individual survival, legality, public policy, and morality. And as this note will eventually argue, they are fundamentally questions about the human potential, drive, and need for learning and growth.

Habitual Ways of Thinking About Difference— Patterns of Duality and Oppositionality

From psychologist Carl Jung to anthropologist Edward T. Hall, from philosopher Simone de Beauvoir to linguist Ferdinand de Saussure,

---

1. Chris Argyris, "Teaching Smart People How to Learn" *Harvard Business Review* (May–June 1991), p. 103.

many scholars have noted the ubiquity, across varied times and cultures, of certain patterns of duality, dichotomy, and binary opposition in human language and thought. Dichotomies in themselves are not a problem; they are simply a pattern of perception. However, the tendency to oversimplify our observations by limiting them to *binary* oppositions as opposed to more complex and multiple perceptions, and the tendency to value one term of the dichotomy over another, whether appropriate or not, creates difficulties. If we require ourselves to self-consciously critique the very reasoning and critical thinking processes that we bring to bear upon questions of diversity, we will see a consistent application of these patterns, a consistency that restricts our answers for such questions to either/or, right/wrong, you/me choices.

In the following pages, we will examine nine descriptions of ways we typically think about difference, in an effort to reveal the dichotomies that shape and constrain our reasoning. Although some of the authors and approaches described below focus exclusively on race or gender or on the United States, the conceptual tendencies they discuss extend to other forms of difference. The objective here is not to explain the origins of racism or sexism or any other form of oppression, but rather to make visible the habitual but often unconscious patterns of thinking that keep us from thinking and acting our ways out of inefficient and destructive behaviors.

Mary Ann Glendon and Rights Talk

In *Rights Talk: The Impoverishment of Political Discourse,* Harvard Law professor Mary Ann Glendon examines the distinctive way in which thinking and talking about rights has developed in America. In particular, she observes an emphasis upon "absolute" rights; that is, there is a tendency to view rights as an "all or nothing" affair. People say that they have the "right to do and live as they choose," and any attempt to place limits around that statement is seen as a "slippery slope," a dangerous assault on freedom that will result in repression. For example, people who themselves would never wish to offend a colleague will bristle at discussions of sexual harassment, arguing that their right to free speech is in jeopardy.

Glendon also observes a tendency in the United States to emphasize the protection of individual rights, but without a balancing emphasis upon responsibilities. She argues that these characteristics are not universal when one looks at other nations' official statements toward human liberties, providing historical and contemporary examples from other countries of a balancing language of duty and commitment to community.

Glendon argues that this emphasis on "absolute" rights and the omission of a balancing emphasis upon responsibilities compromise the United States' ability to move toward reasonable and equitable solutions to inevitable conflicts:

> Our rights talk, in its absoluteness, promotes unrealistic expectations, heightens social conflict, and inhibits dialogue that might lead toward consensus, accommodation, or at least the discovery of common ground. In its silence concerning responsibilities, it seems to condone acceptance of the benefits of living in a democratic social welfare state, without accepting the corresponding personal and civic obligations. In its relentless individualism, it fosters a climate that is inhospitable to society's losers, and that systematically disadvantages caretakers and dependents, young and old. In its neglect of civil society, it undermines the principal seedbeds of civic and personal virtue. In its insularity, it shuts out potentially important aids to the process of self-correcting learning. All of these traits promote mere assertion over reason-giving.[2]

Thus, the tendency toward dichotomous thinking which Glendon observes in American discourse on rights feeds divisiveness and limits our reasoning and problem-solving repertoire.

Self-Definition through Oppositionality

In the introduction to her classic text, *The Second Sex,* Simone de Beauvoir writes about the human tendency to perceive and understand experience as dualities or binary oppositions:

> Things become clear, . . . if, following Hegel, we find in consciousness itself a fundamental hostility toward every other consciousness; the subject can be posed only in being opposed—he sets himself up as the essential, as opposed to the other, the inessential, the object.[3]

In other words, we define ourselves, our identity, in opposition to, or as distinct from, others: I know who I am because I am not you. This self-definition through oppositionality can be problematic as it sets up a chain reaction: my sense of myself is built upon my ability to distinguish myself from you; therefore I value the ways in which I am different from you; therefore I begin to devalue the traits that make you distinct from me.

Michelle Fine, a psychologist who has written extensively on gender and race in education and social policy, provides us with an example of how this process of self-definition through oppositionality works. She was asked to research and testify in the 1993/1994 legal proceedings considering whether or not The Citadel, an all male military college in South Carolina, was constitutionally bound to admit women students. In her observations and interviews at the school,[4] she noticed that male students were regularly exhorted to behave in ways that would prove their

---

2. Mary Ann Glendon, *Rights Talk: The Impoverishment of Political Discourse* (New York: The Free Press, 1991), p. 14.

3. Simone de Beauvoir, "Introduction to *The Second Sex,*" in *New French Feminisms,* ed. Elaine Marks and Isabelle de Courtivron (New York: Schocken Books, 1981), p. 45.

4. Keynote address to Columbia University Teachers College Winter "Roundtable on Cross-Cultural Counseling and Psychotherapy: Race and Gender," February 18, 1994, New York.

masculinity, their strength, their courage, rather than behaving "like a woman." She concluded that the institution was organized around a concept of "oppositional identity," arguing that despite their official exclusion, women were in fact, "omnipresent at the school as [entities] to be reacted against," and that the institution reinforced a "fragile sense of masculinity perched on opposition to women, as 'the other.'"

Fine pointed out that "as they are currently constituted, whiteness and maleness are about denigration of 'the other,' [and what is needed, therefore,] is to give whites and males other ways to see their identity than through oppositionality." Fine has put her finger on one of the ways in which "self-definition through oppositionality" is self-perpetuating and resistant to change: if I begin to see those different from myself in a more positive light, does that mean that I will begin to see myself more negatively? Where is the appeal, or the motivation, in that? It seems that I need to begin to be able to define myself in a more complex way, and not simply in opposition to others along some dimension of difference, be it gender, religion, race, sexual orientation, or something else.

Cultural Generalizations: Dichotomy or Continuum

Deborah Tannen, linguistics scholar and author of the national bestseller, *You Just Don't Understand: Women and Men in Conversation,* has argued that women and men tend to develop and use communication skills for different purposes, often resulting in misunderstanding:

> *Intimacy* is key in a world of connection where individuals negotiate complex networks of friendship, minimize differences, try to reach consensus, and avoid the appearance of superiority, which would highlight differences. In a world of status, *independence* is key, because a primary means of establishing status is to tell others what to do, and taking orders is a marker of low status. Though all humans need both intimacy and independence, women tend to focus on the first and men on the

second. . . . If women speak and hear a language of connection and intimacy, while men speak and hear a language of status and independence, then communication between men and women can be like cross-cultural communication, prey to a clash of conversational styles.[5]

Studies like Tannen's can be very useful in helping us to put ourselves in the shoes of others, to see the world through a different lens. But Tannen herself is among the first to caution against the dangers of generalizing about the behavior of an entire group. She understands that the tendency to value one pole of a dichotomy over another can result in prejudices reinforced: for example, if she describes differences in the conversational styles of men and women, men's style may tend to be valued over women's. Nevertheless, she fears even more the mutual understanding that will be lost if such concerns stop us from trying to understand the degree to which patterns of difference do seem to exist between the genders.[6]

Interestingly, if we take this debate to either extreme, understanding is sacrificed. If we affirm that there *are* differences between identity groups (in this case, between genders), we can get lost in generalizations and stereotypes that keep us from seeing the distinctiveness of individuals and the commonalities between these same groups, and that can reinforce discrimination. On the other hand, if in our efforts to ensure equal treatment and opportunity, we assert that there are no generalizable differences, that men and women differ only as individuals differ, we sacrifice the insights of work like Tannen's, or Carol Gilligan's, or that of any number of anthropologists who study cultural patterns.

In casual conversation about Tannen's work, we are likely to hear variations on the following: "I *did* recognize the patterns she writes about in

---

5. Deborah Tannen, *You Just Don't Understand: Women and Men in Conversation* (New York: Ballantine Books, 1990), pp. 26, 42.

6. Ibid., pp. 14–16.

my male/female friends' behavior. She really had them down. But, you know, I don't think I really fit the pattern she describes for *my* gender." In this instinctive response, we can see the crux of the issue: it is much easier and appealing to generalize about others than to be generalized about ourselves. Similarly, we tend to assume that others will be unaware of, and thus bound by, their gender or cultural conditioning, while being perfectly willing to believe in our ability to see through and therefore escape our own. Both of these tendencies can block true understanding and communication.

Shelby Steele and "Seeing for Innocence"

In his 1990 book of essays, *The Content of Our Character: A New Vision of Race in America,* Shelby Steele offers an analysis of racial dynamics built upon the concepts of power and innocence. He argues that the conflict between races is a conflict over power, and that this pursuit of power is rationalized by an appeal to innocence:

> Your difference from me makes you bad, and your badness justifies, even demands, my pursuit of power over you . . . the human animal almost never pursues power without first convincing himself that he is *entitled* to it. And this feeling of entitlement has its own precondition: to be entitled one must first believe in one's innocence, at least in the area where one wishes to be entitled. By innocence I mean a feeling of essential goodness in relation to others and, therefore, superiority to others.[7]

Steele goes on to explain that while whites in America have historically defended their subjugation of blacks with claims of innocence, blacks in the sixties began to use this equation to their own advantage. Blacks claimed the innocence that derives from being the victims of white racism, thereby gaining some power of their own. Thus, both blacks and whites are invested in

seeing themselves as innocent, and since their innocence is based on the other's guilt, this means that they are unconsciously motivated to see the other in ways that preserve conflict, racial disharmony, and prejudice. Ironically, each group claims the status of "victim," a status that disempowers them with regard to dismantling racism, discouraging individual initiative to get past these issues.[8]

There are several dichotomous thought patterns embedded in this model of behavior. First, individuals are seen and see themselves in terms of a single identification, black or white, as opposed to possessing multiple identities. Second, individuals are seen and see themselves as existing in a state of guilt or innocence, thereby limiting their options for learning, change, and complexity.

Although Steele's analysis focuses on American race relations, the fundamental model aptly describes a pattern of self-defeating dichotomization that can apply to other types of difference as well. His model can shed light on many of the counterproductive behaviors we observe around diversity. For example, sometimes individuals will resist behaving in a more supportive manner toward those different from themselves because such a change implies, in their minds, that they were somehow at fault or "guilty" in the past. Or sometimes individuals will look for ways to maintain their criticisms, even stereotypes, of those who are different from them in an effort to preserve a sense of innocence. And sometimes individuals will resist acknowledging and embracing the successes of other members of their own "identity group" (race, gender, etc.) for fear that such success casts doubt upon their own righteous experience of oppression—their "innocence" in Steele's terms.

Cornel West and "Racial Reasoning"

In his 1994 book, *Race Matters,* philosopher and theologian Cornel West describes a particular

---

7. Shelby Steele, *The Content of Our Character: A New Vision of Race in America* (New York: St. Martin's Press, 1990), p. 5.

8. Ibid., pp. 8, 14.

way of thinking he finds all too prevalent among black leadership in America today. "Racial reasoning," as he names it, is a way of thinking about black progress that tries to promote the race as a whole at the expense of many within its ranks.

The basic line of reasoning that West observes goes like this: since "America's will to racial justice is weak . . . black people must close ranks for survival in a hostile country"; this "closing ranks mentality" depends upon individuals' ability to lay claim to "racial authenticity" because if one is not "really black," or "black enough," he or she would be a threat to the group as a whole (in Steele's terms, they would not possess the entitlement that goes with "innocence"); as soon as one's sense of security and legitimacy is based upon racial authenticity, numerous reasons for exclusion emerge, and before we know it, black progress or "black social order" seems to rest upon the subordination and control of certain other blacks.[9]

West argues that:

> The claims to black authenticity that feed on the closing-ranks mentality of black people are dangerous precisely because this closing of ranks is usually done at the expense of black women. It also tends to ignore the divisions of class and sexual orientation in black America—divisions that require attention if all black interests, individuals, and communities are to be taken into consideration.[10]

He calls for a corrective to this limiting and separatist form of thinking that attempts to correct one form of oppression while participating in another. His antidote is a new form of reasoning that bases its claims to moral authority not on "black authenticity" but on a "mature black self-love and self-respect . . . [based] on the moral quality of black responses" to the experience of racism. This reasoning would replace ex-

clusivity and closed ranks with a "coalition strategy," welcoming the support of those genuinely committed to combating racism regardless of their color or ethnicity, and it would embrace truly democratic ideals rather than justifying the subordination of some blacks in the service of others.[11]

As with Steele's concept of "seeing for innocence," West's model of "racial reasoning" holds lessons for our thinking about other forms of difference as well. It underscores the diversity that exists within identity groups as well as between them. And it illustrates the ubiquity and limitations of dichotomous, us/them patterns of thinking.

Chris Argyris and "Defensive Reasoning"

In his research on organizational behavior, Harvard professor Chris Argyris has observed a pattern of behavior among managers that effectively, if unintentionally, blocks learning, and he calls this pattern "defensive reasoning." Argyris observes that in all his studies, across nation, gender, age, education, race, and so forth, there seem to be four values that guide people's action:

1. To remain in unilateral control.
2. To maximize "winning" and minimize "losing."
3. To suppress negative feelings.
4. To be as "rational" as possible—by which people mean defining clear objectives and evaluating their behavior in terms of whether or not they have achieved them.

The purpose in all of these values is to avoid embarrassment or threat, feeling vulnerable or incompetent. In this respect, the master program that most people use is profoundly defensive.

Defensive reasoning encourages individuals to keep private the premises, inferences, and conclusions that shape their behavior

---

9. Cornel West, *Race Matters* (New York: Vintage Books, 1994), pp. 37, 38.
10. Ibid., p. 41.

11. Ibid., pp. 43, 44.

and to avoid testing them in a truly independent, objective fashion.

Because the attributes that go into defensive reasoning are never really tested, it is a closed loop, remarkably impervious to conflicting points of view.[12]

In numerous case examples, Argyris demonstrates how this dichotomous approach to our role and functioning in organizations—winner or loser, in control or controlled—makes us fearful of new information and new perspectives, solidifying into a profoundly anti-learning stance. His antidote is to propose an alternative approach to action that is based upon making our premises and inferences transparent and discussible, and pursuing free choice rather than control in relation to others.[13] In the service of learning and growth, what was once perceived as a threatening or embarrassing contradiction can then be seen as the source of innovation and new insight.

Argyris's observations have obvious relevance for thinking about differences of identity. Without the willingness to reveal the sources of and assumptions behind our conclusions, we unwittingly reinforce others' tendencies to hear and understand us in terms of their preexisting stereotypes.

Thomas Gilovich and How We Know What Isn't So

In his highly readable 1991 book, *How We Know What Isn't So: The Fallibility of Human Reason in Everyday Life,* social scientist Thomas Gilovich describes and illustrates a series of reasoning errors, both common in human thinking processes and remarkably resistant to corrective factual data. If we examine these frequent reasoning flaws, we readily recognize how they can help to generate and reinforce counterproductive ways of thinking about diversity.

Gilovich examines the following cognitive tendencies:

- Our preference for clear dichotomies when considering options: yes/no, right/wrong, all/nothing. We tend to oversimplify experience in an effort to categorize it into these dualities, and then to hang onto our analysis with excessive confidence.
- Our preference for believing that all experience is controllable, a preference that may lead us to attribute causality or personal choice in situations where there is none.
- Our preference to see structure and consistency in experience rather than pure randomness.
- Our "tendency to be more impressed by what *has* happened than by what has *failed* to happen, and the temptation to draw conclusions from what has occurred under present circumstances without comparing it to what would have occurred under alternative circumstances."[14]

He then suggests a set of corrective cognitive tactics in order to minimize the frequency of reasoning errors:

- Focus not only on the foolishness of basing conclusions upon "incomplete and unrepresentative evidence," but also on the frequency with which "our everyday experience presents us with biased samples of information." We need to ask ourselves, "what do the other three cells look like?" In other words, what are the counter examples, the contradicting evidence that we have not considered, or even attempted to gather?
- Recognize our tendency to ignore the frequency with which our status, position, iden-

12. Chris Argyris, "Teaching Smart People How to Learn" *Harvard Business Review* (May–June 1991), p. 103.

13. Chris Argyris, *Strategy, Change and Defensive Routines* (Marshfield, MA: Pitman Publishing, Inc., 1985), p. 261.

14. Thomas Gilovich, *How We Know What Isn't So: The Fallibility of Human Reason in Everyday Life* (New York: The Free Press, 1991), p. 186.

tity can cut us off from certain kinds of data or overexpose us to others.

- Recognize our "talent for *ad hoc* explanation . . . the facility with which we can explain a vast range of outcomes in terms of our preexisting theories and beliefs. . . . Our beliefs thus appear to receive too much support from equivocal evidence, and they are too seldom discredited by truly antagonistic results." Gilovich suggests we counter this tendency by using "consider the opposite" strategies: "Suppose the exact opposite had occurred. Would I consider that outcome to be supportive of my belief as well? . . . How would someone who does not believe the way I do explain this result? . . . What alternative theory could account for it?"
- Recognize the "uncertainties and distortions of secondhand information."
- Ask ourselves "whether our beliefs are really as widely shared as they appear. The absence of explicit disagreement should not automatically be taken as evidence of agreement."[15]

Although Gilovich is writing about cognitive behavior in general, it is easy to see how these various tendencies can contribute to an adversariality, a resistance to change and to trust, and a closed mind when dealing with questions of difference. Although diversity issues involve emotional, political, historical, and economic levels as well, an understanding of these reasoning errors can aid us in our attempts to unravel their complexity.

Pareto Optimality/Scarcity Thinking

In many cultures, modes of reasoning borrowed from economics have penetrated deeply into our patterns of thinking about other areas of experience. Several of these mental paradigms can constrain our thinking about questions of diversity. There is a sort of "all or nothing," "me or you" quality to these reasoning patterns that can predefine the range of options we might conceive for a particular dilemma.

For example, microeconomic equilibrium models of optimal resource allocation assume as a minimal requirement the condition of *Pareto optimality:* "a situation where no one in the economy can be made better off without someone else . . . being made worse off.[16] Although intended only as a descriptor, we can observe a tendency to evaluate the desirability of action choices in terms of this condition. In other words, if a particular course of action betters the position of some at the expense of worsening the position of others, it is considered suboptimal. This seems sensible enough until we consider the situation where the privilege of some may be a direct result of the exclusion of others. As in the economic markets from which this concept derives, it all comes down to the initial resource distribution. Adhering to this pattern of thinking precludes change.

A preoccupation with resource scarcity, the assumption of a "limited pie" to be divided among all comers, is another example of an economics-based approach to thinking about the choices diversity presents. The point is not that scarcity does not exist, but rather that the *assumption* of scarcity limits our creativity and sense of possibility, and ill positions us for the redefinition of goods and resources that such choices require.

Masking and Overdetermined Terminology

Questions triggered by diversity in the workplace go to the heart of some of our most cherished assumptions about our organizations and perceptions about ourselves: meritocracy, equal opportunity, fair treatment, unbiased standards of performance, and so forth. And painfully, these questions point out seeming contradictions and inconsistencies in those assumptions and perceptions.

---

15. Ibid., pp. 186–189.

16. Stanley Fischer and Rudiger Dornbusch, *Economics* (New York: McGraw-Hill, 1983), p. 521.

These contradictions and inconsistencies are often the result of the way certain concepts and terminology acquire meanings over time, through repeated use and misuse and through association. The concept of meritocracy, for example, is firmly held and valued by many as the preferred and only truly fair, efficient standard by which to evaluate performance. We will often argue about the importance of *continuing* to reward individuals according to their merit, slipping in the assumed premise that this has been the case in the past. Yet we fail to examine the ways and reasons by which individuals are and have been rewarded in actuality.

"Merit" is, first of all, a subjective term. The indicators that cause us to *see* merit are multiple and are based upon many factors besides observable talent: familiarity, comfort, prior relationship, recommendation by a friend, association with familiar schools and institutions, prior commitments or a sense of obligation/guilt/gratitude, and so forth. All of these factors can be masked by the term "merit."

Even with these distorting factors put aside, how do we define "merit"? A candidate may exhibit ability along many criteria and a decision, often subjective, is made about how to prioritize these criteria. And once a few abilities have been defined as primary, how reliable are our measures?

This discussion is not intended to argue against the usefulness of attempts to evaluate "merit," but rather to point out the ways such concepts seem to take on a solidity, a clarity in our rhetoric which they often lack in actual experience.

Reframing Diversity

In all nine of these reasoning models, we have seen that a tendency toward dualism in our thinking can restrict the way we frame and answer questions of diversity. And the most fundamental expression of that dualism is in our self-definition: I define myself as either male or female, gay or straight, right or wrong, and so on. In our earlier discussion of "oppositional identity," we said that I know who I am because I am not you. This is not an affirmation of my own identity or even an understanding of differences, but rather an exploitation of them as a "short-cut" to self-insight and self-esteem.

But let us consider an alternate approach to self-definition and to the consideration of, and interaction with, others. Rather than defining ourselves "in opposition to" someone else, let us incorporate opposition into ourselves. Let us adopt a "multiple perspective" rather than an oppositional and dualistic one—a multiple perspective that can comprehend alternate viewpoints not so as to excuse oppression but rather to clarify it, to expose the pain of one individual group without denying that of another. For ultimately, understanding and *experiencing* "the compelling quality of contradictory realities is the only way, short of violence, to resolve their differences."[17]

What we are talking about here is a new way to approach and address the conflicts and the dilemmas posed by our encounters with differences, based upon a new way of defining ourselves and our own point of view. By defining ourselves multiply, by perceiving others multiply, by generating multiple hypotheses in response to seeming trade-offs, by seeking out and embracing disconfirming data and complexity, we open up the potential for new growth and learning, for creativity, and for breaking the cycle of reductionist dichotomies that keep us locked in a mutually self-destructive pattern of separation, discrimination, oppression, anger, and guilt.

To this end, let us examine the following model for reframing diversity[18] (see Exhibit 1), first in terms of our own identity and then in

---

17. Mary C. Gentile, *Film Feminisms* (Westport, CT: Greenwood Press, 1985), p. 8.

18. Excerpts from Introduction to *Differences That Work: Organizational Excellence Through Diversity*, ed. and introduction by Mary Gentile (Boston: Harvard Business School Press, 1994.) pp. XV–XVII reprinted by permission.

EXHIBIT 1   Reframing Diversity: A Model

1. Multiple Identities
We all have multiple identities, one or another of which we may identify with more strongly at different moments in our lives and in different contexts.

2. Salience
We often experience contradictory urges or needs for a sense of belonging or "fitting in" on the one hand, and for a feeling of uniqueness or "specialness" on the other. Thus in a particular situation, one of our multiple identities may feel more salient to us than others.

3. Costs and Benefits
Some identities exact a higher and/or different cost (or provide greater and/or different benefits) for the bearer in a particular societal, historical, or even situational context than others.

4. Choice
Sometimes individuals have a choice of becoming recognized as members of a particular identity group in a particular setting, and that choice brings certain costs and benefits, as well.

5. Redefinition and Change
Our individual identities are always developing, we are continually negotiating, defining, and redefining the internal coherence of our original values, our new experiences, and our multiple identities.

6. Shared Goals
Identity differences do not preclude the development and pursuit of "shared goals" among and across identities.

---

relation to others, both individuals and groups. This model is really a set of observations, insights, and acknowledgments that can serve as tools for promoting understanding of, and conversation about, diversity.

Our framework consists of the following six observations:

1. *Multiple Identities:* **We all have multiple identities, one or another of which we may identify with more strongly at different moments in our lives and in different contexts.**

For example, we all have our gender, race, ethnic origins, religion, age, sexual orientation, class, educational background, etc. Sometimes we may stress one of these identities over others, and sometimes these identities may be in conflict. For example, we may feel discomfort expressing some of our views in a context where they might feed stereotypes about one of our identities. For example, when I am with a group of women, I may be more cognizant of the commonalities of our experience based upon gender,

whereas when I am with a mixed gender group of colleagues at work, I may identify more strongly as an individual with a particular educational and professional experience held in common with my peers in that context.

From these multiple identities, we can begin to recognize that we each have experienced positions of relative privilege and relative exclusion in different contexts. Nevertheless, we negotiate more or less coherent, if complex, personalities.[19] This internal negotiation of identity can be a model for understanding the negotiation of a group identity and interactions, in social contexts or in business settings. And seeing our own identities multiply can be the beginning of seeing others in more complex, less stereotypical, and ultimately more realistic ways. We will not view women, African-Americans, or white men as all

---

19. C. D. Alderfer, "Intergroup Relations and Organizations," in *Perspectives on Behavior in Organizations,* ed. J. R. Hackman, E. E. Lawler, and L. W. Porter (New York: McGraw-Hill, 1983), p. 410.

alike because we will see ourselves and each other as so much more than just our gender or race.

2. *Salience:* **We often experience contradictory urges or needs for a sense of belonging or "fitting in" on the one hand, and for a feeling of uniqueness or "specialness" on the other.**[20] **Thus in a particular situation, one of our multiple identities may feel more salient to us than others.**

In some contexts, we may tend to emphasize our ethnic identities, for example, in order to feel special or unique. In other contexts—family gatherings for instance—we may emphasize the same ethnicity as a means to feel part of the group. These conflicting urges can trigger complicated reactions of loyalty, rejection, pride, and guilt within the same individual and between different individuals.

Understanding our own mixed desires around a sense of belonging and a feeling of uniqueness can give insight into what may sometimes appear as the desire of other individuals or groups to "have it both ways," to have their particular history of achievement and perhaps oppression recognized, as well as to be treated "just like everybody else." But as this second observation suggests, in a sense everyone wants it "both ways," and that may not be such a bad thing if we are self-aware and realistic about it.

3. *Costs and Benefits:* **Some identities exact a higher and/or different cost (or provide greater and/or different benefits) for the bearer in a particular societal, historical, or even situational context than others.**

In the United States, for example, the historical experience of African-Americans has had very real implications, generally speaking, for access to education, information, and financial resources. In a group of African-Americans,

however, the lone white individual may experience a temporary situational cost for being/feeling different that, if understood and explored, can serve as a foundation for empathy for all present.

Treating this lone white's experience as if it is "the same" as, or somehow equivalent to, the experience of African-Americans is not accurate, but it is also inaccurate and counterproductive to insist that this individual has never experienced the pain of exclusion. It is certainly a different pain, without the historical and institutional and cultural weight of the African-American's experience of racism, but it may serve as the beginning of shared insight. It suggests an appeal to empathy rather than merely guilt.

4. *Choice:* **Sometimes individuals have a choice of becoming recognized as members of a particular identity group in a particular setting, and that choice brings certain costs and benefits, as well.**

Some identities, such as gender, race, and age, *tend* to be immediately evident. Other identities, such as religion or sexual orientation, can be less evident. It is useful to understand the potential advantages and disadvantages of so-called invisible diversity. For example, as a gay or lesbian person, often one can choose to "pass." This choice gives gay/lesbian people greater control over the impression they make on others at the same time that it creates personal and political dilemmas.

On the one hand, they may judge that to be open about their sexual orientation could be unsafe, either professionally, socially, or even physically. But on the other hand, they may wonder if their discretion is actually a manifestation of internalized homophobia and a lack of self-confidence. Or is it a betrayal of gays and lesbians more generally because it allows others to assume they are not working with and depending upon homosexuals in their daily lives? Understanding the advantages and the burdens of having a "choice" about how one's identity is

---

20. Mary C. Waters, *Ethnic Options: Choosing Identities in America* (Berkeley, CA: University of California Press, 1990), p. 147.

perceived is critical to thinking about and addressing questions of diversity.

5. *Redefinition and Change:* **Our individual identities are always developing, we are continually negotiating, defining, and redefining the internal coherence of our original values, our new experiences, and our multiple identities.**

Individual identities—and group identities—are not static. If we remain aware of our own process of self-definition which involves a continual reconciliation of the multiple aspects of our identities, we can be more open to the same process in those with whom we learn and work. We need not be "frozen" in a single role or stance, nor need we "freeze" others. We are more than the sum of our "identities," and our behavior is not predetermined or fixed because of them.

6. *Shared Goals:* **Identity differences do not preclude the development and pursuit of "shared goals" among and across identities.**

Effective response to diversity is dependent upon the acceptance of some primary objectives to which we all are willing to commit. In the workplace, such objectives might include survival of the firm, and therefore a commitment to the productivity and innovation necessary for that survival. This does not imply that a respect for and sensitivity to individual and group differences are not important—after all, the shared objective is *not* the survival of the firm at *any* cost—but rather this suggests that there are at least a few areas where our commonalities are as salient as our differences.

The preceding model—its insights and acknowledgments—can serve as the foundation and the impetus for both internal and external dialogue and inquiry about diversity. It gives us a way to think and talk about diversity as a learning process in which we all are or can be engaged, thereby providing a powerful *motivation* for these discussions.

The model defines diversity *inclusively*, indi-

cating that it is about all of us. It offers a way to understand the behaviors and dynamics of both groups and individuals within them that is *descriptive, rather than judgmental.* Nevertheless it is based upon certain clear values, primarily the value of learning, the desirability of pursuing knowledge about oneself and others, and the acknowledgment that in a diverse and interdependent world, one of the most valuable kinds of knowledge is about understanding and communicating across differences.

Confronting a Decision

With this model in mind, what are some of the key questions we might bring to framing and addressing questions of diversity? How does this model have an impact on our decision making? How does it address the suboptimal patterns of thinking described earlier in this note? [See Exhibit 2 for a checklist of questions that reveals when we are falling victim to the reasoning "traps" described earlier, and that suggests alternate responses to the same decision, based on the model above.]

Let's take a look at an example of the different ways we can approach the same issue, depending upon what types of reasoning frameworks we are using. We will take up an example that is frequently raised as a diversity dilemma and pose it in the words we are likely to hear:

If you have two candidates for a job—a member of the majority identity group in your organization (let's say a white man) and a member of a group "underrepresented" in your organization (let's say a white woman)—and the man is better qualified, whom do you hire?

Some of the responses to this question we are likely to hear, or offer ourselves, include:

- *You always have to hire the "more qualified candidate." If you don't, you are putting the effectiveness, perhaps even the survival, of the organization in jeopardy.*

This argument, and the dilemma itself, are posed using the "masking and overdetermined

EXHIBIT 2 Interrogating Our Thinking

The following checklist of questions can help us to recognize when we are falling into restrictive patterns of reasoning and to push ourselves beyond these common traps.

Mary Ann Glendon and Rights Talk

Traps	*Escapes*
Does my thinking reflect a fearfulness or insecurity about inadvertently "giving away" my rights?	Am I more interested in understanding the reasons why others may feel that insecurity? *and* Does my thinking reflect a security in my own identity and an openness to new ideas that is born of the awareness that my identity is multiple and dynamic, and that change does not necessarily mean loss?
Am I focused only on preserving my own privileges, rather than also understanding my appropriate and necessary responsibilities to the community I inhabit?	Am I trying to understand the different costs and benefits associated with differing identities and positions in that community, including my own?

Self-Definition through Oppositionality

Trap	*Escape*
Do I define myself by the ways in which I am different from others, or in terms of "the ways I am not" (i.e., not ignorant, not guilty, not a failure, not weak)?	Do I define myself more complexly, recognizing the differing and even conflicting aspects of my own multiple identities? Can I admit that I have things in common with the people I most admire as well as with those of whom I am most critical?

Cultural Generalizations: Dichotomy or Continuum

Trap	*Escape*
Do I tend to see people either as representative of and somewhat determined by their group identities, or as distinct individuals completely free of any group identity determination?	Am I able to recognize the conflicting needs for both a sense of uniqueness and also a sense of belonging to a particular group, in myself and others?

Shelby Steele and "Seeing for Innocence"

Traps	*Escapes*
Does my argument focus on justifying the blame or innocence assigned to a group and its individual representatives?	Am I focused on understanding the differential costs and benefits of individual and group identities, and trying to find shared objectives?
Am I locking myself or others into one aspect only of my/their identities?	Am I trying to see the multiple aspects of my own and others' identities, and perhaps finding shared ground by so doing?
Am I invested in proving or holding on to a sense of oppression or a victim status?	Am I open to the changing, dynamic aspects of individual and group identity?

Cornel West and "Racial Reasoning"?

Trap	*Escape*
Does my argument reflect a defensive, "closing ranks mentality," requiring others to prove their group "authenticity" if they are to stand with me? Am I setting up ever-new tests or thresholds of legitimacy for those who "deserve" to share my position?	Am I interested in finding ways to embrace multiple perspectives and ever-wider circles of participation, building a "coalition strategy," to address conflicts and to enable true learning?

EXHIBIT 2   *(concluded)*

Chris Argyris and "Defensive Reasoning"

Traps	*Escapes*
Am I more interested in being "right" than in learning?	Am I open to, or even appreciative of, the potential to change one's mind, to see things in a new way?
Do I present my point of view in a way that discourages negative feedback and questioning?	Do I embrace disconfirming data and multiple perspectives as an opportunity for learning?*

Thomas Gilovich and How We Know What Isn't So

Traps	*Escapes*
Do I tend to frame my decisions as dichotomous, either/or choices?	Am I able to hold multiple options, not all necessarily mutually exclusive, in my mind? Do I think in terms of dynamic and transitional solutions, as opposed to permanent answers?
Do I habitually look for someone to blame or praise for any outcome?	Can I recognize the limits of my own, and others', control?
Do I cut myself off from the conflicting and multiple aspects of my own experience and perceptions, tending to allow only one of my inner voices to dominate?	Do I try to remain in touch with differing perspectives within, as well as those from outside?

Pareto Optimality/Scarcity Thinking

Trap	*Escape*
Do I approach any attempt to improve conditions for some, from a defensive stance of "as long as it doesn't affect me . . ."?	Am I willing to redefine the terms of cost and benefit? Am I willing to consider that some aspects of myself may benefit from a choice that costs other aspects of myself?

Masking and Overdetermined Terminology

Trap	*Escape*
Are my arguments built upon rhetorical appeals to loaded concepts that I do not question and "unpack"?	Am I able to see that the same concept or term may look and feel very different from various perspectives (i.e., the historical perspective versus the eternal present, the individual perspective versus the organizational, or your perspective versus mine)?

*Catherine Bateson talks about this practice as learning skills for changing times, arguing that when we experience discomfort with new information or unexpected reactions, we should recognize that discomfort as a cue to try to learn something, and the *very process of trying to learn cures the discomfort.* (From a reading and lecture on *Peripheral Visions* at the Brattle Theatre, sponsored by Wordsworth Books, Cambridge, Massachusetts, June 21, 1994.)

terminology" discussed earlier. This confident assertion of "who is best qualified" serves to disguise any number of prior choices and unconscious assumptions. It asserts as unambiguous an evaluation that is often sublimely subjective. It assumes a clarity about what constitutes quali-

fication for this job, when that conclusion itself is also often based upon tradition rather than science. And it begs the question of whether decision makers are able to perceive the relative qualifications of the candidates objectively, denying the impacts of stereotyping, historical oppression, and the documented perceptual effects when individuals make judgments about members of a group other than their own.

This argument also illustrates the tendency to analyze and argue only one side of an oversimplified dichotomy that Gilovich describes in *How We Know What Isn't So.* Has the respondent asked himself or herself, "in this case, what are the potential *positive* impacts of hiring the woman, and what are the potential *negative* impacts of hiring the man?"

* *If you don't hire the man, you are trying to right past injustices with current ones. You are trying to counteract discrimination with another form of discrimination, for the only thing working against the man is his gender.*

Aside from continuing to repeat the assumptions about qualification noted above, this argument illustrates Gilovich's concerns about our tendency to oversimplify events into either/or choices and to ignore unstated data. For example, the argument takes as an assumption that in any other situation, the only data considered in making a hiring or promotion decision is this unexplained criterion of "qualification." It ignores the fact that such decisions always involve weighing a number of considerations, such as seniority against targeted experience, depth of expertise against breadth, familiarity with the project against outside experience, and a candidate who brings significant experience in areas that are already represented in the project team against a candidate who brings less experience but in an unrepresented area. Might gender be just another set of criteria in this mix?

This argument also reflects a version of Steele's "seeing for innocence," where somehow "being qualified" is equated with having a right to a particular job and not getting that job is seen as a form of undeserved punishment. Thus, the male candidate's "innocence" is implied, while the female candidate is therefore "guilty" of obtaining a job unfairly. As noted above, this formulation contains all sorts of blurred distinctions and unconscious assumptions, but never-

theless carries an emotional weight that feeds a divisive "us against them" perspective on this dilemma.

Finally this argument (reminiscent of Pareto optimality) blurs individual perspectives, experience, and accountability with group perspectives, experience, and accountability. It asserts that accumulated injustices toward and by groups in the past are being paid for with an individual injustice in the present, ignoring the fact that discrimination was and is always an individual *and* a group experience. We can address discrimination effectively only if we address it at both levels. This realization does not necessarily suggest that either candidate should be hired in this case; it merely suggests that the fact that both individuals and groups are affected by any actions taken is unavoidable.

* *If you hire the man, you are passing up the opportunity to begin to make a change in the demographic mix of the department/organization—a change that will be necessary in order to attract and best support other women and minority members in the firm.*

This argument, like the first one we examined, illustrates the tendency to analyze and argue only one side of an oversimplified dichotomy . . . only it is a different side. It ignores the importance of trying to make a decision that will result in a *successful* hire, regardless of gender, not only for the firm's benefit but also for the benefit of the other women and minorities in the firm now and to come. Additionally this argument, and the dilemma itself, beg the question of why we are concerned with "representation" in the first place. There are legal arguments, moral arguments, and "business" arguments that may underlie this concern [See **Managerial Effectiveness and Diversity: Organizational Choices, in Part III** for a discussion of these arguments, or "motivations."] However, if organizational decision makers do not adequately think through this question, their judgments risk superficiality, cynicism, and self-contradiction—or at least, accusations of the same.

• *If you hire the man, you will demonstrate that the organization is not really interested in diversity.*

Once again, this argument raises only one side of an oversimplified dichotomy; it ignores other data about the company's policies and actions around diversity. The more sophisticated argument might be that "if you hire the man, the organization will *appear* to not really be interested in diversity." This argument suggests something about the kind of consistency and trust the organization needs to build in order to be free to make difficult decisions as it sees fit.

• *If you hire the woman, you are not doing her any service for she will experience negative reinforcement around her performance.*

This argument illustrates our readiness to interpret evidence about an employee's performance in ways that support prior conclusions, what Gilovich refers to as our "talent for *ad hoc* explanation." This tendency can result in self-fulfilling prophecies.

• *If you hire the "less qualified candidate," you are not doing other women any service for you are reinforcing the perception that their successes may be based on identity rather than merit.*

The problem with this argument is that it ignores the fact that this perception can be caused by decisions to hire a woman or "minority" candidate, regardless of their qualifications. It also embodies an unstated and unexamined assumption that other hiring decisions are always based purely on objective qualifications, that this is the desired state of affairs, and that we can and do know what these objective qualifications are. "Merit" in this statement is an instance of "masking terminology."

However, this argument does surface the importance of thinking through and communicating decision criteria clearly. Differing perceptions ought to be respected, considered, and

addressed, but they ought not be a source of tyranny for they always cut both ways.

The point of these observations is not to suggest that any or all of these responses are necessarily wrong, but rather to suggest that each of them is incomplete. The original dilemma, as posed, asks for an either/or choice, when the real take-away from such a decision is the learning, the relationship, and the process created by communicating about it. Ultimately there will be times when the hiring decision will go one way and times when it will go the other, for good reasons, but the test of the decision-making process is whether all parties can keep talking and working together afterward toward shared goals.

Applying the Model for Reframing Diversity

In order to achieve this objective, we need other ways of posing the dilemma that will shed new light on the question. After all, each of us has heard the arguments listed above before and yet many of us are no closer to a comfortable answer to the dilemma.

So let's revisit the original question in light of our model for reframing diversity:

If you have two candidates for a job—a member of the majority identity group in your organization (let's say a white man) and a member of a group "underrepresented" in your organization (let's say a white woman)—and the man is better qualified, whom do you hire?

First of all, the way this question is framed tends to discourage multiple identities, within ourselves, others, or our organizations. Rather we may experience the question as requiring us to define ourselves oppositionally—that is, as for or against "merit" as a basis for hiring decisions. What's more, the oppositional self-definition gets worse, because we may experience this choice as pitting a commitment to "merit" against a commitment to diversifying an admittedly "unrepresentative" or skewed employee pool. Finally, one more link in this chain of dualities aligns white males with a commitment to merit and a disregard for diversity, while white women are aligned with a commitment to diversity and a disregard for merit.

Thus we can see that without an attempt to reveal and unpack the assumed alignments within the framing of this question, the respondent feels himself or herself torn, forced into an artificial choice that fails to reflect the true complexity of any of the parties. Because the choice is framed as a static dichotomy, using masking rhetoric and built upon a denial of shared goals, it literally pushes us into many of the reasoning pitfalls described above.

Now, of course, people and experience present us with challenges and dilemmas on a regular basis, and they are often posed in less than constructive ways. We cannot control the ways in which others identify and frame the questions they ask us. We can, however, restructure these choices in order to avoid some of the impasses we found in the responses above. We can do so by reflecting upon the decisions we face and asking the following questions derived from our proposed model for reframing diversity. With practice, this process of examining and reposing the choices we encounter will enable us to approach all such decisions in a new manner, designed to maximize learning and our openness to innovation and unexpected insights.

I. Multiple Identities

- *What are the aspects of ourselves (of others, of the organization) that are engaged in addressing this decision?*

In other words, are we bringing the full range of our multiple identities to this question? Are we openly addressing the potential conflicts or contradictory responses these different aspects trigger in us, or are we prematurely aligning with a single "side" of ourselves? The goal is not to define ourselves oppositionally, but rather to internalize the oppositionality, to acknowledge and name our internal conflicts, thereby reducing the defensiveness in ourselves and others. That defensiveness blocks openness to new and potentially conflicting ideas, and reducing it allows for the generation of multiple perspectives and multiple hypotheses that boost our ability to see through masking terminology.

In the sample decision presented above, I might ask myself if I feel free to explore all my possible reactions, or if I feel pressure to foreclose my exploration and avoid entertaining a response that might feel as if it positions me as "anti-merit" or as "anti-diversity." If I feel discomfort around examining all aspects of my response, that's a pretty good signal that there is something to examine.

In particular, I would ask myself if I feel as if I have ever been awarded opportunities on any basis other than merit. If so, how do I feel about that? Do I feel I proved the decision sound? Do I feel as if someone else had a "right" to my opportunity, or do I think it is appropriate that other criteria enter into these decisions sometimes?

I might also ask myself if I feel as if others have been awarded opportunities on bases other than merit, particularly when I felt I had a claim on the opportunity. How have I reconciled these experiences of relative privilege and relative exclusion within myself?

Running myself through this exercise of getting in touch with multiple perspectives within myself makes it easier for me to imagine a similar range of responses in others, and in the organization. Such thinking discourages the painting of my own or others' points of view with a single brush. It allows me to consider this decision as both an individual situation facing specific managers, as well as a representative action on the part of the organization—rather than as just one or the other.

II. Salience

- *What aspect of our (others', the organization's) multiple identities feels most salient in this situation?*

To which aspect of our identity do we feel the desire/need to belong or "fit in"? Around which aspect of our identity do we feel the desire/need to "stand out" and be unique? And consequently, which aspects of ourselves are we suppressing? And why? What would be the cost of standing out in one way, or not fitting in another?

In the sample decision presented above, I might ask myself whose approval is most important to me here? Whom do I want to stand with, and why? And how do I want to be recognized around this issue? Once I recognize this experience of "salience" around some specific aspect of my identity, I free myself to stand apart from it, to question it, and to try on other points of view—and, of course, to see the same kind of tendencies operating in the others involved in this decision.

III. Costs and Benefits

- *What are the costs and benefits associated with engaging each aspect of our (others', the organization's) identities in response to this decision?*

By addressing this question, we can begin to unpack the baggage of history (culture and ideology, the experience of dominance and oppression) that comes along with different aspects of our identities. The fact is that not all experiences of relative privilege or relative exclusion are equal.

In the sample decision above, for instance, one might ask whether or not the cost of a single career move to the white man is balanced against the range of career opportunities to which he has and will be exposed. Further, one might ask whether this position may represent one of the relatively few opportunities to which the other candidate has or will have access without the additional experience available in the new opening.

IV. Choice

- *To what extent do we (others, the organization) have a choice about how we will be perceived in this situation?*

In addition to the forms of "invisible diversity" mentioned above, there tends to be a greater range of possible images available to those who are in the numerical majority and/or the "higher power" group in a particular context. Understanding the abundance or scarcity of choices available to ourselves and others enables us to better gauge the impact of our decisions.

In the sample decision above, it appears that the woman has no good choice. She will either be perceived as unqualified for hire and therefore be passed over, or she will be perceived as unqualified for hire and taken on anyway. If she is to be hired, clearly the managers involved and the organization need to communicate about their criteria and goals in such a way as to offer her a fighting chance.

V. Redefinition and Change

- *How might we (others, the organization) redefine our identities so as to facilitate new learning and greater effectiveness within and among our multiple identities?*

For example, since I now have access to that aspect of myself that acknowledges that not all my accomplishments have been solely due to my autonomous effort, I can begin to question and redefine the concept of merit qualification in my organization. I can talk more openly about the variety of criteria I now do, and always have, sought out in candidates for hire. I am not locked into an Argyrean pattern of defensive reasoning that effectively precludes learning and change.

VI. Shared Goals

- *What shared goals can we identify among all parties to this decision?*

For example, all parties can be committed to the hiring organization's efforts to more fully understand their hiring criteria and to their enhanced ability to select candidates who can function effectively to the betterment of the firm and their own careers—in other words, to maximize productive learning and growth.

Conclusion

So finally, we are trying to reframe this question in such a way as to:

- Encourage exploration of all perspectives, both between and within each party to the decision.
- Avoid denying/suppressing aspects of each party. Address and balance the different costs/benefits associated with the identities of each party.
- Maximize choice for all parties.
- Allow change within each party.
- Identify and pursue shared goals among all parties.

Instead of the dilemma as originally posed, we might ask:

How do we assess and communicate merit criteria and representation goals in our organization? What action plan can we develop to ensure meeting both these criteria and goals? When evaluating two candidates for possible hire (one white man, one white woman), how might we position the decision within the context of this plan?

This revised question allows us to position the decision within a history that extends both backward (allowing us to address past inequities) and into the future (allowing us to place each action step within a projected stream of actions, and avoiding the overweighting of any single choice). It acknowledges at least two agendas for the organization and requires an integrated approach to design an action plan, rather than assuming a contest between them. It positions the actual hiring decision within a context that acknowledges issues that go beyond either candidate, creating the opportunity/necessity to communicate about the choice in ways that depersonalize the issues and preventing candidates from being dubbed as qualified or not, deserving or not, and so forth.

Thus we have attempted to both understand the ways in which our habitual ways of naming and reasoning about questions of diversity limit the responses we generate, as well as the ways in which we can begin to break out of those constraints. With practice, this type of analysis becomes a habit as well, and it allows us to think about these challenging issues in fresh ways; it begins to shift our emotional responses to these questions from the realms of frustration, anger, guilt, and blame to those of openness and excitement about the possibility for new understanding.

GENDER DIFFERENCES IN MANAGERIAL BEHAVIOR: THE ONGOING DEBATE*

1. The Debate

Do men and women have distinct leadership styles? Do they approach management differently? Two perspectives have dominated the ongoing debate on gender differences in organiza-

tional leadership and management behavior. Psychological theories emphasize the different outlook, attitudes, and values inculcated in men and women during their development and socialization. In contrast, situational theories argue that gender differences are few, and largely an artifact of differences in opportunity, power, and lack of representation in business and organizational settings. To date, the evidence from

---

* This note was prepared by Kristin Daly and Herminia Ibarra.

research studies has been mixed: Some studies provide support for the psychological perspective, others for the situational, and yet others advocate a combination of the two. Matters have been further complicated by the fact that studies conducted within different paradigms are often not comparable. It is difficult to determine, for example, whether the results of in-depth interviews with a small number of executives are consistent with large-scale surveys of men and women in diverse managerial jobs. Thus, the debate continues.

2. The Psychological Perspective

The psychological perspective suggests that women, on average, differ from men in their approach to managerial jobs. These differences are believed to stem from the different experiences the sexes have growing up. In the process of sex-role socialization boys and girls are involved in different kinds of activities and rewarded for different kinds of behaviors. For example, girls' play tends to be less competitive than boys' play. Consequently, as adults, men and women evince different behaviors and preferences. Advocates of this perspective argue that the central tendency is for women to demonstrate greater affiliation, attachment, cooperation, and nurturance, while men will tend to demonstrate more independent, instrumentally oriented, and competitive behaviors.

Until recently, effective management was presumed to require the "male" orientation: a tough-minded approach to problems and a willingness to set aside personal and emotional considerations in the interest of task accomplishment. It was assumed that men and women were inherently different, and the difference gave men an advantage in the business world, with women more suitable for support roles. Those women who succeeded in ascending the corporate hierarchy adopted the "male" model of successful managerial behavior.

Today, an increasing number of people favor a pluralistic view of managerial talents and contributions, which emphasizes the value of women's "different voice." Proponents of this view suggest a spectrum of dissimilar but complementary managerial styles and argue that women need not reject "female" characteristics to be successful.[1] Further, they argue that traditionally "feminine" qualities such as nurturing and collaboration represent the kinds of leadership and management skills needed today. Among the managerially relevant differences that have been identified are approaches to organizing, leadership, and communication:

• **Organizing.** In one study, men and women managers reported very different approaches to organizing their workgroups. The women tended to favor "centrarchies," that is, webs of inclusion, with themselves at the center of a network rather than at the top of a hierarchy. They viewed themselves at the center of a web of relationships, facilitating the dissemination of information and focusing on building effective teams and groups. The men, by contrast, were more likely to see themselves at the top of a pyramid or hierarchy, with a distinct chain of command and established rules for getting things done within the organization.[2]

• **Leadership.** Another study suggested that women tend to be "transformational" leaders while men tend to be "transactional" leaders. The men were more likely to have an "exchange of rewards for services" view of their relationships with subordinates; the women were more likely to operate by persuading subordinates to transform their own self-interest into the interest of the group and concern for a broader goal. The women in this study were also more likely than the men to encourage participation and to share power and information. The men, in contrast, were more likely to report "command and control" managerial styles.[3]

1. J. Grant, "Women as Managers: What They Can Offer to Organizations," *Organizational Dynamics,* Winter 1988, pp. 56–63.

2. S. Helgesen, *The Female Advantage* (New York: Doubleday, 1990).

3. J. Rosener, "Ways Women Lead," *Harvard Business Review,* November–December, 1990) pp. 119–125.

• **Communication.** Recent research suggests that men and women tend to communicate differently. Women appear to use communication as a means to develop or reinforce a relationship, by establishing a common ground, to a greater extent than men. Men, on average more than women, were found to use communication to transmit factual information and to establish or signal their place in the power structure. When men were speaking in a group, for example, they tended to compete to capture the floor, while women tended to take turns speaking.[4]

3. The Situational Perspective

The situational perspective argues that when men and women are in a similar situations, operating under analogous expectations, they tend to behave in similar ways. Proponents of this view offer a very different interpretation of the findings of the psychological perspective. They argue that presumed differences in the behaviors and attitudes of men and women are better explained by differences in power, status, and opportunity.

A variety of statistics supports the argument that the effects of gender cannot be isolated or studied independently of context. For example, in 1992 women represented 3 percent of corporate officers in Fortune 500 companies, and in 1990 almost 60 percent of working women were employed in sales, administrative support, and services, with women making up the majority of service employees, particularly in low-paying, dead-end positions.[5] Further, men and women enter different industries and occupations and generally perform different tasks within broad occupational categories. Within firms, patterns of sex-segregation are also marked with women predominantly located in staff functions such as human resources and public relations.[6] This societal pattern implies that, in general, women lack institutional power. As a result, they are more likely to use traditionally "female qualities," such as collaboration, to get things done.[7]

The critical study that launched the situational perspective was Rosabeth Moss Kanter's study of a corporate bureaucracy. She found that three factors are pivotal in influencing managerial behavior:

• **Opportunity** is the ability to grow and achieve within a firm, and the access to routes within the company to make this possible. Kanter found that regardless of gender, managers who were "stuck" or "plateaued" behaved very differently from those who were moving up, with the "stuck" less likely to take risks or exhibit a high level of commitment to their firms. Because women tended to be overrepresented in low-opportunity jobs, they did indeed behave differently than men on high-opportunity career tracks. Thus, the expectation that women *in general* were less committed to their jobs and more risk averse than men was easily perpetuated.

• **Power** is defined by the access to resources, information, and political support that is associated with a particular work role. Kanter argued that "powerlessness corrupts." Power increases an individual's visibility and effectiveness within the organization, thus leading to greater power; a lack of power led managers to develop other, non-task-related priorities, including favoring interpersonal relationships over task requirements. Again, because most women held low-power jobs, the view that women favor relationships at the expense of task-related demands was frequently reinforced.

• **Numbers** pertains to the proportion of people in a company who are similar or different

4. D. Tannen, *You Just Don't Understand* (New York: William Morrow, 1990).

5. R. M. Kanter, *Men and Women of the Corporation,* 2nd ed. (New York: Basic Books, 1993).

6. A. M. Morrison and M. A. Von Glinow, "Women and Minorities in Management," *American Psychologist* 45, no. 2. 1990, pp. 200–208.

7. N. A. Nichols, "Whatever Happened to Rosie the Riveter?" *Harvard Business Review,* July–August 1993, pp. 54–62.

along characteristics including gender, race, and ethnicity. Regardless of what group it is, the mere fact of being in the numerical minority produces common dynamics and unique pressures, including stereotyping. People in the minority are more likely to be viewed as representatives of their group when they underperform and as exceptions to the rule when they do well. Again, because managerial women were often in the position of being the "only woman," or one of a very few, they were more likely to be seen as group representatives rather than as individuals.

Since Kanter's study, a variety of investigations has provided support for one or more of her three pivotal factors. Among them are the following:

• In a managerial study, nearly 1,000 men and 1,000 women were matched according to age, rank in their organization, organizational type, and number of people supervised. They were compared on five dimensions: managerial philosophy, motivation, participative practices, interpersonal competence, and managerial style. An average of 2.6 subordinates also rated these managers on their practices. The authors concluded that "women, in general, do not differ from men, in general, in the ways they administer the management process."[8]

• A review of studies conducted in the 1980s concluded that there was little "hard" evidence for the "male" task-orientation or for the "female" relationship-orientation. These studies also failed to provide evidence of gender differences in motivational factors. There was evidence, however, that men and women managers tend to differ in their choice of influence strategies: Men appeared to be more likely than women to exercise influence based on the power of their position and tended to rely on promises and threats significantly more than women;

women, by contrast, seem to be more likely to use sources of influence based on personal relationships and to rely on indirect influence strategies.[9]

• An investigation of 89 workgroups varying in their sex composition from 0 to 100 percent female found that women had the most undesirable social experiences when they were in the numerical minority. They reported isolation from informal interactions, experienced job dissatisfaction, and were subject to greater stereotyping by group members. The results also suggested that men's experiences, when they were in the numerical minority, were not as severe as those of the women when they were in the minority. Women holding superior positions in predominantly male workgroups experienced the most undesirable outcomes of any group.[10]

The Role of Social Norms

Another stream of situational research focuses on social expectations or norms about appropriate behavior, which are often gender-based. It shows that behaviors that are accepted or viewed as desirable in men may be seen as inappropriate in women. Men and women are subtly rewarded for conformity to traditional behavioral expectations, and women in management are sanctioned for violating expectations of female-appropriate behavior. Studies have shown that:

• Women managers using "masculine" leadership styles were judged by both men and women as worse managers than male managers using the same leadership style.[11]

8. S. Donnell and J. Hall, "Men and Women as Managers: A Significant Case of No Significant Difference." *Organizational Dynamics,* Spring 1980, pp. 60–77.

9. G. N. Powell, "One More Time: Do Female and Male Managers Differ?" *Academy of Management Executive,* 4, no. 3 (1990) pp. 68–75.

10. A. M. Konrad, S. Winter, and B. A. Gutek, "Diversity in Work Group Sex Composition: Implications for Majority and Minority Members," Research in the *Sociology of Organizations* 10 (1992), pp. 115–140.

11. V. E. O'Leary and J. R. Ickoviks, "Cracking the Glass Ceiling: Overcoming Isolation and Alienation," in *Womanpower: Managing in Times of Demographic Turbulence* ed. U. Sekeran and F. Leong (Beverly Hills, CA: Sage.) pp. 7–30.

• The characteristics describing the typical "good manager" were similar to those used to describe the "typical man," and different from those used to describe the "typical woman." Women, however, were often evaluated on their qualities as both managers and women. This produced a double bind: They may be sanctioned for either "acting like men," or conforming too closely to norms for female behavior, for example, "not being assertive enough." [12]

• A comparison of men and women managers who "plateaued" before reaching the executive ranks found that a "poor image" was a common factor for women but not for men. Senior executives used phrases like "too whiny," "too cutesy," "too feminine," and "too strong" to describe these women. [13]

Some researchers have suggested that men and women have similar "behavioral repertoires," but tailor their actions to the situation at hand as a function of social expectations. For example, gender differences tend to be more pronounced in group settings but much less so in individual assignments. [14]

4. Implications

• **Valuing Differences.** The psychological perspective suggests that organizations have much to gain from expanding their definition of effective leadership and management to include those methods and orientations that are viewed as more typical of women. Adherents of this ap-

proach suggest that widening the range of acceptable styles and pathways to success will free people to lead in ways that play to their individual strengths and preferences. Traditionally defined "male" and "female" styles are viewed as complementary, and the ideal is for both men and women managers to expand their behavioral repertoires to include skills based on both orientations. By valuing a diversity of managerial styles, organizations will develop the strength and flexibility to survive in a highly competitive and increasingly diverse economic environment. Critics warn, however, that we may be unintentionally perpetuating behavioral expectations by overvaluing differences that stem from traditional views of appropriate male and female behavior.

• **Changing the Power Structure.** The situational perspective suggests that "the job makes the person." Adherents of this approach suggest that valuing diversity is only rhetoric until women have equal access to jobs with opportunity and power, as well as to the career paths that lead there. Instead of pointing to job titles such as vice president or percentages of men and women in aggregate categories, this perspective suggests the need for change in access to the power structure, including jobs with direct influence over company revenues and budgets; the ability to get jobs for others, including hiring employees and directing large supply and consulting contracts; and external contacts and connections, such as seats on powerful corporate boards and civic involvement. For individual women, the implication is the need to develop strategies to counter the subtle barriers to power prevalent today. While differences in preferred leadership styles are accepted, the central concern is building and exercising a broad range of sources of power. Critics of this theory maintain, however, that the movement of women into the upper echelons of power has been hampered by an unwillingness to recognize and accept deep-rooted gender differences.

---

12. M. Heilman et al., "Has Anything Changed? Current Characterization of Men, Women, and Managers," *Journal of Applied Psychology* 74, no. 6, (1989) pp. 935–942.

13. A. Morrison, R. P. White, and E. Van Velsor, The Center for Creative Leadership, *Breaking the Glass Ceiling: Can Women Reach the Top of America's Largest Corporations?* (Reading, MA: Addison-Wesley, 1987).

14. K. Deaux and B. Major. "Putting Gender into Context: An Interactive Model of Gender-Related Behavior," *Psychological Review* 94, no. 3 (1987), pp. 369–389.

RACE AND ETHNICITY*

Taylor Cox, Jr.
University of Michigan, Ann Arbor, Michigan

Stella Nkomo
University of North Carolina at Charlotte, Charlotte, North Carolina

I. Introduction

This reading addresses the impact of racial and ethnic diversity on organizational processes and behavior. There are several reasons for devoting a chapter to this subject. First, in American society at large, race has been shown to influence many categories of life experience, including economic well-being (Morishima, 1981), psychological health (Thomas and Hughes, 1986), availability of health services (Eggers, 1988), sentencing in criminal cases (LaFree, 1980), and housing patterns (Massey and Denton, 1988). It seems reasonable therefore to expect race to also have an impact on behavior and processes in organizations. Second, previous research on the effects of race in the organizational context has generally shown that the work experience of employees varies systematically by race. For example, in our review of 145 empirical studies of the effects of race on organization behavior topics, significant main effects were found in 71 percent of the studies (Cox and Nkomo, 1990). Third, the workforce in the United States and throughout the world is becoming increasingly more diverse in terms of race and ethnicity (Johnston and Packard, 1987; Johnston, 1991; Horwitz and Forman, 1990). Because of this increase in racial heterogeneity in workgroups, the need to understand how race as well as racial

and ethnic differences influence work behavior is greater than ever before.

This chapter will address theory and research on race/ethnicity as a factor in organization behavior (OB). Throughout the chapter, we will use the term *racioethnicity,* as suggested by Cox (1990), to refer to the combination of physical and cultural differences that distinguish Euro-Caucasian members of organizations from minority groups such as African-Americans, Hispanic Americans, Asian-Americans, and American Indians.

Following this introduction, we will review and analyze previous literature on the intersection of racioethnicity with central subject areas in the OB domain.

II. Review and analysis of previous research

In this section we review five central subject areas in OB: job satisfaction/attitudes, performance appraisal, leadership, motivation, and careers (entry and upward mobility). These are the subject areas that have historically been addressed in the literature on racioethnic issues in organizations. For example, in a recent review of 20 of the leading OB journals we found that 88 percent of all articles dealing with racioethnic effects did so in terms of one of these five traditional OB topics, excluding articles on the legal aspects of [Equal Employment Oportunity/ Affirmative Action] EEO/AA (Cox and Nkomo, 1990). We have taken this topical approach because work in this area is not yet sufficiently

* Taylor Cox, Jr. and Stella Nkomo. "Race and Ethnicity." In *Handbook of Organizational Behavior.* ed. Robert T. Golembiewski. Marcel Dekker, 1993, pp. 205–29.

developed to organize our discussion around alternative theoretical paradigms. Throughout the review, we will offer an assessment of the literature focusing on strengths and shortcomings of the work and also offer suggestions for extending it. We conclude the chapter with additional suggestions for future research, focusing on some of the recent work on racioethnic effects that we consider to be particularly promising or important for researcher attention in the coming decade.

A. Job Satisfaction and Job Attitudes

Research in the area of job satisfaction has largely focused on two interrelated questions: Are there racial differences in job satisfaction; and are there racial differences in the importance attached to the facets that determine job satisfaction? There were a number of studies conducted during the 1970s and early 1980s, with a decreasing number appearing during the period from 1986 to 1991. Virtually all of this research addressed satisfactional attitudes of blacks compared to whites. Despite the sizable quantity of this research, the results are largely inconsistent. Some studies report whites as more satisfied than blacks, while other studies report the opposite.

O'Reilly and Roberts (1973) examined the differences in job satisfaction among a matched sample of white and nonwhite females performing the same job in a hospital setting. Using the job description index, the GM faces scale, and the Bayfield-Rothe index, they reported that whites were more satisfied with their jobs and that whites associated overall satisfaction more closely with promotion than nonwhites. The authors concluded that whites and nonwhites approach their jobs with different frames of reference. They argued that since socialization of school, work, and social behaviors is different for whites and nonwhites, it may be expected that attitudes and behaviors toward work will reflect these subcultural differences. The authors do acknowledge the difficulty of explaining

differences without theoretical notions to explain cultural differences.

Consistently, Milutinovich and Tsaklanganos (1976) found significant differences in job satisfaction for workers living in communities with different levels of prosperity. Workers from poor neighborhoods were less satisfied with work, supervision, promotion, and total jobs than middle-income workers. In addition, they reported a significant interaction effect between the race of the worker and community prosperity. For example, blacks from middle-income communities were more satisfied with their work than blacks from either poor or high middle-income communities, while whites from poor communities were less satisfied with their work than whites from either middle-income or high middle-income communities. It would seem that this finding merely underscores the interaction between race and class and the likelihood that workers from poor neighborhoods are more often employed in jobs with lower pay and benefits.

Weaver (1978) found differences in the correlates of job satisfaction factors for whites and blacks. Using data drawn from national surveys he found that family income, supervisory position, and occupational prestige correlated with job satisfaction for whites but were not significant for blacks. Veechio (1980) examined data from the National Opinion Research Center for over 2,000 full-time male workers and found significant main effect differences between blacks and whites on measures of job satisfaction. There were also differences in the manner in which these variables related for blacks relative to whites. A comparison of relationships between age and job prestige and between education and job satisfaction suggested the operation of different labor market processes between the two groups.

In contrast to the aforementioned studies, Gavin and Ewen (1974) compared job satisfaction of black and white male semiskilled employees in the same company. The instrument used to measure job satisfaction examined satisfaction with advancement, job and company, supervision, cooperation among co-workers and supervisors, and pay and working conditions. They found that blacks were more satisfied than whites on all but the supervision dimension; however, the size of the effect was small. The authors interpret their findings to indicate that the work perceptions of blacks may be influenced by external considerations—for example, reference groups or prior personal experiences. Similarly, Jones et al. (1977) compared the job satisfaction of black and white sailors assigned to the same shipboard divisions and found that while there were no differences in general satisfaction levels, black sailors were more satisfied with pay, rules and regulations regarding appearance, opportunities to get a better job, and attitudes toward the navy than their white counterparts. The satisfaction measures used by Jones et al. were the same as those employed by Gavin and Ewen (1974).

Two studies during the early 1980s attempted to explain racial differences in employee job satisfaction (Moch, 1980; Konar, 1981). Moch (1980) measured structural, cultural, social, and social psychological explanations for differential employee satisfaction by race. In addition to race, his analysis distinguished: racial composition of the employee's workgroup; the importance the employee placed on interpersonal relationships, on extrinsic rewards, and on intrinsic rewards; and the employee's social integration and perceived relative deprivation. He found that blacks reported less satisfaction than whites and that Mexican-Americans were more satisfied than whites. Race accounted for 21 percent of the variance in satisfaction beyond that accounted for by all the other factors. The other factors, however, accounted for only 4 percent of the variance in satisfaction beyond that accounted for by race. Moch concluded that structural, cultural, social, and social-psychological factors did not significantly contribute to explaining racial differences in job satisfaction. In

a review of the work, Konar (1981) differed with Moch's conclusion and argued that more research was needed on the structural factors affecting job satisfaction.

The most recent studies examining racioethnic effects on job satisfaction also report mixed results. Dalton and Marcis (1986) examined 1980 youth cohort data from the National Longitudinal Survey and found that satisfaction with the job for males compared to females was closely linked to general background characteristics, including race and ethnicity. Shiflett (1988) investigated the extent of job satisfaction and the importance of various job facets and performance outcomes for white and black enlisted men. He reported that black soldiers rated all facets of job satisfaction substantially more positively than did whites. Blacks seemed to derive greater satisfaction from extrinsic factors while whites tended to be more satisfied by intrinsic rewards. Wright et al. (1987), in a study of job satisfaction among black female public-sector managers found that organizational measures (organization size, type of position, level of government, etc.) accounted for most of the explained variance in satisfaction. Their study did not focus on racial differences per se, but used a sample of black women to test a model of job satisfaction.

Studies examining the relative importance of the different facets making up job satisfaction also report mixed findings. Slocum and Stawser (1972) examined whether or not intrinsic and extrinsic job factors vary as a function of racioethnicity. The black CPAs in their sample reported more need deficiency than white CPAs in the areas of opportunity to help people, opportunity for friendship, feeling of self-esteem, opportunity for independent thought and action, opportunity for growth and development, and compensation. Black CPAs generally felt that their needs were less satisfied by their jobs.

Weaver (1975) investigated preferences for job characteristics among black and white workers and found that blacks prefer high income more than whites, and were less likely to prefer important work and a feeling of accomplishment. Weaver (1975: 441) argued that because a black worker knows that having a job is at best tenuous, he may focus on the tangible, immediate security of income and be less mindful of the intrinsic satisfactions with work. Alper (1975) explored racioethnic differences in desired job characteristics among newly hired college graduates in sales and engineering positions. Overall, there were no differences in the relative importance attributed to job and work characteristics. However, black college graduates gave the hygiene factors (e.g., benefits, job security, and starting salary) significantly higher ratings than did the white sample. Alper (1975) concluded that while newly hired college graduates are highly future-oriented, the newly hired minority college graduate might still have security concerns beyond those of their white counterparts.

Beaty (1990) examined the link between job characteristics and job satisfaction for black and white nurses. He found no differences between black and white nurses on the extrinsic and intrinsic satisfaction measures and overall satisfaction. On the other hand, Shiflett (1988) reported that black soldiers derived greater satisfaction from extrinsic factors while white soldiers tended to be more satisfied by intrinsic factors. For blacks, satisfaction with extrinsic factors was related to intention to reenlist. For whites, satisfaction with work and supervision were related to reported effort and intention to reenlist. Shifflett (1988) also reported that blacks were more optimistic that good performance would lead to a desirable outcome.

Few studies have addressed racioethnic groups other than blacks and whites. Moch (1980) reported that the Mexican-Americans in his sample were more satisfied than blacks. McNeely (1987) investigated 336 black, Hispanic, and white female human service workers to determine whether or not racial/ethnic status was related to job satisfaction among managerial, supervisory, and professional employees.

There were no significant differences among the three race groups on either overall or intrinsic satisfaction. Data indicated that blacks and whites were similar in patterns predictive of their satisfaction, and that Hispanics were influenced by concerns peculiar to those achieving recent professional status. The emphasis for Hispanics was on satisfaction with teamwork. The authors are cautious about their results because of the relative small sample of Hispanics in the study ($N = 20$). Chusmir and Koberg (1990) examined ethnic differences in the relationship between job satisfaction and sex-role conflict among Hispanics and non-Hispanic white individuals. Hispanic subjects scored significantly lower on satisfaction with pay, supervision, and co-workers than did non-Hispanic whites. There was no significant link to any of the five facets of job satisfaction and sex role conflict for Hispanics. The authors did not address the possibility that the sex role conflict scale used in their study may be culture-bound. Since other research has demonstrated that sex roles and gender roles among Hispanics may be unique to their culture (Williams, 1988), this omission is potentially crucial.

In summary, research in this domain is plagued by inconsistency on how (if at all) racioethnic identity affects job satisfaction. There was also a lack of consistency in the instruments used to measure job satisfaction. In addition, only a few studies attempted to identify the underlying factors that might contribute to racioethnic differences in satisfaction. More attention needs to be paid to the social or psychological phenomena that have led researchers to predict or explore intergroup differences in job satisfaction. In this regard, the work of Moch (1980) and the suggestions of Komar (1981) should be revisited and extended.

There are some notable patterns in the approach to studying racioethnic effects on job satisfaction in the studies reviewed. In those studies in which differences were reported in facets of job satisfaction between black and white workers, the finding was that blacks placed more emphasis on hygiene or extrinsic factors than whites. There is a potential danger that the results could be interpreted as a cultural deficiency in that blacks are oriented toward fulfilling lower-order needs. An alternative interpretation may rest in examining the overall economic and historical context of work for black workers. Scholars must also be aware of potential differences in the meaning of the job satisfaction construct as well as in the reference point used by groups. In this regard, it would be helpful to know if the pattern of differences in job satisfaction facets holds across organizational levels and types of jobs.

B. Performance Evaluation

A number of studies have addressed the issue of rater and ratee racioethnic effects in performance ratings. The relatively large amount of research in this area is evidenced by the existence of three comprehensive literature and research reviews on the subject. Landy and Farr (1980) published a traditional literature review in 1980. Dipoybe (1985) offered a critical discussion of the limitations of both the theoretical framework and research methodology employed in most studies. Finally, Kraiger and Ford (1985) reported the results of a meta-analysis of over 70 studies. A brief summary of the major results of the research in this area is presented below rather than attempting to discuss each published study individually.

Several research studies have examined the effect of the racioethnicity of the ratee on job performance ratings. Early findings were often tentative and contradictory. Some studies found that ratees received significantly higher ratings from evaluators of their own race (Cox and Krumboltz, 1958; Dejung and Kaplan, 1962; Crooks, 1972; Landy and Farr, 1976; Schmitt and Lappin, 1980). Other studies reported results that indicated a complex interaction between ratee racioethnicity and ratee performance. Hamner et al. (1974) found that black performance may be rated as average by whites

regardless of the actual level of performance. Similarly, Bigoness (1976) found bias even when objective performance standards had been implemented. Contrary to these findings, other studies failed to support the existence of significant racioethnic effects on performance evaluations (Bass and Turner, 1973; Schmidt and Johnson, 1973; Mobley, 1982; Brugnoli, Campion, and Basen, 1979). A notable distinction in the study by Brugnoli et al. was that race-linked bias was not evident when evaluations were based on observations of relevant job behavior.

Kraiger and Ford's 1985 meta-analysis of this research helped to clarify earlier results. They reported the following findings. First, the racioethnicity of the ratee does have an impact on performance ratings. Racioethnicity explained approximately 3.7 percent of the variance in job performance ratings. Ratees tend to receive higher ratings from raters of the same race. This tendency is equally strong for both black and white raters. The mean correlations between ratee racioethnicity and ratings for white and black raters were 0.183 and -0.220, respectively. Second, racioethnic effects were more likely in field settings than in laboratory studies. Third, racioethnic effects were more likely when blacks composed a small percentage of an organization's workforce.

Research since the Kraiger and Ford analysis has again produced contradictory results. Pulakos et al. (1989) examined ratings collected for 8,642 first-term army enlisted personnel and found that racioethnic effects on ratings were minimal (less than 1 percent). They reported that blacks were rated higher on military bearing but lower than whites on the other two performance dimensions (technical skill and job effort and personal discipline). However, the authors did not explore why blacks were rated higher on military bearing, which was defined as appropriate military appearance and staying in good physical condition. Pulakos et al. (1989) strongly underscored how their results contradicted the findings of Kraiger and Ford (1985). From one perspective, however, their results do not really contradict those of Kraiger and Ford (1985) but are actually consistent with them. Blacks have good representation in the army among enlisted men and this could have moderated the racioethnic effects on performance ratings.

Greenhaus, Parasuraman, and Wormley (1990), in a matched sample of black and white managers in three companies, reported significant racioethnic effects in performance evaluations. Supervisors rated blacks lower than whites on both the relationship and task components of performance. In their study, racioethnicity accounted for 2.5 percent of the variance in the relationship component and 5.5 percent of the variance in the task component. Kleiman, Biderman, and Faley (1987) sought to identify factors related to employee perceptions of the accuracy of subjective performance ratings. The study also examined if perceived fairness and accuracy was moderated by employee sex and/or racioethnicity. They found that the black females in their study perceived the appraisal process as less fair and accurate compared to white males and females. These perceptions were affected by job experience. Black females with more job experience perceived the system as being fair and accurate.

While the studies often contradict one another, the accumulated evidence does indicate that racioethnicity plays a part in performance ratings. The remaining research issues revolve more around how much impact racioethnicity has on performance ratings and in understanding the processes underlying race effects. A few articles have explored this latter issue (Cox and Nkomo, 1986; Dipboye, 1985; Ilgen and Youtz, 1985; Pettigrew and Martin, 1987; DeMeuse, 1987). Cox and Nkomo (1986) explored the possibility that the meaning of performance ratings and the weighting of criteria may differ for members of different racioethnic groups. Data from performance appraisal ratings of 125 first-level managers revealed that among the top 10 correlates of performance ratings, blacks and whites

had only one item in common. Overall results indicated that social behavior factors were more highly correlated with the overall job performance rating of black ratees than for white ratees. These findings suggest the use of different criteria and information based on racioethnicity, and hence black ratees may be confronted with the task of meeting a more complex set of performance criteria than their white counterparts. This point of view is reinforced by survey research suggesting that many black managers believe they are subjected to different performance expectations and criteria (Fernandez, 1981; Jones, 1986; Dickens and Dickens, 1982).

Ilgen and Youtz (1986) discussed the factors affecting the evaluation and development of minorities in organizations. Because their work represents one of the most thorough (and we believe thoughtful) discussions of the *causes* of difference, we will comment on it in some detail here. Drawing heavily from theoretical concepts in social psychology, they examine three possible explanations for the existence of racioethnic effects in the performance evaluation process: (1) rater bias; (2) lost opportunities; and (3) self-limiting behavior.

C. Rater Bias

The first and most obvious explanation for the existence of racial differences is rater bias based on stereotypes of minorities. However, Ilgen and Youtz (1986) argue that the biases that exist in ratings may be the result of complex judgment processes of person perception rather than the simple minority group stereotypes. More subtle effects of group membership on attributions about the causes of performance, the attention that obvious membership in a particular minority group draws to the person, and beliefs about the conditions under which the person was hired for the job are also likely sources of rater bias. For example, good performance for minorities may be attributed to external factors (e.g., luck or the task) rather than ability, while that of majority group members may be more likely attributed to ability or effort (Greenhaus and Para-suraman, in press). Ilgen and Youtz (1986) also argue that the cognitive processing view of performance appraisals suggests that the search for information about ratee performance may be biased. Hypothesis-confirming ratee behaviors tend to be more salient to raters, and thus are more likely to be noticed and recalled by them. For example, if a rater believes that blacks are lazy he or she is more likely to notice instances of "laziness" on the part of black ratees (Ilgen and Youtz, 1986).

Cox and Nkomo's (1986) study also supports the view of differential use of information by raters when rating blacks. Jussim et al. (1987) examined predictions derived from three theories of stereotyping: complexity-extremity theory, assumed characteristics theory, and expectancy-violation theory. They found that the range of whites' evaluation of black applicants was larger than the range of their evaluations of white applicants. In a similar fashion, DeMeuse (1987) argues for more attention to the role of nonverbal cues on person perception. Nonverbal cues are defined as "all communication except that which is contained in words" (DeMeuse, 1987: 208). He suggests that this also includes demographic indicators (e.g., gender, race, and age) that may communicate systematic images to perceivers (raters). Demographic cues often possess widely understood and socially shared meanings (e.g., stereotypes of blacks and other racioethnic groups).

Another possible source of rater bias may simply be due to the novel or "solo" status of the minority group member (Pettigrew and Martin, 1987). In the case of a single minority group member among a majority group, the minority group member stands out. When racioethnicity is a very salient feature, it may be credited with far more relevance with respect to performance judgment than it deserves. This observation, noted by Ilgen and Youtz (1986) and Pettigrew and Martin (1987), is reinforced by Kraiger and Ford's (1985) finding that racioethnic effects in performance ratings are more likely in field settings when blacks are few in number.

D. Lost Opportunities

The second possible source of racioethnic effects in performance evaluation cited by Ilgen and Youtz (1986) was lost opportunities. Lost opportunities as a concept focuses on the role of the treatment of minorities in creating actual differences between groups (Ilgen and Youtz, 1986). These lost opportunities include the absence of mentors, less interesting or challenging work as a result of being in the outgroup, and being left out of the informal social network. While these lost opportunities do not directly affect performance ratings, according to Ilgen and Youtz (1986) they may lead to *actual* differences in performance between groups over time. Similar explanations have also been posited by other researchers. For example, Alderfer et al. (1980), in their landmark study of race relations in organizations, found that the greatest disagreement between black and white managers was on the topic of promotions. In their study, white managers reported sharing career-relevant information with black managers at more than twice the rate that black managers reported receiving such information from white managers. Similarly, Greenhaus, Parasuraman, and Wormley (1990) found that compared to white managers, black managers felt less accepted in their organizations and perceived themselves as having less discretion on their jobs.

E. Self-Limiting Behavior

The final explanation presented by Ilgen and Youtz (1986) is self-limiting behavior on the part of minority group members, which they discuss as a long-term effect of experiencing rating biases and lost opportunities. According to their analysis, self-limiting behavior operates in a two-pronged fashion. First, if minorities continually experience lower performance ratings, negative stereotypes, and fewer job opportunities, they may come to believe that they are less competent and develop a negative self-concept. Second, minority employees continually placed in routine, unchallenging work assignments outside the normal career path may fall behind majority employee cohorts in terms of job knowledge, skill development, and performance. Self-limiting behavior developed as a result of lost opportunities will tend to perpetuate performance differences. We add to their discussion of self-limiting behavior that the extent to which racioethnic minorities engage in such behavior may be influenced by one's level of racioethnic identity. Those minority group members with a strong sense of identity will more likely resist internalizing negative feelings and their self-esteem would remain intact.

In our view, all of these possible explanations warrant further study and research and underscore the importance of focusing research on understanding the processes that lead to differences in performance ratings between minority and majority group members in organizations. Research is also needed on effective ways of minimizing negative rater behaviors and in testing performance evaluation systems that control rater errors grounded in stereotypes and bias.

F. Leadership

Studies examining racioethnicity and leadership have typically focused on differences in leader behavior between blacks and whites, as well as on the effects of racioethnicity on subordinate perceptions of leader behavior. One of the earliest studies on leadership and racioethnicity was Delbecq and Kaplan's (1968) investigation of interactions between black leaders and predominantly black subordinates in a government-sponsored program. They found that the leaders generally reacted by dominating the decision-making process, resorting to coalitions and authority of the office to resolve conflicts, and concentrating on safeguarding their own status and self-image. Unfortunately, there were no comparisons made with white leaders.

Richard and Jaffe (1972) investigated the behavior of biracial workgroups when blacks supervise whites. Results indicated that the performance ratings of black supervisors were significantly poorer than those of white supervisors. Subordinates supervised by blacks behaved differently from subordinates supervised by whites, and some of these behaviors appeared to hinder the effectiveness of the black supervisor. For example, subordinates with a black supervisor gave more suggestions and opinions and disagreed more than subordinates with a white supervisor. Finally, subordinates with negative racial bias gave poorer ratings to black supervisors than subordinates with liberal racial attitudes.

Beatty (1973) used the leader opinion questionnaire to measure supervisor consideration behavior and initiation behavior of black supervisors. Results indicated that the employer's perception of the black supervisors' social behavior tended to be the most important influence in evaluating black supervisors. Interpersonal attributes and cultural awareness were key determinants of perceptions.

Bartol, Anderson, and Schneier (1981) examined the motivation to manage among business students and found that blacks had a lower orientation toward imposing wishes on others and were less assertive. Shull and Anthony (1978), in a study of participants in a supervisory training program, examined black and white supervisory problem-solving styles. Little difference was found in all measures except attitudes toward received discipline. Blacks were less willing to accept harsh criticism for violation of rules, especially if performance was otherwise high. Bartol, Evans, and Stith (1978) conducted an extensive review of the research on black/white differences in leadership between 1964 and 1977, and found that ethnic factors affected leader behavior, leader potential, and leader performance, although blacks and whites were similar in many respects. They argued for more studies of ethnicity in all aspects of leadership research.

Adams (1978) examined attitudes and perceptions of subordinates toward minority versus majority group managers. Black males were perceived as exhibiting more "consideration" behavior compared to other groups. There were no related effects on satisfaction. Ivancevich and McMahon (1977) used the path-goal leadership model to examine the moderating impact of racioethnicity on task-goal attributes and task-effort and performance. They found that blacks reported different goal attributes associated with task effort and performance on an assigned goal. Goal challenge was related to performance for whites but not for blacks. Parker (1976), using Bowes and Seashore's four dimensions of leadership, explored black and white differences in leader behavior as perceived by black, white, and Chicano subordinates. Black supervisors were seen by subordinates as more effective leaders than white supervisors on the dimensions of managerial support, goal emphasis, and work facilitation. There was no evidence that subordinates viewed supervisors of the same racioethnic group more favorably than supervisors of a different race. However, white subordinates of white supervisors in workgroups that were predominantly black saw their supervisors more favorably than white subordinates of white supervisors in workgroups that were predominantly white. Parker (1976) speculated that the differences may have been due to the fact that majority group subordinates are not accustomed to being in the minority. Chicano subordinate rankings differentiated between black and white supervisors only on the goal emphasizing dimension, where black supervisors were rated higher.

Using Allport's intergroup contact theory, Hill and Fox (1973) tested hypotheses of differences in the way black and white supervisors feel and act toward black, white, and Puerto Rican subordinates on dimensions of work that are not task-prescribed. The sample consisted of Marine rifle squads. White leaders praised whites more than blacks. Black leaders showed no differences in the use of praise. Whites gave higher ratings of performance to black versus white subordinates. In general, racioethnic effects were found for white leaders but not for black leaders. Although white leaders often were more favorable to black subordinates, the authors speculated that this finding was affected by a recent emphasis on racioethnic harmony in the army.

Kipnis, Silverman, and Copeland (1973) examined the use of coercion by supervisors with black and white subordinates. First-line supervisors at a steel mill described an incident in which they used delegated powers to correct subordinate behavior. Analysis of these incidents revealed that supervisors used more coercion with black than white subordinates. It was assumed that heightened emotional responses caused by prejudice in the case of black subordinates induced the use of coercion.

It is perhaps noteworthy that we were unable to locate studies of racioethnicity and leadership published in the last 10 years. The amount of research done seems to have peaked in the late 1970s. As evidenced from the review above, there is a good deal of disparity in the nature of the effect of racioethnicity on leader behavior and subordinate reactions. Clearly, there is a profound need for more research in this area, given the forecast of an increasing diversity of racioethnic groups in the labor force. Research is needed that will more fully examine leadership styles of leaders of different racioethnic groups and in different supervisor-subordinate dyads.

In recent years leadership research has focused on examining "substitutes" for leadership. According to Kerr and Jermier (1978), "This research explores factors that neutralize leader behavior—the nature of the task, subordinate ability, and the organizational situation." Future research should take a multivariate approach using these factors in addition to racioethnicity.

Also needed is research that examines the relationship between transformational leadership (Kimberly and Quinn, 1984) and racioethnicity. For example, how do race and ethnicity influence one's ability to be a transformational leader?

Finally, we must incorporate theories of power and domination in understanding racioethnicity and leadership. Ultimately, leadership must be understood as an influence process and we cannot overlook the impact of the historical dominant and subordinate positions of whites and nonwhites in the larger societal context. What does it mean for a white employee who has grown up in society in which he or she holds a dominant and superior status vis-à-vis nonwhites to be in a situation in which he or she is now "subordinate?" Alternately, what are the social-psychological implications of a racioethnic minority manager functioning in a role that places him or her in a superior position relative to members of the white majority group? Traditional examinations of differences in leader behavior do not address the individual, group, societal, and historical factors that may impact leader or subordinate behavior in mixed racioethnic dyads.

G. Motivation

Previous work on racioethnic effects on employee motivation has centered on cross-group comparisons of need structures and on expectancy theory. This focus is consistent with that of motivation theory generally, since it is frequently categorized as *content* (need structure theories such as Maslow's need hierarchy) and *process,* the most prominent being expectancy theory (Arnold and Feldman, 1986).

H. Need Structure Studies

The need structure studies have generally used either Herzberg's motivation-hygiene theory (Herzberg, Mausner, and Snyderman, 1959) or McClelland's achievement, power, and affiliation theory (McClelland, 1961) as their basic framework. The primary research question addressed in this body of research is whether or not the need structures of workers are systematically related to racioethnicity. Two early studies examined growth/higher-order needs (challenging work, advancement, etc.) and hygienic factors (fringe benefits, job security, salary, etc.). Alper (1975) studied need structures among a sample of 70 newly hired African-Americans and 179 newly hired whites. Although the study had no formally stated hypotheses, the author employed a Maslow-hierarchy logic (Maslow, 1954) suggesting that the history of economic disadvantage of nonwhites might lead to a greater emphasis on hygiene factors among nonwhites compared to whites. His results supported this line of reasoning, in that racioethnicity had no effect on the priority assigned to the growth factors, but whites gave significantly lower scores to hygiene factors.

However, a study by Feldman (1973) using the same conceptual framework but a sample of hard-core employed and working-class men, produced contradictory results. Feldman's data did show significant racioethnic effects on certain individual work outcomes, but did not support the pattern of higher priority on hygiene factors for nonwhites. The contradictory findings may have been due to slight differences in operational definitions of some variables. For example, Alper defined the pay variable as the importance of starting salary to initial employment decisions while Feldman defined it as a rating of good pay as a work outcome using a scale of 1 (most positive) to 9 (most negative). In the latter study respondents may have focused on postemployment concerns rather than the initial job decision. One interpretation, therefore, is that pay is a more prominent outcome in the initial employment decision, whereas other factors, such as advancement, become more salient in the frame of reference of ongoing employment.

In another interesting study of racioethnic effects, using the Herzberg framework, Kahoe (1974) found that patterns of correlations between intrinsic and extrinsic job incentives scales differed for black males compared to whites. In particular, he found that although working conditions are normally treated as an extrinsic factor in theory and research, scores on working-condition scales correlated highly with the intrinsic scales in the black male sample. Kahoe offers the interpretation that the data indicate that working conditions may hold different meanings for members of different racioethnic groups. He suggests that working conditions may have self-actualization implications for persons with a history of poor and unequal conditions. Although the description of his work is not sufficiently detailed in the article to judge whether or not his argument is convincing, the idea that members of different racioethnic groups may assign different psychological meanings to job incentives is an intriguing one that we think deserves further exploration.

Several studies have also made cross-race comparisons using the McClelland framework. Watson and Barone (1976) studied achievement affiliation and power motivation levels in a sample of 64 black and 64 white managers using the thematic apperception test (TAT). No a priori predictions were offered about how racioethnic identity would affect the need structures. Their results indicated a significant effect of racioethnicity for power (higher for whites) but not for achievement or affiliation. They concluded that "black managers, as a class, have a remarkably similar need pattern to their white counterparts" (p. 47). Lefkowitz and Fraser (1980) essentially replicated the findings of Watson and Barone (1976) on achievement but did not find any racioethnic effects on power motivation. Their sample was college students and was quite small (31 blacks and 32 whites). Lefkowitz and Fraser (1980) also found that the racioethnicity of the test administrator had a significant effect on verbal productivity scores of both nonwhite and white respondents. Their discussion of this result provides an interesting insight into racioethnic influence. They note that McClelland found this same result and commented as follows on its meaning:

> If interactions (of administrator and respondent racioethnic group) were the rule, the concept of "race" for purposes of interview research could be reduced to the much simpler psychological concepts of same and different. Uniform reactions to black and white interviewers by respondents of both races necessitate conceptualization of race

into black and white, concepts much less explicable and understandable psychologically than same and different (McClelland, 1974: 395).

This observation by McClelland has important implications for racioethnic research and for work on the broader concept of workforce diversity. The generic diversity concept is more appropriate when the group phenomena under study are accurately reducible to the notions of same and different, but there are many phenomena for which the specific racioethnic identities (and roles) of the interacting parties will be crucial. As McClelland has suggested, much of the work on diversity effects will therefore require attention to the social and psychological meaning of specific racioethnic groups represented in a transaction.

An additional implication of the use of the work of both Watson and Barron (1976) and Lefkowitz and Frazer (1980) is that their findings highlight the importance of acknowledging that minority-group managers in corporations are not necessarily representative of the overall population of their group. This was relatively less important when only a few nonwhites were being hired, but with workforce demographic trends indicating that more and more nonwhites will be hired, the profiles of the overall group become more important. Research that is limited to the present cohort of managers and professionals in organizations may not inform us well about the racioethnic issues of the future.

I. Expectancy Theory

Another prominent theoretical framework in the employee motivation area is expectancy theory (Vroom, 1964; Porter and Lawler, 1968). This theory holds that motivation to work will be high when: (1) a person believes that effort and good performance are tightly linked (effort-performance expectancy), and (2) a person believes that a good performance will lead to the outcome that he or she values (performance-outcome expectancy). A series of studies in the

1970s examined the possibility that one or both of these "expectancies," or their ability to predict actual job performance, vary by racioethnicity.

All such studies that we were able to locate focused on comparisons between whites and blacks. Greenhaus and Gavin (1972) explored expectancy-theory differences in a sample of 390 white and 81 black male blue-collar employees of a major airline. They combined the two expectancies into a single variable called effort-reward expectancy. They also examined possible differences in the importance placed on various work rewards. Findings indicated no differences between blacks and whites on the value of rewards. The effort-reward expectancies were significantly different in only 2 of 12 reward categories, and in all cases they were higher for blacks. Perhaps most intriguing, the correlation between expectancies and supervisor ratings of job performance was more often significant for whites than for blacks. However, the correlations were low for both samples, and differences in correlations between blacks and whites were not significant.

Orpen and Nkohande (1977) studied relations between self-esteem, locus of control, and expectancy beliefs in a sample of 59 black and 61 white low-level managers from 10 South African companies. They predicted that whites would have both higher self-esteem and higher internal control scores than blacks, and that both self-esteem and internal control would have a positive relationship with effort-performance and performance-outcome expectancies. Although they did not explicitly address it, this theoretical scheme implies that blacks would have lower expectancies by virtue of lower self-esteem and more external locus of control. Their findings confirmed that the white managers had significantly higher self-esteem and internal locus of control scores, but these variables were significantly correlated with expectancies only in the white sample. Unfortunately, this study was not as informative as it could have been because the authors did not report how the expectancies themselves compared for the two groups, and failed to provide a test of statistical significance for the differences in correlation coefficients between blacks and whites.

In a related study, Feldman (1973) tested the following hypotheses: (1) blacks would have lower performance-outcome expectancies for the behavior of work itself; and (2) blacks would have stronger performance-outcome expectancies for the behavior of not working. His data supported neither hypothesis, however he did find significant effects of racioethnic group on expectancies. Blacks generally had higher expectancies of positive outcomes from working and less negative outcome expectancies of not working than whites. Feldman offers some thought-provoking speculation about the reasons for these results. In part, he argues that blacks may view not working less negatively because of a more realistic view of unemployment (because of their greater experience with it as a group), more ingenuity in finding alternatives to full-time continuous employment as sources of income, and less emphasis on one's work role as the basis of personal respect.

While we would not support an interpretation that the availability of regular, full-time work is relatively unimportant to blacks compared to whites, it does seem plausible that the different sociocultural histories of blacks and whites may convey different meanings for work in terms of personal respect and self-esteem. For example, since blacks were barred from participation in high-status jobs in racioethnically integrated settings for hundreds of years, to accept one's work role as the basis of esteem would have been to severely diminish self-esteem to the entire group. Under these circumstances it seems rational for blacks to resist the use of work roles as the basis for personal respect.

Collectively, these studies seem to suggest that relationships of the expectancy theory framework (i.e., the theory itself and related theories such as linkages with self-esteem and internal control) are not as reliably predicted for non-white samples as they are for whites. Feldman (1973: 20) puts it this way: "These data, while not supporting the original hypotheses, strongly suggest that race and economic class are associated with different views of the world of work."

This leads to questions about why the theory seems to operate differently for different racioethnic groups. Consideration of these questions offers some interesting ideas for further research. For example, one interpretation of the Greenhaus and Gavin (1972) study reviewed above is that the lesser correlation between expectancies and performance ratings indicates that performance ratings are less reflective of work effort for nonwhites compared to whites. As a second example, Orpen and Nkohande (1977) speculated that self-esteem could have been a better predictor of effort-performance expectancy for whites than for blacks because work is less central to the self-concept for the latter group. Still another explanation is suggested by Fernandez (1987), who observes that need structures may vary for people of different races. To the extent that they do, the valence-of-outcomes dimension of expectancy theory will be affected.

While researchers need to continue to give attention to new theoretical schemes for racioethnicity effects in the context of expectancy-theory, we believe that the theory of differential effort-performance expectancies for nonwhites compared to whites deserves special attention. Effort-performance expectancies may be lower for nonwhites because: (1) they have less confidence that their efforts will be recognized with high performance ratings; (2) they have control over fewer resources; and (3) they may have lower self-confidence for performance in organizations that are dominated by whites. The first point is supported by research indicating that some minority groups have a more external orientation to locus of control (Orpen and Nkohande, 1977; Helms and Giorgis, 1980), by research indicating that nonwhites tend to

receive lower performance ratings than whites (Greenhaus, Parasuraman and Wormely, 1990), and also by the possibility of bias against non-whites in performance evaluation processes (Pettigrew and Martin, 1987). The second point is supported by research indicating that nonwhites tend to have less overall responsibility and fewer subordinates than whites at comparable job levels (Mueller, Tanaka, and Parcel, 1989). The third point is supported by research on the self-confidence of nonwhites when there is a history of discrimination against their particular group (Brett and Morse, 1975; Orpen and Nkohande, 1977; Lefcourt and Ladwig, 1965).

One possible explanation for the failure of the previous studies to support the theory of lower expectancies for nonwhites is that these studies were all conducted during the early 1970s when equal opportunity and affirmative action were first emphasized in corporate America. It was a time of optimism for many minorities as the first decade under the Civil Rights Act of 1964 unfolded. Many organizations were sponsoring research and other activities around equal opportunity, which tended to raise expectations of positive change. At such a point in history, non-whites may have been more likely to express strong belief in the meritocracy norm that underlies expectancy theory.

J. Careers: Entry

Research on whether or not white decision makers are less likely to select nonwhites for jobs has produced inconsistent results. Mullins's (1982) study of hiring decisions using white business students to rate hiring favorability of black and white applicants found that the black applicants were actually rated higher than the white applicants and that blacks performing poorly in the interview were rated higher than the low-performing white applicants. A similar conclusion was reached in two studies of racioethnic differences in recruitment that utilized the controversial methodology of sending fictitious résumés of black and white applicants to prospective employers (Newman, 1978; McIntyre et al., 1980). Newman (1978) investigated possible discrimination in recruitment by an analysis of responses of 207 companies to unsolicited résumés from fictitious black and white applicants. Findings indicated a tendency for large companies to favor black applicants. Using a similar methodology, McIntyre et al. (1980) essentially replicated the Newman findings.

Research using different methodologies has produced contradictory results. For example, using a policy-capturing approach, Barr and Hitt (1986) found that both managerial and student decision makers gave higher hiring favorability ratings and recommended higher starting salaries for white applicants than for black applicants. A careful analysis of the Barr and Hitt (1986) study suggests that several methodological differences may have accounted for the contradictory findings. First, in order to reduce the possibility of random or inconsistent decision patterns, they eliminated responses when the R^2 for a given ratee fell below a specified threshold (0.33). Second, they employed a policy-capturing data analysis approach that has a greater likelihood of identifying "theories used" rather than espoused theories (Slovic and Lichtenstein, 1971). Third, they included a visual (video) presentation of candidates as well as written dossiers. These steps may have increased the probability of detecting racioethnic impact. This research suggests that attention should be given to these methodological issues in future research designs testing racioethnic effects on hiring decisions. This is especially true for the issue of whether or not expressed theories and beliefs accurately reflect behavior. The problem of socially desirable responses is especially acute with racioethnic research because unfavorable responses toward nonwhites may be interpreted as racist behavior.

There has also been a considerable amount of research on racioethnic effects in interviews and tests employed in hiring decisions, but the studies we located were inconsistent as to whether or not there is racioethnic bias in interviews. Jackson (1979) studied the factors that affected the selection of managers in government jobs and concluded that interviewees with darker complexions may be at a disadvantage in the hiring process. Mullins (1982) used videotaped stimulus materials to examine interviewer ratings of high- and low-quality candidates role-played by black and white males. This laboratory experiment used business undergraduate students to rate applicants. Results indicated that the most important variable influencing interviewer ratings was applicant quality, but that the black applicant was significantly favored over the white applicant. Finally, Parson and Liden (1984) examined actual interview ratings of candidates for jobs in an amusement park. They found that blacks were rated significantly lower than white applicants on a number of interview dimensions.

The contradictory results in these studies on interviews may be related to the type of methodology employed. Much of the research using lab experiments has found that blacks received higher ratings than whites in interview situations, while studies using field data tend to show the opposite. The confusion here underscores the methodological dilemma faced by researchers. Laboratory experiments facilitate the creation of comparisons in which the candidates differ only by racioethnicity, but they may well increase the likelihood of socially desirable responses. On the other hand, nonexperimental field studies may be less subject to socially desirable response bias (i.e., when actual decisions are examined), but it is more difficult to assure that white and nonwhite applicants in the sample have the identical qualifications.

Research has also shown that interaction effects between the racioethnic identity of the interviewer and the interviewee sometimes influence the interview process. For example, Word, Zanna, and Cooper (1974) and Weitz (1972) found that white interviewers displayed more negative behaviors (e.g., physical distancing or low eye contact) with black interviewees than with white interviewees. Such behaviors can account for less adequate performances of black interviewees (Word, Zanna, and Cooper, 1974).

Additional research is needed in this area, especially on the implications of racioethnic interactions for the interview behavior of both interviewers and interviewees. Such research should include the situation in which whites are interviewed by nonwhites. The potential effectiveness of interviewer training to avoid subtle influences of racioethnic dynamics should also be explored. Traditional interviewer training in organizations has concentrated on the kinds of interview questions that are illegal under Title VII guidelines, with less attention to the possible unconscious behaviors of interviewers toward applicants of other racioethnic groups.

K. Research on Test Validation
A considerable amount of research has been done on the validity of various employment tests for people of different racioethnic groups. The prototypical question in this area has been: Does differential validity exist for specific groups? Once again, nearly all of this research has focused on blacks and whites. The term *differential validity* is used to describe the hypothesis that employment tests are less valid for nonwhites than for whites (Gatewood and Field, 1990). To a lesser extent, researchers have also focused on the single group validity issue— when a test is valid for one group and not the other.

Like most areas of research on racioethnic effects, results on test validity have been mixed. In one of the first studies, Lopez (1966) examined data on 865 black and white female toll collectors, and found that the best method for predicting job performance for the white group of employees differed from the best method for black employees. Kirkpatrick et al. (1968) also found differential validity in tests for different ethnic groups. Carter and Swanson (1990) addressed the extent to which the Strong interest inventory is psychometrically valid for black

samples. After citing research supporting the validity of the Strong inventory for predicting the vocational interests of white samples, the authors review eight studies involving its use with black samples. They conclude that vocational interests are influenced by racioethnic group and also that little evidence supports the Strong inventory as a valid measurement device for black samples. They suggest that the different applicability of the Strong may be due to cultural differences among racioethnic groups.

Other research supporting the differential validity hypothesis for various tests includes Dugan (1966), Bayroff (1966), Ruda and Allrights (1968), Bartlett and O'Leary (1969), Lefkowitz (1972), Toole (1972), and Moore and MacNaughton (1979). In the 1970s, these studies were so influential that the Equal Employment Opportunity Commission altered its guidelines to recognize the possible existence of differential validity (Arvey and Faley, 1988).

Despite the considerable research supporting the existence of differential validity of hiring tests, the evidence is by no means unanimous. Boehm (1972; 1977) reviewed 31 studies involving the differential validity hypothesis and concluded that a majority of the reported findings of differential prediction could be regarded as methodological artifacts resulting from small sample sizes and inappropriate job performance measures. Similarly, Schmidt, Berner, and Hunter (1973) concluded from their review of the research that differential validity is found only by chance. An additional finding was that differential validity was more likely to be found in those studies that used subjective criterion measures (e.g., supervisory ratings).

Finally, three comprehensive reviews of the research available in the mid-1970s concluded that there was no support for the differential validity hypothesis (Hunter and Schmidt 1978; Hunter, Schmidt, and Hunter, 1979; Schmidt, Pearlman, and Hunter, 1980). The Schmidt, Pearlman, and Hunter study was exceptional in that it included Hispanics.

Unfortunately, much of the research and analyses of research on differential validity concentrates on methodological issues in conducting validity studies. More careful and extensive consideration needs to be given as to why one would expect differential validity to occur and why test score differences among certain racioethnic groups for certain types of tests persist (e.g., test differences between blacks and whites on many standard cognitive ability tests; Arvey and Faley, 1988). An idea that we believe deserves further exploration is that differences between minority and majority group members on paper-and-pencil employment tests result from cultural differences. The line of reasoning is that the content of most employment tests is based on white middle-class culture and therefore persons from that culture may be advantaged in taking such tests. A few writers have developed so-called culture-fair tests (e.g., the black intelligence test of cultural homogeneity developed by Williams, 1975, and the Chicano intelligence scale of cultural orientation developed by Ramirez, 1989). However, culture-fair tests have not had wide application (Arvey and Faley, 1988).

In sum, the available research about racioethnic effects on employment tests and interviews does not support concrete generalizations about the presence or absence of such effects. It would therefore seem prudent for organizations to take great care to ensure that the suitability and interpretation of selection tools are specifically assessed for racioethnic effects. It is also important to note that the research to date has been directed toward blacks and whites and has done little to examine validity for Hispanic, Asian, or other nonwhite populations. Finally, research to date has emphasized tests, and to a lesser extent, interviews. There is a need for research on other selection tools, such as assessment centers.

L. Careers: Promotion / Upward Mobility

The effect of being a racioethnic minority on promotion opportunity has been the subject of much commentary but relatively little empirical

research or detailed theory construction. The most prevalent theoretical premise of the published material is that racioethnic minorities have lower opportunities for advancement in white-majority organizations than do whites and especially white males. The most obvious evidence in support of this conclusion is the relative absence of nonwhites from the highest levels of management in U.S. organizations. For example, 995 of the CEOs listed in the *Business Week* 1000 for 1990 are white, and a recent Department of Labor study of senior managers in nine *Fortune* 500 companies found that only 2.6 percent of the top managers were nonwhite (U.S. Department of Labor, 1991).

Since management jobs were effectively closed to racioethnic minorities until fairly recently, it is appropriate to distinguish the issue of arrival at the top from progress toward it. In this regard, Jones (1976; 1986) and Fernandez (1987) report survey data indicating that despite affirmative action, a large percentage of nonwhite employees believe that their race has hindered their advancement. Research that compares actual promotion rates of different racioethnic groups is scarce. Cox and Nkomo (1986) found no significant differences in promotability ratings between black and white lower-level managers in a large public-sector firm. However, in a study comparing the career progress of 26 black MBAs to that of 680 white MBAs of comparable career tenure, Brown and Ford (1977) found that only 31 percent of the blacks had reached middle-management or higher compared to 73 percent in the white sample. Similarly, in their study of 849 managers in three large corporations, Greenhaus, Parasuraman, and Wormley (1990) found that black managers had lower promotability ratings and were more likely to be plateaued (more than 7 years in their current jobs) than their white counterparts. They found that the lower promotion ratings of nonwhites mainly occurred indirectly through lower performance ratings, whereas the plateauing seemed to be a direct effect of racioethnicity.

A small amount of research and discussion has addressed possible causes of lower upward mobility of nonwhites compared to whites in predominantly white organizations. For example, Fine, Johnson, and Ryan (1990) studied 242 employees of various levels in a regional agency of the federal government. Factors cited as obstacles to the upward mobility of nonwhites included the impact of a white/male culture and negative stereotyping of nonwhites.

Another study addressing factors that may underlie upward mobility problems for nonwhites is the work by Greenhaus and Parasuraman (in press) on the effects of race on performance attributions. Their data, taken from 1,628 managers in three companies, indicate that the racioethnicity of employees does affect the types of performance attributions made about their work. In working relationships of less than 1 year, they found that supervisors were more likely to attribute good performance to ability if the subordinates were white instead of black. They also found that supervisors were more likely to attribute good performance to help from others and to job ease if the subordinate was black rather than white. Moreover, they found that advancement prospects for all managers were better if good performance was attributed to ability rather than luck, ease of job, or amount of help from others. This combination of findings strongly suggests that racioethnic effects on performance attributions is a significant cause of glass-ceiling effects on the upward mobility of nonwhite managers in predominantly white organizations. There has been much discussion in recent years about "subtle" discrimination. However, empirical verification that such discrimination actually occurs, and of how it occurs, is scarce. The work of Greenhaus and Parasuraman makes an important contribution in this regard. We strongly urge additional research to replicate and extend their work.

A number of writers have argued that nonwhites have difficulty gaining promotion in predominantly white organizations because of more limited access to the types of job assignments and organizational experiences that are needed for promotion (Nkomo and Cox, 1990; Fernandez, 1975, 1981; Jones, 1986). Although published accounts of empirical research on this argument are scarce, several will be cited here. Mueller, Tanaka, and Parcel (1989) studied spans of both responsibility and control in a sample of 621 white male and 142 black male supervisors. They found that black managers had lower spans of control and less authority over the pay and promotion of subordinates than white managers. This finding suggests that blacks may not be as likely as whites to be selected for middle and senior manager positions because they do not have the same opportunity as whites to control resources at lower levels of management.

The control of resources is important for multiple reasons. First, the ability to control more resources may enable one to accomplish better work results and thereby create a more impressive track record. Second, jobs that control more resources are more likely to gain the attention of senior managers whose support is needed for promotion. Third, demonstrating the ability to handle resources well should improve one's probability of being selected for jobs of greater responsibility.

Another result from the Mueller, Tanaka, and Parcel study that is germane to our purpose here was their finding that social psychological variables, such as achievement orientation and interpersonal trust, were important predictors of spans of control for black supervisors but not for white supervisors. They interpret these results as evidence that nonwhites must be more qualified than whites to gain advancement in predominantly white organizations. Our own conclusion hinges on the interpretation of the phrase "more qualified." To the extent that it refers to judging minority managers on a broader range of criteria than is used with majority managers, we agree with their interpretation. In this respect, their results are reminiscent of our own finding cited earlier that social behavior factors were important predictors of overall performance ratings for black managers but not for white managers (Cox and Nkomo, 1986). Despite the obvious unfairness of such apparent "double standards," it is explainable on both rational and emotional grounds. If senior managers believe that nonwhite supervisors encounter more resistance than whites from peers, subordinates, and perhaps even from some customer constituencies, they may conclude that only very exceptional candidates will be able to succeed in such a position. Also, to the extent that the senior managers themselves (the vast majority of whom are white) feel more comfortable with racioethnically similar peers and direct reports, they may be more prone to give white candidates "the benefit of the doubt" in such areas as achievement motivation and interpersonal trust.

The double-standard discussion inevitably raises the issue of affirmative action. Some would argue that the presence of affirmative action creates a double standard in which nonwhite candidates are subject to *less* rigorous evaluation criteria. Responding fully to this argument would require a lengthy and complicated discussion that is beyond the bounds of this reading. One response, however, is that whatever advantage affirmative action offers to nonwhites must be viewed within the context of the various forms of adverse discrimination that it is designed to address.

Several studies have addressed the extent to which nonwhites are segregated into certain kinds of jobs in predominantly white organizations. In a lab experiment using fictitious job applicant résumés, Terpstra and Larsen (1985) found that some jobs were stereotyped according to racioethnic identities of the applicant. Similar findings are reported by Stone and Stone (1987). Finally, Collins (1989) addressed the question of whether or not nonwhite managers tend to be segregated into staff jobs and particularly human relations, personnel, and community affairs. Based on interviews with 76 of the highest-ranking black managers in majority-white organizations, she determined that 66 percent of the sample entered and advanced through the managerial ranks in "racialized" jobs (i.e., jobs created to handle black consumer issues or civil rights-related matters). For a majority of the sample (51 percent), their last job held in the predominantly white sector was a racially oriented personnel or public relations job. Collins notes that nearly a third of these managers were working in more mainstream functions of their organizations when requested by superiors to accept racially oriented jobs. She further argues that the emphasis on these career paths for black executives made them unlikely candidates for further advancement because top managers in the private sector are rarely drawn from human relations or community affairs functions. Examination of the career paths of CEOs of large American firms (such as is provided in the 1990 annual *Business Week* 1000 profile) makes it clear that the critical career path for senior management positions has historically been finance (24 percent), marketing (25 percent), or operations/engineering (26 percent), but certainly not human resources, (0 percent) and community relations (0 percent). Therefore, Collins' premise that functional segregation of nonwhites is a major cause of their absence from top management seems well founded.

M. Additional Suggestions for Future Research

Much of our thinking on the implications of past research for future theory and research has already been communicated in the process of reviewing the literature. Further, we have noted elsewhere (Cox and Nkomo, 1990) that previous organizational research on racioethnicity has suffered from: (1) an absence of theory or the use of overly simplistic and underdeveloped theoretical frameworks; (2) incomplete or inappropriate operationalizations of the concept of race itself (especially ignoring the cultural significance of race and intragroup differences in levels of racioethnic identity); and (3) failure to use multigroup samples and to address nonwhite samples other than blacks.

This said, we will address here several promising directions for future work that were not identified earlier. As suggested in the introduction to our review, previous work on racioethnicity in the OB literature has tended to address traditional OB topics for two biologically differentiated racioethnic groups (e.g., differences in motivational structures between blacks and whites). We believe that the quest to understand how organizational processes are influenced by racioethnicity will be well served if future work gives added emphasis to: (1) cultural dynamics of race, (2) intergroup theory, (3) the intersection of racioethnicity and gender, and (4) the theory of everyday racism. Each of these will be briefly discussed.

III. The Cultural Dynamics of Race

While the biological aspects of racioethnicity are undeniably important, a considerable literature in social psychology suggests that African-Americans, Chinese-Americans, Mexican-Americans, native Americans, and other minority groups also represent distinct cultural groups. For example, Cox, Lobel, and McLeod (1991) have noted differences in cultural traditions among black, Asian, Hispanic, and white Americans in the extent to which individualistic versus collective behaviors are favored. They found that from a knowledge of these differences they could predict that members of these nonwhite groups would display higher levels of cooperative versus competitive behavior in a two-party mixed motive game. Another example is Kochman's work (1981) on differences in communication styles between cohorts of white and black Americans born in the late 1940s and 1950s. He shows numerous examples of how ignorance of these differences creates potential for misunderstanding and leads to unsatisfying cross-group interactions. Numerous other writers have also addressed the cultural distinc-

tiveness of different racioethnic groups (e.g., Fernandez, 1981; Triandis and Malpass, 1971; 1976; Foeman and Pressley, 1987; Leung and Bond, 1984; de Forest, 1984). Since organizations also represent specific cultural constellations (Denison, 1990; Sales and Mirvus, 1984; Meyerson and Martin, 1987), the issues of cultural intersection and potential culture clash deserve attention. Examples of emerging work that addresses these issues include the work of Bell (1990) on bicultural identity, Cox and Nickelson's (1991) theory of intraorganizational acculturation, and empirical studies that apply ethnology research to the organizational context (e.g., Cox, Lobel, and McLeod, 1991; Farh, Dobbins, and Cheng, 1991; James and Khoo, in press). Additional work of this type is needed.

IV. Intergroup Theory

Various branches of intergroup theory also hold a wealth of relatively untapped potential for work on racioethnic effects on organization behavior. We will mention two that we believe are especially promising. The embedded group theory (Alderfer, 1987; Alderfer and Smith, 1982) has been successfully applied to race-relations research in the organizational context. Alderfer and Smith (1982) argue that relationships between people are embedded in a network of affiliations that include both personal identity groups (e.g., ethnicity, gender, age) and task groups (e.g., organization level, functional specialization). These affiliations, in turn, occur in a context that is a mixture of intraorganizational and external environment. Understanding transactions between individuals therefore requires an understanding of the group affiliation profile of the parties as well as the social-political backdrop within which the parties interact. The theory acknowledges that individuals have multiple identities, and that the meaning of these identities must be understood in the context of the organizational and societal history of interaction of the identity groups. For example, the theory would predict that the relationship between a black manager and a white subordinate would be hindered by the fact that relationships between blacks and whites in America have historically featured the domination of whites over blacks. Understanding the interaction is further complicated by the other group affiliations of the respective parties. For example, if the manager is also a woman and the subordinate is a man, successful interaction will be even more difficult unless there is special attention to the relationship by both parties.

A second line of work within the domain of intergroup theory that we find especially promising for work on racioethnicity in OB is that on minority group density (Kanter, 1977a, b; Blalock, 1967; Pettigrew and Martin, 1987). In general, this work seeks to explicate the impact of proportional representation of a particular minority group identity in the larger group (density) on behavior and work outcomes. Kanter's thesis, which was developed from empirical work on gender and not racioethnicity, is that organizational experience of minorities will become more positive as their density increases. Blalock (following logic originally suggested by Key's studies of voting behavior of whites in the South, 1949; 1964) found that the experience of minorities may actually become more negative as density increases if the majority group feels threatened by the greater representation. Both arguments have received some empirical support. Additional research is needed not only to clarify how density affects behavior in organizations but also to provide guidance on how to respond to these effects. For example, if the Kanter thesis is correct, is affirmative action the most effective response? If the Blalock thesis is correct, how can perceived threat among majority group members be minimized?

V. Racioethnicity and Gender

Few studies have examined the intersection of racioethnicity and gender effects on organizational experiences. Nonwhite women are typically subsumed alternately under the category "women" or "minorities." Their combined identity as black, Asian, or Hispanic women is often invisible, as they fall between the cracks of the two streams of research (Nkomo, 1988). There is an emerging body of literature that indicates that the combined and interactive effects of racioethnicity and gender have a pervasive impact on the lives of nonwhite women (Leggon, 1980; Bell, 1986; Nkomo and Cox, 1989; Thomas, 1989; Greenhaus, Parasuraman, and Wormley, 1990). A central issue in much of this early work has been whether or not the combined effects of racioethnicity and gender produce a double advantage or double disadvantage. While most researchers have recognized the effect as cumulative, they differ on whether it is positive or negative (Bell, Denton, and Nkomo, forthcoming). The double-advantage view holds that minority women enjoy positive effects from their dual identities (Epstein, 1973), while the double-whammy hypothesis suggests the net effect of racioethnicity and gender is negative for minority women (King, 1988; Benjamin, 1982).

In a study of black professionals, Nkomo and Cox (1989) examined the validity of the double-advantage and double-whammy hypotheses for black women managers. Although overall results supported neither hypothesis, the researchers did find that the black women had higher job performance ratings and were at about the same hierarchical level as the black men, but that the women received significantly lower pay.

Woo (1985) examined the notion of advantaged status of Asian-American women. In her study of census data, she found that while education enhanced earnings capability, the relative gains made by Asian-American women were not as great as those made by other women and were well below parity with white males.

Romero (1986) tested the double-advantage hypothesis for Chicano women and found that the slow pace of the movement of Chicanos into higher-paying managerial and skilled positions did not support the claim of "preferential treatment." Other organizational researchers using cross-race, cross-gender designs, have reported significant interaction effects of racioethnicity and gender (Greenhaus, Parasuraman, and Wormley, 1990; Thomas, 1989). The available research suggests that the intersection between race and gender is complex and problematic and that we cannot assume that the experience of nonwhite women is similar to the experiences of nonwhite men, nor can we assume that the experiences of nonwhite women are the same as of white women. Therefore, organizational scholars must increase the utilization of research designs that examine the interactive effects of racioethnicity and gender.

VI. Everyday Racism

Essed (1991) has developed what she calls a theory of everyday racism which combines the daily experiences of individuals with a more structural account of racism. Her theoretical framework draws on work from the literature of macro- and microsociology, social psychology, discourse analysis, race relations theory, and women's studies. According to Essed (1991: 50)

> Everyday racism is the integration of racism into everyday situations through practices (cognitive and behavioral) that activate underlying power relations. This process must be seen as a continuum through which the integration of racism into everyday practices becomes part of the expected, of the unquestionable, and of what is seen as normal by the dominant group.

According to her analysis, racist beliefs and actions permeate everyday life and become embedded in human systems so that they tend to reproduce themselves. Essed (1991) identifies three main mechanisms of everyday racism: marginalization, problematization, and containment. Marginalization is a process in which a sense of "otherness" is perpetuated, while problematization refers to ideological constructions legitimizing exclusion and repression of certain groups. For example, problematization involves the hierarchical ordering of differences between groups according to biological, cultural, or value differences (e.g., European culture as superior to African or Asian culture). Containment suggests efforts by the dominant group to suppress the efforts of dominated groups for equality, justice, and power.

The theory of everyday racism suggests that research on racioethnicity in organizations must identify and examine the rules, policies, conditions, and power relations that tend to reproduce racism in "everyday organizational situations." Concomitantly, we need to explore how racism is systematically represented in events and language (often assumed to be neutral) in the daily routine of organizations. An example of language use is the often-stated emphasis on the word "qualified" when seeking a minority job candidate. Often the hidden belief behind the use of the word is the assumed pervasiveness of the inferiority of members of racioethnic groups.

Everyday racism also suggests that individuals in organizations are involved differently in the process of racism because of their position in the power structure. Gender, class, and other factors determine the content and structure of racism. For example, the experience of racism for African-American women, while similar to that of African-American men, may have qualitatively different features. Essed (1991) has labeled the experience of racioethnic women as gendered racism. In like fashion, the racism of dominant group women may be qualitatively different than that of dominant group men because of the position of women in the power structure. Research drawing upon the concepts of everyday racism may help unmask the subtle and covert nature of racism today and should contribute toward identifying both individual and structural strategies for eradicating racism in organizations.

VII. Conclusion

This chapter has reviewed and analyzed organizational literature on racioethnicity. Suggestions for future research have been described. In conclusion, we offer several summary comments.

First, it seems clear that the base of knowledge about how racioethnic diversity impacts behavior in organizations remains woefully underdeveloped. Second, there is a considerable base of knowledge about the effects of racioethnicity in the society at large that has not been adequately applied to the organizational context. Finally, there is a great need for work that more adequately reflects the complexity of racioethnic phenomena in organizations. We are encouraged that several streams of work in the OB domain have emerged in the last few years that we believe address long-neglected, but critical dimensions of that complexity.

REFERENCES

Adams, A. V., Krislov, J., and Lairson, D. R. (1972). Plantwide seniority, black employment, and employer affirmative action. *Industrial and Labor Relations Review, 26:* 686–690.

Adams, E. F. (1978). A multivariate study of subordinate perceptions of and attitudes toward minority and majority managers. *Journal of Applied Psychology, 63*(3), 277–288.

Alderfer, C. P., Alderfer, C. J., Tucker, L., and Tucker, R. (1980). Diagnosing race relations in management. *J. of Applied Behavioral Science, 16:* 135–166.

Alderfer, C. P., and Smith, K. K. (1982). Studying intergroup relations embedded in organizations. *Administrative Science Quarterly, 27:* 35–65.

Alper, S. W. (1975). Racial differences in job and work environment priorities among newly hired college graduates. *J. of Applied Psychology, 60:* 120–134.

Arnold, H. J., and Feldman, D. C. (1986). *Organizational Behavior.* McGraw-Hill, New York.

Arvey, R. D., and Faley, R. H. (1988). *Fairness In Selecting Employees.* Addison-Wesley Publishing Company, Reading, Mass.

Barr, S. H., and Hitt, M. A. (1986). A comparison of selection decision models in manager versus student samples. *Personnel Psychology, 39:* 599–617.

Bartlett, C. J., and O'Leary, B. S. (1969). A differential prediction model to moderate the effects of heterogeneous groups in personnel selection and classification. *Personnel Psychology, 2:* 1–18.

Bartol, K. M., Anderson, C. R., and Schneier, J. (1981). Sex and ethnic effects on motivation to manage among college business students. *Journal of Applied Psychology, 66:* 40–44.

Bartol, K. M., Evans, C. L., and Stith, M. (1978). Black versus white leaders: A comparative review of the literature. *3:* 294–304.

Bass, A., and Turner, J. (1973). Ethnic group differences in relationship among criteria of job performance. *J. of Applied Psychology, 7:* 101–109.

Bayroff, A. (1966). Test technology and equal employment opportunity. *Personnel Psychology, 7:* 191–209.

Beatty, D. (1990). Re-examining the link between job characteristics and job satisfaction. *J. of Social Psychology, 130:* 131–132.

Beatty, R. W. (1973). Blacks as supervisors: A study of training, job performance, and employers' expectations. *Academy of Management Journal, 16:* 196–206.

Bell, E. (1986). The power within: Bicultural life structures and stress among black women, Ph.D. dissertation, Case Western Reserve University.

Bell, E. L. (1990). The bicultural life experience of career-oriented black women. *J. of Organizational Behavior, 11:* 459–477.

Bell, E., Denton, T., and Nkomo, S. M. (1993). Women of color in management: Towards an inclusive analysis. In *Women in Management: Trends, Perspectives and Challenges* (E. Fagenson, ed.), Sage Publications, Newbury Park, Calif.

Benjamin, L. (1982). Black women achievers: An isolated elite. *Sociological Inquiry, 52:* 141–151.

Bigoness, W. (1976). Effect of applicants' sex, race, and performance on employers' ratings: Some additional findings. *J. of Applied Psychology, 61:* 80–84.

Blalock, H. Jr. (1967). *Toward a Theory of Minority-Group Relations.* John Wiley & Sons, New York.

Boehm, V. R. (1972). Negro-white differences in validity of employment testing and training selection procedures. *Journal of Applied Psychology, 57:* 101–109.

Boehm, V. R. (1977). Differential prediction—a methodological artifact. *J. of Applied Psychology, 62:* 146–154.

Brett, E. A., and Morse, S. J. (1975). A study of the attitudes of middle-class Africans. In *Contemporary South Africa: Social Psychological Perspectives* (S. J. Morse and C. Orpen, eds.), Juta, Cape Town, pp. 154–167.

Brown, H. A., and Ford, D. L., Jr. (1977). An explanatory analysis of discrimination in the employment of black MBA graduates. *J. of Applied Psychology, 62:* 50–56.

Brugnoli, G., Campion, J., and Basen, Jr. (1979). Racial bias in the use of work samples for personnel selection. *J. of Applied Psychology, 64:* 119–123.

Carter, R. T., and Swanson, J. L. (1990). The validity of the strong interest inventory with black Americans: A review of the literature. *J. of Vocational Behavior, 36:* 195–209.

Chusmir, L. H., and Koberg, C. S. (1990). Ethnic differences in the relationship between job satisfaction and sex-role conflict among Hispanics and nonhispanic white individuals. *Psychological Reports, 66:* 567–578.

Collins, S. M. (1989). The marginalization of black executives. *Social Problems, 36*(4): 317–331.

Cox, J. A., and Kr;uboltz, J. D. (1958). Racial bias in peer ratings of basic airmen. *Sociometry, 21:* 292–299.

Cox, T. H. (1990). Problems with research by organizational scholars on issues of race and ethnicity. *The Journal of Applied Behavioral Science, 26*(1): 5–24.

Cox, T. H., and Finley-Nickelson, J. (1991). Models of acculturation for intra-organizational cultural diversity. *Canadian Journal of Administrative Sciences, 8*(2): 90–100.

Cox, T. H., Lobel, S., and Mcleod, P. (1991). Effects of ethnic group cultural difference on cooperative versus competitive behavior in a group task. *Academy of Management Journal, 34:* 827–847.

Cox, T. H., and Nkomo, S. M. (1986). Differential appraisal criteria based on race of the ratee. *Group and Organizational Studies, 11:* 101–119.

Cox, T. H., and Nkomo, S. M. (1990). Invisible men and women: A status report on race as a variable in organizational behavior and research. *J. of Organizational Behavior, 11:* 419–431.

Crooks, L. A., ed. (1972). *An Investigation of Sources of Bias in the Prediction of Job Performance: A Six Year Study.* Educational Testing Service, Princeton, N.J.

Dalton, A. H., and Marcis, J. G. (1986). The determinants of job satisfaction for young males and females. *Atlantic Economic Journal, 14:* 85.

deFrost, M. E. (1984). Spanish-speaking employees in American industry. *Business Horizons, 27:* 14–17.

Dejung, J. E., and Kaplan, H. (1962). Some differential effects of race of rater and ratee on early peer ratings of combat aptitude. *J. of Applied Psychology, 46:* 370–374.

Delbecq, A. L., and Kaplan, S. D. (1968). The myth of the indigenous community leader within the war on poverty. *Academy of Management Journal, 11:* 11–25.

DeMeuse, K. P. (1987). A review of the effects of nonverbal cues on the performance appraisal process. *J. of Occupational Psychology, 60:* 207–226.

Denison, D. (1990). *Corporate Culture and Organizational Effectiveness.* John Wiley & Sons, New York.

Dickens, F., and Dickens, J. B. (1982). *The Black Manager.* Amacom, New York.

Dipboye, R. L. (1985). Some neglected variables in research on discrimination in appraisals. *Academy of Management Review, 10:* 116–127.

Dugan, R. (1966). Current problems in test performance of job applicants: II. *Personnel Psychology, 19:* 18–24.

Epstein, C. F. (1973). Positive effects of the multiple negative: Explaining the success of black professional women, *American Journal of Sociology, 78*(4): 912–935.

Essed, P. (1991). *Understanding Everyday Racism: An Interdisciplinary Theory.* Sage Publications, Newbury Park, Calif.

Farh, J. L., Dobbins, G. H., and Cheng, B. S. (1991). Cultural relativity in action: A comparison of self-ratings made by Chinese and U.S. workers. *Personnel Psychology,* 129–147.

Feldman, J. (1973). Race, economic class, and perceived outcomes of work and unemployment. *J. of Applied Psychology, 58:* 16–22.

Fernandez, J. P. (1975). *Black Managers in White Corporations.* John Wiley, New York.

Fernandez, J. P. (1981). *Racism and Sexism in Corpo-*

rate Life: Changing Values in American Business. Lexington Books, Lexington, Mass.

Fernandez, J. P. (1987). *Survival in the Corporate Fishbowl.* Lexington Books, Lexington, Mass.

Fine, M. G., Johnson, F. L., and Ryan, M. S. (1990). Cultural diversity in the workplace. *Public Personnel Management, 19*(3): 305–318.

Foeman, A. K., and Pressley, G. (1987). Ethnic culture and corporate culture: Using black styles in organizations. *Communications Quarterly, 35:* 293–307.

Gatewood, R. D., and Feild, H. (1990). *Human Resource Selection.* The Dryden Press, Chicago.

Gavin, J., and Ewen, R. (1974). Racial differences in job attitudes and performance—some theoretical considerations and empirical findings. *Personnel Psychology, 27:* 455–464.

Greenhaus, J. H., and Gavin, J. F. (1972). The relationship between expectancies and job behavior from white and black employees. *Personnel Psychology, 25:* 449–455.

Greenhaus, J. H., and Parasuraman, S. (in press). Job performance attributions and career advancement prospects: An examination of gender and race effects. In *Organizational Behavior and Human Decision Processes.*

Greenhaus, J. H., Parasuraman, S., and Wormley, W. (1990). Effects of race on organizational experiences, job performance evaluation, and career outcomes. *Academy of Management Journal, 33:* 64–86.

Hamner, W. C., Kim, J. S., Baird, L., and Bigoness, W. J. (1974). Race and sex as determinants of ratings by potential employers in a simulated work-sampling task. *J. of Applied Psychology, 59:* 705–711.

Helms, J. E., and Giorgis, T. W. (1980). A comparison of the locus of control and anxiety level of African, black American and white American college students. *J. of College Student Personnel,* 503–509.

Herzerg, F., Mausner, B., and Snyderman, B. B. (1959). *The Motivation to Work.* John Wiley & Sons, Inc., New York.

Hill, W. H., and Fox, W. M. (1973). Black and white marine squad leaders' perceptions of racially mixed squads. *Academy of Management Journal, 16:* 680–686.

Hunter, J. E., and Schmidt, F. L., and Hunter, R. (1979). Differential validity of employment tests by race: A critical analysis of three studies. *J. of Applied Psychology, 63:* 1–11.

Hunter, J. E., Schmidt, F. L., and Hunter, R. (1979). Differential validity of employment tests by race: A comprehensive review and analysis. *Psychological Bulletin, 85:* 721–735.

Ilgen, D. R., and Youtz, M. A. (1986). Factors affecting the evaluation and development of minorities in organizations. In *Research in Personnel and Human Resource Management: A Research Annual* (K. Bowland and G. Ferris, eds.), JAI Press, Greenwich, Conn., pp. 307–337.

Ivancevich, J. M., and McMahon, J. T. (1977). Black-white differences in a goal-setting program organization. *Behavior and Human Performance, 20:* 287–300.

Jackson, M. (1979). Racial factors in executive selection. *Public Personnel Management, 8:* 218–222.

James, K., and Khoo, G. (1991). Identity-related influences on the success of minority workers in primarily nonminority organizations. *Hispanic Journal of Behavioral Sciences.*

Johnston, W., and Packard, A. (1987). *Workforce 2000: Work and Worker for the 21st Century.* Hudson Institute, Indianapolis.

Jones, A. P., James, L. R., Bruni, J. R., and Sells, S. B. (1977). Black white differences in work environment perceptions and job satisfaction and its correlates. *Personnel Psychology, 30:* 5–16.

Jones, E. W. (1973). What's it like to be a black manager? *Harvard Business Review, 51:* 108–116.

Jones, E. W. (1986). Black managers: The dream deferred. *Harvard Business Review, 64:* 84–93.

Jussim, L., Coleman, L., and Lerch, L. (1987). The nature of stereotypes: A comparison and integration of three theories. *Journal of Personality and Social Psychology, 52*(3), 536–546.

Kahoe, R. D. (1974). A negro-white difference in psychological meaning of job incentives. *J. of Social Psychology, 92:* 157–158.

Kanter, R. M. (1977a). Some effects of proportions on group life: Skewed sex ratios and responses to token women. *American Journal of Sociology, 82:* 965–991.

Kanter, R. M. (1977b). *Men and Women of the Corporation.* Basic Books, New York.

Kerr, S., and Jermier, J. (1978). Substitutes for leadership: Their meaning and measurement. *Organizational Behavior and Human Performance, 22:* 375–403.

Key, V. O. Jr. (1949). *Southern Politics.* Random House, Inc., New York.

Key, V. O. Jr. (1964). *Politics, Parties, and Pressure Groups.* Thomas Crowell Co., New York.

Kimberly, J., and Quinn, R. (1984). *New Futures: Managing Corporate Transitions.* Dow Jones-Irwin, Homewood, Ill.

King, D. (1988). Multiple jeopardy, multiple consciousness: The context of a black feminist ideology. *Signs, 14:* 42–72.

Kipnis, D., Silverman, A., and Copeland, C. (1973). Effects of emotional arousal on the use of supervised coercion with black and union members. *J. of Applied Psychology, 57:* 38–43.

Kleiman, L. S., Biderman, M. D., and Faley, R. H. (1987). An examination of employee perceptions of a subjective performance appraisal system. *J. of Business and Psychology, 2:* 112–121.

Kochman, T. (1981). *Black and White Styles In Conflict.* University of Chicago Press, Chicago.

Konar, E. (1981). Explaining racial differences in job satisfaction: A reexamination of the data. *J. of Applied Psychology, 66:* 522–524.

Kraiger, K., and Ford, J. (1985). A meta-analysis of ratee race effects in performance ratings. *J. of Applied Psychology, 70:* 56–65.

LaFree, G. D. (1980). The effect of sexual stratification by race on official reactions to rape. *American Sociological Review, 45:* 842–854.

Landy, F. J., and Farr, S. L. (1976). Police performance appraisal, *JSAS Catalog of Selected Documents in Psychology, 6:* 83 (ms. No., 1315).

Landy, F. J., and Farr, S. L. (1980). Performance rating. *Psychological Bulletin, 87:* 72–107.

Lefcourt, H. M., and Ladwig, G. W. (1965). Effect of reference group upon negroes' task persistence in a biracial competitive game. *J. of Psychology & Social Psychology, 1:* 668–671.

Lefkowitz, J. (1972). Differential validity: Ethnic groups as a moderator in predicting tenure. *Personnel Psychology, 25:* 223–240.

Lefkowitz, J., and Fraser, A. W. (1980). Assessment of achievement and power motivation of black and white, using a black and white TAT, with black and white administration. *J. of Applied Psychology, 65*(6): 685–696.

Leggon, C. B. (1980). Black female professionals: Dilemmas and contradictions of status. In *The Black Women* (La Frances Rodgers-Rose, ed.), Sage Publications, Beverly Hills, Calif.

Lueng, K., and Bond, M. (1984). The impact of cultural collection on reward allocation. *J. of Personality & Social Psychology, 47*(4): 805–811.

Maslow, A. H., (1954). *Motivation and Personality.* Harper & Row, New York.

Massey, D. S., and Denton, N. A. (1988). Suburbanization and segregation in U.S. metropolitan areas. *American Journal of Sociology, 94:* 592–626.

McClelland, D. C. (1961). *The Achieving Society.* Van Nostrand, Princeton, N.J.

McClelland, D. C. (1974). Effects of interviewer-respondent race interactions on household interview measures of motivation and intelligence. *J. of Personality and Social Psychology, 29:* 392–397.

McIntyre, S., Moberg, D., Posner, B., and Newman, J. (1980). Discrimination in recruitment: An empirical analysis-comment-reply. *Industrial & Labor Relations Review, 33:* 543–550.

McNeely, R. L. (1987). Predictors of job satisfaction among three racial/ethnic groups of professional female human service workers. *J. of Sociology & Social Welfare, 14:* 115–136.

Meyerson, D. E., and Martin, J. (1987). Culture change: An integration of three different views. *J. of Management Studies, 24:* 623–647.

Milutinovich, J. S., and Tsaklanganos, A. (1976). The impact of perceived community prosperity on job satisfaction of black and white workers. *Academy of Management Journal, 19:* 49–65.

Mobley, W. (1982). Supervisor and employee race and sex effects on performance appraisals: A field study of adverse impact and generalizability. *Academy of Management Journal, 25:* 598–606.

Moch, M. (1980). Racial differences in job satisfaction: Testing four common explanations. *J. of Applied Psychology, 65:* 299–306.

Moore, C. Jr., and MacNaughton, J. (1979). Ethnic differences within an industrial selection battery. *Personnel Psychology, 22:* 473–482.

Morishima, J. (1981). Special employment issues for Asian Americans. *Public Personnel Management Journal, 10*(4): 384–392.

Mueller, C. W., Tanaka, K., and Parcel, T. L. (1989). Particularism in authority outcomes of black and white supervisors. *Social Science Research, 18:* 1–20.

Mullins, T. W. (1982). Interviewer decisions as a function of applicant race, applicant quality and interviewer prejudice. *Personnel Psychology, 35:* 163–174.

Newman, J. M. (1978). Discrimination in recruitment: An empirical analysis. *Industrial and Labor Relations Review, 32:* 15–23.

Nkomo, S. M. (1988). Race and sex: The forgotten case of the black female manager. In *Women's Careers: Pathways and Pitfalls* (S. Rose and L. Larwood, eds.), Praeger, New York.

Nkomo, S. M., and Cox, T. Jr. (1989). Gender differences in the factors affecting the upward mobility of black managers. *Sex Roles, 21:* 825–835.

Nkomo, S. M., and Cox, T. H. Jr. (1990). Factors affecting the upward mobility of black managers. *Review of Black Political Economy, 18.*

O'Reilly, C. A., and Roberts, K. M. (1973). Job satisfaction among whites and nonwhites: A cross cultural approach. *J. of Applied Psychology, 57:* 295–299.

Orpen, C., and Nkohande, J. (May 1977). Self-esteem, interval control and expectancy beliefs of white and black managers in South Africa. *J. of Management Studies:* 192–199.

Parker, W. S. (1976). Black white differences in leader behavior related to subordinates' reactions. *J. of Applied Psychology, 61,* 140–147.

Parson, C. K., and Liden, R. C. (1984). Interviewer perceptions of applicant qualifications: A multivariate field study of demographic characteristics and nonverbal cues. *J. of Applied Psychology, 69:* 557–568.

Pettigrew, T. F., and Martin, J. (1987). Shaping the organizational context for black American inclusion. *J. of Social Forces, 43:* 41–78.

Porter, L., and Lawler III, E. E. *Managerial Attitudes and Performance.* Dorsey Press, Chicago.

Pulakos, E. D., Oppler, S. H., White, L. A., and Borman, W. C. (1989). Examination of race and sex effects on performance ratings. *J. of Applied Psychology, 74:* 770–780.

Ramirez, A. (1989). Racism toward Hispanics: The culturally monolithic society. In *Eliminating Racism* (P. A. Katz and D. A. Taylor, eds.), Plenum Press, New York, pp. 137–153.

Richards, S. A., and Jaffee, C. L. (1972). Blacks supervising whites: A study of interracial difficulties in working together in a simulated organization. *J. of Applied Psychology, 56:* 234–240.

Romero, M. (1986). Twice protected? Assessing the impact of affirmative action on Mexican-American women. In *Ethnicity and Women* (W. A. Van Horne and T. V. Tonnesen, eds.), pp. 135–156.

Ruda, E., and Allrights, L. (1968). Racial differences on selection instruments related to subsequent job performance. *Personnel Psychology, 2:* 31–41.

Sales, A. L., and Mirvis, P. H. (1984). When cultures collide: Issues of acquisition. In *Managing Organizational Transitions* (J. R. Kimberly and R. E. Quinn, eds.), Irwin, Homewood, Ill., pp. 107–133.

Schmidt, F. L., and Johnson, R. H. (1973). Effect of race on peer ratings in an industrial setting. *J. of Applied Psychology, 57:* 237–241.

Schmitt, N., and Lappin, M. (1980). Race and sex as determinants of the mean and variance of performance ratings. *J. of Applied Psychology, 65:* 428–435.

Shiflett, S. (1988). Effects of race and criterion on the predictive ability of beliefs and attitudes. *Psychological Reports, 62:* 527–535.

Shull, F. Anthony (1978). Do black and white supervisory problem-solving styles differ? *Personnel Psychology, 56:* 28–32.

Slocum, J. Jr., and Strawser, R. (1972). Racial differences in job attitudes. *J. of Applied Psychology, 56:* 28–32.

Slovic, P., and Lichtenstein, S. (1971). Comparison of Bayesian and regression approaches to the study of information processing in judgment. *Organizational Behavior & Human Performance, 6:* 649–711.

Stone, D. L., and Stone, E. F. (1987). Effects of missing application blank information on personnel selection decisions: Do privacy protection strategies bias the outcome? *J. of Applied Psychology, 58:* 16–22.

Terpstra, D., and Larsen, M. (1985). A note on job type and applicant race as determinants of hiring decisions. *J. of Occupational Psychology, 53:* 117–119.

Thomas, D. (1989). Mentoring and irrationality: The role of racial taboos. *Human Resource Management, 28:* 279–290.

Toole, D. (1972). The differential validity of personality, personal history, and aptitude data for minority and nonminority employees. *Personnel Psychology, 25:* 661–672.

Triandis, H. C., and Malpass, R. S. (1971). Studies of black and white interracial and job settings. *J. of Applied Social Psychology, 1:* 107–117.

U.S. Department of Labor (1991). A report on the glass ceiling initiative.

Vecchio, R. (1980). Worker alienation as a moderator of the job quality–job satisfaction relationship: The case of racial differences. *Academy of Management Journal, 23:* 479–486.

Vroom, V. H. (1964). *Work and Motivation.* Wiley, New York.

Watson, J. G., and Barone, S. (1976). The self-concept, personal values, and motivational orientation of black and white managers. *Academy of Management Journal, 19:* 36–48.

Weaver, C. N. (1975). Black-white differences in attitudes toward job characteristics. *J. of Applied Psychology, 60:* 438–441.

Weaver, C. N. (1978). Black-white correlates of job satisfaction. *J. of Applied Psychology, 63:* 255–258.

Weitz, S. (1972). Attitude, voice and behavior: Repressed affect model of interracial interaction. *J. of Personality and Social Psychology, 24:* 14–21.

Williams, N. (1988). Role making among married Mexican-American women: Issues of class and ethnicity. *J. of Applied Behavioral Science, 24:* 203–217.

Williams, R. L. (1975). The Bitch-100: A culture-specific test. *J. of Afro-American Issues, 3:* 103–116.

Woo, D. (1985). The socioeconomic status of Asian-American women in the labor force: An alternative view. *Sociological Perspectives, 28:* 307–338.

Word, C. O., Zanna, M. P., and Cooper, J. (1974). The nonverbal mediation of self-fulfilling prophecies in interracial interaction. *J. of Experimental Social Psychology, 10:* 109–120.

Wright, R., King, S. W., Berg, W. E., and Creecy, R. F. (1987). Job satisfaction among black female managers: A causal approach. *Human Relations, 40:* 489–506.

NATIONAL CULTURE AND MANAGEMENT

What is the role of national culture in business and management? Do various cultures differ in their approaches to management, and if so, in what ways? What problems are encountered when doing business across cultures, and what can managers do about them?

These questions are becoming increasingly important as more and more business is conducted across national lines. Just a few years ago, only a small percentage of Americans had direct dealings with managers from other countries. But now, as many American firms have wholly-owned foreign affiliates, as others have

This note was prepared by Philip M. Rosenzweig.
Copyright © 1994 by the President and Fellows of Harvard College.
Harvard Business School note 394-177.

been acquired by foreign firms, and as still others are participating in international joint ventures or strategic alliances, American managers are working directly with people from all over the world. For a growing number of managers, working in a cross-cultural environment is a fact of daily life.

Yet the relationship between culture and management is not clearly understood. At one extreme, some people doubt that culture has any impact on management at all. They find it easier to claim that human behavior is basically the same all over the world, that "business is business everywhere." This view, although convenient, is naive in that it fails to recognize that fundamental differences exist among people around the world. It may also be dangerous in that it does not alert managers to challenges they face in a cross-cultural setting.

At the other extreme, some people exaggerate the importance of culture, using it to explain almost everything that involves more than one country. For example, the superior performance of Japanese firms during the 1970s and 1980s was frequently attributed to some unspecified attribute of "Japanese culture," rather than to manufacturing practices or quality techniques or government policies that may have had little, if anything, to do with culture. Similarly, when frictions arise during negotiations between firms from different countries it is easy to blame "cultural difficulties," when in fact these same frictions may arise in almost any negotiations, whether domestic or international. Just because a conflict involves firms from different countries doesn't mean that the problem is cultural in nature.

Why should it be difficult to understand the relationship between culture and management? Part of the problem can be traced to a lack of clarity about the concept of "culture." Exactly what is culture, anyway? In what ways do cultures differ? If we cannot offer clear answers to these questions, our ability to speak meaningfully about culture will never advance far. A second problem lies in the tendency to assume that all members of a culture behave in an identical fashion—that is, to think in terms of cultural stereotypes. Many people are reluctant to address a topic that involves sweeping generalizations and therefore avoid the topic altogether. Finally, part of the problem lies in a lack of systematic thinking about the ways that culture is manifested in business settings. Even if we believe that cultures differ, and even if we avoid the pitfall of stereotypes, how do cultural differences affect managers? A useful treatment of culture and management should be able to relate culture, at a broad level, to specific aspects of management.

This note takes a systematic approach to the discussion of culture. It begins by offering a working definition of culture, and goes on to explore the many levels at which cultures exist. Next, it identifies some of the ways that national cultures differ by presenting the findings of two leading researchers, Edward Hall and Geert Hofstede. It then suggests a number of ways that these cultural traits are manifested in business settings, and offers some implications for practicing managers. Its goal is neither to deny nor to exaggerate the importance of culture in management, but to offer a systematic way of thinking about culture, and as a consequence, to provide a benefit to practicing managers.

Defining Culture

Culture is a complex concept and eludes a simple definition. Anthropologists, psychologists, sociologists, and organizational theorists have offered somewhat different definitions of culture. Although we cannot provide a single definition that is acceptable to all, we can offer a working definition of culture as a *shared system of meaning, ideas, and thought*. It is a code through which patterns of conduct are communicated and deciphered through the use of words, gestures, and objects. Culture is powerful because it guides our perception and understanding of the world, and in turn it shapes our behavior. One scholar has called culture the "software of the mind" because much like a computer's operating system it provides us with an essential code by which we make sense of the world.[1]

Two leading scholars, John van Maanen and André Laurent, have described the pervasive role that culture plays in our lives:

[Culture] provides members with images of their basic concerns, principles, ethics, and bodies of manners, rituals, ideologies, strategies, and tactics of self-survival, including certain notions of good deeds and bad, various forms of folklore and legends, and a set of ideas that allows something of a "consciousness of kind" to emerge such that the rough boundaries of demarcation can be drawn between (and among) members and non-members.[2]

Culture is acquired naturally early in life through interaction with others. Van Maanen and Laurent continue:

The way we give logic to the world begins at birth with the gestures, words, tone of voice, noises, colors, smells, and body contact we experience; with the way we are raised, washed, rewarded, punished, held in check, toilet-trained and fed; by the stories we are told, the games we play, the songs we sing or rhymes we recite; the schooling we receive, the jobs we hold, and the careers we follow; right down to the very way we sleep and dream. *Our culture is what is familiar, recognizable, habitual, It is "what goes without saying."* (Emphasis added.)

Most of the time we are not aware of our culture at all—what we do seems entirely normal.

1. Geert Hofstede. *Cultures and Organizations: Software of the Mind* (London: McGraw-Hill Book Company, Ltd., 1991).

2. John Van Maanen and André Laurent, "The Flow of Culture: Some Notes on Globalization and the Multinational Corporation," in *Organization Theory and the Multinational Corporation,* ed. Sumantra Ghoshal and D. Eleanor Westney, (New York: St. Martin's Press, 1993).

It is when cultures meet, when we find ourselves in contact with people from other cultures, that we become aware of its existence. At first we may only note that others are somehow "different." With time and practice, however, we may come to see what is distinctive in our own culture, and may learn that what we have long considered "normal" is only one of many ways to organize human experience.

The Scope of Culture

Some cultures are very broad in scope and include a great many people, while others are smaller, including relatively few people. At a very broad level, some cultures include large numbers of people on virtually all continents, such as Islamic culture and Buddhist culture. Members of these groups belong to a common culture in that they share a set of values and a system of meaning. Aside from cultures that have a basis in religion, we can think of other large, pan-national cultures, such as Hispanic culture, which includes the people of Spanish-speaking countries. Although citizens of, say, Argentina and Cuba are different in many ways, they share certain cultural traits owing to their common Hispanic roots. In the same way, gypsies, Arabs, and Scandinavians, are all examples of distinct cultural groups that span nations.

Very frequently we talk about culture as something shared by citizens of a nation, as in Mexican culture or Italian culture or Russian culture. Although cultural boundaries do not coincide perfectly with national boundaries, cultures and nations are often closely related. Some nation-states are the political manifestation of a culture; the French nation, for example, can be thought of as the political embodiment of French culture. Within nations, too, we can identify distinct cultures, such as French-speaking Québecois who share a common national culture with English-speaking fellow Canadians but in other ways are culturally distinct. Similarly, in many African nations there are important cultural differences among tribal groups, such as the Hausa, Yoruba, and Ibo tribes of Nigeria, and the Zulu and Xhosa in South Africa. The nation of India, with 865 million inhabitants, is composed of literally hundreds of distinct cultural groups. Citizens of the United States, too, share a common national culture but may also belong to distinct cultures according to their national origin, their ethnic groups, their religion, and so on.

At an even finer level, there are cultures (or perhaps more accurately, subcultures) composed of people who share a common set of experiences or values. Artists, members of the armed forces, teenagers, residents of small towns, gays, lesbians, lawyers, students, and other groups share specific codes of meaning that make them culturally distinct. Corporations, too, have cultures of their own—IBM, Microsoft, and Hewlett-Packard might all be said to possess a distinct "corporate culture." By the same token, Harvard Business School is in some ways culturally different from, say, Wharton or MIT's Sloan School. And within Harvard's MBA program, first-year Sections develop and maintain somewhat different norms of behavior that mark them as distinct cultures.

Each of us, therefore, is a member of multiple cultures, which may range in scope from pan-national to national to professional to social to organizational. Yet these cultural affiliations are not of equal importance in shaping our experience and behavior—some are critical in shaping our fundamental perceptions of the world and are central to our identity and values, others less so. An IBM employee who changes jobs and finds herself at Microsoft may need a few days or even months to adjust to a new way of doing things, and a soldier returning to civilian life may take some time to get his bearings, but their adjustment process is far less serious than the culture shock experienced by, say, a Cambodian immigrant who arrives in Boston for the first time, or an American who travels to Djakarta or Dakar.

Given that cultures exist at many levels, what is the best way to think about culture and international management? Since international management is, by definition, concerned with differences among nations, it makes most sense to focus on national culture. And in fact, considerable empirical research has shown that significant differences in cultural values and culturally-based behavior are found among citizens of different countries. Cultures may not coincide perfectly with nations, and citizens of a given country may differ substantially from each other, but as a first cut it is helpful to think of cultures at the national level.

Dimensions of National Culture

In what ways do national cultures vary? One anthropologist developed a list of seventy "cultural universals," elements that appear in every national culture, including practices of courtship and marriage, norms of gift giving, body adornment, hospitality, hygiene, funeral rites, and many more.[3] While this comprehensive list may be helpful for the study of entire societies, it is a bit extensive for our interest in management. Two recent studies may be more helpful in showing the relationship between culture and management: the work of an American anthropologist, Edward T. Hall, and the research of a Dutch management scholar, Geert Hofstede.

Edward T. Hall: The "Silent Languages" of Culture

Edward T. Hall has conceived of culture as a means of communication which takes place through symbols, or "silent languages." He identifies five silent languages: the languages of time, space, material goods, friendship, and agreements.

---

3. George P. Murdock, "The Common Denominators of Culture," in *the Science of Man in the World Crises*, ed. Ralph Linton (New York: Columbia University Press, 1945).

a. The language of time Cultures vary in their approaches to time. Some conceive of time as linear, sequential, and rational. People in these cultures tend to be very precise about timing; they schedule activities in detail, they are punctual in keeping appointments, they take deadlines very seriously and are concerned about delays. The use of time is not only an important principle in the organization of daily life, but is an effective means of communication: Matters of priority are dealt with immediately; low-priority matters may be postponed; causing others to wait is rude, and so on. In other cultures, people conceive of time in a more fluid, elastic, or even circular fashion. They take a somewhat less strict view of time, attach less precision to scheduling, and place less importance on postponement or delay. When members of these different cultures interact they may misunderstand each others' use of time. For example, members of one culture may feel insulted to be kept waiting for 30 minutes for a scheduled appointment, whereas no slight may have been intended at all. Similarly, placing a great emphasis on deadlines and schedules may reflect, to one person, the importance of the project, whereas to someone else an emphasis on meeting deadlines may be entirely unrelated to importance.

b. The language of space Cultures vary in the way they use space. For example, each culture has a norm of social distance—the distance at which people naturally stand from each other—which conveys intimacy, friendship, or formality. These distances may vary from culture to culture, so that standing at a close distance may seem normal and sociable to one person but intrusive and uncomfortable to another. Cultures also vary in their queuing behavior—their norms about waiting in line. In some cultures, people take their place at the end of the line and patiently wait their turn, whereas in others queuing is much less orderly or formalized. Less obvious but frequently important is the use of spatial positioning to denote rank or power. In some countries, a delegation of managers will be ar-ranged with great precision so that their positioning indicates relative rank, while in others grouping conveys nothing about rank. Not surprisingly, members of different cultures may experience difficulties when communicating through the language of space. As an example, American businesspeople often pay less attention to spatial arrangements than do their Japanese counterparts, which may be frustrating to the Japanese as they are unable to infer rank from physical position.

c. The language of material goods The use of material goods is an important medium of cultural communication, and is often used to signal status and power. Compared to other cultures, Hall observes, Americans tend to place a high degree of importance on material possessions and the accumulation of goods. This tendency has a historical origin: "Lacking a fixed class system and having an extremely mobile population, Americans have become highly sensitive to how others make use of material possessions. We use everything from clothes to houses as a highly evolved and complex means of ascertaining each other's status."[4] In much the same way, American companies tend to denote power and prestige through the use of material possessions: a corner office, a larger desk, a company car, and a salary that is very large compared to that of other members of the organization. In other cultures, by contrast, less importance may be attached to material goods. In some Japanese firms, top executives share a large open office with little distinction in their physical surroundings, and salaries tend not to vary greatly. In European firms, as well, pay scales are more compressed than in the United States, perhaps reflecting a somewhat lower importance attached to material goods as an indication of status.

d. The language of friendship The ways that people develop and maintain friendships vary

4. Edward T. Hall, "The Silent Language in Overseas Business," *Harvard Business Review,* 1960.

considerably among cultures. In some cultures, relatively low emphasis on material possessions may be matched by greater emphasis on one's personal relationships. A person is known not by what he or she owns, but by his or her place within a social network of family and friends. Because of the emphasis on these relationships, friendships may take long to develop, but are very durable and involve a strong sense of reciprocal obligation. In other cultures, friendships are made and lost more easily. A view commonly held by visitors to the United States is that Americans make friends very quickly and easily, but that their friendships are often transitory, and without the depth or endurance of friendships in the visitors' home countries.

e. The language of agreement How people express agreement and disagreement varies greatly. In some cultures, agreements tend to be explicit and spelled out in writing. An American saying captures this view: "A verbal contract isn't worth the paper it's written on." In other cultures, agreements are based on trust and may be consummated with a handshake and only a brief statement. Similarly, during the process of negotiation leading up to an agreement, norms of expressing agreement and disagreement may vary widely. In some cultures, dissent is voiced quite readily; managers are not hesitant to identify terms that are unacceptable or conditions that must be met for an agreement to be consummated. In other cultures direct confrontation tends to be avoided, and subtle cues are provided to express disagreement. Rather than saying openly that a proposal is unacceptable, a manager might suggest only that the proposal "may be difficult" or that "it raises some concerns."

Hall identified these five "silent languages" in the late 1950s. As he continued his research, Hall found common patterns in the ways that people used these five languages, observing that some people tended to communicate in a relatively explicit fashion, whereas others communicate effectively with much less explicit information. In a subsequent book, co-written with Mildred Reed Hall, Hall offered the distinction between *high context* and *low context* messages. The Halls explained:

> A high context (HC) communication message is one in which *most* of the information is already in the person, while very little is in the coded, explicit, transmitted part of the message. A low context (LC) communication is just the opposite: that is, the mass of the information is vested in the explicit code.[5]

More significantly, the Halls found that some cultures tended systematically to use high-context communication, while other cultures communicated mainly through low-context messages. *High context cultures,* they observed, tend to place great emphasis on friends and networks, and are less formalistic in negotiations, preferring instead to rely on trust and understanding. Members of these cultures were able to communicate effectively despite the absence of much explicit coding because of a high degree of shared understanding. According to the Halls, the Japanese, Arabs, Mediterranean, and Latin cultures were all examples of high-context cultures. By contrast, people in low-context countries tend to be more precise, specific, and required more explicit information in order to communicate effectively. Examples of low-context cultures include Anglo-Saxon countries (for example, the United States, Great Britain, Canada, and Australia), Germany, and Scandinavian countries.

Hall's concepts can be helpful in illuminating the cultural behavior of a few specific countries. Perhaps because the United States is a young country, and is composed of immigrants from many different backgrounds, American culture does not rely on communication deeply embedded in cultural context. It is, as noted above, a

_____

5. Edward T. Hall and Mildred Reed Hall, *Understanding Cultural Differences* (Yarmouth, ME: Intercultural Press, 1990).

low-context culture. Americans tend to communicate in explicit terms: They value candor and frank discussion, and are likely to voice disagreement openly. (A recent biography of Harry S. Truman was called *Plain Speaking,* a trait regarded as a virtue by most Americans.) They also tend to negotiate contracts that are explicit, complete, and literal. Hall describes Americans as monochronic in their approach to time: They think of time as linear and discrete, tend to do one thing at a time, and adhere to schedules. Meeting deadlines and keeping appointments is important; keeping someone waiting is a sign of disrespect. As noted above, Americans tend to place a great emphasis on material goods, and make friends easily and casually, reflecting the absence of a fixed social structure.

French culture, by contrast, is a relatively high context culture. Relationships and social contacts are of great importance. Negotiations are often preceded by a lengthy process of building trust, often with dinners and lunches that are not merely occasions to discuss business but have a ceremonial quality. According to Hall, the French have a polychronic approach to time: They often do many things at once, they tolerate interruptions; they love to talk and communicate with gestures and body language as well as with words. Because the French are polychronic, Hall continues, they may not adhere to schedules as strictly as Americans, and may change plans without much notice.

Japan is a very high context culture, with effective communication possible through relatively little explicit information. An example of high-context Japanese communication is *hara-gai,* a form of guttural speech that seems hardly intelligible to a Westerner but is an effective medium of communication among Japanese. Typical of a high-context culture, in which relatively less overt communication is needed, Japanese negotiations are conducted without explicit statements of agreement and disagreement—in fact, to make an overt and blunt statement when subtle communication would suffice is abrupt and rude. Not surprisingly, this way of expressing agreement and disagreement has at times led to problems of communication. Americans often complain that the Japanese are reluctant to voice direct disagreement—they appear not to say no. Whereas it is true that the Japanese prefer not to say no in the explicit fashion preferred by Americans, it is not correct to say that they do not express disagreement. It would be more accurate to say that their high-context expressions of disagreement are difficult for members of low-context cultures to understand.

Geert Hofstede: Indices of Work-Related Values

Some of the most influential research about national culture has been conducted by Geert Hofstede, a Dutch management scholar. Hofstede studied a rich data set in which thousands of employees at IBM in more than 40 countries answered questions about their jobs and work settings. By analyzing their responses, Hofstede identified systematic differences among countries. He distilled four basic dimensions of work-related values, which he termed *individualism/ collectivism, power distance, uncertainty avoidance,* and *masculinity/femininity.* Countries could be classified along these four dimensions to produce a profile of their work-related values.

a. Individualism/collectivism Individualism describes a tendency of people to see themselves as individuals rather than as members of a group. In individualistic cultures, members tend to be concerned with personal achievement, with individual rights, and with independence. In collectivistic cultures, people tend to see themselves first and foremost as part of a group, and may be more concerned about the welfare of the group than about individual welfare. They may value harmony and equality above personal achievement, and may be more concerned about an obligation and duty to other members of the group than about individual rights.

b. Power distance Power distance captures the degree to which members accept an uneven distribution of power. In high-power-distance cultures, a wide gap is perceived to exist among people at different levels of the hierarchy. Subordinates accept their inferior positions, and are careful to show proper respect and deference to their bosses. Managers, in turn, may issue directives rather than seek broad participation in decision making. In low-power-distance countries, managers may be less concerned with status and more inclined to allow participation, and their employees may be less deferential and more willing to speak out.

c. Uncertainty avoidance Uncertainty avoidance describes the extent to which people seek to avoid, or feel threatened by, ambiguous or risky situations. Individuals in cultures characterized by high uncertainty avoidance may be risk averse in trying new ways of doing things, in starting new companies, in changing jobs, or in welcoming outsiders. They may tend to emphasize continuity and stability rather than innovation and change. In cultures of low uncertainty avoidance, members may more readily embrace change, may show more initiative, and may be more accepting of different views and new ideas.

d. Masculinity/femininity Hofstede used the term "masculinity" to represent a cultural preference for achievement, assertiveness, and material success, and "femininity" to describe a greater importance placed on maintaining relationships, on caring for members, and on a high quality of life. In so-called masculine countries, work-related values tend to favor achievement and competition. In so-called feminine countries, firms provide more extensive services for the well-being of members, and emphasize overall welfare rather than bottom-line performance.

Based on the analysis of his data set, Hofstede calculated a score for 40 different countries on each of these four dimensions. These scores, he stressed, have no absolute value, but are useful only as a way to compare countries. **Table A** shows the scores for 20 countries.

As shown in Table A, the highest scores for

power distance were found in the Latin American countries of Panama (95) and Mexico (81), while the lowest scores were found in the Scandinavian countries of Sweden (31) and Denmark (18), and in Israel (13). Greatest uncertainty avoidance was found in Japan (92) and Spain (86); the lowest scores were again registered in Sweden (29) and Denmark (23). Anglo-Saxon countries scored highest in individualism: the United States (91), Australia (90), and Great Britain (89); whereas the lowest scores came from the Asian countries of Thailand (20) and Indonesia (14). Finally, Hofstede found that Japan rated highest in masculinity (95), while the lowest scores were found in the Netherlands (14) and Sweden (5).

Hofstede's findings, published in 1980, offered important evidence that cultures have clear patterns in their work-related values.[6] Furthermore, the four indices he developed seemed to do a good job of capturing the most important differences among cultures. With the increasing power of East Asian economies during the early 1980s, however, Hofstede wondered if his four indices had adequately captured what he perceived as the distinctive cultural characteristic of East Asian cultures: diligence, patience, and frugality. Based on further research, Hofstede added a fifth dimension which he called Confucianism. Not surprisingly, countries such as Singapore and Taiwan scored high on this index.

Although Hofstede's research has been very influential, it has numerous shortcomings.

> Hofstede's sample was drawn entirely from employees of one company—IBM. Employees of a single company surely do not constitute a random sample of citizens, and probably do not capture fully the traits of their countrymen. Whether Hofstede's findings accurately describe the work-related values in the 40 countries he examined, or whether they merely describe the values of the

---

6. Geert Hofstede, *Culture's Consequences: International Differences in Work-Related Values* (Beverly Hills, CA: Sage Publications, 1980).

TABLE A   Work-Related Values for 20 Selected Countries

	Power Distance	Uncertainty Avoidance	Individualism	Masculinity
Argentina	49	86	46	56
Australia	36	51	90	61
Brazil	69	76	38	49
Canada	39	48	80	52
Denmark	18	23	74	16
France	68	86	71	43
Germany (F.R.)	35	65	67	66
Great Britain	35	35	89	66
Indonesia	78	48	14	46
India	77	40	48	56
Israel	13	81	54	47
Japan	54	92	46	95
Mexico	81	82	30	69
Netherlands	38	53	80	14
Panama	95	86	11	44
Spain	57	86	51	42
Sweden	31	29	71	5
Thailand	64	64	20	34
Turkey	66	85	37	45
United States	40	46	91	62

Adapted from: Geert Hofstede, *Culture's Consequences* (Beverly Hills, CA: Sage Publications, 1980)

IBM employees in those countries, is open to question.

Although the initial survey contained dozens of questions, Hofstede's dimensions were ultimately based on the responses to a very few questions, raising doubts about the robustness of the dimensions. Adding or amending a few questions might significantly alter the results.

Some of the indexes are well-grounded in theory, but others are less clear. Individualism, for example, is a concept that has been widely researched in social psychology and is generally accepted as a meaningful concept. By contrast, masculinity/femininity is less clear: companies that show a high concern for the welfare of their employees are often called "paternalistic," yet are somehow "feminine" in Hofstede's view. Hofstede's use of gender-based terms seems to obscure as much as it illuminates. Quite apart from the name Hofstede has chosen to give this index,

it is questionable that Japan should emerge as the most "masculine" of all countries, given its traditionally high concern for employees and the importance it has placed on group harmony. Similarly, it is not clear that uncertainty avoidance is a single index rather than a composite of several underlying values. Americans may be low in uncertainty avoidance when it comes to starting a new company or changing jobs, but they tend to be rather high in uncertainty avoidance when it comes to wanting clarity in job descriptions and seeking explicit language in contracts. Whether it makes sense to combine these rather different tendencies into a single index, described by a single score, is questionable. A better approach might be to distinguish among a few aspects of uncertainty avoidance and to measure each one.

In sum, Geert Hofstede's research has made a major contribution to our thinking of culture and management, but should not be taken as the final word on the subject. And to be fair, Hofstede never intended that his work should be the final word about culture in management, but expected others to refine and expand upon his work. If his findings are too often cited, and his four indices are overused, the problem lies not with Hofstede but in the uncritical way that others have accepted his findings rather than conducting their own research.

Culture in Management Settings

The research undertaken by Edward Hall and Geert Hofstede has been helpful in identifying specific ways that cultures vary. They are not the only ways to think about cultural differences, but are a good place to begin. They have been important in showing that culture is not some vague, ill-defined concept, but can be shown to have specific dimensions that vary across countries.

What, then, are the lessons for managers? Where might these differences manifest themselves in business settings? Broadly speaking we can think of culture as manifesting itself in two places: in the interactions between firms, and in the interactions among people within a firm.

Interactions between firms

Much of business involves interactions between firms, such as negotiations with suppliers, dealings with customers, and collaborative activities such as joint ventures and strategic alliances. When these interactions take place across national lines, they may be greatly affected by the cultural behavior of the participants. Successful outcomes may depend on the abilities of individuals to communicate effectively with each other.

A first concern emerges at the early stages of interaction, when relationships are developed. In many countries, the specifics of business negotiation can only be broached after a basis of trust and mutual respect has been developed. The process of building trust may take days,

weeks, or longer—and cannot easily be accelerated. Americans, who often prefer to "get down to business" without much in the way of relationship building, may need to adjust their behavior and allow for the development of trust. They should see such interaction not as a mere formality or as an unfortunate waste of time, but as a way to understand a potential business partner and as a way to build a beneficial relationship. Investing time and effort during this stage may pay dividends later in terms of confidence and trust.

Once involved in active negotiations, it is important to pay attention to the "silent languages" of time and of agreement. A manager might ask himself or herself: Do I have an implicit expectation of the time it should take to reach an agreement? Am I imposing a deadline on the proceedings? If so, perhaps exercising greater patience and allowing the pace of negotiations to develop at its own speed would yield better results. How agreement and disagreement are expressed is also important. The manager might ask: How am I used to voicing disagreement or dissatisfaction? In the United States, where candor is a virtue, it might be effective to state one's position explicitly, but in another culture explicit communication may be seen as abrupt and even rude. Phrasing disagreement in a discreet way might still be effective while not upsetting the relationship.

The specificity with which a contract is drawn up may also be important. Americans, coming from a low-context culture, tend to care about the letter of the law, and seek precise terms and clauses to cover explicitly all aspects of the agreement. The result is often a very clear and precise legal document. In some other countries, a shorter agreement, with less emphasis on the explicit terms and more weight on trust and mutual obligation, may be the norm. It may be difficult to word a contract in a way that is comfortable to both sides, but at least it should be recognized that the reluctance of another party to word contracts in explicit language is not necessarily an indication of evasiveness or duplicity, but a reflection of their cultural norms.

Interactions within firms

An entirely different set of cross-cultural issues arises when managing people from multiple cultures within a single organization. Any organization that is composed of members from different cultures, or has affiliates in more than one country, is likely to encounter some challenges in managing cross-cultural relations. Some of the most important issues have to do with power relationships, with norms of participation and decision making, and with views about motivation, performance evaluation, and compensation.

One of the most important aspects of any organization has to do with power relations among members. Cultures described by Hofstede as low in power distance tend to be relatively egalitarian, with relatively few distinctions among members of an organization according to hierarchy, while cultures relatively high in power distance observe greater differences in status. When members of an organization follow the same norms of power distance their interaction may be smoothest, but problems can arise when employees in a single organization have very different ideas about status and hierarchy. For example, one U.S.-based multinational firm instituted a policy that made employees responsible for initiating career development discussions with their managers. The policy was effective in the United States, where employees were relatively comfortable in raising this issue with their managers, but was totally ineffective in foreign subsidiaries where subordinates were much more reticent in initiating discussions with their superiors. It made sense in low-power-distance countries, but not in high-power-distance countries. The firm therefore had to adapt its approach to career development to the cultural norms of its various host countries.

Many American firms take the view that employees are primarily motivated by rewards for individual performance rather than for group performance. This approach may be particularly successful in highly individualistic cultures, but may be less effective in cultures that place a greater emphasis on the collective. In collectivistic cultures, the emphasis on preserving group harmony may be more important than rewarding the individual—indeed, rewarding one person more than another may be a source of embarrassment and chagrin. Rewarding individual behavior may also have unanticipated consequences, as in the anecdote about a servant boy in India who, upon receiving a raise in pay for a job well done, sent his brother in his place the next day. Far from being encouraged to work harder once he had received his raise, the boy's response was to spread the benefit to another member of his family—his collective social unit. Rewarding the individual for his efforts had wholly unexpected results.[7]

Another difference between individualistic cultures and collectivistic cultures was shown by P. Christopher Earley in his study of social loafing.[8] In the United States, loafing is often encountered in the so-called "free rider" problem—the notion that individuals in group settings are tempted to slack off and let others carry the load. To minimize this problem, we often subdivide groups or otherwise structure work in such a way that individuals are held accountable for specific tasks. This approach may make sense in individualistic cultures, but may not be effective in collectivistic cultures, where people feel great responsibility toward each other and to the performance of the group. Earley found that in collectivistic cultures, people tend to work *hardest* when they are part of a group, as they seek to meet the expectations of the collective, quite the opposite of the free-

7. Nancy J. Adler, *International Dimensions of Organizational Behavior* (Boston, MA: Kent Publishing, 1987).

8. P. Christopher Earley, "East Meets West Meets Mideast: Further Explorations of Collectivistic and Individualistic Work Groups," *Academy of Management Journal* 36, no. 2 (1993).

rider problem encountered in individualistic cultures. Earley also found that people from collectivistic cultures tended to loaf the most when they are assigned individual tasks, as the stimulus of group pressure is missing. The free-rider problem, often thought to be universal, turns out to be very much related to cultural norms.

How Important Is Culture, Really?

Most of this note has been devoted to describing ways that cultures differ, and to showing how these differences may be manifested in management settings. It has been argued that cultural differences are real and that they are manifested in many aspects of management, both between firms and within firms. But as noted at the outset, the importance of culture in management can be overestimated just as easily as it can be underestimated. We should therefore ask ourselves: how important is culture, *really*? Is it among the most important things that a manager has to understand, or are there times when it might be low on the list of practical concerns?

To answer this question, it is useful to distinguish between two elements of management: technical systems and social systems.[9] Technical systems comprise mechanical, mathematical, or otherwise inanimate variables, and include financial models, systems of process control, and manufacturing systems, to name a few. Because they do not involve human behavior or interactions among people, they are unaffected by cultural differences. By contrast, such things as leadership, human resource management, and negotiations, are inherently social and may be strongly affected by culture.

As a first caveat, then, national culture is of little importance to technical systems, and affects only social systems. Furthermore, the

real importance of culture in social systems can vary. In some cases, cultural differences may be little more than a minor obstacle, or even a source of amusement. Although we commonly think of cultural differences as a *cause* of poor performance, some recent evidence suggests that "cultural problems" may just as easily be a *symptom* of a firm's performance.[10] Consider, for example, a French corporation which recently acquired two American firms. In one of the acquisitions, managers reported that cross-cultural frictions had been a major problem, while in the other acquisition neither French nor American managers seemed troubled by any cultural differences. Upon closer examination, it was found that the former acquisition involved a business that had been performing poorly, was generating low profits, and was facing sharp cutbacks. Quite possibly the difficult business situation created a tense climate which was attributed to culture. The latter acquisition, by contrast, involved a healthy business unit, with high growth and excellent profitability, and no mention was made of cultural problems. In fact, cross-cultural frictions might not have been very important in *either* acquisition, but became a convenient target of blame in an acquisition that was performing poorly for entirely separate reasons. This example suggests that although it is important to be attuned to cultural differences and to be sensitive to their potential influence in business, we should be careful not to make sweeping attributions wherever we find problems, or to assume that any cross-cultural situation inevitably leads to difficulties.

Conclusion

This note has offered a systematic way to think about culture and its role in management. It has identified some of the differences that exist

---

9. For more on the distinction between technical and social systems, and the ways that culture may affect them, see Philip M. Rosenzweig, "When Can Management Science Be Generalized Internationally?" *Management Science* 40, no. 1 (January 1994).

10. Rosabeth Moss Kanter and Richard Ian Corn, "Do Cultural Differences Make a Business Difference? Contextual Factors Affecting Cross-Cultural Relationship Success," *Journal of Management Development,* Winter 1994.

among national cultures and has shown how they are manifested in managerial settings. Rather than embrace either extreme view—that culture is of no consequence in management, or that it is always of great consequence—this note has tried to show how and when culture may be important. The result, it is hoped, is a more balanced and practical understanding of culture and management.

As more and more business is conducted across national lines, managers will need to develop a better understanding of national culture and its role in management. Rather than merely acknowledging that people from another national culture are "different" in some undefined way, managers should be able to identify specific ways in which various cultural groups may exhibit distinctive behavior. Just as importantly, they should develop an awareness of their own cultural behavior. They should ask: what are *my* implicit assumptions about time, about expression of agreement and disagreement, about individualism, and about power distance? How do my cultural norms manifest themselves in the ways that *I* behave in a business setting? How am *I* likely to be perceived by someone from another country? Culture, after all, is not something that only affects the behavior of others, but is a basic component that shapes each of us.

GLOBAL WORK FORCE 2000:
THE NEW WORLD LABOR MARKET

Today we talk about world markets for cars, computers, and capital. Tomorrow we will talk about a world market for labor.

For more than a century, companies have moved manufacturing operations to take advantage of cheap labor. Now, human capital, once considered to be the most stationary factor in production, increasingly flows across national borders as easily as cars, computer chips, and corporate bonds. Just as managers speak of world markets for products, technology, and capital, they must now think in terms of a world market for labor.

The movement of people from one country to another is, of course, not new. In previous centuries, Irish stonemasons helped build U.S. canals, and Chinese laborers constructed North America's transcontinental railroads. In the 1970s and

1980s, it was common to find Indian engineers writing software in Silicon Valley, Turks cleaning hotel rooms in Berlin, and Algerians assembling cars in France.

During the 1990s, the world's work force will become even more mobile, and employers will increasingly reach across borders to find the skills they need. These movements of workers will be driven by the growing gap between the world's supplies of labor and the demands for it. While much of the world's skilled and unskilled human resources are being produced in the developing world, most of the well-paid jobs are being generated in the cities of the industrialized world. This mismatch has several important implications for the 1990s:

• It will trigger massive relocations of people, including immigrants, temporary workers, retir-

This article was written by William B. Johnston.
Copyright © 1991 by the President and Fellows of Harvard College.
Harvard Business Review, No. 91204, March–April 1991.

ees, and visitors. The greatest relocations will involve young, well-educated workers flocking to the cities of the developed world.

• It will lead some industrialized nations to reconsider their protectionist immigration policies, as they come to rely on and compete for foreign-born workers.

• It may boost the fortunes of nations with "surplus" human capital. Specifically, it could help well-educated but economically underdeveloped countries such as the Philippines, Egypt, Cuba, Poland, and Hungary.

• It will compel labor-short, immigrant-poor nations like Japan to improve labor productivity dramatically to avoid slower economic growth.

• It will lead to a gradual standardization of labor practices among industrialized countries. By the end of the century, European standards of vacation time (five weeks) will be common in the United States. The 40-hour work week will have been accepted in Japan. And world standards governing workplace safety and employee rights will emerge.

Several factors will cause the flows of workers across international borders to accelerate in the coming decade. First, jet airplanes have yet to make their greatest impact. Between 1960 and 1988, the real cost of international travel dropped nearly 60 percent; during the same period, the number of foreigners entering the United States on business rose by 2,800 percent. Just as the automobile triggered suburbanization, which took decades to play out, so will jumbo jets shape the labor market over many years. Second, the barriers that governments place on immigration and emigration are breaking down. By the end of the 1980s, the nations of Eastern Europe had abandoned the restrictions on the rights of their citizens to leave. At the same time, most Western European nations were negotiating the abolition of *all* limits on people's movements within the boundaries of

the European Community, and the United States, Canada, and even Japan began to liberalize their immigration policies.[1] Third, these disappearing barriers come at a time when employers in the aging, slow-growing, industrialized nations are hungry for talent, while the developing world is educating more workers than it can productively employ.

These factors make it almost inevitable that more workers will cross national borders during the 1990s. Exactly where workers move to and from will greatly influence the fates of countries and companies. And even though those movements of people are not entirely predictable, the patterns already being established send strong signals about what is to come.

The Changing World Labor Force

The developments of the next decade are rooted in today's demographics, particularly those having to do with the size and character of various countries' work forces. In some areas of the world, for instance, women have not yet been absorbed in large numbers and represent a huge untapped resource; elsewhere the absorption process is nearly complete. Such national differences are a good starting point for understanding what the globalization of labor will look like and how it will affect individual nations and companies.

Although looming labor shortages have dominated discussion in many industrialized nations, the world work force is growing fast: (Exhibit 1) From 1985 to 2000, the work force is expected to grow by some 600 million people, or 27 percent (that compares with 36 percent growth between 1970 and 1985). The growth will take place unevenly. The vast majority of the new workers—570 million of the 600 million workers—will join the work forces of the developing countries. In countries like Pakistan and Mexico, for example, the work force will grow at

---

[1]Editor's note: As this article was published in 1991, some of these policies have shifted yet again. Although short-term trends may vary, Johnston's broader point about global interdependence is valid.

EXHIBIT 1   The Growing World Work Force (in millions)

Country or Region	Labor Force 1970	Labor Force 1985	Labor Force 2000	Labor Force Annual Growth Rate 1985–2000
World*	1,596.8	2,163.6	2,752.5	1.6%
OECD*	307.0	372.4	401.3	0.5%
United States	84.9	122.1	141.1	1.0
Japan	51.5	59.6	64.3	0.5
Germany	35.5	38.9	37.2	−0.3
United Kingdom	25.3	28.2	29.1	0.2
France	21.4	23.9	25.8	0.5
Italy	20.9	23.5	24.2	0.2
Spain	13.0	14.0	15.7	0.8
Canada	8.5	12.7	14.6	0.9
Australia	5.6	7.4	8.9	1.3
Sweden	3.9	4.4	4.6	0.3
Developing Regions*	1,119.9	1,595.8	2,137.7	2.1%
China	428.3	617.9	761.2	1.4
India	223.9	293.2	383.2	1.8
Indonesia	45.6	63.4	87.7	2.2
Brazil	31.5	49.6	67.8	2.1
Pakistan	19.3	29.8	45.2	2.8
Thailand	17.9	26.7	34.5	1.7
Mexico	14.5	26.1	40.6	3.0
Turkey	16.1	21.4	28.8	2.0
Philippines	13.7	19.9	28.6	2.4
South Korea	11.4	16.8	22.3	1.9
USSR	117.2	143.3	155.0	0.5%

*Totals include some countries not listed in table.

Sources: For OECD nations except Germany: OECD, Department of Economics and Statistics, *Labor Force Statistics, 1967–1987;* U.S. Bureau of Labor Statistics; The World Bank, *World Development Report, 1987.* For developing nations and Germany: International Labour Office, *Economically Active Population, 1950–2025;* The World Bank, *World Development Reports, 1987.*

about 3 percent a year. In contrast, growth rates in the United States, Canada, and Spain will be closer to 1 percent a year, Japan's work force will grow just .5 percent, and Germany's work force (including the Eastern sector) will actually decline.

The much greater growth in the developing world stems primarily from historically higher birth rates. But in many nations, the effects of higher fertility are magnified by the entrance of women into the work force. Not only will more young people who were born in the 1970s enter the work force in the 1990s but also millions of women in industrializing nations are beginning to leave home for paid jobs. Moreover, the work force in the developing world is also better and better educated. The developing countries are producing a growing share of the world's high school and college graduates.

When these demographic differences are combined with different rates of economic growth, they are likely to lead to major redefinitions of labor markets. Nations that have slow-growing work forces but rapid growth in service sector jobs (namely Japan, Germany, and the United States) will become magnets for immigrants, even if their public policies seek to discourage them. Nations whose educational systems produce prospective workers faster than their economies can absorb them (Argentina, Poland, or the Philippines) will export people.

Beyond these differences in growth rates, the work-forces of various nations differ enormously in make-up and capabilities. It is precisely differences like these in age, gender, and education that give us the best clues about what to expect in the 1990s.

Women will enter the work force in great numbers, especially in the developing countries, where relatively few women have been absorbed to date. The trend toward women leaving home-based employment and entering the paid work force is an often overlooked demographic reality of industrialization. (See Exhibit 2.) As cooking and

cleaning technologies ease the burden at home, agricultural jobs disappear, and other jobs (especially in services) proliferate, women tend to be employed in the economy. Their output is suddenly counted in government statistics, causing GNP to rise.

More than half of all women between the ages of 15 and 64 now work outside the home, and women comprise one-third of the world's work force. But the shift from home-based employment has occurred unevenly around the world. The developed nations have absorbed many more women into the labor force than the developing regions: 59 percent for the former, 49 percent for the latter.

More telling than the distinction between the developed and developing worlds, though, are the differences in female labor force participation by country (Exhibit 3). Largely because of religious customs and social expectations, some

EXHIBIT 2   Women Join the Workforce as Nations Industrialize

Percentage of Women Age 15 to 64
Who Hold Paid Jobs

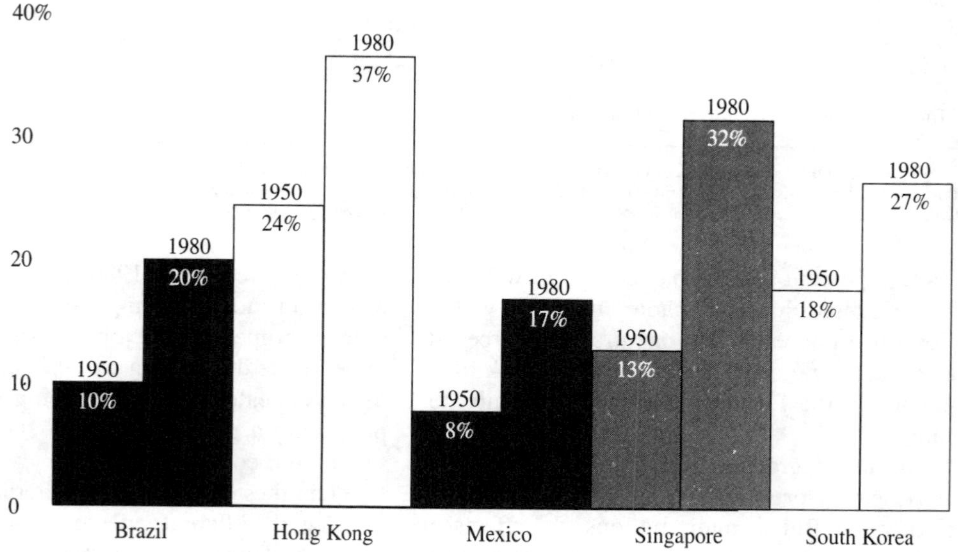

Source: International Labour Organization, *Economically Active Population, 1950–2025,* Table 2.

EXHIBIT 3   Women Hold More Than One-Third of the World's Jobs

Country or Region	Working Women 1985 or 1987* (in millions)	Female Share of Work Force (percentage of total work force)	Female Labor Force Participation (percentage of all females age 15 to 64)
World†	790.1	36.5%	51.3%
Developed Regions‡	156.5	40.9	58.6
United States	53.9	44.1	66.0
Japan	24.3	39.9	57.8
Germany	11.1	39.3	51.3
United Kingdom	11.7	41.4	62.6
France	10.2	42.5	55.2
Italy	8.9	36.9	43.4
Spain	4.8	32.6	37.5
Canada	5.7	43.2	65.4
Australia	3.1	39.7	54.1
Sweden	2.1	48.0	79.4
Developing Regions‡	554.2	34.7	48.6
China	267.2	43.2	75.5
India	76.8	26.2	32.3
Indonesia	19.8	31.3	38.0
Brazil	13.5	27.2	32.2
Pakistan	3.4	11.4	12.1
Thailand	12.2	45.9	74.8
Mexico	7.1	27.0	31.1
Turkey	7.3	34.0	47.4
Philippines	6.4	32.1	39.2
South Korea	5.7	34.0	42.2
USSR (1985)	69.2	48.3	72.6

*For developed regions, 1987 figures were used; for developing regions, 1985 figures.
†Totals include some countries not listed in table.
‡Developed and developing regions as defined by the International Labour Office.

Source: International Labour Office, *Economically Active Population, 1950–2025,* Table 2.

developed countries have relatively few women in the work force, and a small number of developing nations have high rates of female participation. The fact that women are entering the work force is old news in Sweden, for instance, where four-fifths of working-age women hold jobs, or in the United States, where two-thirds are employed. Even in Japan, which is sometimes characterized as a nation in which most women stay home to help educate their children, about 58 percent of women hold paid jobs. Yet highly industrialized countries like Spain, Italy, and Germany have fairly low rates of female participation. And for ideological reasons, China, with one of the lowest GNPs per capita of any nation, has female participation rates that are among the world's highest.

The degree of female labor force participation

has tremendous implications for the economy. Although a large expansion of the work force cannot guarantee economic growth (Ethiopia and Bangladesh both expanded their work forces rapidly in the 1970s and 1980s but barely increased their GNP per capita), in many cases, rapid work force growth stimulates and reinforces economic growth. If other conditions are favorable, countries with many women ready to join the work force can look forward to rapid economic expansion.

Among the developed nations, Spain, Italy, and Germany could show great gains. If their economies become constrained by scarce labor, economic pressures may well overpower social forces that have so far kept women from working. In developing countries where religious customs and social expectations are subject to change, there is the potential for rapid expansion of the work force with parallel surges in the economy.

Women are unlikely to have much effect in many other countries—Sweden, the United States, Canada, the United Kingdom, and Japan, all of which have few women left to add to their work forces. They may be able to redeploy women to more productive jobs, but the economic gains will likely be modest. Also, countries that maintain their current low utilization of women will have a hard time progressing rapidly. It is hard to imagine Pakistan, for example, a largely Moslem country where 11 percent of women work, joining the ranks of the industrialized nations without absorbing more of its women into the paid work force.

As more women enter the work force worldwide, their presence will change working conditions and industrial patterns in predictable ways. The demand for services like fast food, day care, home cleaners, and nursing homes will boom, following the now-familiar pattern in the United States and parts of Europe. Child rearing and care for the disabled will be increasingly institutionalized. And because women who work tend to have more demands on them at home than men do, they are likely to demand more time

away from their jobs. It is plausible, for example, that some industrialized nations will adopt a work week of 35 hours or less by the end of the 1990s in response to these time pressures.

The average age of the world's work force will rise, especially in the developed countries. As a result of lower birth rates and longer life spans, the world population and labor force are aging. The average age of the world's workers will climb by more than a year, to about 35, during the 1990s.

But here again it is important to distinguish between the developed and the developing countries. The population of the industrialized nations is much older. Young people represent a small and shrinking fraction of the labor force, while the proportion of retirees over 65 is climbing. By 2000, fewer than 40 percent of workers in countries like the United States, Japan, Germany, and the United Kingdom will be under age 34, compared with 59 percent in Pakistan, 55 percent in Thailand, and 53 percent in China. (See Exhibit 4.)

The age distribution of a country's work force affects its mobility, flexibility, and energy. Older workers are less likely to relocate or to learn new skills than are younger people. Countries and companies that are staffed with older workers may have greater difficulty adapting to new technologies or changes in markets compared with those staffed with younger workers.

By 2000, workers in most developing nations will be young, relatively recently educated, and arguably more adaptable compared with those in the industrialized world. Very young nations that are rapidly industrializing, like Mexico and China, may find that the youth and flexibility of their work forces give them an advantage relative to their industrialized competitors with older work forces, particularly over those in heavy manufacturing industries, where shrinkage has left factories staffed mostly with workers who are in their forties and fifties.

Most industrialized nations will have 15 percent or more of their populations over age 65 by the year 2000, compared with less than 5 percent

EXHIBIT 4 The World's Work Force and Population Are Aging

Country or Region	Share of Work Force under Age 34		Share of Population over Age 65		Labor Force Participation of Workers over Age 65
	1985	2000	1985	2000	1985
World*	57.1%	51.7%	5.9%	6.8%	32.8%
Developed Regions†	46.9	40.7	11.2	13.3	9.0
United States	50.4	39.5	12.3	12.9	10.3
Japan	33.8	33.9	11.1	15.8	26.0
Germany	45.7	37.4	14.2	16.0	3.2
United Kingdom	43.6	38.8	15.5	15.4	4.6
France	47.0	41.5	13.6	15.6	3.0
Italy	48.0	44.6	14.0	16.7	3.9
Spain	49.9	49.0	9.1	11.5	3.8
Canada	50.9	39.7	11.1	13.1	7.1
Australia	50.7	44.4	10.7	11.6	5.1
Sweden	38.7	36.3	16.9	17.2	5.4
Developing Regions†	60.7	54.9	4.2	5.1	26.3
China	63.7	53.3	5.5	7.3	16.0
India	55.6	52.0	3.4	4.1	40.1
Indonesia	55.7	52.7	2.8	4.2	38.3
Brazil	62.5	42.1	4.0	4.9	17.7
Pakistan	63.3	59.2	4.1	3.9	33.7
Thailand	62.8	55.2	3.9	5.2	27.2
Mexico	61.4	51.9	4.1	4.9	42.1
Turkey	59.6	54.4	4.3	5.2	10.9
Philippines	59.2	54.8	3.3	3.8	44.8
South Korea	54.7	44.2	4.5	5.9	26.5
USSR	50.2	42.9	9.3	11.9	4.4

*Totals include some countries not listed in table.
†Developed and developing regions as defined by the International Labour Office.

Sources: International Labour Office, *Economically Active Population, 1950–2025* and *Yearbook of Labour Statistics, 1988.*

for most developing nations. The challenge that industrialized nations may face in preserving their competitive positions as their work forces age may be stiffened by the high costs of older workers and older societies. Older workers typically have higher wages because of seniority systems, and their pension and health care costs escalate sharply during the later years of their work lives. As more workers in industrialized nations retire toward the close of the century, national health and pension taxes in these nations may rise as well. Unless these rising costs are offset by productivity gains, employers and nations that have older work forces may lose their competitive leadership in industries with standardized production technologies. This could be especially challenging for Japan, where the aging of the population is proceeding even more rapidly than in other industrialized nations.

One silver lining to this cloud of higher costs

may be the higher rates of personal saving that come with older populations. As workers age, they tend to save a bigger chunk of their paychecks. This could increase the capital available for investment in industrialized countries and give them more money to buy productivity-enhancing equipment. (Of course, in a world of mobile capital, these funds could just as easily flow to the developing nations if economic conditions were more promising there.)

Wealth could be redistributed in another way too. As the number of retirees in industrialized countries rises, more of them are likely to cross national borders as tourists or immigrants. Traditionally, few retirees have settled outside their home countries. But cross-border retirements and travel are likely to burgeon in the 1990s: Japanese retiring to Hawaii, Americans receiving Social Security checks in Mexico, and English pensioners sunning themselves on the coast of Spain. As Algerians, Turks, and Mexicans return home bringing retirement checks with them, these flows could mirror the movements of young workers.

People worldwide will be increasingly well educated. The developing countries will produce a growing share of the world's high school and college graduates. Educational trends are hard to track because school and college systems differ so much from country to country and because the linkage between years of school and work skills is indirect and hard to document. Even the national data on years of education are often incomplete.

Still, the data reveal important developments. Based on the numbers of high school and college graduates, the world's work force is becoming better educated. In the decade and a half between 1970 and 1986, world high-school enrollments grew by some 120 million students, or more than 76 percent. College enrollments more than doubled during the period—from 26 million to 58 million. This trend is likely to continue, as nations and individuals increasingly recognize the economic value of education. By the year 2000, it is likely that high school enroll-

ment could grow by another 60 percent, reaching nearly 450 million, while college attendance could double again to top 115 million.

Today, higher percentages of children in industrialized nations attend high school and college. Most of them educate nearly all children through high school and typically further educate about one-third of college-age youths. (Germany and Italy are notable exceptions; only three-quarters of children between ages 12 and 17 go to secondary school; See Exhibit 5). Most of the developing nations have less than half their young people in high school, and they seldom place more than one-fifth in college (although South Korea, Argentina, and the Philippines enroll more than one-third in college).

But an important shift is under way: the developing world is producing a rapidly increasing share of the world's skilled human capital. This trend has been under way for some time and will accelerate through the turn of the century. In the decade and a half between 1970 and 1986, the United States, Canada, Europe, the Soviet Union, and Japan saw their share of world high-school enrollees shrink from 44 percent to 30 percent. If current trends continue, their share is expected to drop to only 21 percent by the year 2000.

U.S. high-school students made up 9 percent of world enrollees in 1970 but only 5 percent in 1986. Not only is their relative number shrinking but also U.S. students are performing worse relative to the rest of the world. International standardized tests suggest that high-school students from many other nations are now better prepared, at least in mathematics and science. In tests given to high-school students worldwide during the mid-1980s, for instance, U.S. seniors ranked thirteenth among 13 nations in biology, twelfth in chemistry, and tenth in physics. The U.S. performance looks even weaker, considering that only small fractions of American students took the tests, while greater percentages of non-U.S. students did.

The developed world is also losing ground when it comes to higher education. (See Exhibit

EXHIBIT 5   Developed Countries Send More of Their Young to School

Country or Region	Percentage of Age Group in High School* 1986	Percentage of Age Group in College* 1986
OECD†	93.0%	39.0%
United States	95.0	59.0
Japan	96.0	29.0
Germany	72.0	30.0
United Kingdom	85.0	22.0
France	95.0	30.0
Italy	76.0	25.0
Spain	98.0	32.0
Canada	103.0	55.0
Australia	96.0	29.0
Sweden	83.0	37.0
Developing Regions†	40.0	7.0
China	42.0	2.0
India	35.0	9.0
Indonesia	41.0	7.0
Brazil	36.0	11.0
Pakistan	18.0	5.0
Thailand	29.0	20.0
Mexico	55.0	16.0
Egypt	66.0	21.0
Turkey	44.0	10.0
Philippines	68.0	38.0
South Korea	95.0	33.0
USSR	99.0	22.0

*Ratio of those enrolled to total school-age population. For high school, population base is typically age 13 to 17. For college population, age 20 to 24 is used. Gross enrollment level can exceed 100% if people from outside these ages are enrolled.
†Totals include some countries not listed in table.

Sources: United Nations Educational, Scientific, and Cultural Organization (UNESCO), *Statistical Yearbook, 1988;* U.S. Department of Education, National Center for Education Statistics, *Digest of Education Statistics, 1989.*

6.) Between 1970 and 1985, the share of the world's college students from the United States, Canada, Europe, the Soviet Union, and Japan dropped from 77 percent to 51 percent. The share of college students in the developing world leaped from 23 percent to 49 percent, and these figures may be understatements because many students in Western universities are citizens of other countries and will return home when they graduate. By the year 2000, students from developing nations will make up three-fifths of all students.

It's true that in absolute numbers, the United States, the Soviet Union, and Japan are still the leading producers of college graduates of all kinds, but a growing number of the world's college graduates originate outside the traditionally highly educated countries. Four of the next

EXHIBIT 6   The Developing Countries Supply a Growing Share of the World's Educated People (*share of enrollees*)

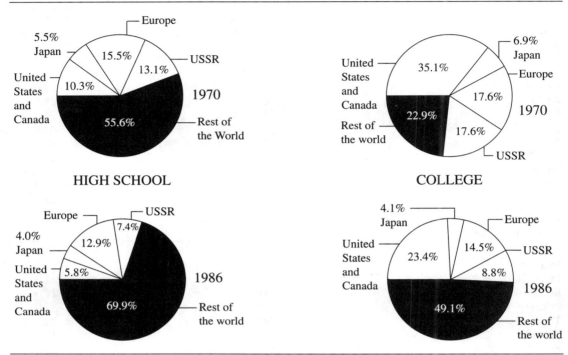

Source: U.S. Department of Education, National Center for Education Statistics, *Digest of Education Statistics, 1989,* Table 341, pp. 386–87.

six greatest sources of college graduates are developing countries: Brazil, China, the Philippines, and South Korea. Differences in the numbers of graduates are especially intriguing when sorted by discipline. China and Brazil rank third and fifth in numbers of science graduates, followed by Japan. For engineering graduates, Brazil, China, Mexico, Korea, and the Philippines all place ahead of France and the United Kingdom.

What makes the rising levels of education in developing countries especially significant is the link between education and economic growth (see Exhibit 7). Those developing nations that educate large proportions of their young have achieved above average rates of growth and

higher standards of living. Among the 42 nations labeled by the World Bank as "low income," only one, Sri Lanka, sends more than half of its high school-age children to school. Among those labeled "upper middle" or "high income" (excluding the oil producers), all but two send more than 60 percent of teenagers to school. Only Brazil and Portugal send less.

The Pressures to Emigrate

The link between the education levels of the work force and economic performance argues that some well-educated, middle-income nations may be poised for rapid growth in the 1990s. In Eastern Europe, for example, Poland, Hungary,

EXHIBIT 7   Many Developing Countries Send More Than Two-Thirds of Teenagers to High School (*percentage of students age 12 to 17 enrolled in secondary school in 1989*)

South Korea	95%	Romania	79%	Hungary	70%
Greece	88%	Trinidad and Tobago	76%	Chile	70%
Yugoslavia	82%	Argentina	74%	Philippines	68%
Poland	80%	Uruguay	71%	Egypt	66%

Source: The World Bank, *World Development Report, 1989,* Table 29, p. 221.

and Czechoslovakia are especially well positioned for development because of their relatively well-educated work forces coupled with their relationships with other European countries. The Philippines, Egypt, Argentina, Peru, Cuba, and Mexico also have huge growth potential because they too have relatively well-educated work forces. But their fragile political and economic infrastructures and sometimes foolish economic policies make their development far less certain.

The tentative economic prospects of these well-educated nations illustrate the risks and opportunities facing countries whose educational systems outperform their economies. During the 1990s, workers who have acquired skills in school will be extremely valuable in the world labor markets. And if job opportunities are lacking in their native lands, better jobs will probably be only a plane ride away. Countries that fail to find a formula for growth can expect to become exporters of people. In Eastern Europe, for example, if the post-Communist rebuilding process stretches on for many years, hundreds of thousands—if not millions—of Poles, Czechs, and Hungarians will seek better opportunities in Western Europe or the United States. Similarly, if South America cannot find ways to restore investor confidence, the northward flow of economic refugees will accelerate.

Although most governments in industrial nations will resist these movements of people for social and political reasons, employers in the developed world are likely to find ways around government barriers. The combination of slow work force growth, fewer women left to enter the work force, earlier retirements, and a shrinking share of high school and college graduates virtually guarantees that many industrialized nations will face labor shortages at various points during the economic cycles of the 1990s. When they do, a growing array of occupations and labor markets will become internationalized.

Not all workers are equally likely to emigrate—or equally likely to be welcomed elsewhere. The image of the labor force as a large pool of similar workers competing for jobs is inexact. There are actually many smaller labor pools, each defined by occupational skills. Patterns of immigration will vary, depending on the conditions of markets that are defined by specific skills.

Typically, unskilled workers—janitors, dishwashers, or laborers—are recruited locally. At higher skill levels, companies often search across states or regions. Among college graduates, national labor markets are more common: New York banks interview M.B.A.s from San Francisco; Midwestern manufacturers hire engineers from both coasts. At the highest skill levels, the labor market has been international for many years. Bell Laboratories physicists, for example, come from universities in England or India as well as from Princeton or MIT. At Schering-Plough's research labs, the first language of biochemists is as likely to be Hindi, Japanese, or German as it is English.

When labor markets tighten and become even more specialized, however, many employers will expand the geography of their recruitment efforts. Recent trends in nursing and software design suggest the emerging patterns of the 1990s. As the shortage of nurses at U.S. hospitals became acute during the 1970s and 1980s, health care providers began to recruit in ever-widening circles. What was once a local labor market became regional, then national, and finally international. By the end of the 1980s, it was routine for New York hospitals to advertise in Dublin and Manila for skilled nurses. Similarly, in systems development, the shortage of engineers led rapidly growing companies to look to universities in England, India, and China to fill some of their U.S. job openings.

Government policies and corporate needs are likely to focus most on the immigration of younger, higher-skilled workers filling specific occupational shortages. But while such flows of higher-skilled workers will predominate, even unskilled jobs may become more internationalized in the 1990s. Indeed, during the 1970s and 1980s, some of the largest international movements of workers were relatively low-skilled workers immigrating to take jobs natives didn't want: Turks to Germany, Algerians to France, Mexicans to the United States. Although these movements of low-skilled workers generate explosive social and political tensions, the economic realities of the 1990s argue that the numbers will grow.

Gains from Trade in People

The globalization of labor is good for the world. It allows human capital to be deployed where it can be used most productively. Countries that recognize it as a positive trend and facilitate the flow of people will benefit most. (See Exhibit 8.)

When workers move to a developed country, they become more productive because an established economic infrastructure can make better use of their time. A street corner vendor of tacos in Mexico City would be lucky to gross $50 for a day's work, while the same worker at a Taco Bell in Los Angeles might sell 10 to 50 times as much in a day. The higher output translates into higher wages. Even at minimum wage, the new Taco Bell employee will earn 10 times his or her former daily income.

For highly skilled workers, the effects are magnified. An engineer once relegated to clerical work in Bangkok may design a new computer system when employed by a Boston electronics company. A Filipino nurse can go from poverty to middle class by taking a job at a hospital in Atlanta. The positive impacts of immigration are visible in robust economies of Southern California and South Florida.

Immigration will be especially good for advanced nations with high levels of capital per worker but constrained labor. In particular, immigration may boost the economies of the United States, Canada, Germany, and other European nations.

The United States is likely to fare particularly well for a number of reasons. For one thing, its wages are among the world's highest, so they attract top talent. Also, political barriers have always been low, and opportunities for immigrants to advance are great. Further, its higher education system draws a large number of students from around the world. In 1987, U.S. universities

EXHIBIT 8   Much of the World's Scientific Brain Power Comes from Developing Countries

Country or Region	Thousands of College Graduates in 1986			
	Total College Graduates	Scientists	Engineers	Ph.D.s
United States	979.5	180.7	77.1	394.3
USSR	839.5	61.7	352.3	na*
Japan	378.7	33.5	74.5	23.5
Brazil	**244.6**	**34.1**	**20.0**	**8.9**
China	**227.7**	**44.7**	**72.7**	**14.2**
Philippines†	**212.0**	**26.3**	**23.4**	**na***
Germany	172.5	35.4	30.2	22.3
France	164.4	30.6	15.0	53.9
South Korea	**155.0**	**16.9**	**21.9**	**20.7**
United Kingdom	132.7	31.4	17.0	37.4
Canada	118.9	21.1	8.4	19.8
Mexico	**112.8**	**20.4**	**25.3**	**8.0**
Egypt	**101.0**	**11.4**	**9.3**	**10.4**

*Not available.
†Estimated.
■ Developing countries.

Source: United Nations Educational, Scientific, and Cultural Organization (UNESCO), *Statistical Yearbook, 1988,* Tables 3–10, pp. 3–306.

granted to foreigners some 51 percent of doctorates in engineering, 48 percent in mathematics, 32 percent in business, and 29 percent in physical sciences. Many of these graduates return home, but many stay. Either way, they stimulate the U.S. economy—by enhancing trade relationships or by increasing the U.S. supply of human capital.

Australia, New Zealand, and some European nations—notably, Germany—are also likely to gain from the international flow of people. Historically, political and cultural obstacles have constrained emigration to Europe. But language and political barriers are weakening (English and German are becoming the languages of business), and the integration of formerly Communist states in Eastern Europe into the OECD trading regime suggests that Europe will increasingly welcome people who want to cross its borders. During the summer of 1990, for example,

five nations in Western Europe agreed that they would eliminate all restrictions on the rights of their citizens to live and work anywhere within their five borders. In Germany, there has been a sharp political backlash against the guest worker program that allowed many Turkish workers into the country during the 1970s. Germany remains committed to preserving its ethnic identity and plans to tighten restrictions on immigration by non-Germans, but it continues to accept thousands of German-speaking people from Russia, Poland, and other East European countries. These workers are likely to strengthen the German economy during the 1990s.

While the politics of accepting more foreigners are unfavorable in virtually every industrialized nation (and may grow worse during the coming recession), the demographic and economic trends will create pressures in most nations to accept greater flows of people. Only

EXHIBIT 9   High School Students in Other Countries Outperform Americans in Science

Country or Region	Science Test Scores*		
	Biology	Chemistry	Physics
Singapore	**66.8**	**66.1**	**54.9**
England	63.4	69.5	58.3
Hungary	**59.7**	**47.7**	**56.5**
Poland	**56.9**	**44.6**	**51.5**
Norway	54.8	41.9	52.8
Finland	51.9	33.3	37.9
Hong Kong	**50.8**	**64.4**	**59.3**
Sweden	48.5	40.0	44.6
Australia	48.2	46.6	48.5
Japan	46.2	51.9	56.1
Canada	45.9	46.6	48.5
Italy	42.3	38.0	28.0
United States	37.9	37.7	45.5

*Scores normalized to a mean of 50, with a standard deviation of 10.
■ Developing countries.

Source: U.S. Department of Education, *Digest of Education Statistics, 1989,* Table 348, p. 391.

Japan is likely to reject increased immigration, regardless of its looming labor shortages. Japan's enormous language and cultural barriers and its commitment to preserving its racial homogeneity virtually rule out the acceptance of many foreign workers. For the foreseeable future, Japanese economic growth will depend on native Japanese human resources. This may pose a stiff challenge for Japan because its work force is among the oldest in the world and its work force growth rate is among the lowest. One opportunity for Japan to pursue may lie in its female labor force: Although a high proportion of Japanese women have paid jobs, many are underemployed and therefore not as productive as they could be. This may also be true for many—if not all—developed economies, but it seems to be especially true of Japan.

Leaders of developing nations often express concern that mass migration of their young people will harm their economies, but there is little evidence to support these fears. The large numbers of Korean, Taiwanese, and Chinese scientists and engineers who have emigrated to the United States do not seem to have had any appreciable impact on the economies at home. Indeed, many immigrants have returned home at some point in their careers, and the cross-fertilization seems to have boosted both economies. Nor have larger movements of less-skilled workers harmed the economies left behind. Actually, the earnings sent home from Mexicans in the United States, Turkish guest workers in Germany, Algerians in France, and Egyptians throughout the Middle East have stimulated growth in labor-exporting countries.

A demonstration of the gains from trade in people occurred in Kuwait in 1990, when the gains were suddenly extinguished. When Iraq invaded, Kuwait's economy ground to an immediate and almost complete halt. Kuwait could no longer export oil, the occupying military force looted many businesses, but most important, the Asian and Middle Eastern workers who had made up two-thirds of the work force left for home. Hospitals lacked doctors and nurses,

EXHIBIT 10 Developed Countries Use Labor More Productively (*output per worker*)

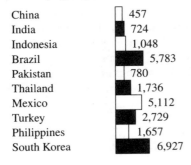

Country or Region	Gross Domestic Production Value per Worker, 1987 (in dollars)
World*	$6,755
Developed Regions	
United States	37,821
Japan	39,143
West Germany	38,066
United Kingdom	20,900
France	35,004
Italy	32,579
Spain	20,557
Canada	28,758
Australia	24,110
Sweden	32,318
Developing Regions	
China	457
India	724
Indonesia	1,048
Brazil	5,783
Pakistan	780
Thailand	1,736
Mexico	5,112
Turkey	2,729
Philippines	1,657
South Korea	6,927
USSR	14,244

*Total includes some countries not listed in table.

Sources: World Bank, *World Development Report, 1989*, Table 3, pp. 168–169; International Labour Office, *World Labour Report, 1989*, Table A-1, pp. 152–55.

buses had no drivers, stores had no clerks. In the space of a few weeks, most of Kuwait's economy disappeared. Kuwait is not the only country to suffer. The huge repatriation of hundreds of thousands of Pakistani, Filipino, and Egyptian workers was equally traumatic for those nations. Not only did these workers and their families return to economies with few jobs available but their foreign earnings (a great part of which had been sent home from Kuwait) were also suddenly missing from the local economy. The gains from trade in people had been lost, and both the sending and the receiving nations were poorer because of it.

The developing countries can thrive despite massive emigration. The real test of whether they will realize their economic potential is how well they can combine their human capital with financial backing, sensible economic policies, and a sound business infrastructure. As always, they must win investors' confidence if they are to make any real progress.

From Globalization to Standardization

The globalization of labor is inevitable. The economic benefits from applying human resources most productively are too great to be resisted. At least some countries will lower the barriers to immigration, and at least some workers will be drawn by the opportunity to apply their training and improve their lives. But more likely, many countries will make immigration easier, and many workers will travel the globe. By the turn of the century, developing countries that have educated their young and adopted market-oriented policies will have advanced faster than those that have not. Developed countries that have accepted or sought foreign workers will be stronger for having done so. As the benefits become more obvious, the movement of workers will become freer.

The world will be changed as a result. As labor gradually becomes international, some national differences will fade. Needs and concerns will become more universal, and personnel policies and practices will standardize. As developing nations absorb women into the work force, for example, they are likely to share the industrialized world's concern about child care and demand for conveniences.

Two forces will drive workplace standardization: companies responding to global labor markets and governments negotiating trade agreements. For a global corporation, the notion of a single set of workplace standards will eventually become as irresistible as the idea of a single language for conducting business. Vacation policies that are established in Germany to attract top scientists will be hard to rescind when the employees are relocated to New Jersey; flexible hours of work that make sense in California will sooner or later become the norm in Madrid; health care deductibles and pension contributions designed for one nation will be modified so that workers in all nations enjoy the same treatment. Typical of most innovations in corporate personnel practices, the benefits of most importance to high-wage, highly valued employees (who will be the most often recruited internationally) will be standardized first.

Government efforts to harmonize workplace standards will accelerate these market-based responses. Currently, for example, officials from most EC countries are seeking to draft a single set of rules to govern workplaces throughout Europe, beginning in 1992. These will cover such things as wage and hour standards, employment rights, and worker safety. While the comprehensive European process is not likely to be repeated elsewhere, standardized working conditions and reciprocal work rules may become an element in many trade negotiations in the 1990s, particularly those relating to services. If Mexican and U.S. truck drivers were to be freely employed by companies on both sides of the border, for example, a U.S.-Mexico free trade agreement would need to cover driver licensing standards, hours of work, and fringe benefits.

Like the process of globalization of product and financial markets, the globalization of labor will be uneven and uncertain. Governments will play a greater role in world labor markets than in other markets, and governments often will be motivated by factors other than economic gain.

But for companies and countries that accept the trends, the 1990s and beyond can be a time of great opportunity. For countries seeking to maximize economic growth, strategies that develop and attract human capital can become powerful policy tools. For companies prepared to operate globally, willingness to compete for human resources on a worldwide basis can be a source of competitive advantage.

PART II

Individual Choices

Managerial Effectiveness and Diversity: Individual Choices

When we consider diversity's impact on our individual lives in the workplace, we typically conjure up specific interactions with co-workers who are different from us in some way, and the challenges, opportunities, or confusion which those differences trigger. Although the word *diversity* tends to jog memories of interactions across race or gender, we would do well to broaden our set of illustrations to include functional differences, differences of educational background and learning styles, of communication styles or senses of humor, and so forth. By broadening our definition in this way, we begin to recognize the array of skills and techniques we already possess for responding to difference, a repertoire of abilities that we seem to forget or deny when we find ourselves interacting across the more politicized of our differences.

In an effort to organize our choices around individual experiences of difference, we will focus this discussion around three ubiquitous and fundamental types of workplace interaction: entry into an organization or a workgroup, performance development, and individual conflict. We have chosen these three interactions because they allow us to examine just about every experience of and reaction to individual difference that we will find in organizational life, and to do so in a relatively concentrated context with relatively immediate consequences. The first two of these organizational moments—entry and performance development—are inevitable *stages* in any individual's work life. The third example—individual conflict—is a *type of interpersonal interaction* that can and does occur at any stage of one's work life.

As we consider these three topics, some may protest that many of the decisions and challenges of diversity are, in actuality, exacerbations of the same decisions and challenges that exist across seemingly homogeneous interactions. In other words, it is difficult to give negative performance feedback to an employee whether you are, for example, of the same race, gender, or ethnicity or of a different one. To the degree that this is true, it is a valuable recognition. It allows us to avoid attributing discomfort to identity differences when they may actually be the result of situational realities.

And as suggested above, it also helps us to reconnect with the skills we already possess for handling such situational challenges.

On the other hand, as we increasingly interact with colleagues from backgrounds different from our own, we may observe behavioral distinctions that arise from their membership in different groups, be they organizational groups (based on common job assignments and work contexts) or identity groups (based on common biology, physical attributes, and/or sociocultural backgrounds).[1]

Obviously, individuals can and will vary in the degree to which they share these behavioral distinctions with other members of their own groups, if only because we all belong to numerous groups, some of which may be more salient for us at certain times than others. Further, an awareness of the existence of these types of distinctions as central tendencies in a group, but not as necessary behaviors in an individual, can help us make more effective choices about our individual interactions. Nevertheless, it seems clear that in some cases diversity itself can be the occasion of potential, although often avoidable, conflict.

In the following discussion of individual choices related to entry into an organization or workgroup, to performance development, and to individual conflict, we will focus on the potential challenges and opportunities that diversity can present. Additionally, we will attempt to examine these situations from as many points of view as possible: that is, from the point of view of the individual entering a group and that of the existing group members; from the point of view of both the giver and the recipient of performance development input; from the points of view of all parties to a conflict; and from the points of view of both majority and minority representatives and high- and low-power group members within a particular organizational setting and/or the larger societal context.

ENTRY INTO AN ORGANIZATION OR WORK GROUP

Upon entering a new work environment, individuals encounter a variety of contextual factors and realities that affect their comfort levels, their sense of belonging, their ability to perceive and be perceived objectively, and ultimately, their behaviors and effectiveness. For example, just as individuals have "multiple identities" such as gender, race, ethnicity, religion, or functional background, so also are organizations composed of multiple, overlapping groups.[2] The new individuals not only join an organization, they join any number of groups (e.g., the M.B.A.s at ABC Co., the women at ABC Co., the Hispanics at ABC Co., the Hispanic women at ABC Co., the marketing professionals at ABC Co., the "minority" marketing professionals at ABC Co., the women in middle management at ABC Co.).

In order to understand the potential impact of these multiple group memberships on the entering individuals, it is useful to consider what the history of each group has

---

1. David A. Thomas and Clayton P. Alderfer, "Influence of Race on Career Dynamics: Theory and Research on Minority Career Experiences," in *Handbook of Career Theory,* ed. D. Arthur, T. Hall, and B. Lawrence (Cambridge, England: Cambridge University Press, 1989).

2. See *Ways of Thinking About and Across Difference,* in this volume.

been within the organization; whether each group comprises a majority or a minority within ABC Co. and in the broader community context; and whether each group is perceived and/or experiences itself as a high- or low-power group within the firm and in the community.

Numerical prevalence obviously plays a significant role in the entry experience of individuals. If we are one of a very few members of a particular group, we face all the challenges of tokenism as described by Rosabeth Moss Kanter. For example, we are easily stereotyped because there are so few of us that the majority tends to draw generalizations based on limited data.[3] We may feel the need for a support and mentoring network of people who share the same group membership, precisely because we want help in understanding the challenges and available strategies for succeeding as a "minority" in the organization, but again, precisely because we are in a minority, there are few such mentors to whom we can turn.

If we are members of a numerical majority within the firm, we may encounter early acceptance and the assumption that we belong and "fit in" from our co-workers. At the same time, we may begin to realize that this acceptance is based on a set of expectations about who we are and how we act that we are not wholly comfortable with. For example, just because an individual is male does not necessarily mean that he shares the general attitudes and expectations of the majority of men in the firm. Nevertheless, as a member of a majority at ABC Co., he has more room to maneuver; there is wider range of behavioral options because it is difficult to draw such tight generalizations around a large and varied group.

Numbers alone do not determine an individual's experience of group membership within an organization. The relative power and status attached to a group, both within the firm and in the broader community, is also critical. For example, one can be in a numerical minority within a firm along some experience, but membership in the group that has that experience may confer high power and status (for example, being one of the only managers in a start-up venture who has prior entrepreneurial experience). Thus, uniqueness can bring greater behavioral latitude and respect from one's colleagues. Similarly, an individual may be a member of a numerical majority within a profession (for example, women in the field of social work in the United States) and, nevertheless, find that positions of power within that field are held most often by men, the gender that is often attributed with having greater power in the wider societal context.

The origins of power and status attributions are often a matter of social, economic, and political history in the wider societal context, and an awareness of this background is valuable. However, for the individual entering an organization it is equally important to attend to the power and status attributions unique to that firm's culture.[4] Such awareness is important not only for members of "low-power" groups so that they might better understand their entry experiences, but also for members of "high-power" groups. Otherwise they may never become aware of judgments, behaviors, and attitudes that *derive* from the shared experience of their group but *appear* to be

---

3. Rosabeth Moss Kanter, *Men and Women of the Corporation* (New York: Basic Books, 1977).

4. See the discussion of cultural audits in *Managerial Effectiveness and Diversity: Organizational Choices* in this volume.

universal truths—by virtue of the fact that they are unquestioned, save by those from groups of lower organizational status and fewer numbers.[5] Thus these members of "high-power" groups miss the learning that comes from undistorted self-assessment and may find themselves inadvertently participating in the exclusion of those who represent other, equally valid, points of view.

In addition to a sophisticated awareness of the contextual factors that may have an impact on their entry experience into an organization, individuals will do well to consider their own behavioral tendencies. For example, one of the ways we cope with new situations which present us with great amounts of new information and sensory input is to try to sort these data into our preexisting categories of experience, categories we have learned and developed from prior relationships and experience. This is a wonderful coping mechanism and can provide great efficiencies around making judgments and predictions under conditions of uncertainty and limited data. The problem is that these generalizations are themselves usually based upon limited data, represent no rigorous investigation, and tend therefore to simply replicate the errors as well as the accurate judgments of the past.

Such generalizations often inform our so-called first impressions of people and situations, impressions in which we tend to place a great deal of confidence. Some will argue that our first impressions tend, in fact, to be *that* accurate, while others contend that we have a "talent for ad hoc explanation,"[6] that we stick with our first impressions because they become, in effect, self-fulfilling prophecies. A great deal of social psychology research supports the idea that we tend to fit the facts to our preexisting interpretations, and while this does not totally discredit the adaptive value of our ability to make generalizations and quick judgments about people and experiences, it does suggest the importance of questioning and checking our basis for those generalizations and judgments.

Although many of our previous examples address the reception new members experience when they join an organization or work group, the same realities and tendencies apply to the experiences of those individuals who already belong to the group. New members' expectations about how existing employees will perceive and receive them can be based on inaccurate generalizations or they can turn into self-fulfilling prophecies that impact the comfort and effective functioning of both parties.

Questions to Consider

Given the issues raised above, what are some of the questions that new entrants face, vis-à-vis their "differences," as they join an organization (and of which existing members of the organization would do well to be cognizant)?

5. David A. Thomas, "Doing Diversity: Effectively Managing Identity Group Differences in Organizations, "*Work Force Diversity: Management Challenges and Ethical Dilemmas. Business Ethics Forum* Vol. 7, No. 1, Harvard Business School, Spring 1994, p. 24.
6. See discussion of Thomas Gilovich in *Ways of Thinking About and Across Difference* in this volume.

- *If I am a member of a minority or lower power group in this organization, to what extent are my colleagues' reactions to me derived from this fact, and to what extent are they merely reactions to my being new?*

There is so much new information being received and processed both by the new entrants and by their colleagues, it is sometimes difficult to sort out the causes and motivations. It becomes critical to question our assumptions and generalizations about others and about their reactions to ourselves. What is our evidence? Can we generate alternate explanations? Is the experience isolated or repeated?

- *To what extent should I call attention to my "differences" by naming them; by talking about my experiences and values as being derived from my gender, race, ethnicity, etc.; by revealing parts of my identity that may not be obvious (for example, religion or sexual orientation); or by questioning behaviors and policies that feel exclusionary to me?*

There are trade-offs around being explicit about the experience of difference. If colleagues do not already know and trust us, they may become defensive, feel betrayed, or use our comments to feed negative generalizations about our ability to "fit in" to the group and become team players. On the other hand, if we do not set limits on inappropriate behaviors or unfair practices right from the start, colleagues may take later objections less seriously, and we ourselves may feel increasingly less able to shift our stance as time goes on.

For many, at a time when we already feel tentative about our place in a new environment, it is difficult to say or do anything that seems to set us further apart. Others of us may feel that our individual identity is at stake and that its importance outweighs the benefits of "belonging." For the entrant, it is important to recognize our own tendencies and to ask ourselves, how important is this issue, for me and for others? (In other words, to conserve our own energy as well as credibility, we may want to choose our battles carefully, rather than take on every issue.) How likely am I to be able to make change? Would the chances of my effectiveness increase at a different time? What is the cost to my personal integrity and to my career if I speak up, postpone action, or remain silent?

For the existing members of the organization, it is important to consider these conflicting pressures on new entrants and to ask ourselves: Am I really open to the substance of their concern? Or am I simply reacting defensively, "circling the wagons" against new ideas, against an awareness of my own limitations, or against simple change?

PERFORMANCE DEVELOPMENT

Performance development is a critical managerial activity, from both the point of view of the individual receiving the feedback and the individual providing it. The stakes are high: wasted potential, wasted resources, lost productivity, legal risks. Careers are made and careers can be stalled, even ended. And we are not talking solely about the individuals receiving the input. If managers cannot develop their reports, if turnover is unacceptably high and/or productivity is low in their areas, they have a problem, too. Central to effective performance development across differences is the ability to distinguish between judgments based on differences of ability versus differences of identity.

Obviously, many of the issues we raised in the previous section on entry into an organization or work group also apply here. To the degree that the provider and/or the receiver of performance feedback holds inappropriate or unverified assumptions and generalizations about the individual on the other end of the relationship, the developmental process will be compromised. First impressions and self-fulfilling prophecies can affect these interactions, as can the organizational context and the numerical prominence of different groups within the firm. Nevertheless, a number of issues deserve separate attention here.

For example, we have already discussed the ways in which numerical prominence of one identity group over another can contribute to the assumption that the majority group's general tendencies are, in fact, universal and desirable norms. We have noted that this phenomenon can be invisible to those who accept it.

However, at times we do encounter instances of conscious effort to exclude the members of some groups from access to resources and power. Depending on the cultural and political context, these efforts may be overt or covert. For example, in the United States today it is illegal and usually unacceptable to explicitly base a decision to exclude someone from employment or promotion on race or gender, even if that is the case. Some identity groups, however, are more overtly excluded, as the recent controversy over homosexuals in the military demonstrates. Although some will debate the relative costs and benefits of overt versus covert exclusion and resistance, it is clear that the developmental process of changing attitudes toward targeted groups almost always involves a period when hostility goes "underground."

Obviously this type of conscious exclusion and resistance, whether overt or covert, can wreak havoc with the performance feedback and development process, with regard to the quality and quantity of both the feedback provided and the developmental activities encountered (for example, job rotations, promotions, visibility, and learning opportunities). The individuals who believe themselves victims of such bias will do well to monitor and record their experiences, seek confirmation from "safe" and neutral parties, and pursue guidance from trusted parties both within and outside the firm (mentors, Human Resource staff, legal counsel, etc.). Individuals who demonstrate this exclusionary type of behavior may find it increasingly difficult to reconcile their biases and behaviors with their new insights if they become part of an organizational learning process that critiques the reasoning pitfalls and emotional barriers to innovation discussed earlier.[7] Organizations have a responsibility to both the target and the source of biased behavior, to support the former and to educate and/or discipline the latter.

Conscious exclusion aside, the performance development process is still vulnerable to our inability to respond well to differences. For example, social scientists have observed the "ultimate attribution error," a tendency for us to find situational reasons

---

7. See *Ways of Thinking About and Across Difference* in this volume.

for failure and to credit individual talent or virtue for success when the actors are members of a group to which we ourselves belong. Conversely, we tend to blame individual flaws for failure and to credit situational factors for success when the actors are members of a targeted or out-group.[8] Obviously such tendencies can lead us to be either more or less optimistic, and therefore helpful, when providing performance feedback to individuals whom we perceive as similar to or different from us. In the same way, we may be either more or less open and receptive to feedback received from individuals we perceive as similar to or different from ourselves.

Having discussed both conscious and unconscious bias, there are still other ways in which difference may impact the performance development process. Assuming good faith efforts to understand and check our own assumptions as both the givers and receivers of feedback, we may also encounter barriers to effective feedback that derive from differences in communication styles—both verbal and nonverbal, differences in motivation, and differences in our attitudes toward authority. For example, patterns of eye contact (direct or indirect), preferred methods of receiving praise (publicly or privately), and preferred learning styles (orally or visually) can vary widely.

Social scientists have studied such phenomena across racial, gender, and cultural groups, and although some patterns have been revealed, it is important to recognize these patterns as general tendencies and continua rather than categorical inevitabilities. As stated earlier, an individual's behavior is influenced by numerous group memberships, one of which may be more salient at one moment than another, as well as by distinct individual experiences. It is useful to familiarize oneself with such behavioral continua as behavioral cues to observe or as questions to ask, rather than as a sort of guidebook for understanding the actions and attitudes of others.

Perhaps the most important learnings here are twofold:

- *Do not assume that everyone is motivated by the same things as we are or prefers to interact in the same ways as we do.*
- *Do not let an awareness of the first learning become an excuse for not hiring, promoting, and giving feedback to, or receiving feedback from, individuals different from ourselves. Most individuals will give us the benefit of the doubt if they sense respectfulness and a good faith effort to understand and to be sensitive to differences.*

Aside from the more general tendencies regarding differences and performance development discussed above, there are some distinct realities for both the recipient and the provider of feedback and developmental guidance that should be noted. Research has suggested that women and members of minorities within organizations may encounter greater difficulties in gaining access to mentors and career networks.[9] To the degree that these newer employees desire mentors and networks of individuals

---

8. T. F. Pettigrew, "The ultimate attribution error: Extending Allport's cognitive analysis of prejudice." *Personality and Social Psychology Bulletin* 5, 1979, pp. 461–76.

9. H. Ibarra, Personal networks of women and minorities in management. *Academy of Management Review* 1993, No. 1, pp. 56–87; B. R. Raggins, Barriers to mentoring: The female manager's dilemma. *Human Relations,* 42, No. 1, 1989, pp. 1–22; D. A. Thomas, Mentoring and irrationality: The role of racial taboos. *Human Resource Management,* 28, No. 2, 1989, pp. 279–90; D. A. Thomas, (1990). The impact of race on managers' experiences of developmental relationships: An intraorganizational study. *Journal of Organizational Behavior,* 1, No. 6, 1990, pp. 479–92.

who share their group identities, difficulties can arise because of the often smaller numbers of women or minority managers from whom they can draw mentors and among whom they can build networks. If they desire a mentor who is highly placed within the organization, they may need to draw from the usually larger pool of white men in such positions. In such cases, the relative comfort and skills of both the mentor and the mentee in responding to differences will determine the effectiveness of the developmental relationship.[10]

Majority and/or in-group members may encounter challenges to providing effective performance guidance to minority members for a variety of reasons. They may experience conflicting pressures: being aware of institutional and individual biases in the organization and in themselves, being dependent upon the performance of their direct reports, wanting to be totally "fair" (and not being certain what that means in this context), and feeling rather risk-averse.

For example, sometimes managers may be leery about hiring or promoting an individual perceived to be "different" within the firm because such a decision may be seen as risky. If they hire someone who *appears* to fit in and that person fails, it would more likely be chalked up to "just one of those (unforeseeable) things." If they hire someone who appears to be an unusual hire, they call attention to their decision and if that person fails, that failure is more likely to be attributed to a poor choice that could have been anticipated.

On the other hand, when majority or in-group members report to minority members within an organization, other tensions can arise. Questions about, and discomfort with, authority and difference can occur on both sides of the relationship.

Although awareness of the tendencies and pitfalls described above does not necessarily protect a manager or an employee against them, it raises the odds of their ability to anticipate, recognize, respect, and respond to them. And in all the cases raised, the process of building effective performance development across differences enhances the learning and communication abilities of all parties.

INDIVIDUAL CONFLICT

Individual conflicts are always about difference, whether it be difference of race and gender and ethnicity, or differences of perception, experience, analysis, and values, or some combination of the above. Often, conflicts over one of these are mistaken for the other, thus changing and sometimes raising the stakes. Many of the challenges and opportunities of entry and performance development described above can result in conflict, but the term covers much wider territory.

A completely conflict-free organization is probably an organization of somnambulists. In fact, constructive conflict is necessary for growth and innovation and learning, for how do we learn anything new except by confronting the limits of our previous knowledge—a process that involves conflicting ideas and perceptions and analyses,

10. D. A. Thomas, Racial dynamics in cross-race developmental relationships. *Administrative Science Quarterly* 38, 1993, pp. 169–94.

as well as, not infrequently, conflicts between the individuals who hold those different ideas, perceptions, and analyses.

We can structure our reflections on conflict and difference in several ways. For example, we can try to consider all the times when conflict emerges in organizations: in racial or sexual harassment complaints; over performance evaluations across difference; over the accessibility of promotion and career paths for all employees; within work groups over personal styles and attitudes; and so on. The problem with this approach is that the list is interminable.

Therefore, in the following material we will organize our thoughts around six ways of thinking about conflict, ways of thinking that might apply in any or all of the situations listed above. These six perspectives can provide a sort of mental checklist for self-insight and insight into others, around situations of individual conflict.

1. Intent versus Perception

In many instances of individual conflict, the disagreement boils down to a question of one person's intention set against another's perception or experience of the first individual's behavior. For example, in some workplace harassment complaints, the targets of the behavior will experience it as demeaning, threatening and/or disempowering, while the accused will protest that they were just trying to be friendly, that they were treating the targets the way they would treat any of their colleagues, that they actually wanted to be inclusive and welcoming.

First of all, of course, there is the question of credibility. Do we believe the claimed "good intentions" of the accused? But assuming that we do, how does one proceed in these situations? From a legal perspective, the use of the "reasonable woman" standard in sexual harassment cases, as opposed to the "reasonable man" standard, suggests the importance of the target's perception and experience. But in day-to-day managerial situations where we hope to avoid the need for legal recourse, how do we deal with experiential reality of the "perception versus intent" debate?

Both parties feel that they are "right." Those accused of questionable behavior feel they should not be held accountable for, or be penalized for, the perceptions of another: perceptions beyond their foreknowledge or control. The targets of the behavior feel that ignorance is no excuse, and that the behavior has the same negative impact whether intended or not.

In such situations, individuals do well to reframe the question from a determination of "who is to blame?" to a search for "what can be learned?" For example, individuals who are accused of insulting or offensive behavior will want to ask themselves what their assumptions were concerning the needs and desires of the offended parties. Did they consider how their comments or behavior would be experienced? Are there reasons why the offended parties may experience the behavior differently than themselves? Have they made assumptions about the needs and interests of the offended parties without bothering to check them out? If they truly intend no harm, are they open to hearing about the reactions of the offended parties and to trying to change their own behavior?

The offended individuals will want to consider their assumptions about the offender's intentions. What is their evidence for these assumptions? Have they tried to explain their concerns? Do they feel there is a way to express their reactions without putting themselves at risk? It is useful to bear in mind that the personal and organizational costs of ignorance about what may offend individuals in underrepresented or low-power groups may differ from the costs of similar behavior directed toward individuals in majority or high-power groups.

uninsentional?

2. Power and Access

We talked above about the potential for education when a conflict is the result of ignorance rather than of malice. There are also instances where the conflict, although apparently over a particular comment or some interpersonal behavior, is actually about organizational power and access to resources and career possibilities. For example, many women have noted that seeming social interactions that tend to be exclusively male (e.g., sporting events, men's clubs) often are also an opportunity for professional exchanges. The men's reluctance to alter this reality can be motivated both by a resistance to change and by a conscious or unconscious desire to limit access to decision making. The stakes in such situations may not be explicit, although individuals who experience themselves as having lower power in such a conflict (due to organizational position or identity-group membership) are quite likely to be aware of them.

intentional?

For these individuals, explicit efforts to educate their offender may not be the most effective course of action. Because the offense appears to be intentional and the stakes are directly and primarily organizational, then organizational solutions are likely to be most effective, either internal (through Human Resources departments or other senior management) or external (through legal complaint).

3. Is Equal Fair?

Sometimes individuals will become conflicted over differing conceptions of what constitutes "fair" treatment. Some will argue that all our attention to "diversity" in the workplace would be unnecessary if we just treated everyone in the same way. This raises several problems, however.

First, there is the question of whether the way we treat everyone is chosen as optimal because it is the way in which the majority would choose to be treated. In other words, is there already an inherent bias in the way organizational decisions are made? We naturally want to work for and among individuals with whom we feel comfortable, but does that comfort preclude differences? We can justify our decisions to exclude others by claims that they just don't "fit in," or we can learn to be comfortable with people of a variety of backgrounds, styles, and so forth.

The second problem with treating everyone the same brings us to our next topic.

4. Creative Conflict

Here we ask, will treating employees "equally" maximize everyone's potential productivity and contribution to the organization, as well as the organization's ability to learn and innovate? Homogeneity in the workforce may expedite some processes and smooth communication, but such convenience may be at the expense of creativity that is triggered through controversy and differences of opinion and approach. Differences among individual employees, if ignored or handled poorly, may hinder workplace effectiveness, but if managed well they can enhance performance.

5. Bystanders and Third Parties

Frequently we may witness workplace conflicts triggered by or around diversity issues, but we may not be direct parties to the controversy. In such cases, we face two questions, one of obligation and the other of personal impact. First we may ask ourselves if we have any obligation to become involved in someone else's conflict? Our answers to such a question may differ in different situations, but some of the issues we will want to consider include: the severity of the situation and the stakes for all parties; our position within the organization (i.e., if we are in senior positions, we may have greater responsibility for the organization's broader behavior); our personal power within the organization; our personal beliefs and values; the potential impacts, positive and negative, of our taking action.

Second, we may ask ourselves if or how diversity conflicts may impact us, even if we are not directly involved? Does the practice of discrimination and prejudice in my organization, for example, affect me if I am not the target? Are there ways in which my organization's greater or lesser ability to accommodate diversity will have an impact on my experience there?

Finally, when it comes to so-called bystanders and third parties to diversity conflicts, it is critical that we consider the potential consequences of any actions we may take on those directly involved. For example, if I speak out against a perceived injustice to another, am I helping that individual or putting them in a more difficult, politicized, and embattled position than they already face? Due diligence is always required in such decisions.

6. Freedom of Expression

Many debates around diversity are framed as debates around freedom of expression. Both parties to a conflict often feel that their views are unfairly restricted. It becomes important here to make several distinctions:

- To distinguish between the freedom to hold and express our views, as opposed to the right to have others comply with them.

- To distinguish between the freedom to express our views for the purpose of constructive dialogue and learning, as opposed to the purpose of silencing or harassing others.
- To distinguish between personal values and beliefs versus values and beliefs germane to the workplace. (For example, we may have strongly held views concerning abortion and a co-worker may have just as strongly held but contrary views, but that does not preclude our working together on a soup marketing campaign. The issue is not germane.)

Understanding these distinctions does not resolve all controversies over freedom of expression, but it can serve as a place to start the conversation, a place that focuses around process rather than the embattled content.

CONCLUSION

The preceding has been an attempt to flag some of the most important and common ways in which differences can affect individual interactions in the workplace, and to suggest some potential ways of framing and addressing the questions these interactions raise. The hope is that it has become clear there are opportunities for all individuals to take productive action to enhance their individual interactions across difference, and that such actions can enhance the learning and the performance of all parties.

ENTRY

ANNE LIVINGSTON AND POWER MAX SYSTEMS (A): INTERVIEWING WITH THE *POWERPLAYER* SOFTWARE ENGINEERING TEAM

Senior technical manager with successful track record in management, leadership, and operations for commercial software product development, release, and support. Innovative leader, experienced with a breadth of complex assignments requiring strong organizational, problem solving, communication, analytical, and decision-making skills. Capable of shaping and motivating a creative technical team to establish and meet objectives.

Résumé background summary, Anne M. Livingston, December 1990 (See Exhibit 1.)

Anne Livingston knew that Power Max Systems was one place she did not want to work. Among her ethnically diverse personal and professional network, Power Max's reputation was that of a primarily white male environment that was especially recalcitrant about integrating a diverse workforce. She had also heard about several lawsuits, in particular the recent government-initiated Federal Labor Commission suit filed against Power Max for some questionable labor practices in their Texarkana, Texas, plant. When Ed Martin, a professional recruiter, called Livingston in the winter of 1990 to discuss opportunities in general at Power Max, she candidly shared her thoughts, not only about Power Max but also about headhunters, and dismissed them both.

Much to her surprise, Martin called back a couple of weeks later. This time, he expressed interest in Livingston's managerial background and experience in interactive media for a specific software engineering manager position with

Power Max's New Product Development Group (NPDG). As Martin attempted to sell her on Power Max's new product venture, Livingston recalled recent newspaper articles and analyst speculation that the Power Max, if successful, would "inherit the mantle of the next revolutionary mass media product." Based on her extensive interactive media background, she sensed that Power Max was working on interesting technology she should see firsthand.

Power Max Systems

Austin, Texas, was the corporate headquarters for Power Max Systems. Its activities were spread throughout the world with products, systems, and services in the fields of consumer electronics, small domestic appliances, music and film, communications systems, industrial electronics, components, and semiconductors. Power Max employed 250,000 employees worldwide and had $28 billion in annual sales.

Power Max had been a world leader and product innovator in consumer electronics and communications systems, but by 1990 the market for these products was experiencing difficulties. Gerald Gertz, the Chairman and CEO of Power Max, was quoted in the 1990 annual report: "It

---

This case was prepared by Pamela J. Maus under the supervision of Mary C. Gentile.

Harvard Business School case 395-067 (Rev. February 6, 1995).

EXHIBIT 1   Résumé of Anne Livingston, December 1990

Anne Livingston
341 Estes Way
Austin, Texas

Professional Summary

Senior technical manager with successful track record in management, leadership, and operations for commercial software product development, release, and support. Innovative leader, experienced with a breadth of complex assignments requiring strong organizational, problem-solving, communication, analytical, and decision-making skills. Capable of shaping and motivating a creative technical team to establish and meet objectives.

Technical Leadership

- Managed the ExperTech Software engineering team, taking the team from technology research phase into product development and release of Soft School Learningware.
- Organized teams of software and hardware engineers to design commercial product technology.
- Collaborated with engineers to create new technology—software, hardware, integrated systems, and distributed systems. Results included patentable and licensable technology.
- Worked with international technology partners to embed and integrate co-developed technologies.

Department Management

- Recruited and formulated motivated teams of software engineers and technical managers for commercial product development. Teams varied from small teams to department of 60 engineers and managers.
- Created and optimized software development, testing, and maintenance processes.
- Administered annual budgets up to $50 million.

Organizational Leadership

- Collaborated with senior management to establish, communicate, and achieve corporate objectives and corresponding departmental objectives.
- Worked with senior management to coordinate product development, announcement, release, and support. These responsibilities included working with members of executive management team, as well as staff in marketing, business development, public relations, legal, product operations, and customer support.
- Experienced with a variety of organizational structures, including traditional and matrix management. Experienced with a variety of tools and innovative techniques for building teams and for motivating staff.

Employment History

ExperTech, Inc., 1984–1990
Director of Product Development; Director of Product Operations

Managed Product Development department, and eventually product operations, for several commercial interactive media software products in a company which grew from 30 to 240 employees. Working with engineering, product marketing, licensing, and industrial design, this engineering team designed, developed, released, and supported system software and applications for the Soft School Learningware product line in conjunction with parallel hardware development to create fully-integrated consumer products.

Education

Massachusetts Institute of Technology

Master of Science awarded in Electrical Engineering and Computer Science, 1984.
Thesis topic: Data Structures for Optimized Interactive Media and Intelligent Graphics

Northwestern Univerity

Bachelor of Science degree awarded in Electrical Engineering and Computer Science, 1980.
Electives and independent study in Interactive Telecommunications.

gives us little consolation that all the companies in the field of consumer electronics are experiencing a dramatic fall in earnings. We have no alternative but to further attack the cost base of the Consumer Electronics and Components divisions. This will be done by measures such as streamlining sales organizations, closing factories, pruning product lines, intensifying cooperation with other companies, and being more selective in product development."

Among the short list of highly select products under development was the interactive multiplayer. Given Power Max's product streams and broad electronics and communication systems base of technology, it was in the optimum position for developing what was being purported as the next generation of technological innovation—the convergence of electronics and computers.

Power Max, as well as its current competition—Nintendo, Sega, Philips, Commodore, and Tandy—all had interactive video game players in the entertainment market, but none had achieved a market standard. Power Max hoped to set that standard by introducing an interactive media product that would go well beyond the current targeted 6–25 year-old male consumer to a broad-based consumer market of all ages, genders, and ethnic groups. The interactive multimedia player would house a sophisticated integration of hardware and software that would utilize computer compact discs (CDs) and the family television to provide an access to not only video games, but also full-length movies, music, instruction, and CD-stored photographs. A network version that would be able to access new services, such as video on demand provided through fiber-optic or telephone wires, was also being planned for a later introduction. Its proprietary design would surpass the current medium by using a 32-bit compressor that would increase speed by 50 times and create a superior quality of 3D graphics with texture mapping, color, audio, and interface capability. Gertz saw the multiplicity and variety of functions having the potential to make *PowerPlayer* a household staple.

The competition was stiff and the race was on, but Power Max was betting on being first to the market with its revolutionary design. Power Max was continuing to ride a wave of confidence from its 1986 entry into the interactive video game player market, the highly successful *PacPlayer*. As one business information analyst reported, "Power Max seems to have a better understanding of what the user wants in this market than any of its competitors." Since several engineers who had worked on the *PacPlayer* development were assigned to *PowerPlayer*, Gertz hoped to repeat the same success with the consumer. Gertz was concerned though because he had seen little evidence of progress. In the fall of 1990 he sent Paul Dixon, senior vice president of NPDG and highly regarded for his technological contributions, to evaluate what was happening with the *PowerPlayer* project and assess whether they should continue to commit resources or to abandon the venture.

What Dixon found impressed him. The engineers were exploring technology that had never been applied before to a consumer product, particularly the broad-based market for which the *PowerPlayer* was intended. But they lacked decisive leadership and were having trouble making selections about which features would be attractive to the customer. Far from recommending that the project be abandoned, Dixon felt confident that he could bring the focus and direction that was needed. He recommended that he take over its leadership and made a commitment to ship the product by fall of 1992. Dixon's confidence was bolstered because he was convinced that a new programming language he had been working on himself would be the perfect application programming language for the *PowerPlayer*.

The *PowerPlayer* Culture

Dixon came to *PowerPlayer* with a reputation. Some of the people on the team had worked with Dixon before and did not want to work with him again. They recalled that he often flew off the handle and directed his rage at whomever was present. Others felt that he would add value because of his background in programming language design. As one engineer said, "If it weren't for Paul's support, the whole project would have been canceled and we wouldn't have a job. But he's just not someone you can push off in a corner and say 'sit there and be a figurehead.' Paul is involved in everything."

The *PowerPlayer* project consisted of two distinct teams, each reporting to Dixon. Don Jones was the manager for the hardware team and his counterpart for the software team was Marc Murray. While the hardware team was highly structured and goal directed, the software team was characterized, even within the Power Max environment, as chaotic.

Murray joined the six-member PowerPlayer software team in 1989, along with 15 others who had worked together on the original *PacPlayer* development team. Murray was promoted to manager in June of 1990 and because of his previous relationships with many on the team, he was surprised at how resistant the team was to being managed. Making the transition from team member and friend to leader was difficult for him. Livingston later observed that Murray had a high need to be liked and the blurred line between professional and personal relationships made it hard for him to make unpopular decisions. Nevertheless, the 22 engineers worked with intensity and routinely devoted 90-hour weeks to their endeavor. Their extraordinary prior achievements on the *PacPlayer* encouraged an arrogance and independence that was reinforced by their separate location away from the main Power Max Systems campus. A strong bond evolved and the software team enjoyed a family-like atmosphere.

Given Gertz's renewed commitment to the development of *PowerPlayer,* Murray knew that the software team's membership would increase and that another manager who would report to him and help shift the team to product mode would be needed if they were to ship the product by fall of 1992.

Although it was the company tradition to hire from within, the *PowerPlayer* team was reluctant to be managed by anyone from elsewhere in Power Max. The team interviewed several internal candidates and summarily rejected each of them. One member of the team told Livingston "Everyone else here is a bunch of idiots." But, as the pressures and complexity of the new product grew along with demands from Dixon and the staff, so did Murray's resolve to hire a manager to take on part of the load.

By this time, Ed Martin had persuaded Livingston to interview with Power Max.

Livingston's Background

Livingston was born in South Carolina to African-American parents and moved at a young age with her mother and three sisters to Michigan. Her mother worked two or three jobs at a time to single-handedly rear her four daughters. Mrs. Livingston's strong faith provided spiritual guidance and inspiration to Livingston and her sisters. Livingston attributes her life successes to the affirmation of self that her mother bestowed on her and her sisters. "Holding down two jobs meant that very early on my mother counted on us to get things done. She assumed that we would make decisions and taught us how by encouraging us to do the things that we each did best. I got to be the nerd in the family and rewire the doorbell and fix the toaster."

It was not long after Livingston entered public schools that she was identified for her intellectual potential. As she put it, "I maxed out on somebody's scales. Because I was black and a girl, the social workers and counselors seemed to see me as a special case and didn't know what to do with me." One suggestion, although it did not happen, was to remove her from her family and place her in an academically-oriented foster home where it was presumed that she would have a better opportunity to cultivate her potential.

As a child, the Apollo moon missions influenced Livingston's decision to become a scientist. She pursued electrical engineering at Northwestern University in Evanston, Illinois, followed by computer science graduate studies at the Massachusetts Institute of Technology where she studied interactive media in its infancy phase. Afterwards, she joined ExperTech where she worked closely with corporate clients to employ interactive media to develop new products. One particularly satisfying project was collaborating with a scientist at a *Fortune* 500 company to turn his in-depth knowledge of systems concepts into an educational product to develop the thinking and learning skills of primary-school children. After seven years managing product development with ExperTech, Livingston was ready to take some time off. First, she traveled throughout Bali, and then took time to explore options for her next career move.

Interviewing at Power Max

Livingston had no trouble remembering the January 1991 date of her first interview with Power Max since she did not usually work on Martin Luther King's birthday. Neither did William Benjamin, the Human Resources Manager, who was among the people Livingston met that day.

Murray and Livingston met briefly before Dixon, who was both Murray's boss and a member of the software team, joined the interview. The meeting continued with Murray and Dixon asking Livingston questions about her interactive media background and how it might fit with some of the situations that were challenging the team. Livingston offered details about how she thought her expertise would contribute to their work. She particularly noted issues related to programming language choices and their impact on interactive media applications. Her assessment of the *PowerPlayer* project was so accurate that Dixon's face turned red and he became visibly agitated. Murray had a different response and immediately started to dive into the technical problems. Livingston later articulated her observation.

Dixon was very uncomfortable when Murray started to get into the technical details. He

seemed irritated that I already knew more than I should. Dixon was short with Murray, trying to shut down the conversation, but Marc hung in there justifying why they should pursue the line of inquiry even though Dixon was getting very angry. They were soon involved in a heated discussion that didn't involve me. Although I didn't know the specifics, it was becoming clear to me that they were entrenched in different design camps and that my expertise was fueling Murray's preference and Dixon's anger.

When the interview resumed, they provided Livingston with an overview of the software team, explaining its responsibility for the design, testing, and release of all system software and describing the five technical groups that composed it: Operating Systems, Network, Media Streaming, Interface, and Applications (Exhibit 2). Each of the 22 members was part of at least one group and in some cases more than one. As was the norm on the *PowerPlayer* software team, there were no formal leaders, but in some of the groups informal leadership had emerged. The problem, as she learned from Murray, was that the software team was having difficulty moving into product mode. He also told her that he expected the team to grow substantially and that he wanted someone who would take over the management for half of the team and provide an operational strategy across all of the groups. Paul Dixon revealed his mandate to introduce the product just in time for the 1992 Christmas season. Soon, Murray and Dixon began another off-line discussion of whether or not the team needed a manager. "The friction was amazing. I'm sitting there thinking, do you or don't you want a manager. Wow, these guys need to talk."

When the interview came back on track, Livingston asked about the degree of ethnic diversity in the team, particularly in leadership roles. Murray, as Livingston saw it, fell all over himself telling her about Melda Amjad, a woman and the informal leader of the Network group, who was originally from Turkey. Livingston then asked more specifically, "Are there issues here for women in leadership roles? Since this is

EXHIBIT 2   The *PowerPlayer* Software Engineering Team, January 1991

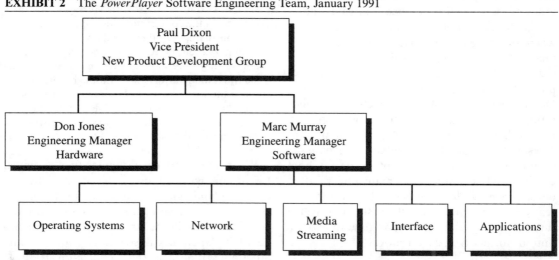

primarily a white male team that already has reluctance to being managed, what do you think I would face as a woman engineer of color in a leadership position?" Again, Murray interrupted her to respond that that just was not an issue, adding that there were two other women in the software team. Dixon backed up Murray with comments about how Power Max was a very open company, progressive and working on diversity. Livingston went on to mention that she had heard about a suit initiated and settled with the Federal Labor Commission over discriminatory hiring practices. Both Murray and Dixon explained the situation as one of misunderstanding, poor communication, and media exaggeration. Livingston wondered whether she should question them further.

Reflecting on her interviews, she noted, "I was puzzled about what I could believe of what they were saying. They were in their sales mode. They were trying to be nice, but it was a veneer."

Interviews with the Engineers

Livingston had not been told that she would be interviewed in teams of two, but she figured it out by the time the third of 11 teams of software engineers rotated in and out of the conference room where she spent the day. The process for most of the teams was similar. They would briefly check out her technical skills and quickly conclude that she was a peer. Beyond that, they quickly ran out of steam and struggled to keep the interview going. Sometimes they would look at each other and ask if the other had more questions, or they would revert to the résumé in search of the next topic. Livingston later told her friend Janet:

> I don't mean to be condescending, but they didn't have a clue about what questions they wanted to ask me. I started to do what I do as a manager, draw people out and get them to talk about things that mattered to them. Pretty soon they were telling me all about their work and we'd end up having a great discussion. The technology they were developing was clearly cutting-edge and exciting.

Livingston was puzzled by a line of questioning that came up repeatedly in the interviews—she was asked whether she played basketball. While posed in a joking manner, "We never hire anyone who doesn't play basketball," it was clear that she was expected to answer. She wondered if the references to basketball were racial.

She was also asked whether she wore shorts to work. She had never been faced with such inappropriate questions and wondered how she should take them. She also wondered how she would handle these behaviors should she come on board as a manager of this team.

Livingston's last interview of the day was with John Gunn one of the senior engineers on the team. He came to the interview yawning, rubbing his eyes, pushing his hands through his hair, and sliding down in his chair. He did not ask her any questions, but by this time, Livingston had honed her interviewing approach and tried it on Gunn. Gunn responded with very little information. Sensing his cue, Livingston decided to cut to the chase: "Do you think you need a manager here at all?" This time Gunn answered her question: "Managers don't have any use on this planet, but if everyone else on the team thinks we do, I'll go along with it. We're just going to ignore them anyway."

The day was long and Livingston had a lot to digest. She recognized that she had come to Power Max with preconceived expectations, so everything she experienced supported the worst stories she had heard from the outside. On the other hand, the best stories she had heard about the technology were also true.

The Offer

When Livingston returned two weeks later for her final interview with Murray and Dixon, she felt confident that they would make her an offer. The team had been unanimous about hiring her, and although she did not know that at the time, she would not have been surprised. She had felt a genuine connection with the engineers and was impressed by their work.

Livingston collected her thoughts. Presuming an offer, she not only considered whether she would take the job, but under what circumstances.

Although Murray and Dixon were still debating the team's resistance to having a manager, they agreed that the position would report to Murray and include managerial responsibility for half the groups. It would also encompass the development of both an across-the-board operational strategy and a consumer orientation for the team.

Given the concern about the team's resistance to having a manager, she considered suggesting that she come in reporting to Murray as a member of several groups rather than as a formal manager. Livingston was not hung up on titles and it was her expectation that she would emerge as their leader. By doing this, though, would she make herself vulnerable to being taken advantage of later?

Livingston admired the expertise of the engineers and expected she could move them forward by factoring in consumer requirements for marketing, diversifying the composition of the software team, and focusing the engineering decision making on closure. She did not have good feelings about Dixon and Murray. They had good reputations in the industry for their technical contributions, but she was concerned about the tension that she had observed in her interviews with them. She figured she could probably work things out with Murray. Dixon was another matter. He had a temper and she was very leery of people with tempers in authority positions. She considered them high risk. As she told Janet,

On the other hand, the technology is extremely cool. What they are trying to do is ambitious and has incredible potential. Some of the things I got a glimpse of showed me that they were erasing the whiteboard and starting all over—not basing it on any stuff that is already entrenched, and that is a very intoxicating thing for a technologist who has always worked within the constraints of other peoples' technology. We could do anything we wanted.

ANNE LIVINGSTON AND POWER MAX SYSTEMS (B-1): INITIAL ENTRY

"I must be slightly crazy for taking this job." During early 1991, Livingston had several job offers including one from Power Max Systems. She weighed the pros and cons of all the offers, and the lure of working on a completely new consumer product using her expertise in interactive media won out. She would come into the *PowerPlayer* software team reporting to Murray with the same title as him, Software Engineering Manager, but at a lower pay grade. Her responsibilities would include membership on several groups with formal responsibility for operational strategy for all the groups moving them into product mode and increasing their understanding of consumer needs.

Livingston had questions about some of the things that had come up in her interviews and was concerned about the importance of first impressions and how she would be received. She thought about the group's resistance to being managed and how she might reduce barriers. Given the informality of the environment, she decided to re-introduce herself on the first day of work by her nickname "Annie 'B'." The name immediately stuck and from that day forward she would be Annie "B" to the *PowerPlayer* family.

In contrast, Livingston remembered another introduction during those first few weeks that did not go as well:

> Some Japanese executives from an important hardware vendor were visiting. Gertz and Dixon personally brought them over to meet our team. Murray introduced everyone before coming to me.

This case was prepared by Pamela J. Maus under the supervision of Mary C. Gentile.

Harvard Business School Case 395-068.

When he reached me he started stammering, "Uhhh what is your title?" which was especially ironic since we had the same one. This is a real no-no when you are trying to establish lines of communications and working relationships, and particularly in the Japanese culture where introductions are very important.

The Power Max culture was a complex integration of casual work norms contrasted with the high energy and stress of working on cutting-edge technology in a context of cyclical changes in the workforce. During Livingston's early weeks there, a companywide layoff was announced. As was the custom at Power Max, the electronic mail system was busy with E-mail debates: "Why do we spend all this money on off-sites when we could be spending it on salaries." "If Gertz didn't make $22 million a year we could afford to keep enough engineers on *PacPlayer II* to get it shipped."

One day Livingston was in the coffee area among some people who were discussing the looming layoffs. A senior hardware engineer, looking at Livingston, offered his assessment of why they were happening: "The reason we're having all these layoffs is because we've been doing all this equal opportunity hiring." Immediately, everyone else in the group was looking at Livingston too. Without responding, she shrugged, poured some coffee and returned to her office, not sure what to think about this comment.

Livingston was also struck by the informality of the culture, reflected in attire and spontaneous group activities. The Power Max workplace was a T-shirts environment. Everything got celebrated with a special T-shirt. Murray even kept a score card on the *PowerPlayer* team's achievements:

T-shirts   7
PowerPlayer   0

And, T-shirts and shorts were common workplace attire. John Gunn wore them all year long. During her interviews she had been asked whether she wore shorts and she had answered "not at work." Livingston typically wore long pants and long sleeve shirts buttoned to the collar. She was frequently teased about her choice of attire. Eventually, Livingston told them that she preferred long pants and sleeves because of the air conditioning.

The team members also continually pursued Livingston to play basketball with them: "Hey Annie "B", come play basketball. Everyone's playing, come on." But she had watched their games and concluded that they played too roughly and she did not want to get injured. Still Livingston did not tell them this because she feared hurting their feelings.

She remembered the day the issue finally came to a head: "Here I am with five men standing over me in my cubicle going at me about why I didn't play basketball with them. One of them finally said, 'Oh, you just don't want to play basketball with a bunch of white boys.'"

Livingston was getting tired of the persistent nagging from her co-workers, but she was sensitive to her relationship with them and wanted to maintain a balance between her managerial role and her budding work relationships.

ANNE LIVINGSTON AND POWER MAX SYSTEMS (C-1): BUILDING ROLE CREDIBILITY

A week before Livingston's start date of April 3, 1991, she had stopped by Power Max to drop off some new-hire paperwork and sat for a moment with Murray. They discussed Livingston's first responsibility for creating a schedule for the *PowerPlayer* software team. Murray, like the other members of the team, did not believe that software could be scheduled. There was still uncertainty about the end product and the discovery process would uncover findings that were impossible to anticipate. He chuckled as he told her how he would jab the engineers, "Just wait until Livingston gets here. We're going to get a schedule. You guys told me you wanted her, so you'd better get ready."

This case was prepared by Pamela J. Maus under the supervision of Mary C. Gentile.
Copyright © 1994 by the President and Fellows of Harvard College.
Harvard Business School case 395-070.

On the other hand, Dixon was a strong proponent of a well-developed schedule much like the one that the hardware team had achieved. It covered an entire wall and indicated detailed events for the next two years. Livingston recalled her interview with Dixon and Murray: "One of the first questions they asked me was: 'Can you build a schedule?' And Dixon added, 'If you can, we need you here.' The schedule the software team was working with had only about three general milestones—Alpha, Beta, and Top Dog, the code name for the project." Livingston later reflected: "everyone knew that this schedule wasn't going to cut it, but they didn't know how to get something that was more real, more credible."

Livingston began the scheduling assignment by interviewing both individuals and teams, encouraging them to tell her everything they were doing. The team's five groups operated independently of each other. She decided to build a bottom-up schedule, collecting data from each group: How did they define their unique contribution? How long did they need to accomplish it, and where did it fit with other aspects of the project? The time frame and target date would be revealed when the schedule was completed.

The scheduling task proved to be easier to talk about than implement. Livingston recalled three incidences that characterized her challenge:

"Creativity cannot be scheduled." Livingston's first scheduling meeting was with Robert Jordan. From the beginning he had made it explicit that he did not want to work on the schedule. He told her, "creativity cannot be scheduled."

Jordan had recently lost his engineering partner to another company and, by his own assessment, did not work well by himself. He was responsible for the operating system (OS) kernel that was key to all other parts of the system and essential to the early development process. He understood his area of expertise in great depth, but without a partner he had difficulty translating his vision into a workable application. Livingston knew very little about the technology of the OS kernel, but she became Jordan's *de facto* partner, taking lengthy walks with him, sometimes for a whole day with only brief breaks along the way. He would talk while Livingston listened and crafted more of the questions that would help Jordan work out his design.

"There is a lot of history here that you don't know." Melda Amjad had already tried and failed to lead the Communications group in creating a schedule. When Livingston organized a meeting with the Communications group to get them started, Amjad reported the group's previous feedback to her—that there were too many uncertainties facing the group to schedule milestones at this time. Instead of backing Amjad up, the group surprised her by immersing themselves in the scheduling activity. Amjad confronted the group on why they were now supply-

ing information that they had told her could not be predicted. Soon the discussion became an argument about history. When Livingston intervened to pull the group back to the present she found herself the object of Amjad's next remark, "We've been working on this stuff for the last year. There's a lot of history here that you do not know, and you do not get to stand there and act like it is not important."

"If you want to provide leadership for this team . . ." Not long into the scheduling project, Livingston met with Dixon after a stressful design meeting where the engineers could not agree on anything.

> Dixon said to me, "You seemed to be very apathetic in that design meeting about which programming language we should use. Do you or don't you have an opinion?" I assured him, knowing that he had a strong preference, that I had an opinion on just about everything. He went on to say that "You didn't seem engaged and if you want to provide leadership for this team, you have to engage. You have to send a message to this team that you care by emphatically arguing for your opinion. You'll never have credibility if you don't."

But nevertheless, by June, Livingston's work with the team resulted in a PERT chart replete with parallel sequences of boxes, diamonds, arrows, linkages, and benchmarks that represented the schedule of events that would produce the *PowerPlayer* software. The much-anticipated wall-sized software-development schedule was presented at a special meeting of the *PowerPlayer* team, including Murray and Dixon. Despite Livingston's requests, neither Murray nor Dixon had reviewed the copies she sent them days before the special meeting. According to the schedule, the product would be ready for unveiling in two years, October of 1993. Livingston knew that the time frame would not be acceptable to Dixon, but she decided to present what she believed would be realistic. She knew, as did everyone else, that Dixon had never in his 12 years at Power Max shipped a product.

Without benefit of discussion, Dixon exploded, "Wrong answer. The time frame for the product is wrong. Do what you have to do. Add resources. Cut features. We're shipping *next* October."

Dixon's outburst sent the team into rounds of doubting and second guessing. Old arguments reemerged. Disgruntlements such as "I told you so" and "What a waste of time" were repeated. Livingston quietly listened and observed as the team poked holes in their own work. She was also watching the demise of her first three months on the job. All the work she had done building the team's confidence in her and their own ability to work to a schedule was unraveling before her eyes.

ANNE LIVINGSTON AND POWER MAX SYSTEMS (D-1): BUILDING THE *POWERPLAYER* SOFTWARE TEAM

At the time Livingston joined the *PowerPlayer* team, there were 22 engineers, all of whom reported to Murray: 18 Caucasian males, three Caucasian females, and one female of color. Eighty percent of them had previous Power Max experience. The team was expected to grow significantly over the next several months (see Exhibit 1).

Livingston shared Murray's concern about the composition of the team and its difficulty shifting into product mode. The team had tended to hire people that they already knew from within Power Max and the result was that most of the team's skills were skewed toward a few areas of technical expertise. Product discussions revolved around the limitations of the team's knowledge and represented a narrow understanding of the customer's needs.

As Livingston assessed what would be needed to reorient the team, she considered some of the areas where leadership needed to be strengthened.

This case was prepared by Pamela J. Maus under the supervision of Mary C. Gentile.

Copyright © 1994 by the President and Fellows of Harvard College.

Harvard Business School case 395-072.

Focus and Goal Setting

The team dynamics, Livingston observed, had become complicated by Murray's personal friendships on the team:

> Marc socialized a lot with members of the team which created a dilemma for him. He would try to make a decision about some feature of the product and later during a social outing, he'd hear about it, "Hey, I thought you were my friend. Why did you turn on me at that meeting?" So he'd shy away from making the kind of leadership decisions that the team desperately needed. Consequently, the team had a long list of priorities for the product and no one to help them with decision making.

Livingston saw the long list of priorities as further indication of how little perspective the team had on what would be attractive to the customer. She remembered the discussions the engineers would get into when they were trying to define the product:

> These guys were infatuated with bells and whistles technology and really could design just about whatever they set their mind to, but they didn't have a clue about what the customer needed. There were always arguments about all the features the product would need "if it were going to

EXHIBIT 1   *PowerPlayer* Software Team, March 1991–December 1993

	March 1991	September 1991	January 1992	June 1992	December 1993
Total Staff (including technical, managerial, and administrative)					
Caucasian males	18	23	34	35	35
Caucasian females	3	5	8	9	10
People of color—males	0	3	12	12	14
People of color—females	1	1	4	4	5
Totals	22	32	58	60	64
Staff by Previous Power Max Experience					
Previous experience—males	16	21	33	34	35
Previous experience—females	2	1	5	5	5
No previous experience—males	2	5	13	13	16
No previous experience—females	2	5	7	8	8
Totals	22	32	58	60	64

be a *PowerPlayer.*" They would spend hours trying to convince each other, and instead of paring the list, they'd make it longer. At the rate they were going, the *PowerPlayer* was going to cost about $8,000 and our target price was under $1,000. Jordan was one of the people who literally had 1,000 things on his list. I told him that he had to choose one, and only one, item to develop. Then, when he finished that, he could choose another one.

Leadership Potential

Other than Murray and herself, there were no other formal leaders on the team. Informal leadership had emerged within some groups, but to be effective, it had to be accepted by support from Murray and the senior engineers among the team or within the particular group. In consideration of the increasing complexity of the project and the growing membership, Livingston took inventory of the leadership talent in the team.

Melda Amjad had emerged as the unofficial leader of the Communications group but she

was having trouble maintaining this role. The scheduling debacle was just one example of the group's resistance to her leadership. She attributed much of the problem to Murray, characterizing his support for her as "spotty and unpredictable." Consequently they were engaged in daily arguments. Eventually Amjad issued an ultimatum to Murray, "Either make me a manager or I'm leaving." If Amjad got an offer from another company, Livingston was concerned that she might take it. Murray had resisted making Amjad a manager because he was concerned that if he did, it would keep Lance Ellis, the senior member of Amjad's group from taking a leadership role.

Ellis had been at Power Max for 12 years. As a member of the *PacPlayer* development team, he had been a powerful and quietly influential leader. His style was to work steadily on his projects, fixing problems as they occurred and before they became project threats, earning him a reputation for being one of the best debuggers within Power Max. Livingston said, "Ellis writes, tests, and designs his code so that when it's done it is rock solid." Ellis had been working with Human Resources to create a position and title of "distinguished engineer" to recognize individual contributors with a track record of extraordinary and consistent achievements.

When Livingston arrived at Power Max, Murray was concerned about Ellis's productivity. Given the combination of Ellis's just coming off an intense *PacPlayer* press tour and some bad history with Murray, Livingston believed, "He was just burnt out, really in a bad slump."

John Gunn, another senior engineer and former member of the *PacPlayer* development team, represented a third potential leader on the team:

> One very important part of Power Max's culture is "heroics" and Gunn provided the heroics for the *PowerPlayer* team. He would let the small problems go while he focused on other issues. Then when a problem grew out of control, Gunn would rush in, put out the fire and take care of the problem at a level where everyone would notice. He'd be a hero! Heroics are rewarded. You get money. Seriously, like major bonuses. You get recognition. You get raises. You get promotions.

Gunn was awarded the first distinguished-engineer title at Power Max.

Increasing Staff Diversity

The team was steadily increasing its size and Livingston believed that if the team were going to achieve its mission, it would need to enlarge its perspective by adding people with knowledge of consumer products, technical expertise not presently in the group, and sensitivity to working with foreign vendors. The *PowerPlayer* team was working with Japanese and German engineers from two vendors to develop a version of the hardware. Livingston was concerned about the possibility of offending the foreign engineers because of a basic insensitivity to their cultures: "We couldn't continually offend them because of cultural things that we just refused to acknowl-edge, not if we were going to get the software to come together with the hardware. There were zillions of reasons that the work wouldn't come together and very few reasons why it could."

Broadening the skill composition of the team would mean looking in new places to recruit staff. It would require the team's sensitivity and willingness to consider people other than ones they already knew. And Livingston believed that getting the best "blend" of talent and the broadest understanding of their market also meant diversifying the mostly white male homogeneity of the current team with a new gender and ethnic mix.

Reflecting on her own experience of the interviewing process with the *PowerPlayer* team, she said, "We will never be able to attract the talent and diversity this project needs if people are subjected to the awful interviews that I went through. I was able to get past the questions about basketball and my clothing, but some people would be put off by that." In order to build the team's skills, she scheduled a workshop on interviewing which created a forum for team members to discuss Livingston's agenda for enhancing the composition of the team:

> One of the team members asked me if I was specifically hiring people of ethnic minority backgrounds since he had noticed that the last three hires were black engineers. I was pleased that he was asking, but I was concerned that the staff was still struggling with how to value diversity and its relationship to understanding and building a consumer product. I told him that I was interested in having a variety of dimensions—backgrounds, perspectives, and cultures—dimensions that would help us build products for the variety of consumers on broad band networks. I reminded him that the millions of potential customers would not all be nerds like us and that we need to have people to remind us to keep looking at the broader view. I assured him that while ethnic diversity often comes along with other differences such as backgrounds, perspectives, cultures—dimensions that help us build products for the variety of consumers out there, which I think is a

good thing—I'm not specifically looking for a black engineer or an Hispanic engineer if they don't bring the skills that are needed for the group.

Chris Leung was among the candidates interviewed that first summer. Leung was a small, quiet person of Chinese heritage, and, as Livingston later described him: "He cranks out serious code." Before making him an offer, one member of the team raised a concern: "I'm not sure that Leung has the stamina to make it here. I don't think that he would be able to take the stress." Others chimed in; they, too, shared the concern.

Leung later called Livingston to discuss what it might be like to work with the group: "That

was a really weird interview. I'm not sure I can come to work there. I like to look forward to coming to work. If I feel as if everyday is going to be a struggle, it wouldn't be fun."

Livingston thought about the commitment she wanted to make to Leung if he were to come on board. She valued Leung's work and knew that he could help increase the team's customer orientation. She also knew that while she was making headway in building and diversifying the team, she had very little support from above or below and that progress would be slow.

She wondered if she could make Leung an offer in good faith.

ANNE LIVINGSTON AND POWER MAX SYSTEMS (E-1): LIVINGSTON TAKES FORMAL AUTHORITY

Everyone, including Livingston, was shocked when Murray resigned the third week of September in 1991. The tension between Murray and Dixon had continued to grow to the point where Murray was fighting with Dixon every day. Murray told Livingston that he was tired of the tension and wanted to take some time to do other things, "like be with my family." Ironically, when Livingston had raised her concerns about Dixon's temper with Murray before signing on with Power Max, it had been Murray who had reassured her that Dixon was "manageable."

Murray, given unrelenting pressure from Dixon to create more structure and leadership for the software team, appointed five senior engineers to managerial roles across several of the

This case was prepared by Pamela J. Maus under the supervision of Mary C. Gentile.

Copyright © 1994 by the President and Fellows of Harvard College.

Harvard Business School case 395-074.

groups right before he left. They did not have Livingston's cross-group responsibility but would still serve to complicate her authority after Murray was gone. Of the five individuals he promoted, Lance Ellis alone had previous managerial experience, and was the only one that Livingston would have considered for a managerial role. Murray and Livingston had had several discussions about how to bring more leadership into the group and Livingston was opposed to the decision he made as a strategic and a tactical error.

I was concerned that Marc didn't really understand the issues in the group. He chose managers because they were senior engineers and had proven to be brilliant individual contributors. But they didn't have the skills that would provide leadership for the groups, much less diversifying the team's composition and building a customer focus. When he bailed and I had to inherit this mess, I was really mad. But, the deed was done. The only thing I could do was let the new managers sink or swim so that I could then put a more effective leadership team in place.

The team had grown to 32 members by the time Murray departed, and from where Dixon stood, they were no closer to meeting the October '92 ship date than they were before Livingston had come on board. On the other hand, Livingston was seeing real progress. Meeting the September 1 deadline had provided the team with much needed project focus. More important, the individual groups had succeeded, for the first time, at integrating the components of the system.

Livingston and Dixon argued for three months about whether or not she was going to take on formal leadership of the team. She felt that her authority had been muddled with the appointment of the five new managers, and yet she assumed herself to be responsible for the work of the software team. Dixon bluntly told Livingston that he did not believe her style of leadership would work, and that she was not tough enough to embody the decisive leadership that the team required.

Simultaneously Dixon and Livingston were in conflict over the programming language that Dixon favored. Livingston recalled:

Dixon had this pet programming language he'd been working on for years that he was convinced was the language for the *PowerPlayer*. I was open to an alternative because his language was way beyond the scope of the product. He just refused to entertain that it wouldn't work and that we were wasting valuable time trying to make it fit.

Livingston remembered that Dixon revisited the programming language argument in another meeting to express dislike for her leadership style:

At a typical *PowerPlayer* meeting everyone yells at each other. I never took part because no one was listening anyway. My style was to have these discussions off line with the individual. At this meeting where his programming language was still taking flack, Dixon all of a sudden shouted: "It's

Annie "B'"s fault. She's not taking a stance that supports this technology choice. Her people are following her lead and that is why it isn't gaining acceptance." Ellis, Gunn, and others in the meeting were quick to come to my defense, but Dixon went on, "No, it *is* her fault because she doesn't engage in the meetings."

At a two-day design meeting that Livingston referred to as the "damned idiot offsite," Dixon took his disapproval of Livingston's leadership style and her resistance to his programming language to new heights:

As was usual, everyone was screaming, yelling, and disagreeing about the viability of using the programming language that Dixon championed. The discussion had escalated to the point that Dixon was standing and having a shouting match with one of the engineers. Then when Jack, a bright young junior engineer, merely started to say something, Dixon lashed out at him, "And you, you're a damned idiot if you think you know anything about programming language!" Utterly stunned, Jack broke down in tears. I had said nothing throughout the argument but when I said, "Let's take a break," the room cleared quickly.

During the break I was standing in front of my car when Dixon and Benjamin approached me. Dixon said: "This is all your fault. You pamper these engineers, spoil and coddle them." I'm standing there shocked, looking back and forth at Dixon and Benjamin thinking to myself, "Benjamin, you're Human Resources. Jump in here and facilitate this." Benjamin said nothing, so I said to Dixon: "You owe Jack an apology." Dixon went on at me: "You owe *me* an apology. I told you that I don't believe in your management style." And, pointing emphatically at me he added: "I don't believe in your philosophy of life." He went on with a few more personal things that I can't even remember now. By this time I was completely floored, saying "Wait, wait, wait. What are we talking about!?" Can you believe it! Dixon was offended by my "Peace" license plate. He told me that he did not like that "everything should be peaceful and happy" kind of approach to things, because you can't make progress without people engaging in some kind of tension. Tension brings about progress.

Shortly thereafter, Livingston decided to confront Dixon with the reason she suspected he was reluctant to give her Murray's position. She explained that her approach to building diverse perspectives into the team was in part because she brings a different background and culture. She pointed out that a different cultural background influences how she responds in meetings and her choice to make decisions collaboratively rather than in an authoritarian fashion.

Dixon disagreed with Livingston, telling her that he considered himself a liberal and offered, as proof, that he had several friends who were black.

Livingston vented to Janet: "It was like talking to a wall. I got nowhere with him." Livingston then took her concern to Benjamin, who listened to her case, but explained that he worked for Dixon and would have to abide by Dixon's decision. He suggested that Livingston take her concerns to the Multicultural Programs whose charter was to promote diversity within Power Max.

The representative of the Multicultural Programs validated and helped reinforce Livingston's case, suggesting that Livingston let one of their investigators review it with Dixon. They also advised Livingston of the escalation procedure for matters in which employees did not think that they were being treated fairly by their manager. In Livingston's case, this meant going to the CEO, Gerald Gertz.

The Multicultural Programs investigator failed to make headway with Dixon. She told Livingston: "He threw me out of his office." Livingston decided to review the situation with him one more time. Only when Dixon refused to budge did she tell him of the process for airing her grievance: "He blasted me and foolishly backed up his words with an E-mail flame: "The more I think about this, the angrier I get. I just want to let you know, that if you take this to Gerald Gertz, you no longer have a career here.'"

Livingston printed this message, added it to others she had gotten from Dixon, and took them to two different lawyers. Both lawyers agreed that Livingston had a strong discrimination case and, as she put it, were "lathering to get at it." But she was not yet ready to pursue it.

In January of 1992, Dixon gave Livingston the responsibility for the entire software team but with neither an increase in pay nor a promotion in level. Livingston knew that Murray had been making $45,000 per year more than she was when he held the same responsibility.

Livingston weighed what she should do. She had a solid case against Dixon and Power Max. She was concerned about the lack of acceptance for ethnically diverse people and felt that she had a responsibility to come forward. At the same time, she was conscious of her commitment and responsibility to the people she had brought into the *PowerPlayer* team.

Livingston reconsidered her goals for joining Power Max and thought hard about what she should do.

THURGOOD MARSHALL HIGH SCHOOL

On July 15, David Kane became principal of the Thurgood Marshall High School, the newest of the six high schools in Great Falls, Illinois. The school had opened two years earlier amid national acclaim for being an important breakthrough in inner-city education. Among its many features, the school was specially designed and constructed for the "house system" concept. Marshall High's organization was broken down into four "houses," each of which contained 300 students, a faculty of 18, and a housemaster. The Marshall complex was designed so that each house was in a separate building connected to the "core facilities"[1] and other houses by an enclosed outside passageway. Each house had its own entrance, classrooms, toilets, conference rooms, and housemaster's office. (See Exhibit 1 for the layout.)

Kane knew that Marshall High was not intended to be an ordinary school. It had been hailed as a major innovation in inner-city education, and a Chicago television station had made a documentary about it shortly after it opened. Marshall High had opened with a carefully selected staff of teachers; many were chosen from other Great Falls schools and at least a dozen had been especially recruited from out of state. Indeed, Kane knew his faculty included graduates from several East and West Coast schools such as Stanford, Yale, and Princeton, as well as several of the very best Midwestern schools. Even the racial mix of students had been carefully balanced so that African-Americans, whites, and Hispanics each constituted a third of the student body (although Kane also knew—perhaps better than its planners—that Marshall's students were drawn from the toughest and poorest areas of the city). The building itself was also widely admired for its beauty and functionality and had won several national architectural awards.

Despite these careful and elaborate preparations, Marshall High School was in serious difficulty by the time Kane became its principal. It had been wracked by violence the preceding year, having been closed twice by student disturbances and once by a teacher walkout. It was also widely reported (although Kane did not know for sure) that achievement scores of its 9th and 10th grade students had actually declined during the last two years, while no significant improvement could be found in the scores of 11th and 12th graders' tests. Marshall High School had fallen far short of its planners' hopes and expectations.

David Kane

An athletic man who stood over 6 feet 4 inches tall, David Kane was born and raised in Great Falls, Illinois. His father was one of the city's first African-American principals; thus Kane was not only familiar with the city but with its school system as well. After serving a tour of duty with the U.S. Marine Corps in Viet Nam, Kane decided to follow his father's footsteps and went to Great Falls State College, from which he received both his bachelor's and master's degrees in education. Kane was certified in elementary and secondary school administration, English, and physical education. Kane had taught English and had coached in a predominantly

This case was prepared by John J. Gabarro.

Harvard Business School case 494-070.

[1]The core facilities included the cafeteria, nurses' room, guidance offices, the boys' and girls' gyms, the offices, the shops, and auditorium.

EXHIBIT 1

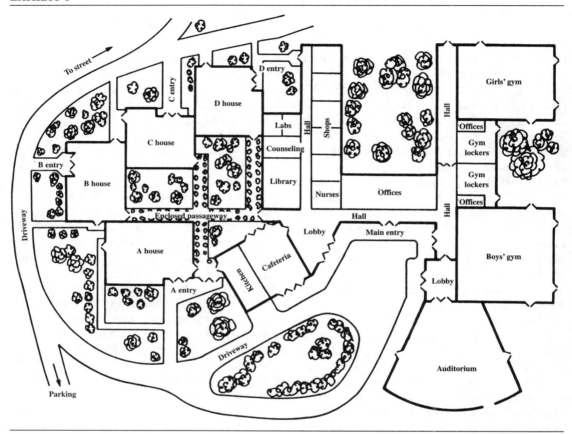

African-American middle school until 10 years ago, when he was asked to become the school's assistant principal. After five years in that post, he was asked to take over the George La Rochelle Middle School, which had 900 pupils and was reputed to be the most difficult middle school in the city. While at La Rochelle, Kane gained a citywide reputation for being a gifted and popular administrator and was credited with turning La Rochelle around from the worst middle school in the system to one of the best. He had been very effective in building community support, recruiting new faculty, and raising academic standards. He was also credited with turning out basketball and baseball teams that won state and county middle school championships. Kane knew that he had been selected for the Marshall job over several more senior candidates because of his ability to handle tough situations. The superintendent had made that clear when he offered Kane the job.

The superintendent had also told him that he would need every bit of skill and luck he could muster. Kane knew of the formidable credentials of Dr. Louis Parker, his predecessor at Marshall High. Parker, a white, had been the superintendent of a small, local township school system before becoming Marshall's first principal. He had also written a book on the house system concept as well as a second book on inner-city education. Parker had earned a PhD from the University of Chicago and a divinity degree from Harvard. Yet despite his impressive background and obvious ability, Parker had resigned in disillusionment and was described by many as a broken man. In fact, Kane remembered seeing the physical change that Parker had undergone over that two-year period. Parker's appearance had become progressively more fatigued and strained until he developed what appeared to be permanent dark rings under his eyes and a perpetual stoop. Kane remembered how he had pitied him and wondered how Parker could find the job worth the obvious personal toll it was taking.

History of the School

The First Year. The school's troubles became apparent in the school's first year. Rumors of conflicts between the housemasters and the six subject-area department heads were widespread by the middle of the first year. The conflicts stemmed from differences in interpretations of curriculum policy on required learning and course content. In response to these conflicts, Parker had instituted a "free market" policy by which department heads were to encourage housemasters to offer certain courses, while housemasters were to convince department heads to assign certain teachers to their houses. Many observers in the school system felt that this policy exacerbated the conflicts.

To add to this climate of conflict, a teacher was assaulted in her classroom in February. The beating frightened many of the staff, particularly some of the older teachers. A delegation of eight teachers asked Parker to hire security guards a week after the assault. The request precipitated a debate within the faculty about the desirability of having guards in the school. One group felt that the guards would instill a sense of safety within the school and thus promote a better learning climate, while the other group felt that

the presence of guards would be repressive and would destroy the sense of community and trust that was developing. Parker refused the request for security guards because he believed that symbolically they would represent everything the school was trying to change. In April a teacher was robbed and beaten in her classroom after school hours and the debate was rekindled, except this time a group of Latino parents threatened to boycott the school unless better security measures were instituted. Again Parker refused the request for security guards.

The Second Year. The school's second year was even more troubled than the first. Because of budget cutbacks ordered during the previous summer, Parker was not able to replace eight teachers who resigned during the summer; it was no longer possible, therefore, for each house to staff all of its courses with its own faculty. Parker therefore instituted a "flexible staffing" policy whereby some teachers were asked to teach students from outside their assigned house; thus, students in the 11th and 12th grades were able to take some elective and required courses in other houses. During this period, Wesley Chase, one of the housemasters, publicly attacked the move as a step toward destroying the house system. In a letter to the *Great Falls Times,* he accused the Board of Education of subverting the house concept by cutting back funds.

The debate over the flexible staffing policy was heightened when two of the other housemasters joined a group of faculty and department chairpersons in opposing Wesley Chase's criticisms. This group argued that the individual house faculties of 15 to 18 teachers could never offer their students the breadth of courses that a schoolwide faculty of 65 to 70 teachers could offer and that interhouse cross registration should be encouraged for that reason.

Further expansion of a cross-registration or flexible staffing policy was halted, however, because of difficulties encountered in the scheduling of classes in the fall. Several errors were found in the master schedule that had been planned during the preceding summer. Various schedule difficulties persisted until November, when the vice principal responsible for the scheduling of classes resigned. Burt Wilkins, a Marshall housemaster who had formerly planned the schedule at Central High, assumed the scheduling function in addition to his duties as housemaster. The scheduling activity took most of Wilkins's time until February.

Security again became an issue when three sophomores were assaulted because they refused to give up their lunch money during a "shakedown." It was believed that the assailants were from outside the school. Several teachers approached Parker and asked him to request security guards from the Board of Education. Again he declined, but he asked Bill Jones, a vice principal at the school, to secure all doors except the entrances to each of the four houses, the main entrance to the school, and the cafeteria. This move appeared to reduce the number of outsiders in the school.

In May a disturbance occurred in the cafeteria that grew out of a fight between two boys. The fight spread and resulted in considerable damage to the school, including the breaking of classroom windows and desks. The disturbance was severe enough for Parker to close the school. A number of teachers and students reported that outsiders were involved in the fight and in damaging the classrooms. Several students were taken to the hospital for minor injuries but all were released. A similar disturbance occurred two weeks later and again the school was closed. The Board of Education then ordered a temporary detail of municipal police to the school despite Parker's advice to the contrary. In protest of the assignment of the police detail, 30 of Marshall's 68 teachers staged a walkout that was joined by over half the student body. The police detail was removed from the school, and an agreement was worked out by an ad hoc subcommittee of the Board of Education with informal representatives of teachers who were for and against assigning a police detail. The compromise called for the temporary stationing of a police cruiser near the school.

Kane's First Week at Marshall High

David Kane arrived at Marshall High on Monday, July 15, and spent most of his first week interviewing individually the school's key administrators. (See Exhibit 2 for a listing of Marshall's administrative staff as of July 15.) He also had a meeting with all of his administrators and department heads on Friday of that week. Kane's purpose in these meetings was to familiarize himself with the school, its problems, and its key people.

His first interview was with William Jones, who was one of his vice principals. Jones, an African-American, had previously worked as a counselor and then as vice principal of a middle school. Kane knew that Jones had a reputation as a tough disciplinarian and was disliked by many of the younger faculty and students. However, Kane had also heard from several teachers, whose judgment he respected, that Jones had been instrumental in keeping the school from blowing apart in the preceding year. It became clear early in the interview that Jones felt more stringent steps were needed to keep outsiders from entering the building. In particular, Jones urged Kane to consider locking all of the school's 30 doors, except for the front entrance, so that everyone would enter and leave through one set of doors. Jones also told him that many of the teachers and pupils had become fearful of being in the building and that "no learning will ever begin to take place until we make it so people don't have to be afraid anymore." At the end of the interview, Jones told Kane that he had been approached by a nearby school system to become its director of counseling but that he had not yet made up his mind. He said he was committed to Marshall High and did not want to leave, but that his decision depended on how hopeful he felt about its future.

As Kane talked with others, he discovered

EXHIBIT 2 Administrative Organization, Thurgood Marshall High School, Great Falls, Illinois

Principal	David Kane, 42 (African-American) B.Ed., M.Ed., Great Falls State College
Vice Principal	William Jones, 44 (African-American) B.Ed., Breakwater State College M.Ed. (counseling), Great Falls State College
Vice Principal	Vacant
Housemaster, A House	Burtram Wilkins, 47 (African-American) B.S., M.Ed., University of Illinois
Housemaster, B House	Frank Kubiak, 36 (white) B.S., University of Illinois M.Ed., Great Falls State College
Housemaster, C House	Wesley Chase, 32 (African-American) A.B., Wesleyan University B.F.A., Pratt Institute M.A.T., Yale University
Housemaster, D House	John Di Napoli, 26 (Italian-American) B.Ed., Great Falls State College M.Ed., Ohio State University
Assistant to the Principal	Vacant
Assistant to the Principal (for community affairs)	Vacant

that the "door question" was one of considerable controversy within the faculty and that both pro and con feelings ran high. Two of the housemasters in particular—Wesley Chase, an African-American, and Frank Kubiak, a white—were strongly against closing the house entrances. The two men felt that such an action would symbolically reduce house autonomy and the feeling of distinctness that was a central aspect of the house identity and pride they were trying to build.

Wesley Chase, master of C House, was particularly vehement on this issue as well as on the question of whether students of one house should be allowed to take classes in another house. Chase said that the flexible staffing program introduced the preceding year had nearly destroyed the house concept and that he, Chase, would resign if Kane intended to expand the crosshouse enrollment of students. Chase also complained about what he described as interference from department heads in his teachers' autonomy.

Chase appeared to be an outstanding housemaster from everything Kane had heard about him—even from his many enemies. Chase had an abrasive personality but seemed to have the best operating house in the school and was well liked by most of his teachers and pupils. His program also appeared to be the most innovative of all. However, it was also the program that was most frequently attacked by the department heads for lacking substance and for not covering the requirements outlined in the system's curriculum guide. Even with these criticisms, Kane imagined how much easier it would be if he had four housemasters like Wesley Chase.

During his interviews with the other three

housemasters, Kane discovered that they all felt infringed upon by the department heads, but that only Chase and Kubiak were strongly against locking the doors and that the other two housemasters actively favored crosshouse course enrollments. Kane's fourth interview was with the housemaster of A House, Burtram Wilkins, an African-American in his late forties who had been an assistant to the principal of Central High before coming to Marshall. Wilkins spent most of the interview discussing how schedule pressures could be relieved. Wilkins was currently involved in developing the schedule for the new school year until an administrative vice principal was appointed. (Marshall High had allocations for two vice principals and two assistants in addition to the housemasters. See Exhibit 2.)

Two pieces of information concerning Wilkins came to Kane's attention during his first week there. The first was that several teachers were circulating a letter requesting Wilkins's removal as a housemaster because they felt he could not control the house or direct the faculty. This surprised Kane, since he had heard that Wilkins was widely respected within the faculty and that he had earned a reputation for supporting high academic standards and working tirelessly with new teachers. However, as Kane inquired further he discovered that although Wilkins was greatly liked within the faculty, he was generally recognized as a poor housemaster. The second piece of information concerned how Wilkins's house compared with the others. Although students had been randomly assigned to each house, Wilkins's house had the largest absence rate and the greatest number of disciplinary problems. Jones had also told him that Wilkins's drop-out rate for the previous year was three times that of any other house.

While Kane was in the process of interviewing his staff, he was called on by Francis Harvey, chairman of the social studies department. Harvey was a native of Great Falls, white, and in his late forties. He was scheduled for an appointment the following week but asked Kane if he could see him immediately. Harvey had heard that a letter was being circulated asking for Wilkins's removal and therefore wanted to present the other side of the argument. He became very emotional during the conversation and said that Wilkins was viewed by many of the teachers and department chairpersons as the only housemaster who was making an effort to maintain high academic standards; his transfer would be seen as a blow to those concerned with quality education. Harvey also described in detail Wilkins's devotion and commitment to the school and the fact that Wilkins was the only administrator with the ability to straighten out the schedule, which he had done in addition to all his other duties. Harvey departed by saying that if Wilkins was transferred, then he, Harvey, would write a letter to the regional accreditation council telling them how standards had sunk at Marshall. Kane assured him that it would not be necessary to take such a drastic measure and that a cooperative resolution would be found. Kane was aware of the accreditation review that Marshall High faced the following April, and he did not wish to complicate the process unnecessarily.

Within 20 minutes of Harvey's departure, Kane was visited by a young white teacher named Tim O'Reilly, who said he had heard that Harvey had come in to see Kane. O'Reilly said he was one of the teachers who organized the movement to get rid of Wilkins. O'Reilly said he liked and admired Wilkins because of his devotion to the school, but that Wilkins's house was so disorganized and discipline so bad that it was nearly impossible to do any good teaching. O'Reilly said that it was "a shame to lock the school when stronger leadership is all that's needed."

Kane's impressions of his administrators generally matched what he had heard about them before arriving at the school. Wesley Chase seemed to be a very bright, innovative, and charismatic leader whose mere presence generated excitement. Frank Kubiak seemed to be a highly competent though not very imaginative administrator, who had earned the respect of his faculty and students. John Di Napoli, a housemaster who was only 26, seemed very bright and earnest but unseasoned and unsure of himself. Kane felt that with a little guidance and training, Di Napoli might have the greatest promise of all. At the moment, however, Di Napoli appeared to be uncertain, and tentative, and Kane suspected that Di Napoli had difficulty simply coping. Wilkins seemed to be a sincere and devoted person who had a good mind for administrative details but an incapacity for leadership.

Kane knew that he would have the opportunity to make several administrative appointments because of three vacancies that existed. Indeed, should Jones resign as vice principal, Kane could fill both vice principal positions. He knew that his recommendations for these positions would carry a great deal of weight with the central office. The only constraint Kane felt in making these appointments was the need to achieve some kind of racial balance among the Marshall administrative group. With his own appointment as principal, the number of African-American administrators exceeded the number of white administrators by a ratio of two to one, and Marshall did not have a single Latino administrator, even though a third of its pupils had Hispanic surnames.

The Friday Afternoon Meeting

In contrast to the individual interviews, Kane was surprised to find how quiet and conflict-free these same people were in the staff meeting he called on Friday. He was amazed at how slow, polite, and friendly the conversation appeared to be among people who had so vehemently expressed negative opinions of each other in private. After about 45 minutes of discussion about the upcoming accreditation review, Kane broached the subject of housemaster–department head relations. The ensuing silence

was finally broken by a joke Kubiak made about the uselessness of discussing that topic. Kane probed further by asking whether everyone was happy with the current practices. Harvey suggested this was a topic that might be better discussed in a smaller group. Everyone in the room seemed to agree with Harvey except for Betsy Drobna, a white woman in her late twenties who chaired the English department. She said that one of the problems with the school was that no one was willing to tackle tough issues until they exploded. She said that relations between housemasters and department heads were terrible, and it made her job very difficult. She then attacked Wesley Chase for impeding her evaluation of a nontenured teacher in Chase's house. The two argued for several minutes about the teacher and the quality of the experimental sophomore English course that the teacher was giving. Finally, Chase, who by now was quite angry, coldly warned Drobna that he would break her neck if she stepped into his house again. Kane intervened in an attempt to cool both their tempers and the meeting ended shortly thereafter.

The following morning, Drobna called Kane at home and told him that unless Wesley Chase publicly apologized for his threat, she would file a grievance with the teachers' union and take it to court if necessary. Kane assured Drobna that he would talk with Chase on Monday. Kane then called Eleanor Dodd, one of the school's math teachers whom he had known well for many years and whose judgment he respected. Dodd was a close friend of both Chase and Drobna and was also vice president of the city's teachers' union. He learned from her that both had been long-term adversaries but that she felt both were excellent professionals.

She also reported that Drobna would be a formidable opponent and could muster considerable support among the faculty. Dodd, who herself was African-American, feared that a confrontation between Drobna and Chase might create tensions along race lines within the school even though both Drobna and Chase were generally quite popular with students of all races. Dodd strongly urged Kane not to let the matter drop. She also told him she had overheard Bill Jones, the vice principal, say at a party the preceding night that he felt Kane didn't have either the stomach or the forcefulness necessary to survive at Marshall. Jones further stated that the only reason he was staying was that he did not expect Kane to last the year. Should that prove to be the case, Jones felt that he would be appointed principal.

PERFORMANCE DEVELOPMENT

JENSEN SHOES: LYNDON TWITCHELL'S STORY*

Jensen Shoes, established in 1943, prided itself on being a trendsetter and the leading marketer in the United States of high quality athletic and casual footwear for children and adults. Kenneth Jensen, the founder, was fond of saying "At Jensen Shoes we value our employees as much as our products. Employees who find their work worthwhile and satisfying do their best. In turn, the company profits while providing high-quality, well-priced shoes to the customer." Jensen managed with an open-door policy that became a model for other managers. Over the years, sensitivity to employee issues, both work and personal, became a hallmark of the Jensen Shoes culture.

For many years Jensen Shoes enjoyed a highly profitable position, to the point where one manager said, "We only have finance people to count the money." By 1994, it was a $65 million company with 4,500 employees worldwide. It was making significant progress creating a presence in international markets and had targeted off-

---

This case was prepared by Pamela J. Maus under the supervision of Mary C. Gentile.

Copyright © 1994 by the President and Fellows of Harvard College.

Harvard Business School case 395-121.

*This case should be used in conjunction with Jensen Shoes: Jane Kravitz's Story, No. 395-120.

shore growth as an objective. Casual wear made up 45 percent of company revenues in recent years. Athletic shoes accounted for 30 percent of the 1993 revenue and children's wear accounted for the other 25 percent. Return on Equity was 20 percent in 1993. Although this represented a slight decline from previous years, it was competitive with industry leaders.

Sales had grown steadily in athletic and children's wear during the last decade, but casual wear had begun to flatten, necessitating the need to diversify product lines and strengthen long-term industry viability. In January of 1994, Jensen Shoes' executive management charged Sally Briggs, 44, female Caucasian, Vice President of the Marketing Division, to define opportunities for new markets and new products. In turn, Briggs assigned Chuck Taylor, 47, male Caucasian, Director of Strategic Marketing, to develop a major marketing strategy within the next six months, just in time for the annual board of director's meeting.

Taylor set about the assignment by reorganizing his group. He established three Strategic Product Managers who would be key to developing the plan. Jane Kravitz, M.B.A., 40, a Caucasian female with the company for 12 years, would be responsible for casual wear. Kyle Hudson, M.B.A., 39, male Caucasian, and Robert

Murphy, M.A., 45, male Caucasian, were assigned, respectively, athletic shoes and children's shoes. As strategic product managers, they would be responsible for developing a marketing plan including strategies for advertising, new-product development, positioning, revitalizing existing products, and greater penetration into international markets. Each manager would supervise a team of marketing professionals.

In the area of casual wear, changing consumer tastes had demanded a wider selection of styles beyond the traditional offerings. Kravitz's strategic performance objectives (S.O.s) included the completion of a comprehensive marketing plan for several vertical markets: African-American, Latino, Mature, College, Pre-teens, Men, and Women. Kravitz would inherit a staff of three: Lyndon Twitchell, M.B.A., Ph.D., 37, an African-American male with the company three years; Larry Bunton, M.B.A., 29, a Caucasian male with five years at the company; and Cheryl Abbott, B.S.B.A., M.A., 35, a Caucasian female with nine years seniority.

Lyndon Twitchell

Lyndon Twitchell grew up in Wilmington, Delaware, where he attended integrated schools. He credits his ability to do well academically and socially to his parents, who taught him the value of always doing his best and to respect all people, regardless of race or religion. After being aggressively recruited, Twitchell received a full scholarship to attend Howard University, a predominately black institution in Washington, D.C. His academic achievements caught the attention of one of his professors, who encouraged him to continue his education and suggested that graduate study in business would be a good fit with his undergraduate degree in science. He attended Georgetown University and attained a dual degree, the M.B.A. and a Ph.D. in Sociology. As a result of his doctoral studies on trends in consumer buying habits for over-the-counter health care products, he landed a job in consumer marketing at a major health care company.

Twitchell joined Jensen Shoes in 1990, after eight years professional marketing experience (see exhibit). He had been promoted regularly throughout his career and was excited about joining Jensen Shoes as a manager in its newly formed Special Promotions group, reporting to Chuck Taylor. Unfortunately the assignment was fraught with difficulties, and Twitchell and his team were not able to complete all of their strategic objectives (S.O.s).

Twitchell's Career History

Jensen Shoes, 1990–present
Strategic Marketing, casual wear
Promotions, Manager, ethnic markets
Healthcare USA, Consumer Products, 1987–1990
New Product Development
Becton Dickinson, Marketing Research, 1982–1987
Market Research Manager, consumer products
Associate Manager
Research Associate
Georgetown University, Ph.D., Sociology; M.B.A., 1982
Howard University, B.S., Chemistry, 1977

When he heard that he would be reporting to Jane Kravitz as a result of Taylor's reorganization, Twitchell was of two minds. He felt that losing his staff was punishment for not completing his S.O.'s in the Promotions job, but he also felt that a fresh start was what he needed. He knew Kravitz from some committee work and thought that she would be a reasonable person to work for. When she assigned him the African-American and Latino vertical markets, however, he grew concerned that he was being categorized as an ethnic specialist. He feared that this, coupled with his previous problems with inadequate resource and time allocation, were limiting his promotional opportunities. He called Mitch Lawson, 45, vice president of Operations and Twitchell's sponsor from the Black Senior Manager's Network, to request a confidential career discussion. Lawson invited Twitchell to come to his office and tell him what was going on.

Twitchell Tells His Story

The following story was told from memory by Lyndon Twitchell to Mitch Lawson. The time frame was the first three months of 1994.

I came to Jensen Shoes with a lot of enthusiasm. Everything that I'd heard about the company was positively reinforced during my initial interviews. There was talk about how committed the company was to the development of its employees and particularly to building a diverse workforce—even to the point of assigning people of color a sponsor, like yourself. I intended to rise to the top rungs of a medium-to-large company and saw Jensen Shoes as a place where I could achieve some of my career goals.

I knew at the time I accepted the job to help build Special Promotions that the group was unformed—a big part of my attraction to the job was being part of a start-up. I was offered and accepted the position as one of a team of Product Promotions Managers. The target populations had not been selected at the time that I accepted the offer. During my interviews, Chuck and I had talked about what they might be and I had suggested some ideas, fully expecting that I would be part of the decision process once I was on board. I'm sure you can appreciate what a surprise it was when I arrived on the job to not only find that the markets had been selected, but also that I had been put in charge of ethnic promotions. I wondered whether or not this would be a good career move, since I had never had any professional experience working with ethnic groups. It occurred to me that the assignment was deliberate, but I convinced myself that a stint in ethnic marketing would broaden my background. Besides, I was brand new to the company. I'd uprooted my family to come here. I figured that the smartest thing I could do was give it my best, do a good job, gain some credibility and move up in the company. Unfortunately, that isn't the way things went.

First, I was assigned a fairly inexperienced staff, so I had to spend quite a bit of time getting them up to speed. There were some bumpy points along the way, but with persistence we worked things through. Then, about six months into the program I found out that when everyone's budget was cut, mine was cut the deepest. It was hard not to yell "foul," but I was still working on building a track record, so I let it go. The good news was that my staff had a lot of raw talent and energy, and what we did, we did well. But we didn't achieve all of our strategic objectives. I knew from the beginning that we'd have trouble, given the severity of the budget cuts and the inexperience of the staff. Although I raised my concerns with Chuck, he didn't seem to take them seriously. He said something to the effect of "do your best" and left me saddled with the original S.O.s. I left his office wishing that he'd been more responsive, but I was under the impression that it wasn't the end of the world if we didn't achieve all of them. I was not at all prepared for what happened next. At the end of a critical phase of the project, Chuck called me into his office. Our discussion went something like this:

Chuck

> Twitchell, there is a reorganization coming down. With the start-up of Special Promotions under way, I've decided to do some streamlining. You'll be moved to Strategic Product Marketing.

Me

> I assume I'll be taking my group with me. We've really formed a solid team. It sounds like this could be a good opportunity.

Chuck

> Well, no, your group is going to be divided among the other managers in Promotions. You'll be reporting to Jane Kravitz.

Me

> It sounds like I am being demoted?

Chuck

> No, no, no. I wouldn't look at it like that. It's just that we feel that you need some time learning

your way around our products here since you didn't complete all of your S.O.s. You also had some difficulties with your staff. Some time as an individual contributor would probably be a good move for you now.

As much as I wanted to challenge him, I needed to think about what he said. No one else completed their S.O.s, but none of them lost their jobs. He didn't provide any feedback on the S.O.s we had completed and I disagreed about the difficulties with the staff. From where I stood, that was one of my most significant achievements. Simultaneously, I felt that I had failed and that I had been failed. The internal conflict made it difficult for me to find the appropriate words. I never did say anything in my defense. I do remember that I welcomed the change of reporting to Jane. Yeah, it smelled like a demotion, but Jane seemed like a decent person and I was banking on the opportunity to prove myself in another arena.

I was prepared to appreciate Jane's management style. She had a good track record and I figured I could have done a lot worse. At her first staff meeting, she laid out the time line for the proposal process. Jane was expected to present her proposal to Taylor and Briggs in five months. She charged us with completing our individual strategic objectives in four months. Just as I was thinking so far so good, the roof fell in and I had this *déjà vu* sinking kind of feeling. Jane presented the assignments and there it was next to my name: Twitchell: African-American and Latino Vertical Markets. This would mean two assignments in a row doing ethnic marketing. I couldn't help thinking that I was being relegated to a stereotype. I was also concerned that she assigned me two S.O.s, since I was bringing a special project with me that I was expected to complete in addition to my work with Jane. I'd been through that wringer when I didn't complete my S.O.s in Promotions and didn't want to make the same mistake twice.

My anxiety grew as I tried to think of a way to get out of this situation. I needed to get back into line management if I were going to achieve

my career goals. I didn't know Jane well enough to be certain how direct I could be with her. I liked her; she seemed like a reasonable person. But I needed some good press and raising my concerns might sound like I was complaining or put her on the defensive. On the other hand, if I didn't raise my concerns, I'd set myself up to fail and I couldn't afford another bad performance review.

I decided to feel my way through. When Jane and I sat down one-on-one, I had planned to steer the meeting to the special project on environmental buying trends that the executive vice president (EVP) had assigned me before the re-org. My background in consumer buying trends had caught the EVP's attention and I saw it as an opportunity to avoid the "ethnic marketing" label. I also thought that I might be able to grow the environmental project into a full-fledged job. In any case, I was counting on it to buy me some time. I hoped to find another position in the company. I liked the product and my family was settled here.

As I recall, Jane started the meeting by giving me the opportunity to raise some concerns:

Jane

First let me welcome you to the department. I've been looking forward to working with you. I realize, though, that this assignment represents a change for you and wanted to know how you feel about being here?

Me

Please don't take this personally, because it isn't meant that way, but I really prefer to be in a management job. Leading is where my talents lie, and something like the environmental project is more up my alley. I can see where it could turn into a full-fledged undertaking and I'd like to lead it for the company. In any case, I would like to get back into line management as soon as possible.

Jane

I can understand that. I've been in that situation before. If there is any way that I can help you get a new job, I will. I've been here for 12 years now, so I know quite a few people.

We talked some more about the special project. She provided me some information about how the company was already using recycled materials in shoes. The meeting was going well so I raised my concerns about the strategic objectives. To the best of my memory, here's how the conversation went:

Me

> I would like to talk about my assignments for the next four months. I expect that it will take me a couple of months to complete the special project. That would leave me only two months to do two strategic objectives.

Jane

> Are you saying that you don't think you'll be able to carry the load?

Me

> I noticed that you had allotted two months per S.O. for the other markets.

Jane

> Yes and no. I see the African-American and Latino market as having a lot in common and thought that you would be able to do them together. I suggest that we put that on hold while we see how the environmental project takes shape. Let's talk again then.

It wasn't the answer I was looking for. It was vaguely reminiscent of my conversation with Chuck when I raised my concerns regarding the budget cuts and inexperienced staff. I also didn't agree that the two markets could be collapsed. They were much more different than she realized.

At least we had gotten some things on the table. I wouldn't be leaving her totally in the dark about my intentions or my concerns. I decided against raising my concerns about the ethnic typing. That can be such a loaded issue. I was also somewhat uncomfortable that she seemed so eager to help me find a new job. But, I wanted to think of her as an ally, someone that I could count on. Maintaining a good relationship with Jane was important, since I would

need her for a reference. In any case, I was feeling better than I had for a long time and encouraged that I might be able to get back on track toward the career I'd intended.

That taken care of, I got going on the special project. It just so happened to be one that I was excited about—the impact of environmentally conscious consumer buying trends in the footwear industry. This was a hot topic. Although, I had never done environmental research, I knew a lot about consumer buying trends. I had some contacts and ideas about how to get going. Jane started me off with some leads. They weren't quite what I needed for the project, but I appreciated her support. I went over and above the call of duty to do a good job. For one thing, I needed a win, but more importantly, I was hoping that the networking would lead me to a new assignment either with the environmental project or something else.

When I completed the project, Jane seemed to go a little overboard recognizing me. Sure I'd done a good job, but she wrote a memo to Chuck, sent copies to his peers, Briggs, the EVP, and me. She even took me out to lunch at a fancy restaurant to celebrate. Hey, I like a nice meal as well as the next person, but a more low-key form of recognition would have seemed more appropriate. I was somewhat embarrassed by it. All the same, I decided to capitalize on the good press and met with Chuck for a little face-to-face visibility. I hoped the successful completion of the project would turn around my relationship with him. I opened the meeting with a comment intended to elicit his interest:

Me

> I thought I'd check in with you since this environmental project revealed some cutting-edge opportunities.

Chuck

> So, you think this stuff is new?

Me

> Well, not new, but definitely gaining momentum. I think we'd be wise to take the findings further.

Chuck

> You know, Twitchell, I'm not sure that you're in your element with this kind of project. While your report has merit, it falls short in terms of technical depth. I suggest that you put it behind you and get going on your S.O.s. The African-American and Latino markets have a tremendous unrealized potential, and you're the obvious choice to make it happen.

This conversation only strengthened my resolve to get out of Chuck's organization! I didn't need to hear any more. I also knew why Jane seemed so patronizing. After all, Chuck was her boss. I was convinced that he could only see me in ethnic marketing, no matter what other expertise I had. "Obvious choice" was just code for "you're the only black guy here." And that comment about me being out of my element was ridiculous—consumer buying trends was one of my areas of expertise. The gap between Jane and Chuck's feedback was so wide that you could drive a truck through it. I went from feeling on top of the world to scraping the bottom of the barrel. I wished that there had been someone in marketing that I could talk to, but marketing is pretty thin when it comes to black men.

I told Jane about my conversation with Chuck and expected her to go to bat for me. We both knew that I'd done a good job. Instead she sent me a memo requesting a proposal for my preliminary research on the two S.O.s. You know the kind of thing—goal statement, resources, contacts, time line—the whole nine yards. It seemed excessive, like micro-managing. Given her praise on the environmental project, I thought she'd give me some latitude. I was feeling let down by Jane and wasn't very committed to doing either S.O.

As much as I needed to raise my concerns about my prospects for advancement, I was feeling wary of Jane by this time. I thought that if I could stall the S.O.s by a week that we'd both be in a better frame of mind for negotiating something more realistic. I suggested that I start the project with some hands-on research by at-

tending a trade show in San Diego and then spending time at the West Coast sales offices. I figured they would have some good information. I also wanted to check out some job leads outside the company. To be fair, I saw the extra time as part my agenda and part the company's so I was willing to stay on my own nickel instead of racking up company expenses. Jane, as I recall, was uncharacteristically curt with me:

Jane

> I don't get this trip to San Diego. How can you even imagine going for a week to the West Coast when you are late getting started on your S.O.s. The trip sounds like a boondoggle to me.

Me

> Starting late on my S.O.s? Jane, I just completed the environmental project.

Jane

> That may be true, but you only have two months until the deadline for the S.O.s if I'm going to meet my deadline for reporting to Chuck.

Her reaction took me by surprise. It was as if we'd never talked about renegotiating the S.O.s. She went on about Chuck breathing down her neck, something about which I could certainly sympathize. It irked me though when she referred to the San Diego trip as a boondoggle. I swear, her behavior toward me seemed to run so hot and cold. I can't count on anyone in this place.

Are You Telling Me You Are Going on Strike?

I didn't know why she was going on about the San Diego trip. Everyone here builds comp time into a business trip. That's common knowledge. Besides that, it wasn't even going to cost the company extra lodging expenses. I just stood there and let her rant; there didn't seem to be any use trying to say anything. After she was done, I tried to tell her that I would be taking some of the time and expense as my own, but she wasn't listening. It seemed like we weren't getting anywhere, so I went back to my office.

If only she had let it drop there. Instead, she came down a while later and started all over again. She carried on about how I had to understand her position and she couldn't afford to have me out of the office and away from my work for a week. She even said something about how I was penalizing her and how this wasn't just jeopardizing my career but hers, too. Then I specifically remember her saying, "Unfortunately, it's my boss who is insisting that these things get done. I need to get you to get them done. That's my responsibility as your supervisor." When she finished I said to her:

Me

It sounds like you're taking this personally. From the very beginning, I told you that I didn't think this assignment was realistic. I wanted to be fair to both of us.

Jane

Are you telling me you're going on strike?

I don't know what she meant by the strike thing. I could see that she was under a lot of pressure, maybe more pressure than I realized. So was I and at least I'd tried to be up front with her about my career and the S.O.s. Now I was feeling on the verge of being hung out to dry.

I had to push on the issue of the two S.O.s. I'd already been through that set up with the Promotions job. After going back and forth a few times, she finally agreed that one S.O. made more sense. She suggested the African-American S.O., saying something about how that would take me less time. I'm thinking "Here we go again. The black man is the African-American expert." I was working hard to keep my cool and I didn't want to push her too far. I told her about some work I'd done in the Promotions job with Latino focus groups and how we went beyond the domestic agenda and discovered some things that could expand our offshore presence. I'd be losing all of my momentum if I did the African-American S.O. With the Latino market I'd still be the "ethnic expert," but at least it would provide me the opportunity to build my expertise in expanding international markets. Jane agreed to assign the African-American S.O. elsewhere.

We talked more about the Latino S.O. She asked me some questions and by the time the meeting ended, I thought we were in a good place. But then I got this "contract" outlining the terms of our agreement. It made me uncomfortable. The content was what we agreed to, but it was a real affront to my integrity—like she didn't trust me. On top of that, the last time I met with Jane, she seemed to be really ticked. She dragged out my past performance reviews and then she said something about it being hard to find me a new job in the company.

Mitch, things are a mess here. It seems like every time I make some progress something gets in the way. Things are starting to build up. First it was the ethnic marketing, which I thought I'd made peace with until I got assigned to the same markets in Jane's group. Then it was unrealistic strategic objectives. And, on top of that, the interactions going on among Jane, Chuck, and me are strange. I'm not sure who to trust, including myself. I have to keep reminding myself that I'm good at what I do, because the longer I stay here, the more I lose sight of that. As things stand now, I don't see a future for myself at Jensen Shoes.

JENSEN SHOES: JANE KRAVITZ'S STORY*

Jensen Shoes, established in 1943, prided itself on being a trendsetter and the leading marketer in the United States of high quality athletic and casual footwear for children and adults. Kenneth Jensen, the founder, was fond of saying "At Jensen Shoes we value our employees as much as our products. Employees who find their work worthwhile and satisfying do their best. In turn, the company profits while providing high-quality, well-priced shoes to the customer." Jensen managed with an open-door policy that became a model for other managers. Over the years, sensitivity to employee issues, both work and personal, became a hallmark of the Jensen Shoes culture.

For many years Jensen Shoes enjoyed a highly profitable position, to the point where one manager said, "We only have finance people to count the money." By 1994, it was a $65 million company with 4,500 employees worldwide. It was making significant progress creating a presence in international markets and had targeted off-shore growth as an objective. Casual wear made up 45 percent of company revenues in recent years. Athletic shoes accounted for 30 percent of the 1993 revenue and children's wear accounted for the other 25 percent. Return on Equity was 20 percent in 1993. Although this represented a slight decline from previous years, it was competitive with industry leaders.

Sales had grown steadily in athletic and children's wear during the last decade, but casual wear had begun to flatten necessitating the need to diversify product lines and strengthen long term industry viability. In January of 1994, Jensen Shoes' executive management charged Sally Briggs, 44, female Caucasian, Vice President of the Marketing Division, to define opportunities for new markets and new products. In turn, Briggs assigned Chuck Taylor, 47, male Caucasian, Director of Strategic Marketing, to develop a major marketing strategy within the next six months, just in time for the annual board of director's meeting.

Taylor set about the assignment by reorganizing his group. He established three Strategic Product Managers who would be key to developing the plan. Jane Kravitz, M.B.A., 40, a Caucasian female with the company for 12 years, would be responsible for casual wear. Kyle Hudson, M.B.A., 39, male Caucasian, and Robert Murphy, M.A., 45, male Caucasian, were assigned, respectively, athletic shoes and children's shoes. As strategic product managers, they would be responsible for developing a marketing plan including strategies for advertising, new product development, positioning, revitalizing existing products, and greater penetration into international markets. Each manager would supervise a team of marketing professionals.

In the area of casual wear, changing consumer tastes had demanded a wider selection of styles beyond the traditional offerings. Kravitz's strategic performance objectives (S.O.s) included the completion of a comprehensive marketing plan for several vertical markets: African-American, Latino, Mature, College, Pre-teens, Men, and Women. Kravitz would inherit a staff of three: Lyndon Twitchell, M.B.A., Ph.D., 37, an African-American male with the company three

This case was prepared by Pamela J. Maus under the supervision of Mary C. Gentile.

Copyright © 1994 by the President and Fellows of Harvard College.

Harvard Business School case 395-120.

*This case should be used in conjunction with Jensen Shoes: Lyndon Twitchell's Story, No. 395-121.

years; Larry Bunton, M.B.A., 29, a Caucasian male with five years at the company; and Cheryl Abbott, B.S.B.A., M.A., 35, a Caucasian female with nine years seniority.

Jane Kravitz

Jane Kravitz had proven herself to be a well-respected manager and individual contributor. She had been in a staff position for the last 18 months and was pleased to be getting back onto the line (see exhibit). She considered the new job a perfect one for her, important to her career development and an opportunity for advancement to the next level.

Kravitz's Career History

Jensen Shoes, Casual Wear, 1982–present
    Senior Strategic Marketing Manager
    New-Product Development Manager
    Market Research Program Manager
Procter & Gamble, Personal Care, 1978–1982
    Brand Manager
    Associate Brand Manager
Johnson & Johnson, Infant Care, 1976–1978
    Associate Brand Manager
    Brand Assistant
University of Michigan, M.B.A., 1976
Michigan State University, B.S., Sociology, 1973

She was excited about her new staff. Not only did she consider them a perfect mix, given the assignment, but she also prided herself on being particularly sensitive to the needs of a diverse workforce. As a white woman, she believed she had faced her share of adversity "making it in a white man's world" and felt a responsibility to use her learning to help others advance in their careers.

After considering the strengths of the staff, she assigned each member two vertical markets. The College and Men's markets went to Bunton. Abbott, the mother of two pre-teens, was assigned the Pre-teen and Women's markets. Kravitz took on the Mature market, and assigned the Latino and African-American markets to Twitchell, a fit she thought was a natural.

Kravitz had been in her new job less than three months when she approached Patty Russell with concerns about Lyndon Twitchell. Russell, 33, an African-American, was the human resources professional assigned to Kravitz's group. Russell had been with the company for only a short time, but had already developed a reputation for effectively handling sticky situations. Russell encouraged Kravitz to tell her the story from the beginning. Afterwards, they could develop a strategy for handling it.

Kravitz Tells Her Story

The following story was told from memory by Jane Kravitz to Patty Russell. The time frame was the first three months of 1994.

When Chuck reorganized his group, I became a Strategic Marketing Manager and inherited a staff of three. Chuck gave me glowing reports about Cheryl and Larry, but when he came to Lyndon, he was less than enthusiastic. Lyndon had been with the company for about three years and it seemed as though he hadn't received very good performance reviews. Frankly, I wasn't that concerned about the assessment because Chuck could be a little quick to judge. Besides, I knew myself to be a good manager. I'd had some challenging situations, but I knew how to cajole, nurture, beg, direct—whatever it took to get the job done. I'd also worked with Lyndon on a couple of committees and found him to be very professional. I decided to come into the situation with an open mind, giving Lyndon the benefit of the doubt.

Having said that though, I was caught somewhat off guard in my initial conversation with Lyndon. He had barely sat down in my office before he was saying something like "don't take this personally, but I don't intend to be here for long. I want to get back to managing a staff." I had some ideas why he might be saying that.

Lyndon is well educated, good looking, and makes no bones about his desire to get ahead. I also thought that he might have felt it a comedown to report to me since he had had a staff prior to the reorganization. That was cool. I could understand that. I had even been in that situation before. I told him that I'd been here a few years now, knew a lot of people and, if he wanted, could help him get his next position. I also figured that that wouldn't be a problem since he was a black man and everyone was looking for diversity on their staff. I was glad that he opened up because it gave us the chance to get off to a good, direct, and honest start.

As with my meetings with Cheryl and Larry, I discussed Lyndon's strategic objectives with him. We talked about what I would be expecting in terms of his particular vertical markets, how the work should be organized and that I expected it to be ready in four months. I had asked the staff to prepare a proposal for how they would approach their S.O.s. In addition to Lyndon's strategic objectives, he would be conducting a special project on environmental consumer buying trends that he was expected to get under way immediately. The project had been handed down to Lyndon through Chuck from the Executive Vice President (EVP). It seemed as though the EVP wanted to tap into Lyndon's background in consumer buying trends. You don't argue with senior management, so we agreed that he would go ahead and get it completed before starting his S.O.s.

Lyndon did raise his concern that two S.O.s might be an unrealistic assignment, given his special project. Still, I didn't want to rule out his doing both of them. I wanted to see how he did with the environmental project first. I told him that I saw a fair amount of overlap in his two vertical markets and was thinking of them more like one. I suggested we wait and see how things went.

The environmental aspect of the project was something that Lyndon had never done before,

so I spent quite a bit of time coaching him. I was impressed with how diligently he took on the project. He spent time researching new material and took advantage of the resources that I suggested, which I also thought would provide him with some good visibility. He completed the project on time and, in my estimation, with top quality. I would have preferred that he'd been a little more communicative about what he was doing and his interim reports were sketchy, but I figured that that was all part of getting on board with each other. In recognition, I took Lyndon out to lunch to celebrate and reward his performance. To be truthful, I was conscious of wanting to keep him happy. After all, his performance was my performance, and since I knew that he wasn't all that eager to be in the job, I wanted to reinforce anything that I considered positive.

Lyndon was hoping that this project would develop into something more, so I made a point of reporting Lyndon's accomplishments to Chuck who, to my dismay, was less than impressed. All he had to say was "anyone could have done that project. What I want to know is how's he doing on his S.O.s?" Chuck's urgency raised a flag for me. He didn't have much faith in Lyndon, which meant that I was going to have to work that much harder to get Lyndon up to speed in Chuck's estimation.

I had already planned to meet with Lyndon the next day when I expected to review his proposal on how he intended to carry out the assignment. Since the assignment had outlined a fairly extensive proposal process, I was expecting a well-developed execution plan. Lyndon should have done this kind of thing a zillion times; it was Marketing 101. Instead, all he came prepared with was some information about a trade show in San Diego that he wanted to attend the next week. He also planned to be gone the entire week. Since the trade show was only for two days, I wanted to know how he planned to spend the remainder of the time. The conversation was bizarre. As best as I can summon my memory, it went something like this:

Me

> I don't have any problems with you going to the trade show as long as you get your S.O.s done. But since the trade show is only on Monday and Tuesday, what else do you plan to do?

Lyndon

> I thought I would drop by the San Diego sales office and talk to some people that I know there.

Me

> Oh. How do you think that will help you with your S.O.s?

Lyndon

> Well, I know some of the people and I thought that they might have some information that could help me.

Me

> A week seems like a long time just to stop by the sales office. What do you expect to accomplish?

Lyndon

> I won't exactly know until I'm there, but, I'm sure that these guys will be able to help me out.

We went around a couple more times, and soon I was frustrated with the exchange. He seemed evasive. I also wondered why he wasn't more concerned about the deadlines for his S.O.s. This just wasn't a good time for him to take a week off and he should have known it. Had he become a little too comfortable with some of the negative aspects of the company's culture? I'm all for giving people the benefit of the doubt, and all that open-door stuff managers are expected to do, but some people take advantage of it. I hated to think that Lyndon might be doing that. He's got too much going for him— well manicured, erudite, and black. I thought that I needed to be extra direct with him, just in case he was starting to slough off. Here's how I remember our conversation:

Me

> Let me tell you how things work around here. Your S.O.s are the most important thing you do. If you don't meet your deadlines, everyone up the ladder is in trouble.

Lyndon

> Is this about my traveling?

Me

> Traveling isn't the issue. I don't have any trouble with you traveling, but this trip doesn't make sense. It would help me if you could just explain to me what you're doing for work out there for a week since the trade show is only on Monday and Tuesday. I don't have trouble with your taking comp time, but you've got two S.O.s due soon and you haven't even started them. Lyndon, this is sounding like a boondoggle. As a manager I can't justify a week's time, to say nothing of hotel and other expenses.

Lyndon

> It wouldn't cost the company anything. I'd be staying with my brother.

Then I got it. He wanted to combine the business trip with a personal trip. Obviously he knew what he was doing wasn't quite kosher and that was why he wasn't being up front. But if he'd just told me what he wanted to do, we could have negotiated something. I'm not that inflexible. There have been times when I've signed off for a staff member to do some training in Chicago because her fiancé lived there or to attend a trade show in Miami in the middle of winter. I don't care if people want to combine a business trip with personal plans, but as his supervisor I thought I had a right to know what he was doing. And finally, his S.O.s weren't getting done and that was the heart of the matter. Lyndon was falling behind.

I wasn't done with our discussion, but I didn't know what to say next. He seemed so reluctant to get on with his work. I couldn't figure it out. Maybe he didn't know how to do what I was asking. That seemed ludicrous, because I knew that he could do good work. Before I could say anything else, he abruptly left my office.

There is so much at stake if he misses the deadlines for the S.O.s. Neither of us will get a bonus. I really needed him to focus on a plan. I couldn't afford for my boss to think I couldn't manage my staff. This is my biggest concern. And I was beginning to have doubts. This can be a great place to work but sometimes the company style can be a headache for a manager. I'm expected to get my S.O.s done, but I can't just tell an employee to do their job—it's like I'm supposed to humor them.

I let things ride for a couple of hours before going to his office, thinking he would come around if I gave him time to think. I also thought he might feel more comfortable in his own office. I started off by asking Lyndon what was going on. I wasn't asking him to stay here until 10:00 at night doing extra projects. That would probably stress me, too. I offered to help him put the proposal together. Then he said something like "I told you from the beginning that I don't want to be here and that the two S.O.s were a big load on top of the environmental project." By this time I was concerned that he didn't intend to do any of his work. I didn't need this. Supporting Lyndon was starting to feel very risky. Just to make sure I understood him, I asked point blank, "Do you mean to tell me that you are going on strike?!"

Upping the Ante

At this point, I felt as though I had been backed into a corner and, as much as I didn't want to face Chuck's "I told you so," I had to bring him up to date on this situation. After all, this isn't just Lyndon's performance, it is mine, too. I should have guessed Chuck wouldn't be terribly surprised. He made some crack about "the *brothers* never being happy" and told me to start documenting his performance.

I hated being in this position. I've always taken a special interest in minority populations as I've moved up the ladder. Even if they didn't report to me I would do what I could to give them extra visibility and go out of my way to coach them. Chuck's lack of support toward Lyndon complicated matters, too. I had to find some way to motivate Lyndon. I was beginning to feel that I was managing by trial and error. I sat down with Lyndon again and I specifically remember saying to him:

Me

> Lyndon, look, I feel bad. Obviously I didn't mean to upset you, but you have to understand my position. I have to get the S.O.s done and you have to help me. We're nearing completion deadlines and I don't see any progress. I can't afford to have you out of the office and away from your work for a week if you can't work on your S.O.s.

I offered him some time off when we finished the proposal. I even tried to appeal to him on the grounds that he wasn't just hurting himself when he resisted doing his S.O.s, but that he penalized me as well. I also threw in the pressure I was getting from Chuck to get the S.O.s done. I finished by saying "I need to get you to get your work done. That's my responsibility as your supervisor."

We talked for a long time. Lyndon seemed to resist. He said that he only wanted to do the one S.O. His position was that while the environmental project wasn't an S.O., it did add to his work load. Reluctantly, I agreed to the one S.O., but I preferred that he do the African-American one since I thought that market had more potential. I also thought he could complete it faster. In the back of my mind, I still hoped that he could make progress on both of them. He, on the other hand, wanted to do the Latino S.O. At this point, I was getting worn down, so I decided to take what I could get. I wrote up an agreement and we both signed it.

I've tried to keep him motivated. I even threw him a birthday party. I didn't do that for anyone else. But, when I would check in with him to see if there were ways I could help, he sort of indicated that he had things under control without providing much in the way of details. So, I would ask him for written updates which he'd provide sparingly. While they were better than nothing, they gave me little to go on. I am beginning to have serious doubts about whether he will even complete the one S.O., much less the two I hoped for.

In the meantime, I was doing what I could to find him a new job. I'm buddies with Ron Johnson who is the director of Distribution and an influential member of the Black Senior Managers Network. I remember a conversation we had while walking out of a meeting:

Me

> Hey Ron, I noticed you've got a few openings in your group. You know Lyndon Twitchell don't you? Well, he's working for me now and he wants to get back into managing. Would you consider hiring him into your group?

Ron

> I'd like to help, but his background is marketing, not distribution. Who have you talked to in marketing? It seems like that would be a better fit for him.

I resisted saying much about the problems I was having with Lyndon. I didn't think that would help either of us. I was hoping that since Ron and Lyndon were part of the Black Senior Manager's Network that he would take Lyndon under his wing and was surprised that he didn't take more of an interest.

I'm At My Wit's End

In one final attempt, I remember sitting down with Lyndon and putting it to him straight.

Me

> What gives here? I know you've got what it takes to do these S.O.s. In your last job's two performance reviews it was the same story: the S.O.s that you completed met expectations, but for whatever reason, you didn't complete all of them. And, you haven't made much progress on the one S.O. that we agreed to. This is catching up with you.
>
> Just do the S.O. and do it well and you'll be fine; no one will complain. But the way it is now, getting you a job elsewhere here is becoming a slim possibility.

I thought for a moment about whether I should tell him that I had been documenting his performance since that is the first step toward termination. If he doesn't get the message now, he's going to be without any job. I don't want to demoralize him. I really want to help him. I just wish that he would get the message and get on with his work. I'm at my wit's end. I'm losing sleep and weight. I don't know what to do next.

KAREN LEARY (A)

It did not surprise Karen Leary that her lunch with Ted Chung had turned into a somewhat uncomfortable experience. Although a year had passed since she hired Chung to be a financial consultant (FC), Leary sensed that there was a wide gulf between them. She had tried to get to know him better, but Chung had always distanced himself from her and the other FCs in the office. Leary had hired the Taiwan-born Chung to attract customers from the thriving community of Taiwanese entrepreneurs that had sprung up around Elmville, a Chicago suburb. In his first year at Merrill Lynch, Chung opened the $6 million account of a Taiwanese industrialist and had traded the account actively, generating substantial commissions.

Over lunch, Leary and Chung reviewed Chung's performance during the past year. Leary told him that she was pleased that he had opened such a big account. She reminded him of her concern about the appropriateness of some of his trades. The client was new to the American market, and she questioned Chung's investments in risky stocks and his use of margin. She also cautioned Chung not to spend all his time with this one account; she expected him to develop other Taiwanese customers.

Chung explained that he had been actively developing relationships with wealthy Taiwanese businesspeople and expected to bring in more accounts soon. He also reassured Leary that the Taiwanese industrialist was fully aware of how his account was being handled. Chung then said, in reviewing his own performance, that he was

certainly going to be one of the most important producers in Leary's branch, and therefore, he deserved and needed a private office.

Leary was taken aback by Chung's request. Of the 45 FCs at the Elmville branch, only eight had private offices and they were the best and most experienced brokers. Even FCs doing substantial business in their 20th year sometimes did not have private offices. Although Chung appeared headed toward a successful career at Merrill Lynch, several elements in Chung's performance over the past year worried Leary. Given her expectations of the Taiwanese market's potential and her aggressive goals for the office, Leary wondered how she should respond to his request.

Merrill Lynch Background

In 1985, Merrill Lynch, one of the nation's largest wirehouses, found itself in the midst of a fiercely competitive battle in the retail financial services industry. Government deregulation of major financial institutions and increased innovation in financial instruments had unleashed a head-on clash among a diverse group of players. Merrill Lynch, Citicorp, Prudential, American Express, and Sears had built up impressive arrays of consumer financial services through expansion and acquisition.

From the 1940s when Charles Merrill had pioneered the concept of bringing "Wall Street to Main Street," Merrill Lynch had been in the forefront of bringing one-stop financial shopping to all Americans. The core of Merrill's approach to providing financial services had always been the tight bond that brokers formed with their clients. The company had set up a large network of branch offices and supported its brokers with extensive training and top-notch

This case was prepared by Jaan Elias under the supervision of Linda A. Hill.
Copyright © 1986 by the President and Fellows of Harvard College.
Harvard Business School case 487-020.

research. Through its efforts, Merrill created the mold for the modern professional broker.[1] FCs responded by showing fierce pride in the company. Most of senior management, including many of the past CEOs, had started out as brokers.

The increased competition, however, had Merrill's top management leading its brokers in new directions. The decision to retitle account executives *financial consultants* was more than cosmetic; it reflected a transition in the way Merrill marketed its services. (Brokers at Merrill Lynch were first called *account executives* by Charlie Merrill in the 1940s. In 1983, they were retitled *financial consultants.*) According to the Merrill Lynch 1985 Annual Report, the company had been moving toward a customer-oriented rather than a product-centered structure. Services were to be "wrapped around the customer." Accordingly, the company introduced a menu of new products, ranging from real estate investments and insurance to centralized cash management accounts. Salaried product specialists had been dispatched to branch offices to aid FCs in pinpointing the proper mix of financial instruments to respond to a client's needs. The new lineup of products necessitated additional training in financial planning practices and profiling the customers' long-term financial goals.

Increased competition and consumer sophistication had also meant smaller margins, and concern about the high fixed cost of operating a large brokerage system. (Merrill Lynch estimates that it takes $100,000 a year to support one broker.) Upper management had targeted goals of cost control and increased productivity per broker while continuing to offer the most professional financial advice possible to the client. The compensation system was restructured to reward asset gathering and top brokers. To be profitable, Merrill's management believed the company must enhance an FC's ability to add

value by recognizing and properly satisfying a customer's long-term financial objectives.

Some industry analysts, however, provided a sharp counterpoint to the new strategies being employed by financial service firms. One commented, "People still do business with brokers because they like them. You need the entrepreneurial type of guy. What happens if some of a firm's big ideas don't work?" Another observed, "For most brokers, trading remains the most glamorous part of the business; it provides the high-stakes financial rewards and excitement that motivated them to become brokers." Many thought trading would always be a broker's bread and butter. One broker commented, "The industry is always restructuring. It'll probably happen again in a few years, but the bottom line will still be how much you can bring in with commissions."[2]

Taking Over the Branch Office

Leary's Background
Leary joined Merrill Lynch as a financial consultant in 1975, after having managed a family business for several years. Besides quickly building her own client list, Leary took on various leadership roles, such as product coordinator, in the San Francisco branch where she worked.

> I truly enjoyed working with my clients and helping them fulfill their dreams, such as getting the money for a new home or funding the investments that would make it possible for a child to go to college. But I always knew that I wanted to go further in the industry.

After six years as an FC, Leary went to the Merrill Lynch assessment center and passed the

---

1. *Business Week,* January 16, 1984.

2. At large wirehouses, brokers received between 30 percent and 45 percent of the business they generated. Branch managers were compensated as a percentage of what the brokers they managed produced. Brokers prized relationships with large customers since over 80 percent of the commission dollars were produced by 20 percent of the customers.

grueling set of exercises designed to evaluate management skills. She was assigned to a downtown Chicago branch as sales manager. In 1983, she became resident vice president and general manager at the Elmville branch, a substantial office for a first-time branch manager.

> When I took over the office, there was a large group of people here who had been in production for maybe 10 years or more. Many were average producers who did a lot of options and small trades. A few were oriented toward just getting a commission dollar and were having difficulty implementing a financial planning approach. I felt I would have to change this, that the culture was one that would not allow growth. I knew that even if I brought in new, good people their growth would be inhibited by the prevailing culture. . . . Some managers have the philosophy: "If a person is moderately profitable for the firm and no trouble, then fine." I'm not saying that is a bad approach. The firm makes money, the FCs make money, and the manager makes money. It is just that I am more aggressive and my goals are higher. I wanted to build a winning team that would be recognized for the quality and professionalism of its people, that would excel in matching clients with the products, and that would utilize the full range of Merrill Lynch services. I don't want to be a little country office out in Elmville.

Leary terminated eight of the FCs that she inherited, some of whom had been with Merrill Lynch for over six years. She believed that these were people who could not follow the firm's strategy. In many instances it was a difficult decision, and Leary helped some FCs find positions with other brokerage houses.

Leary initially focused on hiring experienced brokers to fill the vacancies.

> I interviewed some younger people who had been brokers with other firms. They were already fully registered and for one reason or another had not fit into their firms. To train a person with no experience, it costs Merrill Lynch $30,000, and it is at least six to eight months before an inexperienced

person is at all productive. So it is a long-term, expensive proposition. The people I interviewed were fully registered and knew a little about the business. So I took a risk. It was a business decision; it cost Merrill Lynch little. I hired four or five of them and two made it. . . . But I learned you really can't do it that way and build what I want. It exposes the rest of the office to unsuccessful people and the office needs to view themselves as a collection of successful professionals. So, while it did not cost the firm financially, I think it cost the firm in other areas.

Leary's Management Style

Leary made a point of getting out of her office and on to the floor of the boardroom as often as she could. For at least two hours every day, she navigated among the cubicles, where the FCs were talking with clients on the phone and monitoring market indicators and current events on Quotron screens.

> I do a lot of coaching and counseling informally. I find it's effective and less threatening than to be called into the manager's office and asked to explain yourself. So, I'll frequently sit down at a person's desk and just say "Hi. How's it going. Let me see what you're working on. That looks interesting. Have you seen the new tax-free bonds up on page eight of the Quotron?" or I will ask them about a problem they had or a stock that they are watching.

"Karen is by far the most sales-oriented manager I've ever seen," a veteran Merrill Lynch FC commented. "Literally every day, she finds just the right investment for a client. Now a good broker can get on the phone and use that immediately. . . . Some managers are content to just check the mail and do the administration. Not Karen. She really is very aggressive in trying to motivate the FCs."

Leary's superiors praised her development of innovative sales and training programs. She created a voluntary program of partnerships/internships for FCs both to motivate top, older producers and to help young FCs get started.

Some of these older people are doing five or six hundred thousand a year in production and have their business set. They get kind of complacent. At that point in their career, it is very difficult to get these people to prospect or develop new business. On the other hand, younger people need strong role models who are willing to teach them more about the business. I think this program provided a unique opportunity for less-experienced FCs to learn firsthand about superior customer service and prudent money management.

Leary persuaded a few of her more experienced FCs to take on younger brokers or trainees as junior partners. The young brokers agreed to make the cold calls and draw up the client profiles needed to gather more assets, while the older FCs helped with the clients and with servicing the accounts. Leary hoped that the program would help reinvigorate the careers of some of her older producers while giving younger ones much-needed experience and supervision.

Leary stressed training her corps of younger brokers. She often came in before the market opened or on Saturdays to lead seminars designed to familiarize young FCs with financial planning techniques. Through case-by-case review, Leary led spirited discussions of Merrill Lynch products and techniques for profiling customer needs. She also leaned on her young FCs, keeping tabs on their cold calling (they were expected to make 200 calls a day) and overseeing the development of their own customer strategies.

Overseeing brokers' trades was an important part of a Merrill Lynch manager's responsibilities, and many of the FCs in Leary's office gave her high marks for staying on top of compliance issues.[3] The branch manager was considered the key to a brokerage house's compliance effort, since he or she was in the best position to monitor brokers. Branch managers were charged with

guarding against a wide range of broker malfeasance, including churning (doing more trading in an account than warranted), misrepresentation (failing to properly convey the risks of an investment), unauthorized trading, and unsuitability (recommending investments not in keeping with an investor's financial position).

One of Leary's first moves on taking over the Elmville office was to bring in a new chief compliance officer, one she felt would get to know brokers better and evaluate their trades. Daily, Leary reviewed all of her FCs' account activity and often questioned FCs about their trades. Leary observed, "There is a great deal of concern about protecting our customers. So it is very important to me that we do quality business for them and make sure their investments are right and proper. We deal with money and are very tightly regulated."

Leary's aggressive approach to sales and compliance appeared to have paid off. During her first year, business increased by 30 percent. However, her style had some FCs grumbling. "She rides all the FCs hard," one commented, "She is always pushing you and looking over your shoulder." Leary hoped her innovative approach to management would be beneficial to, and recognized by, Merrill Lynch. From the Elmville office, her specific goals in 1985 included completing an office renovation, opening another satellite office, and developing the small business trade. Generally, she wanted to build "a high-producing, successful group of professionals who help one another and work together to provide clients with complete service in meeting their long-term financial goals. All recognizing, of course, that we're dealing with egos and that it takes a very strong ego to be successful."

Developing the Taiwanese Market

Hiring and Training Ted Chung

Leary hired Chung to develop the Taiwanese market for Merrill Lynch. "The Taiwanese are not really assimilated into the American system, so we needed a person with a Taiwanese back-

---

3. *Compliance* is the name given to surveillance against broker fraud and to the maintenance of integrity in the brokerage industry.

ground who spoke Chinese to begin to develop this market. I put some general ads in the paper, and Ted Chung was one of many who answered the ad and one of several Taiwanese." Numerous Taiwanese-owned and -operated businesses had sprung up throughout the Chicago area during the 1970s. Unlike other waves of immigrants to the United States, these Taiwanese had a strong network of contacts and sufficient capital to set up businesses. Through hard work and determination, family-run, first-generation Taiwanese businesses had built up substantial positions in a relatively short time. Many active Taiwanese community organizations had formed, and businesses tailored to the Taiwanese had opened their doors.

The other Taiwanese applicants were young, and Leary felt she needed a more experienced broker to work with Taiwanese businesspeople.

Chung was in his early forties and he appeared mature, stable, and responsible. He was married with four children, and his wife was a computer programmer. In his seven years in the United States, he had been a very successful salesman for a real estate company and had owned his own moving business. He was independently wealthy. He had been born in Taiwan, yet he was westernized in many ways.

Leary described hiring new FCs as one of the most important functions of a branch manager. She frequently interviewed people three or four times before making a final decision. She met with Chung eight times in various settings before hiring him.

I felt I didn't really know the whole person, but I wrote that off to the fact that he was Asian and I was not, or maybe there was some concern over my being a woman (though he never expressed any concerns). So after a period of time where I could not put my finger on anything that was wrong, I made the decision to hire him because I felt there were so many areas where he fit. I knew his wife, met his children, knew where he lived, and investigated his background, and there was nothing there that appeared negative.

Newly hired FCs went through an intensive four-month training program. During the first two months, they prepared for the rigorous General Securities exam, and in their third month they learned additional subjects such as portfolio management and selling techniques. The first three months of the program were spent in the branch office, and Leary saw this as a time when trainees could learn how the office operated. Trainees were often asked to fill in for sales assistants or to help in operations.

Chung studied hard and did well on his tests; however, Leary noticed that he bristled and found other things to do when staff members asked for his help.

I called him in and said, "You were asked to sit at the sales assistant's desk this morning, and it appeared that you were uncomfortable with this request, and you found some way not to fulfill it. Let's talk about that." He then described how his feelings were hurt. It came out that he didn't like to do those things; that he frankly considered it to be beneath him, particularly if an underling asked him. He told me that if I asked him he would do it for me. I said, "Well, Ted, this is an office and a business. As a trainee, you are here to learn and to develop, and I would like you to do that."

In their fourth month of training, FCs were sent to the Merrill Lynch training center at One Liberty Plaza in New York City. (Merrill Lynch opened a training center in late 1985 in Princeton, New Jersey.)

When Ted went there, he was very well prepared. He had received excellent scores on all of his tests. Before he went, he and I discussed strategies. I told him there were very fine research people there and gave him names of those people and told him he should develop relationships. And he did.

Leary noted that Chung was very good at establishing contacts with the Merrill people in New York:

Whenever he would go in to meet with a research person, he would bring them something to eat: coffees for both of them, and a doughnut or a bagel. He always made sure to call the person's secretary to find out how they took their coffee and any other preferences. After the meeting, he would send a note along with a little gift, such as a Merrill Lynch pen or cup. He had gone out and bought a whole slew of Merrill Lynch paraphernalia, and he used it effectively.

Bringing in the Big Account

After four months as trainees, FCs began the often arduous process of gaining clients. Most FCs spent their first months back from training making up to 200 cold calls a day. They also gave and attended seminars on personal investing, identifying clients who could benefit from their expertise. Chung, however, felt that the Taiwanese market had to be developed differently.

> Ted felt that he could develop the Taiwanese market, but that it was a different market and had to be approached according to Taiwanese tradition. He assured me that in time he would develop very substantial accounts, but that he wouldn't do a lot of business in the beginning, opening what he called "chicken-feed" accounts. I said fine. This is a responsible person who wants to be successful. This is the game plan he wants to use, and it makes sense to me.

Unlike his peers, Chung did not make cold calls and spent much of his time outside of the office, attending events in the Taiwanese community. He felt that the way to develop the Taiwanese market was to increase his own visibility and prestige. In the first three months after he had completed his training, Chung had yet to open his first account. Leary became increasingly concerned about his lack of prospective clients and business. She met with him occasionally, and he reassured her that he was developing relationships that would lead to substantial accounts.

Over time, Leary was becoming more aware of Chung's stiff formality and need for privacy. Leary noted:

> Everything about his desk was spotless. He brought in all kinds of items from past lives,

framed pictures of himself from magazines and other displays of his importance. No one was allowed to use his desk. People here can be a little touchy [about their desks], but he was really excessive. He didn't want people using his phone, he didn't want people working at his desk. Normally, an FC will have his desk the way he wants it, and if we are going to have someone else sit there, we usually do the person a courtesy and ask them. But sometimes you just can't. Nobody usually minds. . . . Once you sat at Ted's desk, nothing was an informal meeting. If I sat down there to chat with him, he'd get up and clear all of his papers away and arrange his coat and get everything all set before he would start to talk.

In his fourth month after training, Chung set the office buzzing by bringing in a $6 million account.

> I congratulated him, and we made sure that the account was set up properly. I then made calls to New York to three very good Merrill Lynch analysts and set up some private meetings to support him. I talked to him about the possibility of having the account managed by Merrill Lynch Asset Management, a Merrill Lynch subsidiary that manages substantial amounts of money. I was very uncomfortable with the idea of a brand-new FC handling that kind of money. He insisted the client only spoke Chinese, that there was no way he would allow anyone else to work with him. Chung said he had come to Merrill Lynch only because of him and the fact that they were from the same village in Taiwan. Chung insisted that he could do it.

Leary and her administrative manager, Fred Lewin, began watching the account closely. (The administrative manager is also the chief compliance officer at the branch.) At Leary's request, Chung wrote a letter, in Chinese, to the investor detailing a financial plan that Leary had approved. Chung proposed a conservative stock purchase plan and option-writing program with money (which was coming out of CDs [certificates of deposit] held at a local bank) equally distributed between equities and a conservative fixed-income strategy. Leary commented:

Initially, the investments were pretty good. His first five or six investments were appropriate: they were fixed income and good quality stocks. Then he began to get into takeover stocks. It was an explosive time in the market when takeover rumors about many stocks were booming. While most of the stocks he was purchasing had takeover rumors circulating about them, he initially made sure that the stock was still a Merrill Lynch-recommended security. The stocks Merrill recommends are fundamentally fine, well-managed companies, and have nothing to do with the rumor mill. But the direction he was going in was becoming clear. I'd see his purchases show up on the computer screen and call him in. He would swear, "No, no, no, he's buying it because it's good quality stock, love the earnings," et cetera.

More and more of the account was being invested in equities, and Chung actively used margin borrowing. He also began purchasing stocks not recommended by the Merrill Lynch research department. FCs were not allowed to recommend these stocks to their clients and could not buy them unless the purchases were unsolicited. After making non-Merrill Lynch-recommended purchases, Chung presented typed, signed, certified letters to Leary from the client attesting that Chung had not suggested the stock and that the purchase order had come at the customer's insistence.

> When Chung's handling of the account departed from the initial strategy, I told Ted I would need to meet the customer. The customer, a Taiwanese industrialist, spoke little English. Chung brought the customer in, but it was a fairly uncomfortable meeting because our communication was limited. The customer smiled and indicated that he was pleased with Chung's work. Ted interceded after about five minutes and said the industrialist had to catch a plane. Translating for him, Chung told me the client had enjoyed meeting me and thanked me for my hospitality.

Leary was now checking Chung's trades every morning. The account was trading actively, and Chung had generated a substantial amount of commissions. Chung was careful to document all of his trading activity formally and to fulfill standard compliance procedures. As time went on, however, Chung became more annoyed with Leary and Lewin's monitoring. He resisted questioning and occasionally became angry at Lewin's inquiries.

The other FCs were very impressed with Chung's achievement. In handling the account, Chung had made some good trades and had followed compliance procedures. Although he had not brought in any other accounts, Chung hinted that additional substantial accounts were on the way.

Leary commented:

> When the trades were good, I would call him in and tell him he was doing a good job. I also kept urging him to try to develop other areas. I was always available to him if he needed consultation, and I got him through to people in New York who could help him with the account. These were people most first-year FCs don't ever get to sit down with.

Back at Lunch

Following Chung's request for an office, Leary mentally reviewed the situation. She felt uncomfortable with several aspects of his performance, and the lunch was doing little to ease her worries. She did not know how involved Chung's client was with the account, and because of the language barrier and Chung's close relationship with the client, she could not check with the client more directly. Chung's growing displays of "ego and temper" also worried her. His request for a private office was totally inappropriate. Leary observed:

> It usually takes a person a substantial amount of time to get a private office here. They go to very special people who have really earned their spurs through a lot of good quality business and longevity with the firm. So while the FCs in the office were amazed by the business Ted was doing, they also needed to think of the office as their family, where things were basically fair.

FCs frequently stated that they considered a private office an important success symbol and worked hard to achieve it. One private office was available, and Chung clearly had his eye on it.

Leary talked with Chung on numerous occasions about her expectations and about her views on how FCs should build their business. Chung never openly disagreed with her, but it was difficult to gauge exactly what he was thinking. Although she once had some qualms about Chung's slow start, he was now a strong producer (with this one account), and Leary knew that the Taiwanese market could be further developed. Leary wondered how she should respond to Chung's request, and what impact her answer would have on the rest of the office.

STEVE FINDLEY

Two months after graduating from Harvard College and starting work as a financial analyst at Putnam & Peters in September 1985, Steve Findley found this message on his desk. It was from Michael Gordon, a managing director of the firm:

Findley, please see me ASAP. Wetstone and Brown have an oral presentation to the Delaware Resource Redemption Authority tomorrow. Webster has to go to St. Louis. We need to know if you can take his place.

This case presents, in Steve Findley's own words, his reaction to the message and the steps he took after receiving it.

The message was a major surprise. Putnam and Peters (P&P), a major investment banking firm headquartered in New York, had an unwritten policy against including analysts in any oral presentations or client meetings. Moreover, the Delaware Resource Redemption Authority (DRRA) was a potential client that was selecting bond underwriting managers for its multiyear bond issue program. This request from the head of the department sounded almost too good to

be true. Rob Wetstone and Pete Brown were vice presidents in the utilities group and I was a first-year analyst in the general markets group. Moreover, I knew very little about resource recovery, which was a fairly specialized area of municipal ·finance.

While I was elated at the chance to quickly impress my superiors, I wanted to completely understand why I was selected for this opportunity over the four analysts and three associates in the utilities group. I decided to discuss the situation with Andrew Webster, a vice president in the general markets area and good friend over the past two years.

Andrew Webster

Andrew Webster was the highest ranking, black professional at Putnam & Peters. He was a second-year vice president. These two facts alone conveyed the limited opportunities that historically had been available for minorities at the major investment banks.

Black investment bankers were rare until the early 1980s. Their numbers had steadily increased during the first half of the decade due to an increase in the number of blacks attending business school and the rise of a summer internship program for gifted minority students started by a nonprofit organization called the Sponsors for Educational Opportunity (SEO). Still, the absolute and relative numbers remained small and were overrepresented in the lower rungs of the professional ladder (analysts, who were college graduates, and associates, who were freshly minted business school graduates).

One area of investment banking was becoming very progressive with regard to black professionals: municipal finance. Unlike corporate finance, which involved the issuance of stocks and bonds for corporations, municipal finance focused on structuring and issuing bonds for governmental entities. Over the past 10 years, blacks had been elected or appointed to an increasing number of high-ranking political offices, and they could influence the selection of investment bankers, just as corporate treasurers and CEOs traditionally influenced the selection of investment banking firms in corporate finance. Recognizing an opportunity both to add talented professionals and capitalize on a political trend, the top firms started to increase their hiring of black professionals.

Mr. Webster and I had become good friends in 1983 when I participated in the SEO Wall Street intern program the summer between my sophomore and junior years of college. I was randomly assigned to P&P's municipal finance department that year and had returned to work there the following summer. In August 1985, upon graduation, I started full-time work at the firm. Andrew had been my mentor during the two summers, though I rarely worked with him on any projects during the second summer. Since

my initial summer, I also had worked frequently with Mike Gordon and Steve Glick, the head of the department and second-in-charge, respectively, and had become good friends with them. To the consternation of many other analysts and associates, I was frequently selected to work with them on some of the department's most important projects. This trend had continued upon my return in 1985.

"Webby, what's the deal with DRRA? Did you know that Mike asked me to go to the orals?" I asked him anxiously. I was hoping that he would tell me that Mike simply had decided to accelerate the progress of "Golden Boy" (as I had been called by another summer intern the previous year).

"Steve," he responded, "let me tell you what's happening. Look at us. What similarities are there? Let me tell you that the new state treasurer of Delaware also is black.

"Listen, I hate for you to be introduced to this side of the business so soon. The state treasurer wants to see at least one black professional or the firm has no chance of being named a manager. I'm used to these situations, but if you feel uncomfortable, you don't have to go. I'll either try to reschedule with St. Louis or neither of us will go. If you decide to go, Brown will tell you what part they want you to give. It's your decision, but I'll support you either way."

That explanation confirmed my suspicions. While I may have been Gordon's "Golden Boy," I still was black and that carried certain burdens and responsibilities in the investment banking field. Andrew was correct; I was not used to this type of situation and had never thought about how I would respond. As I sat in his office, I realized that this was a real dilemma.

If I accepted, I had to justify this decision to myself and define the role I wanted to play in the presentation. If I rejected this request, I certainly needed to rationalize my decision to Mike and Steve, who were white and might not understand why a first-year analyst refused to be a "team player." Furthermore, it would be necessary to justify this decision to myself in light of the potential career risk, and given the imminence of the presentation, to respond within the hour.

Background

Both of my parents were high achievers. My mother attended Radcliffe College and my father earned his doctoral degree in history from Harvard University. When they obtained their education in the early 1950s, one could count the number of black students at Harvard on two hands. As a result of their achievements, they preached advancement through hard work and personal development. They refused to accept any excuses for failure or laziness.

While they did not pressure their only child to pursue any particular career path or extracurricular activities, they believed in "doing" rather than "protesting" or "complaining." During the Civil Rights movement, for example, they were active members of the NAACP and National Urban League and believed in advancement through equal educational opportunities and racial integration.

Their philosophy of "action over words" also influenced their day-to-day actions. In 1960, when my father was teaching at the University of California at Davis, they attempted to go to dinner at a local restaurant which reputedly refused to serve blacks. Having made reservations under my father's name, they showed up at the establishment and were told that there was some mistake and their reservations must have been lost. Although the restaurant was virtually empty, the hostess would not seat them because they had no reservation. My mother realized the establishment could have knowingly canceled the reservation because my father was very well known in Davis, having grown up there and starred athletically for the local high school and college.

Instead of complaining or staying home, my mother went home and made another reservation at the restaurant under her maiden name.

Since she has a Boston accent, there was no suspicion on the part of the restaurant. When they returned to the restaurant an hour later, they were seated by the same hostess without a problem.

While I never confronted the blatant racism experienced by my parents, I did encounter several situations where race was clearly an important factor in another person's actions. In each instance, I chose to adopt their philosophy of "action over words." The following are several examples of such occasions:

• In 1980, I was selected to attend the Wilkes-Johnson Memorial Cancer Institute summer science program for highly qualified high-school juniors and seniors. My application was pushed strongly by a black chemistry teacher at my high school and I became the first black to be admitted to this program. As a result, there were questions in my mind, and in the minds of the admissions committee as I later discovered, about my "true" qualifications. This required a decision about whether I wanted to go as a possible "token."

• During my senior year in high school, while I was pitching for my high-school team against a rural school in upstate New York, several of their players consistently heckled me with cries of "watermelon picker." There was nothing that could be done to stop these comments, but my coach gave me the choice of either continue as pitcher, changing positions, leaving the game, or filing a protest with the league after the game.

• During the spring of my senior year in high school, the Knights of Columbus, a civic group in Buffalo that sponsors an award luncheon for all of the valedictorians of the area high schools, offered to present me with an award for being the salutatorian of my high school. This was highly unusual, since no other salutatorians were given this opportunity. The organization may have been asked by the school system to do so because I was the first black to achieve either honor in that area in recent years. Again, I had to make a decision about whether this type of award was an honor or patronizing.

Almost every racial dilemma that I have confronted concerns the recognition of achievement rather than blatant rejection due to race. In each instance, I chose to accept the challenge or award as a method of instilling self-discipline and confidence.

My experiences and upbringing were characterized by an ethic of hard work and achievement. I was highly competitive, sometimes impatient, and always self-confident. This self-confidence had been reinforced greatly by success in several areas and disciplines. Like my parents, I wanted to reject any external reasons for failure and believed that one could accomplish almost anything through dedication and talent.

My First Job

I had two summers of experience at Putnam & Peters before returning full time in August 1985. I considered and treated Mike Gordon, Steve Glick, and Andrew Webster like older brothers or mentors. Consequently, I had a tremendous amount of loyalty to these individuals and had turned down a greater amount of money from another major investment bank to return to this firm.

I was apparently well-positioned within the department. I also believed that this job met all of my medium-term career requirements. It was fast-paced and very competitive. Furthermore, the industry rewarded performance very well. In addition to a high starting salary and huge potential bonuses, I could possibly earn a business school scholarship from P&P if I was a top performer. Most important, I believed that investment banking was becoming increasingly color-blind as the desire for profit drove every firm to recruit the most talented individuals available. Municipal finance investment banking in particular seemed to offer blacks the most immediate opportunity for long-term advancement. Given these trends, I was sure that my talents would be judged fairly and equally.

September 1985

I took a look at the glorious view from Andrew Webster's office, turned to the door, and walked back to my own little cubicle. At least two conflicting impulses surged through me. One was to walk straight to Mike Gordon's office and either make up an excuse why I could not go ("too much work") or simply tell him that this was not acceptable. ("Surely," I thought, "given our relationship, he'll understand.") Another was to stop making such a big issue of this and be a team player. (Part of me was saying, "stop fooling yourself, just make the best of it.") I picked up the phone to dial my father's office, before remembering he and my mother were at a meeting of the American Historical Association in Honolulu. Even if they had been around, I'm not sure they could have helped me. This decision had to come from within.

LAURA WOLLEN AND ARPCO, INC.

Laura Wollen, group marketing director for ARPCO, Inc., a manufacturer of small electrical tools and appliances, telephoned London from her Columbus, Ohio, office. She was getting ready to recommend her best product manager, Charles Lewis, for a position in the London office, a job that would give Lewis the international exposure he would need to progress toward senior management. She and David Abbott, her counterpart in the United Kingdom, had had several conversations about Lewis's candidacy, and Abbott had seemed impressed. Wollen simply wanted to touch base with him before making her recommendation formal.

Only two candidates were serious contenders for the U.K. product manager job: Frank Billings and Charles Lewis. Billings had joined ARPCO the previous year as a product manager for the housewares division. Before that, he had been a sales representative for one of ARPCO's main competitors. Wollen knew Billings fairly well because he had reported to her for several months on a special project. She found him to be intelligent and hardworking.

Yet she believed that Lewis, who had reported to her for three years, had the same innate talents but was better prepared for the job and possessed a creative spark that Billings did not. With a bachelor's degree in business administration and two years of experience selling financial services, Lewis had joined ARPCO as a sales rep in the Midwest. He immediately proved himself a winner. Marketing often recruited high fliers from the sales force, so Lewis was soon offered a job as product manager for power saws.

This case was prepared by Mary C. Gentile.

Copyright © 1992 by the President and Fellows of Harvard College.

Harvard Business School case 393-003.

This case was adapted from an earlier version published in the Harvard Business Review, July–August 1991.

Within a year, Lewis had such command of his product management job that Wollen asked him to head the introduction of an electrical charging system for ARPCO's new line of cordless power tools. The assignment required more than the usual amount of interdependence and collaboration, but Lewis worked carefully and cautiously to develop the relationships that he needed. The product introduction was a smashing success.

Now in 1990 the company wanted to launch the charging system along with several cordless power tools in the United Kingdom. It was ARPCO's first entry into the British home workshop market. Its success was important because the last few years—the late 1980s—had brought high interest rates and inflation that slowed consumer spending in the housewares division. Entry into the do-it-yourself home maintenance market was seen as a way to benefit from a slowing economy as consumers turned toward household projects to save money. ARPCO hoped to expand its revenues and to maintain its visibility in the United Kingdom, while waiting for the economy to pick up and for the opportunities that Europe 1992 would bring.

Jobs outside the United States were highly prized at ARPCO, and only very strong performers made the cut. When an opening occurred, marketing directors reviewed their product managers and selected appropriate candidates. They then discussed the candidates informally with the director who was doing the hiring, and each could recommend one candidate to his or her divisional vice president. The vice presidents typically reviewed the recommendations and passed them on unchanged to the director in the host country. ARPCO encouraged managers to recommend their best people; it rewarded managers for the number of people they put on the fast track and for the performance of the fast trackers in their first six months on the job.

To Wollen's mind, Lewis was a natural for the job. Although she hated to lose him, she was glad he would have the opportunity to demonstrate his ability in such a visible position, and she was eager to play a role in his professional development. But her friendly conversation with Abbott suddenly took an unexpected turn as she learned that Abbott no longer shared her enthusiasm for Lewis.

"You're the group marketing director, Laura, so I can't tell you who to recommend for the position, but I'll go on record as preferring Billings to Lewis." Abbott's British enunciation had an insistent edge.

"That really surprises me," she responded. "I know Billings is bright and motivated and all of that, but his experience is in housewares, just as yours is. Lewis, on the other hand, has three years in the home workshop division. His experience can get the launch off to a good start, and I know how important that is to you."

"You're right, I do have a lot riding on this launch, and it will require a lot of coordination. That's why I'm trying to pull together a team of professionals who can work together in the British environment. I need people who are comfortable with our sales force, our research and support staff, and our buyers. When Billings was here on temporary assignment last fall, he demonstrated that ability. I'm sure he can learn the product line."

"But let's face it," Wollen said. "That assignment was a three-month fill-in in housewares and didn't include any client contact. Besides, Billings has been on line as a product manager for only 11 months. Compared with Lewis, he's less mature, less creative—"

"If you insist on recommending Lewis, fine. I won't refuse the hire," Abbott said crossly. "But I need someone who will fit in, someone who can work comfortably and constructively with the team I've put together, not some individual contributor whose main concern is the next rung on the career ladder."

Wollen hesitated, then trusting her instincts, said, "We're not really talking about the same thing here, are we, David? This isn't about mar-

ket knowledge or ego. It's about race. You're concerned because Lewis is black, aren't you?"

"You didn't even mention it in our earlier conversations! If one of my managers hadn't mentioned it, I wouldn't have known until he walked in the door for the interview two weeks from now."

"Does it matter? Is it relevant here?" Wollen asked.

"The only thing that matters is that my new product manager is able to work well with the other managers and that he—or she—is able to adjust to the culture. Other managers like Lewis have been uncomfortable here, and we can't afford to botch this introduction. It's the key to our presence in the whole market."

"Look, David," Wollen reasoned, "in the three years Lewis has worked for me, he's had to work with all kinds of co-workers and customers, and they all had their own concerns and assumptions about him. But he managed to build productive relationships despite all those things. If you think he's too sensitive or inflexible, I can point to—"

"Don't misunderstand me, Laura. Lewis looks very good on paper. I'm certain he's very talented and will go far with ARPCO. I just don't believe that he is the most appropriate candidate for this position at this time. And when a manager doesn't last, everyone suffers from the loss of continuity. It will set the product line back months. Our group can recover from that kind of setback, but what about you? A failed recommendation will become part of your record. And just think what it will do to Lewis's career."

Wollen winced. "What would have happened to my career if Ralph Jordan hadn't been willing to take a chance by putting a woman product manager in the home workshop division for the first time? That's all I'm asking of you, that you give Lewis the chance to show what he can do."

"Perhaps this one is a bit too close to home, Laura. Are you sure this isn't just a personal issue?"

Wollen regretted giving Abbott that opening and closed the conversation coolly: "I'll think about what you've said and submit my recommendation by the end of the day."

Wollen hung up the phone and rushed from her office up to the eighth floor conference room for a meeting with the rest of the home workshop marketing directors and Ralph Jordan, their divisional vice president. Much as she tried to shift gears, she kept thinking about Abbott's question, "Are you sure this isn't a personal issue?"

ARPCO

ARPCO was a $2.5 billion business, based in Columbus, Ohio, that produced small appliances for the home and workshop, as well as larger equipment for the yard and garden. With over 200 products, the company was organized into three divisions:

Housewares. This was ARPCO's original business, representing $1.25 billion in sales. It included three product families—Food and Beverage Preparation, Personal Care, Cleaning and Garment Care.
Home Workshop. This division represented $750 million in sales and included the Power Tools, Garden Aids, and Watering and Lighting product families.
Groundskeepers. This was the newest division, representing $500 million in sales. It included two product families—LawnCare and WinterCare.

Throughout the 1980s, as the Housewares market matured, ARPCO relied more heavily on growth from new-product development, expansion into the two newer divisions, and international markets. By the close of the decade, operations in Europe, the United Kingdom, Latin America, and Canada represented 30 percent of ARPCO's revenues. Although recession and economic uncertainty were slowing consumer spending in many of their markets, ARPCO managed to maintain modest growth in both 1989 and 1990 through innovative product introductions and expansion into new global markets.

This emphasis underlay the company's strong, explicit commitment to the development of international managers. ARPCO had a tradition of careful career tracking and attention to performance management and mentoring. Its leadership was convinced that the key to their continued competitiveness was in their people, so career management systems had been modified to include opportunities for international assignments.

In the Marketing area, line management career tracks followed a fairly straightforward progression. Product manager positions were the entry point for candidates recruited from several pools, including new MBAs who were hired directly into these positions and BA degree holders who distinguished themselves over a five-year period in several positions, typically Sales as well as other marketing-support areas such as Research, Distribution, or Support Services.

Successful product managers were circulated through different product families, different divisions, and/or different regions. Over the past five or six years, international assignments had become clearly necessary for promotion to the next level—Product Group Marketing Director—and competition for these posts was intense.

Performance evaluations for product managers were based upon product performance as well as upon supervisors' review. Evaluations for product group marketing directors were based upon product group performance as well as supervisors' (in this case, marketing vice president) review. Among the criteria evaluated by the vice presidents was a marketing director's effectiveness in developing new managerial talent. This evaluation was based upon both the number of product managers placed upon the circulating track, as well as their performance during the first six months of their new assignments.

Wollen's Career

Wollen had been with ARPCO for nine years, and although she knew the company had its problems, she was proud of it. It was known for making high-quality tools and appliances and

EXHIBIT 1   ARPCO, Inc.—Organization Chart

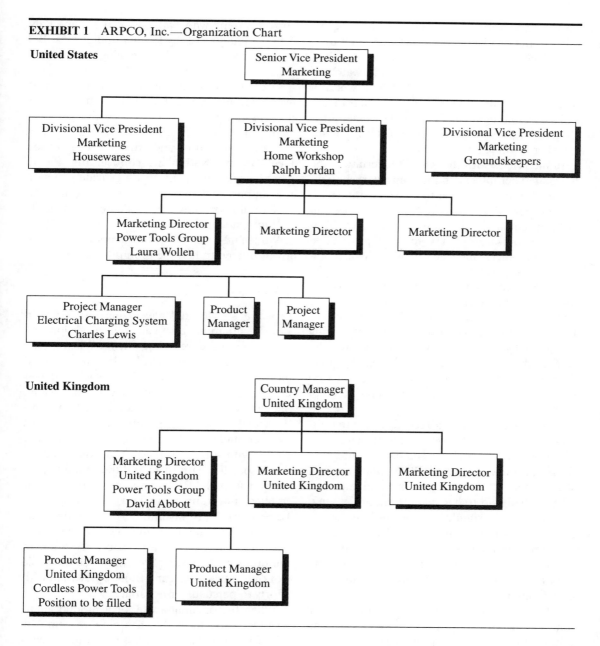

United States

- Senior Vice President Marketing
  - Divisional Vice President Marketing Housewares
  - Divisional Vice President Marketing Home Workshop Ralph Jordan
    - Marketing Director Power Tools Group Laura Wollen
      - Project Manager Electrical Charging System Charles Lewis
      - Product Manager
      - Project Manager
    - Marketing Director
    - Marketing Director
  - Divisional Vice President Marketing Groundskeepers

United Kingdom

- Country Manager United Kingdom
  - Marketing Director United Kingdom Power Tools Group David Abbott
    - Product Manager United Kingdom Cordless Power Tools Position to be filled
    - Product Manager United Kingdom
  - Marketing Director United Kingdom
  - Marketing Director United Kingdom

for being a responsible employer. The company was full of bright, dedicated people, many of whom had been with ARPCO for more than 20 years. But by the time Wollen reached Jordan's office, she found herself thinking about the time five years earlier when she nearly left in disillusionment and defeat. It was Jordan who convinced her to stay.

Having joined ARPCO fresh from her MBA program, Wollen came ready to make her mark on the organization. She was particularly interested in the relatively new home workshop division. Her father was a carpenter, and she had spent many evenings and weekends watching and helping him. She loved that time working quietly beside her father and was proud of the skills he had taught her. She saw the home workshop division as the perfect place for her to combine her talents and interests.

In interviews with the ARPCO recruiters, she had stated her interest in the home workshop division, but they urged her to take a position with housewares. They assured her that if she did well, she could circulate into another area. That began a four-year stint with food processors, vacuum cleaners, and electric knives. Wollen improved the performance of every product she managed, and whenever she learned of an opening in the home workshop division, she notified her supervisor of her interest. Nevertheless, she was consistently passed over. Finally, after being overlooked yet again, she was ready to leave. Before she did, she made a last-ditch effort by going over her director's head to Ralph Jordan, who was then the divisional vice president of housewares.

Jordan knew Wollen's record, and after listening to her story, he looked into the situation. Six days later, he told her she had an interview for product manager of ARPCO's power drills if she wanted it. She still remembered much of what he had said to her that afternoon: "Laura, you have an outstanding record in housewares, and you deserve to be circulated among other divisions and regions. You have potential to do well here, both for yourself and for the company. And I'm committed to developing talent whenever I find it.

"But I want you to listen to what I say to you now. Home workshop has never had a woman product manager before, partly because of a lack of interest on the part of our women product managers and also because of a lack of imagination on the part of our marketing directors. At any rate, you'll be working with managers and customer reps who will find you an anomaly. You're taking a risk by leaving housewares. But if you succeed, you will be opening a whole new set of doors for yourself.

"I can't guarantee that you'll succeed. I can't even guarantee you a level playing field. That's just the nature of the market you've set your sights on.

"What you do—and the challenges you face—are not within my control. But I'll do what is within my control: I'll provide you with the support and the authority you merit—just as I would with any other talented manager—no more, no less."

Wollen interviewed for the position, and when it was offered to her, she promptly accepted.

Wollen and Lewis

In a way, Wollen did have a personal stake in Lewis's situation. She had embraced Jordan's philosophy of developing talent. When Lewis first went to work for her, Wollen had reflected on the fact that he was the only black manager in her group and one of very few in the division. She was aware that he was not as well knit into the social fabric of the group as other managers hired around the same time. Although Lewis got along with his colleagues professionally, he didn't socialize with them and their families, except for formal ARPCO events. Wollen had felt stymied, uncertain as to how she could assist Lewis to work his way into the organization. She believed she couldn't change people's attitudes and so she looked for a structural solution to the problem. She was always more comfortable working with systems and frameworks than with efforts to persuade or negotiate.

When the opening arose for a product manager to introduce the charging system for ARPCO's new line of cordless power tools, Wollen had some concern that Lewis's outsider status would cause problems for the project if it meant that he couldn't work himself into the information loop with the other product managers. On the other hand, the social distance could give him a balanced perspective, free of personal loyalties that might complicate the task. Finally, she thought the charging system assignment might be just what Lewis needed to hook into the product managers' informal network.

The posting provided the opportunity for Lewis and Wollen to begin to develop a close mentoring relationship. Wollen was open and accessible to Lewis, and she made a point of checking in frequently with him during the first few months of his new assignment. This support was an important signal to Lewis and to the other product managers as well. They were made aware of how important the collaborative project was to the entire group. And in fact, this cordless segment of the power tools market had been growing at a rate five times that of the rest of the group over the past two years.

At about the time Wollen had begun to look around for an international assignment for Lewis, she learned of ARPCO's plan to enter the British home workshop market with the cordless line. The timing and fit seemed perfect.

Although he had no prior international experience, Wollen felt that Lewis was by far her strongest candidate. When considering any manager for an overseas assignment, ARPCO encouraged their executives to conduct extensive conversations with candidates, detailing the benefits and the challenges of such posts: financial and career implications, cultural barriers, family implications, reentry considerations, and so forth. Wollen had called Lewis in several weeks earlier and had raised the topic with him. She had encouraged him to view the series of video training programs that ARPCO's HR team had developed to help managers anticipate the issues they might face overseas.

Back in her office after a difficult lunch discussing cuts in the research budget, Wollen tried to prepare for a 1:30 meeting with Charles Lewis. Lewis had requested the meeting hastily, which meant one thing: He wanted to get to Wollen before she submitted her recommenda-

tion. The two of them had discussed the position at great length when it first opened, and initially Lewis was excited but concerned—excited about the implications of such an assignment, concerned about the impact on his family. After many long conversations with his wife, who had just rejoined her law practice after a year-long maternity leave, Lewis had told Wollen that he was willing to make the one-and-a-half to two-year commitment.

As Lewis entered the office, Wollen could see that the concern was back.

"Thanks for seeing me on such short notice," Lewis started. "It's about the U.K. position, of course. I know you haven't promised me anything. . . ."

"But I told you you're high on the list. Go on."

"It's just that I've heard rumors from some of the guys over in housewares, and I don't know how much credence to give them."

"What exactly did you hear?" Wollen asked.

"Vague comments, really. When they found out I was being considered for the London slot, they shook their heads and said things like 'I hear it's real conservative over there' and 'Don't expect a lot of warmth.' I thought they were jealous. But then they got more explicit. They told me about a product manager who was assigned there—a black manager. He found the environment very difficult."

"You know we can't promise that all your client contact will be smooth sailing," Wollen said. "You deal with that all the time, and you've always been able to establish your credibility firmly and quietly."

"But that's just it," Lewis replied. "With this other manager, the customers weren't the problem, or not the only one. It was the other managers and even the supervisor, David Abbott. I know I can deal with difficult clients, but I've always counted on my boss's—on your—support. I've got to know there's some authority behind me. I'll need David Abbott's support."

Wollen hoped Lewis couldn't read her face. She knew Lewis was right about needing

Abbott's support, and she was undecided about how to handle Abbott's message from the morning's call. She was also concerned about putting ARPCO in legal jeopardy.[1]

Wollen didn't know how much candor she could afford, so she proceeded cautiously. "You know, Charles, when U.S. companies send expatriate managers overseas, there are bound to be obstacles. Sometimes people are outright hostile, if only because they think you're taking opportunities away from them. When you—"

"That's not what I'm talking about," Lewis interrupted. He sat silent for a long, uncomfortable moment, then said, "I've given this opportunity a great deal of thought. My wife and I have considered the pros and cons for both of our careers, for our marriage, and for our daughter. We don't expect it to be easy, but we're ready to face the challenge."

"I'm not asking for any guarantees of success," Lewis continued. "But I am asking you to consider whether or not you think I truly have a shot in this slot. Is this a suicide mission? If it is, then don't recommend me. I'll trust your judgment. Maybe I don't have the right to ask that of you, but you know more about the situation than I do, and I don't see that I have a choice."

Lewis and Wollen ended the meeting with a

---

1. As of November 21, 1991, the Civil Rights Act of 1991 extended protection from discrimination in employment to U.S. citizens working in foreign countries while employed by U.S. firms. This act extended the coverage of Title VII of the Civil Rights Act of 1964 and of the Americans with Disabilities Act to such employees. Before this, the applicability of Title VII to U.S. employees on foreign soil had been a contested area of the law. In March of 1991, the Supreme Court upheld an earlier decision in *Boureslan v. Arabian American Oil Co.* and ruled that Title VII did not apply outside U.S. territory. The new Civil Rights Act of 1991 addressed and changed that situation.

solemn handshake. Wollen's forced smile faded when Lewis closed the door.

Earlier in the day, Wollen thought nothing could dissuade her from recommending Lewis. Now she sat at her desk poring through the personnel files, looking for a reason to change her mind.

The company policies were clear: "promote the most qualified person, regardless of race, gender, or ethnic background" and "capitalize on the considerable investment ARPCO makes in its people by applying their skills in ways that will maximize benefit to the company and the individual." In Wollen's opinion, Lewis was the most qualified, and making him product manager in Britain would leverage his training and experience in the United States. She also wondered how long he would remain at ARPCO if he didn't get this opportunity. Lewis knew international circulation was critical to his career there and he was very ambitious.

The criteria used to evaluate her performance were also clear. Her vice president would consider the number of product managers she placed on the circulation track and how those managers performed in the first six months of their new assignments. Lewis was her best—virtually her only—shot.

But policies and her own career aside, there were other considerations, such as the realities of the London office and Lewis himself. Could he succeed in the United Kingdom without Abbott's support? Could she—or the firm—provide support for Lewis once he was in Abbott's shop? And finally she wondered: Should she just make the recommendation and let Lewis decide for himself whether or not to accept it?

Wollen glanced back at the recommendation papers she held in her hands. It was 5:00 P.M. and Ralph Jordan was waiting for her.

A CASE OF AIDS

How should an HIV-infected employee be managed over time?

I. The Hiring Decision, 11-1-89

Greg van de Water leafed through the applications one more time. After weeks of interviewing, he had narrowed the field to two young men, both of them internal candidates seeking promotion to Greg's sales and customer service team.

Hiring, he believed, was the most important decision he made as team leader. Since taking over three years ago, he had hired four of the six team members, and he had chosen well. Now again he was faced with a choice that would affect team performance for better or worse. Subjective judgments about how people would work together, how they would feel about each other, how deeply they would buy into company values like openness, honesty, mutual respect, and support were just as important as the sales ability, communication skills, knowledge of the industry, energy, and enthusiasm that the job called for on paper. Greg also knew that teamwork and attitude produced results and that members of a sales team could easily become destructively competitive unless their commitment to each other was genuine.

The folder on top belonged to Peter Kroll. Peter had worked his way up through the company and understood its products and its product strategy. He was bright, eager, and came highly recommended. Greg was confident that he could handle the job and handle it well.

This case was prepared by Richard S. Tedlow and Michele S. Marram.

Harvard Business Review, No. 91611, November–December 1991.

The second folder was Joe Collins. On paper, Joe and Peter looked much the same, but after meeting them both, Greg preferred Joe. On the minus side, Joe hadn't been with the company as long—only two years. On the plus side, Joe had worked well under the kind of group-compensation system Greg's sales team utilized. Moreover, Joe seemed to have more self-confidence than Peter. Joe also struck him as a better listener and a more sensitive person—important qualities in teamwork and communication. Finally, although neither had much sales experience, Joe somehow seemed a natural salesman.

So that was that—except for one thing. In the strictest confidence, Joe had revealed that he was HIV infected. Greg was not panicked by the news. He knew there was no danger of contagion from casual office contact, and he knew an HIV-positive person could live and work productively for years without developing an active case of AIDS. Moreover, the company guidelines stated clearly that "physical disabilities and chronic health conditions" were not to be considered in hiring and promotion decisions unless they interfered directly with performance.

But was it really that simple? Joe had shown no symptoms yet, but Greg was worried about hiring him and then having his health deteriorate. How could Joe work up to speed if he was recovering from a bout of pneumonia? Wasn't there at least a chance that the pace and the pressure of this job would be detrimental to his health? Moreover, how could Joe keep his secret from the other people on the team?

Except for HIV, the choice was easy: hire Joe. But was there any such thing as "except for HIV"?

Jonathan Mann

Jonathan Mann is professor of epidemiology and international health at the Harvard School of Public Health, director of the International AIDS Center of the Harvard AIDS Institute, and chair of the Eighth International AIDS Conference to be held in Amsterdam in 1992.

Greg van de Water should hire Joe Collins—with or without his HIV infection. Like all other people, some HIV infected are excellent workers and some are not. It is wrong to assume that when people become HIV infected, they immediately and irrevocably fall into a category of people who can't work well. Joe proves that HIV infection need not handicap one's performance.

Obviously, the "hidden" issue here is transmission. Will other workers be safe in the workplace? In this case, the answer is absolutely unanimous and unequivocal: there should be no concern for transmission in the workplace. (The exceptions are professions that involve exposure to blood and, in two instances that transcend the workplace but that I mention for the sake of completeness, people having sexual intercourse and sharing needles.) So it's important to put that concern to rest.

It's also important to put the hiring decision into the context of the expected lifespan of a person who is infected with HIV. The facts are that 10 years after being infected, half of HIV-positive people will develop AIDS, while half will not—and this is without treatment. With treatment, depending on a number of factors related to individuals that we don't fully understand, that picture is improved in several ways.

There is an issue of a potentially reduced work life. While that's a real concern, consider how important any condition—HIV infection, hypertension, smoking, a family history of cancer—should weigh upon a hiring decision where there is a clear, or felt, superiority of a candidate. HIV infection doesn't tell you whether someone can or can't do a job well.

The employee's ability counts most. Greg should hire Joe because Joe is the most qualified candidate. At the same time, he should discuss the future with Joe. Finally, having the information that he does, Greg should find out if the company has an AIDS policy in place. If it doesn't, he should push for one. Because in the United States, with over one million people who are HIV infected, the idea that it won't happen in your company is fantasy. It's just a matter of time.

James W. Nichols

James W. Nichols was an assistant vice president of the American Security Bank in Washington, D.C. Diagnosed as HIV positive in 1985, Nichols had lectured and written extensively on AIDS in the workplace. He died of AIDS-related complications in October 1991.

Greg van de Water should not take Joe Collins's HIV infection into account when hiring him. He should hire on abilities, not disabilities. Besides, who is to say that Peter Kroll, the other candidate, isn't HIV positive as well?

I know that many of the roughly 1.2 million people infected with the AIDS virus in this country are productive workers. For five and a half years after receiving my HIV diagnosis, I continued to contribute to my company as an employee and a manager. My company knew my health status throughout. In allowing me to continue working, the company not only benefited from my work but also fueled my will to live.

My experience taught me that the only way for companies to handle the issue of HIV infection is for the company and the employee to work together. Like work, AIDS takes place in the context of personal relationships. It needs to be *co-managed,* not merely managed. When Greg hires Joe, then, he should establish that he will work with Joe as his illness develops or when other considerations arise. Greg could say, "Joe, I can't tell you how important your honesty has been to me, and I believe that knowledge of your

HIV status should be held in the strictest confidence.

"But when you are ready to tell people you have HIV, or if your productivity slips to the point that people approach me, I would hope, Joe, that you and I can work together to solve the problem."

It is absolutely critical for HIV-positive employees to know that they're going to have the support of their company. When I tested positive, I had a very good relationship with the head of my division. After I told him of my infection shortly after I was diagnosed in the spring of 1985, he said to me, "Jim, I have to tell you this makes me very sad."

He went on to say that the bank was ready to deal with AIDS. It had already rewritten its life-threatening illness policy to include AIDS. It was willing to support me in my work. My boss said: "We want the decisions made about you to be decisions that *we* make about you, not decisions that the bank is going to make for you, not decisions that you're going to make on your own."

As I began living and working with HIV, my company continued doing its work behind the scenes. The bank produced an AIDS-in-the-workplace training program for all employees. It provided brochures on AIDS for the home and workplace, directed toward both singles and families, and produced them in several languages.

All this made me feel like a million dollars. I don't believe the bank kept me because it liked me—but because keeping me was fair.

Lee Smith

Lee Smith is president of Levi Strauss International, a wholly owned subsidiary of the San Francisco-based apparel manufacturer Levi Strauss & Co.

Joe Collins should get the job. In terms of professional skills and "fit," he is the most qualified. And perhaps as important, there is no reason *not* to pick Joe. His HIV status should not count against him for the same reason we don't consider the projected health status of an older employee or the possibility of pregnancy for a female employee. Also, the Americans for Disability Act of 1990 now includes HIV infection as a disability, which means it is illegal for Greg to use HIV as a basis for not hiring Joe.

Once Greg hires Joe, he must respect Joe's confidentiality. Unfortunately, HIV-positive individuals today are subject to terrible discrimination in the workplace and in the rest of their lives. They face fear and stigmatization from colleagues, friends, even family, and as a direct or indirect result, they lose their jobs, their insurance, and other work-related benefits.

On the other hand, disclosure represents the first step for a company and an individual to manage HIV together. I encourage people like Joe to be open about their illness. A partnership of concerned individuals can manage this illness far more effectively than can individuals on their own.

Disclosure is not an easy step: I am not sure that I could follow my own good advice if faced with this situation. Disclosure, moreover, doesn't work without a supportive and well-informed workplace. Levi Strauss & Co. took its first steps toward establishing its AIDS corporate policy in 1982, when the epidemic was in its early stages. It was evident that an appropriate AIDS strategy had to be included in Levi's philosophy about the treatment of employees with any life-threatening illness: all employees are to be treated with dignity and respect. This clearly included an employee with HIV. Employee groups began volunteer activities and fundraising to support people with AIDS. This effort created opportunities for communication and education about the disease, about fear, and about people living and working with the virus.

Since then, we have rolled out a companywide policy of education, support, and involvement in AIDS causes. These education efforts go beyond the company to the employees and their families, to other businesses and community organizations. Initially, we designed a program for managers and employees that we customized to regional and cultural differences.

Today AIDS education is ongoing: most Levi employees in the United States have attended, on company time, a minimum of a one-hour education program about AIDS in the workplace. New employees attend AIDS awareness trainings. Managers and work groups receive specialized training and consultation as needed.

II. The Confidentiality Crisis 11-1-90

Greg van de Water looked up in surprise. Harry Lopez, who'd been a member of the sales team for four years, had come into Greg's office and was closing the always-open door.

"Greg," he began as he turned to face him, "I've got to talk to you about Joe."

"Sit down, Harry," Greg said casually, trying to remain expressionless and hide his concern. "What seems to be the trouble?"

"Well, I don't know exactly, but something's wrong. I hate to say it, but Joe's been letting us down. Now, don't get me wrong. We all like him. We liked him the moment he came on board last year. He was fun and easy to work with, he contributed more than his share of new leads, he knows the merchandise. He pulled his weight and then some. He made us look better than we'd ever looked before. And with sales up, we were making more money than ever before."

Lopez paused, took a deep breath, and went on. "But that's all changed. I want to be fair, but lately he's been, well, taking advantage of the team. You know what I'm talking about. He comes in late or he leaves early—not every day but two or three times a week. A couple of times last month, and again yesterday, he didn't come in at all. No phone call, no explanation, just never showed up.

"Worse yet, he's preoccupied and unpredictable. I heard him yell at a customer last week, and Friday we had a real argument about who would take care of one last caller. I ended up handling it myself.

"It's reached the point where we're all having to work harder because of Joe's behavior. We're still a team, so we still cover for him, but nobody likes doing it. And nobody can talk to him anymore. Greg, he's just not himself. You know what I'm talking about. You've got eyes."

Harry paused for a moment and cleared his throat. "In fact," he went on, "I wonder if you know something about Joe that you're not telling the rest of us."

"Like what?" Greg said lamely. He'd been trying hard not to see Joe's increasing delinquencies. He dreaded the prospect of talking to Joe and addressing the issue of his apparently emerging illness—if that's what it was. And then there was the issue of Joe's privacy to consider. Of course he'd known when he hired him that this day would probably come sooner or later, but who would have thought Joe would get sick so soon?

"You tell me," Harry said. "Maybe there's a family crisis. Maybe he's got a drinking problem. For all I know, he could have AIDS—and I've been sharing a cubicle with him for a year. Whatever it is, you owe us an answer. This team lives and dies on honesty and openness and mutual respect. We've never kept secrets from each other. Whatever it is that's going on violates everything we stand for."

Greg needed time. "You're right, Harry," he said. "I'm glad you brought it up. I have noticed some of the things you're talking about, but I didn't know it was this serious. I'll talk to Joe. Thanks, Harry. We'll work it out."

Jonathan Mann

Forget HIV infection for a second. Greg's got an employee who's dysfunctional. The question is: What's really going on? Jumping to the conclusion that Joe has AIDS is premature. Though his behavior could be related to the symptoms of HIV infection, I can think of many reasons why someone would be unreliable or irritable—and they have nothing to do with HIV.

The point is that Greg does not have to diagnose the condition. He just has to help Joe do his job. As a first step, he needs to open up the channel of communication. Greg could approach Joe in a supportive way and point out that his work has been suffering. It's unlike him to miss work, Greg could say. Is there anything he could do to help? Greg thus begins a process of easing Joe toward the evaluation and care he might need.

At the same time, Greg needs to become what I call "literate about AIDS." People at his level in a corporation should know what the disease is, how it spreads, how it acts in the body. Most important, Greg should know how and where to learn about AIDS. He needs access to accurate and updated AIDS information independent of Joe—a doctor, for instance, whom he can call to ask any and all questions without embarrassment. Because AIDS is a constantly evolving health and social issue, it mandates access to sound and up-to-date technical information in order to make informed decisions.

Facts are important; leadership is equally vital. Harry's aside shows that Greg should also start pushing the company to develop an ongoing educational program on AIDS in the workplace. He needs to take a leadership role so that company discussion is a coming together and not a witch hunt. Greg might make a symbolic gesture such as walking into the educational meeting with his arm around Joe.

Greg should not tell Harry about Joe's situation without Joe's consent. First of all, Joe deserves to have his immediate problem evaluated and brought under control. Then he and Greg can discuss disclosure. Given that transmission is not an issue here, neither Greg nor Joe has a legal or public health obligation to disclose that Joe is HIV infected. But for the sake of group

dynamics, Greg and Joe might want to consider informing the team about Joe's health status, which can be done in a way that builds on the supportive environment of the team.

James W. Nichols

Greg van de Water needs some fundamental training on how to manage people. No one can make a positive contribution to AIDS in the workplace unless teamwork already exists. And teams are built by professional managers who respect and build the self-esteem of their employees. Clearly, Greg has not learned this.

As a general rule, managers should attack problems, not employees. Greg did the opposite by agreeing with Harry that Joe's work has suffered. He should have merely thanked Harry for offering his opinion. And rather than playing the paternalistic manager who fixes employee's problems, Greg could have asked Harry for his solution.

When Greg does talk to Joe he should focus on his failing productivity and show him the same respect he shows Harry—that is, give him the chance to solve the problem. Asking Joe what he thinks should be done may force him to concede that HIV has slowed him down, but it also respects his abilities.

Let me add that Joe's declining productivity may be AIDS related but does not necessarily reflect his own health. My own productivity dropped so low at one point that the bank could have fired me in 30 seconds. I was performing so poorly primarily because I was suffering from bereavement overload.

Bereavement overload and grief are two of the biggest problems for employees who have AIDS. My brother was the thirty-fifth person I knew who died of AIDS. After him I quit counting. It got to the point where one day I exploded at work over an incident that had nothing to do with work and everything to do with my anger; it took a sympathetic worker to say to me, "Jim, it's not the teller you can't take. You can't take having lost so many friends." Her reaction, which was to gather the troops and tell them I was having personal troubles—without mentioning my health—helped me immensely.

You don't have to be infected to be affected by AIDS. The HIV factor is a hidden productivity crippler to the brothers, sisters, parents, friends, and lovers of those who have the disease. Unfortunately, the stigma associated with AIDS forces those people to cope with AIDS privately, secretively, and from a distance.

Lee Smith

Greg van de Water's missed opportunities are coming back to haunt him. Because Greg didn't develop a plan, educate his work team, or work with Joe more openly, he now faces a volatile situation.

He has abrogated the stated company standards of honesty, openness, and forthrightness and chosen the path of avoidance. There's absolutely no question that the best approach with this disease is proactive rather than reactive. It is easier for people to grapple with the issues surrounding an HIV-infected co-worker before he or she begins showing symptoms and performing poorly.

Of course Greg is dealing with a thorny issue: balancing Joe's right to confidentiality with the expectations, needs, and rights of the other team members. First of all, Greg should talk with Joe about his situation; after all, Greg can't be sure that the recent performance delinquencies are due to the illness. Then Greg should use all his skills to convince Joe of the benefits of confiding in the work group. Much can be gained by sharing this information. A team can manage this situation far better than one individual fighting it quietly, secretly, alone. Work teams really mount an effort to help individuals in trouble: there are times in all of our lives when colleagues cover for us, whether the problem is AIDS or something else. Sharing information that affects

the work group can bring out the best in everyone.

At Levi Strauss, I work with an HIV-positive man by the name of Alan Philip. Right now he is asymptomatic. In fact, he's a marathon runner. With his input and participation, we disclosed Alan's HIV status to selected managers and are running small, informal meetings with Alan and his close co-workers to discuss any issues involving HIV and their own work group. We want to provide a safe place for everyone on the staff to be informed and to be able to explore their own feelings.

Greg and Joe shouldn't miss this opportunity to teach the work team about HIV infection in all its complexities. Talking about AIDS is very different from watching it happen to someone you know. Few people turn their backs on the person who sits next to them day after day.

I remember how Keith Coppin, a Levi Strauss employee who recently died of complications related to HIV infection, was apprehensive about telling his work group about his illness. When he did, people were initially scared and uncertain; some were angry with his manager for not revealing his condition earlier. But Keith and his manager, Paula Dueball, worked to create an environment where people could talk about their feelings and clarify assumptions they had made about what Keith could and should do. Eventually, Keith felt there was a normalcy to his daily working life.

III. The Long-Term Question 11-1-91

Joe Collins was sitting in Greg van de Water's office, grinning broadly. "Tell me the truth, Greg," he said. "Have you ever had a better sales team? Or a better salesperson? Admit it, I'm 110 percent of my old self, and those numbers prove it!"

Greg laughed at Joe's good humor as he scanned Joe's most recent sales figures. "No question about it, Joe," he said. "You've really bounced back from last year. I don't know if it's the medication or if it's just you and your attitude, but I have to admit, the work you've done in the last six months has been super."

"I was hoping you'd say that," Joe said. "As a matter of fact, that's what I came to talk to you about." He paused briefly to signal the beginning of a more serious discussion. "I've been here two years now, and frankly, Greg, I think that I'm ready for a change."

Greg nodded attentively, so Joe went on. "I feel as though I've pretty much done everything I can do here. I was looking through the job listing sheets, and I think I came across one that's right up my alley. It's right here," Joe said, handing him the internal job listings. "I've got it circled."

Greg read the job description: "Senior Sales Representative, Western States Region. Top-level sales and customer service job covering our fastest growing markets. Requires full knowledge of our product line. Candidate must be prepared for extensive travel and fast-paced customer demands. As the company grows, we will look to this individual—and the team that comes together under his/her leadership—to form long-term relationships with Western customers and to steer us into the markets of the future. Compensation commensurate with contribution to the company's future! Who wants it???"

Greg looked up. "I don't know, Joe," he said slowly, trying to hide his surprise. "When you said you wanted a change . . . I was expecting . . . well, I kind of thought that after the rough time you had last year, you might want to slow down a bit."

Greg knew he had to be gentle. Joe had confirmed he had AIDS and was likely to get sick again, and he seemed to be in denial. But Greg also knew he couldn't recommend Joe for a job he couldn't handle. That would hurt the company, and it wouldn't do much for Greg's reputation, either.

"It seems to me," Greg said carefully, "that this job calls for the kind of long-term commit-ment you might not want or be able to make right now. Tell me the truth, Joe, do you really want to add all this stress to your life? And all that travel?

"You're such a good salesman," he went on, "I was thinking we could design a special job just for you—maybe a training and teaching job so you could help some of our younger people. You know, a chance for you to pass along some of your ideas and techniques. The hours would be flexible, you could work whenever you felt like it, and you could design the course to meet your own health needs. But this job," Greg looked back down at the job description in his hands. "I don't know about this job. This isn't slowing down, Joe. This is going into overdrive."

Joe fixed Greg with a long, searching look. "Greg," he said, "I know what you're thinking, but I'm not kidding myself. I'm just a long, long way from giving up—or from having to. I've still got a life to live. God knows I've still got drive. And I still do terrific work, which matters a lot to me and ought to matter to the company. I want my career."

He sat back in his chair and grinned. "I'll tell you what, Greg. Stop and think about it again. I'm going to give you another chance."

Jonathan Mann

HIV workers who are not ill should be handled like all other workers who are not ill; HIV-infected workers who are ill should be handled like all other workers who are ill. Greg's problem is that he is operating on what he expects rather than what the facts of the disease and the infection indicate. He sees a worker working well. Why should Greg assume Joe wants to slow down?

Even for people who have developed clinical AIDS, survival can be quite long. I have a friend who had clinical AIDS diagnosed almost 10 years ago. And though he is the exception rather than the rule, it is important to know that exceptions exist. We're talking about biology, not mathematics.

If Joe can do the job and is the most qualified, Greg should recommend him. For Joe's sake, if he believes he'll be happy with the extra work and travel, if he'll be satisfied and fulfilled, then this job might actually be more important than eight hours of sleep. Stress is *not* necessarily unhealthy for Joe: some people work better and are in fact happier with a certain amount of external stress.

Greg's alternative comes across as a way of "parking" Joe. The real question is: What does Joe's future look like? Will he live longer and be healthier if he feels his career's over or if he's working extra hours as the head of a team? I think the answer lies somewhere between the two extremes: maybe what works for him now is the high-stress travel, and later he'll take another position with less stress and fewer hours.

Above all, Greg and Joe must use the facts of Joe's condition to make the decision. Now if Joe is clinically ill and can work only two days a week, the situation is easier to resolve: How could he possibly take this job? But until then, I recommend Greg follow this principle: if Joe's clinically sick, treat him like any other sick worker. If he's well, treat him that way.

Can Joe handle a long-term commitment? The question for me is, How long is long term? In today's workforce, where mobility has become the norm, even a five-year commitment is considered long term. When you start to think about a job with a ten-year or fifteen-year commitment, then I would ask another question: How do you make decisions about the long term? Would it matter if Joe smoked or had hypertension? We don't figure those questions into the equation now, why should we with AIDS?

That is especially true today, as one can legitimately offer hope to a person who develops AIDS. It used to be that a person diagnosed with AIDS had an average life expectancy of about one year. Now it's a couple of years. And with the ability to prevent some life-threatening illnesses, it is becoming quite common to see people who have suffered their first AIDS-related illness return to relative health for a long period of time.

James W. Nichols

Greg has offered Joe the ultimate in reasonable accommodation. Again, I speak from the perspective of an employee with HIV and AIDS. Greg has offered Joe a training position with flexible hours, with no cut in pay or benefits, without the stress of sales goals, and without competition from his peers.

As manager, Greg's role is to assess Joe's work performance and then provide choices. It certainly is his right to offer, or push for, reasonable accommodation. I was appalled when Joe offered Greg "a second chance." Joe has got it backwards. Employees don't give managers second chances. Besides, Greg has already given Joe a second chance. When his productivity declined, Greg gave him the opportunity to stay with the company and keep his job.

Joe appears to be very poorly educated about how HIV operates. I say this because I agree with Greg's original assumption: Joe is in serious denial. Joe seems to be denying the spiraling health-care costs associated with AIDS. He appears not to know that stress is a major cofactor in the replication of the virus and that fatigue is a major symptom. Beyond that, if he takes the new job and fails, he could be fired on the spot—losing his salary and benefits. Joe's hope for the future is overshadowing his assessment of the present.

Greg has given Joe options—and only with options can Joe still maintain control. In fact, Greg's offer sounds exactly like the deal my bank offered me two and a half years ago. At that time, my boss said I had a decision to make. My productivity had gone to hell, and I was not acting as a good manager. I had the choice of quitting—or turning my attitude around and keeping a job at the bank. I was not given the choice of keeping my old job, however. The bank offered me a new job, at the same salary and benefits, yet without the stress of managing people or meeting sales goals.

The way the bank handled my illness was vital to my continued productivity. If employees want to work and can, companies should let them. If you take away a person's job unnecessarily, you not only rob the company of potentially valuable work, you also take away much of what sustains that person's will to live.

Lee Smith

Greg should take the "second chance" Joe's offering him by putting Joe up for the promotion. If Joe can perform, has shown the ability to do so, and is qualified for the promotion, I can think of no other relevant consideration. AIDS or not, he is entitled to his career.

Joe may not be able to work indefinitely, but I'm betting that he can perform well in this job for a reasonable amount of time, providing a return on the investment. If he becomes too ill to work, then reasonable accommodation can be worked out by all parties.

But it's not only Joe that worries me. I'm also concerned about Greg. He talks about the company's openness and honesty, and yet he still seems to be acting solely to protect himself. Although I applaud him for being more explicit with Joe, he is still making assumptions about Joe's *future* health.

Ultimately, this situation is an opportunity for the company to find out whether it really cares about individuals in the organization or whether it cares strictly about output. Joe's situation presents the company with a tremendous chance to educate fellow employees, to bring compassion to the workplace, and to treat people with dignity in the face of a life-threatening illness.

There are also solid business reasons to keep and promote people in Joe's condition. First of all, employees in companies such as ours stay for an average of five or more years. We have a huge investment in those people, and losing them suddenly to disease means an absolute loss. We also incur the expense of training replacements. So it is cost-effective to leave HIV-positive workers in place as long as they continue to be productive. And we benefit in terms of insurance and medical outlays by intervening earlier to help individuals stave off the higher costs of the later stages of the disease.

Additionally, we have an opportunity to educate people about the disease and in so doing help prevent the spread of AIDS. For many adults, the workplace is the only place they receive this lifesaving information. We gain financially if we save even one employee from becoming infected. And by creating a more supportive work environment, we allow people who might otherwise be fearful to get on with their jobs and work side-by-side with someone who is HIV positive.

CONFLICT

MANAGING CONFLICT IN A DIVERSE WORKPLACE

I. Intent versus Perception

Antoinette Mayer[1]

In 1994 DigiSys was an $840 million technology company. Its principal client was the U.S. Department of Defense, and many of the company's senior managers were retired military officers.

In the early autumn of 1994 Antoinette Mayer, a senior software engineer with some management responsibilities, was leaving her office a little later than usual. Her boss, Jay Strong, saw her leaving, asked if she was headed to the same parking lot as he was, and volunteered to walk with her. During the five-minute walk to the parking lot Strong's conversation moved from business topics to more personal conversation about Mayer's recent marriage. Mayer, who felt the remarks were somewhat flirtatious and unprofessional, steered the conversation back to business matters. Once they reached the parking lot, Mayer said good-bye to Strong "coolly" to indicate her discomfort with the conversation.

The walk troubled Mayer for several days. She considered confronting Strong about it, but he was out of town. When he returned, Mayer felt that Strong's manner toward her had changed; he was "warmer," seemed to encounter her more in the company cafeteria, and requested more frequent updates about the work that she was doing for him.

This case was prepared by Sarah B. Gant under the supervision of Mary C. Gentile.

Copyright © 1995 by the President and Fellows of Harvard College.

Harvard Business School case 395-090 (Rev. June 1, 1995).

Strong was a gregarious "rising star" at DigiSys. He was also the CEO's protégé. Armed with free run of DigiSys's corporate boxes at sporting events, use of the company's country club memberships, and a budget for after-hours socializing, Strong was rotating through company divisions in order to become more familiar with both the operations and key employees within each. Strong had been Mayer's manager for three months, and would continue within her division for another nine months before his next assignment.

About a month after their walk to the parking lot, Strong left Mayer a voice mail asking her to come by his office at 3 PM with some information pertaining to her primary project. She returned the voice mail confirming that she could make the meeting with the data he requested. At 2:45, however, Mayer picked up another voice mail from Strong saying that something had come up, but that he really needed the information in order to prepare for a meeting early next morning. He asked if Mayer would mind meeting him at 6:30 at Oliver's, a quiet restaurant and bar near the office.

Mayer was irritated when she entered Oliver's. Strong was seated at the bar and grinning broadly as he slapped Mayer on the back and steered her toward a stool. As Mayer pulled a file folder from her briefcase, Strong leaned toward her, said his meeting had been postponed, said he had tried to call her before she had come to meet him, but, having failed that, would she stay for a drink? Mayer was irritated, said she did not drink, left the file folder, and left the bar saying, "I think there is a problem here."

Strong was dumbfounded. As a key engineer at DigiSys, Mayer was on his "get to know" short list. He had hesitated asking Mayer and her husband to the recent Army-Navy game, believing that they might still want their post-honeymoon privacy. But, the CEO had recently sent him an article about how senior women in organizations felt "out of the loop" because they did not "bump into their male supervisors in the washroom." Strong thought he was being particularly attentive to reducing this barrier; he had eagerly sought opportunities to chat with Mayer casually, and had thought those interactions had gone well.

The morning after meeting Strong at Oliver's, Mayer demanded a meeting with Cecil Groves, DigiSys's Human Resources vice president charged with investigating sexual harassment complaints. Groves listened to Mayer's chronology of events and request to have Strong formally warned about his behavior.

Groves and Mayer had known each other for many years, both at DigiSys and at the historically black college that they attended together. At the end of the meeting, Groves said, "Antoinette, I'm talking to you as an old friend—completely off the record—and I'll never admit to saying any of this. But, I don't think you have much of a case here. I'm telling you this for your own good. And hold on before you call me another 'chauvinistic, paternalistic S.O.B.' This place is full of military types, and they haven't quite gotten the hang of having women in the workplace. Strong may be a 'boy's boy' and not have the least clue of what is appropriate or inappropriate behavior with a professional woman, and you may think there's no excuse for it in this day and age, but Strong's well-connected and going to be CEO some day. He has five kids, an at-home wife, and a house in an affluent, white suburb. He's not hustling you, he's just a well-meaning jerk. As a black and a woman, an engineer, and a senior corporate type, I know you've done your share of educating and are probably pretty tired of it. But, it just isn't worth your career here to try and prove me wrong by asking for an investigation. You'll be fine, just lighten up a little."

. . . . .

Discussion Point 1. . . . men and women often widely disagree regarding more ambiguous behavior, such as staring, telling sexually explicit jokes, and flirting. For example, in one recent study, 46 percent of the men surveyed said women would be flattered by flirting; in contrast, only 5 percent of women agreed.

Terry Morehead Dworkin, "Harassment in the 1990s"[2]

Discussion Point 2. Because women are disproportionately victims of rape and sexual assault, women have a stronger incentive to be concerned with sexual behavior. Women who are victims of mild forms of sexual harassment may understandably worry whether a harasser's conduct is merely a prelude to a violent sexual assault. Men, who are rarely victims of sexual assault, may view sexual conduct in a vacuum without a full appreciation of the social setting of the underlying threat of violence that a woman may perceive. . . .

Ellison v. Brady, 924 F. 2d 872, 879–80 (9th Cir. 1991).

Discussion Point 3. . . . even in the best-intentioned and most progressive companies, women are usually kept out of the informal channels of information, where important decisions sometimes crystallize. Female managers, for example, are left behind when male peers go out to lunch, or to a sporting event, or on a good old-fashioned pub crawl. "Men don't do this on purpose, [Nancy] Hamlin[, a consultant,] says. "They just don't *think* about it."

She and other diversity experts add that, since the Anita Hill-Clarence Thomas debacle, fear and confusion have multiplied. As she says, "Male executives will think, 'Hmmm, wouldn't it be easier, and safer, to take this business trip, or go on that client dinner, with another guy?'" But the most pervasive problem, and perhaps the most intractable one, is that a lifetime of social conditioning has trained many men to think of women as sweethearts, wives, daughters, secretaries—not as equal colleagues. Muses Hamlin, "It's hard to completely re-socialize people."

Anne B. Fischer, "When Will Women Get to the Top?"[3]

Discussion Point 4.   The chivalrous man who holds a door open or signals a woman to go ahead of him when he's driving is negotiating both status and connection. The status difference is implied by a metamessage of control: The woman gets to proceed not because it is her right but because he has granted her permission, so she is being framed as subordinate. Furthermore, those in a position to grant privileges are also in a position to change their minds and take them away. This is the dimension to which some women respond when they protest gallant gestures as "chauvinist." Those who appreciate such gestures as "polite" see only the connection: He's being nice. And it is also the dimension the man performing the generous gesture is likely to see, and the reason he may be understandably incensed if his polite gesture sparks protest rather than thanks.

Deborah Tannen, *You Just Don't Understand*[4]

Discussion Point 5.   At a time when efforts are being made to eradicate discrimination between the sexes in the search for social equality and justice, the differences between the sexes are being rediscovered in the social sciences. This discovery occurs when theories formerly considered to be sexually neutral in their scientific objectivity are found instead to reflect a consistent observational bias. Then the presumed neutrality of science, like that of language itself, gives way to the recognition that the categories of knowledge are human constructions.

. . . since it is difficult to say "different" without saying "better" or "worse," since there is a tendency to construct a single scale of measurement, and since that scale has generally been derived from and standardized on the basis of men's interpretations of research data drawn

predominantly or exclusively from studies of males, psychologists "have tended to regard male behavior as the 'norm' and female behavior as some kind of deviation from that norm . . ." [David C. McClelland, *Power: The Inner Experience* (New York: Irvington Publishers, 1975), p. 81.] Thus, when women do not conform to the standards of psychological expectation, the conclusion has generally been that something is wrong with the woman. . . .

. . . The psychology of women that has consistently been described as distinctive in its greater orientation toward relationships and interdependence implies a more contextual mode of judgment and a different moral understanding. Given the differences in women's conceptions of self and morality, women bring to the life cycle a different point of view and order human experience in terms of different priorities.

Carol Gilligan, *In a Different Voice*[5]

Discussion Point 6.   A woman who runs a counseling center noted that when she meets with women on her staff, it is not unusual for them to spend 75 percent of their time in personal talk and then efficiently take care of business in the remaining 25 percent. To men on the staff, this seems like wasting time. But the director places value on creating a warm, intimate work environment. She feels that such personal talk contributes to a sense of rapport that makes the women on her staff happy in their jobs and lays a foundation for the working relationship that enables them to conduct business so efficiently.

Deborah Tannen, *You Just Don't Understand*[6]

II. Power and Access

Nikki Bliss

Nikki Bliss, the daughter of Pentecostal missionaries, was used to rough treatment and adventure. During her parents' overseas assignments in Southeast Asia, Bliss even had been harangued for spreading "Western imperialism." But nothing yet had equaled the trading floor of the brokerage firm where she worked. Strongly independent, Bliss always knew she wanted to be a trader. She believed that the frenetic pace of trading floors rivaled the seeming chaos of the Asian bazaars that she had frequented and loved as a teenager.

Bliss attended a women's college. After graduating with honors in economics in 1990 and earning an M.B.A. at Harvard two years later, she joined the training program at Haskell and Higgins, a Wall Street brokerage firm. She worked directly with Bertram Law, the partner who oversaw Haskell and Higgins's trading floor.

Bliss had been eager to work for Law. Not only would she be on the trading floor that she had dreamt of for years, but she would be working directly with one of Wall Street's legends. Law was the firm's "rainmaker," bringing more money into the firm than any other two partners combined. He was frequently written up in the business press both for his economic prowess and his "colorful" character.

Law was a big man. Over six feet tall and tipping the scales at 300 pounds, under Law's tutelage Haskell and Higgins's trading room environment resembled that of a disorganized fraternity house. One trader referred to it as "a perpetual food fight." In general, language on the trading floor was vulgar, and Law commonly called Bliss "bitch" rather than by name. At various times he had left pornographic photographs, a sexual aide, and a riding crop on her desk. All of this was done publicly; the trading floor was entirely open, everyone was always in public view.

Law had never physically assaulted Bliss—and Bliss was not fearful of it happening—but Law would ask her about her sexual interests, the color of her underwear, whether she liked groups, etc. several times a day and in front of others.

At first Bliss found her environment intellec-

tually challenging and was able to ignore its less pleasant aspects. She was the only woman and only trainee on the trading floor. She had made friends with several of the young male traders. After several weeks, however, Bliss was tired of the daily onslaught of raunchy jokes and provocation. Three months after joining Haskell and Higgins, she found herself angry. She felt that the atmosphere of the trading room created several barriers to her learning. She was realizing that she hesitated to ask questions, or draw any attention to herself, out of fear of ridicule and harassment.

One morning Bliss and the senior partner who had recruited her stepped into the elevator alone together. Asked how she was liking her work, Bliss wondered how to respond. If she complained, would she be considered weak? Would her comments get back to Law? Would that be a good thing or bad? Frankly, she had been thinking of quitting or transferring to another area. But just thinking of that made her mad; she wanted to be on the trading floor.

Discussion Point 7.   . . . [The securities industry] remains subject to old-boy customs that many women see as a hindrance, from their first raunchy hazing until their final bump against the still-fixed glass ceiling . . .

. . . To be sure, Wall Street's record may be no worse than that of corporate America as a whole, and in fact, the Street is one of the few arenas in which a woman with enough drive and skill can break into the seven-figure income bracket . . . Women hold 40 percent of the jobs in Wall Street's 10 largest securities firms, but they make up just 4 percent of all partners and managing directors.

. . . More than many industries, the brokerage business is based on personal relationships, steeped in prankish humor, and reliant on clannish favor-swapping . . . Lawyers who represent Wall Street women in sex discrimination cases say that it is a rare woman who will stand up and publicly charge she has been harassed. "You really do get blackballed in the securities industry," says Boston lawyer Beville May. "It's such an old-boys network." . . .

. . . "Wall Street is a woman-unfriendly environment, says Barbara Roberts, a former capital markets executive and director of Dean Witter Reynolds Inc., who left the industry and now heads the Financial Women's Association of New York. "If you're not comfortable with a certain level of lewdness, you shouldn't be there."

But the larger issue, many women on Wall Street say, is that some of the men who run the firms simply don't believe that women belong in high-powered jobs there.

Laurie P. Cohen, William Power, and Michael Siconolfi, "Wall Street Women: Financial Firms Act to Curb Office Sexism, With Mixed Results"[7]

Discussion Point 8.   . . . [Sexual harassment] has less to do with sex than with power. It is a way to keep women in their place; through harassment, men devalue a woman's role in the workplace by calling attention to her sexuality.

The use of harassment as a tactic to control or frighten women, researchers say, explains why sexual harassment is most frequent in occupations and work places where women are new and in the minority.

. . . [According to Dr. Nancy Baker, a Los Angeles psychologist who studies workplace harassment], "The more nontraditional the job for women, the more sexual harassment. Women surgeons and investment bankers rank among the highest for harassment."

. . . [According to Dr. Louise Fitzgerald, a psychologist at the University of Illinois], "Men see women as invading a masculine work environment. These are guys whose sexual harassment has nothing whatever to do with sex. They're trying to scare women off a male preserve."

Daniel Goleman, "Sexual Harassment: It's about Power, Not Lust"[8]

Discussion Point 9.   Hazel O'Leary, 55, [in 1992] an executive vice president at Northern

States Power in Minneapolis [and in 1993 appointed federal Energy Secretary, says]: "Whatever you're asked to do, make sure you do a better job of it than the man next to you." But while you're at it, don't neglect to form friendships. "Without losing your own personality, it's important to be part of the prevailing corporate culture," she says. "At this company, it's golf. I've resisted learning to play golf all my life, but I finally had to admit I was missing something that way." O'Leary has bought a set of clubs and tees up with an instructor on weekends.

Anne B. Fischer, "When Will Women Get to the Top?"[9]

Discussion Point 10.   According to professionals, 90 percent of sexual harassment incidents—including explicit propositions—still go unreported.

Why? Because women are afraid of reprisal and a loss of privacy. They are afraid of a society that wants to slander the messenger and ignore the message. They are afraid of losing their jobs.

"Women are silenced from reporting sexual harassment because they feel they will end up shouldering the blame," said Judith Jordan, director of women's studies at McLean Hospital [in Boston]. "They feel if they bring charges, they will be seen as provocative, over-reacting, a troublemaker, and out of touch with reality."

And, "if they do speak up," Jordan said, "they are met with a backlash from co-workers. They feel discredited, doubted, and often end up leaving their jobs. There is an unspoken rule out there that tells women to put up with harassment and not make a fuss."

Patti Doten, "Why Women Don't Speak Out"[10]

Discussion Point 11.   The powers of Salomon Brothers relied on the training program to make us more like them . . . The relevant bits, the ones that I could recall two years later, were the war stories, the passing on of the oral tradition of Salomon Brothers . . . All the while there was a hidden agenda: to Salomonize the trainee. The trainee was made to understand, first, that inside

Salomon Brothers he was, as a trader once described us, lower than whale shit on the bottom of the ocean floor, and, second, that lying under whale shit at Salomon Brothers was like rolling in clover compared with not being at Salomon at all.

. . . There were a million little rules to obey. . . . At Salomon Brothers men traded. Women sold. No one ever questioned the Salomon ordering of the sexes. But the immediate consequence of the prohibition of women in trading was clear to all: It kept women farther from power.

Michael Lewis, Liar's Poker[11]

Discussion Point 12. . . . the employer should use its power to control its workplace so that employees are not forced to tolerate abusive conditions to earn a living. Failure to use this power to control employees' verbal or physical conduct (usually of a sexual nature) that unreasonably interferes with an employee's work, or that creates an intimidating, hostile, or offensive working environment, will subject the employer to liability.

Terry Morehead Dworkin, "Harassment in the 1990s"[12]

III. Is Equal Fair?

Moses Wu

Moses Wu badly wanted to break into the inner circle of senior managers at Colorado-based Environmental Technologies (ETech). ETech, a nine-year-old engineering venture, had recently taken its innovative ground-water decontamination technology public to wide acclaim.

Wu, raised in New York's "Chinatown" neighborhood, had both a B.S. and Ph.D. from the Massachusetts Institute of Technology by the time he was 23. He also had an M.B.A. from Northwestern University's Kellogg School of Management. Wu had been an early recruit of ETech's founding partners and had been at the firm since its establishment. Now 36, Wu was ETech's most senior engineer and had led ETech's single-product technological development team. With that success behind him, he wanted to get out of the lab. Wu felt that he had the credentials for senior management, he certainly knew ETech's technology better than anyone. But Wu sometimes felt he was hitting the "glass-ceiling"; he was, as his Asian-American peers from MIT called it, a "tech coolie" destined to quietly grind out new technologies from a lab bench for the rest of his life. It had been three months since he had mentioned his goals to the firm's founder and he had heard nothing, not even the promised request to talk.

ETech had 80 employees in 1993. Wu was the sole Asian and very nearly the only employee not born and raised in the West. Not surprisingly, Wu felt "different" in ETech's offices and at the company's many after-hours events. But he never felt "less." His work was respected, he was respected. He did not find the office jokes about his race offensive—things like calling the company basketball team "The Cowboys and Moses." It seemed to him a natural way to deal with the obvious.

Of more concern to Wu as he considered the likelihood of becoming a senior manager at ETech, were the "compliments" about his management style. Wu was not an aggressive person. He had often been complimented for bringing ETech's product to market without once "screaming, cursing, or slamming a door." At brainstorming sessions, as "cowboys" pounced on ideas and talked over one another, Wu's opinion was typically "sought." He frequently settled arguments, brought out important points of fact, and very often had the last word.

While he was complimented for it, Wu wondered whether his management style was the most significant barrier to his promotion out of the lab. Cowboys ran the company and only cowboys had moved from the lab to the senior management circle. Since he produced, Wu did not think that using "cookie cutter" criterion to judge potential success at the most senior level was fair. He knew he was respected and vital; he also knew he was the "other." The question was, even in this small company where he felt nothing less than "loved," was he too "other" to be let out of the lab?

Julia "Mack" MacKenzie

Julia "Mack" MacKenzie was a marketing hot shot at Jensen and Rigby (JR), a multinational consumer products company. MacKenzie was on what JR executives called the "Re-Re Team." MacKenzie and seven others, all male, from the JR marketing department specialized in assessing products on long sales declines. The highly creative Re-Re Team was a group of equals with no hierarchical structure and access to both the senior VP for marketing and JR's CEO. After a rigorous assessment period the Re-Re Team would either recommend that a product be "killed," or the team went to work on the product's repackaging and relaunching.

MacKenzie had always thought of herself as "one of the guys." She loved the Re-Re Team's elitism, casual atmosphere, and cohesiveness. She especially loved the group's late-night and all-night "think ins."

It was at one of these "think ins" that MacKenzie announced that she was pregnant. Everyone laughed and congratulated her—several of them had young children about whom they loved to tell stories. But for days she could not shake what one of the guys on the team had said: "Mack, I didn't even know you were a girl. But that's great. Now we'll get a 'Mom's eye view' of the products."

MacKenzie was thrilled to be pregnant and, to the extent that it was possible, had planned her pregnancy and postpartum child care help so that she could be a "hands-on Mom" without jeopardizing her career development or the Re-Re Team workstyle. Now she wondered if group dynamics would change forever simply because she was "doing this totally female thing." She began to wonder if being "one of the guys" for so many years had carried unforeseen costs that she was only now beginning to understand.

. . . . .

Discussion Point 13. Another subtle form of institutional bias is defining effective leadership or management traits in a way that is not identity-neutral. Sometimes, such as when traits like aggressiveness and ability to work independently are specified in performance rating forms, this form of bias is explicit in the criteria used. In other cases it occurs more informally through the images that supervisors hold about the ideal manager and the translation of such images into management actions such as performance ratings and rankings for promotion.

. . . findings have consistently shown that both men and women define good management in ways that are decidedly biased toward traditionally male traits. Based on his analysis of earlier research and his own data [Gary] Powell concludes, "In summary, despite the increase in female managers, and no matter what questionnaire or study design has been used . . . people have described men as more like good managers than women, and good managers as higher in stereotypically masculine traits than stereotypically feminine traits. Men and women at all career stages examined, including practicing managers . . . share the same biases about management." [G. Powell, *Women and Men in Management* (Newbury Park, CA: Sage, 1988), p. 148.]

Taylor C. Cox, *Cultural Diversity in Organizations*[13]

Discussion Point 14. . . . In the United States, norms of participation in meetings often favor those who are very forceful in getting their points heard. Typically, one obtains airtime by jumping in as soon as the current speaker pauses. Since a pause may or may not signal the completion of a person's intended contribution to the discussion, people are routinely cut off prematurely. This type of communication is difficult for many people, but it is especially difficult for those from cultural backgrounds where speech anxiety resulting from modesty or reserved behavior is operative. There may also be a gender effect here in that men, more so than women, are culturally conditioned to use communication to gather and hold attention in groups (Tannen 1990) and are more prone to dominance behavior in groups (Adams and Landers 1978) . . .

. . . Brainstorming is a popular problem-solving and creativity technique used in interactive groups in which members, often extemporaneously, offer whatever ideas come to mind in a random, uncritical fashion. The objective is to surface as many relevant ideas as possible. Although this technique may be experienced as empowering and even fun by many workers, cultural traditions and language factors may make it more difficult to use effectively with members of some . . . groups.

Taylor C. Cox, *Cultural Diversity in Organizations*[14]

Discussion Point 15. . . . Men and women do continue to be socialized differently so that when women join a management culture populated predominantly by men, they must adapt in ways that are often alien to them. If women want to be part of the management ranks, and if the management ranks want to admit them, these differences must be identified and addressed openly.

Karen A. Geiger, Vice President and Director of Career Development, NCNB Corporation, "Letters to the Editor," *Harvard Business Review*[15]

Discussion Point 16. . . . Skewed groups are those in which there is a large preponderance of one type over another, up to a ratio of perhaps 85:15. The numerically dominant types also control the group and its culture in enough ways to be labeled "dominants." The few of another type in a skewed group can appropriately be called "tokens." . . .

Numerical skewing and polarized perceptions left tokens with little choice about accepting the culture of dominants. There were too few other people of the token's kind to generate a "counterculture" or to develop a shared intergroup culture. Tokens had to approach the group as single individuals. They thus had two general response possibilities. They could accept isolation, remaining only an audience for certain expressive acts of dominants. This strategy sometimes resulted in friendly but distant peer relations, with the risk of exclusion from occasions on which informal socialization and political activity took place. Or they could try to become insiders, proving their loyalty by defining themselves as exceptions and turning against their own social category . . . To turn against others of one's kind (and thus risk latent self-hatred) can be a psychic cost of membership in a group dominated by another culture.

Rosabeth Moss Kanter, *Men and Women of the Corporation*[16]

Discussion Point 17. We adopt the perspective of a reasonable woman because we believe that a sexblind reasonable-person standard tends to be male-biased and tends to systematically ignore the experiences of women. A gender-conscious examination of sexual harassment enables women to participate in the workplace on an equal footing with men.

From the groundbreaking decision in *Ellison v. Brady*, 924 F.2d 872, 879–80 (9th Cir. 1991) which found, in effect, that justice ought not to be blind.

IV. Creative Conflict

Cassandra Barton

Cassandra Barton, one of the first female design team leaders at a major U.S. car manufacturer, was widely known throughout her organization, and indeed the whole of the automotive industry. She was a tough boss, an innovative manager, and had an enviable record of delivering her products on time and under budget.

Barton's first product as a team leader was the Atalanta, a sporty sedan targeted to—and designed specifically for—women. The Atalanta's touted design features allowed women to drive comfortably and safely even when wearing high heels, constricting skirts, long fingernails, and with their hair gathered on the back of their necks or piled high on their heads. At first the automotive press scoffed, but dealers found it hard to keep Atalantas on their lots. And not just women bought them. The lighter interior and exterior colors of the Atalanta sold well throughout the South, Southwest, and on the West Coast. And, though designed for women, its interior proportions also worked well for the elderly and men who were smaller in stature than Detroit's model American male driver. In 1994 the Atalanta was well on its way to being among the five best-selling, U.S.-made cars in the United States.

Riding on her Atalanta success, Barton wanted a new challenge—no less than redesigning how her company created products. In the past, designers, engineers, and marketers had all worked in isolation. To Barton's mind, this caused senseless and costly delays. For example, when Barton's Atalanta team had come up with an interior design to fit women's stature and dress restrictions, engineers greeted the specs with a resounding "no way;" it would not fit into the exterior shell that they had been working on for months. Engineers believed that their concerns for aerodynamics and safety took precedence over anything from the design team. Barton was frustrated by time delays as designers and engineers negotiated trade-offs. Similar delays and frustrations occurred again as marketers were brought on board later still in the process and when, in fact, they could have virtually no input.

In early 1995 Barton got her second challenge as a design team leader—a truck, the Phoenix, for blue-collar women. She also got her wish. From the start, her design team would include designers, as well as people from engineering and marketing.

At the first formal meeting of the Phoenix team, Barton laid out the truck's consumer profile and a tight schedule of deadlines. Before opening the floor to brainstorming, Barton ordered her team "to forget about departmental allegiances without forgetting about the best work your department ever did. With the Phoenix, we're not only designing a truck, we're redesigning how we get a product from drawing board to show room. I have no intention of failing and the Phoenix will be on deck in 20 months. There's no room in our schedule for defending turf or political agendas. We're a team with a single goal from here on out."

For the next 90 minutes, the Phoenix team generated ideas—some were excellent, some were even feasible, but most were delivered with gratuitous jokes and stereotypes of engineers, designers, or marketers. When the session was over she was not sure that anyone heard any of the good ideas that were generated unless they came from someone who shared a team member's area of expertise. It was not at all unusual for brainstorming sessions to get quite boisterous. Barton, in fact, thought creative antics and jokes could build group rapport and help the team make it through the inevitable long hours and late nights that lay before them—but not if the antics got in the way of hearing others.

It was obvious to Barton that her "little team spirit lecture" was not going to be enough to dispel the deep suspicions and disrespect that existed across functions. The Phoenix would never fly on schedule if the intolerance continued. Barton recognized that the first few Phoenix team encounters would likely be rocky; she needed to find a way to rein in the spirit of the brainstorming without crushing it. She knew that the sooner she "managed past all that turf garbage" and got designers to think like engineers, engineers to think like designers, and everyone to think like marketers, the sooner she would have her first prototype on the test site and in front of focus groups.

Despite her success with the Atalanta, Barton was also hearing resistance to the make up of her design team around headquarters. Most troubling to her was a conversation she had with Peter Watson, vice president of North American sales. Watson was Barton's mentor and, in her mind, the most forward thinking car executive in the country. As Barton was mulling how to get her cross-functional team to come together around the Phoenix, and how to defend the promise of the cross-functional approach around headquarters, she kept hearing Watson's words:

"Cassandra, this cross-functional stuff is not much more than the latest buzz-word from business schools and management 'gurus.' It has some merit, of course. I've heard the marketing people are thrilled to be dropping their reams of research on your desk and thinking it will have an impact on something more meaningful than colors; it can't do any harm getting them to buy into the product this early on. But once the Phoenix is out of the showroom, the only thing that's going to keep it on the road and developing customer loyalty is engineering. The engineers have got to lead the design and you can't muck with them. Engineering is the science here, not design, not marketing. Let's say there are enough girls in construction to make the Phoenix a reasonable seller, a truck is a truck is a truck. It's got to haul, it's got to handle, and no construction worker is going to have long fingernails. All those nice girl features were OK for the Atalanta, but they're not going to mean 'squat for a truck. Make a real truck—an engineer's truck—Cassie, and put some nice detail work on it. That's my advice."

Discussion Point 18. . . . in establishing planning teams or product groups, organizations often filter diversity by removing potentially disruptive elements, selecting people who think alike, proceeding quickly in the absence of awkward numbers, and so on. The process results in quick plans and actions, but these soon meet resistance in the face of reality. Creativity thrives

on the tension created by diversity, and it is essential that steps be taken to ensure organizations build enough tension and variety into processes where innovation is required.

Gareth Morgan, "Endangered Species: New Ideas"[17]

Discussion Point 19. . . . powerful social pressures are brought to bear by the members of a cohesive group whenever a dissident begins to voice his objections to a group consensus . . . I use the term *groupthink* as a quick and easy way to refer to the mode of thinking that persons engage in when concurrence-seeking becomes so dominant in a cohesive ingroup that it tends to override realistic appraisal of alternative courses of action.

. . . groupthink type of conformity tends to increase as group cohesiveness increases. Groupthink involves nondeliberate suppression of critical thoughts as a result of internalization of the group's norms, which is quite different from deliberate suppression on the basis of external threats of social punishment. The more cohesive the group, the greater the inner compulsion on the part of each member to avoid creating disunity, which inclines him to believe in the soundness of whatever proposals are promoted by the leader or by a majority of the group's members.

. . . The mutual enhancement of self-esteem and morale [in cohesive in-groups] may have functional value in enabling the members to maintain their capacity to take action, but it has maladaptive consequences insofar as concurrence-seeking tendencies interfere with critical, rational capacities and lead to serious errors of judgment.

Irving L. Janis, "Groupthink"[18]

Discussion Point 20. Although diversity in workgroups holds strong potential performance advantages, it is also clear that cultural diversity in workgroups presents some potential problems for organizations.

... work on group dynamics has consistently indicated that highly cohesive groups have higher member morale and better communications than less cohesive groups (Lott & Lott, 1965; Randolph & Blackburn, 1989) ... diversity in workgroups potentially lowers member morale and makes communications more difficult. In addition, at least one empirical study has shown that heterogeneous groups experience higher member turnover than homogeneous groups (Jackson et al., 1991).

... there is reason to believe that the presence of cultural diversity does make certain aspects of group functioning more problematic. Misunderstandings may increase, conflict and anxiety may rise, and members may feel less comfortable with membership in the group. These effects may combine to make decision making more difficult and time-consuming. In certain respects, then, culturally diverse workgroups are more difficult to manage effectively than culturally homogeneous workgroups.

Taylor Cox, *Cultural Diversity in Organizations*[19]

Discussion Point 21.   ... [numerical] minority influence, on the other hand, appears to involve quite a different process. At first, the disagreeing minority is regarded with derision. When the minority refuses to compromise but, rather, insists on its position with consistency, he/she is perceived less negatively and, in fact, is accorded dynamic perceptions of confidence. After the passage of time which allows the behavioural consistency to become evident, sometimes one person from the majority moves over to the minority position. When that occurs, the process "snowballs" and members of the majority tend to move together. However, there are a number of groups in which no public movement to the minority position is evident. We assume this is due, in part, to the unfavorable consequences of being in the minority position. How-

ever, the influence still occurs, though at a latent level. Many subjects who show no public movement will nonetheless show substantive private change in related beliefs or in the perception of the stimulus.

Thus we hypothesize that subjects exposed to a minority view will be under considerably less stress than those exposed to the majority view. The minority simply does not have the immediate impact of the majority. However, we assume that their impact is related to behavioral consistency. If the minority is that confident, if they are willing to incur the unfavorable consequences of nonconformity, perhaps there is something to their position. The consideration of that viewpoint and its correlate of reconsideration of one's own viewpoint is, we believe, a starting point for creativity.

Charlan Jeanne Nemeth and Joel Wachtler, "Creative problem solving as a result of majority vs. minority influence"[20]

V. Bystanders and Third Parties

Everett Evans

Everett Evans was a marketing VP at Stone Bank in Massachusetts. In 1992 Evans was disturbed to learn that his company's annual off-site "Family Day" and softball game would be held at a local country club notorious for denying memberships to people of color.

Twelve of Stone's 47 mid- and upper-level managers were women or people of color. Evans, a white male, spoke to several women at the bank and to the two African-American VPs informally to understand if they were as disturbed as he was about the location of "Family Day." Evans's intention was to gather support for a memo to Stone's CEO to demand that "Family Day" be moved to a different location or be canceled.

Few of the people Evans polled shared the strength of his sentiments. One female executive told him to "relax. Things change slowly and there is no sense making waves. I'm a woman, I should know." One of the African-American

VPs noted that the country club's membership rules were currently being litigated. He was certain "that old boys' club would soon be opened up." He had been a guest of club members many times and thought it was a great place for "Family Day." "Besides," he said, "it could only be a good thing for the club to see me and my family there."

Dwight Stewart
Dwight Stewart had lived and worked in the Midwest all his life. Stewart grew up on a farm and loved the decency and "family values" of small-town America. Now in his early 40s, he was a well-liked partner at Eckert & Eckert, a management consulting firm in Kansas City, Missouri. Stewart had joined the firm straight out of college, had always felt comfortable there, and had moved easily through the ranks into the partnership of 15. For the first time in his life at Eckert & Eckert, Stewart was disturbed by office politics.

It was time to make a partnership decision about Donald Cumberland. The decision-making meeting was still three months off, but Cumberland was increasingly the focus of casual discussion when Eckert & Eckert partners were together. Stewart thought Cumberland was "a good man." His work was "solid," and he had brought the firm significant business. Cumberland was somewhat quiet, socializing less perhaps than some of the other senior consultants. But to Stewart's mind "people have different commitments and are free to make their own decisions about social connections."

The problem for Stewart was the increasing conjecture about why Cumberland was unmarried, why he socialized less, and where he went on his frequent weekends out of town. Cumberland never talked about family—about wanting one or having one. Clearly, the partners were coming closer and closer to suggesting that Cumberland was a homosexual—and the unspoken assumption was that no homosexual belonged at Eckert & Eckert. The founder of the firm, some 20 years Stewart's senior and the man who had recruited him and been his mentor, led the low-level campaign against Cumberland.

Stewart was an active lay minister in his Methodist church. He did not believe that God or scripture condoned homosexuality, but he did believe God loved everyone, even the sinners. Stewart, as far as he knew, had met only one homosexual—a boy from his hometown and a close friend of his youth, Michael Gerrard. Stewart and Gerrard had been frequent companions on hunting and fishing trips. Gerrard had gone to college out of state, but he and Stewart wrote often and always looked each other up during vacations.

Over one Christmas holiday Gerrard had told Stewart that he was "gay." Stewart was "disgusted" by this revelation, no longer wrote to Gerrard, and only politely followed his comings and goings when mention was made of him at the town diner and at church. Several years had past when Stewart bumped into Gerrard at the funeral of a mutual friend, another hunting and fishing companion, who had died in a rafting accident.

The emotion of the burial service and funeral, and their mourning the premature death of a friend, brought Stewart and Gerrard together again briefly. During a long walk following the funeral, they talked openly about feelings of disgust and betrayal. Gerrard's "lifestyle" still made Stewart uncomfortable, but he knew he loved his friend.

At Eckert & Eckert the partners told the "usual sorts" of jokes when socializing. Stewart did not tell the jokes about Jews, blacks, homosexuals, and others that the other partners did, but sometimes he thought the jokes were funny and would laugh at them. To Stewart, what the founding partner was doing was not funny, however. Even if Cumberland was a homosexual, he was quiet about it and did his work. It was unjust to jeopardize the man's reputation and career—one that he had worked hard for. Stewart was clear that the "rabble rousing" against Cumberland was wrong, the question was what role did he have in addressing it? Certainly he could live with being called a "homo lover" for a while, but what would be the longer-term impacts of speaking out?

Discussion Point 22.   First they came for the Jews and I did not speak out—because I was not a Jew. Then they came for the Communists and I did not speak out—because I was not a Communist. Then they came for the trade unionists and I did not speak out—because I was not a trade unionist. Then they came for me— and there was no one left to speak out for me.

Martin Niemöller[21]

Discussion Point 23.   While blatant bigotry is a problem in organizations, neutrality may be an even greater obstacle to blacks. While an estimated 15 percent of white Americans are extremely antiblack, 60 percent are more or less neutral and conform to socially approved behavior. According to Joseph Feagin, a sociologist at the University of Texas at Austin, "Those managers and executives who are the biggest problem are not the overt racial bigots. They are the people who see discrimination and do nothing about it. These are the people who let racially motivated behavior go unnoticed, unmentioned, or unpunished. These are the people who won't help."

Edward W. Jones, Jr., "Black Managers: The Dream Deferred," in *Differences that Work*[22]

Discussion Point 24.   In 1950 . . . I enrolled at Howard University Law School in Washington, D.C., because it was the center of the civil rights law I intended to practice, and because I realized I had never lived and worked among Negroes in circumstances where we were on an equal footing. I was Howard's first white law student since the days when women suffragists attended, unable to get degrees elsewhere. My parents were terribly upset, fearing for my career . . . to stop me from enrolling in a predominantly Negro university [my grandmother] pleaded, "You can go there to teach them, to help them, but you can't go and be a student with them."

Harris Wofford, elected to the U.S. Senate from Pennsylvania in 1991, was Special Assistant to President Kennedy for Civil Rights, Associate Director of the Peace Corp, and a close colleague of Martin Luther King, Jr. From his memoirs, *Of Kennedys and Kings*[23]

Discussion Point 25.   The victim does not have to be the person harassed but could be anyone affected by the offensive conduct.

From "Facts About Sexual Harassment," a brochure published by the U.S. Equal Employment Opportunity Commission, which defines various circumstances under which sexual harassment can occur.[24]

VI. Freedom of Expression

Jillian Reese

Just before recruiting period during her third year at Harvard Law School in 1993, Jillian Reese and several other African-American women students spent a great deal of time talking about their hair.

Unlike most African-American students at the school who straightened their hair and adopted "white, majority" hairstyles, Reese and two other African-American women, Lynn Banks and Jodie Griffith, wore their shoulder-length hair plaited in hundreds of tiny braids, a popular "ethnic" style. The three women felt intense pressure from a "faceless, white corporate world" and even from other African-American students to adopt more "traditional" hairstyles.

After attending a cocktail reception hosted by a New York law firm, Banks said that she "felt judged. I stuck out like a sore thumb." Feeling that her "hair was not worth jeopardizing landing the best possible job I can get," she changed her hairstyle and advised Reese and Griffith to do so as well. When they argued that their hair was a symbol of pride in their ethnic heritage and was "worth fighting for," Banks reasoned: "You can do a whole lot more for African-Americans by making a lot of money and being a role model for young blacks in a corporate law firm than you can by hanging on to your hair and flipping burgers for the rest of your life. Your hair is not worth a job, and honey, you're not going to work at any Manhattan law firm with that hair." Griffith cut her hair.

Reese, who had graduated from Yale *magna cum laude,* had grown up in Manhattan. Her mother, a civil rights attorney, and her father, a retailing executive, had instilled Reese with pride in her racial heritage. She had always excelled— in school, in sports, and in the government relations division of a major chemical company following graduation from Yale. She had always felt well-liked and respected, and felt she moved easily among racial groups. She had only worn her hair braided as a student, but was confidant she could make it in a corporate setting without being untrue to her ethnic identity.

Jacqueline LaRue
New York-based Graham-LaRue Consulting Group (GCG) prided itself on the diversity of its workforce. GCG had three U.S. offices and seven foreign offices. Forty percent of its 800 consultants were women, 20 percent of the total were nonwhite, and 12 percent were not U.S. citizens. The 15-person board of directors which governed GCG was similarly diverse.

In August 1993 Jacqueline LaRue, daughter-in-law of one of GCG's founding directors and a well-respected, senior consultant, came to the New York office for an extended stay to lead a project for an important client account.

LaRue had spent all of her five years with GCG based in Europe. Her New York assignment was designed to help her build stronger connections with the U.S. side of the business. LaRue knew that success in New York would increase the potential of her being named a GCG director.

Toward the end of August LaRue attended an informal meeting at the offices of her client. During lunch the client's CFO glanced at LaRue's legs and said, "I don't know whether your legs are hairier than mine or not." Rolling up his pant leg he said, "Wanna compare?" Ev-

eryone but LaRue laughed and the meeting continued.

LaRue was furious. As soon as lunch was over she went to speak with the director who managed the New York office. The director, Rebecca Barnes, had been wanting to talk with LaRue since her arrival in New York. Two directors and some consultants had spoken to Barnes about the fact the LaRue did not shave her legs. She had also overheard secretaries chatting about LaRue's "European style." The director had hesitated to speak to LaRue about her appearance and now LaRue was in her office demanding that the client apologize to her for "diminishing her authority in front of her project team."

Nahum Prager
Christopher Stern, publisher of *The Daily Times,* was unsure how to respond to Nahum Prager's memo. Earlier in the week, Stern had asked Prager to manage the *Time's* coverage of the upcoming presidential elections. Prager, an award-winning reporter whose national news coverage was widely quoted and who had personal connections to several of the leading candidates, had accepted the role immediately.

Now Prager was informing Stern of a significant condition. The memo read, in part, ". . . having grown in my faith since my father's death earlier this year, and having wrestled with my conscience, I know I must observe the Sabbath laws." Prager informed Stern that he would no longer be available to work from sundown on Friday until sundown on Saturday. He would no longer answer telephone calls or respond to his pager during that time.

Terry O'Leary
Terry O'Leary, vice president for new-product development at TechToys, Inc., felt that he had been excoriated for "telling the truth and making a valid management decision." The CEO had just informed him of a reorganization that left him with his title, but took him out of the loop of senior decision makers at the company.

Two months before, O'Leary had sat listening

to four of his managers debate who should lead the Robo-Boy project team. It was nine months before Robo-Boy, a voice-activated, solar-powered robot for pre-adolescents, needed to be in the warehouse if the company wanted a Christmas launch of the product.

Each of the two candidates under discussion had a stellar track record with the company— they delivered on schedule, worked well under pressure, were great managers. O'Leary was listening because he found it hard to say what he felt had to be said, but a decision had to be made. No matter everyone else's concern for "doing the right thing," his longevity at the company depended on Robo-Boy making a killing at Christmas. Finally he spoke:

"Look, you're all a great bunch of white, male, bleeding hearts and it's real decent of you. But the Robo-Boy project is a pressure cooker. Doris Grand is a black woman and Reggie Burke's a white guy. All of the designers are white guys— for better or worse, that's the way it is. The Robo-Boy group is going to be in the shop day and night for months. We cannot afford any glitches, any time spent with the team working through what it's like working for a woman, working for a black, working for a vegetarian, whatever Doris is. I agree, she's great. They'll be some other project for her to be great on. This one goes to Reggie."

The comments had gotten back to Grand, who brought them to the attention of the CEO. Her letter to him had ended: "I'm not going to make a stink about this, although we both know I could." The CEO himself talked with O'Leary about how he had made his decision. Although O'Leary outlined his concerns about intergroup dynamics more carefully this time, he still had been "benched. It was nothing less than censorship."

Discussion Point 26. America is oppressive, imposing subservience on various victim groups. The culture is permeated with racism, sexism,

heterosexism, classism (oppression of the working class), so the first task of universities is "consciousness-raising." This is done with "diversity education," which often is an attempt to produce intellectual uniformity by promulgating political orthodoxy.

Such "value clarification" is a moral reformation of young people who are presumed to be burdened with "false consciousness" as a result of being raised within the "hegemony" of America's "self-perpetuating power structure."

The universities' imprimatur is implicitly bestowed on a particular view of American history, a political agenda, and specific groups deemed authoritative regarding race, sex, class, etc.

This orthodoxy is reinforced—and enforced—by codes of conduct called "anti-harassment" codes, under which designated groups of victims are protected from whatever they decide offends them. To cure the offensiveness of others, therapists and thought police are proliferating on campuses, conducting "racial awareness seminars" and other "sensitivity training."

These moral tutors have a professional interest in the exacerbation of group tensions, to which university administrators contribute by allowing, even encouraging, group identities— black dorms, women's centers, gay studies, etc.

The status of victim is coveted as a source of moral dignity and political power, so nerves are rubbed raw by the competitive cultivation of grievances. The more brittle campus relations become, the more aggressive moral therapy becomes, making matters worse.

George F. Will, "Radical English" in *Debating P.C.*[25]

Discussion Point 27. Freedom is another word for having nothing left to lose.

Kris Kristofferson, "Me and Bobby McGee"[26]

Discussion Point 28. . . . As a child I heard the same chant over and over: "Why are you trying to act like a white person?" I was threatened and harassed because I liked to read, for using correct English, and for striving to articulate my words . . . then, as now, the idea that these skills are the domain of white people infuriates me. . . . Painting American success as a white attribute smacks of white supremacy . . . Who's setting the standards? I consider myself quite Afrocentric, quite aware of my blackness. . . . Basically, what I am is an articulate, professional black woman. . . . So am I trying to act white?

Rachel L. Jones, "Striving for Success Doesn't Make Us 'White'"[27]

Discussion Point 29. What became clear to me is that people like myself, my friend, and middle-class blacks in general are caught in a very specific double-bind that keeps two equally powerful elements of our identity at odds with each other. The middle-class values by which we were raised—the work ethic, the importance of education, the value of property ownership, of respectability, of "getting ahead," of stable family life, of initiative, of self-reliance, et cetera—are, in themselves, raceless and even assimilationist. They urge us toward participation in the American mainstream, toward integration, toward a strong identification with society, and toward the entire constellation of qualities that are implied in the word *individualism*. These values are almost rules for how to prosper in a democratic, free-enterprise society that admires and rewards individual effort. They tell us to work hard for ourselves and our families and to seek our opportunities whenever they appear, inside or outside the confines of whatever ethnic group we belong to.

But the particular pattern of racial identification that emerged in the sixties and that still prevails today urges middle-class blacks (and all blacks) in the opposite direction. This pattern asks us to see ourselves as an embattled minority, and it urges an adversarial stance toward the mainstream and an emphasis on ethnic con-

sciousness over individualism. It is organized around an implied separatism . . .

. . . Clearly, the two indispensable parts of my identity were a threat to one another . . . I moved back and forth like a bigamist between the demands of class and race.

Shelby Steele, *The Content of Our Character*[28]

Discussion Point 30. . . . "There's a backlash" . . . "When a female or minority or some combination is appointed to a particularly prestigious job, there's always the comment that the reason they were selected is that they were a women or minority. That's one of the statements white males still aren't afraid to make in public," says Sara Kelsey, vice president and assistant general counsel at Chemical Bank in New York.

Michele Galen and Ann Therese Palmer, "White, Male & Worried," *Business Week*[29]

VII. The Implications of Involvement

Andie Ottway

Andie Ottway, a popular child movie actor in the late-1950s was a successful senior studio executive in 1994. Well-known around Hollywood, Ottway had always protected his private life. Although his partner was active in the gay rights movement, Ottway was not "out" as a gay man.

Ottway considered his work environment to be quite homophobic; he had often sat silently at meetings where the sexuality of actors was debated and often derided. Ottway was pleased to have made the career move from in front of the camera to behind it as easily as he had, enjoyed his success, was comfortable in his private life, and had never felt particularly political.

In 1992 and 1993 several movies that portrayed gays or lesbians in a negative light had been released to wide popular acclaim. At the end of 1994, Ottway was approached by a well-respected, national gay rights organization to lend his name and inside clout to a campaign to have movies produced by major studios that portrayed gays and lesbians positively.

Maggie Reynolds, Letitia Spiller, and Abby Addams

It was the usual meeting of the Wednesday Night Club—a weekly event when Maggie Reynolds, Letitia Spiller, and Abby Addams got together to talk over dinner at one of Boston's ethnic restaurants—but with a special theme. Reynolds had been on the most recent cover of *Fortune* magazine and been featured in an article, "The Women of Bio-tech." Reynolds, the founder and CEO of a closely-watched bio-tech venture; Spiller, a surgeon; and Addams, a senior administrator at the hospital where Spiller worked, had gotten together to celebrate. The conversation soon turned to the number of phone calls, faxes, and E-mail requests that Reynolds had gotten since the magazine went on sale just days before.

Reynolds: "I think the attention's great. Lord knows black women could use a little positive feedback. But then again, some people are probably thinking the only reason I'm getting any attention at all is because I'm a black woman. Who knows?

What troubles me most, though, is that if I responded to a quarter of the invitations I get to speak, I'd have no time to run my business, it would go down the tubes, and the next *Fortune* piece I appeared in would be, 'Why Blacks Can't Manage Success.' I can't tell you how many people out there are just waiting to pounce on my first wrong move and say, "I told you so." I'd like to help other blacks, I'd like to help other women, but I've got to run my company—and it *is* harder for me than it would be for a white guy. And then the accusations start: Elitism, or 'you're too white for your own good.'"

Spiller: "I hear what you're saying. Every time I go to another business forum or minority business conference to be the 'show-and-tell' success story, I think, 'What am I doing here?'. My colleagues aren't here; they're smoozing with the big corporate types and developing some breakthrough drug to address Alzheimer's or a laser to move surgery forward into the next century. There are costs to doing this 'help your people' stuff. And, you're right, you can't say you're not interested or you're too busy. It sound real bad. It's not allowed."

Addams: "You're right there. What gets me are the assumptions people make every time I get a request like that. Just because I'm black, just because I'm female—folks go assuming I'm pro-choice and a Democrat. Because I'm those things *and* successful, they assume I'm straight, married, have legitimate children, live in suburbia, and grow tomatoes in my free time. I can't tell you how many times I've come too close to giving someone a nasty lecture about these assumptions and what that is doing to 'the people'."

Discussion Point 31. It has always annoyed me to hear from the mouths of certain arbiters of blackness that middle-class blacks should "reach back" and pull up those blacks less fortunate than they—as though middle-class status was an unearned and essentially passive condition in which one needed a large measure of noblesse oblige to occupy one's time. My own image is of reaching back from a moving train to lift on board those who have no tickets. A noble enough sentiment—but might it not be wiser to show them the entire structure of principles, effort, and sacrifice that puts one in a position to buy a ticket anytime one likes? This, I think, is something members of the black middle-class can realistically offer to other blacks. Their example is not only a testament to possibility but also a lesson in method. But they cannot lead by example until they are released from a black identity that regards that example as suspect, that sees them as "marginally" black; indeed that holds *them* back by catching them in a double bind.

Shelby Steele, *The Content of Our Character*[30]

Discussion Point 32. Asking gay men and lesbians to check their private lives at the door leaves a part of your company's workforce isolated and afraid. In surveys, about two-thirds say they have witnessed some form of hostility toward gay people on the job, and discrimination based on sexual orientation is still legal in much of the United States. So most [gays and lesbians] hide . . .

Gay executives . . . fear a "glass ceiling" beyond which known or suspected homosexuals cannot rise. In a 1987 survey by *The Wall Street Journal,* 66 percent of major company CEOs said they would be reluctant to put a homosexual on management committees; while attitudes may have changed since, there's no evidence of a revolution.

Hundreds of employers, including dozens of Fortune 500 companies, have pledged not to discriminate on the basis of sexual orientation, but gay and lesbian executives are under no illusion that they will soon win mainstream acceptance in corporate America. The organizers of a conference on gay and lesbian workplace issues held [in 1991], who sent invitations to CEOs and Human Resources directors at 9,400 companies, received one reply—not on letterhead—that began: "To all the fags, gays, homos, and lezzies. Do not mail me any of your fag shit lezzie homo paperwork to my business." . . .

Thomas A. Stewart, "Gay in Corporate America"[31]

Discussion Point 33. It is often said that unlike African-Americans, gay people can hide their identity; like light-skinned blacks of an earlier era who "passed" for white, gays can "pass" for straight. This analogy does point out a difference: Gay people can hide. But the condition of hiding or passing is a surrender of freedom, of identity, and ultimately of life itself. Like the secret Jews of Inquisition Spain, and like those rare people of color who did pass for white, the unsuspected homosexual, trapped in an unwanted heterosexual lifestyle, pays the trib-

ute of his or her own life to the system of oppression. Such a person courts dysfunction, misery, and shame without escaping intolerable oppression and special vulnerability to persecution.

Michael Nava and Robert Dawidoff, *Created Equal: Why Gay Rights Matter to America*[32]

NOTES

1. Each of the vignettes contained in this case is loosely based on a composite of information from public sources. While each vignette is designed to portray a realistic business situation, no vignette is based solely on the particulars of any one company or individual.

2. Terry Morehead Dworkin, "Harassment in the 1990s," *Business Horizons,* March-April 1993, pp. 52+.

3. Anne B. Fischer, "When Will Women Get to the Top?" *Fortune,* September 21, 1992, p. 48.

4. Deborah Tannen, *You Just Don't Understand: Women and Men in Conversation* (New York: Ballantine Books, 1990), p. 34.

5. Carol Gilligan, *In a Different Voice: Psychological Theory & Women's Development* (Cambridge, MA: Harvard University Press, 1982), pp. 6, 14, and 22.

6. Tannen, p. 118.

7. Laurie P. Cohen, William Power, and Michael Siconolfi, "Wall Street Women: Financial Firms Act to Curb Office Sexism, with Mixed Results," *The Wall Street Journal,* November 5, 1991, pp. A1, A12.

8. Daniel Goleman, "Sexual Harassment: It's about Power, Not Lust," *The New York Times,* October 22, 1991, pp. C1, C12.

9. Fischer, p. 56.

10. Patti Doten, "Why Women Don't Speak Out," *The Boston Globe,* October 9, 1991, pp. 73, 78.

11. Michael Lewis, *Liar's Poker: Rising through the Wreckage on Wall Street.* (New York: W.W. Norton & Company, 1989), pp. 47–49, 51, and 67.

12. Dworkin, p. 52+.

13. Taylor C. Cox, *Cultural Diversity in Organizations: Theory, Research & Practice* (San Francisco: Berrett-Koehler, 1993), pp. 220–21.

14. Cox, pp. 126 and 214.
15. Karen A. Geiger, Vice President and Director of Career Development, NCNB Corporation, "Letters to the Editor," *Harvard Business Review,* May-June 1989, p. 190.
16. Rosabeth Moss Kanter, *Men and Women of the Corporation* (New York: Basic Books, 1977; 1993 ed.), p. 208, 230.
17. Gareth Morgan, "Endangered Species: New Ideas," *Business Month,* April 1989, p. 76.
18. Irving L. Janis, "Groupthink," *Psychology Today,* November 1971, pp. 43–44, 76.
19. Cox, pp. 36–39.
20. Charlan Jeanne Nemeth and Joel Wachtler, "Creative problem solving as a result of majority vs. minority influence, *European Journal of Social Psychology,* Vol. 13 (1983), p. 48.
21. Attributed to Martin Niemöller (1892–1984). A pastor and critic of National Socialism, Niemöller spent eight years in Nazi concentration camps.
22. Edward W. Jones, Jr., "Black Managers: The Dream Deferred," in *Differences That Work: Organizational Excellence through Diversity,* ed. Mary C. Gentile (Boston, MA: Harvard Business School Press, 1994), p. 73.
23. Harris Wofford, *Of Kennedys and Kings: Making Sense of the Sixties* (New York: Farrar-Strauss-Giroux, 1980), p. 110.
24. U.S. Equal Opportunity Commission, January 1992, Ref. EEOC-FS/E-4.
25. George F. Will, "Radical English" in *Debating P.C.,* ed. Paul Berman, pp. 259–60.
26. Kris Kristofferson and Fred Foster, "Me and Bobby McGee," Combine Music Corporation, New York, October 31, 1969.
27. Rachel L. Jones, "Striving for Success Doesn't Make Us 'White'," *The Boston Globe,* September 6, 1994, p. 11.
28. Shelby Steele, *The Content of Our Character: A New Vision of Race in America* (New York: St. Martin's Press, 1990), pp. 95–97.
29. Michele Galen and Ann Therese Palmer, "White, Male and Worried," *Business Week,* January 31, 1994, p. 50+.
30. Steele, pp. 108–9.
31. Thomas A. Stewart, "Gay in Corporate America," *Fortune,* December 16, 1991, pp. 44–45, 56.
32. Michael Nava and Robert Dawidoff, *Created Equal: Why Gay Rights Matter to America,* (New York: St. Martin's Press, 1994), p. 18.

TOM REESE

Don't waste your time talking to the Accounting Department. That bunch of faggots doesn't do anything but count beans and play with each other all day.

Roy Mallick

Tom Reese, a consultant for Creative Insights Group (CIG), had endured comments like this from his client contact, Roy Mallick, throughout the first six weeks of his current assignment. Mallick was the production manager at Motor Technologies, CIG's most important new client. Since Mallick was Reese's primary contact within the client's organization, Reese had to spend as much as two hours a day with him.

While Tom Reese was accustomed to keeping his personal opinions to himself in order to facilitate client relationships, he had never before felt so frustrated and angry about staying silent. Tom explained:

> After holding it in for a month and a half, I really felt like the pressure was building up inside me. I didn't just want to say to him, "Look, that kind of comment really bothers me," I wanted to say, "Look, I'm *gay* and that kind of comment really bothers me." Imagine if you were Jewish and someone said something anti-Semitic in front of you because they assumed you weren't Jewish. You wouldn't just want to tell them you were offended—you'd want to tell them you're Jewish—and you're proud of it. You'd want to make a point to them so that maybe they'd think twice the next time.

This case was prepared by Jay Steele under the supervision of Joseph L. Badaracco.

Harvard Business School case 391-145.

Tom Reese

Tom Reese grew up in the Boston area, where he attended public high school and graduated with top honors. He majored in psychology at Yale University, again attaining honors and distinguishing himself in varsity baseball and track. Upon graduation from Yale, he secured a job with a financial consulting firm. After working with this firm for two years in New York City, he attended the Harvard Business School and received his M.B.A. in 1987. He then joined the Creative Insights Group, a strategic consulting firm, and began work in their Washington, D.C. office. Tom considered his years at CIG:

> For the most part it was a terrific experience. I really liked the work we were doing and I think I had a pretty good reputation in the firm. After working with a variety of managers in my first couple of years, I took pride in being one of the more sought-after consultants—and that was critical if you wanted to get promoted. I'd made a number of friends at CIG, but I really believed in keeping my private life to myself—I wasn't open with my co-workers about being gay.

Occasionally Tom felt the pressure of hiding his sexual orientation:

> I tried to walk a fine line by lying as little as possible about myself. I didn't talk about any of the men I dated, but I didn't make up stories about having girlfriends either. Usually this wasn't a problem. Most people just accepted the fact that I wasn't talkative about my private life—they didn't pressure me with questions. Whether this meant

they *res*pected me or *sus*pected me I don't know. In any case, I got along with almost everyone in the office. The people who made me uncomfortable—the ones who were too nosy or made a lot of homophobic remarks—I just avoided to the extent I could. But they were a small minority.

Problems at Motor Technologies

Initially, Tom Reese was excited to be assigned as a project team leader on the Motor Technologies case because he knew what an important opportunity it was for CIG. His boss, Anthony Ryland, made it clear that he was "expecting a lot" from Tom in handling Motor Technologies, so Tom felt more than the usual pressure to make the client happy. Tom's hopes for an enjoyable assignment dissolved as soon as he started spending time with his contact, Roy Mallick. Tom recalled:

> It was unbelievable. I never met anyone who made such incessant homophobic remarks. Roy Mallick's derogatory term for any man he disliked was "fag" or "faggot." He constantly brought up the subject, too—if he happened to spot two male co-workers walking down the hall together more than once in the course of a day, he'd say something like, "What are you two guys, faggots or something? You're always together. I'm going to stay away from you!"
>
> Unfortunately, there was no way around dealing with Roy. He was the key source for contacts and information in my case assignment. Nothing went on in manufacturing without his knowing it.

And to make matters worse, he had a lot of influence with the division general manager who had commissioned our consulting work. If I said the wrong thing to Roy, I knew it would find its way back up the ladder to the G.M., then to my boss, then down to me.

Tom Reese thought at first that he would be able to simply "grin and bear it," but after the first six weeks of what would likely be a four-month study, he realized that something had to be done.

> Some days I felt like I was going to explode. I started to hate my job—and myself.
>
> I felt like I really needed to make a statement—not sidestep the issue, but address it right in the face. The problem was that it was such a big unknown. And I had no way of knowing beforehand how my company would react. Once they found out I was gay, there was no reversing my steps. For God's sake, I'd worked hard to get where I was!
>
> A million things went through my mind as I tried to sort it all out. I remembered an incident with my boss that happened around the time of the Gay Pride March last year. Ironically, the CIG offices are in the Du Pont Circle area of Washington, which is home to a lot of gay people. My boss was looking out his window at a group of outrageously dressed men who were hanging out across the street. He said to me, "Geez, will you look at the faggots!"
>
> Was that the kind of reaction I would get? Or was he just not thinking?

STAR DISTRIBUTORS, INC. (A)

May 1, 1989
Dear John Heyman:
After much deliberation, I have come to the conclusion that the main problem relative to morale at Star Distributors is you. As witnessed by our current opinion survey, your cruel and inhumane attitude toward certain blacks is a disgrace for a man of your intelligence and position . . .

Paul Logan

On the morning of May 2, 1989, John Heyman, part owner of Star Distributors, a soft drink distributorship, could hardly believe his eyes as he read a copy of the letter his partner, Paul Logan, had sent to corporate headquarters. The letter frankly accused Heyman of discriminatory practices. It explicitly stated that his actions had been detrimental to the company's well-being by targeting its black sales personnel for disciplinary action. As he read the closing statements, pacing the floor, Heyman wondered how their relationship had deteriorated to this point (see Exhibit 1). He believed that his actions had been aimed at addressing the performance problems at Star.

In March 1983, Logan, an African-American, and Heyman, a white American, had entered a partnership under which they owned and operated Star Distributors. Located in Detroit, Star was a newly independent but troubled distributorship of Belmont Beverages, Inc. Each partner owned 50 percent of Star. Logan was president but had the additional responsibility of overseeing sales and marketing activities. Heyman, vice president of operations, managed administration, delivery, and the warehouse.

This case was prepared by Deborah J. Evans under the supervision of David Thomas.

Copyright © 1992 by the President and Fellows of Harvard College.

Harvard Business School case 493-015 (Rev. December 1, 1993).

Both men had been committed to improving the distributorship's performance. But after six years, the company still had not come close to achieving the owners' projected goals: Market share had continued to drop (see Exhibit 2) and sales had declined. Up to this point, Belmont had taken a hands-off approach to the distributorship's problems, merely cautioning the partners that if solutions were not forthcoming, the company would be forced to buy back the franchise—at a nonnegotiable price. It now seemed almost certain that Logan's letter would prompt headquarters to intervene—or worse, force it to make an offer dissolving the partnership. As he stared blankly at the office walls, John Heyman did not know quite what to expect from headquarters.

John Heyman

John Heyman grew up in Detroit. He lived in a racially integrated part of town and attended public schools. In 1969, after graduating from high school, Heyman was hired as a driver at Belmont Beverages, Detroit, which later became Star Distributors (see Exhibit 3). He worked his way through college, receiving a bachelor's degree and an M.B.A. from the University of Michigan at Dearborn in 1973 and 1975, respectively.

Between 1969 and 1978, Heyman made it his priority to learn the different facets of the

---

EXHIBIT 1

May 1, 1989

Dear John Heyman:

After much deliberation, I have come to the conclusion that the main problem relative to morale at Star Distributors is you. As witnessed by our current opinion survey, your cruel and inhumane attitude toward certain Blacks is a disgrace for a man of your intelligence and position, and especially as it relates to Larry Simms. You have belittled and harassed this man beyond any human understanding.

However, when it comes to evaluating white management and personnel, you exhibit patience and understanding beyond belief (i.e., Rick Talley, Warehouse Manager; Bob Hargrove, Delivery Manager; Carol Willis, Sales Administrator; and Timothy Cirelli, former Office Manager). All of the aforementioned, by your own admission, were not qualified for the position they held, or are currently holding.

The obvious conclusion is that you put them in their respective positions with the thought that if they were dismissed it would be an admission of your bad judgment.

Now to add insult to injury, you come to me seeking my support in discharging Larry Simms, Peter Smith, William Patterson, Cheryl Johnson—all blacks—and Chris McKinney . . . immediately. I strongly believe that this was a retaliatory act based on the fact that you felt they told the truth regarding your character during our opinion survey.

On two occasions, Larry Simms has come to you regarding the performance of Pre-Salesman Mori Lee (Asian) only to be blamed for his substandard performance. It should be noted that Mr. Lee, himself, recognizing that he could not meet the demands of his position, insisted on resigning from Star Distributors. However, his resignation was not acceptable to you, due to the negative effect it might have on the Asian community, which represents 60 percent of all small-store owners, and less than 1 percent of Detroit's population. However, on the other hand, you are prepared to discharge (4) Blacks immediately with no concern as to how it would affect the Black community which represents 63 percent of Detroit's population.

Larry Simms (Black) takes time off to go to his aunt's funeral in California and you strongly suggest that we consider docking his pay.

Bob Hargrove (White) takes off to go to a funeral (his wife's cousin, I believe) and you say nothing.

Michael Scott (White) walks around the office in shorts and a T-shirt after being told on numerous occasions that this attire is improper, and you say nothing.

Tom Hayes (White), Pre-Salesman, got his driver's license impounded for a DWI charge, an incident that

(continued)

---

beverage distribution business. Recruited by the corporate office as a market analyst in 1978, he moved to Milwaukee, Wisconsin. "I was pleased yet somewhat insecure when headquarters recruited me along with M.B.A.s from Ivy League Universities," Heyman admitted.

Heyman found that the culture of the corporate office was a perfect fit for him and was thrilled to be "in the heart of the action." He progressed rapidly through the company, aiming always to surpass the standards that Edward M.

Jones, the company's president and CEO, set for his employees. Heyman's hard work paid off when Jones selected him as his personal administrative assistant.

Privately, Heyman had hoped someday to rise to the level of vice president. Jones, on the other hand, felt that a partnership would present Heyman with a greater opportunity to sharpen his managerial skills and selected him as a partner of Star, the newly independent Detroit distributorship. Heyman had often pondered owning a

---

EXHIBIT 1   *(concluded)*

---

you were made fully aware of from the start. Later, after I find out about the incident, you wanted to blame Larry Simms for not knowing about it. I am perplexed as to your rationale relative to this issue. I am sure that as your Partner, I should have been informed by you, but again nothing was said by you until the issue was forced to the surface.

Timothy Cirelli (White), former office manager, screwed up the books and the office in general. Again, by your own admission, you stated that he would be let go. Instead, he was promoted to the position of Dispatcher, with, I strongly believe, no reduction in pay. Finally, Timothy left the company to work for a traveling marketing campaign as Star's liaison with that company.

Could all of these acts be construed as Racism?

As bad as we need sales, you allow and approve of a program that says if the salesman sells over a given amount on certain days, they will have to find a way to participate in delivering that product, as if they can totally control the retailer's request for product. Well, in my opinion, this is a delivery function, and as long as I am at Star Distributors, no salesman will assist in that function, unless he elects to do so.

The end result is that I am fed up with watching the morale of this company and my life savings and efforts go down the drain due to your attitude.

John, in my opinion, you are not qualified to run anything that involves people. Computers and machines are your forte, and it is a field you should confine yourself to, as they require no concern for their emotional well-being.

Having brought many of these issues to you in prior conversations and being an eternal optimist, I thought that you might change. However, I sincerely think that is an impossibility.

John, I am fed up with the partnership, and due to the 50–50 equity position we currently hold, I am requesting that Belmont Beverages intervene in this matter to clear the air, with the end result being one person controlling Star Distributors 100 percent. Please bear in mind I have no plans for leaving or relinquishing my stock.

Sincerely,

Paul Logan

cc: Edward M. Jones
    Chairman of the Board and President
    Belmont Beverages

---

distributorship, but in a somewhat less urbanized area than Detroit. Partially out of deference to Jones, Heyman accepted the offer. But his long-term objective was "to put a good management team in place and hope that Paul Logan, his partner, would buy him out some day."

Paul Logan

Paul Logan was raised in Philadelphia. As a teen he had dreamed of becoming the world's greatest saxophone player. Realizing that playing the sax might not pay the rent, Logan enrolled in junior college and later enlisted in the military. In 1963, with some help from his uncle, Logan landed a sales job with Belmont Beverages, Philadelphia (see Exhibit 4).

Logan's skill at marketing and enthusiasm enabled him to move up in the company. He used his appreciation for cultural diversity to help wholesalers gain a better understanding of ethnic markets, thereby strengthening the company's position in minority communities.

EXHIBIT 2

	Belmont Total Market Share	Star Detroit Market Share	
		Projected	Actual
1983	32.9%	24.4%	24.7%
1984	35.0	25.2	25.4
1985	37.1	26.6	26.8
1986	38.6	27.1	27.0
1987	40.6	27.7	26.4
1988	41.8	28.4	25.8
1989	43.3	29.1	26.7

Logan began to think about owning a distributorship in the early 1970s. After a string of successful assignments, Logan was promoted to general manager of Belmont Beverages' Detroit distributorship. Three years later, in 1983, his dream of becoming a distributorship owner became a reality when John Heyman joined him to acquire the Detroit operation.

Belmont Beverages hailed the newly incorporated distributorship as a significant accomplishment in minority business and circulated flyers publicizing Logan's rise to ownership. His success also drew the attention of national black-owned magazines. But Logan had even "higher hopes of one day becoming sole owner of the partnership," and passing his business on to his sons, giving them opportunities he had missed.

History of Star Distributors, Inc.

Before Star became an independent franchise, the distributorship had been owned and operated by Belmont Beverages, Inc. The company prided itself on the quality of its soft drinks. Under the leadership of Jones, 49, Belmont had expanded its beverage product line and diversified into nonbeverage businesses. The company was also vertically integrated into new can manufacturing, syrup production facilities, and container recovery. The company compensated its employees well in return for a high degree of loyalty. Turnover in the company was low and lifetime employment was assumed by many.

**Problems at Belmont Beverages'
Detroit Distributorship**

In 1980, when Logan arrived in Detroit as general manager at Belmont Beverages, the operation was fraught with problems: poor product positioning, ineffective inventory controls, inadequate distribution systems, employee pilfering, and a sales force that had not adapted to changes in the retail sector. As a result, market share and sales had deteriorated, and profits had plummeted. Speaking from a wholesaler's perspective, an employee in Detroit explained:

> We blame Belmont's top-down management structure and one-way communication for these problems. Detroit is a unique market. Headquarters tries to hold us to the same standards as its other distributorships. Decisions are made by the bureaucrats in Milwaukee instead of by the sales representatives who interact with the retailers and customers. The lack of locally structured programs, promotions, and competitive discounting hurts us when the competition's doing on-premise programs and giving discounts.

A supervisor concurred:

EXHIBIT 3   Background of John Heyman

Age: 40
Race: White

Career Chronology

1969	Joined Belmont Beverages, Detroit, as driver; sold and delivered beer.
1971	Promoted to warehouse crewman; maintained inventory.
1972	Transferred to an independent Belmont Beverages wholesalership in Columbus, Ohio, as the warehouse manager.
1974	Promoted to office manager.
1977	Rejoined Belmont Beverages, St. Louis as a district manager.
1978	Hired as a market analyst at Belmont Beverages headquarters in Milwaukee, Wisconsin.
1979	Promoted to Assistant to the Vice President.
1981	Promoted to Assistant to the President, Edward M. Jones.
1983	Became an owner of Star Distributors, Inc., in a 50/50 partnership.

EXHIBIT 4   Background of Paul Logan

Age: 56
Race: African-American

Career Chronology

1962	Joined Belmont Beverages, Philadelphia, in Sales; displayed merchandise and advertisements.
1963	Promoted to salesman; coordinated promotional materials and trained drivers.
1968	Served as the regional representative for New Jersey. Assisted wholesalers in understanding the African-American market.
1969	Became the district manager for New England; supervised wholesalers in Massachusetts and Rhode Island.
1979	Promoted to sales manager at Belmont Beverages, Denver.
1980	Promoted to general manager at Belmont Beverages, Detroit.
1983	Became an owner of Star Distributors, Inc., in a 50/50 partnership.

We needed to improve communication with Belmont regarding the composition of our market. I thought we had some unique opportunities that headquarters saw as problems. We're in a culturally diverse market, with a wide range of incomes, but mainly a black population base. When we ran Belmont six-packs on sale, headquarters didn't make any $1.99 price signs and that hurt us, because they only promoted $6.99 a case. In a low income ethnic market they don't buy by the case. Why is Belmont Beverages trying to sell cases to consumers who buy by the can or six-pack?

A sales rep added that:

Belmont's products are targeted at white middle-class suburbanites. There is a lack of congruence between Belmont's image and the African-

American community. For example, African-Americans have unique purchasing patterns when buying beverages. Beverage purchases by blacks are either at the very high end of the product line or the low end. And soda is often purchased by the can instead of in cases, which is what Belmont Beverages often promotes.

Pressure from the African-American Community[1]

In the early 1980s, only a few corporations had minority-owned franchises. In many cities, African-Americans rallied for broader inclusion into the franchise opportunities of selected industries, such as fast food, liquor, and soft drinks. Because African-Americans made up a disproportionately large percentage of the consumer base in these industries, the case for greater inclusion was compelling. Business and community leaders began to mobilize black consumers and inform them about the influence they could exert through their collective purchasing power.

A major source of such organized pressure was Operation PUSH. Led by the Reverend Jesse Jackson, the goal of PUSH (People United to Serve Humanity) was to secure jobs for blacks and to support the growth of black-owned businesses. Selective boycotting of some of the largest national corporations persuaded companies such as Seven-Up, Burger King, and Heublein to sign "covenants" with Reverend Jackson promising greater economic opportunity to blacks. These corporations agreed to hire more blacks, to increase procurement with black businesses, to award franchises to blacks, to deposit money in black-owned banks, to use black-owned publications for advertising, and to donate money to black colleges and organizations.

The sheer idea of a boycott prompted other companies to follow suit without even signing covenants. Indeed many executives believed

---

1. Ernest R. House, *Jesse Jackson and the Politics of Charisma: The Rise and Fall of the PUSH/Excel Program* (Boulder, Colorado: Westview Press, 1988), p. 13.

PUSH could harm virtually any corporation it wanted. It was under the influence of such pressure from the black community that Star Distributors was created.

Belmont Beverages' Minority Distributorships

When Logan and Heyman formed their partnership Belmont had one minority-owned franchise out of approximately 1,000 independent distributorships. In response to the pressure from the African-American community, Belmont transformed its St. Louis, Philadelphia, and Chicago operations into minority-owned distributorships. The company hoped these newly independent operations would both increase its market share and defuse possible protest.

But the way Belmont awarded and structured Star's partnership differed from its other franchises. First, each owner's share could not exceed 50 percent. Second, Belmont's franchises were generally sold as perpetuities, permitting one generation of a family to transfer its equity down to the next upon retirement or death. In contrast, property rights in Star were structured in a way that discouraged intergenerational transfers. If one owner retired, died, or sold his equity, the partner—not the family—had the first right to buy. Moreover, Belmont maintained the right to approve or veto all buy-out decisions and could purchase all or part of the partnership itself. Finally, Belmont franchises were usually awarded on the basis of ability, though political influence and seniority often played a role as well. Like the other minority franchises, however, Star was formed under community pressure.

From Belmont Beverages Detroit to Star Distributors, Inc.

Belmont also saw the partnership between Logan and Heyman as a strategic move because Royal Beverages, its major competitor, already had a minority-owned distributorship in Detroit. Logan recalled:

We were virtually given the distributorship and, I must admit, from a very generous credit standpoint. Neither of us had a lot of money. What little money there was we were able to get it together and get them to give us a deal. We would have gotten it even if we had no money. They wanted a minority-owned distributorship in Detroit. So Belmont had to get a black in there. I guess they figured I was the best guy because I was already here. They wanted to get Heyman up here because he was from here originally. So it worked out well.

Star's operating funds were tight because of its incurred debt; each partner had put up $50,000, with Belmont covering the rest, to be paid off through profits. Logan and Heyman assumed roles according to their managerial strengths (see Exhibit 5). "We were hands-on managers. We could have put other managers in positions of responsibility but it would have cut the profit very thin," Logan said. "We had to learn the operations ourselves, so that when we hired a manager we would know what they were doing."

Logan and Heyman needed to turn things around quickly, but they faced new and unexpected challenges. "You have to understand the situation; headquarters basically had run the distributorship out of Milwaukee," explained Heyman. "When we came in we had to take over legal, administrative, and accounting functions that Belmont had supplied. At the time we were losing 500 cases a month; they were disappearing out of the warehouse. We had to get a computerized accounting system and insurance," Heyman said.

Logan and Heyman also inherited all of the existing personnel from Belmont. The staff was very diverse racially. Sixty percent of the employees were black, 30 percent were white, and the remainder included Asians and Puerto Ricans. Two of the three sales supervisors were black, while both the warehouse manager and administration manager were white. Such diversity was rare in the industry and Logan and Heyman were happy their organization reflected the community.

With all the changes it was difficult for some employees to adjust to the newly independent status of the company. "Perks and base salaries

EXHIBIT 5   Star Distributors, Inc.—Organization Chart, 1983

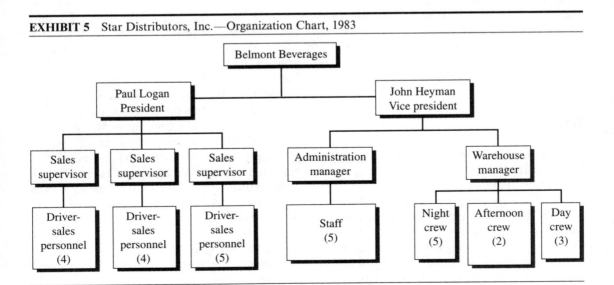

were better under Belmont," one said. "You knew what your raises were going to be. All sales reps had company cars. The company had more resources then."

Moreover, employees now had to report to two owners instead of one manager. "There was at least protocol at that time. Logan was the general manager then and everyone reported to him. When the company was sold, we had two owners, one black and one white. What happened was all the white sales representatives went to the white owner and all the black sales representatives went to Paul," a white employee said.

One employee believed the alignment between employees and owners had nothing to do with race. "The sales reps quickly learned which decisions Logan would approve and those Heyman would approve," he said. "It was basically a thing where you knew how Logan was; he wasn't giving up a penny to do anything. If it was a case of money you knew not to ask him, you knew to go to Heyman because he would give it to you. . . . This is where the thing of bypassing whoever you needed to to get the answer you wanted started."

A black employee summed up his feelings after the company's transition: "Logan going from general manager to owner wasn't really the problem at Star. He was well respected. But at that point nobody really knew Heyman. The question was how to take in someone that nobody knows."

The Partners

Logan's Managerial Style
Being African-American was an important source of Logan's motivation to excel as a franchise owner: "My thing was to prove to Belmont and Star that a black person can do the job, that he is not a lazy, idle person trying to shift and shamble his way through. I work, it does not matter—Saturday or Sunday, all day. I believe you have to represent yourself well." But, Logan added, "it's a shame I have to go through all of this to get acceptance or prove a point."

Logan had two guiding principles. The first was to lead by example: "If I expect employees to work 12 hours a day I'm going to be here with them even though I don't have to, so they can see that I am actually doing and not just talking." His second principle was to be accountable and to hold others accountable: "I have no respect for people who don't keep their commitments. Why should I spend an hour of my life sitting here waiting for someone?" Logan said. "Habitual lateness shows a disrespect for the other guy. Whether black or white, let's do what's right."

Even though he was regarded as a "good street salesperson," someone with "a good gut feeling about what is going on in the market," Logan gave his sales representatives the independence to make their own decisions about their accounts. Said one sales rep, "He basically focused on his expertise; projecting sales, and that type of thing. But on a day-to-day account basis, that was left up to the reps to handle."

A sales supervisor who had worked for Logan for several years portrayed him this way: "Paul Logan is easy to get along with. When he needs to make his point, he's to the point. He lays down the law when it has to be laid. Once it is over with he forgets about it, he doesn't hold grudges. He's well respected and thought of very highly by most of the people here."

Logan made it a point to attend Detroit's political and civic functions, and volunteered for community projects representing Star and Belmont. Although his employees recognized his growing political influence, they did not feel it made him lose touch with them. "He is different in the business and out of the business," one said. "When he's out of the business, he is one of the guys."

Heyman's Managerial Style
One reason Heyman was selected for the partnership was his superb analytical skills. He

prided himself on his number-crunching capabilities and on his ability to take into account multiple factors. An employee commented on Heyman's decision-making style: "He is broad-minded about the decisions that are made. Before he says yes or no he wants to look at things 25 different ways."

Some Star employees, however, regarded Heyman as somewhat "lacking in interpersonal skills." Said one, "He has a hard time dealing with people. It's not like him to be one of the guys." Another observed that "Heyman believes he is right most of the time." Heyman summed up his own managerial philosophy: "Try it my way first and if it doesn't work then let's talk about it."

Heyman attributed the development of this style to the time he had spent at Belmont headquarters and, in particular, to working directly with Jones. He believed that Logan's style would complement his. "Logan would perform all of the public relations and marketing tasks while I oversaw operations and administration."

In comparing the owners' styles, one employee provided the following illustration:

> If each owner had to sell 20 cases of soda to 20 accounts they would do it in two totally different ways. Logan's style of selling would be to hit every account, selling one case to each retailer, while Heyman would identify his one big volume account and sell all 20 cases to the one retailer. They would both end up selling the same amount of soda. But the difference in how they got there would be like night and day.

Problems at Star

Distribution

Prior to 1988, Star's driver-sales representatives would load each type of beverage on the truck and drive around to their retailers, selling directly out of the truck and returning to the warehouse to restock if needed. But "pedal selling," as it was called, was fast becoming an anachronism in the industry because driver-sales representatives could not manage the increasing assortment of packages from Belmont's expanded product line. This put new strains on Star's delivery system. "The business has gotten more complicated," Heyman explained. "When I first started we had two brands. Probably each of them had three or four packages. So driver-sales reps had probably six packages that they were selling; now we have 70 packages. We had to have a more professional salesperson, accomplishing things at a different level."

In early 1988, Logan and Heyman decided to change the distribution system from pedal selling to pre-sales, in effect separating the delivery function from the sales function. Instead of selling directly to the retailers, drivers would now be paired with sales reps. The sales rep would take orders on one day and the driver would deliver the beverages the next. A driver commented on the change: "The driver-sales rep had more freedom. He handled merchandising the accounts, deliveries, displays, and pricing. He was also the account representative and serviced the account. He made money." Although salaries remained commission-based, one's earnings now depended on joint efforts between a sales rep and a driver. Under the pedal sales system, driver-sales reps, most with only a high school diploma, earned $50,000 to $60,000 a year. Under the pre-sales system, drivers' salaries fell below $40,000 a year.

Under the new system, some driver-sales reps were promoted to sales representatives while others continued to deliver. Many drivers resented not being selected as sales reps. "Not all driver-sales reps were considered the best professionals. There was a suggested list given to the sales department recommending who should go from driver to sales rep," Heyman said.

Star's delivery manager explained how the shift from pedal selling to pre-sales affected the company's overall performance: "When we went to pre-sales, sales declined. According to the data, we should have started to rebound in two to three months. There was no rebound. Sales

EXHIBIT 6 Star Distributors, Inc.—Organization Chart—Presales System, 1988

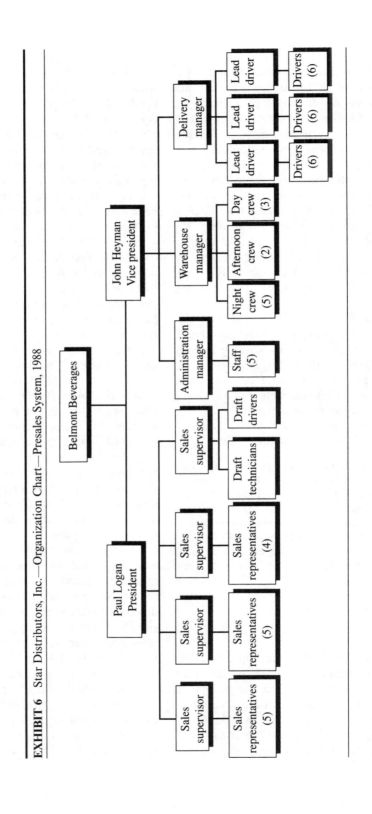

kept deteriorating for six months. And if you are managing sales you have to explain why sales are continuing to go down."

The new "marriage arrangement between sales and delivery" also altered the organizational structure (see Exhibit 6). Sales reps now reported to Logan while drivers reported to Heyman.

Managerial Involvement in the Retail Sector

In an attempt to bolster sales, Logan and Heyman separately strengthened their relationships with certain retailers by visiting their stores, offering them special deals, and assuring them that they were concerned about their accounts. Both attended company-sponsored promotions held at clubs and sporting events. Most of the accounts Logan visited were located in the African-American community, while those Heyman visited targeted white consumers.

Although sales rose slightly through these efforts, a sales supervisor described how the owners' involvement in the retail sector brought unexpected tension between the owners and the sales representatives, and ultimately between Logan and Heyman:

> Heyman began visiting sections of Detroit that were white. He would mingle with the different accounts in those areas. He was in and out of sales. At some points he got into sales and at some points he didn't. Whatever he wanted to do he did. John Heyman did things the reps would not know about. He would have his own thing going with retailers and nobody would know about it. And when he would decide to get out of sales the ball would drop back to the reps. The same thing was true for Paul Logan. He would visit accounts in the black community. That's when the friction started coming between John and Paul.
>
> The tension started when they were out visiting accounts and no knowledge would come back to the reps who actually saw the accounts more often than Logan and Heyman did. So what happened was the owners of the stores said to the reps, "We don't need to deal with you, we will

deal with the owners." The reps really didn't have any responsibility. They felt like they were not a part of the program, but they still had to hit the accounts and do their jobs.

Sales reps expressed their dissatisfaction with the owners' direct involvement in retail, confiding in the owner to whom they felt closer. This tended to be divided on racial lines and, moreover, it led to conflicting advice. "Heyman would tell a salesman one thing, then Logan wouldn't find out or maybe he'd find out a month later when it's thrown up in his face because it is a sales deal," a sales rep explained. "That's when Logan said everything that goes on in sales must come through him. If you don't go through him forget it. It was at this point that Heyman decided he would take himself out of sales."

Internal Management

Less gregarious than Logan, Heyman developed close relationships with a few trusted employees, sometimes providing favors for them. Unaware of Heyman's informal agreements, Logan would eventually hear of them through the company grapevine. An employee described one of these situations:

> We had a driver here, Tom, who was white. He had been convicted of a DWI driving while intoxicated. There was an incident where Tom was out drinking. He had a little bit much to drink and was stopped by the police. Unfortunately, his license was suspended. The only way he could keep his job and keep working was to deliver out of another guy's truck. So Tom ended up staying on with the company just route-riding with the other driver. Heyman knew about it and did not tell Logan. It caused a lot of friction.

But Heyman also commented on this incident, offering a different perspective:

> I admit not telling Paul was a mistake. I allowed the situation because Tom told me his license would be reinstated within a week. I eventually told Paul I was wrong.

The tension between the owners heightened as Logan got word from others of the preferential treatment Heyman gave a few employees, all of whom were white. When Logan found out Heyman had loaned $70,000 of company funds to a manager, he felt he could no longer trust Heyman, and that he should personally "look out for" black employees.

Headquarters Involvement

Many executives at headquarters had developed close relationships with Heyman. He had earned their respect as the administrative assistant to the vice president and, subsequently, to Jones. They thought he was disciplined and loyal, and they admired his quantitative approach to decision making. When they had questions about Star, they talked to Heyman, regardless of issue.

This offended Logan, who was unpersuaded by Heyman's explanation that the reason the executives sought his advice was because he managed the company's operational and administrative concerns: "The financial stuff frustrated Logan—dealing with the corporate office in Milwaukee and the administrative workload. Logan ran the sales; it was his strength. He believed that if we were to get Star turned around it had to be out on the street. We had to get more sales and he was right. Everyone at Star and in Milwaukee knew Logan was better at doing the external boundary work—marketing, public relations, and civic and community responsibilities." Logan, however, felt he had been bypassed by headquarters, although he did acknowledge that Heyman's relationship with headquarters brought some benefits. Says Logan: "When I was the general manager and Belmont owned the distributorship, the corporate guys were in here all the time. Once John came they backed off. This gave us some breathing space."

Communication

As Star entered its sixth year, communication between the owners had deteriorated markedly; they spoke to each other only when necessary.

"We would have meetings where Logan would stand on one side of the room and Heyman on the other. They would air their disputes in the meetings and hope to come to an agreement. They would do this instead of going into one of their offices to solve their problems . . . In my opinion they put too much out in the open. Everyone in the room saw they were not agreeing," said an employee. By the end of 1988, the interpersonal crisis had reached a peak. "It became a power struggle between Logan and Heyman. So everything became a challenge to them," a salesman said.

Heyman's Recommendation

One morning in April 1989, Heyman sat down in his swivel chair, pen in mouth, and reviewed the sales data for that quarter. As usual sales had fallen and market share had dropped. "Something has to change," Heyman concluded. The company could no longer afford to perform that poorly. "I know sales always takes the beating if things don't go right, but . . . that's sales," Heyman said to himself. He decided to consult Logan. Logan explained that he too had reviewed the company's sales report and was deeply concerned.

Heyman had believed all along that the ultimate reason for the company's poor sales performance was the incompetence of the sales force. Now thoroughly frustrated with the impasse, Heyman recommended to Logan that the sales supervisors be terminated. He explained that despite Logan's effort, the sales force—especially the supervisors—had not improved. To him, this proved that they lacked the skills to work under the new pre-sales structure. Logan admitted that one or two of his supervisors had been performing poorly, and that some of the sales reps had not achieved their quotas. But he also believed that incompetence ran throughout the company and wondered why his area was drawing all the negative attention.

Logan had often said to Heyman that "if anyone in sales was going to be terminated for incompetence, every incompetent person in the company should be terminated." Privately, Logan felt that Heyman's allegiances prevented him from holding all employees to the same standard. He believed that a fairer standard would force Heyman to terminate most of the employees for whom he had provided favors. Many of them were well known for their attitudinal problems, poor attendance, and below-average performance.

Logan's Response

Rising to leave the room, Heyman asked Logan for a response to his proposed solution to the company's problems. Logan politely told Heyman he had to think about it for a few days and would get back to him. Three days later, he handed Heyman a copy of the letter he had written in response to his recommended solution. A copy of the letter had also been sent to Edward M. Jones.

ANN HOPKINS (A)

The general method of maintaining an informal executive organization is so to operate and to select and promote executives that a general condition of compatibility of personnel is maintained. Perhaps often and certainly occasionally men cannot be promoted or selected, or even must be relieved, because they cannot function, because they "do not fit," where there is no question of formal competence.

Chester I. Barnard *The Functions of the Executive,* 1938, 1964.

Many of the best companies really do view themselves as an extended family.

Thomas J. Peters and Robert H. Waterman *In Search of Excellence,* 1982

Ann Hopkins was nominated for partnership at Price Waterhouse in August 1982. A senior manager in the firm's Office of Government Services

---

Ilyse Barkan, J. D., prepared this case under the direction of Joseph Badaracco, Jr.

This case is based on approximately 6,500 pages of legal documents relating to the case of *Ann B. Hopkins* v. *Price Waterhouse,* 618 F. Suppl. 1109 (D.D.C. 1985), 263 U.S. App. D.C. 321, 825 F.2d 458 (1987), reversed and remanded in 490 U.S. 228 (1989), on remand, *Price Waterhouse* v. *Hopkins,* 737 F. Supp. 1202 (D.D.C. 1990), affirmed, *Hopkins* v. *Price Waterhouse,* (U.S. App. D.C.) 920 F.2d 967 (1990). The quotations in the case are taken from courtroom testimony and pretrial depositions in the public record.

Copyright © 1991 by the President and Fellows of Harvard College.

Harvard Business School case 391-155 (Revised 1991).

(OGS) in Washington, D.C., Hopkins specialized in large-scale, computer-based systems designed for government agencies. Her 1982 partnership class included 87 other candidates; Hopkins was the only woman in the group. Price Waterhouse offered partnerships to 47 of them, rejected 21, and placed 20, including Hopkins, on hold.[1]

Soon afterward, Hopkins met with the firm's chairman to discuss the decision and the admissions committee's recommendations. It had suggested that she be given more work with partners and undertake a quality control review in order to demonstrate her skills and allay concerns about her. In 1983, however, one of her original supporters at OGS said he opposed her renomination and a second OGS partner joined him. Shortly afterward, Hopkins was told it was unlikely that she would ever become a partner at Price Waterhouse.

Hopkins then had four options. She could leave the firm. She could join the international area "on the hope of slim chance" she would be proposed for partnership the next year. She could continue working with Price Waterhouse as a career manager, without any chance of partnership.[2] The final option, which she ultimately pursued, was to leave the firm and initiate a lawsuit charging Price Waterhouse with sex discrimination. She also asked the courts to order the firm to make her a partner.

Ann Hopkins

Ann Hopkins was born December 18, 1943. She described herself as "third-generation, small-town Texas" and as an "army brat" who "learned from her childhood how to be an outsider."[3] She said her mother taught her that "when you shake hands, you should always shake hands firmly, and when you walk into a room, you should walk in as if you owned it." Her father, she said, was an "army career officer who disapproved of army wives working." Hopkins's mother, however, worked as a nurse and believed her career was important. Press reports said Hopkins used phrases such as "hills to die on" and said setbacks were "opportunities to manage." "I think of myself," she said, "as tough-minded, which is different than tough. To be tough-minded is to challenge whatever the assertions are."[4]

Hopkins graduated from high school in 1961 at the age of 17. She majored in mathematics at Hollins College in Roanoke, Virginia, where she earned a B.A. in 1965. Two years later, she received a master's degree in mathematics from Indiana University. Hopkins then returned to Hollins College to teach mathematics.

After a year, Hopkins left her teaching position to join IBM. In her early months there, she worked as a mathematical physicist and managed a seven-person project for NASA's Goddard Space Flight Center.[5] In 1972, Hopkins joined Computer Sciences Corporation where she continued to work on NASA accounts. About two years later, she moved on to Computer Usage Corporation. Although she continued to develop business at NASA, she began work in marketing and split her time between working for NASA and developing and installing computer systems for banks in New York and Chicago.[6]

In 1976, Hopkins joined Touche Ross, a major public accounting firm, as a systems management consultant. Her projects included the development of a system for payroll, personnel, and budgeting for the Federal Home Loan Bank Board. She also implemented a health claims processing system for the United Mine Workers. This project took more than two years, and Hopkins headed a team of as many as 20 Touche Ross consultants and UMW consultants and programmers. During this period, she married the man she called "the love of her life." Hopkins and her husband had three children.

In late 1977, when her husband came up for partnership at Touche Ross, she left the firm because it would not consider anyone for partnership whose spouse worked there. Hopkins joined American Management Systems (AMS) in 1978 and soon recognized that the move was a mistake. "I realized I basically preferred a multiproject environment and a broader focus," Hopkins said. Touche Ross referred her to Price Waterhouse.[7] In August 1978, Hopkins left AMS and began working at Price Waterhouse as a manager in the Management Advisory Services (MAS) department of OGS.[8]

Price Waterhouse was a professional partnership that specialized in auditing, tax, and management consulting services. Its principal clients were private corporations, including many Fortune 500 companies. It also worked for government agencies. In the early 1980s, in its 90 offices across the United States, Price Waterhouse had

662 partners.[9] The partnership worldwide had approximately 2,600 partners.

The firm was divided into three departments. Accounting and auditing represented 46 percent of the business; tax services, 20 percent; and management advisory services, the remaining 34 percent. Unlike auditors and accountants, who usually came to Price Waterhouse directly from college or the military, consultants typically had five or more years' experience and additional academic training.[10]

The Partnership Admission Process

The senior partner of Price Waterhouse and a policy board managed the firm and elected all new partners through a formal, annual nomination and review process that culminated in a partnershipwide vote. There was no formal limit on how many partners could be elected in a year.[11]

Partnership was, in essence, a lifetime appointment. "One of the great risks of admitting partners to our firm," said Timothy Coffey, the partner in charge of MAS, "is that, one, they're less supervised, and, secondly, they are more tenured and therefore people that have a likelihood or potential of abusing authority can cause serious long-term problems for the firm."[12] In practice, if the management committee decided to drop a partner, they negotiated with the individual. If the person objected, a 75 percent vote of the entire partnership was required to force a partner out.[13] In the history of the firm, there had been two mandatory withdrawals.[14]

Partners had unlimited personal liability and were exposed to substantial legal and financial risks.[15] Information about partners' incomes was closely guarded. Estimates suggested that partners at Price Waterhouse earned on average about $125,000 a year in the early 1980s. As a senior manager, Hopkins earned approximately $65,000. At the trial, one expert estimated that she would have earned approximately $107,000 had she become a partner in 1983.

The partnership candidates in a particular year were called a class, and the firm prepared a booklet for each class member. Its first page was the candidate's photograph. This was followed by an application for admission to partnership. Notes on counseling sessions, staff performance evaluations, partners' evaluations, statistical analyses of the quartile rankings for the candidate in each of the evaluation categories, and comparative rankings of the class candidates were typically included with the application.

Candidacy and review for partnership began when the partners in a local office proposed a candidate to the admissions committee.[16] The committee then invited every partner in the firm to submit written comments on each candidate.[17] Partners who had significant and recent contact with a candidate submitted a long-form evaluation; those with more limited contact used a short form.[18] Occasionally, the committee interviewed partners who had submitted comments to learn more about the basis for their comments.[19]

The admissions committee met for three days in early December 1982 for its initial consideration of candidates.[20] The committee member who had visited each candidate's office summarized the results of the visit, the strength of the nominating office's support, and important material from the candidate's personnel file, and then described the candidate's strengths and weaknesses for the Admissions Committee.[21] Questions followed. The absolute number of positive and negative evaluations was not decisive, and negative votes were given more weight, often leading to "no" or "hold" decisions. The committee ultimately made recommendations on each candidate and forwarded these to the policy board.

The policy board reviewed the admissions committee's recommendations and then voted on whether to include each candidate on a firmwide partnership ballot, "hold" the candidate, or reject the candidate.[22] According to one partner, "the board could override the recommendations of the admissions committee and approve candidates on the basis of individual merit or the firm's business needs."

Some candidates had been held because of concerns about their interpersonal skills. According to testimony from Price Waterhouse partners, the firm had "consistently placed a high premium on a candidate's ability to deal with subordinates and peers on an interpersonal basis and to promote cordial relations within a firm which is necessarily dependent on team effort." Other testimony stated that "[t]he Policy Board takes evaluations or a negative reaction on this basis very seriously," even if the negative comments on short-form evaluations were based upon less contact with the candidate than glowing reports on long-form evaluations based on more extensive contact. The policy board had, however, recommended and elected two candidates "criticized for their interpersonal skills because they were perceived as being aggressive, overbearing, abrasive, or crude." The reason was that the firm had a specific need for their skills and feared it would lose by putting them in the "hold" category.[23]

Approved candidates' names appeared on a ballot for partnership-wide election. For admission to partnership, two-thirds of the entire partnership had to approve a candidate.[24] Sixty percent of the female candidates and 68 percent of the male candidates who reached the final balloting had been elected to partnership.[25] Price Waterhouse had, however, only seven female partners.[26] It gave two explanations for this. One was the relatively recent entry of large numbers of women into accounting and related fields. The other was the success of clients and rival accounting firms in hiring away female potential partners.[27]

Hopkins's Candidacy

OGS nominated Hopkins for partnership in August 1982. According to Hopkins and the nominating proposal, OGS praised her "outstanding performance," said it was "virtually at partnership level," and underlined her "key role"[28] in connection with a large State Department project. No other 1982 candidate's record for securing major contracts was comparable.[29] Hopkins had also billed more hours (2,442 hours in 1982 and 2,507 in 1988) than any other candidate and generated more business than any other candidate considered for partnership in that year.[30] The proposal strongly urged her admission to the partnership."[31]

OGS had written several drafts of Hopkins's nomination proposal. Thomas Beyer, the partner in charge of consulting services at OGS, testified:

> The proposal is terribly important because it is the only document offered to the partners which demonstrates or shows what the individual has done and is the only place in time where we are allowed, [sic] the unstated rules of the firm to . . . politic . . . , to campaign for an individual. That's the only chance you have. In fact, it's well known and well understood in the firm that anybody trying any other method is clearly in violation of the unstated law and is terribly frowned upon. So we had to have this right. It had to be done just exactly right. Every word. Every nuance.[32]

Four partners were involved in the drafting and redrafting of Hopkins's proposal. Beyer did the final review himself.[33]

The admissions committee then circulated long and short forms to all Price Waterhouse partners. Thirty-two partners, all male, responded about Hopkins.[34] Of the 32 initial evaluations, 13 supported her for partnership, 3 recommended that her candidacy be put on hold, 8 stated that they were uninformed as to her suitability for partnership, and 8 opposed making her a partner. (See Exhibit 1.)

During the fall, Donald Ziegler, the head of the admissions committee, followed up the evaluations by interviewing respondents at the two offices where Hopkins had worked, OGS and the St. Louis office.[35] Another member of the committee, Roger Marcellin, also visited OGS.[36] He summarized the contents of Hopkins's file for the admissions committee, encapsulating her

EXHIBIT 1   Summary of Short Form and Long Form Comments

A.B. HOPKINS	MO12
SHORT FORM	
#1	

No comments. (Yes)   *Kelly*

My only contact with Ann was on the FMHA proposal this past July/Aug.   *Green*
   She tended to alienate the staff in that she was extremely overbearing. Ann needs improvement in her interpersonal skills. She also demonstrated an apparent lack of tech skills. (Insuff)

Ann's performance at the State Dept can only be described as "fantastic." She knows   *Laughlin*
how to deliver superior, distinctive client services. (Yes)

Ann has the "will" to get things done. There is no question as to who leads the proj-   *Lohneis*
ects she is responsible for. Ann has very high strength of conviction. (Yes)

   I am bothered by the arrogance & self-centered attitude that Ann projects.   *Haller*

Also while she may be admired by some she appears to be simply tolerated by others.
She may not be of value outside current (OGS) environment. (Insuff)

Observation through office association. (Yes)   *Simonetti*

Ann is hardworking, determined & relentless.   *Hartz*
She can also be abrasive in dealing with staff members. I have no question about her
tech competence.
I believe the key question regarding her admission is, "Will her personality limit her
   ability to successfully market work, retain staff, & maintain satisfactory relations
   with her ptrs?" (Insuff)

I have known Ann for the last 2 yrs. Her office is next to mine. I have not worked with   *MacVeagh*
her, but have been an interested observer of her mgmt of the 1st State Dept project &
her rapid growth as a professional & as a person. She unquestionably has the scope,
stamina, skills, & experience to run successfully the very large projects that contributed
so much to our present & potential growth. As a person she has matured from a
tough-talking somewhat masculine hard-nosed mgr to an authoritative, formidable, but
much more appealing lady ptr candidate. She should now become a lady ptr. (Yes)

A.B. HOPKINS	MO12
SHORT FORM	
#2	

I was second on a large project for Bureau of Indian Affairs. Ann was project mgr.   *JB Adams*
(Yes)

   I believe Ann does *not* possess the leadership qualities we desire in our ptrs. Also, in   *Wheaton*
   my exposure to her, albeit about 3 yrs ago, I seriously questioned her tech knowledge
   of data processing. (No)

A.B. HOPKINS	MO12
SHORT FORM	
#3	

Known through frequent in-office interaction & review of proposals prepared by her.   *Jones*
(Yes)

continued

EXHIBIT 1 *(continued)*

During the QCR Ann demonstrated a high degree of independence & impartiality of mind & courage of her convictions in evaluating the jobs she was assigned. She is however somewhat lacking in the congeniality dept. (Yes)	*PR Powell*
I have observed Ann on a casual in-office basis for the period 8/79–12/81. I have been impressed & would be pleased to have her as a ptr. (Yes)	*Gross*
Strength—ability to "pull together" the details into the QCR report, take charge attitude. Weaknesses—not good communicator, seemed "rough." (Insuff)	*Kercher*
I have no first-hand working relationship with Ann. All my input comes through 3–5 MAS sr mgrs who have worked with her extensively—it is uniformly *negative*. She is not tech respected & her interpersonal relationships are extremely poor. (Insuff)	*Docter*
Relationship—Has offered to teach numerous times & has taught some MAS seminars, which is my only relationship to Ann. She appears to me to be articulate, tough minded, supportive of PW as opposed to being self-serving. (Insuff)	*Markstein*
While I have only *limited* exposure to Ann as a result of work in the OGS office, I do not want her as my ptr. I cannot comment on her technical skills, however she is universally disliked by the staff and, in my judgment, does not possess the interpersonal skills or personal attributes that are critical. (No)	*Everett*
Basis of evaluation—exposure to candidate at firm mtgs. (No)	*Carroll*
I know Ann through: attending a CE course she instructed; attending a MMGS seminar with her; having several discussions with her relating to government pricing. (No)	*Brugos*
Ann is a "tough cookie." She is no nonsense. (Yes)	*Hart*

A.B. HOPKINS   MO12
SHORT FORM
 #3—Page 2

In 1980 I conducted an ASR (QCR) in OGS; which included reviewing a project for the Bureau of Indian Affairs which Ann served as project mgr. During my review of the BIA engagement, I was informed by Ann that the project had been completed on sked & within budget. My subsequent review indicated a significant discrepancy of approx $35,000 betw the proposed fees, billed fees, & actuals in the WIPS. I discussed this matter with Ann, who attempted to try & explain away or play down the discrepancy. She insisted there had not been a discrepancy in the amount of underrealization. Unsatisfied with her responses, I continued to question the matter until she admitted there was a problem but I should discuss it with Krulwich. My subsequent discussion with Lew indicated that the discrepancy was a result of 500 additional hrs being charged to the job (at the request of Bill Devaney . . . agreed to by Krulwich) after it was determined that Linda Pegues, a sr consultant from the Houston off working on the project, had been instructed by Ann to work 12–14 hrs per day during the project but to only charge 8 hrs per day. The entire incident left me questioning Ann's staff mgmt methods & the honesty of her responses to my questions.	*Fridley*

continued

EXHIBIT 1 *(continued)*

In July/Aug 82 Ann assisted the St. Louis MAS practice in preparing an extensive proposal to the Farmers Home Admin (the proposal inc 2,800 pgs for $3.1 mil in fees/expenses & 65,000 hrs of work). This proposal was completed over a 4-w period with approx 2,000 plus staff/ptr hrs required based on my participation in the proposal effort & sub discussions with St. L. MAS staff involved.

Ann's mgmt style of using "trial & error techniques" (i.e., sending staff assigned off to prepare portions of the proposal with little or no guidance from her & then her subsequent rejection of the products developed) caused a complete alienation of the staff towards Ann & a fear that they would have to work with Ann if we won the project. In addition, Ann's manner of dealing with our staff & with the Houston sr consultant on the BIA project, raises questions in my mind about her ability to develop & motivate our staff as a ptr. (No)

A.B. HOPKINS   MO12
SHORT FORM
#3—Page 3

My contact is limited to a few conversations. She is very intelligent but appears to be weak in interpersonal skills. (Insuff)   *FR Johnson*

Ann participated in Houston QCR in 82. Prior to that she managed a job that I provided a staff consultant to work for her (the 79–80 Bureau of Indian Affairs)—where the staff worked 10 or more hrs/day & reported 8 hrs.   *Devaney*

This classic OGS technique blew up in my face when, upon return, the staff said what do I do to get paid for the 500 + hrs worked & not reported? (No)

I worked with Ann in the early stages of the 1st State Dept proposal. I found her to be *(a)* singularly dedicated,   *Whelan*

(b) rather unpleasant. I wonder whether her 4 yrs with us have really demonstrated ptr qualities or whether we have simply taken advantage of "work-aholic" tendencies. Note that she has held 6 jobs in the last 15 yrs, all with oustanding companies. I'm also troubled about her being (having been?) married to a ptr of a serious competitor. (Insuff—but favor hold, at a minimum)

Ann's exposure to me was on the Farmers Home Admin proposal. Despite many negative comments from other people involved I think she did a great job and turned out a first class proposal. Great intellectual capacity,   *Blythe*

but very abrasive in her dealings with staff. I suggest we hold, counsel her and if she makes progress with her interpersonal skills, then admit next year. (Hold)

A.B. HOPKINS   MO12
LONG FORM
VI.

She can write, sell, perform, & collect systems assignments like I've ever known. This gal will bring in far more than she could ever hope to take out of the firm. (Yes)   *Beyer*

Ann has many superior qualities. She is innovative, highly intelligent, articulate, self-confident, & assertive. She has worked long & hard in a difficult environment & has gained the respect of the client. She has played *the* key role in our PD activities at the State Dept.   *Epelbaum*

continued

EXHIBIT 1   *(concluded)*

At times, however, she can be abrasive, unduly harsh, difficult to work with &, as a result, causes significant turmoil.

Nonetheless, she has made an almost unprecedented contribution to the firm & deserves to receive our serious consideration for admission. (Yes)

Outstanding MAS professional in fastest growing area of MAS (+ OGS) practice—systems design & implementation. First rate in handling the *most* difficult client asignments (Dept of State) & is very creative & analytical in developing & conducting work. Excellent in training & assisting staff. I trust Ann's judgment on both tech & business matters & believe she can become the "big job" client service partner we need. With her husband & family, she is a fine person with a high sense of integrity. (Yes)   *Krulwich*

A.B. HOPKINS   MO12
LONG FORM
    VII.
——————————

Hopkins is aggressive, bold, & mesmerizing of clients and ptrs.   *Statland*
    Staff does not like working for her. Her judgment is not always good, i.e., she will bend to client demands too easily.
Writes & speaks well; commands authority—little substance—potentially dangerous. (No)

Ann needs a chance to demonstrate people skills.   *Coffey*
She has a lot going for her,
    but she's just plain rough on people. Our staff did not enjoy working for her. There is a risk that she may abuse authority. (Hold)

While Hopkins has made a major contribution to the firm, she still has a few rough   *Warder*
spots which need to be corrected. (Hold)

A.B. HOPKINS   MO12
LONG FORM
    VIII.
——————————

Hopkins is probably too bright; she probably drives too hard.   *Beyer*
    On occasion, she'll forget herself & lose sensitivity for staff.
But . . . not one staff member ever suggested, throughout State project over 2 yrs in duration, that Ann was not an outstanding leader & should be replaced. Ann should be a ptr. (Yes)

A.B. HOPKINS   MO12
SHORT FORM
    #3
——————————

Contacts with Ann are only casual—several mtgs at OGS and MMGS sessions.   *CG Hoffman*
    However, she is consistently annoying and irritating—believes she knows more than anyone about anything, is not afraid to let the world know it. Suggest a course at charm school before she is considered for admission. I would be embarrassed to introduce her as a ptnr. (No)

performance reports, brief letters about her accomplishments, and other miscellaneous materials in her file. (See Exhibit 2.)

The admissions committee also tabulated the results of the evaluations for all the candidates and prepared quartile rankings of the class.[37] (See Exhibit 3.) Hopkins received very few "yes" votes and more "no" votes than all but two of the 88 candidates that year. These no votes and negative comments, mostly from partners outside OGS, placed Hopkins near the bottom of the class.[38]

Hopkins's Record at Price Waterhouse

The day before Hopkins was to start work, the partner who hired her called and said that firm policy prohibited hiring anyone who was married to a partner or had a close relationship with a partner in a national accounting firm.[39] Hopkins was told that, nevertheless, Price Waterhouse would stand behind its offer[40] and she began work as planned. For the first few months, she was not assigned to any client work.[41]

Hopkins's initial project began in the fall of 1978. It was one of four major assignments during her Price Waterhouse career. The first was for the Department of Interior. It consisted of two contracts worth approximately $200,000 each, one of which she later managed. The second client was the Department of State. Hopkins was in charge of developing a proposal, in competition with 11 other contractors, that led ultimately to a State Department contract whose long-term value to Price Waterhouse was $35 million. The third project was for the Department of Agriculture, a proposal valued at $2.5 million[42] for work for the Farmers Home Credit Administration.[43] The fourth was also for the Department of State and involved implementing a worldwide real property management system, valued at $6 million.

Department of the Interior
At the Interior Department, Hopkins worked on a computer conversion project for the Bureau of

Indian Affairs (BIA). An OGS partner later called her performance on the project "outstanding." He added "She had to manage the project at a remote site (Albuquerque), using staff from Denver and Houston and work with a difficult client. Her project management skills are excellent."[44]

There were, however, criticisms of her work. Some came from Robert Kaplan, a consultant who worked with Hopkins in Albuquerque, New Mexico, on the BIA project. He cited problems with Hopkins as the reason he left the firm a few years later. According to Thomas Beyer, Kaplan called Hopkins from Albuquerque to review the BIA job, and Hopkins got into a violent argument with him, screaming obscenities at him for about 45 minutes. Kaplan believed Hopkins prevented him from advancing in the firm.[45]

Another problem surfaced when Hopkins's BIA work was reviewed by a partner in 1980. His report said:

I was informed by Ann that the project had been completed on sked within budget. My subsequent review indicated a significant discrepancy of approximately $35,000 betw[een] the proposed fees, billed fees [and] actuals in the WIPS. I discussed this matter with Ann who attempted to try [and] explain away or play down the discrepancy. She insisted there had not been a discrepancy in the amount of the underrealization. Unsatisfied with her responses, I continued to question the matter until she admitted there was a problem but I should discuss it with Krulwich [A partner at OGS]. My subsequent discussion with Lew indicated that the discrepancy was a result of 500 additional hours being charged to the job (at the request of Bill Devaney . . . agreed to by Krulwich) after it was determined that Linda Pegues, a senior consultant from the Houston off[ice] working on the project had been instructed by Ann to work 12–14 hrs per day during the project but only to charge 8 hours per day. The entire incident left me questioning Ann's staff management methods and the honesty of her responses to my questions.[46]

EXHIBIT 2 Review of File

OFFICE VISIT

Ann B. Hopkins	Dept: MAS
	Years of Service: 5
November 17, 1982	Age: 39
	Contract Year: 1978

REVIEW OF FILE   PRIVATE
ANN HOPKINS

10–25–82   Memorandum to the file. Effective October 1, 1982, Ann assumes responsibility for the 10 people in word processing. She will manage the department, evaluate performance, determine compensation, and obtain high quality productivity. Ann is delighted to be able to assume this responsibility, particularly as this will demonstrate her ability to manage subordinates effectively. Memorandum signed by Beyer.

10–12–82   Report by Beyer on Foreign Buildings Operation—State Department. 1's and 2's. Very good report. The only suggestion for improvement being she could delegate a little more.

9–14–82   Report by Epelbaum on US Department of State. Chiefly 1's and 2's. A 3 in utilization of reference material, involvement in community and professional activities, and inter-personal skills—associates. Overall assessment was exceptional. Comments: performance has been outstanding. She is bright, imaginative and assertive, and an asset to the firm. By focusing on being more sensitive to others, she will become an extremely productive partner.

9–28–82   Report by Beyer on State Department. 1's and 2's except for 3's in interest in promoting full service to clients and involvement in community and professional activities. Exceptional overall assessment. A comment that she does believe that taff should have same dedication as herself. This is not always possible and sometimes leads to problems.

9–15–82   Report by Coffey on Farmers Home Administration proposal. 1, 2's and 3's, with a 4 in interpersonal skills–associates. Comments: she should devote more time to communicating what she expects at task assignment time and dealing effectively and motivationally with staff is Ann's primary apparent weakness. It may be that our staff in St. Louis are used to being coddled but I suspect this is the one area where Ann needs to show improvement to become a partner. Overall assessment was "higher than expected."

          Summary comment: The big question with Ann is people skill. The St. Louis staff did not enjoy their experience on this proposal but certainly sympathized with Ann's position (full responsibility while working with those with whom she had never worked). We need partners with her technical and intellectual capacity, but she must demonstrate people skills. I believe we should help her do so.

          Tom Beyer has added a note to this report saying: "Not at the risk of sloppy work or missed deadlines. I disagree after reviewing situation with Tim and Ann."

6–16–82   Report by Kercher on Houston MAS quality control review. All 1's and 2's. No adverse comments.

continued

EXHIBIT 2 *(continued)*

6–22–82   Counseling session with Epelbaum. Ann agreed that she is sometimes overly assertive and needs to be more tolerant of others. Disagreed that she needs to place greater focus on staff development. Her feeling is she needs to work with staff that have a future.

1–15–82   Report by Statland on US Department of State. All 1's and 2's. Comments: Ann is excellent on her client relationships, ability to organize work materials, ability to utilize staff ability to grasp the complex issues. Ann is sometimes overly critical of people's work, has relatively light technical (EDP) and accounting systems knowledge, and often allows judgment to be clouded by casual statements. She is dynamic but needs to learn how to execute under more control. Also not everything is to be made to appear black or white.

9–20–81   Report by Beyer on State Department. All 1's and 2's. Ann is the consummate professional and obvious partner candidate for next year. Needs time to increase maturity. Needs to be patient with superiors who are slower than she is.

6–17–81   Counseling session by Fred Laughlin. Mentions cleaning up her office and keeping partners informed. Bulk of the session devoted to people technique. Needs to soften her image; careful with her language—not just avoiding profanity but also guarding against unprofessional language and expressions. Ann agreed she would attempt to be more observant about whether her personality was threatening to the individual.

11–13–79   Report by Lewis Krulwich on Bureau of Indian Affairs. All 1's and 2's. No unfavorable comments.

Other material in the file indicates she has been with Price Waterhouse since 1978, with American Management Systems 1977–78, with Touche Ross from 1973–1977 and with several other positions data back to 1968 with IBM.

2–26–81   Memorandum by Tom Beyer indicates a midyear compensation increase was affected in order to stave off a threatened termination for purposes of higher compensation.

Ann B. Hopkins
DISCUSSION WITH PARTNERS

MacVeagh—Remarkable change in last year or two. Apparently she has been counseled and is taking it to heart. On State Department job, she knew she was over her head on the EDP side; she held herself out as a project manager. Beyer wanted to staff out of OGS. In final analysis we won.

Haller—Has broad gauged abilities. Questions personality. Brings kids into office. Sees no evidence of change but she is worth saving.

Krulwich—Has not worked on State Department engagement but knows fairly well. Large systems area is key to growth. She is one of the best. She beat the feathers off of other firm on State Department. Would trust Ann with financial assets. Ann has a clearly different personality—outspoken, diamond in the rough. Many male partners are worse than Ann (language and tough personality). Her husband is no longer a Touche partner. Velvet glove with clients. Tom wants in the worst way to admit Ann. Ann does not hold herself out as a DP specialist. Thinks O.T. issue is irrelevant. Krulwich says responsibility was his. Thinks subject was discussed in general with PG early on. Krulwich told Ann to pass the buck to him. Thinks he sees improvement.

Gross—Good worker. Is in the office early in the mornings. Critical comments regarding personal characteristics come as a complete surprise. Would guess above average. Have to be tough to get along with her boss.

continued

EXHIBIT 2   *(continued)*

Wheaton—Spent about 40 hours with her on metro proposal. Several times told Dick that she didn't think her technical capabilities were up to that job. Dick did not see that job as a very complex job. She and Pshyk did not get along. Dick has reservations.

Kelly—I didn't see anyone quitting during course of state job. She will not change. Five minutes into discussion, client probably forgets she's macho. If you get around the personality thing, she's at the top of the list or way above average.

Lohneis—One of the two strongest—writing ability, quickness on feet, ability to sort out masses of opinions. Personal comments: she will not change.

Beyer—Conscious of problems. Ranks her #1. Very hard worker. Very bright. FPC specialist (not intended to be EDP specialist). Outstanding ability to sell a client on her ability, on firm ability. Brings home profits. She is the partner on the job in the client's mind. On second phase of State Department work client specified Ann Hopkins. Has done a marvelous job demonstrating to Tim Coffee that she is a great technician. Ann went through hell writing St. Louis proposal. She couldn't even get word processing help. Coffee will change his original comments. Beyer told Hopkins he would have trouble proposing her for partnership. She came back and said, "I quit." Beyer got back and said, "I didn't say you don't have a chance." Her husband a partner at Touche was a problem. Her husband was not enamored with Touche. Two weeks later came in and left Touche. Ann came back and withdrew her request to terminate. Subsequent to that asked partners to increase compensation for 2 people because of hours worked and because of success to date. Under government contract hours over 2.030 reduce rate per hour. As practical matter would collect rate increase. In three weeks Ann got results out of word processing that Fred Loughlin and Hunter Jones had not been able to achieve. No longer any backlog—no people have quit.

Flamson—One tough lady! Very competent. Needs to be tough to supervise the type of people that have been working on her project.

Hartz—Was previously with Touche and had put in a system at UMW which had its faults but I don't know if Ann was necessarily responsible for those faults.

Epelbaum—Impressions based on daily and even hourly contact in the April to June period. I believe I know her well. Her accomplishments are unprecedented. Her management style is one of perpetual crisis. If she can't convince you there is a crisis, she will go out and create one. Ann could be a great success or a great failure. She sold a $20 million job. Neither Steve Higgins nor I could have done it. She apparently can work well with Beyer; I'm certain she could not work with everyone. [Ann wants to win; I don't know where she would draw the line.] I don't enjoy working with her. I avoid her socially.

PRIVATE   No. MO 12

ANN B. HOPKINS

(OGS)

DISCUSSION WITH ST. LOUIS PARTNERS

Blythe—Observed her in FMAA proposal effort. Had heard negatives about her before she came to St. Louis for proposal effort. In final analysis, she got the job done. May have some minor holes in it, but was a massive effort. She is very capable and bright. Within the OGS environment she is probably exceptional. She left town with a favorable impression. Has a reputation of being tough on staff, but Tom didn't see it.

continued

EXHIBIT 2   *(concluded)*

Coffey—Worked closely with Ann on proposal for Farmers Home Administration accounting system. Had two concerns: she tends to be tough on people (runs over people) and uses trial-and-error type management techniques. May have overcompensated for being a woman. St. Louis would not have had a chance on proposal without her help. Will be a 65,000 hour job if we get it and it looks good. She is one of the brightest people Tim has met. He now switches his "Hold" to a "Yes" and fully supports her.

Fridley—Fridley reviewed one of her jobs, Bureau of Indian Affairs, in 1980 when he performed a quality control review of OGS. Felt she wasn't honest with him with respect to a number of matters. Ann said she had no problems with respect to fees, billings, etc. but couldn't reconcile inconsistencies. There was $30,000 excess written off, then the planned underrealization. Despite this, she insisted everything was OK and had tried to mislead John for 15 minutes. Apparently, Ann had told female consultant from Houston to work 12 hours per day, but charge only 8. Some 500 hours were charged back by Bill Devaney when he found out about this. Her style seemed to be—work what it takes to get the job done, but charge only what the budget will allow. Overall reaction now is that she does have substance. She came to help on Home Farm Mutual proposal. Final product was massive, but not quality. In the process, she alienated almost everyone who worked on the project. She seemed to be unorganized and worked as if it were a Chinese fire drill. No one wants to work with her on project if we get it.

D. R. Ziegler

The State Department

At the end of the Interior Department project in late 1979, Hopkins volunteered to write a proposal for developing a financial management system for the State Department. The proposal was the first phase of a competition with other firms. The winners would be paid to write a second proposal describing how they would implement their plans. Many Price Waterhouse people worked on the first-round proposal. The multi-volumed document, which included a technical proposal with appendices and a cost proposal, was submitted on time in February 1980. In May, Price Waterhouse learned it was one of two finalists.[47] The State Department held an award-signing ceremony in May 1980, and its chairman, Joseph Connor, came down from New York to attend.

From May 1980 until February 1982, a Price Waterhouse team varying from 4 to 12 people and composed of consultants, managers, accountants, and computer specialists worked on the second proposal. An OGS partner was the partner-in-charge for the proposal; Hopkins worked as project manager. The work required fieldwork at 20 to 30 overseas posts.[48] Partners from Price Waterhouse's international firm and personnel from embassy staff were also involved. Hopkins traveled to Asia for five weeks and then to Europe. Team members often worked from eight in the morning until late at night and on weekends.[49] During the project, Hopkins received a raise and was promoted from manager to senior manager.[50]

In early 1982, when the proposal was nearly due, Hopkins summoned the team to decide together whether to make the deadline or to request an extension. Hopkins said she played a game called "chicken," telling the team that they had two choices, to ask for the extension or to make the date. She warned them that the second alternative was "not going to be pleasant." According to Hopkins, the team decided to make the deadline.[51]

Hopkins believed the project group developed a sense of team spirit. She noted, for example,

EXHIBIT 3   Statistical Summary

Candidate MO12		Long-Form Summation			
		Top Quarter	Second Quarter	Third Quarter	Bottom Quarter
Conduct of work:					
As an auditor	(1)	—	—	—	—
As an accountant	(2)	—	—	—	—
As a tax specialist	(3)	—	—	—	—
As a MAS specialist	(4)	2	2	1	1
As an industry specialist	(5)	—	—	—	—
As other specialty	(6)	—	—	—	—
Imagination—creativity	(7)	3	2	1	—
—analytical	(8)	3	3	—	—
Consultation with others	(9)	1	1	3	1
Communication skills—speaking	(10)	2	3	1	—
—writing	(11)	5	1	—	—
—listening	(12)	2	1	3	—
Total conduct of work		16	13	9	2
Management skills:					
Client related:					
Independence and impartiality	(13)	3	2	1	—
Business sense—underst. client's needs	(14)	4	1	1	—
—decision-making ability	(15)	4	1	1	—
—promotes full service	(16)	—	2	1	—
Leadership	(17)	2	2	—	1
Administration—planning	(18)	2	3	1	—
—delegating	(19)	2	1	2	1
—supervising	(20)	2	1	3	—
—training	(21)	2	—	2	2
Financial mgt.—billing	(22)	2	2	—	—
—collecting	(23)	2	2	—	—
Total client related		25	17	12	4
Firm related:					
Practice development	(24)	1	3	2	—
Sells services outside own specialty	(25)	—	3	1	—
Willingness to accept assignment	(26)	6	—	—	—
Accepts non-client resp.—recruiting	(27)	1	3	1	—
—counseling	(26)	1	2	2	—
—contin. ed.	(29)	1	2	2	—
Total firm related		10	13	8	—
Profession related:					
Activity in professional organizations	(30)	—	—	2	1
Civic activities	(31)	—	—	2	1
Acceptance by—partners	(32)	2	2	1	—
—staff	(33)	—	3	1	1
—clients	(34)	3	1	—	—
Total profession related		5	6	6	3

continued

EXHIBIT 3 *(continued)*

Candidate MO12		Long-Form Summation			
		Top Quarter	*Second Quarter*	*Third Quarter*	*Bottom Quarter*
Personal attributes:					
Basic intelligence	(35)	4	2	—	—
Outside interests	(36)	—	3	1	1
Judgment	(37)	2	2	2	—
Integrity	(38)	2	2	2	—
Tolerance	(39)	1	1	2	2
Practicality	(40)	2	3	1	—
Authority	(41)	5	1	—	—
Maturity, poise	(42)	2	3	1	—
Sensitivity, tact	(43)	—	2	2	2
Adaptability	(44)	2	3	1	—
Stamina	(45)	5	1	—	—
Perseverance	(46)	6	—	—	—
Sense of humor	(47)	2	2	2	—
Self-organization	(46)	2	2	2	—
Total personal attributes		35	27	16	5

		Short-Form Summation			
		Top Quarter	*Second Quarter*	*Third Quarter*	*Bottom Quarter*
Conduct of work:					
Technical competence	(1)	3	6	2	—
Communication skills	(2)	5	10	3	1
Total conduct of work		8	16	5	1
Management skills:					
Independence and impartiality	(3)	7	5	1	1
Business sense	(4)	8	5	1	1
Leadership	(5)	6	6	3	3
Administrative ability	(6)	6	4	1	—
Practice development	(7)	6	4	—	—
Dedication to the firm	(8)	9	4	—	—
Outside activities	(9)	—	1	1	4
Total management skills		42	29	7	9
Personal attributes:					
Intellectual capacity	(10)	8	9	1	—
Integrity and judgment	(11)	5	9	—	2
Poise, authority, maturity	(12)	5	10	4	1
Stamina	(13)	7	5	—	—
Congeniality	(14)	1	5	10	7
Total personal attributes		26	36	15	10

continued

EXHIBIT 3   *(concluded)*

Candidate MO12	Long Forms	Short Forms
Favor admission this year	3	10
Favors hold	2	1
Do not favor admission	1	7
Insufficient basis for opinion	—	8
Total	6	26

	Long-Form Percentages			
	Top Quarter	*Second Quarter*	*Third Quarter*	*Bottom Quarter*
Conduct of work	43%	31%	21%	5%
Management of skills:				
Client related	43%	29%	21%	7%
Firm related	32%	42%	26%	—
Profession related	25%	30%	30%	15%
Total	37%	33%	24%	6%
Personal attributes	42%	33%	19%	6%
Overall evaluation	33%	17%	50%	—

	Short-Form Percentages			
	Top Quarter	*Second Quarter*	*Third Quarter*	*Bottom Quarter*
Conduct of work	27%	53%	17%	3%
Management skills	48%	33%	8%	10%
Personal attributes	29%	43%	17%	11%
Overall evaluation	16%	32%	26%	26%

	Long-Form Percentages			
	Top Quarter	*Second Quarter*	*Third Quarter*	*Bottom Quarter*
Conduct of work	18	13	9	2
Management skills:				
Client related	25	17	12	4
Firm related	10	13	3	—
Profession related	5	6	6	3
Total	40	36	26	7
Personal attributes	35	27	16	5
Overall evaluation	2	1	3	—

	Short-Form Percentages			
	Top Quarter	*Second Quarter*	*Third Quarter*	*Bottom Quarter*
Conduct of work	8	16	5	1

that Steve Higgins, one of the Price Waterhouse consultants, had a drink with her after work or dinner every other week.[52] Higgins sometimes brought his children from New York to the dinners at Hopkins's house. She was also with him when one of his children was born during the project.[53]

Thomas Beyer later recalled personnel problems on the project.[54] During one meeting of the project team, a consultant, Patricia Bowman, attempted to present some ideas in her area. "Ann struck out at her," Beyer said, "Inasmuch as to smother her commentary and say we don't need that now . . ." Bowman "struck right back and said something to the effect you can't treat me that way. Don't you dare treat me that way." Beyer said Hopkins accepted it and continued the meeting.[55]

Beyer also said that Karen Nold, one of the senior managers, "was quite depressed about things . . ." Beyer said Nold "just felt that Ann's overbearing style was smothering her attempts to . . . bring forth her ideas, her conclusions, her recommendations, and suggestions." Beyer recommended that Nold speak up because her contributions were important.[56] Nold, however, characterized her conversation with Beyer as him telling her to become assertive.[57] Despite this incident, Nold praised Hopkins for some things.[58] "Ann is very smart, very to the point, very directed at getting good results . . . she cares about the people who work with and for her . . ." Nold said that Hopkins taught her about self-confidence, how to apply her knowledge and skills without self-doubt, and how to support her presentations with facts and numbers. She found working with Hopkins "very stimulating." "Did I enjoy it?" she said, "Yes and no."[59]

Other positive reports came from some State Department personnel. Robert Lamb, later the State Department's Assistant Secretary of Administration and Security, was the Counselor for Administration in the American Embassy in Bonn, Germany, when he first worked with Hopkins on the project. "I had a lot of respect for her," Lamb said, "I thought she was a very good project manager. In fact, I've subsequently tried to hire Ann for the State Department because I thought she was so good. I thought she provided a good sense of direction, a good sense of leadership for the team." Lamb referred to Hopkins as decisive but not dictatorial,". . . quite interested in competing points of view . . . somebody that would hear her staff out on a question. I never saw her cut anyone off . . ."[60]

Beyer, however, recalled difficult moments during this period. In the summer of 1981, Hopkins, Beyer, and Krulwich had lunch at the Mayflower Hotel. "They were eating and just kind of passing time . . . and something happened to Ann," Beyer said. He continued:

> I wasn't quite sure what. But she began to criticize a number of people in the office at different levels. In different fashions. At first I passed it off thinking well, this is, this is Ann. She's probably tired . . . But Ann kept up with it. Lew was silent and—not saying anything and Ann kept on talking . . . And it got more vitriolic. More striking. [A]fter awhile I began to get quite angry . . . At that point, Lew, kind of trying to settle the situation, said, look, let's quit and go back to work. They walked back to the office in silence.

Beyer was angry and Krulwich upset. When they spoke about the incident back at the office, Beyer reminded Krulwich that despite her problems with people, Hopkins was an integral part of the office and they needed her skills.[61]

That summer, Hopkins had her first session with Fred Laughlin, the partner assigned to counsel Anne Hopkins. (One such partner was assigned to each staff member.) This was part of a mandatory annual counseling policy instituted in 1981. Laughlin, Hopkins recalled, counseled her "to be more careful with my language . . . I think he probably meant tone of voice, profanity, to some extent what I said, also in other instance[s], how I said it." During the last stages of the State Department work, Hopkins said she "renewed [her] efforts to be sensitive to the cares, concerns, and well-being of the people that she worked with." "I still use a measure of profanity . . . ," she said, "I made an attempt to not intimidate, if you will, or be overbearing with little people, people who are innocent bystanders or people with whom we had no contact and I took that to heart."[62]

Near the end of the work, Beyer told Hopkins that he expected Price Waterhouse to win the proposal competition. He told her to write the proposal for implementing the firm's recommendations. Although she would not be the project manager, he said, she should write herself in "in an administrative, transitional kind of position."[63] Price Waterhouse won the contract, and Connor attended another award ceremony.

Despite their work on the proposal, neither Hopkins nor the partner-in-charge was involved in the rest of the project. The State Department's director of financial systems, who was principally in charge of conducting the work, had asked Price Waterhouse to remove the partner. The reason, according to Roger Feldman, then Comptroller of the State Department, "had to do with his performance, attitude, his presentation, and the lack of constructive contribution on his part to that point . . ."[64] In contrast, Feldman said Hopkins's replacement had nothing to do with her performance or her personal skills. "[T]he committee and team that determined the selection," he said, "were very favorably impressed with her performance during the orals and were also very favorably disposed to the written proposals that came from Price Waterhouse."[65] Feldman described her as "extremely competent, intelligent, a very capable person. Strong and forthright, very productive, energetic, and creative" with a sense of humor.[66] He and his staff worked extensively with Hopkins, and Feldman stated he had not seen Hopkins behave in any abusive, dictatorial, or unfair ways with her staff.[67]

Nevertheless, the Department thought the project manager should be a partner because this would lend greater prestige to the project. According to Feldman, the Department's director of financial systems also thought "the project was going to reach a dimension that was very large in anybody's terms of organization and structure . . . there would be a need to require top flight talent to be brought forth on throughout the firm and that a partner would be presumably well positioned to be able to tap on the different resources of the firm."[68]

In mid-1982, Beyer told Hopkins over lunch at the International Club that he would propose her as a partner in the admissions cycle about to begin.[69] Beyer then had the first of a series of conversations with Hopkins about how she could improve her chances for partnership, and gave her advice about her hair, makeup, clothing, and jewelry. Hopkins said she found these conversations offensive. When Beyer suggested that she style her hair, Hopkins explained to him that she already got up at five or six in the morning, had a lot to do, and didn't have the time. Beyer answered that Sandy Kinsey, another woman in OGS, managed to find the time.

By the summer of 1982, Hopkins was focusing her time on projects other than the State Department work. She participated, along with several partners, in an MAS Quality Control Review in the Houston office.[70] Hopkins later complained to one of them about his writing obscene anatomical references, such as "This is where our balls are on the line," in the margins of his work papers.[71] According to Hopkins, another confrontation with this partner occurred during a meeting in his office. The partner sat at his desk, repeatedly raising a stiletto letter opener and stabbing his desk with it. When Hopkins asked him to stop, he said, "Why, is it making you nervous?" Hopkins said, "Yes." "Well, if you think that makes you nervous," the partner responded, turning to pull a gun from a credenza behind his desk and turning back around to face her, "What do you think about this?" He pointed the gun into the air. When she later described this incident, Hopkins insisted that she had not been threatened with the gun.[72]

Farmers Home Credit Association

Beyer next assigned Hopkins to manage the St. Louis office's proposal for the design of an automated accounting system for recording and tracking loans to farmers. The client was Farmers Home Credit Association, a U.S. Department of Agriculture agency with major data processing operations in St. Louis. Arthur Anderson had done extensive work for the agency, and Beyer believed it was getting ready to work on the loan accounting project.[73]

From July through August 1982, Hopkins helped the St. Louis MAS department prepare a 2,000-page proposal for the work.[74] At stake were $3.1 million in fees and expenses[75] in a contract for 65,000 hours of work. Price Waterhouse partners and staff worked over 2,000 hours during the four weeks it took to complete the proposal.[76] Hopkins spent 260 hours on the project.[77]

Along the way, she experienced two major problems. The first was getting the St. Louis office to prepare the proposal in the way she preferred. The local staff was accustomed to working on fixed-price contracts, while this was a cost-plus contract.[78] Hopkins had to convince the staff that they should abandon their familiar way of preparing a proposal and that her way was correct; then would show them how to do it and get the work completed on time. The problem had deeper roots, mainly the office's inexperience with this type of client. As Beyer later explained, "In OGS we had developed a streamlined fashion for efficiently dealing with proposal developments for generating deliverable on jobs. It became a way of life. It had to. It was the only way we could survive. The St. Louis office was not used to this. They had dealt more in the private sector and in state government work."[79]

Several members of the St. Louis office staff

later complained about Hopkins. One consultant she said was "direct, abrupt, sometimes insensitive. And demeaning at times."[80] He recalled an exchange between Hopkins and the office's graphics contractor. "Ann wasn't pleased at all and expressed herself fairly directly . . . ," the consultant said. Afterward, feeling that he had done the work badly and that he was going to lose the Price Waterhouse account, the contractor called back. The consultant said that he assured him this was not the case.[81] The consultant also complained that "[T]he development of a fairly detailed work plan and assignment of responsibilities really didn't occur." Hopkins prepared an outline "as to what she envisioned the document to look like," which he thought inadequate. He also said she was unable to direct staff members on improving their work. This lack of direction resulted in chaos,[82] and he said his co-workers expressed similar feelings to him.[83]

Hopkins and the staff ultimately produced a four-volume proposal and then helped two St. Louis partners prepare for oral reviews.[84] One of those partners, Timothy Coffey, said that the "[f]inal project was massive but not quality." He added that Hopkins "alienated almost everyone who worked on the project. She seemed to be unorganized and worked as if it were a Chinese fire drill. No one wants to work with her on the project if we get it."[85] He also said, "Ann needs a chance to demonstrate people skills. She has a lot going for her but she's just plain rough on people. Our staff did not enjoy working for her. There is a risk that she may abuse authority."[86] Coffey also suggested that Hopkins "[m]ay have overcompensated for being a woman." But he also said that "St. Louis would not have had a chance on [the] proposal without her help" and that she was "one of the brightest people he had met."[87]

In December 1982, the Association awarded the contract to Price Waterhouse. Beyer sent Connor a letter telling him about how successful

Hopkins had been.[88] Later, without OGS assistance, the St. Louis office wrote a successful federal government proposal worth several million dollars.[89]

Department of State

In October 1982, Hopkins got two new assignments.[90] One was managing the OGS word processing center. The other was developing a proposal for managing the real estate administered by the State Department abroad. When the State Department's Comptroller contacted Beyer seeking Price Waterhouse's help in developing a system to manage its overseas service post properties, Beyer assigned the work to Hopkins. As for the word processing assignment, Beyer reported in Hopkins partnership admissions file that "Ann is delighted to be able to assume this responsibility particularly as this will demonstrate her ability to manage subordinates effectively."[91]

The 10-person word processing staff that Hopkins took over had been very troubled under its prior manager, with staff members complaining about inadequate compensation adjustments and a lack of consideration in relating staff skills to workloads and priorities.[92] Hopkins "went right to the core of those problems," Beyer said. "She cleaned up the backlog in the unit. Nobody quit. She addressed the personnel problems of people on the staff." "I give Ann a lot of credit for keeping the department on a fairly even keel," Beyer said. "[I]t was one of the first times you had seen someone at that level of partner or manager get involved with the people themselves."[93]

The Partnership Decision

In March 1983, the admissions committee recommended that Hopkins be held "at least a year to afford time to demonstrate that she has the personal and leadership qualities required of a partner."[94] The policy board adopted the admissions committee's recommendation and sug-

gested that Hopkins participate in a quality control review.

Hopkins learned from Lew Krulwich that she had not been promoted. The reason, he said, reporting what Connor had told Beyer, was that she had irritated some senior partners.[95] Hopkins said neither she nor Krulwich knew what that meant. Another partner suggested that she should probably not come to the office on the day the partnership list was posted. Hopkins believed he was concerned that she might lose control emotionally. According to her, the partner added that some of the names posted were "not competent to lick her boots."[96] The other two candidates OGS had nominated became partners. One had worked for Price Waterhouse for less time than Hopkins.

Hopkins went to New York to meet with Joseph Connor, the firm's chairman, and discuss the decision. She asked him how to overcome the "hold" and make it an "admit." Connor told her that she had to undergo a quality control review and come out of it with no negative comments. He also told her that OGS had to continue to be profitable. When Hopkins asked what her prospects were, Connor replied, "Fifty-fifty."[97] Connor also advised her to relax and "to take charge" less often.[98]

Beyer also advised Hopkins.[99] According to Hopkins, he suggested she "soften her image in the manner in which she walked, talked, dressed . . ." He later said that "when she comes into the office or starts walking down the hall, it is with a lot of authority and forcefulness. I admire that quality. I respond to it. It does not always appear in the same view or in the same manner to other people." She also said he advised her to use less profanity and to alter her voice tone, to "look more toward appearing more feminine," to wear more jewelry and make-up, to style her hair, and to dress less in 'power blues.'"[100] He also suggested that she stop smoking, not drink beer at lunch, . . . not carry a briefcase."[101] Hopkins said she explained that carrying a briefcase was easier for her than managing a handbag, a suitcase, and a briefcase simultaneously. She later said she did not wear make-up because she was allergic to it. Even if she weren't she said, "applying make-up would be difficult because she can't see without her trifocals."[102]

Soon after this, two of the OGS partners who had nominated Hopkins withdrew their support for her. The reason one of them gave was the difficulty he had with her as a senior manager and his concern that problems would grow worse if she acquired the power and authority of a partner. He complained that she routinely barged into his office, got her business done, and barged out again. The incident that changed his mind, he said, occurred at a time when he was understaffed and Hopkins offered him one of her staff members, only to withdraw the offer the next day. According to the partner, she had insisted on making the offer without qualification, refused his suggestion that she think it over for a day, then told him the next day that he could not use the staff member she had offered.[103]

During the next few months, according to Hopkins, the firm failed to give her opportunities to demonstrate her abilities and gain more exposure. Four months after the policy board's recommendations, with two OGS's strong support, it was felt that her candidacy could not possibly be successful. Hopkins was advised that it was very unlikely that she would be admitted to partnership.

Reviews of her work on the State Department Real Estate management project were, on balance, favorable. An initial review by the partner who had been removed from the large State Department project was negative, but the subsequent Quality Control Review conducted on the State Department work, including REMS, was a "strong positive."[104] It also suggested some changes which Hopkins and the rest of the REMS team later made.

Hopkins later wrote that she was "the *only* candidate who was not admitted to Price Waterhouse—initially or after being put on hold—who was criticized solely for deficiencies in inter-personal skills."[105] Similarly situated men, she says, were admitted.[106] Hopkins was at the bottom of overall quartile rankings and only 13 of 32 partners favored her admission, but the firm had admitted one candidate who had support from 14 of 30 partners and another who ranked 39th of 42 in overall quartile rankings.[107]

In December 1983, she learned she would not be reproposed for partnership. Hopkins tendered her resignation and left Price Waterhouse in January.[108] In 1984, she started her own management consulting firm. She also filed suit against Price Waterhouse claiming that she had been denied a partnership because of sex discrimination. She sought an award of backpay for lost wages and reinstatement at Price Waterhouse as a partner.

NOTES

1. 825 F.2d 458 at 462.
2. Plaintiff's Testimony, Tr. 112.
3. Tamar Lewin, "Winner of Sex Bias Suit Set to Enter Next Arena," *New York Times,* May 19, 1990 (National edition, p. 7).
4. William Galberson, "Determined to be heard: Four Americans and their journeys to the Supreme Court," *The New York Times Magazine,* October 2, 1988 (Sunday), 33–40 at p. 38.
5. Plaintiff's Testimony, Tr. 7.
6. Plaintiff's Testimony, Tr. p. 7–9.
7. Plaintiff's Testimony, Tr. 12–13; See also, Plaintiff's Deposition, Vol. I, p. 25.
8. Plaintiff's Testimony, Tr. 13–14.
9. 825 F.2d 458, citing 618 F. Supp. 1109, 1111 (D.D.C. 1985); See also, 109 S. Ct. 1775, 1781 (1989).
10. Connor's Deposition of March 12, 1985, for Trial, p. 3, 8, 10.
11. 825 F.2d 458, 461 (D.C. Cir., 1987); See also, 618 F. Supp. 1109, 1111 (D.D.C. 1985).
12. Coffey's Testimony in 1990 Trial, Tr. 346.
13. Coffey's Testimony, Tr. 346.
14. Connor's Testimony for 1990 Trial, Tr. 255.
15. See, 1990 Trial, Tr. 346–48.
16. 109 S.Ct. 1775, 1781 (1989); Pet. App. 41a.

17. 109 S.Ct. 1775, 1781 (1989).
18. 825 F.2d 458 at 462; See also Defendant's Exhibits 21, 22, and 23.
19. 825 F.2d 458 at 462; See also Ziegler Testimony and Defendant's Brief, p. 5.
20. Ziegler Testimony, Tr. 257.
21. Ziegler Testimony, Tr. 258.
22. Price Waterhouse Brief, p. 5.
23. Testimony.
24. Testimony of Ziegler or Coffey.
25. 618 F. Supp. 1109 (D.D.C. 1985).
26. See Note 12 above.
27. Ibid; Testimony of Partner.
28. 109 S.Ct. 1775, at 1782.
29. 109 S.Ct. at 1782, citing Plaintiff's Exhibit 15.
30. 825 F.2d 458 at 462; See also, 618 F. Supp. at 1112.
31. 825 F.2d at 462; Plaintiff's Exhibit 15 cited therein.
32. Beyer's Testimony, Tr. 207.
33. Beyer's Testimony, Tr. 208.
34. Trial Testimony (Ziegler).
35. Trial Testimony (Ziegler).
36. Defendant's Exhibit 30; See Testimony or Deposition (Ziegler).
37. See Trial Record, p. 002012ff, Exhibits 17ff which were not necessarily ready for the December meeting.
38. 618 F. Supp. 1109 (D.D.C. 1985).
39. Plaintiff's Deposition, Vol. I, p. 24.
40. Plaintiff's Testimony, Trial or First Deposition, Tr. 84–85; See also, Plaintiff's Deposition, Vol. I, p. 24–26.
41. Plaintiff's Testimony, Tr. 13–14; See also, Plaintiff's Deposition, Vol. I, p. 27.
42. Plaintiff's Brief on Remand, p. 3.
43. Plaintiff's Complaint; See Coffey evaluation in Supreme Court lodging.
44. Defendant's Exhibit 7, Krulwich's Annual Manager Personnel Report, April 4, 1980.
45. Beyer's Testimony in 1985 Trial, Tr. 193.
46. Fridley, in Short-Form Partner Evaluation, Comments #3, p. 2, Trial Record, p. 002004. This is from one of the documents in the Supreme Court Lodging.
47. Plaintiff's Deposition, Vol. I, p. 43.
48. Tr. 34–35; Deposition, p. 48; The number of sites given in Plaintiff's Deposition is 23, but at trial the number of sites was reported as 20 to 30.
49. Deposition, Vol. I, p. 50. Hopkins estimated her billable time that year at approximately 20,000 to 24,000 hours, Tr. p. 34–35.
50. See Partner Admission File, Summary, November 28, 1982.
51. Trial Testimony, Tr. 46–47.
52. Trial Testimony, March 15, 1985, p. 56–57.
53. Testimony at Trial, p. 53, 56.
54. Beyer's Testimony, Tr. 192.
55. Beyer's Testimony, Tr. 196.
56. Beyer's Testimony, Tr. 194–196.
57. Nold's Testimony, Tr. 421.
58. Tr. 417–419.
59. Tr. 420.
60. Testimony of Robert Lamb, Trial or Deposition.
61. Tr. 197–197A.
62. Tr. 52–53.
63. Tr. 136–137.
64. Tr. 149.
65. Tr. 146–152.
66. Tr. 149–152.
67. Tr. 146–149.
68. Tr. 149.
69. Plaintiff's Deposition, Vol. I, pp. 53, 57.
70. See, Short-Form Evaluation Notes in the Partnership Admission File.
71. Plaintiff's Deposition, Vol. II, p. 24.
72. Plaintiff's Deposition and Trial Testimony.
73. Letter of December 2, 1982, from Beyer to Connor, Plaintiff's Exhibit 14.
74. Fridley's Short-Form Evaluation, repeated in Lodging, Short Form 3, p. 2. The project was also known as the Hom Farm Mutual proposal and the FMH Association proposal; Fridley in Ziegler's Notes in Partnership Admission File.
75. See, Ziegler's Notes 1982.
76. Fridley, Ibid.
77. Coffey's Evaluation, Performance of MAS Contract Staff.
78. Coffey's Testimony at Trial, Tr. 342–343.
79. Beyer's Testimony at Trial, Tr. 171.
80. Tr. 363.
81. Boehm's Testimony, Tr. 367–368.
82. Tr. 363.
83. Boehm's Testimony, Tr. 364–365.
84. Letter, Beyer to Connor, December 2, 1982; Plaintiff's Exhibit 14.
85. Ziegler's summary of discussion with St. Louis Partners, Defendant's Exhibit 31, p. 003845.

86. Ziegler, Long-Form Summary, 20006; Coffey later qualified himself. He said, "I would be highly surprised if I said she abuse[s] authority. I probably said she had the potential of abusing authority which is a concern that I [have]." Tr. 346.

87. Ziegler's summary discussion with St. Louis Partner, Defendant's Exhibit 31. See Ziegler's Notes on Discussions with St. Louis partners in Review of File, Long-Form Summaries, p. 002206, November 17, 1982.

88. Beyer to Connor, December 2, 1982, Plaintiff's Exhibit 14.

89. Tr. 371.

90. Plaintiff's Remand Brief, p. 4.

91. Ziegler in 1983 partnership admissions file, citing memorandum of October 26, 1982, signed by Beyer, Ziegler, p. 003841, Private and Protected.

92. Beyer's Testimony at Trial, Tr. 210.

93. Trial Testimony.

94. Pet. App. 43a quoting Plaintiff's Exhibit 10; Tr. 267–268.

95. Plaintiff's Deposition, Vol. I, p. 59.

96. Plaintiff's Deposition, Vol. I, p. 70.

97. Plaintiff's Deposition, Vol. I, p. 64–65.

98. Plaintiff's Deposition, Vol. I, p. 65.

99. Plaintiff's Trial Brief, p. 12; See also, Plaintiff's Deposition, Vol. I, p. 67.

100. Plaintiff's Trial Brief, pp. 12–13; For a definition of the term "power blues," and Hopkins's attorneys' comment, "Sometimes you just can't win," See, Plaintiff's Trial Brief, p. 13, n. 5.

101. Plaintiff's Deposition, Vol. I, p. 68.

102. Jaclyn Fierman, "Why Women Still Don't Hit the Top," *Fortune,* July 30, 1990, p. 40–62, at p. 50.

103. Epelbaum's Deposition or Trial Testimony in 1985.

104. Plaintiff's Answer to Interrogatories, Interrogatory 10; See also, Protected Document, Exhibit 12 in Beyer Deposition, March 7, 1985, pp. 2–3.

105. Plaintiff's Remand Brief, p. 20, n. 2 citing Defendant's Exhibit 64.

106. Plaintiff's Remand Brief, p. 20, no. 2.

107. Plaintiff's Remand Brief, p. 20, n. 3 citing Defendant's Exhibit 73 at 1102 and Defendant's Exhibit 36 at 3859, No. A 228 is Puschaver.

108. 618 F. Supp. 1109 (D.D.C. 1985).

PART III

Organizational Choices

MANAGERIAL EFFECTIVENESS AND DIVERSITY: ORGANIZATIONAL CHOICES

If we take a look at even a short list of key trends facing business organizations today—the growth of global business competition; the changing demographics of the workforce; the questioning of business, government, and community roles and relationships; trends in organizational structures toward more interdependent, cross-functional, flexible, and less-layered forms; rapidly evolving technologies; shifts in the nature of work toward more service and information-based jobs—it becomes apparent that the diversity of the workforce, of the customer base, and of the business context is both a common element or influence in these trends, and also a critical lever for responding to them.

We can define this diversity in individual terms, organizational terms, and/or societal terms, but we are really talking about a complex set of interlocking issues, frames of reference, and points of leverage. While recognizing this interconnectedness, this note will define diversity in organizational terms and provide a framework for understanding the ways organizations identify and respond to the challenges and opportunities diversity presents.

Defining Organizational Diversity

Some might argue that once we understand the nature and impact of differences within and between individuals, the question of organizational diversity is answered: that is, if managers and

employees understand and manage their own reactions to individual differences, there would be no challenges left for organizations to address. But that perspective not only oversimplifies the challenge to individuals, it fails to acknowledge the ways in which past perspectives, values, and assumptions are embedded, maintained, and reproduced in organizational structures, systems, and culture, influencing the various forms of diversity individuals are able to perceive and how they respond to them.

So how do we define diversity in organizational terms? Efforts to understand interpersonal diversity have suggested that we can most effectively understand and respond to the differences *between* individuals if we begin to understand and respond to the diversity *within* each individual and within so-called homogeneous groups. Similarly, organizations are confronted by diversity both internally and externally.

By defining diversity in broad and varied terms that encompass both the internal and external manifestations, we gain several advantages. First, we begin the education process that helps organizations to frame diversity in proactive terms as a business opportunity, as well as in reactive terms as a social or legal imperative. Second, we make it possible for *all* managers and employees to perceive the firm's diversity initiative as having "something in it for them," and we avoid the resentment and backlash that can be triggered by efforts that appear to serve only certain groups. Third, as R. Roosevelt Thomas puts it, we create opportunities for "economies of learning," where the organizational competencies and mindset developed to respond to one form of diversity better prepare

EXHIBIT 1   Model of Organizational Diversity

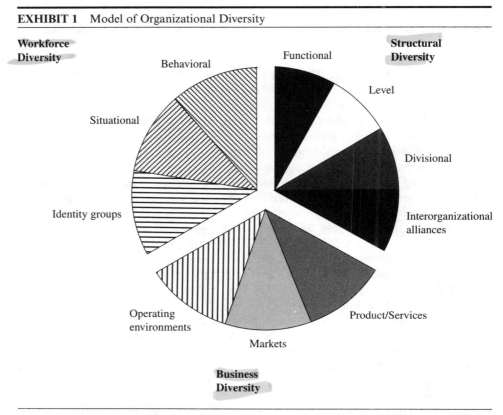

Adapted from "Managing Diversity: A Strategic 'Grass-Roots' Approach" by Joel M. DeLuca and Robert N. McDowell in *Diversity in the Workplace: Human Resource Initiatives* by Susan E. Jackson and Associates, the Guilford Press, 1992.

the organization to respond to another.[1] Fourth, such a capacious definition of organizational diversity highlights its ubiquity, its inevitability, and the degree to which all members of the organization have both differences and similarities in *common.*

Exhibit 1 provides an illustration of just such a broad and varied definition of organizational diversity, organizing its various interdependent and sometimes overlapping aspects into three

categories: workforce diversity, structural diversity, and business diversity.

Workforce diversity encompasses group and situational identities of the organization's employees (i.e., gender, race, ethnicity, religion, sexual orientation, physical ability, age, family status, economic background and status, educational background and status, geographical background and status) as well as behavioral diversity (i.e., learning styles, communication styles, work styles, aspirations). Changes in the labor market demographics, as well as changes in attitude and expectation on the part of employees, contribute to this type of diversity.

Structural diversity encompasses interactions

1. R. Roosevelt Thomas, Jr., President of the American Institute for Managing Diversity, Inc., "The Diversity Paradigm," working paper, ©*The American Institute for Managing Diversity, Inc.* (1993), p. 5.

across functions, across organizational levels in the hierarchy, across divisions and between parents and subsidiaries, and across organizations engaged in strategic alliances and cooperative ventures. As organizations attempt to become more flexible, less layered, more team-based, and more multi- and cross-functional, this type of diversity is gaining greater attention.

Business diversity encompasses the expansion and segmentation of customer markets, the diversification of products and services offered, and the variety of operating environments in which organizations compete (i.e., legal and regulatory context, labor market realities, community and societal expectations/relationships, business cultures and norms). Increasing competitive pressures, globalization, rapid advances in product technologies, changing demographics in the customer bases both within domestic markets and across borders, and shifts in business/government relationships all signal a need to examine an organization's responses to business diversity.

Although by applying this holistic "diversity lens" to their operations, organizations can gain the self-insight and the synergies mentioned above, many do not do so. They often view the various forms of diversity outlined in Exhibit 1 as discrete realities presenting unrelated challenges. In fact, sometimes organizations point to the potential friction and competing agendas of various distinct groups within the firm as a reason to define diversity more narrowly, as focused upon only a few specific identity groups (for example, women, African-Americans, and Hispanics). However, this very real possibility for tension demonstrates the value of clearly communicating—as a frame—a broad definition of diversity and its potential for synergistic learning, while at the same time identifying the need to break down any actions into specific, measurable, and sequenced goals. Gender conflicts, for example, are trivialized and confused if they are equated with functional conflicts. But at the same time, it enhances our ability to respond to both concerns if we recognize that they require some of the same skills and tactics.

Understanding Organizational Responses to Diversity

The remainder of this note will outline a descriptive framework for recognizing and understanding the range of organizational responses to different forms of diversity, as well as their strengths and their limitations (see Exhibit 8). The four components or lenses of the framework are:

- MOTIVATORS: What motivates a company (or a unit of a company) to begin to recognize and address behaviors or trends that, given the definition of diversity posited, we would identify as diversity-related? More subtly, what are the *felt* motivators, and what are the *espoused* motivators? Examples include: legal pressures; competitive pressures around the attraction/retention of employees or around the appeal to a broadening customer base; internal conflict; external pressures from community groups; a leader's commitment; and so forth.

- MINDSET: What are the philosophy and the assumed values revealed by the different choices companies make around how to approach diversity-related issues? For example, some approaches are individual-based whereas others are more focused on building a community; some emphasize education while others stress structural drivers; some are control-oriented while others are learning-oriented. What are the different implications of these choices? What works best in what context, and in a related vein, how does a particular company/industry/national context influence the mindset adopted?

- METHODS: What are the range of methods and approaches that managers and firms utilize to address diversity-related issues, once motivated? Typically, who is the source or driver of such efforts? What types of mechanisms have been tried and in what circumstances are they effective? Examples include: training, diversity task forces, caucus groups, numerical goals and/or controls, cultural awareness building, and so forth.

- MEASURES: What is the firm trying to achieve? What, if anything, is measured to assess the effectiveness of the methods used? How does a manager know if he or she is being successful? What are the implications of diversity initiatives that are designed without measures of effectiveness?

MOTIVATORS

We can generate a fairly extensive list of motivators that have been observed to move organizations to think about and respond to diversity. Seven of them are discussed below. It is useful to note that some of these motivators are responses to the diversity that *already exists* in an organization and its operating environment; some of them are responses to the diversity that *will exist* in the near future; and some of them are responses to a vision of the diversity that individuals believe *should exist* in their organizations. These distinctions raise the question, "Do organizations want to have more diversity, or merely manage that which they have?" and they have implications for:

- The degree of urgency individuals feel around the issue of diversity.
- The ease with which individuals can maintain their denial around the need for change.
- The amount of guilt that the topic triggers in individuals (important because although guilt can serve as an initial catalyst to action, it quickly becomes counterproductive by triggering resentment and blocking creativity).

Thus, although we have argued that there are advantages to defining diversity broadly, it nevertheless is essential to think rigorously about the distinctions between various forms of difference and also about the motivators which drive organizations to address diversity.

Let's turn now to a discussion of some of the motivators that have been observed to trigger organizational responses to diversity.

1. Legal and Regulatory Pressures

In many organizations, legal and regulatory pressures serve as a catalyst for attending to diversity-related issues. However, the actual legal requirements related to equal opportunity and the zeal with which they are enforced differ from country to country. These differences may reflect a number of factors in an individual country:

- Workforce demographics.
- Employment availability.
- Changing political environment.
- Cultural norms, values, and traditions (emphasis on individual rights versus community rights; traditional roles of men, women, and family; etc.).

Obviously, the law is a contingent, reactive, and often blunt instrument, but nevertheless, it represents a pressure that is sometimes effective in gaining the attention of those organizations which may not otherwise experience the challenges or the opportunities of diversity.

In the United States, legal and regulatory pressures fall roughly into three categories: suits brought by individuals or groups of individuals, government investigations of suspected illegal business practices, and government rulings, sometimes expressed as threshold requirements for access to various contracts and/or liberties. The first category includes complaints of discrimination in hiring, compensation and promotion practices, wrongful discharge, and harassment charges. The second category includes charges filed by the Equal Employment Opportunity Commission (EEOC), charges that may be triggered by the complaint of the claimed victim or by the EEOC itself. Two illustrations of the third category include President Johnson's Executive Order 11246 which strengthened earlier efforts by Roosevelt and Kennedy to deny discriminating companies federal contracts, and Congress' 1988 decision to strengthen the Community Reinvestment Act of 1977 (a law that prohibited "redlining") by stating that only those banks which had strong community reinvestment records would be allowed to take advantage of new opportunities to expand into the securities business.[2]

The degree to which such legal pressures affect companies is dependent upon a number of factors such as enforcement records, settlement sizes, employees' likelihood to bring complaint (in turn dependent upon their sense of their own career options and the possibility of organizational retaliation), societal and organizational climate, and so forth. In the United States, for example, the threat of significant penalties can influence organizational behavior. These penalties can include financial settlements, often quite sizable;[3] exclusion from government contracts or other liberties as noted above; and negative publicity among potential employees (for example, books and periodicals now rate company environments for women and minority employees), among customers, among investors (for example, some investment researchers publicize company records on the hiring and promotion of women and minorities), and within the larger community.

As a comment upon the U.S. environment, we should note that complaints filed under the Americans with Disabilities Act of 1990 were up to almost 1,000 a month by 1993, and federal

charges of sexual harassment doubled in 1992.[4] The Civil Rights Act of 1991 granted discrimination victims the right to pursue compensatory and punitive damages awarded in jury trials. Prior to this law, they could only obtain job reinstatement and back compensation. Between October 1, 1992, and September 30, 1993, there were 89,942 charges of employment discrimination filed with the Equal Employment Opportunity Commission, and recovered monetary benefits came to $161 million. This was an almost 22 percent increase in the number of complaints filed (due largely to the Americans with Disabilities Act) and a decrease in monetary benefits from the 1992 total of $188.8 million.[5] (See Exhibit 2.)

Issues and Questions

When considering any of the motivators that trigger organizational attention and responses to diversity, it is useful to consider the costs and benefits, the advantages and disadvantages of approaching diversity from this vantage. When legal and regulatory pressures are the motivators, a number of issues are raised:

- **Legal and regulatory pressures can trigger a reluctant compliance or an adversarial mindset in organizations, resulting in game-playing and a focus on the "letter of the law" only.**

In reaction to U.S. affirmative action initiatives, some organizations have tried to take the "easy out,"[6] as Patrick Davol, the U.S. assistant attorney general for civil rights, called it: adopting short-term measures to address numerical goals without attacking the systemic barriers to equal opportunity that may exist, or looking for

---

2. Redlining is the practice of systematically denying mortgage loans or property insurance in certain communities perceived by the banks or insurance companies as bad risks.

3. Taylor Cox, Jr., *Cultural Diversity in Organizations: Theory, Research & Practice* (San Francisco, CA.: Berrett-Koehler Publishers, Inc., 1993), p. 13.

4. Barbara Berish Brown, "Status of Legislative and Regulatory Agenda Charges Filed Under ADA and Civil Rights Act of 1991," *Employment Relations Today.* 20, no. 2 (Summer 1993), pp. 215–218.

5. "Record Number of EEOC Charges Filed in Fiscal Year 1993," *BNAC Communicator,* 14, no. 2 (Spring/Summer 1994), p. 5.

6. Patrick Davol, "On Affirmative Action," *Boston Globe* (March 10, 1992), p. 3.

EXHIBIT 2   Bases of Alleged Discrimination in EEOC Charges

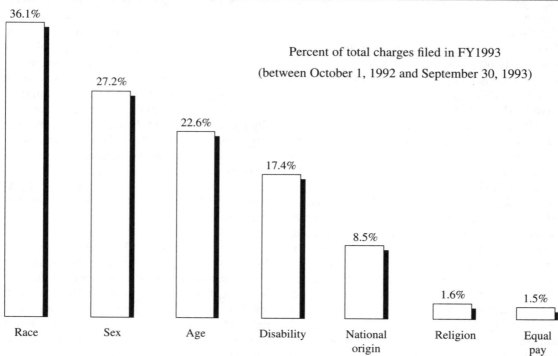

Percent of total charges filed in FY1993
(between October 1, 1992 and September 30, 1993)

Race	Sex	Age	Disability	National origin	Religion	Equal pay
36.1%	27.2%	22.6%	17.4%	8.5%	1.6%	1.5%

Source: Equal Employment Opportunity Commission.

ways to locate or develop new sources of qualified employees. Such actions reinforce stereotypes, feed resentment, and fail to address professional development issues.

A recent example of the impact of an adversarial mindset was reported in *The Wall Street Journal.* Some companies are requiring, as a condition for employment or advancement, that employees agree to submit any discrimination complaints, including sexual harassment, to binding arbitration rather than to the courts. The U.S. Congress is looking into this practice and its possible impact on, and viability under, federal law enforcement.[7]

- **Sometimes legal pressures can trigger creative, constructive responses on the part of organizations.**

When Chicago's Commonwealth Edison Co. settled a gender discrimination complaint in 1994, they agreed not only to a $3.3 million payment to certain women who unsuccessfully applied for meter-reading jobs during the 1980s, but also to developing a $300,000 training program "for women who are interested in nuclear operating and other technical jobs . . . not traditionally held by women."[8]

In another example of creative response to le-

7. Steven A. Holmes, "Some Workers Lose Right to File Suit for Bias at Work," *The Wall Street Journal,* March 18, 1994, p. A1+.

8. "Payment of $3 Million by Commonwealth Edison Ends Bias Case," *The Wall Street Journal,* December 30, 1993, p. A10.

gal and regulatory pressure, some banks have developed a variety of ways to respond to the Community Reinvestment Act of 1977's requirements for investment in all sectors of the community, including low-income areas. Such measures range from targeted telemarketing and marketing surveys to working through community churches to identify and reach potential borrowers.[9]

- **Legal and regulatory pressures on organizations can result in an ambiguous or mixed commitment to diversity, both because laws and their enforcement change with the political climate and because they vary between countries and, in the United States, even between states.**

Sometimes companies adapt to these mixed signals by adopting a policy of "when in Rome, do as the Romans do." This can result in cynicism on the part of employees and managers. For example, a company that works toward gender pay equity in one country in compliance with equal compensation regulations (such as those in the United Kingdom, Canada, or the United States) while disregarding such a commitment in unregulated environments, undercuts the message of respect and equal value that it might send both its women and men employees.

On the other hand, an effort to be consistent in the treatment of women employees in all settings may fly in the face of cultural norms regarding gender roles in some countries. (Not to mention the competitive implications a firm may face if it compensates employees at much higher levels than its peers in a particular country.) How can a company be responsive to both a commitment to gender equity and a sensitivity to cultural value differences? A reliance on the "legal minimum" in each context may appear to be a way out of this thorny dilemma. It may seem to take the clashes between the rights and values of women and the rights and values of a particular cultural group out of the company's realm of responsibility.

However, as in any values clash, an organization's failure to attempt to think through the conflicting points of view and build communication among its own members will limit its abilities to address the role of women in *any* context and feed cynicism and resentment. There may not be easy answers, but a reliance on minimal compliance ensures that the debate is never even engaged.

2. Labor Market Demographics

Much has been made of the demographic shifts expected in the workforce by the year 2000, particularly in the United States.[10] The often-cited reports put out by the Hudson Institute, *Workforce 2000* (1987) and *Opportunity 2000* (1988), announced increasing diversity in the country's labor pool and have served as a catalyst for discussion in the government, the media, and among corporate leaders. In order to understand the ways in which demographics have and can serve as a motivator for corporate attention

---

9. Elizabeth Leech, "Huntington Bank Maps a Path for Increased Community Lending," *Bank Management* 69, no. 2 (February 1993), pp. 51–54; Eunice Cooper, "Going Beyond CRA Requirements: Community Banks Reaching Out," *ABA Bank Compliance* 13, no. 7 (July/Summer 1992), pp. 23–25; and Mark Borowsky, "Mortgaging Home Lending's Future," *Bank Management* 69, no. 5 (May 1993), pp. 16–23.

10. It is useful to consider demographic shifts in other parts of the world, as well. In *Human Resources Outlook in Europe,* The Conference Board reports: "Europe faces a very sharp reduction in the number of young people entering the labour force over the coming years and an ageing population profile . . . Statistics from the EC's [European Community] Eurostat show the peak year [for the labour market] was in 1981 with 968,000 net new entrants. In 1989, the figure was 350,000 . . . By 2000 around 300,000 more employees will leave than join." Companies use a variety of tactics to deal with this shortage including efforts to attract more women and older workers, to train existing employees, and to hire the long-term unemployed. "The Corporate Response to the Demographic Crunch," *Human Resources Outlook in Europe: A Survey for the European Human Resource Conference 28–29 November 1990* by Andrew Tank, Research Associate, ©*The Conference Board Europe,* November 1990, pp. 4, 5, 6.

to diversity, let's take a look briefly at the key predictions about the coming workforce, as well as some of the challenges to these findings that have been raised.

Most basically, the Hudson Institute reports predicted the following for the United States workforce as it enters the next century:

• A shrinking labor pool, due mainly to slower population growth.
• An aging workforce, as the Baby Boom generation grows older and fewer young workers enter the pool.
• More women in the workforce.
• More minorities in the workforce.
• Increasing numbers of immigrants.
• Changes in the nature of jobs available, from manufacturing to service and information sectors, and from lower to higher skill requirements largely because of new technologies.[11]

A number of significant challenges have been addressed to these predictions. For example, many have pointed out that the manner in which the demographic changes were described in these reports, both verbally and especially in graphic form, was misleading. For example, by reporting the significant differences between the rate of growth for minority populations and for non-Hispanic white males, they underplayed the fact that the absolute population numbers were still so skewed as to temper the implied impact of growth rate differences. Misunderstandings aside, we are still looking at a decrease in the percentage of non-Hispanic white males in the labor force, from 43 percent in 1990 to 38 percent in 2005 although absolute numbers are still expected to increase.)[12] (See Exhibit 3.)

Commentators DiTomaso and Friedman point out that the decrease in the percentage of non-Hispanic white males in the United States labor force has been occurring for 50 years and that rather than "heating up" in the last decade of the twentieth century, it is slowing slightly. They attribute this to the leveling off of new women entrants into the workforce. Finally they point out that "the United States has had a diverse population without a diverse labor force for most of its history," and therefore demographics alone do not determine workforce representation or opportunity.[13]

Other critics raise additional questions. Harris Sussman reminds the reader that the "Workforce 2000" reports focused on those who would be entering the labor force between 1987 and 2000, a relatively small group when compared to the existing workforce. This emphasis, he argues, skews corporate attention toward recruiting, releasing it from concern in times of cutbacks as has been the recent case for many large employers.[14]

Mishel and Teixeira of the Economic Policy Institute argue that slow growth in the population and the labor force does not necessarily lead to labor shortages, as demand growth tends to slow as well.[15] They also suggest that the shift toward higher skills requirements in available jobs will not be as dramatic or as widespread as suggested by the earlier reports.[16]

What this summary of predictions and critiques suggests is not that the "Workforce 2000" predictions should be dismissed, but rather that they are incomplete, that it is important to understand demographic shifts in the context of continually shifting policy and practice as well as the context of longer term demographic

11. *Opportunity 2000 Creative Affirmative Action Strategies for a Changing Workforce.* Prepared for Employment Standards Administration, U.S. Department of Labor, Submitted by Hudson Institute, Indianapolis, Indiana (September 1988), pp. 3–14.

12. Judith Friedman and Nancy DiTomaso, "What Managers Need to Know about Demographic Projections." (unpublished manuscript, Rutgers University, December 1993), Figure 3, p. 11.

13. Ibid., p. 4.
14. Harris Sussman, "Workforce 2000—Five Years Closer," *Managing Diversity* (June 1992).
15. Lawrence Mishel and Ruy A. Teixeira, *The Myth of the Coming Labor Shortage: Jobs, Skills, and Incomes of America's Workforce 2000* (Washington, D.C.: Economic Policy Institute, 1991), p. 29.
16. Ibid., p. 5.

EXHIBIT 3　Workforce Changes, 1985–2000

Based on Hudson Institute projections
current, net additions, and projected labor force

(*numbers in thousands*)

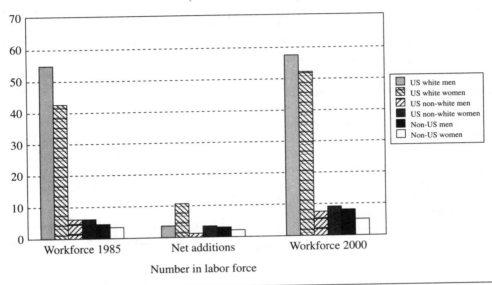

Number in labor force

Source: Judith Friedman and Nancy DiTomaso, *What Managers Need to Know about Demographic Projections (unpublished manuscript, December 1993).*

trends and a broader-based review of organizational experience. What follows is a list of some of the key factors that ought to be considered when reviewing labor force demographic projections:

- **Demographic trends ought to be considered in a global context.**

In his 1991 article, "Global WorkForce 2000: The New World Labor Market," William B. Johnston states "While much of the world's skilled and unskilled human resources are being produced in the developing world, most of the well-paid jobs are being generated in the cities of the industrialized world."[17] He goes on to ex-

plain that this "mismatch" will increase the mobility of labor pools, exerting pressure on both government (i.e., immigration policy, labor practices) and corporate policies (i.e., language policies, recruiting practices). Thus, labor markets in one area of the world can sometimes very much affect the labor markets in another.

- **Demographic trends in a particular country will be affected by that country's immigration policies, the ways in which those policies interact with immigration policies in other countries, as well as the level of illegal immigration.**

Most experts predict continued high levels of immigration to the United States, primarily Hispanics and Asians, for the rest of this century. Obviously, changes in immigration policy and trade agreements can shift these trends. In many countries, social pressures to limit immigration

17. In Mary C. Gentile (ed.), *Differences that Work: Organizational Excellence through Diversity.* (Boston, Mass.: Harvard Business School Press, 1994), p. 3.

are strong, but these pressures are affected by shifting economic realities; they increase in times of recession and unemployment and lessen in times of labor shortage.

- **Projected demographic trends should be considered in relation to the economic trends, shifts in job availability, and changes in the nature of work in a particular industry and/or region.**

Although the Hudson Institute predicted labor shortages and a dramatic shift to higher skill jobs as the United States approached the year 2000, a February 1993 *Fortune* article stated: "Since 1989, 440,000 defense industry workers have been laid off, 300,000 soldiers, sailors, and fliers have been mustered out of the service, and 100,000 civilian Defense Department employees have lost their jobs. . . . over the same period [there were cutbacks] at GM (105,000), IBM (104,000), AT&T (60,000), and Sears (50,000)."[18] Changes in Defense policy and widespread corporate downsizing have affected the number, age, experience levels, and goals of the available labor force.

In addition, although Mishel and Teixeira argue that the predicted "upskilling" of jobs in the United States is exaggerated, they do concede that: "jobs today are more likely to require at least threshold levels of literacy and numeracy . . . Employers . . . view these skills as a necessary condition for flexible use of employees (i.e., retraining) in work situations," and "some jobs in 'best practice' firms within certain industries (i.e., banking, insurance, textiles, apparel, metalworking, etc.) are being substantially upgraded." Though these firms are "are not the norm in the U.S. economy today . . . they are becoming numerically more important over time."[19]

- **Projected demographic trends ought to be considered in light of government and corporate policies regarding family care, health care, and retirement issues.**

The availability and cost of quality child and elder care, the flexibility of employers around work schedules and location, the availability of affordable health care, and changes in pension practices and Social Security rules all have an impact on participation rates for various segments of the potential workforce.[20]

Issues and Questions

- **An oversimplified and generic use of predicted demographic shifts in the labor pool as the motivator for organizational attention to diversity can trigger a backlash effect, triggering anxiety, cynicism, and/or denial.**

In an effort to tie organizational diversity to tangible and quantifiable business concerns, many managers, educators, policymakers, and journalists have seized upon demographic trends as a useful tool. However, our earlier discussion illustrates that such trends are multifaceted, changeable, and easily misunderstood.

For example, the misreading of the Hudson Institute findings about rate of change among new entrants in the coming workforce was double-edged. On the one hand, it drew attention and new energy to organizational diversity initiatives. On the other, it triggered expectations and anxieties about immediate and sweeping change. If these changes do not become visible at the expected rate, employees can become cynical and engage in a denial of those changes that may yet be imminent but perhaps less apparent.

Obviously, broad demographic trends will not necessarily affect all organizations in the same

---

18. Lee Smith "Can Defense Pain Be Turned to Gain," *Fortune,* February 8, 1993, pp. 84–96.

19. Lawrence Mishel and Ruy A. Teixeira *The Myth of the Coming Labor Shortage: Jobs, Skills, and Incomes of America's Workforce 2000* (Washington, D.C.: Economic Policy Institute, 1991), p. 23.

20. Judith Friedman and Nancy DiTomaso, "What Managers Need to Know about Demographic Projections," (unpublished manuscript, Rutgers University, December 1993), pp. 19, 20, 21.

ways at the same rate. A few observations about the United States 1993 workforce are thought-provoking: "The Fortune 500 are the fastest-declining sector of the workforce. Less than 10 percent of the U.S. workforce work in the Fortune 500. Women-owned businesses employ more people than the Fortune 500. The fastest-growing sector of the workforce is people who work from home."[21] Facts such as these help to put the individual manager's experience of a changing workforce into context and suggest the importance of a careful, specific, and *customized* expression of the expected impact of demographic trends on a particular organization.

- **Still, demographic pressures are a very real and *felt* motivator for organizational attention to diversity in a number of specific situations.**
- **Some industries have experienced real shifts in the characteristics of those candidates in the educational pipeline for their entry-level positions.** The numbers of women earning accounting degrees and law degrees has increased significantly, for example.
- **Some organizations are located in communities or regions where the demographics of the available labor pool are shifting rapidly, where populations that used to be in the minority are approaching or have reached equal or majority representation.** For example, in Miami, Florida, "since 1970, the Hispanic population has tripled, and in 1990, it accounted for nearly half of the metropolitan area's population of 1.9 million."[22]
- **The demographics of a population shift, and so too do the demographics of an organization's customer base.** Some organizations feel this reality more acutely, because they are located in a community where the population is shifting

rapidly and they focus on a local market, because their product has come to appeal to a new population, or because they have specifically targeted a particular population in their product design and marketing.

- **In times of labor shortage, organizations tend to think more creatively, more expansively about potential pools for new employees.**
- **As Rosabeth Kanter has argued in her classic *Men and Women of the Corporation*, the internal demographics of an organization can also influence its policies, practices, and culture with regard to diversity.** She argues that women retain a "token" status in an organization until they reach a critical mass in numbers.[23] One might argue the flip side of this point, suggesting that in those organizations where women or minorities reach a certain critical mass, they can trigger corporate motivation to attend to diversity issues. Of course, numbers alone do not guarantee such an effect. The relative power of the individuals' organizational positions, as well as their individual and group dispositions are critical.

Two of the important lessons to be culled from workforce projections are the importance of attending to both short- and long-term trends in the labor pool[24] and the importance of developing the organizational and managerial flexibility and skills necessary to tap and develop the potential of a workforce that may be significantly different tomorrow than it is today.

3. Globalization of Business
By now it has become commonplace to refer to the increasing globalization of business, but the figures can still startle us with the magnitude of that growth. From 1980 to 1989, investment

21. Harris Sussman, "The U.S. in Perspective," unpublished paper.
22. Gail De George and Antonio N. Fina, with Irene Recio, "Latin America's Newest Capital City: Miami," *Business Week,* September 30, 1991, p. 120.

23. Rosabeth Moss Kanter, *Men and Women of the Corporation* (New York: Basic Books, Inc., 1977), pp. 207–209.
24. Harris Sussman, "Workforce 2000—Five Years Closer," *Managing Diversity,* June 1992.

EXHIBIT 4 Globalization of Business (All figures in billions of US$)

	Germany		Japan		United States	
	Exports	Imports	Exports	Imports	Exports	Imports
1980	178.8	174.3	144.7	157.6	225.6	257.0
1981	176.0	163.7	152.2	143.1	238.7	273.4
1982	180.0	158.4	146.5	139.0	216.4	254.9
1983	158.7	143.3	150.3	129.3	205.6	269.9
1984	155.1	137.9	160.6	128.7	224.0	346.4
1985	218.2	188.4	209.3	155.0	218.8	352.5
1986	271.2	213.2	221.8	135.5	227.2	382.3
1987	333.5	259.0	269.8	176.0	254.1	424.4
1988	318.9	246.9	269.6	190.8	322.4	459.5
1989	377.6	298.3	263.7	202.0	363.8	492.9
1990	442.2	372.2	308.5	251.9	393.6	517.0
1991	439.4	425.7	338.3	254.8	421.7	508.4
1992	408.0	389.2	344.8	236.7	448.2	553.9

Source: *International Monetary Fund Blance of Payments Yearbook, 1980–1992.*

from abroad into the United States rose from $83 billion to $401 billion; during the same period, U.S. direct investment abroad rose from $215 billion to $373 billion.[25] The U.S. Council of Economic Advisors reports that by the end of the 1980s, United States exports increased to almost 11 percent of the Gross National Product.[26] By 1994, European multinational corporations employed over 2.9 million Americans.[27] (See Exhibit 4.)

This globalization has many implications for managers and can serve as yet another motivator for organizations to recognize and respond to the impact of diversity. For example, with growing proportions of a business' revenues coming from foreign sales, the ability to understand the market needs and preferences of different cultures is essential. In an effort to tap into foreign markets, more and more firms are engaging in joint ventures or acquiring foreign subsidiaries, creating the demand for managers who can understand, negotiate with, and work creatively with managers who reflect different cultural values and often speak a different language. Experts suggest that 20 percent–25 percent of U.S. expatriate managers fail in their attempts to adapt and function effectively in a non-U.S. setting, representing a significant loss for their organizations.[28] Truly global firms face not only the challenge of functioning themselves in contexts foreign to their own, but also the struggle to enable their representatives from a variety of different countries to work together to the employing organization's benefit.

Some of the kinds of challenges individual

25. Mary Lou Egan and Marc Bendich, Jr., "International Business Careers in the United States: Salaries, Advancement and Male-Female Differences," *The International Journal of Human Resource Management* 5, no. 1 (February 1994), p. 33.

26. Ibid

27. Philip Rosenzweig, "Why Is Managing in the United States So Difficult for European Firms?," *European Management Journal,* 12, no. 1 (March 1994), p. 31.

28. Charlene Marmer Solomon, "Success Abroad Depends on More Than Job Skills," *Personnel Journal,* April 1994, p. 51.

managers and organizations may face in international activities include:

- Understanding and complying with different legal and regulatory requirements.
- Overcoming the often subtle misunderstandings that occur when communicating in a second or third language.
- Understanding and showing respect for cultural norms of etiquette, social interaction, and business behavior.
- Understanding and overcoming the personal biases, often quite unconscious, that can be triggered when dealing with individuals who seem "different" from oneself.

Issues and Questions

- **Sometimes cultural differences become a convenient scapegoat, blamed for organizational failures that are actually caused by other unaddressed problems, "such as a failure to respect people, group power and politics, resentment at subordination, poor strategic fit, limited organizational communication, or the absence of problem-solving forums."[29]**

It is often easier to blame a seemingly preexisting and unalterable concept like cultural difference, than to take personal or organizational accountability for failures. Nevertheless, this very phenomenon of scapegoating "difference" would be addressed by organizational efforts to educate managers about diversity.

- **It is useful and necessary to examine the ways in which cultural differences sometimes overlap with, are similar to, and distinct from, other forms of diversity (such as race, gender, religion, and so forth).**

Thus it is important to understand the origins, manifestations, and functions of various perceptual and interactive dynamics, such as stereotypes, in-group and out-group dynamics, and attribution errors, and to recognize the ways in which these dynamics can be and often are applied to any form of difference—gender-based, racial, or cultural. Nevertheless, it is also important to understand the different historical and ideological bases for various forms of exclusion, oppression and oppositionality. For example, cultural differences can be compounded by racial differences between countries, such as the United States and Japan, when there is a history of racial intolerance in one or both nations. On the other hand, cultural differences can be mitigated by past histories of political alliance or by ideological similarities such as a shared religious tradition.

Recognizing these distinctions and similarities allows us to avoid the trap of equating various forms of difference, leading to unrealistic expectations and the exaggeration or trivialization of genuine oppression.

- **In order to anticipate and understand the impacts of cultural difference on organizational and managerial interactions, it is important to look at the reasons or catalysts for the cross-cultural contact.**

In their study of foreign acquisitions of United States firms, Kanter and Korn noted that a significant influence on the relative ease of cross-cultural cooperation was the *felt* "desirability of the relationship."[30] When organizations had a history of cooperative ventures or when the acquired firm perceived the acquisition as rescuing it from financial distress or a hostile takeover attempt, cultural friction appeared only mildly troublesome and relatively easy to overcome.

Similarly, organizational and managerial attitudes toward their foreign hosts will be influ-

---

29. Rosabeth Moss Kanter and Richard Ian Corn, "Do Cultural Differences Make a Business Difference?: Contextual Factors Affecting Cross-Cultural Relationship Success." © 1993 by R. M. Kanter and R. I. Corn, p. 6. To be published in *Journal of Management Development*, Special Issue on Cross-Cultural Management Winter 1994.

30. Ibid., pp. 10, 11.

enced by their reasons for being there. Firms seeking inexpensive human and natural resources may have very different attitudinal and behavioral postures toward their host countries than firms who are courting a strategic partnership based on the host's advanced technological or research capabilities—and these differences in attitude and behavior are likely to trigger very different responses in the companies and labor pool of the host countries.

4. Diversifying Customer Base

Just as the demographic trends discussed above affect the available labor pool, they also affect the potential consumer base. In the United States, for example, as the population ages, as immigrant populations expand, as African-American and Hispanic American populations increase as a proportion of the total population, it behooves companies to examine their product mix and marketing/distribution systems in light of the customer base they are trying to reach.

In 1992, the estimated buying power of African-Americans in the United States was $290 billion, of Asian-Americans was $88 billion, of Hispanics was $180 billion, of gays and lesbians was $500 billion, and the estimated buying power of United States women was 85 percent of the total buying power.[31] Targeted market research and consulting practices are springing up to advise firms on how best to attract and retain specific customer pools, reporting on income distributions, brand loyalties, response patterns to differing advertising media, shopping patterns, and so on. In addition, companies are beginning to recognize the benefits of employing a marketing and sales force that understands and reflects the diversity of the populations they are trying to attract. In some communities, a bilingual or multilingual sales force can be important, for example.

Similarly, as a firm reaches out to a more international customer base, it will need to respect and understand their preferences and requirements. For example, as the European Union permits open trade borders between its member countries, new challenges emerge. As Shari Caudron comments in "The Myth of the European Consumer:" "Though Europeans are becoming more similar in their tastes—thanks in part to the mass-media outlets [Sky TV, CNN, MTV]—it will take generations for them to become a truly homogenized group of consumers, assuming that it happens at all . . . If anything, the unification of the 12 European countries has increased nationalistic tendencies, not reduced them. . . . When there was little trade across borders—when Italian products were sold only in Italy, for example—there wasn't much national feeling."[32] Thus, marketers from other areas of the world must try to understand and respond to the distinctive tastes of a European Union that remains, nevertheless, quite diverse.

Issues and Questions

• **Although employing a diverse marketing and sales force can aid in efforts to understand and appeal to different racial, gender, and ethnic groups among consumers, there may be a danger of taking targeted marketing to its literal extremes, creating a segregated approach both to consumers and to employee career development.**

For example, African-Americans who began their career contributing to the firm's efforts to

---

31. Adam Geller, "It's Just Good Business Upscale Market Expo First to Tap Gay and Lesbian Consumers," *The Record,* April 16, 1994, p. A14; Nancy Harvey, "Glass Ceiling: Dallas Must Dismantle It," *The Dallas Morning News,* July 11, 1993, p. 6J; Carol Sowers, "Retailers Cash in on Minorities' Buying Power," *The Arizona Republic,* December 20, 1993, p. 1, Sec. A.; and Kimberly Blanton, "Pitfalls in the Ethnic-Ad Minefield," *The Boston Globe,* August 22, 1993, p. 75.

32. Shari Caudron, "The Myth of the European Consumer: Despite the Open Borders, Nationalism Still Thrives in the Marketplace," *Industry Week,* February 21, 1994, p. 29.

customize product policy, targeting a predominantly Black consumer group, might run the risk of being typed and restricted to "Black marketing" efforts, rather than being developed for other companywide positions. This need not necessarily occur. If organizations look upon their employees as part of a team where each individual's expertise enriches all the others, the insights of individuals about a particular racial or ethnic identity can be taught to the entire team, whether that may be insights about marketing to African-Americans, Hispanics, or non-Hispanic Caucasians.

- **In a related vein, targeted products for a particular population run the risk of crossing a subtle line into the exploitation, or perceived exploitation, of that same population.**

For example, R. J. Reynolds faced an outcry before it canceled plans to launch Uptown cigarettes, targeting urban Blacks, and Dakota cigarettes, targeting young women. G. Heileman Brewing Company canceled its launch of Colt 45 PowerMaster malt liquor, with its unusually high alcohol content, after much resistance from the Bureau of Alcohol, Tobacco, and Firearms, organized alcohol opponents, and minority advocates who complained that the product was targeted at lower income, urban Blacks. And the producers of high-end athletic shoes have faced organized opposition from those like Operation PUSH who claim that the marketing campaigns prey upon the social ills and limited opportunities of minority youth.

A number of different issues are involved in these cases. Certainly, the fact that a product is seen as harmful to its user (i.e., cigarettes, alcohol) triggers greater objection when that product is targeted to a population that is perceived to have fewer resources and opportunities to empower its resistance.[33] Some will argue that such complaints are merely paternalism, reflecting the majority population's greater willingness to restrict individual choices among minority populations than among the wider public. Others will counter that such a defense is the height of naiveté or cynicism, that many if not most of those who object to these campaigns are members of the targeted groups themselves, and that these targeted marketing efforts are nothing more than blatant exploitation. Interestingly, public objections to the targeted marketing of harmful products may be the leading edge of a shifting societal perspective regarding the age-old debate between a philosophy of caveat emptor and a more protective public policy stance.

When the product is not perceived as harmful in itself, such as sneakers, the objections have more to do with a sense that business is supposed to function as part of a reciprocal relationship with consumers, where the dollars spent by consumers for desired products in turn fuel an economy that produces jobs and opportunities for those consumers. In the case of certain disadvantaged populations, critics perceive that this reciprocity loop has been broken.

- **Firms sometimes fear that efforts to design marketing campaigns that reflect and appeal to a wider representation of the consumer population may be greeted by a backlash from other consumer segments.**

For example, Ikea, a Swedish furniture chain created a 1994 television advertising campaign for the United States that featured a gay couple shopping together for furnishings. Still the executive vice president at the agency which created the spot, Linda Sawyer commented: "I don't know if we'd run this ad in less-cosmopolitan places, but then, Ikea isn't in less-cosmopolitan places."[34]

However, companies run the risk of basing such conclusions upon stereotypes, sacrificing

---

33. N. Craig Smith and John A. Quelch, *Ethics in Marketing* (Boston, MA: Richard D. Irwin, 1993), p. 192.

34. Bernice Kanner, "On Madison Avenue: Normally Gay," *New York Magazine,* April 4, 1994, p. 2.

potential market opportunities due to a failure to actually research their assumptions as they would with any other marketing decision. If their research supports their worst fears concerning potential backlash, creative thinking may yield ideas for targeted media outlets, at a minimum, or for other ways to take a leadership role in shifting consumer responses.

5. External Pressure from Community, Religious, and/or Political Groups

As noted above, sometimes organizations are motivated to address diversity-related issues in response to external pressures from the communities in which they are located, or to whom they are marketing their products and services. Above we mentioned several examples of such organized pressure from groups and coalitions objecting to particular products and/or the ways in which these products are promoted and priced for a particular population. Similarly, some companies have been pressured to employ and promote more representatives from the populations who purchase their products.

On the other hand, organizations sometimes face negative reaction to their efforts to respond positively to employee diversity from communities, religious, or political groups. For example, in 1993, Apple Computer, Inc., encountered resistance to their plans to build a new plant in Williamson County, Texas, when "county commissioners spurned Apple's request for tax relief because of Apple's policy supporting partners of its gay employees."[35] A week later, however, the county commissioners changed their position and offered Apple comparable concessions.

These situations bear some similarities to those instances when firms are motivated to take action around diversity as a result of legal and regulatory pressures. For example, responses to external pressures can sometimes reflect the re-

luctant compliance and cynical game-playing alluded to earlier in this note. If a company hires or promotes members of a particular population solely to appease external pressure groups, the organizational fate of those employees may well be in question. On the other hand, such external pressures can sometimes trigger creative and constructive changes in the way an organization does business with a particular population. Much depends upon the mindset of the organization's leadership and the ability of its representatives to listen to and communicate genuinely with the groups exerting pressure.

6. Internal Employee Pressures

Internal pressure in the form of employee complaints and/or behaviors (turnover, lower productivity, absenteeism, conflict, etc.) can serve as the motivator for many organizations to begin to attend to diversity issues. Examples of such pressures include:

- High **turnover** rates, especially among women and/or minorities, resulting in lost productivity and higher recruiting and training costs.
- Inefficiencies in **performance development and mentoring** across race, gender, ethnicity, etc.
- Employee dissatisfaction and complaints over **barriers to promotion, or a "glass ceiling,"** for women and/or minorities, resulting in lost productivity, turnover, potential future difficulties in recruiting.
- **Harassment** incidents.
- Challenges to **effective communication,** based in cultural differences (norms, expectations, motivation styles, attitudes toward authority, etc.) and language differences.
- Individual and group **conflicts,** especially in organizations that are moving to a greater reliance on team processes.
- Employee requests for more **flexible schedule and benefits policies,** responding to changing work/family issues (i.e., flex/time, job sharing, elder and child care, domestic partner benefits).

---

35. Marilyn Chase, "Apple's Commitment to Gay Employees Upsets Texas County," *The Wall Street Journal,* December 1, 1993, p. A14.

Issues and Questions

- **When organizations respond to these kinds of pressures, it becomes important to distinguish between organizational needs/reactions and individual needs/reactions.**

In many cases, both organizational and individual needs must be addressed: analysis needs to be conducted at both levels, and reactions should be explicitly addressed to each.

For example, when an individual raises concerns about barriers to promotion or about a lack of mentoring for women, organizations can sometimes get bogged down in trying to measure the prevalence of the phenomenon reported throughout the organization. The individual's issues can get lost in time-consuming research, giving the impression that the individual's concern will only be valid if a clear and prevalent pattern of similar behavior is proven.

On the other hand, if an individual who complains of a "glass ceiling" for women is perceived by her manager to be unqualified for promotion, organizations can sometimes release themselves from seriously considering the ways in which she may be the victim of the manager's bias, or the organization can sometimes draw the conclusion that all employees who complain of such barriers are similarly unqualified.

- **Sometimes organizations respond narrowly to the internal employee pressures described above and to the individuals who name them—at best, perceiving the pressures and the individuals as unique in their difficulties and requiring "special" assistance; at worst, perceiving the pressures and the individuals as irritants to be eliminated.**

If, however, organizations view these challenges as leading indicators of organizational learning and development opportunities, their efforts are more likely to enhance the performance and conditions of *all* employees and less likely to raise resentment from individuals who feel left out.

7. Personal Commitment

The personal commitment of individual leaders—at all levels of the organization—can focus attention and resources on diversity issues. In fact, as we have noted, many of the other motivators discussed above can cut in contradictory directions depending upon the context, and many of them have been ignored by organizations undisposed to attend to them, often at significant cost. The clarity, consistency, and strength of personal commitment on the part of key leaders is often the factor that enables an organization to develop effective, consistent, diversity initiatives and to minimize backlash.

This personal commitment can take a number of forms but among the most frequently observed are:

- **A vision of interdependence:** individuals who take a broad and long-term view of their organization's place in society, and who have an almost *visceral* sense of the interlocking destinies of individuals and organizations. These individuals are drawn to intersections: the intersection of our work lives and the rest of our lives, the intersection of the workplace and the economic/social viability of the community in which it is located, the intersection of our national identities and our global citizenships. These individuals see attention to diversity as a matter of survival.
- **A commitment to learning:** individuals who are energized by and drawn to new points of view, opportunities to enrich their view of their work and their world. These individuals are excited by the potential for innovation and surprise represented by each new individual and task they encounter.
- **A commitment to fairness:** individuals who feel inequity palpably and who draw personal satisfaction from promoting behaviors and environments that foster fairness.

Just as the forms of personal commitment to diversity can vary, so too do their sources in the individual. Most often, an individual has had some sort of personal experience that has triggered this response. Sometimes they have had the experience of feeling marginalized, or of seeing their own options constrained. They may wish to improve conditions for themselves, and others who have had similar experiences. Other times, they have been powerfully affected by observing this marginalization or constraint in the life of others, especially those close to them. For example, as ambitions and opportunities for women have expanded, more fathers have been confronted with the reality that their daughters may encounter greater barriers than their sons or the sons of others.

Some of these individuals have been influenced by the example of a parent, a teacher, or an employer who was strongly committed to similar values. Others have been changed by an unexpected confrontation with difference: for example, some managers have been influenced by a prolonged international assignment or by an assignment to a multifunctional team project.

Issues and Questions

• **The personal commitments of individual leaders in an organization may conflict with other commitments, just as deeply held by others.**

This is, in itself, another challenge of diversity. It underscores the importance of explicit discussion of fundamental values and premises that underlie an organization's culture, distinguishing

between "true requirements [as opposed to] . . . preferences, conveniences, or traditions."[36]

• **It is useful to understand that the motivations which cause individuals to take a leadership stance with regard to diversity in an organization may vary greatly.**

Understanding these differences can enhance the effectiveness of organizational diversity initiatives. For example, individuals who are drawn to the work because of a potential for new learning and innovation may not be as responsive to appeals to equity and fairness. It may be important to develop multiple ways of communicating the organization's goals.

Linking diversity programs to practical business goals makes it easier for many individuals to respond positively, allaying fears that their employer may be getting involved in the realm of personal values and beliefs and eliminating resentment of an employer perceived to be reprimanding them for inappropriate behaviors. Nevertheless, as noted above, business motivations can be interpreted as sometimes cutting in contradictory directions if an organization has not thought through its underlying commitments.

* * * * *

The preceding discussion of motivators is not exhaustive, but it does raise the most frequently noted impetuses for diversity initiatives and notes some of the issues and questions that influence the timing, sense of urgency, consistency, and effectiveness of an organization's response.

MINDSET

Examining what motivates an organization to begin to think about diversity begins to tell us how that organization will *define* the subject:

• Is it a *discrete problem to be solved?* (i.e., how do we find the employees we need?)
• Is it a *discrete competitive opportunity* to be tapped? (i.e., how do we attract the Hispanic market to our product?)
• Is it a *potential threat to be avoided?* (i.e., how

do we protect ourselves from potential liability?)
• Is it a *cluster of interrelated challenges and opportunities?* (i.e., how do we thrive with an increasingly diverse labor market and customer base?)

---

36. Thomas R. Roosevelt, Jr., President of the American Institute for Managing Diversity, Inc., "The Diversity Para-

- Is it experienced as a *primarily external (to the organization)* or *primarily internal* reality?
- *How broadly is diversity defined* as a concern and an opportunity for certain groups within the organization or its market, for all individuals in the organization, or for the organization as a whole? (i.e., do we design training programs to help women learn how to manage their careers, OR do we design training programs for all employees to learn both personal career management and how to better assist subordinates in career development?)
- Are the *points of leverage* seen as primarily person-based, or embedded in the organizational systems and culture? (i.e., do we think we need to change the people in the organization, or the organization's influence on its people?)
- Is it seen as a *time-limited, time-bounded* agenda (often engendering a "quick fix" mentality), or as a recent insight into a lasting organizational reality?
- Is the critical *focus on power relations or on education?* (In Clayton P. Aderfer's work with race relations advisory groups, he found this distinction to influence the type of initiatives organizations adopted: "The power emphasis stated that race relations problems occurred because whites in the predominantly white corporation had much more formal authority and informal influence than blacks. The education focus stated that race relations problems occurred because people (primarily whites) did not adequately understand race relations. . . . Upward mobility interventions were primarily directed to reduce the power imbalance between blacks and whites, and the race relations competence workshop was aimed mainly at increasing the understanding of race relations."[37]

- Is the *focus on controlling behavior or on tapping sources of learning and innovation?*
- Is it experienced as a *moral imperative or a business imperative?*
- Is the motivation *fundamentally reactive and defensive, or fundamentally proactive and goal-oriented?*

The answers to these questions of definition will tell us a great deal about the implicit goals embedded in an organization's motivations; about the primary targets of its efforts (i.e., workforce versus market focus: organizational systems and culture, senior managers, middle managers, lower-level employees, customers, external influence groups); and about the methods the organization will select to address its issues. The answers to these questions flesh out a picture of an organizational mindset toward diversity.

There is no single set of "right answers" to the questions above. An organization may appropriately and effectively answer them in different ways at different times. For example, R. Roosevelt Thomas has developed a taxonomy for analyzing an organization's diversity mindset. He lists eight possible attitudes/approaches toward any type of organizational diversity (Exclude, Deny, Suppress, Segregate, Assimilate, Tolerate, Build relationships, Foster mutual adaptation) and he argues: ". . . there is no inherent positive or negative value associated with the options. Whether an option is appropriate depends on the circumstances. As an illustration, consider the case of a company buying a healthy enterprise that is substantially different. Segregation of the acquired company as a subsidiary would be appropriate."[38]

Nevertheless, there are some general trends in the responses that can serve as guidelines, the

digm," working paper, ©*The American Institute for Managing Diversity, Inc.*, (1993), p. 5.

37. Clayton A. Alderfer, "Embedded in Organizations: Report on a Long-Term Project with the XYZ Corporation" in *Diversity in the Workplace: Human Resources Initiatives,*

Susan E. Jackson and Associates (New York: The Guilford Press, 1992), p. 145.

38. Thomas R. Roosevelt, Jr., President of the American Institute for Managing Diversity, Inc., "The Diversity Paradigm," working paper, ©*The American Institute for Managing Diversity, Inc.* (1993), pp. 5–9.

most important being that an organization needs to have or develop the capacity and willingness to answer the above questions in multiple ways, to approach diversity in multiple ways. For example, although some individuals and organizations tend to be more effectively motivated by risk avoidance and others by seeking opportunities, over the long haul it is important that a diversity mindset incorporate both motivations, not only as a means of encouraging "buy-in" from all employees but also as a means of reaping the full benefits of a diverse labor and consumer context.

Similarly, if diversity is defined narrowly, as a discrete issue, an organization and its members will do well to consider the potential and impact of defining it more broadly. The discrete "presenting issue" may still be first priority, but an integrative vision may suggest more effective, long-lasting responses. For example, pressure from the government may cause an organization to identify the hiring of more women or minority group members as a priority (i.e., diversity defined as a discrete problem to be solved). Nevertheless, without a broader vision of what happens to recruits once hired, this is destined to be a recurring and escalating challenge.

Finally, it is useful to consider the degree to which an organization's mindset links diversity to the "bottom line" or business viability of the firm. This does not mean that a commitment to broader values, like fairness, are not also important, but rather that an organization implicitly and explicitly integrates such values into its definition of business success, that its operating norms reflect a belief that such values contribute to productivity and innovation. Such a mindset makes the organization much more likely to recognize and pursue the potential opportunities of a diverse workforce and customer base.

We must remember that the choices, decisions, and attitudes reflected in the answers to the above questions are actually the choices, decisions, and attitudes of those individuals with decision-making power, as constrained and directed by the organization's culture. Therefore, without specific effort to the contrary, the very individuals that an organization may need to better understand, empower, manage, and market to, often have limited (or perhaps only a criticism-based) influence on an organization's mindset toward diversity.

As we review some of the most common methods chosen by organizations to address diversity (see Exhibit 5), consider the answers to the above questions implicit in these choices and whether these answers will lead the organization where it wants/needs to go.

METHODS

As with motivators, we can generate a fairly extensive list of methods that have been used by organizations to respond to one or more of the challenges and opportunities of diversity. Each of these methods raises its own set of implementation questions and some of the most critical are raised below.

1. Cultural Audit

Reflections on the questions of mindset listed above are the beginning of a cultural audit around diversity. Answering these questions requires organizational members to discover and examine their own assumptions about diversity and it provides an opportunity for the discussion and generation of a *shared agenda,* a set of goals that support the organization and therefore can be accepted by all employees. (When organizations have a narrowly defined motivation for addressing diversity—perhaps searching for a "quick fix" for a specific felt problem—they often omit this diagnostic stage altogether.)

The cultural audit not only requires answers

EXHIBIT 5 Programs and Practices Supporting Diversity Initiatives

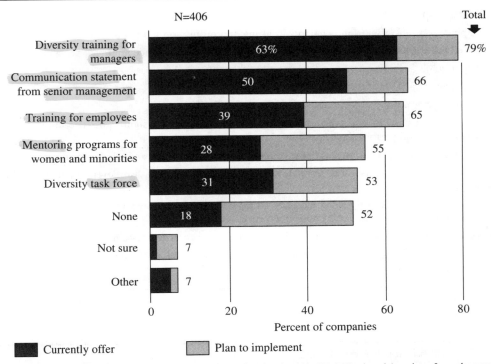

N=406

Total

	Currently offer	Plan to implement
Diversity training for managers	63%	79%
Communication statement from senior management	50	66
Training for employees	39	65
Mentoring programs for women and minorities	28	55
Diversity task force	31	53
None	18	52
Not sure		7
Other		7

Percent of companies

■ Currently offer ▢ Plan to implement

Source: Unpublished data from a 1991 survey of 406 U.S. corporations conducted by Louis Harris and Associates, Inc., who were commissioned by the Conference Board under a grant from the Commonwealth Fund, a private nonprofit foundation.

Source: *Work Force Diversity: Corporate Challenges, Corporate Responses,* Report No. 1013, by Mary J. Winterle, © 1992 by the Conference Board, Inc., New York, p. 21.

to questions about one's explicit mindset toward diversity, as revealed by the questions above, but also insight into the implicit values, assumptions, and norms for dealing with people and getting the work done in the organization, which support or hinder an inclusive environment. On the surface, many of these values, assumptions, and norms appear to have little or nothing to do with diversity. Taylor Cox describes these phenomena as "institutional bias," explaining that: "Institutional bias refers to the fact that preference patterns inherent in how we manage organizations often inadvertently create barriers to full participation by organization members from cultural backgrounds that differ from the tradi-

tional majority group."[39] Cox goes to discuss a suggestive, but not exhaustive, list of common behaviors that contribute to such bias. (See Exhibit 6.)

A cultural audit makes such norms and assumptions visible and uncovers their differential impact and potential for limiting some employees' contributions. Such an audit usually involves employee surveys and confidential interviews. Some sample questions are listed in Exhibit 7. While protecting confidentiality, it be-

39. Taylor Cox, Jr., *Cultural Diversity in Organizations: Theory, Research & Practice* (San Francisco, CA: Berrett-Koehler Publishers, Inc., 1993), p. 207.

EXHIBIT 6   Common Organizational Practices That Tend to Create Institutional Bias

1. The 50-hour-plus workweek and scheduling of weekend and evening meetings.
2. The emphasis on self-promotion behaviors in hiring and promotion interviews.
3. The use of self-evaluations/statements of accomplishment in performance appraisal processes.
4. A policy of maintaining separation of work and personal/family life.
5. The tendency toward standardization of all types.
6. The use of brainstorming as a common idea-generation device.
7. The use of verbal glibness and polished English in presentations as a significant criterion in promotion, job assignments, and performance appraisal.
8. The tendency toward institutional support of monolingualism in work and educational institutions.
9. An orientation in appraisal and reward systems favoring individualism over collective action and teamwork.
10. Reliance on interviews (mostly using majority-group interviewers and informal recommendations and referrals as prime tools in hiring and promotion processes.
11. The use of a payback period as a criterion in promotion decisions and retraining.
12. The tendency to define effective leadership in terms that reflect traits typical of the dominant group.
13. Physical workplaces that assume a fully able-bodied workforce.

Source: Taylor Cox, Jr., *Cultural Diversity in Organizations: Theory, Research & Practice* (San Francisco, CA: Berrett-Koehler Publishers, Inc., 1993), p. 209.

EXHIBIT 7   Cultural Profile Interview: Sample Questions

- What's valued in your organization? What's rewarded?
- What traits/behaviors are most often praised?
- What traits/behaviors are most often criticized?
- What are perceived as the greatest challenges/threats to the organization's success?
- What is taken for granted in your organization?
  (working conditions, abilities, attitudes, values, beliefs, style, etc.)
- Describe typical supervisor/supervisee relationships.
- Describe performance management efforts.
- How are promotion decisions made? What factors are considered? Whose input is considered?
- How is organizational information shared? With whom?
- How are business decisions made? Who is involved?
- How are conflicts expressed? (What kinds?)
- How are conflicts resolved?
- What's important to your organization's recruiters?
- Who does the recruiting/hiring?
- How are they trained/prepared to do so?
- How are new people oriented to the organization?

---

comes important to consider the characteristics of individuals expressing different views: for example, do differences in perceptions and reported experiences break down along race or gender or cultural lines, or by organizational function or level? At best, such an audit can be a powerful tool for organizational self-reflection and insight generation, laying the groundwork for designing effective diversity initiatives. At worst, its findings can fuel internal conflict, or simply be shelved and unaddressed. In order for these efforts to be effective, an organization needs to think through a series of preliminary questions:

- Who will be responsible for analyzing the audit's findings? Often an external consultant is used, to ensure greater objectivity.
- Who will have access to the findings? It is important to recognize that employees who participate in such a study will naturally be interested in the results. Expectations are raised by simply embarking upon the audit.
- Who will be responsible for considering what responses and action steps are called for? It is useful to include representatives of different points of view in such deliberations.
- Perhaps most importantly, is there real commitment on the part of organizational leaders to respond to the audit's findings?

2. Training

Training is one of the most frequently selected methods for responding to diversity in organizations, utilized in some form by 40 percent of U.S. companies according to *The New York Times.*[40] It is frequently designed and provided by outside consultants, sometimes working collaboratively with the firm to design customized programs and sometimes simply implementing "canned" seminars. There are many types of diversity training:

---

40. Heather MacDonald, "The Diversity Industry," *New Republic,* July 5, 1993, p. 23.

- **Introductions to diversity and its implications for business generally and one's own firm in particular.** Such training usually involves the presentation of some demographic statistics about a changing workforce and customer base; a brief overview of historical approaches to diversity in organizations, making distinctions between affirmative action and "valuing diversity;" some basic self-awareness building, using exercises to help individuals see the ways in which they may unconsciously harbor and act upon various stereotypes. The purpose of this type of program is to begin to develop a shared definition and vocabulary around diversity, to share the organization's rationale and goals, and to create a sense of positive interest in further individual training. In addition, this type of workshop can provide an initial forum for discussing diversity outside the firm in the customer environment, and not only among the organization's employees.

- **More in-depth and focused awareness development.** Such programs feature more individual and small group interactions pushing an understanding of the nature, functions, and prevalence of various stereotypes in the organizational setting. Sometimes such efforts will focus on race or gender or ethnicities in particular. The purpose of such programs is to expand individual understanding as a means to changing behavior in relation to other employees and those in the business environment.

- **Skill-building workshops.** Such programs teach specific skills, such as listening across differences, conflict resolution, interviewing, and mentoring—with an emphasis on the ways racial, gender, cultural, or other differences may affect these processes.

- **Targeted workshops for specific groups.** Such programs might target individuals in a minority in the organization for specific training; for example, some companies have developed training programs for their middle-management-level women to try to counteract perceived "glass ceiling" effects. This type of program can have negative effects if it is seen as indicating that members of the targeted group are less prepared than others to advance in the organization, or if it is perceived by nontargeted individuals as "extra or special" assistance. In some organizations these problems have been resolved when such targeted workshops have been developed *by* members of a particular group *for* members of that same group, as a function of a special support network, sometimes using firm resources.

It is also useful to recognize that the skills being communicated in such workshops are useful to all employees and may more effectively be offered in generally available programs that include references to differential impacts on individuals in a minority. For example, if an organization in an area with a large Hispanic population makes English-language training available to its employees, it may also choose to make Spanish-language training available, recognizing that bilingualism will be valuable to both native Spanish and native English speakers.

• **Workshops on sexual or other forms of harassment.** Such programs usually focus on communicating the legal definition of harassment and the organization's policies and practices for dealing with occurrences. Sometimes these efforts also involve discussions where conflicting feelings and concerns about the definition of harassment can be aired and discussed.

• **Integrated diversity training.** Such programs integrate the appropriate diversity issues into the course of preexisting and new training efforts that target specific functional skills or business goals. For example, in a customer-service training program, the particular opportunities and challenges of serving a diverse customer base would be introduced. Such integrated efforts have the benefit of continually linking diversity to the business activities and viability of the organization and of ensuring that the issues are raised often and in varying forums, making it more difficult to compartmentalize and dismiss them.

Questions To Consider

• **What is the purpose of the training? How will we know it has been successful? Are we looking for a change in specific behaviors (if so, which?) and/or the communication of specific information (if so, what?)?** It is useful to define the purposes of such training so as to focus upon the *various* relationships within the organization (employee/manager, employee/employee, manager/manager) and also relationships with those outside the firm (with customers, with vendors, with host communities and countries, etc.) This emphasizes the importance of this work for the survival and functioning of the organization.

• **Who will be trained, and in what sequence?** It is valuable to begin at the top of the organization and cascade training downward, thereby building and communicating commitment.

• **Who will provide the training?** If outside consultants are used, it is critical to screen them carefully. This field has been growing rapidly and reports of poor practices are numerous. If internal trainers are used, how will they be selected and trained? Skillful facilitation is critical in these efforts.

• **How long and frequent will training programs be?** Many participants in diversity training efforts complain that these issues are difficult and require more than a single afternoon to make any progress. Jeffrey A. Sonnenfeld and Catherine Ellis recommend sequenced ongoing programs, rather than one-shot interventions that often open painful issues up without providing closure, let alone learnings and skills for addressing them.[41]

• **How does training fit into a more comprehensive diversity agenda in the organization? And how will this agenda be communicated and have an impact upon individual employees?** A training pro-

---

41. Catherine Ellis and Jeffrey Sonnenfeld, "Diverse Approaches to Diversity," *Human Resource Management Journal* 33, no. 1 (Spring 1994), p. 100.

gram that stands alone and does not appear to have any actionable and measurable implications for an employee's daily experience will have limited impact.

• **How will the organization respond to employees who feel resentful or victimized in response to the training efforts?** Even with the best of plans, some individuals will experience these feelings and it is useful to provide opportunities for such individuals to express their concerns and know they are being taken seriously.

• **How will confidentiality be handled?** It is important to consider who will be present in a particular workshop and how a safe environment may be ensured. Depending upon the content and purpose of the program, it may or may not be appropriate to attend with one's own workgroup or with individuals who share reporting relationships with each other.

3. Recruiting/Hiring Initiatives

Organizations may identify the attraction and hiring of individuals from certain target groups as a priority for a variety of reasons, as discussed above (i.e., to comply with government regulations; to respond to internal pressures from employee groups; to expand and enhance the labor pool available for particular positions). Some of the methods used to achieve these goals include:

• **Expand recruiting sites.** The sites currently chosen for recruiting efforts usually represent traditional sources for the current mix of employees in a particular organization. In order to change that mix, an organization must think creatively about new sources. For example, to locate African-American candidates with certain degree backgrounds, it may be appropriate to consider recruiting at historically Black colleges or at schools with a larger percentage of African-American students than the usual recruiting sites.

• **Review job prerequisites.** Such an action is sometimes criticized as a lowering of standards, when it actually may be simply a revisiting of job prerequisites to determine which ones represent "bonafide occupational requirements" and which may be simply a matter of tradition or unexamined bias. For example, the preferred path to certain leadership positions may be perceived to be through a certain functional area. Often such a pattern develops because a particularly influential leader came from that area and so tends to promote those lower-level managers most known to him or her. Over time, it is assumed that a background in that area is necessary for senior leadership, whether true or not. In a similar way, certain degree requirements or industry background or specific job experience may be seen as a necessary prerequisite for certain positions, thus narrowing the candidate pool, especially when one is looking for "nontraditional" candidates.

• **Enhance the pipeline.** Organizations sometimes develop internship programs and scholarships as a means of attracting candidates to a particular field which may not have been previously seen as offering many opportunities. In particular, this method may be used by organizations or in fields which have a reputation for a homogeneous workforce or for an inhospitable climate for "nontraditional" employees (that is, "nontraditional" within that context).

• **Train organizational interviewers/recruiters.** As mentioned above, interviewers can be trained to be more self-aware of unconscious biases, stereotypes, communication patterns and interaction styles which can skew their assessments of candidates toward a traditional, but not necessarily required, recruit profile.

• **Develop, monitor, and evaluate performance on hiring goals.** Hiring goals or targets can be a very controversial topic in organizations, triggering fears and resentments about fairness and sometimes reinforcing stereotypes about candidate qualifications. Nevertheless, hiring plans are sometimes required by government regulation to demonstrate efforts to balance employee representation across various groups. And in some situations, organizations choose to set such targets because they want to prepare for anticipated changes in the labor pool or to create a more diverse, flexible, and open working environment for existing employees.

In addition, targets speak strongly of senior management intent and commitment, particularly if the goals are set in a thoughtful and realistic way, with input from affected hiring groups and based on a realistic assessment of existing and developable pools of qualified candidates. Opportunities to explain the rationale and to discuss concerns and objections for such a process are important. In particular, clarification of the commitment to rigorous qualifications and the difference between "quotas" and targets are in order. Finally, success in meeting these targets must be monitored and acknowledged. If the targets are unrealistic, unilaterally set, and carry no consequences, they can contribute to cynicism and end up triggering all the negative aspects of hiring goals with none of the positive.

The research on tokenism in organizations, particularly Rosabeth Moss Kanter's classic *Men and Women of the Corporation,* argues that relative numbers of employees from traditionally less represented identity groups are a significant factor in changing organizational dynamics and career experiences.[42] Similarly, David Thomas's research on mentoring suggests additional challenges present in mentoring across racial differences.[43] This type of research can be marshaled to support strong arguments for some sort of systematic and structural mechanisms to effect a change in the proportional representation of identity groups among employees.

• **Signal a hospitable, inclusive environment**

through benefits and employment policies, mission statements, and other visible means.

• **Finally, recruit and/or promote individuals from target groups into senior level positions within the organization—positions that carry hiring and promoting responsibility.** Often organizations focus on entry-level recruiting in their efforts to expand certain populations in the firm, but these attempts alone do not address the challenges of "glass ceilings," a scarcity of women and minority mentors and sponsors, and other institutional biases. In addition, the time needed from entry into the organization to promotion to middle- and senior-level management positions where these individuals can influence decision-making processes is often long. Efforts to locate senior managers, either from within or more often outside the organization, can pay faster and greater dividends.

4. Networks, Discussion Groups, and Task Forces

A variety of group initiatives have been used extensively in organizational diversity initiatives:

• **Networks and support groups.** As a means of counteracting some of the exclusionary experiences of being in a minority within an organization, formal and/or informal networks or support groups are sometimes developed (i.e., women employee networks, African-American employee networks, Hispanic employee networks, Asian-American employee networks, gay/lesbian employee networks). These groups are often created by their members, but occasionally an organization will encourage their formation by explicitly requesting that a manager do so, or by providing resources (for example, program funding) for those who do. Obviously the supportive organization needs to strike a balance between demonstrating support and openness to the groups' input on the one hand, and avoiding efforts to control or thwart their autonomy, on the other.

42. Rosabeth Moss Kanter, *Men and Women of the Corporation* (New York: Basic Books, Inc., 1977), p. 20.

43. David Thomas, "Mentoring and Irrationality: The Role of Racial Taboos," *Human Resource Management* 28, no. 2 (1989), pp. 279–290.

These groups can have a variety of functions. They can serve as a *social network,* bringing employees together who otherwise may not meet, counteracting feelings of isolation and powerlessness. They can also develop an *educational and self-development function,* as members identify shared interests and needs and decide to provide training support to each other. In addition, as research suggests that employees who are in a minority within an organization may be excluded from access to informal information networks, these groups can serve as a mechanism for members to pool and share their own information.[44]

They can serve to empower individuals as they begin to understand that some of their experiences are shared and may, in fact, derive from their minority status in the organization. At this point, networks sometimes begin to take on an *advisory and/or an advocacy function* as representatives seek to inform and recommend policy or behavior changes to the organization's leaders.

• **Advisory task forces.** As mentioned above, support groups and networks sometimes take on an advisory role. However, organizations often choose to create a formal task force to study and discuss all the interrelated implications, challenges, and opportunities of diversity within the firm, and to make recommendations to senior management. Membership of such task forces is usually intentionally selected to reflect the different forms of diversity represented in the organization, and as Taylor Cox points out, these groups are one of the only places where membership may follow "equality norms" rather than "proportionate norms" of representation (for example, although African-Americans may make up only 6 percent of the firm's employees, they may compose a third of the voices in the

group), thereby affecting the group's internal dynamics.[45]

Other important questions of task force membership include efforts to ensure that different functional areas are represented and that at least some members of the group are of sufficiently senior rank and that the group reports to senior levels within the organization, ensuring a serious hearing for their findings. Given the complex and sensitive nature of the issues such groups discuss, since their members often have had little or no contact with each other prior to the group's formation, and given that they come from varying positions of formal and informal power within the organization, it is important to attend to norms of communication and issues of group dynamics. If these groups can work out their differences, their members will serve as models for what the organization can and needs to achieve. If not, the outcomes are certain to be limited.

Finally, these groups have a critical task in determining what their working definition of diversity will be and how they will define and measure their success in affecting the organization's practice. Our earlier discussions of the benefits of defining diversity broadly and of assessing and evaluating an organization's diversity mindset are properly among such a group's first areas of focus. (Such a group is often the appropriate impetus for a cultural audit, as well.) Finally these groups need to develop mechanisms to communicate their findings and to extend their dialogue throughout the organization in an effort to minimize resistance and misunderstanding of any initiatives they recommend.

• **Discussion groups.** In the late 1970s, Digital Equipment Corporation, with Barbara Walker, developed a process for ongoing discussion among small groups of mixed gender, mixed race, mixed level employees. These are "core

---

44. Taylor Cox, Jr., *Cultural Diversity in Organizations: Theory, Research & Practice* (San Francisco, CA: Berrett-Koehler Publishers, Inc., 1993), pp. 196–198.

45. Ibid., pp. 178, 179.

groups" of "seven to nine employees who commit to coming together on a monthly basis to examine their stereotypes, test the differences in their assumptions, and build significant relationships with people they regard as different."[46] These groups provide organizational members with an opportunity that many of them do not have anywhere else: a chance to talk about difficult topics of difference with people who *are* different from themselves, and the assurance that the conversation will be ongoing, that they will have the chance to change their mind, to learn and to grow if they choose to do so. Such a situation is rare in life generally, and especially in organizational life.

This type of initiative reflects a diversity mindset that stresses the individual, but certainly is not limited to that emphasis. Digital, for example, couples their core groups with other initiatives, and individuals who participate in these groups are expected to apply their new understandings to the ways they manage and to the organizational policies and structures they create. Core groups also reflect a mindset that emphasizes learning, as it is posited on the assumption that contact with difference is enriching and will fuel productivity and innovation.

5. *Performance Development/Career Management*

Organizations may identify performance development and career management as a primary emphasis in their diversity initiatives for a number of reasons:

• Individuals in a minority in the organization may experience the negative consequences associated with token status, as mentioned above (isolation, lack of access to informal information networks, lack of mentors, lack of role

models, etc.), contributing to inadequate performance feedback and career guidance and resulting in a glass-ceiling effect, lowered productivity, and lowered morale;

• Conversely, if members of majority groups in the organization are uncomfortable with managers from less represented groups, they can cut themselves off from their own performance development.

There are a number of methods that organizations use to address these issues:

• **Improved performance appraisal systems.** Since the manifestations of discomfort, bias, prejudice and stereotypes are often invisible to those who act upon them, informal performance appraisal systems, based on a "good word" from a colleague one knows and is comfortable with, are often the carriers of inequitable career opportunities. Thus a variety of methods have been tried to counteract these tendencies. Performance feedback guidelines and performance development opportunities have been *formalized* and made *explicit,* ensuring that every employee knows they will receive formal feedback on key dimensions of their work at least a certain number of times per year. In some organizations, *multiple sources of feedback* are considered in making rating and promotion decisions, including feedback from subordinates, peers, and various superiors.

• **Employee development included as a managerial performance objective.** When a manager's track record in developing employees is evaluated as part of his or her own performance evaluation, the organization signals its commitment. In particular, some organizations monitor and consider the number of employees from less represented groups who are hired and promoted. As with all quantifiable measures, it is important that these evaluations do not become simply a numbers game. These measures must be carefully designed, with demonstrable performance development and qualification criteria, as well as

46. Barbara A. Walker and William C. Hanson, "Valuing Differences at Digital Equipment Corporation," in *Diversity in the Workplace: Human Resources Initiatives.* Susan E. Jackson and Associates (New York: The Guilford Press, 1992), p. 121.

a realistic time horizon for the promoted employee's success.

- **Career path assessment and monitoring.** Some organizations have set out to better understand the typical paths individuals take as they move up through management. What are the critical areas of knowledge, of exposure and visibility, the critical skills, the critical relationships needed for career growth? As they come to understand these factors, they can do two things: first, evaluate which of these implicit requirements is actually necessary, rather than simply the traditional or comfortable way of operating; and second, monitor the entry points and career paths of employees to understand if there are common obstacles or plateaus that some employees reach unnecessarily. For example, if there are fewer women candidates for positions which require a certain nontraditional degree for entry, and those positions are a typical path to middle and upper management, we can consider whether there may be other suitable degrees which might substitute as entry criteria, or whether there may not be other equally suitable paths into management.

- **Mentoring programs.** Through their internal research and audit process, some organizations note that women and/or other employees who are in a minority within the firm may find it more difficult than their majority peers to find mentors. As mentors are important to both performance feedback and career sponsorship, several methods have been used to address this issue. Some organizations have attempted to set up formal mentor assignments for new employees. In some cases these assignments are targeted to individuals in a minority within the firm, while in others they are set up for all new employees.

There are a variety of potential difficulties with such programs, such as the fact that mentoring relationships work best when they are entered voluntarily by both parties. In addition, assigned mentors may or may not have the interest or skills to function effectively in this role. Finally, targeted mentoring programs may trigger resentment among those employees not included. Researchers recommend that efforts to facilitate voluntary pairs are superior to forced assignments, and that relationships ought to be evaluated and possibly reassigned if they do not work out. Finally, training for both the mentors and the mentees on giving and receiving feedback, communication skills, and so forth is recommended.[47]

6. Working Conditions and Benefit Policies

As mentioned previously in the discussion of culture audits, there are implicit norms and assumptions that are reflected in the working conditions of an organization and which impact the way in which it views and responds to differences among its employees and its customers. (See Exhibit 6.) These impacts can be revealed through such an audit and through diversity networks and advisory task forces. A few of the many methods used to address such issues include:

- **Flexible work schedules.** In an effort to become a more hospitable working environment for employees with families and in two-career relationships, some organizations adopt strategies such as job sharing, telecommuting, flextime, part time, and so forth. In many cases, such strategies involve rethinking both the way work is structured, and also the way in which employees are evaluated. For example, if "face time" is an important implicit value in the organization, many of these approaches will not be effective.

- **Flexible benefits policies.** Providing choices within the benefits programs for employees to select their priorities implicitly recognizes the differences among workers' living situations. In addition, some organizations are beginning to offer spousal equivalent benefits for the partners

---

47. Taylor Cox, Jr., *Cultural Diversity in Organizations: Theory, Research & Practice* (San Francisco, CA: Berrett-Koehler Publishers, Inc., 1993), p. 205.

of unmarried heterosexual and gay/lesbian employees. Some organizations have also begun to develop resources and referral networks for employees with dependent care responsibilities.

7. External Programs

Some organizations become involved in efforts, often jointly sponsored with community or educational groups, designed to develop their potential labor pool or supplier pool. *Internship* *and scholarship programs* are targeted to individuals who typically would not have access to the education or experience required to be considered as an entry employee. *Technical assistance and start-up loans* are used to encourage the development of women and minority-owned supplier firms. Such programs are sometimes triggered by government requirements, or by a recognition of changing needs in the community which hosts the organization.

MEASURES

Obviously, what an organization chooses to measure sends strong signals about its commitments and exerts a shaping influence on how corporate initiatives are interpreted and how managerial efforts are allocated. Many of the methods described above are very difficult to evaluate in terms of immediate and/or tangible outcomes. For example, training programs often address attitudes and skills that are subtle and manifest themselves over time. For these reasons, diversity efforts are sometimes measured in terms of number and reach of interventions (for example, 12 training sessions of one day in length that reached 30 managers each), rather than in terms of behavior changes or productivity outcomes.

Although it is useful to monitor the number and reach of efforts, an absence of attention to other outcomes perceived as more closely linked to the actual business functions of the firm may fuel employee cynicism. On the other hand, if unrealistic expectations are set up, the same cynicism may result. It therefore becomes important to communicate to employees the goals of a diversity program, their timeframe, and the measures by which they will be monitored.

Examples of such measures are included below:

• Number of hires and promotions, retention rates, and managerial level distribution of employees by demographic group. Some of the advantages and challenges of setting target goals were discussed above, but once set, they must be monitored. Success or failure in meeting these goals must be noted and addressed. There may be extenuating circumstances, but without serious attention these targets become another cause for cynicism and disgruntlement.

• Individual performance on management objectives related to diversity, such as hiring and promotion records, employee ratings on feedback, mentoring relationships, and initiation of other diversity efforts. Measuring and rewarding (or not) performance on diversity criteria can ensure managerial attention and accountability.

• Number and level of managers involved in various diversity initiatives, such as training, advisory task forces, discussion groups, goal-setting, and so forth.

• Frequency and type of communication regarding the importance and role of diversity in the organization. Examples include insertion into mission statement or values statement, emphasis in internal and external speeches by the CEO and other leaders, emphasis in employee orientation programs, integration in other training programs, and so forth.

• Changes in policies, systems, structures (benefits, work flexibility guidelines, performance evaluation systems, etc.).

• Usage levels of programs and policy changes. How many employees take advantage of flexible schedules or new benefits? Are these numbers in line with expected interest, based on internal and external research? If not, are there structural or cultural factors that make the programs unattractive?

• Number of complaints, grievances, lawsuits, and their trend.

• Existence of networks, advisory and discussion groups, number of participants, frequency of meetings, type and extent of initiatives.

• Existence, usage, and impact of internship and scholarship programs.

• Existence, usage, and impact of supplier development programs.

• Number, scope, frequency, length, costs, and emphasis of training programs. Evaluation ratings of same programs at close of program and again some months later.

• Diversity of representation (along different criteria such as gender and race, as well as function and level) in various key committees and team projects.

• Changes and trends over time in culture audit surveys and interviews.

• Customer service evaluations with special attention to results by demographic group.

• Outside recognition, such as awards and mention in "10 best" lists.

• Scope of effort. Has it been rolled out throughout the entire organization (levels, division, regions, countries)?

• Productivity measures. There can be a lot of "noise" in such measures, and it is difficult to sort out what is related to diversity and what is not. It is useful to note and question any signifi-

---

EXHIBIT 8   Organizational Responses to Diversity

A Descriptive Framework

MOTIVATORS

• What motivates a company (or a unit of a company) to begin to recognize and address behaviors or trends that we would identify as diversity-related?
• More subtly, what are the *felt* motivators, and what are the *espoused* motivators?

MINDSET

• What are the philosophy and the assumed values revealed by the different choices companies make around how to approach diversity-related issues?
• What are the different implications of these choices?
• What works best in what context?
• How does a particular company/industry/national context influence the mindset adopted?

METHODS

• What are the range of methods and approaches that managers and firms utilize to address diversity-related issues, once motivated?
• Who is the source or driver of such efforts?
• What types of mechanisms have been tried and in what circumstances are they effective?

MEASURES

• What is the firm trying to achieve?
• What, if anything, is measured to assess the effectiveness of the methods used?
• How does a manager know if he or she is being successful?
• What are the implications of diversity initiatives that are designed without measures of effectiveness?

cant differences in reported experience and results between demographic groups. If absenteeism is significantly higher among women employees, for example, it would be useful to determine what may be influencing the situation. However, often the most interesting productivity changes related to diversity are embedded in qualitative and anecdotal data (i.e., the manager who reports greater creativity the more all employees are empowered to contribute). Thus it becomes important to gather and attend to such data, even though it is hard to quantify. It may point the way to questions that ought to be asked in a more systematic fashion on future surveys, or contributing factors that *can* be quantified.

* * * * *

The preceding has been a general overview of some of the most common motives, mindsets, methods, and measures adopted by organizations in response to the diversity in the workforce and the marketplace. Some of the most significant questions to be asked and guidelines to consider have been noted. Although the issues and examples raised are not exhaustive, they provide a sense of the range and scope of options and considerations facing today's organization.

ACCOUNTANTS AND BUSINESS ADVISORS, INC., CITY OFFICE

It was the summer of 1989, and William Shaughnessy, office managing partner in the City Office of the large public accounting firm of Accountants and Business Advisors, Inc. (ABA) was frustrated with the report he had just received from his director of human resources. For many years, more than half of the entry-level professional audit staff in the firm's City Office had been female. However, although turnover was high in the business generally, attrition of women continued to exceed that of men. In the late 1980s the office had instituted a variety of part-time work schedules, arranged on a case-by-case basis. Shaughnessy, committed to taking all reasonable steps to accommodate his staff's family obligations, ensured that staff requests for changes in work schedules received swift and careful consideration. But despite these initiatives, the retaining of women remained problematic, particularly with respect to keeping them in the firm long enough to be eligible for promotion to partner. Shaughnessy wondered what else he could do.

The Business

ABA, a large public accounting firm with offices and affiliates around the world, had 1990 worldwide and domestic revenues in excess of $4.1 billion and $1.4 billion, respectively. ABA's three main services—audit, tax, and various consulting services—accounted for 60 percent, 20 percent, and 20 percent, respectively, of 1990 domestic revenues.

The audit practice rendered opinions on the financial statements of, and served as business advisers to, companies, not-for-profit organizations, and state and local governments. Opinions were rendered on the basis of audit procedures designed to inform on the fair presentation of financial results and to provide analysis of business systems, organization, and some particular transactions. Such audit procedures ensured that the accounting was consistent with professional standards, such as the "Generally Ac-

This case was prepared by Gary Loveman.

Copyright © 1990 by the President and Fellows of Harvard College.

Harvard Business School case 490-033 (Rev. March 2, 1994).

cepted Accounting Principles," promulgated by professional organizations and regulators.

The tax practice provided tax advice, worked with auditors to determine the tax liability, and prepared tax returns for its business clients and personal returns for their senior management. Finally, the consulting practice provided a wide range of technical and management consulting services, which were frequently integrated within an overall client service strategy.

Most large metropolitan offices had all three practices. Audit and tax reported to the office managing partner (OMP), who had considerable discretion in managing the office, within nationwide parameters. For example, the OMP had almost complete authority over hiring, dismissals, compensation, acquisition of office space, and many other operational issues, and was responsible for the office's bottom-line performance. Audit and accounting procedures were established at the firm level. The consulting practice rented space from the OMP and had a separate reporting structure.

The nature of the auditing business changed in the 1980s, as public accounting firms moved from providing particular audit services to serving as general business advisers. In this new and broader capacity, they sought to leverage a more thorough understanding of the client's business to improve their audit's quality and reliability. Furthermore, the beginning of vigorous competition among the Big Eight in the 1970s meant that when client service was unsatisfactory, clients would seek a new auditor. Previously, clients rarely had changed auditors, and professional ethics had prevented active competition for clients. The pressure for auditors to meet professional standards for quality also increased as a consequence of the remarkable rise in lawsuits against public accounting firms. Rare in the 1960s, lawsuits arising from client failures and financial irregularities became common for Big Eight firms in the 1980s.

Finally, the audit business at ABA became increasingly seasonal: billable hours in the months of January, February, and March as much as doubled those of the other nine months. Clients' demands for timely service in these months created severe scheduling problems requiring auditors to work very long hours.

Career Path at ABA

Like all major accounting firms, ABA was a partnership, albeit a very large one. In 1990 the partnership exceeded 4,000 worldwide, and more than 1,300 in the United States. ABA had four professional job titles: associate, senior associate, manager, and partner (see Exhibit 1). Each audit had an engagement team, typically composed of at least one person at each of the four levels, that conducted the audit and client-relation activities. Associates performed the basic audit procedures, usually at the client's offices, under the immediate supervision of the senior associate. They tested transactions, documented systems, and identified anomalies in the client's financial records and systems. Promotion to senior associate typically occurred after two or three years. The senior associate, in charge of the engagement team at the audit site, analyzed the risks in each client environment and developed approaches to test for and analyze manifestations of these risks. The senior associate also performed more complex audit procedures, evaluated the staff, and served as the liaison between the client staff and the audit manager. Senior associates who had passed the CPA exam soon satisfied the public accounting experience requirements for certification. Once certified, they were more marketable in private industry, and many who did not wish to remain in public accounting would quit at this point.

EXHIBIT 1   Career Path at ABA, Inc.

Job Title	Average Number of Years in Job
Associate	2–3
Senior associate	2–3
Manager	1.5–2
Partner	

The level of manager was attained normally in the fifth year. Managers had overall responsibility for an engagement, which included planning, budgeting, staffing, and staff evaluation, issuing reports to clients and regulators, resolving high-level accounting issues, coordinating the engagement with senior client staff, and billing. The manager was the central operational figure in the conduct of audits. The year or two before consideration for promotion to partner was exceedingly demanding; an experienced manager was expected to perform more complex tasks, and a significant failure in any one of them could delay promotion.

Promotion to the partnership generally occurred after at least eight years. Partners had ultimate engagement responsibility, and only they could sign the firm's name to opinions and other official records. They met with senior client staff to resolve outstanding accounting issues, determined fees, offered general business advice, and worked with audit managers to plan and review the audit work. Much of their time was spent with client senior management to understand the client's business issues and evaluate its decision making. Significant time was spent also on practice development, which included a panoply of outside activities to attract new business, and administrative and technical duties internal to the firm.

New partners had to make a capital investment in the firm to obtain ownership shares; they could also acquire additional shares as their career progressed. Their compensation was a function of the number of ownership shares, which were repurchased by the firm when a partner left or retired. Most new partners were under 40 years of age, and they retired at about age 62.

Performance Evaluation and Compensation

Across all levels of the firm, work was organized by client engagement, with everyone working on several clients throughout the year. Because managers and partners dealt with many clients concurrently, each employee had several bosses, each of whom was concerned primarily with performance on a particular engagement. Formal performance evaluations were given for each client engagement, and all those below the partner level had a file of performance evaluations prepared by many different people. Managers, partners, and Human Resource staff reviewed the evaluations and made promotion decisions; and partners and Human Resource staff decided compensation.

Benefits at ABA were similar to those offered at other large professional services firms. Maternity leave was eight weeks, and unpaid leave could, on request, be much longer. Although no explicit flexible work policy existed, City Office made a variety of arrangements with managers and those below on a case-by-case basis; for example, some managers only taught internal classes or worked on one client, whereas others worked only during the busy season. These arrangements often slowed career progression until the individual returned to a full-time schedule.

Gender Composition

The gender composition of professionals in public accounting varied with position in the job hierarchy. The supply of college graduates with accounting degrees shifted significantly, in relative terms, toward women in the years 1978 to 1989 (see Exhibit 2). Likewise, the hiring patterns of public accounting firms experienced a similar shift (see Exhibit 3). In City Office, at least 50 percent of new staff accountants had been female since the early 1980s (see Exhibit 4).

However, female partners were much more scarce. In 1991, only 6.2 percent of ABA's domestic partnership was female, and in City Office only 5 of 48 audit partners were female. The trend, however, was up, as 13 percent of 1991's new partners in the United States and one of the four new audit partners at City Office were women. Attrition was very high overall, but varied by gender (see Exhibits 5 and 6). Female attrition was about equal to that for males in the first five years of tenure, but was higher in subsequent years.

EXHIBIT 2 Accounting Graduates by Gender: 1978–1989

Year	Percent Male	Percent Female
1978–1979	66%	34%
1982–1983	60	40
1988–1989	49	51

Source: American Institute of Certified Public Accountants.

EXHIBIT 3 Public Accounting Firm's Demand for Accounting Graduates, by Gender: 1978–1989

Year	Percent Male	Percent Female
1978–1979	69%	31%
1982–1983	66	34
1988–1989	53	47

Source: American Institute of Certified Public Accountants.

EXHIBIT 4 Recruiting Trends at City Office: 1981–1989

Year	Number of Entry-Level Hires	Percent Females of Total Hires
1981	95	45%
1982	83	48
1983	79	52
1984	82	52
1985	97	50
1986	105	54
1987	120	56
1988	126	56
1989	114	56

EXHIBIT 5 Attrition at City Office: 1981–1989

Year	Number of Hires	Percent Remaining in 1989	Females as Percent Remaining in 1989
1981	95	11%	10%
1982	83	6	40
1983	79	11	0
1984	82	1	46
1985	97	33	50
1986	105	63	52
1987	120	73	57
1988	126	94	58
1989	114		

EXHIBIT 6 Female Staffing by Practice in City Office: 1989

Practice	Percent of Total Staff	Percent of Managers
Audit	51%	29%
Tax	46	32
Consulting	32	14

To further his understanding of the issues, Shaughnessy had the human resource director interview each of the four female audit partners in City Office (the fifth female partner had not been promoted at the time of the interviews). The four partners were asked to describe their experiences in the firm and to discuss their views on the problem of retaining women. Synopses of the four interviews follow.

Susan Robinson

Susan Robinson joined the partnership in 1988, at the age of 33, after eight years with the firm. She received a B.A. in Accountancy in 1977 and, after three years as a computer programmer with an insurance company and successful completion of the CPA exam, joined the firm as a senior. Susan's progression through the ranks followed the normal pattern: 18 months as senior, 18 months as supervisor, and five years as manager. She was promoted to manager in 1983 while on a six-week maternity leave with her first child. After her second child was born in 1985, she took leave for eight weeks. In 1988 Susan was the first female candidate for promotion to partner in the audit practice in four years.

Susan married during college, and her husband, Bill, was an insurance underwriter. She said,

Together with day care providers and occasional help from our families, we have maintained a very delicate balance that has allowed me to make partner while raising two small children. To make this all work, I've had to prevent my work from becoming all-consuming. I limit myself to a 45- to 50-hour week by being exceedingly well organized and striving to get the most out of both my time at work and my time with the family. Bill works a predictable 40-hour week, and he generally handles the problems caused by the time demands of my job: sick kids, day care problems, and the like. He has made career sacrifices to support my career and to maintain the day care arrangements we want for our children.

Susan emphasized just how delicate the balance was: It could be thrown off by a wide variety of factors. In 1989, after several years of the same day care provider, Susan had trouble finding stable, high-quality day care and had to change providers three times in two years. She said, "I feel guilty about the problems the recent day care changes have caused the children. I guess the other sacrifices caused by this lifestyle have been my husband's career progression and the stress from packing so much work and family into each day."

Susan never felt that her position here was vital to her identity, and she did not devote much time to worrying about the inherent competition for promotion. Though concerned that many of the senior partners' main female influences were their wives, who did not work outside the home, she did not believe that gender impacts work and promotion in City Office up through the partner level. She believed the higher attrition rate for women to be the result of lifestyle decisions, arguing,

> Female managers are at prime child-bearing age, and many do not think the very demanding and unpredictable time commitments of the job are consistent with motherhood. Competent candidates for partner make it. The problem is that there are often no female candidates.

However, all the senior partners who managed the firm were male, and Susan feared that gender could be an issue at this level.

Susan did feel that increasing women's participation in the partnership was an important business problem, particularly in the long term, as demographics favored hiring more women, and a greater portion of clients' senior staff were women. She believed management had trouble knowing what to do about retaining women because the firm had not spent much time critically evaluating engagement management. "If we had done so," she thought, "we would have found better ways to organize the work, thereby reducing the length and unpredictability of working hours and making the job more attractive to women with children." Even without changing the way the work was organized, Susan felt that the gradual increase in female partners and managers, and male partners and managers with working wives, would change work habits in ways that would make the job more compatible with dual-career family life.

Cynthia Noonan

Cynthia Noonan received her M.B.A. from a prestigious university in 1976. Thinking that she would join a Big Eight firm for a broad exposure to business, she joined City Office as a staff accountant. Cynthia progressed quickly through the ranks, spending the minimum time at each level, and was made a partner in 1984, at the age of 35. As a partner, she spent the vast majority of her time on audit engagements and relations with existing clients and roughly 10 percent on practice development.

Cynthia, who was single, did not feel she had encountered any gender bias in her career here, and did not think such a problem existed in the office (with rare exceptions on the part of a few people). She said,

> I think the lack of bias here results from the leadership of our office. Over the years, the OMPs have been dedicated to equal treatment for women, and they expect the same from everyone in the firm. There have been a few clients who do not want women in the senior positions of the audit engagement team, but it hasn't caused me any problems.

Cynthia felt very comfortable with the networking and client relations component of her job. She often invited clients to sports or other social events, but suspected that they were activities her female peers sometimes found difficult. Although there was not yet much data upon which to judge, Cynthia did not believe that promotion into the senior partner positions (i.e., management) would be affected by gender.

Believing the long and unpredictable hours for managers and partners to be due to the firm's emphasis on client service, Cynthia described the job as flexible part of the time and completely inflexible at other times. She noted,

> When a client needs service—for example, for a public offering of securities—I work whatever hours are necessary to meet the client's deadlines. But most weeks there are no such crises, and work hours are more flexible.

Overall, Cynthia worked an average of 45 to 50 hours from April to December and from 60 to 65 hours during the "busy season" of January to March. Special projects tended to occur outside of the busy season, and they required short periods of long hours.

Cynthia felt that retaining women was an important business problem facing the firm.

> Since more than half of our new hires are women, we will have long-run staffing problems if we fail to keep many of them. Our problem is the loss of women who do not wish to raise children while working as a manager or partner. Because managers and partners have to work into the evening or on the weekends, traditional day care is inadequate: live-in help or some other flexible situation is required. No one can cover for the partner; therefore, this sort of flexibility is critical to the job.

Cynthia did not see an easy solution to the retention problem. She thought flexible work schedules were a failure as a general solution.

> The drawback is that for important and challenging clients, managers and partners must be able to work when called upon to do so, and the part-

time workers simply can't be counted on when the need arises. Consequently, part-time managers wind up working on "second tier" clients, such as not-for-profits or small, private companies, which do not make such unpredictable demands on our time. I also don't think that ideas such as "two-tier" partnerships will be successful, since it will be difficult to find people to accept the lower tier. But we need some new ideas, because as we increasingly become business advisers with extensive interaction with the client, and as firms continue to move their year-ends to December 31, the problem of retaining women will get only worse.

Theresa Stevens

Theresa Stevens spent two years with an investment firm after college and returned to school to earn an M.B.A. from a prestigious East Coast university. She joined City Office in 1980, looking for broad professional training and exposure to business practice. Theresa was admitted to the partnership on October 1, 1989, in her ninth year with the firm, at the age of 34.

Theresa progressed relatively quickly through her career path.

> As I began each new level, I worried to some extent that gender may be an issue in the conduct of my new job. However, I subsequently found at each level that any anxiety was largely unnecessary. In fact, I think my clients had respect for women who had persevered up through the partner ranks. Therefore, gender was not a serious obstacle to me.

At the manager level and above, she found that nearly all of her client contacts, who were senior managers, were male; it was not uncommon for her to be the only woman at business meetings. Nonetheless, Theresa did not view being female as an obstacle to progression in the firm, because it could be overcome by quality client service and hard work. As a partner, she did not think her role in a management position generally would be affected by gender.

A self-described "recreational worker," Theresa worked very hard during her career there. She estimated having averaged 60 hours per week during the off-season, and slightly more during busy season. Through the supervisor ranks, she was often near the top of the overtime list in the office, due at least in part to her work on several very large engagements. Theresa believed there was some correlation, at levels below partner, between hours worked and success, as good performance brought greater responsibilities and more work.

Theresa married another member of the audit practice in 1985, and her husband made partner in 1987. She had her first child in 1986, while in her second year as a manager. She worked up to the time of the birth, worked sporadically during a four-week leave thereafter, and then returned full time. Her second child was born early in 1989, near the day that she was notified of her selection by the office as a candidate for admittance to the partnership. In the period before promotion to partner, which included her second pregnancy, Theresa felt pressure to work very hard and prove herself worthy of promotion. Whereas other women with children had shifted to part-time positions, thereby slowing their progression to partner, Theresa preferred to stay on full time.

After their first child was born, Theresa and her husband hired an au pair, who is still with them. The au pair is generally available to work whatever hours are necessary to care for the children when the parents are working. Theresa said,

> This has been a very successful arrangement. My oldest child has benefited from having the positive influence of three "parents" and seems to be very happy. I do regret not having as much time as I would like with my family, and I find it very challenging to fit all that needs to be done into each day. Fortunately, my husband is very sensitive to the demands of my job and has provided tremendous emotional support all along the way in my career.

Theresa viewed the loss of women at later stages in their career paths as an important business problem for the firm, but she was pleased with the steps management had taken to address it. She commented,

> The firm has made investments in the people who have made it to manager, and clients value ongoing relations with the same audit staff. So, the loss of women, who account for more than half the new hires, is costly. The problem results from women choosing to have children and not wishing to devote the long hours that the manager and partner jobs require. I think the part-time arrangements offered by the firm are a great idea, and I mention them in my recruiting work with prospective women hires. The firm is also beginning to offer some administrative help in locating nannies.

Theresa felt that these were the most important steps necessary to improve the number of women staying on through manager to become candidates for partner.

Allison Harding

When interviewing with Big Eight firms in 1971, Allison Harding found that some of them were not hiring women for professional positions. She recalled,

> At that time, the public accounting profession was just beginning to introduce women into the business, and progress was uneven.

Allison joined a midwestern office of ABA and spent five years there before leaving to work as a controller for a client organization. She spent three years out of public accounting, during which time she married a Methodist minister. In 1978 she moved to another large city and interviewed again with Big Eight firms. She found that, although the profession had clearly made large gains in its assimilation of women, ABA was the only office that had a significant number of female managers. She rejoined the firm as a supervisor and, after only three years as a manager, was made a partner in 1982, at the age of 33. After specializing in the firm's health care practice, Allison became its regional director.

On the role of gender in her career, Allison said,

I have not experienced any gender-related differential treatment since returning to the firm in 1978, and I do not foresee problems ahead for women partners wishing to move into management. I credit the office's management with setting a tone that supports equal treatment for all. The management's promotion of equal opportunity has not been manifested in edicts or overt actions, but rather has consisted of taking personal interest in the career progression of the women staff, assigning them to important engagements, and, at the entry level, selecting those capable of making it some day to partner. Moreover, the partners in the office are quite diverse, and it is not necessary to fit any particular mold to be successful. In my specialty, health care, the client senior management is predominantly male, but the individuals tend to be strong proponents of the advancement of women.

Allison described herself as a compulsive worker. Her husband was very understanding of the demands of her job; in fact, the couple had an understanding all along that careers came first in terms of time commitment. He had children—and some grandchildren—by a previous marriage, but the two decided some time ago not to have additional children. They engaged live-in help to handle the cooking and housekeeping chores; Allison reported not having cooked a meal in 11 years of marriage.

When asked about her lifestyle, Allison replied,

I do not think my lifestyle has involved personal sacrifices. Instead, it has involved making careful choices and planning to carry them out. I have enjoyed tremendous rewards from my career, including stimulation, satisfaction, accomplishment, and financial rewards. I think career women, irrespective of their choices, must be very intentional in their planning. Women pursuing demanding careers need a support network, which in my case is mainly my husband, but for women with children includes flexible child care.

The retention of women was, in Allison's opinion, an important business issue for the firm. As she expressed it,

Females now account for the majority of accounting graduates, turnover is costly, and the firm is already short of more senior staff. The problem is that the firm hires high-quality women, but loses many within a few years because they choose other careers, including motherhood.

An advocate of the part-time arrangements the firm had structured with particular women, Allison believed that making available such positions, which slow, but do not stop, career progression was an important initiative in the firm to reduce the attrition of high-quality female staff. Overall, Allison thought that the office, and the firm, were among the most progressive in the public accounting profession in addressing the problem of retaining women.

KURT LANDGRAF AND DU PONT MERCK PHARMACEUTICAL COMPANY (A)

In the first week of December 1993 just after taking over as president and CEO of Du Pont Merck Pharmaceutical Company, Kurt Land-

graf read a "troubling" letter and several electronic mail messages from African-American scientists in the Research and Development division.

The scientists charged that their division dis-

This case was prepared by Sarah B. Gant under the supervision of Mary C. Gentile.

Copyright © 1994 by the President and Fellows of Harvard College.

Harvard Business School case 394-202 (Rev. March 13, 1995).

criminated against African-Americans; they
were not hired, developed, or promoted at the
same rate as their Caucasian colleagues. They
described workdays punctuated by overt racism
and equally demoralizing indifference. One
Ph.D. had been without a lab assistant for more
than a year. He said his work suffered in comparison with white colleagues of equal and less
seniority who had such help. Some of the E-mail
was strident; the authors of the less angry E-mail
sounded worn out by as many as 14 years of employment in an environment which they said did
not value their contributions to it.

Landgraf had known his first several months
on the job would be difficult. He would begin
his tenure by downsizing his workforce by 15
percent. As Landgraf reviewed the letter and
E-mail, downsizing anxiety around headquarters in Wilmington, Delaware, was palpable.
Landgraf was known as a tough boss; one of his
most quoted slogans was "Performance—No
Excuses." He was also known for his unswerving
commitment to a workplace that valued all employees who performed, regardless of their race,
gender, ethnicity, or religion.

In the messages, several scientists from R&D,
calling themselves the African-American Core
Team, requested time with Landgraf to outline
their concerns. Given the impending layoffs,
they wanted an early hearing. They believed that
years of subtle racism had impacted annual
review processes and that African-Americans
would be among the first employees to receive
termination notices. They had been in dialogue
with the executive vice president of Research
and Development, Dr. David Martin, and with
Landgraf's predecessor, Dr. Joseph Mollica, for
several months regarding issues of discrimination.

One of them had even taken steps to start legal action against Du Pont Merck with the Civil
Rights division of the U.S. Justice Department
and with the Equal Employment Opportunity
Commission (EEOC). News of his actions
spread, and enough African-American employ-

ees were interested in pursuing a suit to make
class-action proceedings possible. Now that
Mollica had retired and Martin, in an unrelated
move, had resigned two weeks after him for a
position with another company, the Core Team
turned to Landgraf.

The situation was similar to one Landgraf had
faced in 1988 when he took over as director of
the Worldwide Pharmaceuticals and Imaging
Agents Division at Du Pont. According to
Landgraf, his division then had just completed
a period of rapid expansion and "overhiring,"
was still feeling the impacts of a difficult merger
with American Critical Care, and was torn by
accusations of promotional and pay discrimination, particularly against women. Landgraf describes that time as "a manager's nightmare, in-
heriting someone else's garbage."

As he turned from his computer monitor,
Landgraf weighed how best to address the twin
imperatives before him: to resolve the equity issues inherent in the allegations of racial discrimination and the possibility of a costly, time-
consuming, and damaging lawsuit, and to meet
the increased financial demands placed on his
company, a joint venture between Du Pont and
Merck, despite downsizing, reorganization, and
a rapidly changing business climate within the
pharmaceutical industry. Increasing the output
of Du Pont Merck's R&D drug pipeline was critical to the financial success of the venture. How
would addressing or ignoring the concerns of
the African-American scientists in R&D at this
particular juncture impact pharmaceutical development?

Kurt Landgraf at Du Pont

Kurt Landgraf had moved through a variety of
sales and marketing positions at Johnson &
Johnson and Upjohn before joining Du Pont in
1980. In the early 1980s Du Pont struck him "as
a typical, big U.S. company—conservative, prej-
udiced, and closed. I felt that this kind of environment didn't contribute to tapping people's

energies and contributing to the company's growth."

From 1983 through 1986, he headed Du Pont's pharmaceutical operations in Europe. In his three years abroad, he turned around an operation that had overexpanded and that was torn by internal, nationalistic bickering. Landgraf's European experience opened his eyes to the ways that distrust of "the other" can undermine teamwork and business success; his successful management of the situation also suggested the "effectiveness of a diverse team that worked well together."

Landgraf returned from Europe to spend a year as the planning manager of Du Pont's Corporate Plans Department. There he focused on his company's long-range, strategic vision. In 1988 he was named director of Pharmaceuticals and Imaging, and in 1991 his division was wholly absorbed into the Du Pont Merck joint venture. It was renamed Worldwide Pharmaceuticals and Landgraf oversaw everything in the new organization except research and development. Landgraf was not a Ph.D.-level scientist but, according to him, "senior managers who are trained in the social sciences are far better managers than those with technical, hard science, or engineering degrees," particularly since "there is no right answer to lots of questions."

Du Pont's chief adviser on advanced technology seemed to agree when he noted, soon before Landgraf was named president and CEO of Du Pont Merck, that "the best candidates to minimize risk in new ventures were not necessarily outstanding scientists but practical problem-solvers and team players. In general, personnel with multidisciplinary skills do better than specialists."[1] Landgraf had graduate degrees in economics, business administration, and sociology. Of them, he thought sociology best prepared him to lead a business.

---

1. Ashok K. Gupta and Arvind Singhal, "Managing Human Resources for Innovation and Creativity," *Research Technology Management*, May–June 1993, p. 42.

Diversity in Du Pont's Pharmaceutical Division

According to Landgraf the pharmaceutical division was a $50 million business when he took it over in 1988; it had grown tenfold by 1991. One reason for its success, he says, was his management by "establishing a vision of where you want the organization to be, and a set of principles that can act as guidelines." Landgraf, who grew up in an orphanage, saw the Catholic church as a good example of how such a vision could work. The establishment of the vision was top-down and implementation bottom-up. Once a culture was established, he believed, "you don't need to control people through rules." Overcontrolling behavior, he thought, "leads to real failure." By 1991 his philosophy was codified as the "Du Pont Merck Corporate Behavioral Guidelines" (see Exhibit 1). But, Landgraf's "covenant," as many people called the guidelines, were well-known by many within his division, from senior managers to packers, years before they were formally written down and presented to the organization.

Landgraf's vision, as well as his behavioral guidelines and management skills, were challenged when he was presented with the cultural "powder keg" of Du Pont's pharmaceutical division in 1988. Two years before, Du Pont had

---

EXHIBIT 1   Du Pont Merck Behavioral Guidelines

DMPC Corporate Behavioral Guidelines   *negativity*

- Performance—No Excuses
- Open—Honest—Direct
- Not a Prison Camp
- No Arrogance—Interpersonal Skills
- Caring (Loving) Management
- Equitable Hiring—Promotional Treatment
- Recognition/Holistic Life
- Respect for Local/Geographic Custom
- Teamwork
- Everyone Gets Special Treatment

Source: Du Pont Merck Pharmaceutical Company.

acquired American Critical Care. It was, according to Landgraf, "the most poorly handled acquisition in the history of mankind." Du Pont's pharmaceutical operation and American Critical Care were "two warring factions . . . they couldn't stand each other."

The situation reached a crisis point on October 3, 1988, when Landgraf received a letter written to David Mooberry, the group vice president to whom he reported. In the pervasive atmosphere of dissatisfaction at Du Pont Pharmaceuticals at the time, long overlooked issues of discrimination and harassment were now being articulated. The unsigned letter from "women and minority representatives" at Du Pont Pharmaceuticals outlined perceived discrimination within the organization, particularly related to promotional opportunities for women, and warned that "a class-action suit would give some protection."[2]

 Landgraf asked Mary Ann Kummert, the highest ranking woman in his division, to head a task force to investigate the charges in the letter. Kummert, regional sales director for the Northeast, came to Du Pont through the American Critical Care acquisition. Even though she "didn't share feelings of being put upon" with the letter's authors, she understood that its charges "really disturbed" Landgraf. He gave her until March 1, 1989, to come up with recommendations and promised to implement "everything within reason."

The task force included 10 people: 5 Caucasian women, 1 African-American woman, 2 African-American men, and 2 Caucasian men. Kummert "wanted [the white men] to be a part of the party . . . so they could tell us what they were thinking." She could not find a consultant to develop strategies that "came from the heart of the organization," so she took the task force off-site and worked to identify issues related to gender and race that stood in the way of fulfilling the business goals of the division. In the course of this work, the task force also unearthed significant pay inequities. Over a period of years, several individuals had received promotions that raised their titles and increased their responsibilities, but, because Du Pont had a policy which limited the number of pay grades that one could move up at any one time, some individuals who had the same titles and similar responsibilities received less pay for their work.

After several weeks of research and refinement, the task force reported its recommendations to Landgraf. He immediately began to implement the strategies that the report outlined. He brought salaries for similar job functions up to parity, imposed strict guidelines on overt forms of harassment, mandated sensitivity trainings, and institutionalized the diversity task force.

On a single day Landgraf signed 188 pay changes to bring all individuals who share job functions up to the same grade level and into the same pay scale. According to Landgraf, the majority of women in the division were "paid less for the same work." Some individuals received as much as $2,000 dollars more each month after the increase. According to Kummert, the move impacted the salaries of more men than women because there were, at that time, a greater percentage of men within the organization (see Exhibit 2).

Discriminatory jokes and other forms of harassment were no longer tolerated. The company spent $250,000 on mandatory "sensitivity training" workshops to get the message out, and company literature and videos promoted Landgraf's behavioral rules. It was not until one senior manager was fired and another demoted for breaching the rules, however, that "harassment stopped," according to Landgraf.

Landgraf institutionalized the Diversity Task Force and appointed a full-time "consultant on diversity"—Kirson Herbert, an African-American male with more than 20 years experience in various positions and managerial assignments at Du Pont and a member of Kummert's original team. The Task Force would meet at

---

2. Letter to David Mooberry from "Women and Minority Representatives in DP," October 3, 1988.

EXHIBIT 2 Race and Gender Breakdown of U.S. Sales and Marketing Personnel at Du Pont's Pharmaceuticals Division in 1988

Grade Level	Percent White Men	Percent White Women	Percent Minority Men	Percent Minority Women
5A+	90%	5%	5%	–
5	84	16	–	–
4A	83	11	6	–
4	60	30	7	3%
3A	53	32	6	9
3	49	41	8	2
2–2A	46	54	–	–
Total all levels:	66%	27%	5%	2%

Sources: Du Pont.

least three times a year, serve to keep diversity issues constantly before Landgraf's division at all levels, and seek solutions to crises before they occurred. Herbert understood his task to be threefold. He was to "level the playing field, create awareness regarding cultural sensitivity, and create systems of accountability." The third piece, he felt, was especially critical. There needed to be "financial disincentives to not performing."

Kummert's task force recommended that the Diversity Task Force be a Du Pont-wide effort. The reactions, however, of other Du Pont executives to Landgraf's work on gender and race issues ranged from non-support to non-interference so long as his division performed. Although no division head replicated the pharmaceutical division's Diversity Task Force *per se,* some instituted modified versions of its recommendations, such as a 360 degree evaluation system.

One of the early recommendations of Herbert's task force, the "360 degree" evaluation, was an annual review supported by recommendations from both above and below. Its goal was to make reviews more objective through diverse input into a person's performance, team work, commitment to diversity, etc. The objective of the new review process also was to provide more

complete feedback on managers. Herbert's task force also "recommended hiring goals to mirror the demographics of the U.S. population," 50 percent women and 25 percent minority. Those managers who did not meet their goals or failed to actively promote a diverse workforce found their salaries and promotional opportunities impacted. "You only get what you measure," according to Herbert.

Jerry Gaylord, who oversaw Du Pont's pharmaceutical salesforce, saw divisionwide change between 1988 and 1989 when 150 new hires, about 60 percent of whom were women (up from the previous female hire rate of about 30 percent), joined his existing 300 domestic sales representatives. Gaylord believed that changes in the general hiring pool would have changed the gender mix of his salesforce even without Landgraf's policy initiatives and hiring goals. More women, and more highly qualified women, were applying to Du Pont for sales positions. Gaylord believed, however, that minority candidates were more difficult to find and that without hiring goals for them, they would not have been brought into the salesforce quickly.

According to Gaylord, the salesforce became notably more female, younger, and included far more ethnic and racial minorities over the two-year period. Gaylord's goal was to develop "a population mixture to match that of our customers." Physicians were not exclusively white men and the growing managed-care industry required a team sales approach. The sales team needed to talk with physicians, medical directors, benefits managers, and others within a managed-care organization with diverse educational, ethnic, racial, and religious backgrounds. The added benefit of the changing salesforce mix, according to Gaylord, was that the newcomers "asked more questions and raised the energy level" of the organization. They were "better performers" because they did not have access to the "old boys' network" and needed to find creative ways to make sales.

Mike George, Du Pont's director of Worldwide Marketing in 1989, was very receptive to the hiring and promotional changes Landgraf was making. He had developed a personal appreciation for diversity, growing up in a small town where "you recognized that you needed everyone" to accomplish any large project, and in the U.S. Army which he called "the most diverse organization in the world." He learned about diversity in the workplace while working as a district sales manager for another company in the late 1970s.

He was pleased to have women join his team at that time, although he remembers his all-male sales team as diverse in its own way—some stayed out all night, others played poker—"few wanted to do anything together and few prepared appropriately." At his first off-site area sales meeting with women present, George asked the women to role play around a particular sales situation. The women "blew the men away." The men, according to George, were "embarrassed." Many had been out late, were still yawning themselves awake, and had yet to look at sales materials delivered weeks before.

George saw the 15 individuals he managed develop into a 15-person team over the following year and a half. As individuals, they had done fairly well, but "the more diverse team was more professional." According to George, the women

led the way toward group thinking. People started to have dinner together, and the dinners became brainstorming sessions for approaching new or difficult customers.

Du Pont Merck Pharmaceutical Company

On January 1, 1991, E. I. du Pont de Nemours and Company, the third largest chemical manufacturer in the United States, and Merck & Co., Inc. the largest U.S. pharmaceutical maker, entered into a joint venture to establish Du Pont Merck Pharmaceutical Company.

In 1991, Du Pont's sales and earnings had plunged to the lowest level since 1985. Revenues shrank $1.35 billion to $38.7 billion while earnings fell 39 percent to $1.4 billion. Return on equity saw an equally dramatic decline as it fell over eight percent from an average of 16 percent.[3] The response of Du Pont CEO Edgar S. Woolard, Jr., was to sell off diverse businesses that he had once touted as Du Pont's future engines of growth.

For 20 years Du Pont had tried to make it in the health care business. The company established life sciences research in X-ray technology, clinical chemistry, radiopharmaceuticals, and pharmaceuticals without establishing a viable presence in any of these markets. Additionally, with the mergers of Bristol-Meyers with Squibb, and SmithKline with Beecham driving industry consolidation, Du Pont was under pressure to promote a global strategy to realize a return on its investment in research and development.

Du Pont considered an acquisition to bolster its existing drug business, but stock prices were still steep from the many pharmaceutical mergers of the late 1980s and "an acquisition would have been highly dilutive for Du Pont," according to Mollica, then a vice president in charge of R&D at Du Pont and the eventual

---

3. Joseph Weber, "Du Pont's Trailblazer Wants to Get Out of the Woods," *Business Week,* August 31, 1992, p. 70.

champion of the Du Pont Merck joint venture.[4] By 1990, amidst troubling times in both the chemical and pharmaceutical industries, Du Pont determined to concentrate on its core chemical business. Mollica suggested a joint venture with Merck to Woolard as a possible solution.

Du Pont and Merck had collaborated on a few projects in the late 1980s and Merck faced challenges similar to those at Du Pont—namely establishing an international presence to offset the pressures of a changing domestic pharmaceutical industry. Together, as Du Pont Merck, they could supplement existing product lines and markets of the two parents without creating dependencies on foreign subsidiaries or participating in disruptive mergers.

In July 1990 as it became certain that the joint venture would come to fruition, Mollica set Landgraf's Diversity Task Force to writing statements outlining the new company's vision, purpose, and shared values (see Exhibit 3). When the ink was dry on the joint venture agreement, Du Pont Merck was 50–50 co-owned with a six-person board drawn equally from the two parents. Du Pont brought its entire pharmaceutical and radiopharmaceutical imaging businesses, an R&D pipeline, 1,500 scientists (including 400 at the Ph.D. level), 600 salespeople, and an administrative staff. Merck brought about 10 employees, European marketing rights to several prescription medicines, development funds, international marketing expertise, cash, and some drugs awaiting international marketing approvals.

For an undisclosed period of time, all profits would go into the joint venture; the company was "not expected to produce significant commercial results until the late 1990s."[5] 1991 sales of $795.4 million and assets of $1.06 billion put Du Pont Merck at number 400 on *Fortune* maga-zine's "Fortune 500" survey of the largest U.S. industrial corporations. After one year, Du Pont Merck was the fourteenth largest U.S.-based pharmaceutical company. Sales in 1992 hit $972 million on assets of $1.1 billion (see Exhibit 4). Merck products accounted for 35 percent of sales, and Du Pont products accounted for 65 percent of sales.[6] Du Pont Merck products sold in 80 countries; 70 percent of sales were made in North America with the remainder coming from Europe.

In 1991, $235.9 million, 30 percent of sales, went back into R&D, nearly double the industry average. R&D efforts focused on Acquired Immune Deficiency Syndrome, arthritis, cancer, and cardiovascular and Alzheimer's diseases. Believing that "our future is our [drug] pipeline,"[7] Mollica's first step as CEO of Du Pont Merck was to invest in new R&D facilities and emphasize research for breakthrough drugs. He also strove to address the changing drug delivery system both in the United States and abroad. The 10 top U.S. pharmaceutical makers had, on average, 1,000 domestic and 3,000–6,000 overseas sales representatives.[8] Mollica increased Du Pont Merck's salesforce of 600 by 20 percent and encouraged Landgraf, now executive vice president of Worldwide Pharmaceuticals for the joint venture, to build a force that was more responsive to a changing customer base.

Du Pont Merck continued to serve individual physicians, put greater emphasis on high-volume managed-care providers, and followed the emerging industry practice of marketing directly to patients. Given this changing strategy, the marketplace was vastly more diverse—more international, multiracial, multiethnic,

4. Suzanne C. Moore, "From Zero to 400 in Two Years," *NCC Business,* April 1993, p. 12.

5. Merck & Co., Inc., 1991 *Annual Report.*

6. "Benchmark Study," unpublished company document, July 2, 1993.

7. Joseph A. Mollica, "Face Forward," *Galaxy,* Winter 1993, p. 10.

8. Mollica, untitled, undated speech delivered at the Fifth International Symposium on Recent Advances in Drug Delivery Systems, Salt Lake City, Utah.

EXHIBIT 3   Du Pont Merck Vision, Purpose, and Shared Values

Our Vision

We will be a pharmaceutical industry leader. A multinational, multibillion-dollar, research-based company recognized worldwide for superior service to customers and contributions to mankind. Our efforts will be at the leading edge of science, medicine, and technology in bringing novel solutions to major unmet medical needs.

Our Purpose

We will improve the quality of human life by dedicating ourselves to a spirit of innovation as we discover, develop, and deliver pharmaceuticals.

- To our customers, we pledge to treat you with integrity and fairness and become your partners as we strive together to improve human health.
- To society, we pledge to be a valued member of the communities where we operate, a responsive employer, and a good corporate citizen.
- To our founding partners, we pledge to provide you with superior returns on your investment and manage our company in a manner upholding your proud traditions.
- To ourselves, we pledge to be diligent in the care of our culture, speak up when we see a better way, and curtail actions harmful to our values. We pledge to create a supportive and challenging environment which fosters continuous improvement and excellence in everything we do.

Our Shared Values

Quality. Quality comes first in everything we do. We will strive to do it right the first time, on time, every time, meeting specifications and customers' needs. We view each activity as a process to be continuously improved driven by our customers' needs.

By recognizing and understanding our customers' needs and values, we will anticipate, meet, and exceed their expectations before and better than competition.

Recognition. We will aggressively seek out opportunities to recognize, reward, and celebrate accomplishments in support of our values and achievements toward our Vision.

Performance. We will be accountable for meeting our commitments and delivering results. Each of us individually bears a responsibility—to ourselves, to each other, and to our company—to keep our promises and achieve our objectives.

Innovation. We will break down barriers to creativity and risk-taking, encourage compulsive curiosity, and foster innovative approaches to meeting our customers' needs.

Action. A bias for action will drive everything we do. We will be impelled by individual initiative and a sense of urgency and continuously improve our ability to act swiftly and decisively.

Individual Growth. Individual growth and business success are inseparable. We will individually take responsibility to develop our talents and skills to their full potential to increase our contributions to the success of our business.

Mutual Support. We will trust, encourage, and support each other and develop relationships enabling us to enjoy and share accomplishments—our own, our colleagues, and our business.

Teamwork. We will encourage and reward collaboration and teamwork because teams can far exceed what can be accomplished individually.

Diversity. We must establish an environment where differences are recognized, understood, and valued as adding enrichment to our people and our global business. Our workforce will include diversity of race, gender,

---

(continued)

EXHIBIT 3   *(concluded)*

religion, and culture. While each individual is unique, all will be enabled to contribute, grow, and compete for advancement.

Safety. We will work safely and produce safe products to protect each other, our customers, communities, and the environment.

Ethics. We will always do what is right and fair as responsible individual and corporate citizens.

Contribution to Society. Working to improve the quality of life by fulfilling healthcare needs gives greater meaning to our jobs. We are committed to make a difference in the world.

Source: Du Pont Merck Pharmaceutical Company.

increasingly female, of varying ages, economic, religious, and educational backgrounds—than ever before.

The Changing Pharmaceutical Industry

The U.S. pharmaceutical industry produced 45 percent of all drugs marketed in the world in 1993.[9] It was a highly fragmented industry; no single company had more than a 5 percent share of the market and the top 25 manufacturers controlled 75 percent of the market.[10] Due to increased pressure from growing numbers of managed-care health plans and the Clinton Administration's health care reforms, pricing pressure was intense.

At the beginning of 1994, analysts predicted that the 10 largest U.S. drug companies would be "lucky" to earn $12.7 billion, up 4 percent over the previous year. Sales were not expected to rise more than $3\frac{1}{2}$ percent to $64.7 billion.[11] As profits grew at less than half the annual average of the 1980s, pharmaceuticals companies shed jobs. More than 30,000 were lost in 1993 alone.[12]

Drug companies that had maintained enormous sales forces to call on the nation's 635,000 physicians were rapidly cutting sales and marketing personnel—as well as related expenses which consumed 30 percent of revenues. Sales staff now needed to address the informational needs of the few thousand managed-care buyers who limited doctors' prescription choices and kept price hikes on drugs below the rate of inflation in both 1992 and 1993.[13]

In 1993, 85 percent of prescription dollars were spent on drugs less than 10 years old.[14] R&D spending increased 13.5 percent in 1993 but analysts expected the rate to drop to as low as 4 percent in 1994.[15]

Just two dozen drugs completed the 10–12 year development process to receive federal approval in 1993; 80 percent of drugs in development did not make it. According to the U.S. Office of Technological Assessment it took $230 million to bring a new drug to market in 1993, four times the cost of doing so 10 years before.[16] Greater focus on these costs caused drug makers to grow adverse to risk. More companies focused on symptom relief and "me-too" drugs that provided slight benefit in comparison to rival products, rather than attempting to develop breakthrough medicines.

9. Landgraf, "Government Influence and Its Potential Impact on the American Pharmaceutical Industry," undated speech delivered at the Institute for Pharmaceutical Economics, Philadelphia, PA.

10. Moore, p. 13.

11. Weber, "A Big Dose of Uncertainty," *Business Week*, January 10, 1994, p. 85.

12. "Kicking the Habit," *The Economist*, December 25–January 7, 1994, p. 90.

13. Weber, "A Big Dose of Uncertainty," p. 85.

14. Landgraf, "Government Influence."

15. Weber, "A Big Dose of Uncertainty," p. 85.

16. Landgraf, "Global Pricing," *Galaxy*, Winter 1993, p. 6.

EXHIBIT 4   Du Pont Merck Pharmaceutical Company, Sales and Income

	1991	1992	1993
Sales/other revenues	$795.4 million	$972 million	$1.035 billion
After-tax operating income			
% increase/(decrease)	0	75%	104%

Source: Du Pont Merck Pharmaceutical Company.

There were other financial pressures as well. Patents expired on 42 major drugs in 1992 and 1993, opening the way for cloning by the rapidly expanding generic drug industry and cutting deeply into long-held profits of established manufacturers. In 1993, 36 percent of all U.S. prescriptions were written for generic substitutes costing a third the price of name brands, a practice fueled by the cost-conscious managed-care industry.[17]

Some brand manufacturers established generics divisions in the early 1990s to offset competition from clone manufacturers, or entered into joint ventures with rivals. "Sleeping with the enemy"—as the business press called Merck's $6 billion purchase in 1993 of Medco Containment Services, a mail-order drug distributor handling 95 million prescriptions a year—was seen as a 1990s solution to the quest for diversification and high unit volume.

Clinton Administration health care reforms, particularly a proposed compulsory discount of 17 percent on all drugs purchased by Medicare and plans to establish a National Health Review Board to judge whether drug pricing was "reasonable," caused further alarm within the pharmaceutical industry. Political negotiations surrounding both the discounts and the Board would continue for some time; nevertheless, pharmaceutical company executives had to face the reality that the Medicare discount could slice $2.5 billion off of industry profits annually, and the NHRB could call into question the practice

of charging premium prices for new drugs in order to bankroll future R&D.[18]

In the early 1990s prescription costs represented only 5 percent of the nation's total health care spending.[19] For many consumers, however, drugs (unlike doctor's visits and hospital stays) were nonreimbursable expenses. Public opinion soured as the media and federal government exposed profit margins of pharmaceutical companies during debate over health care reform (see Exhibit 5).

Kurt Landgraf as CEO: Going Forward at Du Pont Merck

In January of 1994, in the first of what he promised would be monthly communications to all Du Pont Merck employees from him as CEO, Landgraf outlined the "strategies we intend to pursue to reach our vision."[20] The first strategy related to performance and the fact that "every employee must understand and be committed to this ongoing effort." He emphasized his commitment to "aggressively" support R&D, "the lifeblood of successful pharmaceutical companies," as well as new sales and marketing efforts.

He also noted that Du Pont Merck would be "fully functioning, but not fully integrated." Begun with just over 2,000 employees in 1991, the company employed 5,000 in 1993. According to Landgraf it had "all the infrastructure of a huge

17. Weber, "A Big Dose of Uncertainty," p. 85.

18. "Kicking the Habit," *The Economist,* December 25–January 7, 1994, p. 90.

19. Merck & Co., Inc., 1991 *Annual Report.*

20. Landgraf, letter, January 4, 1994.

EXHIBIT 5   Profit Margins of U.S. Pharmaceutical Industry

(a) *American Consumer Prices*

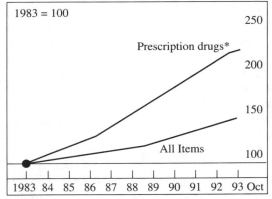

*Figures for 1992–93 lower on some estimates.

(b) *American Drug Companies*

Spending and profits, % of total sales, 1991

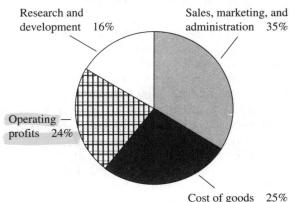

Sources: U.S. Bureau of Labour Statistics; Wilkerson Group; Price Waterhouse (from *The Economist*, December 25, 1993–January 7, 1994, p. 90).

corporation. It had gotten way ahead of itself" at a time when the pharmaceutical industry faced dramatic change.

Landgraf needed to downsize his organization while meeting the increased financial demands of the parent companies, fill David Martin's position as R&D head with someone who shared his vision, and address the concerns of African-American employees regarding hiring and promotional practices companywide.

African-Americans at Du Pont Merck

There was more than one African-American employees' group, as well as an E-mail network for African-Americans, at Du Pont Merck in 1993. Some of the groups were social, others committed to career development and promoting diversity within the company. Because the groups were informal, they typically followed employment and location patterns. Scientific labora-

tories were isolated from corporate headquarters, as were field sales offices. Even for those African-Americans based in Wilmington headquarters, divisions were spread across several low buildings in the Du Pont industrial complex.

Typically, communication among the groups increased around special events, such as the celebration of The Reverend Dr. Martin Luther King's birthday, or around special issues. Increasing activity around the possibility of filing a class-action suit against Du Pont Merck for racial discrimination was an issue that brought African-Americans across Du Pont divisions together.

Class-Action Suit

Wendell Wilkerson joined Du Pont in 1979 with a Ph.D. in chemistry. Throughout the late 1950s and 1960s, Wilkerson had been involved in the Congress of Racial Equality (CORE) and other civil rights causes. He worked directly with King and was committed to creating social change. When he interviewed for positions following post-doctoral research, he had "definitely not been interested in Du Pont" because of its reputation as a "conservative and racist" organization. A professor convinced him to interview however, and Wilkerson soon believed "that if I worked my ass off, I could run the place."

Wilkerson's manager for his first two years was "a tremendous human being." After the manager took another position, however, Wilkerson began to feel that his work was no longer championed in the same way, that he did not receive the attention or resources that others in the research labs received, and that he was the subject of overt racism. When he had joined Du Pont there was only one other African-American Ph.D.; by 1993 there were fewer than a dozen. Wilkerson wanted the African-American employees groups to leave social activities behind and challenge the racial climate at Du Pont Merck. After "12 or 15 years of complaining loudly," on January 28, 1993, Wilkerson wrote a letter to Joseph Mollica outlining his concerns and "threatening a class-action suit."

As the idea of a class-action suit gained momentum, managers in Human Resources and R&D worked to investigate charges, address allegations, and prevent legal action. For many of the African-Americans involved in the discussions, the process was discouragingly slow; when both Mollica and Martin left Du Pont Merck it seemed that progress might end altogether. On December 1, 1993, the African-American Core Team wrote to Landgraf. Their letter congratulated him on his promotion and laid out the "many concerns about the mistreatment and lack of promotional opportunities of African-Americans within the Du Pont Merck Company, especially in R&D."[21]

---

21. Letter to Kurt M. Landgraf from The African-American Core Team, December 1, 1993.

Landgraf Responds

Landgraf's immediate inclination after receiving the letter was to set up a meeting with the letter's authors. His commitment to diversity was well-known and deeply held. His pharmaceutical division had faced many of the challenges that Wilkerson and the angry E-mailers from the research labs described. He believed he could manage a solution to the problems and Du Pont Merck would be a more productive and competitive company for the effort. When he learned through Herbert that Wilkerson's Core Team was not a companywide group he hesitated, however.

Landgraf directed Herbert to work with Gloria Hammond, Du Pont Merck's employment compliance officer, and several other African-American managers to organize a forum to discuss employment issues that African-American employees faced from across the entire organization.

The African-American Employees' Forum

On January 14, 1994, more than 100 African-American employees of Du Pont Merck, drawn from all divisions and all employment grades, met for four hours with Landgraf and the company's Management Committee of division executives. Duane Holland, Du Pont Merck's first African-American vice president, led the Forum.

Holland, one of the few Merck employees to come into Du Pont Merck, had moved from the mail room to senior management in Human Resources over a 20-year history with the companies. He was named vice president for Workforce Development and Diversity, with direct access to Landgraf, only days before the Forum and given a seat on the Management Committee. While heralded as the first African-American on the Management Committee, he was the only one of the 13 senior managers on it who did not have a division reporting to him.

Holland and Landgraf framed the Forum as a celebration of Martin Luther King's values.

EXHIBIT 6A Du Pont Merck Pharmaceutical Company—African-American Hires (selected divisions)

	1991		1993	
	Total	Number Black (%)	Total	Number Black (%)
Worldwide Pharmaceuticals				
≥ 17	2	–	1	–
15–16	2	–	4	–
10–14	15	4 (27)	19	9 (47)
≤ 9	107	19 (18)	24	6 (25)
Total	126	23 (18)	48	15 (31)
Research and Development				
≥ 17	1	–	5	–
15–16	5	–	5	–
10–14	69	4 (6)	27	2 (7)
≤ 9	127	8 (6)	47	2 (4)
Total	202	12 (6)	84	4 (5)
Radiopharmaceuticals				
≥ 17	–	–	–	–
15–16	–	–	1	–
10–14	8	–	20	–
≤ 9	26	–	27	–
Total	34	–	48	–

Source: Du Pont Merck Pharmaceutical Company.

Hammond showed overhead projections of employment statistics broken down by company division (see Exhibit 6), a panel discussed perspectives on the employment issues facing African-Americans at Du Pont Merck, and then discussion was opened to the floor.

Comments were personal and specific; participants told their stories of good and of nonexistent mentoring, of the inconsistency of development processes across divisions, and of review processes that were highly subjective and of one's design to make an employee grow into greater responsibilities. There was a new employee who "already felt less valued" than her white co-workers. There were also several who

had been at Du Pont for more than a decade, many rising from entry-level positions, who were on a successful career track and who felt valued and rewarded.

As in Hammond's statistics, there was a clear division in the comments. Those who worked in Worldwide Pharmaceuticals, Landgraf's former division, were more positive about their experiences and the company than were the scientists in R&D and radiopharmaceuticals. A significant segment of the Forum focused on these two scientific divisions. But no one on the Management Committee was able to respond to questions asked about employment for African-Americans within the scientific divisions, be-

EXHIBIT 6B   Du Pont Merck Pharmaceutical Company—Ph.D. Hires

	White Men	White Women	Black Men	Black Women	Other Minority Men	Other Minority Women
1991	11	7	–	–	4	2
1992	9	5	–	1	6	4
1993	25	11	1	–	4	2

Source: Du Pont Merck Pharmaceutical Company.

Not a priority

cause a successor to Martin had yet to be named, Pieter Timmermans, senior vice president of Research, was absent, and Ken Kasses, president of Radiopharmaceuticals, arrived late. Wilkerson's description of the African-American Scientist Program, expanded on by several others involved in its development, became a lightening rod for the underlying anger at the Forum.

The African-American Scientist Program
In the late 1980s, Mollica spoke with Wilkerson's boss about having Wilkerson recruit African-American scientists for Du Pont, a role that Wilkerson had championed unofficially for several years. Wilkerson accepted the recognition and sought résumés through professional networks, educational ties, and recruiting trips. According to Wilkerson, he brought "dozens and dozens" of résumés to the attention of senior managers within R&D with limited results.

In 1992 Holland and David Grandison, the director of Worldwide Medical Affairs, formalized Wilkerson's efforts by creating the African-American Scientist Program. It established relationships with deans and senior faculty members at major U.S. scientific institutions and historically Black colleges to recruit African-American scientists for Du Pont Merck. In 1993 contacts recommended 14 African-American scientists to Du Pont Merck R&D executives. Of the 14, three were interviewed and none received job offers.

Several associated with the program found it a demoralizing experience. Some attributed its failure to a lack of established hiring goals. Some felt that the experience added to Du Pont Merck's image as a poor environment for African-American scientists and undermined the possibility of any further efforts to recruit African-American scientists.

The Bi-Modal Workplace
At the end of the Forum, Landgraf referred to Du Pont Merck as a "bi-modal workplace." While the hiring and development of African-Americans within Worldwide Pharmaceuticals was not all that it should be, he noted, the environment for African-American scientists at Du Pont Merck was far worse.

The experiences of Donna Jones, an African-American medical writer who worked in the Medical Affairs division, illustrated both the bi-modality of Du Pont Merck and some of the barriers to building an organization where bi-modality was not the norm.

Jones's group moved from the R&D division and was reorganized within marketing. After the move she noted a significant difference in the level of diversity around her, in the way that she was treated, and the way that she felt about coming to work everyday. No longer one of the isolated few minorities in R&D, she no longer was "interrogated" about what it was like to be African-American. In R&D, she said, white scientists had few contacts with educated, middle-class Blacks. She was treated as a novelty by those more receptive to her being there and ignored by those less receptive to her being there. In either case, the "ignorance and fear" about

EXHIBIT 6C Du Pont Merck Pharmaceutical Company—African-American Promotions (selected divisions)

	1991		*1993*	
	Total	*Number Black (%)*	*Total*	*Number Black (%)*
Worldwide Pharmaceuticals				
≥ 17	11	2 (18)%	19	2 (11)%
15–16	26	3 (12)	20	–
10–14	175	20 (11)	178	19 (11)
≤ 9	31	6 (19)	35	7 (20)
Total	243	31 (13)%	252	28 (11)%
Research and Development				
≥ 17	8	–	3	–
15–16	36	–	24	–
10–14	122	3 (2)	112	4 (4)
≤ 9	9	–	90	2 (2)
Total	175	3 (2)%	229	6 (3)%
Radiopharmaceuticals				
≥ 17	5	–	3	–
15–16	9	–	2	–
10–14	36	–	46	–
≤ 9	21	–	75	–
Total	71	–	126	–

Source: Du Pont Merck Pharmaceutical Company.

African-Americans made her very uncomfortable; she would "never go back to R&D."

Barriers to Success

By the end of the Forum, its organizers were already suggesting companywide hiring and promotional goals, a system of accountability to encourage managers to meet the goals, a review of the 360-degree review that was not meeting its intended goals, and mandatory, companywide diversity training. Landgraf expected Holland to pull together a task force to make clear recommendations to him by the end of the quarter. Landgraf was determined to see results in R&D in the very near future. Managers, scientists, and other employees saw significant barriers to Landgraf's achieving this.

Critics argued that R&D was an elitist, degree-driven division. Landgraf, not being a scientist and not having a Ph.D., was already discounted there. Scientists would not look favorably on efforts that took them away from their lab benches and did not produce quantifiable results. Diversity training, for example, might not receive the same response in R&D as it would in sales where "people skills" were considered more important to job function.

One thing quantifiable to managers in R&D was the number of African-Americans who earned Ph.D.s each year. Of the 25,759 doctor-

EXHIBIT 6D   Race and Gender Breakdown of Du Pont Merck Employees (selected divisions)

1991

Grade Level	White Men (Percent)		White Women (Percent)	Black Men (Percent)		Black Women (Percent)	Other Minority Men (Percent)		Other Minority Women (Percent)
Worldwide Pharmaceuticals									
≥ 17	81%		9%	2%		3%	3%		2%
15–16	67		19	3		3	7		1
10–14	49		36	4		4	4		3
≤ 9	23		52	6		12	3		4
Total %	44	(82)	38	4	(11)	7	4	(7)	3
Research and Development									
≥ 17	81		6	2		–	11		–
15–16	67		11	1		–	20		1
10–14	49		32	2		1	10		6
≤ 9	34		54	3		5	2		2
Total %	44	(85)	41	2	(5)	3	7	(10)	3
Radiopharmaceuticals									
≥ 17	87		13	–		–	–		–
15–16	85		12	–		–	3		–
10–14	72		24	1		1	1		1
≤ 9	56		39	1		1	1		2
Total %	64	(96)	32	1	(2)	1	1	(2)	1

1992

Grade Level	White Men (Percent)		White Women (Percent)	Black Men (Percent)		Black Women (Percent)	Other Minority Men (Percent)		Other Minority Women (Percent)
Worldwide Pharmaceuticals									
≥ 17	76%		12%	3%		3%	6%		–
15–16	67		20	3		3	6		1%
10–14	49		36	3		5	4		3
≤ 9	22		53	6		13	3		3
Total %	44	(82)	38	4	(11)	7	4	(7)	3
Research and Development									
≥ 17	84		6	–		–	10		–
15–16	70		9	1		–	18		2
10–14	47		35	2		1	8		7
≤ 9	33		53	3		5	3		3
Total %	44	(84)	40	2	(5)	3	7	(11)	4

(continued)

EXHIBIT 6D   *(concluded)*

	1992 (continued)					
Grade Level	White Men (Percent)		White Women (Percent)	Black Men (Percent)	Black Women (Percent)	Other Minority Men (Percent)	Other Minority Women (Percent)

Radiopharmaceuticals

Grade Level	White Men		White Women	Black Men		Black Women	Other Minority Men		Other Minority Women
≥ 17	82		18	–		–	–		–
15–16	77		18	–		–	5		–
10–14	67		28	2		1	1		1
≤ 9	58		37	2		–	1		2
Total %	63	(95)	32	2	(2)	–	1	(3)	2

	1993					

Worldwide Pharmaceuticals

Grade Level	White Men		White Women	Black Men		Black Women	Other Minority Men		Other Minority Women
≥ 17	70%		15%	3%		6%	6%		–
15–16	66		23	2		1	6		2%
10–14	46		36	4		5	5		4
≤ 9	23		53	6		13	2		3
Total %	48	(81)	38	5	(12)	7	4	(7)	3

Research and Development

Grade Level	White Men		White Women	Black Men		Black Women	Other Minority Men		Other Minority Women
≤ 17	86		6	–		–	8		–
15–16	66		10	1		–	21		2
10–14	46		37	3		1	7		7
≤9	47		41	3		4	2		3
Total %	51	(85)	34	2	(5)	3	6	(10)	4

Radiopharmaceuticals

Grade Level	White Men		White Women	Black Men		Black Women	Other Minority Men		Other Minority Women
≥ 17	82		18	–		–	–		–
15–16	75		18	–		–	7		–
10–14	65		30	2		1	1		1
≤ 9	59		37	1		–	1		2
Total %	63	(95)	32	2	(2)	–	2	(3)	1

Source: Du Pont Merck Pharmaceutical Company.

ates awarded in the United States in 1992, just 951 went to African-Americans.[22] And, of those, only 26 percent were awarded in physical and life sciences.[23] With less than one percent of all Ph.D.s awarded to African-American scientists, R&D was drawing from a limited labor pool. In comparison, sales and marketing employees came from diverse educational backgrounds and

22. Catherine S. Manegold, "Fewer Men Earn Doctorates, Particularly among Blacks," *The New York Times,* January 18, 1994.

23. Carole Feldman, "Study Finds Fewer Blacks Get Ph.D.s Even as Degrees for Minorities Rise," *The Boston Globe,* January 17, 1994.

typically had only a bachelor's degree. In 1990, by comparison, 61,074 African-Americans graduated with bachelor's degrees. Sales and marketing managers attracted them easily at minority job fairs, through employee recommendations, and "over-the-transom" applications.

Timmermans, the most senior manager in R&D while Martin's position remained unfilled, argued that even if there were a larger pool, there had been "limited opportunities to hire" at all in R&D over the past several years. It was a different situation than the one Landgraf faced in 1988 when he could create gender equity through hiring.

In addition, according to Timmermans, whenever there was "pressure and urgency to hire" the results were "disastrous." He argued that what Du Pont Merck's labs made were medicines and that poor science could cost lives. Du Pont Merck had a responsibility to hire only the best scientists to assure that medicines were effective and safe and that there would be no surprises after patients took a drug for 10 or 20 years. Unlike in sales and marketing, there was not as much room for overseeing an individual's learning curve in R&D, Timmermans believed.

What Timmermans could do, he believed, was continue to develop the African-American Ph.D. pipeline as Du Pont Merck had been doing, by sponsoring graduate and post-graduate research, as well as a student intern program that brought young scientists, many of whom were minorities, into Du Pont Merck's labs for a summer. Timmermans argued, however, that you could not force someone who accepted a Du Pont Merck grant to work for the company after their research was completed.

Timmermans was "committed" to a diverse workforce, but found himself "constantly criticized because we cannot deliver quickly." His critics, he said, needed to be "realistic" about the pressures that he faced as a scientist working in a business environment.

Arguments

One manager who worked on the diversification effort within Du Pont Merck's sales and marketing workforce dismissed many of Timmermans's concerns. Even in the toughest economic times, she said, there are "things you can take care of. You can talk about what gets into people's way. If you decrease the negatives, you end with a powerful motivator. It's simplicity that works; Ph.D.s can't understand this simplicity."

Mike George believed one of the greatest motivators he offered the African-American sales representatives who worked for him was attention to career goals, and opportunities to show what they could do. Ask African-American scientists to make presentations, lead internal work committees, make decisions about resource allocations, establish formal mentoring relationships so their concerns were heard quickly and responded to, he suggested. None of this, he believed, would jeopardize patient health.

David Grandison, who held both an M.D. and a Ph.D., argued that there was "no insurmountable barrier" to hiring similarly credentialed African-Americans like himself. R&D managers spent "most of their time looking in the wrong places," he argued. Rather than looking only at "MIT, Harvard, and other elite institutions," they could find qualified minorities graduating from historically Black colleges and universities, on the faculties of other scientific institutions, and among industry competitors.

Grandison financed his education through part-time employment and fellowships that required him to teach and work in the African-American community after graduation. Du Pont Merck should not hesitate to tie potentially good African-American scientists to itself through educational support programs, he argued. In his opinion R&D managers "believed [in diversity], but didn't really work on it in an ongoing process." As with the sales and marketing division, he believed, committed leadership on diversity issues was the only way to change the R&D culture.

Landgraf's Decision

Because his success at addressing discrimination and harassment issues within Du Pont's pharmaceutical division in 1988 was well known at

Du Pont Merck, many individuals now looked to Landgraf for a swift resolution to the problems outlined at the Forum. Landgraf was keenly aware of the expectations put on him, and on his long-stated, personal commitment to diversity. Further, he did not want his company involved in a discrimination suit.

He was also keenly aware that the business climate in 1994 was quite different from that of 1988. Landgraf was under pressure to meet the financial growth schedule set for his organization by its parent companies. Business success or failure rested largely on the success or failure of Du Pont Merck's R&D pipeline. How would addressing the concerns of Core Team members in R&D impact that pipeline?

Landgraf needed to proceed with downsizing as equitably as possible. How would he simultaneously demonstrate the organization's commitment to attracting, retaining, and promoting a diverse workforce? Landgraf noted at the Forum

"that the worst thing that we could do for the diversity effort was play the numbers game," yet he supported numerical goals as "short-term" answers until corporate culture made them unnecessary.

New to his position as CEO, distrusted by senior scientists because he did not share their educational background, and determined to drive diversity down throughout all the ranks of all Du Pont Merck's divisions, Landgraf was faced with several management problems—all to be solved during downsizing and significant changes within the entire pharmaceutical industry. He was determined that Martin's replacement would share his commitment to diversity and that downsizing would not impact women and minorities unjustly. He already had one African-American man in mind for Martin's position and he would personally review the employment records of every individual laid off during downsizing.

THE BALANCED WORKFORCE AT XEROX CORPORATION

In the decade following the creation of the black caucus system in the early 1970s,[1] "affirmative action" became fully institutionalized at Xerox. A large number of minorities and women were spread (albeit unevenly) throughout the ranks and divisions of Xerox, most managers became sensitive to the concerns of minority and female employees, and meeting affirmative action goals was made an element of every manager's annual review. More recently, affirmative action was re-

This case was prepared by Raymond A. Friedman.
Copyright © 1991 by the President and Fellows of Harvard College.
Harvard Business School case 491-049 (Rev. March 21, 1991).

1. See cases *Black Caucus Groups at Xerox Corporation (A), No. 491-047* and *Black Caucus Groups at Xerox Corporation (B), No. 491–048.*

placed by the "balanced workforce." *Balance* meant that the representation in all categories (including majority male) at all levels should match the availability estimates for that job and level. It also involved a new formula for calculating those estimates—which ensured that promotion goals for minority and female employees in the higher ranks of the company reflected the availability in the lower ranks.

These recent changes, however, were the source of some debate. Some minority employees worried that the balanced workforce philosophy would limit their opportunities; the way that availability estimates were calculated and the data upon which those calculations were based were great sources of controversy; and because the company was growing at a slower rate and reducing levels of hierarchy, there were fewer promotions than in the past and more competition for the promotions that were available. The balanced workforce was a part of how Xerox did business, but its implementation required continual effort and adjustment.

The Historical Evolution of Equal Employment Rules

On August 28, 1963, 250,000 people protested against racial discrimination in one of the largest gatherings ever at the nation's capital. It was during this "March on Washington" that Martin Luther King, Jr., made his historic "I Have A Dream" speech. Three months later President Kennedy was assassinated. Seven months later, with the memory of both President Kennedy and the March on Washington fresh in the public mind, Congress passed the Civil Rights Act forbidding racial, religious, or sexual discrimination. Eighteen months later, President Johnson announced Executive Order 11246, which required government agencies and government contractors to not only avoid racial discrimination but also to be proactive in ensuring fair representation of blacks and other minorities in the workforce by establishing affirmative action plans.[2] The order was later expanded to include women.

By the late sixties, the Office of Federal Contract Compliance Programs developed a method for assessing contractor compliance with government regulations. Each company had to develop an Affirmative Action Plan for each facility of more than 50 people. The plan had to include specific goals and timetables to correct any underutilization of women or minorities that existed. Underutilization was determined by comparing the actual numbers of women and minorities in each type and level of job to the "availability estimates" for those types and levels of job. The availability estimates were based on eight factors:

1. Population
2. Unemployment
3. Total workforce
4. Requisite skills (immediate area)[3]
5. Requisite skills (recruitable area)[4]
6. Internal availability
7. External training sources (e.g., college graduates)
8. Internal training

Each company had to find out, using various private and public sources of data, the percentage of women and minorities in each of these categories. Then, based on accepted practices and company needs, each of the factors was assigned a weighting factor for each type and level of job. The actual percentage representation in each factor was multiplied by the assigned weight, and those totals were added together to generate a bottom-line estimated availability for each job type and level.

Availability Estimates at Xerox

This was the system that Xerox began using in the 1960s. Although additional calculations were later added, these basic calculations remained the foundation of Xerox's EEO planning. Exhibit 1 shows the factor weights used at Xerox as of 1990 and the logic for each weight. Exhibit 2 shows an example of current Xerox availability estimates for finance jobs in one district in Washington D.C. The exhibit is divided into four pages, each representing different job grade levels. Levels 1–6 are jobs in the $22,000–$35,000 range; levels 7–9 are $35,000–$50,000; levels 10–12 are $50,000–$64,000; levels 13–14 are $65,000–$74,000. Levels 15–18 and the executive pay group are not shown.

For entry-level finance jobs, no weight was

---

2. The order, and most corporate policies that followed, are expressed in terms of "minorities," although in the initial decade of Equal Employment Opportunity this referred primarily to blacks.

3. "Requisite skills" were determined by the actual jobs that people held in that area as recorded by the U.S. Census, such as "sales," "accounting," or "finance."

4. An example of an "immediate area" is Washington, D.C. An example of a "recruitable area" is the Metropolitan Washington, D.C. area.

given to population or unemployment. The greatest weights were given to college graduates and requisite skills in the area. No weight was given to internal hiring because there was no level below this one from which they could recruit. Moving to level 7–9, internal hiring was weighted most heavily, while requisite skills and college graduates (the external labor market) decreased in importance. This trend away from the external labor market continued for higher job grades, so that for job grades 13–14 internal promotions from levels 10–12 were expected to provide 75 percent of the new people hired into those jobs. This weighting reflected Xerox's philosophy that the majority of upper-level jobs should be filled through internal development and promotion from the "feeder base" of new hires at the bottom of the organization.

One result of this approach and this way of calculating the availability factors was that actual hiring at a given level strongly influenced the hiring goals for the next level above it. In the case of minority females in finance in Washington, D.C., for example, the job family availability for job level 1–6 was 9.8 percent, but the actual percentage hired (listed in the tables as the percentage of minority females in the promotion/transfer pool for job grades 7–9) was 21.6 percent. As a result, the job family availability of minority women at the next level was boosted to 15 percent. The effect on the minority male hiring goals for level 7–9 was the opposite: because the actual hiring results at levels 1–6 were 5.4 percent (which was lower than the job grade 1–6 availability estimate of 10.1 percent), the job availability number for minority males in finance job grades 7–9 was reduced to 8.5 percent.

Because this formula was used to make the calculations, failure to reach representation objectives at one level negatively impacted representation goals at the next higher level. Moreover, since these goals were used to assess the performance of managers throughout the company, lower goals would take pressure off of managers to develop and promote minority and female employees.

Indeed, this was exactly the problem that Xerox was having: throughout much of the 1970s Xerox was oversubscribed with minorities and women at its lower levels, but far fewer were moving up the organization. According to Ted Payne, Equal Opportunity manager for Xerox, "we initially thought of affirmative action as hiring, but then realized that we needed a plan to get minorities and women up the line."

The Pivotal Job Concept
The first attempt to ensure that minorities and women moved up the line after entering the internal feeder pool at the bottom of the Xerox career ladder was the "pivotal job" concept initiated in 1972. Key executives, with the input of the newly-forming black caucus groups, looked at the 50 senior people in a division such as U.S. Sales and realized that they all had similar career paths. They found that there were three or four jobs that nearly all senior managers had held, such as first-line sales manager, branch manager, and a regional-level job. If someone did not have these jobs, it was clear, they could not reach the highest level of U.S. Sales at Xerox. These key jobs were called "pivotal" jobs.

After these jobs were identified, executives met with the managers responsible for filling them. They were asked how many minorities held those jobs, who was slated to be hired for the next opening, and whether there were any minorities ready to take the job. For example, there were some sales regions where none of the 100 sales managers were minorities and regional managers had no intention of promoting any minority salespeople into those jobs. These regional managers were encouraged by top executives to identify their best minority salesperson and to prepare him or her for the job.

The key to this approach was, first, to have enough minorities in the entry-level feeder pool (in this case salespeople) to be certain that at least some would be qualified to be promoted and, second, to ensure that these people had access to pivotal jobs. This strategy did ensure that a number of minorities would reach the highest

EXHIBIT 1 Eight-Factor Analysis

Factor	Source/Scope	Weighting	Logic
1. Population Minority—The minority population of the labor area surrounding the facility. Female—the availability of women seeking employment in the labor or recruitment area surrounding the facility.	U.S. Census/State data	0%—all exempt positions 5%—all nonexempt and hourly positions	Accepted practice is to limit use of this factor to entry-level minimum-skill positions because data is too broad, including persons who are not prospects for employment (i.e., children, military, prisons, etc.).
2. Unemployment The size of the minority and female unemployment forces in the labor area surrounding the facility.	U.S. Census/State data	0%—all positions except hourly 10%—hourly positions: laborer, operatives, and crafts	Accepted practice is to limit use of this factor to entry-level unskilled positions because data is too broad, difficult to determine types of people included.
3. Total Workforce The percentage of the minority and female work forces as compared to the total work force in the immediate labor area.	U.S. Census/State data County/SMSA data (Standard Metropolitan Statical Area	5–10%—all positions except hourly 20%—hourly positions: laborer, operatives, and crafts	The data provided for this factor is substantive and relates to the Xerox workforce population.
4. Requisite Skills—Immediate Area The general availability of minorities and females having requisite skills in the immediate labor area.	U.S. Census/County SMSA data	0–35%—all exempt positions 50–65%—all nonexempt and hourly positions	Same as Factor 3. Xerox practice use of County/SMSA data in lieu of city data based on experience.
5. Requisite Skills—Recruitment Area The availability of minorities having requisite skills in a reasonable recruitment area.	U.S. Census/County SMSA data	0–20%—all exempt positions 15–25%—all nonexempt and hourly positions	Same as Factor 3.
6. Internal Availability The availability of promotable and transferable minority and female employees in the feeder base jobs.	Xerox promotion & transfer data	0%—all entry-level exempt positions; 30–95%—all other exempt positions 0%—all nonexempt and hourly positions, except senior CSE—90%	Empirical internal Xerox data.

(continued)

EXHIBIT 1   *(concluded)*

Factor	Source/Scope	Weighting	Logic
7. External Training Institutions			
The existence of training institutions capable of training persons in requisite skills.	College Placement Council, U.S. college enrollment	0–40%—all exempt positions 0%—all nonexempt and hourly positions	Data has been made available through the College Placement Council.
8. Internal Training			
The training available to prepare minority and female employees to move into all job classifications.	Data not used	0%—all positions	Minority and female employees get the same training as majority male employees, therefore this factor has no relevance.

---

echelons of Xerox, but the job-by-job, individual-by-individual nature of the process limited the impact of pivotal job approach. The manual calculations that this strategy depended on were difficult to extend throughout the company to large numbers of people.

Xerox needed to be able to aggregate availability data across its individual facilities. This would enable executive managers to set and measure overall goals for minority and female representation across large numbers of units. In doing so however, the company had to be careful to avoid the tendency, inherent in the government's formula for calculating availability estimates, to produce limited minority and female representation goals at higher levels of the company.

The "Balanced" Workforce Strategy

The solution, introduced in 1984, was to calculate a different set of numbers than those required by the government. These numbers would be different in two ways: the feeder base would be used to drive goals for upper-level jobs, and numbers would be added across functions and locations.

This balanced workforce (BWF) approach changed the formula by which actual representa-

tion results at one level of job were used to calculate the job availability numbers for people at the next level. Before (and for government reporting purposes still), the availability numbers for job grades 10–12 were heavily influenced by actual hiring at levels 7–9. But the 7–9 level might already show a decrease or increase of minority representation compared to the estimated availability at the 1–6 level. Therefore, the internal hiring pool for levels 10–12 was calculated as an average of the actual employment numbers at *both* job levels 1–6 *and* 7–9, weighted by the total size of the two job level populations. More importantly, this number was applied not only to job grades 10–12, but to *all* job grades up the hierarchy. This approach to calculating the numbers meant that the percentage minority and female representation found in the lowest level feeder pool should be reproduced at higher levels at Xerox as well. This aspect of the balanced workforce calculations is represented in the first five steps of Exhibit 3.[5]

---

5. These calculations did not replace the calculation of availability estimates. Most managers still used the availability estimates as targets. The BWF approach has an impact primarily on top-level managers who are responsible for the hiring and promotion of employees into high job grades (i.e., 10 and above).

EXHIBIT 2 Eight-Factor Analysis (District of Columbia Level = 01 +; Family = FIN)

Factors	Weight		Minority Female	Majority Female	Minority Male	Black	Asian	American Indian	Hispanic	Total Minority	Total Female
							2% of Population				
1. Min/WMN	0.0	Percent Rep	40.8	14.5	35.1	70.3	2.6	0.2	2.8	75.9	55.2
		WTD Factor	0.0	0.0	0.0	0.0	0.0	0.0	0.0	0.0	0.0
2. Unemployment	0.0	Percent Rep	37.0*	11.1	44.4	81.5	0.0	0.0	0.0	81.5	48.2
		WTD Factor	0.0	0.0	0.0	0.0	0.0	0.0	0.0	0.0	0.0
3. Total Labor Force	0.10	Percent Rep	16.3	30.4	15.7	26.0	2.6	0.2	3.0	31.9	46.6
		WTD Factor	1.6	3.0	1.6	2.6	0.3	0.0	0.3	3.2	4.7
4. Req/Skills/Loc	0.30	Percent Rep	12.3	29.1	10.6	16.6	3.3	0.2	2.9	22.9	41.4
		WTD Factor	3.7	8.7	3.2	5.0	1.0	0.1	0.9	6.9	12.4
5. Req/Skills/Recr	0.20	Percent Rep	12.3	29.1	10.6	16.6	3.3	0.2	2.9	22.9	41.4
		WTD Factor	2.5	5.8	2.1	3.3	0.7	0.0	0.6	4.6	8.3
6. Promo/Trans	0.00	Percent Rep									
		WTD Factor									
7. Comm/Training	0.40	Percent Rep	5.1	34.0	8.0	8.2	2.0	0.4	2.4	13.1	39.1
		WTD Factor	2.0	13.6	3.2	3.3	0.8	0.2	1.0	5.2	15.6
8. Inter/Training		Percent Rep									
		WTD Factor									
Job Family % Availability =			9.8	31.2	10.1	14.2	2.7	0.3	2.7	19.9	41.0

Report date: 07/10/90.

*This means that 37 percent of the unemployed in D.C. are minority females.

EXHIBIT 2 (continued)   Eight-Factor Analysis (District of Columbia Level = 07 +; Family = FIN)

Factors	Weight		Minority Female	Majority Female	Minority Male	Black	Asian	American Indian	Hispanic	Total Minority	Total Female
						% of Population					
1. Min/WMN seek empl.	0.00	Percent Rep	40.8	14.5	35.1	70.3	2.6	0.2	2.8	75.9	55.2
		WTD Factor	0.0	0.0	0.0	0.0	0.0	0.0	0.0	0.0	0.0
2. Unemployment	0.0	Percent Rep	37.0	11.1	44.4	81.5	0.0	0.0	0.0	81.5	48.2
		WTD Factor	0.0	0.0	0.0	0.0	0.0	0.0	0.0	0.0	0.0
3. Total Labor Force	0.10	Percent rep	16.3	30.4	15.7	26.0	2.6	0.2	3.0	31.9	46.6
		WTD Factor	1.6	3.0	1.6	2.6	0.3	0.0	0.3	3.2	4.7
4. Req/Skills/Loc	0.20	Percent Rep	12.3	29.1	10.6	16.6	3.3	0.2	2.9	22.9	41.4
		WTD Factor	2.5	5.8	2.1	3.3	0.7	0.0	0.6	4.6	8.3
5. Req/Skills/Recr.	0.10	Percent rep	12.3	29.1	10.6	16.6	3.3	0.2	2.9	22.9	41.4
		WTD Factor	1.2	2.9	1.1	1.7	0.3	0.0	0.3	2.3	4.1
6. Promo/Trans	0.40	Percent Rep	21.6	53.5	5.4	20.0	3.2	0.0	3.8	27.0	75.1
		WTD Factor	8.6	21.4	2.2	8.0	1.3	0.0	1.5	10.8	30.1
7. Comm/Training	0.20	Percent Rep	5.1	34.0	8.0	8.2	2.0	0.4	2.4	13.1	39.1
		WTD Factor	1.0	6.8	1.6	1.6	0.4	0.1	0.5	2.6	7.8
8. Inter/Training		Percent Rep									
		WTD Factor									
Job Family % Availability =			15.0	40.0	8.5	17.2	2.9	0.2	3.2	23.5	55.0

Report date: 07/10/90.

EXHIBIT 2 *(continued)* Eight-Factor Analysis (District of Columbia Level = 10 +; Family = FIN)

Factors	Weight		Minority Female	Majority Female	Minority Male	Black	Asian	American Indian	Hispanic	Total Minority	Total Female
								2% of Population			
1. Min/WMN seek empl.	0.00	Percent Rep	40.8	14.5	35.1	70.3	2.6	0.2	2.8	75.9	55.2
		WTD Factor	0.0	0.0	0.0	0.0	0.0	0.0	0.0	0.0	0.0
2. Unemployment	0.0	Percent Rep	37.0	11.1	44.4	81.5	0.0	0.0	0.0	81.5	48.2
		WTD Factor	0.0	0.0	0.0	0.0	0.0	0.0	0.0	0.0	0.0
3. Total Labor Force	0.05	Percent Rep	16.3	30.4	15.7	26.0	2.6	0.2	3.0	31.9	46.6
		WTD Factor	0.8	1.5	0.8	1.3	0.1	0.0	0.2	1.6	2.3
4. Req/Skills/Loc	0.10	Percent Rep	12.3	29.1	10.6	16.6	3.3	0.2	2.9	22.9	41.4
		WTD Factor	1.2	2.9	1.1	1.7	0.3	0.0	0.3	2.3	4.1
5. Req/Skills/Recr	0.10	Percent Rep	12.3	29.1	10.6	16.6	3.3	0.2	2.9	22.9	41.4
		WTD Factor	1.2	2.9	1.1	1.7	0.3	0.0	0.3	2.3	4.1
6. Promo/Trans	0.60	Percent Rep	14.7	47.7	9.3	13.7	6.4	0.3	3.5	23.9	62.4
		WTD Factor	8.8	28.6	5.6	8.2	3.8	0.2	2.1	14.4	37.4
7. Comm/Training	0.15	Percent Rep	5.1	34.0	8.0	8.2	2.0	0.4	2.4	13.1	39.1
		WTD Factor	0.8	5.1	1.2	1.2	0.3	0.1	0.4	2.0	5.9
8. Inter/Training		Percent Rep									
		WTD Factor									
Job family % Availability =			12.8	41.1	9.7	14.1	4.9	0.3	3.2	22.5	53.9

Report date: 07/10/90.

EXHIBIT 2 *(concluded)* Eight-Factor Analysis (District of Columbia Level = 13 +; Family = FIN)

Factors	Weight		Minority Female	Majority Female	Minority Male	2% of Population				Total Minority	Total Female
						Black	Asian	American Indian	Hispanic		
1. Min/WMN seek empl.	0.00	Percent Rep	40.8	14.5	35.1	70.3	2.6	0.2	2.8	75.9	55.2
		WTD Factor	0.0	0.0	0.0	0.0	0.0	0.0	0.0	0.0	0.0
2. Unemployment	0.0	Percent Rep	37.0	11.1	44.4	81.5	0.0	0.0	0.0	81.5	48.2
		WTD Factor	0.0	0.0	0.0	0.0	0.0	0.0	0.0	0.0	0.0
3. Total Labor Force	0.05	Percent Rep	16.3	30.4	15.7	26.0	2.6	0.2	3.0	31.9	46.6
		WTD Factor	0.8	1.5	0.8	1.3	0.1	0.0	0.2	1.6	2.3
4. Req/Skills/Loc	0.10	Percent Rep	12.3	29.1	10.6	16.6	3.3	0.2	2.9	22.9	41.4
		WTD Factor	1.2	2.9	1.1	1.7	0.3	0.0	0.3	2.3	4.1
5. Req/Skills/Recr	0.10	Percent Rep	12.3	29.1	10.6	16.6	3.3	0.2	2.9	22.9	41.4
		WTD Factor	1.2	2.9	1.1	1.7	0.3	0.0	0.3	2.3	4.1
6. Promo/Trans	0.75	Percent Rep	7.5	22.7	12.4	12.2	4.7	0.9	2.1	19.9	30.1
		WTD Factor	5.6	17.0	9.3	9.1	3.5	0.6	1.6	14.9	22.6
7. Comm/Training	0.00	Percent Rep	5.1	34.0	8.0	8.2	2.0	0.4	2.4	13.1	39.1
		WTD Factor	0.0	0.0	0.0	0.0	0.0	0.0	0.0	0.0	0.0
8. Inter/Training		Percent Rep									
		WTD Factor									
Job Family % Availability =			8.9	24.3	12.2	13.7	4.3	0.7	2.3	21.1	33.2

Report date: 07/10/90.

EXHIBIT 3 Methodology

The following example (greatly simplified) is intended to demonstrate the principles and logic used in the actual calculation of BWF goals.

Step 1. The first step in calculating BWF Goals is to get an accurate count of employees in the organization:

- For each location (facility)   City, county, or metropolitan area
- By job function   Such as engineering, sales, or financing
- By grade band   1–6 for positions in grades 1 through 6
                       7–9 for positions in grades 7 through 9
                       10–12 for positions in grades 10 through 12
                       13–14 for positions in grades 13 and 14
                       15–18 for positions in grades 15 through 18

For this example, let's assume this organization has operations in Los Angeles and Rochester, and that all employees are either in engineering or finance.

City	Grade Band	Job Function	Number of Employees
Los Angeles	15–18	Finance	7
Los Angeles	13–14	Finance	13
Los Angeles	10–12	Finance	14
Los Angeles	7–9	Finance	12
Los Angeles	1–6	Finance	6
Los Angeles	15–18	Engineering	31
Los Angeles	13–14	Engineering	106
Los Angeles	10–12	Engineering	444
Los Angeles	7–9	Engineering	488
Los Angeles	1–6	Engineering	131
Rochester	15–18	Finance	14
Rochester	13–14	Finance	42
Rochester	10–12	Finance	48
Rochester	7–9	Finance	23
Rochester	1–6	Finance	8
Rochester	15–18	Engineering	62
Rochester	13–14	Engineering	125
Rochester	10–12	Engineering	690
Rochester	7–9	Engineering	983
Rochester	1–6	Engineering	201

Step 2. The next step is to get the availability estimates (from the government requirements) by job family and location for grade bands 1–6 and 7–9. There will be different availability estimates for each of the four employee groups:

- Minority females are abbreviated:Min Fem
- Majority females are abbreviated:Maj Fem
- Minority males are abbreviated:Min Male
- Majority males are abbreviated:Maj Male

Following through on our example, the availabilities for the finance and engineering functions in Los Angeles and Rochester are as follows:

(continued)

EXHIBIT 3   *(continued)*

City	Band	Function	Min Fem	Maj Fem	Min Male	Maj Male
Los Angeles	1–6	Finance	14.8	30.5	17.4	37.3
Los Angeles	7–9	Finance	17.9	43.7	12.3	26.1
Los Angeles	1–6	Engineering	3.7	6.6	23.5	66.2
Los Angeles	7–9	Engineering	6.9	11.1	23.9	58.1
Rochester	1–6	Finance	4.5	36.8	4.8	53.9
Rochester	7–9	Finance	11.2	47.9	4.2	36.7
Rochester	1–6	Engineering	1.3	7.9	7.0	83.8
Rochester	7–9	Engineering	5.0	12.3	12.2	70.5

These availability estimates are, by definition, the balanced workforce goals for the 1–6 and 7–9 grade bands. There are different goals for each location and job family. In the above example, the goals for minority females in finance in Los Angeles, grade bands 1–6 and 7–9, are 14.8 percent and 17.9 percent, respectively.

In actual practice, availability estimates are also calculated for the four minority categories: Blacks, Asians, Hispanics, and Native Americans. The totals of these four categories equals the total of Min Fem and Min Male.

Step 3. The third step is to multiply employee headcount (in Step 1) times the corresponding availability estimates for 1–6 and 7–9 grade bands and add the resultant products for each job family by location.

City	Band	Function	Min Fem	Maj Fem	Min Male	Maj Male
Los Angeles	1–6	Finance	6(14.8)	6(30.5)	6(17.4)	6(37.3)
Los Angeles	7–9	Finance	12(17.9)	12(43.7)	12(12.3)	12(26.1)
Los Angeles	1–6	Engineering	131(3.7)	131(6.6)	131(23.5)	131(66.2)
Los Angeles	7–9	Engineering	488(6.9)	488(11.1)	488(23.9)	488(58.1)
Rochester	1–6	Finance	8(4.5)	8(36.8)	8(4.8)	8(53.9)
Rochester	7–9	Finance	23(11.2)	23(47.9)	23(4.2)	23(36.7)
Rochester	1–6	Engineering	201(1.3)	201(7.9)	201(7.0)	201(83.8)
Rochester	7–9	Engineering	983(5.0)	983(12.3)	983(12.2)	983(70.5)

For example, applying this step to the *minority female* population in the *finance job family* in Los Angeles we would get the following result:

- $6(14.8) + 12(17.9) = 88.8 + 214.8 = 303.6$

Step 4. The fourth step is to calculate a weighted average of the balanced workforce goals for grade bands 1–6 and 7–9, for each job family. It is calculated by dividing the resultant sums by the total job family headcount in location (18).

Extending this step to the same population in the above example we generate a result that is called the *weighted 1–9 balance workforce estimate:*

- $303.6 \div 18 = 16.9$

Like availability estimates in the government requirements, the balanced workforce estimates in each row total 100 percent.

Xerox uses this weighted estimate for upper-level positions, rather than the standard availability estimate, to reflect the fact that the vast majority of jobs in grades 10 and above are filled by Xerox people promoted from lower grades. Using these estimates, therefore, results in more realistic balanced workforce goals for upper-level positions.

(continued)

EXHIBIT 3   *(continued)*

City	Grade Band	Function	Min Fem	Maj Fem	Min Male	Maj Male
Los Angeles	1–6	Finance	88.8	183.0	104.4	223.8
Los Angeles	7–9	Finance	214.8	524.4	147.6	313.2
	18		303.6	707.4	252.0	537.0
Los Angeles	1–9	Finance	16.9	39.3	14.0	29.8
Los Angeles	1–6	Engineering	484.7	864.6	2,078.5	8,672.2
Los Angeles	7–9	Engineering	3,367.2	5,416.8	11,663.2	28,352.8
	619		3,851.9	6,281.4	14,741.7	37,025.0
Los Angeles	1–9	Engineering	6.2	10.1	23.8	59.8
Rochester	1–6	Finance	36.0	294.4	38.4	431.2
Rochester	7–9	Finance	257.6	1,101.7	96.6	844.1
	31		293.6	1,396.1	135.0	1,275.3
Rochester	1–9	Finance	9.5	45.0	4.4	41.1
Rochester	1–6	Engineering	261.3	1,587.9	1,407.0	16,843.8
Rochester	7–9	Engineering	4,915.0	12,090.9	11,992.6	69,301.5
	1,184		5,176.3	13,678.8	13,399.6	86,145.3
Rochester	1–9	Engineering	4.4	11.6	11.3	72.8

Step 5. Step five is to apply the 1–9 weighted estimates to grade bands 10–12, 13–14, and 15–18, by corresponding job families and locations. This is the same procedures used in step three, except that the *availability* estimate has been replaced by the *weighted* 1–9 estimate.

City	Band	Function	Min Fem	Maj Fem	Min Male	Maj Male
Los Angeles	10–12	Finance	14(16.9)	14(39.3)	14(14.0)	14(29.8)
Los Angeles	13–14	Finance	13(16.9)	13(39.3)	13(14.0)	13(29.8)
Los Angeles	15–18	Finance	7(16.9)	7(39.9)	7(14.0)	7(29.8)
Los Angeles	10–12	Engineering	444(6.2)	444(10.1)	444(23.8)	444(59.8)
Los Angeles	13–14	Engineering	106(6.2)	106(10.1)	106(23.8)	106(59.8)
Los Angeles	15–18	Engineering	31(6.2)	31(10.1)	31(23.8)	31(59.8)
Rochester	10–12	Finance	48(9.5)	48(45.0)	48(4.4)	48(41.1)
Rochester	13–14	Finance	42(9.5)	42(45.0)	42(4.4)	42(41.1)
Rochester	15–18	Finance	14(9.5)	14(45.0)	14(4.4)	14(41.1)
Rochester	10–12	Engineering	690(4.4)	690(11.6)	690(11.3)	690(72.8)
Rochester	13–14	Engineering	125(4.4)	125(11.6)	125(11.3)	125(72.8)
Rochester	15–18	Engineering	62(4.4)	62(11.6)	62(11.3)	62(72.8)

Step 6. The sixth step is to consolidate the data for each grade band, by pooling across job function and work location. The procedure, similar to that used in Step 4, is to add the products and divide by total headcount. The results are the balanced workforce goals for grade bands 10–12, 13–14, and 15–18.

City	Grade Band	Function	Min Fem	Maj Fem	Min Male	Maj Male
Los Angeles	10–12	Finance	236.6	550.2	196.0	417.2
Rochester	10–12	Finance	456.0	2,160.0	211.2	1,972.8
Los Angeles	10–12	Engineering	2,752.8	448.4	10,567.2	26,551.2
Rochester	10–12	Engineering	3,036.0	8,004.0	7,797.0	50,232.0
	1,196		6,481.4	15,198.6	18,771.4	79,173.2
			5.4	12.7	15.7	66.2

(continued)

EXHIBIT 3   *(concluded)*

City	Grade Band	Function	Min Fem	Maj Fem	Min Male	Maj Male
Los Angeles	13–14	Finance	219.7	510.9	182.0	387.4
Rochester	13–14	Finance	339.0	1,890.0	184.8	1,726.2
Los Angeles	13–14	Engineering	657.2	1,070.6	2,522.8	6,338.8
Rochester	13–14	Engineering	550.0	1,450.0	1,412.5	9,100.0
	286		1,825.9	4,921.5	4,302.1	17,522.4
			6.4	17.2	15.0	61.4
Los Angeles	15–18	Finance	118.3	275.1	98.0	208.6
Rochester	15–18	Finance	133.0	630.0	612.6	575.4
Los Angeles	15–18	Engineering	192.2	313.1	737.8	1,853.8
Rochester	15–18	Engineering	272.8	719.2	700.6	4,513.6
	114		716.3	1,937.4	1,598.0	7,151.4
			6.3	17.0	14.0	62.7

In summary, the balance workforce goals for grades 10 and above are:

Grade Band	Min Fem	Maj Fem	Min Male	Maj Male
10–12	5.4	12.7	15.7	66.2
13–14	6.4	17.2	15.0	61.4
15–18	6.3	17.0	14.0	62.7

As in the case with all other goals, the total for the four employee groups equals 100 percent.

The balanced workforce approach was also used to calculate overall minority and female representation goals for large divisions within Xerox. This meant that, for a given job level, the (now modified) availability numbers for different locations and different functions were combined. This aspect of the balance workforce calculations is represented by the sixth step of Exhibit 3. (The example in the exhibit is greatly simplified. The actual calculations require a computer to calculate.) The final result, seen at the end of Step 6 of Exhibit 3, was a set of goals that were clear and succinct enough to guide and evaluate top-level managers. These calculations also helped to make visible the current representation of minorities and women at high levels of the company, where the small number of total jobs involved made it difficult to see patterns within single locations.

However, this procedure did produce some quirky results. The process of aggregation sometimes produced higher minority and/or female representation goals for the higher job grades than for the lower ones. Xerox's corporate HR personnel were exploring alternative methods of calculating the numbers to address this issue.

Adding the "Majority Male"

The second major aspect of the BWF approach was to ensure, not only promotion of minorities and women, but a balance between all employee categories. To achieve this balance, majority males would also become a category to be tracked and included in the calculation of availability estimates and targets. Whereas in the past, a manager's affirmative action goals were met if employment of minorities and females was at or above target levels, now, overachieving in one category meant, by definition, that goals for other categories were not being met. According to Al Fagan, Vice President and Region General Manager for the Coastal Region:

> The advantage of BWF is that it includes all people. In the past, under AA objectives you could look good by overachieving in the protected

classes and that would be just terrific, but it had to come out of another wedge of the pie that was not focused on—the majority male community. Now balance means that each of those groups will be in balance. I think it is an excellent approach, and a positive step forward for all people.

This aspect of BWF was not visible for several years because majority males were at or above targets in all cases. By the late 1980s, however, majority males were underrepresented in some jobs at some levels. Entry-level sales jobs in some districts, for example, were below targets for majority males. When this happened, tensions rose. Minority males, in particular, worried that their career opportunities would be limited in the divisions of the company where they had been performing well and advancing in large numbers. This aspect of the balanced work force sparked new debates. As Fagan put it,

> Then the battleground becomes what share of the pie should our particular group have and enjoy. It would be hard to disagree with the concept of a balanced workforce, but where the disagreement will come now is how do you determine what size piece of the pie each group has. That gets into things like the 1990 census—where is that taking us and should we anticipate where it is taking us in our 1991 targets? Since [there may be more Hispanics and women], should we anticipate that and build them in?

A number of black managers also worried that alleged systematic undercounting of blacks in the census would affect Xerox hiring goals. In addition to the problem of population estimates was the problem of unit of analysis. Al Byrd, Vice President, Region Manager, Sales, explained that "Washington is 75 percent black, but if you include Metropolitan areas where the large portion is white you get to the point where the representation of blacks is lower. In Atlanta, if you include Cobb county, it dilutes the numbers."

Meeting the Goals

Once BWF goals were set, each manager was responsible for achieving those targets. Xerox's performance appraisal system evaluated managers in four areas: customer satisfaction, business results (profit and market share), quality process, and employee satisfaction. Employee satisfaction included morale, turnover, and BWF. From the top of the company to first line managers, BWF goals were understood and were a part of business. Ed Stanek, Regional Operations Manager, Customer Service, explained that targets and clear leadership from the CEO of Xerox were critical to that understanding:

> [The critical factors were] the leadership that Kearns took in establishing direction, that has to be first, the targeting—expectations that were cascaded down—and then holding people accountable and saying this is something that is part of our business. It is an element of business that will help us be successful. That evolves to the point where you are not going to be successful here if you do not perform in all four areas.

To achieve these goals, managers had to develop ongoing relationships with schools and black community organizations and actively recruit top black graduates. They also maintained ongoing training programs to develop majority and minority employees after they had joined Xerox. The most developed, formalized, and important mechanism to help managers meet their BWF goals was the management resources process (MRP), which identified and tracked people who could. be promoted to and within management.

MRP began with a process of identifying employees who had potential for promotion within the managerial ranks of Xerox. After someone was identified, he or she was labeled as "ready within one year" or "ready within three years." After the people and the time frame had been identified, explained Ed Stanek,

> The next step is that your immediate manager sits down and talks with you about what your specific strengths and weaknesses are and where you need to develop and enhance your capabilities. An action plan will be put in place for specific things for you to do: it might be schooling, it might be an opportunity to make presentations—if you are

not real good on your feet we'll give you some opportunities to get on your feet in front of groups, it might be an analytic shortfall, in which case we will send you to specific schools or have you work with our support managers—whatever it happens to be.

In some cases, developmental positions were made available for 12–18 months to increase the person's exposure and give them more experience. If the appropriate next job was not available after that time, the person would be put back into their previous job, but he or she would be a stronger and more visible candidate when a job did open. The MRP inventory was updated annually, and each individual's progress towards their goals was monitored.

It was this earlier stage in the management of promotions, not the actual point of hiring, that made the difference in terms of meeting BWF goals. Stanek explained:

> If you look and see who your candidates are—ready in one year and ready in three years—if that is your inventory and you don't have the right mix in that inventory, then you have got to do some things inside your region or district to help people develop so that you do make the representation. You can pretty much predict what your representation is going to be based on the inventory. . . . If your inventory is balanced and your existing population is balanced then you can make that decision without considering race. If you're existing population is not balanced, and you have several candidates, then race is going to be an element of the decision.

When internal promotion systems were not enough to bring the population at a management level into balance, outside people were hired directly into management. This was called "premium hiring."

Remaining Problems

Although Xerox had made great strides in its management of diversity, a number of new problems interfered with their ability to accomplish the goal of having a fully balanced workforce by 1995, including: changes in the company's rate of growth, changes in technology, changes in lifestyle throughout society, and the BWF process itself.

During the 1970s and early 1980s, Xerox grew rapidly. There were always opportunities for promotion for those who performed well, including talented women and minorities. By the late 1980s however, Xerox had reached a stable size and was trying to reduce layers of hierarchy in order to remain responsive and competitive. Now, there might not be a job open for those who deserved promotion. The overall pace of promotion would be significantly slower for all employees in Xerox than had been true a decade earlier. As Ed Stanek put it, "the opportunities will be less, as far as people moving up the ranks. That causes some consternation, and the ones that do occur become more precious." Any effort to reshape the demographics of the company would be much slower and more contentious than before.

Even where opportunities did exist, people were now less likely than a decade ago to want to move to places that provided those opportunities. As Fagan complained, the "problem is location, the job, the desire, and the availability—who will move who will not move—that's what makes it more difficult rather than the numbers of candidates." In one example, a woman was ready to become a district manager, but was unwilling to relocate her family. This was a problem not only for women, but for dual-career families and single parents. In sum, Fagan explained, "the big problems are the number of opportunities, and the flexibility of the right kind of candidate to go to the need areas or the areas where the opportunities are."

These uncontrollable factors influenced the expectations put on managers to meet their BWF goals. Lynn Weaver, Region Personnel manager, explained: "in most cases we were able to identify potential candidates for moves, assuming the opportunity presented itself, but if we do not have opportunities, that is taken into considerations as to your achievement. If you don't have anything that happens to allow you to achieve, we aren't going to hold a manager accountable for that." They would, however, still be responsible for developing employees and creating a positive environment for all employees.

Sometimes the goals that were set seemed overwhelming to managers. Al Fagan worried about the "vast number of targets and levels":

> If you take each organization sales, service, and administration, you take each grade level within it, you take each class within that level and all the puts and takes and you are dealing with tens upon tens of targets of which unfortunately it is too easy to miss some here and some there. It is almost an impossibility to get balance because of the large number of targets.

And, Fagan added, even though the targets were now anchored to the demographics of the first-level feeder pool, higher-level demographics were difficult to change without change in the prior level:

> What the feeder base at each level lets you do is say how much can you realistically expect to achieve at the next level. I know I won't be able to get [a balanced population of] 13-pluses, if I don't have adequate representation at the 10-pluses. I just can't get there.

"Small numbers" were particularly difficult to follow. For Hispanics in a given job grade, Fagan added, you had "a one or two number here, a one or two number there, when you add it up around the region it was a 10 or 12 number that was way off the mark. The numbers are so small that nobody's focusing on it." More broadly, small numbers pushed the responsibility for assessing BWF goals up to higher levels: "where a district may have one or two of a particular type of job, to target them on that small a number does not seem appropriate." Yet without targets "it is easy for somebody to not feel accountable to get the job done." It becomes "'situational'— in this situation you have to place a person of type A."

With so many groups and so many levels, it was easy for managers to take their eye off of one ball or another. For example, in the process

of focusing on females and minorities, the company forgot to ensure enough representation of white males in some of the feeder pools. Another example was the relative focus on hiring versus promotion. After initially trying, as Weaver explained, to "just get representation" by hiring minorities and women at the bottom, her office focused on "bringing them through." But later, while helping bring people through, they "took their eye off of the intake piece." She explained: "I realized I had a couple of places that hadn't hired any minorities. I said how in the heck did this happen! We were so focused on the BWF objectives and moving people through, that we were surprised."

In addition to concerns about representation at each *level* within Xerox, minority and female employees worried that access to premium product programs might be not balanced. Xerox was undergoing a major shift from optical-based machinery to electronic "systems." Systems would be the primary "area of opportunity" within the company in the next decade. Weaver explained:

> In the past whether it was conscious, or unconscious—or subconscious!—oftentimes when you have new programs you do not have blacks participating in those programs. And if those are the programs of the future, then you have to have black representation there and female representation there. The 9200 was a big product for us. It revolutionized copying. It wasn't technically more difficult than what we were selling, but it was a new product—we needed sales people to sell it and service people to service it. What we found was that majority males were the ones in that program. Some of it was just comfort: If I am a sales manager or a district manager and I'm making a decision of someone going into that area, I'm probably going to go with my more experienced people who at that time happened to be majority, and I'm doing it in the likeness of myself because that's who I'm more comfortable with. It just kind of happened.

At the time the company was tracking total numbers of employees by category, but participation in the 9200 program was not broken out.

Weaver explained: "we were looking at total numbers, not at that population, and it just happened."

Results as of 1990

1990 balanced workforce results for the U.S. Marketing Group are shown in Exhibit 4. Throughout the group, minority male employees were at or above the BWF goals. At the highest levels of the group, females were underrepresented. And at the entry level, white males were underrepresented. As a result, Xerox was trying to enhance its white male recruiting efforts for entry-level sales jobs. In areas outside of U.S. Marketing several "white islands," such as finance and engineering still remained.

Overall, however, the BWF process has become a way of life at Xerox. There was some resentment among white male employees, but it was not pervasive.

It is well accepted now because it has been in place for so many years; if you start it today in a predominantly white male organization it would be more difficult.

Ed Stanek

People now accept the AA targets as a way of life at Xerox, so I don't see open resentment. That's our goal and we state it; you do it for 17 or 18 years and it's part of the culture, people don't resent it. There is a level of understanding. You try to talk about it and have open dialogue. You have resentment if it's not talked about. When we started [AA] people were doing crazy things, be-

ing outright racist, it made [black employees] active. Now you don't have as much of that, its not as obvious. Part of it is the management process.

Al Byrd

I'm not going to say that every manager's heart is pure on this issue; I won't say that there's not a tremendous amount of prejudice. What's in somebody's heart versus how you act and behave and conduct your business, that's absolutely taboo. Are you going to change people's beliefs—probably not. We never say that we try to do that, but we do hold them accountable for their behavior.

Al Fagan

The balanced workforce goals and processes were a source of constant debate and tension. Should the population at "intake" be balanced, or skewed to help more quickly correct imbalances at higher levels of the company? What would Xerox do if the newly released census data and information on college graduates showed, as some expected, a decrease in availability of black males? Should top black male executives who were "overrepresented" in the U.S. Marketing Group move laterally into equivalent high-level positions in other divisions with lower representation?

These issues were not just necessary to meet government requirements, they were considered a critical element in Xerox's future success. As Fagan put it, "we know that the workforce is going to continue to become more diverse by the year 2000. We have many more different employees and employee needs than we have had over the past years."

EXHIBIT 4 Balanced Workforce Performance (as of April 30, 1990)

EPG		01/01/90 Cnt	01/01/90 Rep %	04/30/90 Cnt	04/30/90 Rep %	1990 Target	1990 Target Achievement	End Point BWF Goals %	Goals	Goal Window	Goal Window Status	Opportunities* Cnt	Opportunities* %	Terminations Cnt	Terminations %
EPG	Maj Fem	2	4.8%	1	2.4%			15.0%	13.1	—	16.9 Under	0	0%	0	0%
	Maj Male	26	61.9	25	61.0							1	33	0	0
	Min Fem	1	2.4	1	2.4			5.0	3.1	—	6.9 Under	0	0	0	0
	Min Male	13	31.0	14	34.1							2	67	1	100
	Total	42		41								3		1	
	Hispanic	1	2.4	1	2.4							0	0	0	0
15–18	Maj Fem	43	13.4	46	13.8	16.7	83	29.0	28.2	—	29.8 Under	5	17	0	0
	Maj Male	212	65.8	224	67.1	GA		56.0	55.2	—	56.8 Over	20	69	7	88
	Min Fem	14	4.7	15	4.5	4.4	100	6.1	5.3	—	6.9 Under	0	0	0	0
	Min Male	52	16.1	49	14.7	GA		8.9	8.1	—	9.7 Over	4	14	1	13
	Total	322		334								29		8	
	Hispanic	10	3.1	10	3.0	3.0	100	4.1	3.3	—	4.9 Under	0	0	0	0
13–14	Maj Fem	137	17.3	152	17.9	19.9	90	25.7	25.1	—	26.3 Under	21	23	3	33
	Maj Male	511	64.5	539	63.4	GA		57.8	57.2	—	58.4 Over	46	50	4	44
	Min Fem	42	5.3	46	5.4	5.9	92	5.9	5.3	—	6.5 Within	6	7	1	11
	Min Male	102	12.9	113	13.3	GA		10.6	10.0	—	11.2 Over	19	21	1	11
	Total	792		850								92		9	
	Hispanic	25	3.2	31	3.6	3.9	92	4.6	4.0	—	5.2 Under	8	9	0	0
10–12	Maj Fem	412	17.9	432	18.6	18.4	100	20.1	19.6	—	20.6 Under	54	30	8	32
	Maj Male	1,384	60.1	1,403	60.3	60.9	99	61.9	61.4	—	62.4 Under	92	51	13	52
	Min Fem	156	6.8	159	6.8	GA		4.6	4.1	—	5.1 Over	15	8	1	4
	Min Male	349	15.2	332	14.3	GA		13.4	12.9	—	13.9 Over	21	12	3	12
	Total	2,301		2,326								182		25	
	Hispanic	114	5.0	113	4.9	5.0	98	5.2	4.7	—	5.7 Within	11	6	1	100

7–9															
Maj Fem	513	37.4	517	36.9	GA	93	32.5	32.0	—	33.0	Over	69	34	8	42
Maj Male	571	41.6	581	41.5	44.4		48.9	48.4	—	49.4	Under	84	41	7	37
Min Fem	131	9.6	141	10.1	GA		8.4	7.9	—	8.9	Over	29	14	2	11
Min Male	156	11.4	161	11.5	GA		10.4	9.9	—	10.9	Over	21	10	2	11
Total	1,371		1,400									203		19	
Hispanic	54	3.9	52	3.7	4.0	92	4.9	4.4	—	5.4	Under	10	5	1	100
1–6															
Maj Fem	191	40.1%	213	42.7%	GA	83	30.4%	29.6	—	31.2	Over	59	48%	4	29%
Maj Male	168	35.2	169	33.9	40.6		55.5	54.7	—	56.3	Under	38	31	4	29
Min Fem	71	14.9	64	12.8	GA		6.6	5.8	—	7.4	Over	10	8	4	29
Min Male	46	9.7	53	10.6	GA		7.6	6.8	—	8.4	Over	15	12	2	14
Total	476		499									122		14	
Hispanic	26	5.5	28	5.8	GA		3.8	3.0	—	4.6	Over	6	5	0	0
SLS															
Maj Fem	1,467	31.1	1,454	30.9	GA	95	25.5	25.0	—	26.0	Over	320	33	67	35
Maj Male	2,236	47.4	2,236	47.6	50.3		61.2	60.7	—	61.7	Under	436	45	84	44
Min Fem	448	9.5	436	9.3	GA		4.8	4.3	—	5.3	Over	92	10	10	5
Min Male	570	12.1	573	12.2	GA		8.5	8.0	—	9.0	Over	113	12	31	16
Total	4,721		4,699									961		192	
Hispanic	228	4.8	222	4.7	GA		4.2	3.7	—	4.7	Within	33	3	5	100

1990 AA Class Goals/Target

Total measured categories (EPG not included)	24
Categories achieving balanced workforce goals	15
Total annual targets	9
Categories achieving annual targets	2

1990 Hispanic Goals/Targets

Total measured categories (EPG not included)	6
Categories achieving balanced workforce goals	2
Total annual targets	4
Categories achieving annual targets	1

Note: GA = BWF goal achieved.

*"Opportunities" are new hires, promotions into a grade cluster, or promotions to higher grades within a cluster.

BLACK CAUCUS GROUPS AT XEROX CORPORATION (A)

We [black employees] do not have the luxury of mediocrity. You hurt yourself and you hurt the group. If mediocrity is your goal, Xerox is not the place for you to work.

Barry Rand, president of U.S. Marketing Group, Xerox

It was September of 1974, and David Kearns, president of Xerox's largest division, the Information Systems Group (ISG), was flying to Toronto to meet with seven black managers from around the United States. His purpose was to discuss the prospect of a national black caucus meeting at Xerox. Since the 1960s, Xerox had made great strides toward integrating blacks into the company (see Exhibit 1). Much of this progress was due to the efforts of the first group of black employees. Through local caucus groups, they had fought to gain equitable treatment of black employees by middle management and had helped to recruit, teach, and advise the black employees who had followed them at Xerox. Kearns had previously effected policy changes and implemented management actions that were supportive of black employees. The caucus structure had played a central role in these changes.

However, a number of legal specialists, Human Resource specialists, and middle managers were worried about the consequences of having a national meeting that could lead to a companywide caucus group for black employees. They feared the power such a group might gain and its potential for being viewed as a union. Kearns had to balance the opinions of his superiors and his advisers against his own experience with the caucus groups. He had to decide how to direct the forthcoming Toronto meeting, which would set the tone and direction for the relationship between Xerox and the black caucus groups for many years.

Background of Xerox Corporation

During the 1960s, Xerox held a virtual monopoly on the office copier market as its product was shielded by several hundred patents. Consequently, the company was able to take full advantage of the explosive growth occurring throughout the market—both domestically and internationally (see Exhibit 2).

This dramatic success dated back to 1946 when the Haloid Corporation, a small specialty photographic paper and film company in Rochester, New York, had acquired permanent and exclusive rights to the experimental new process of "xerography." Haloid—renamed Xerox in 1961—poured money into research and development. By 1952, Haloid had spent $4.3 million on the development of a xerographic copier and was $400,000 in the red. In 1953, however, the research began to pay off, and by 1956 xerographic products accounted for 40 percent of Haloid's revenues (over $9 million.) These successful products included a xerographic machine to make master sheets for offset printing, a xerographic microfilm printer, and a xerographic facsimile reproduction system.

In 1959 the first xerographic office copier was introduced. It was revolutionary. Previous copiers had used expensive chemically coated paper and had tended to produce copies that emerged wet, faded when exposed to light, were difficult

This case was prepared by Caitlin Deinard under the supervision of Raymond A. Friedman.

Copyright ©1990 by the President and Fellows of Harvard College.

Harvard Business College case 491-047 (Rev. November 3, 1994).

EXHIBIT 1 Minority Representation at Xerox: 1964 and 1974

1964

	Total Employees	Total Minorities	
		Number	Percent
Officials and managers	592	5	1%
Professionals	2,013	52	3
Technicians	599	35	6
Sales	3,113	40	1
Office and clerical	2,576	52	2
Other (hourly)	2,434	114	5
Total =	11,327	298	3%

1974

	Total Employees	Black		Asian		Native American		Hispanic		Total Minorities	
Officials and managers	5,925	268	4.5%	53	.9%	8	.13%	80	1.3%	409	6.9%
Professionals	8,003	363	4.5	196	2.4	11	.13	96	1.2	666	8.3
Technicians	11,206	976	8.7	194	1.7	50	.45	175	1.56	1,395	12.4
Sales	6,548	530	8.1	75	1.1	11	.17	111	1.79	727	11.1
Office and clerical	10,126	1,184	11.7	61	.6	31	.3	262	2.6	1,538	15.2
Other (hourly)	12,439	2,020	16.2	192	1.5	38	.3	943	7.6	3,193	25.7
Total =	54,305	4,341	7.9%	716	1.3%	149	.27%	1,667	3.07%	7,928	14.6%

to write on, and were difficult to read. The Xerox machine, on the other hand, used inexpensive, untreated paper, did not use a chemical bath, and produced copies difficult to differentiate from the original.

Since its technical complexity made the Xerox copier too expensive for most businesses to buy outright, Xerox developed an innovative leasing system—pricing for use—which charged businesses by the amount of paper they used. This strategy demanded a large sales force to place the machines and a large technical support staff to maintain them and repair them on site. In fact, in the early 1970s, approximately 12 percent of all domestic Xerox employees were salespeople and approximately 20 percent were technicians.

Xerographic copiers quickly became the firm's dominant product line, producing an estimated 60 percent to 70 percent of revenue as early as 1962. Xerox also expanded internationally, setting up joint ventures with Rank-Xerox to operate in Europe, Africa, and Asia, and with Fuji-Xerox to operate in Japan and other East Asian markets.

The 1960s at Xerox

In 1963, there were a number of violent race riots in Rochester, New York, the city in which Xerox's corporate headquarters was located (see Exhibit 3 for chronology). The shock of this violence in their own "backyard," as well as the other events of the 1960s Civil Rights movement, helped awaken senior Xerox managers to the seriousness of the racial inequities and conflicts in the United States. Joe Wilson, Xerox's

EXHIBIT 2   Summary Income Statements

Year	Total Operating Revenue ($000,000)	Profits after taxes ($000)
1960	40.2	2,610
1961	66.2	5,476
1962	115.2	13,894
1963	176.0	23,001
1964	317.8	43,725
1965	548.8	65,689
1966	752.5	86,700
1967	983.1	106,384
1968	1,224.4	128,950
1969	1,482.9	161,368
1970	1,718.6	187,691
1971	1,961.4	212,610
1972	2,419.1	249,507
1973	2,989.7	300,484
1974	3,576.4	331,083

first chairman and CEO, and Peter McColough, then president of Xerox, shared a common belief in fairness and a moral commitment to affirmative action. Their personal philosophy helped form the company's culture and reputation.

In 1968, Wilson and McColough wrote a letter to all Xerox managers, condemning racial discrimination (see Exhibit 4). They committed the company to intensive minority recruitment and made line managers directly responsible for the success of this recruitment. Cy Wright, a black sales representative who started at Xerox in 1970, recalled how Xerox's overall commitment to racial equity influenced his decision to work there:

> Everything that I'd heard about the Peter McColoughs there caused me to feel that they were at least fair. So, I thought that there was a certain amount of security in that arena even when the managers between me and them did not necessarily share or exhibit the same traits. You knew that they knew that the ultimate decision makers were fair.

Xerox also took other actions under Wilson and McColough. It funded and provided man-

agement consulting to a minority-owned and -operated plant in Rochester's black community. Xerox hoped that the plant, which produced parts for Xerox, would provide jobs for the community's unemployed. Xerox also sponsored and funded television programs, such as "Of Black America," designed to raise public awareness of racial problems and black history and culture.

San Francisco: The "Tan Territory" Issue

Xerox hired the first sizable groups of black sales representatives in the late 1960s (the very first black sales representative was hired in 1967 in New York City). One of the largest groups was located in the San Francisco/Oakland area. Despite Xerox's reputation and efforts to hire blacks for entry-level jobs, things were not easy

EXHIBIT 3   Chronology for Development of Black Caucus Groups

1963	Rochester riots.
1964	Congress passed Civil Rights Act, outlawing discrimination.
1965	President Lyndon Johnson issued Executive Order 11246, establishing affirmative action for all government contractors.
1967	Xerox hired first black sales rep.
1968	Chairman Joseph Wilson and President Peter McColough's letter to all Xerox managers.
1969–1974	Xerox caucus groups independently emerging around the country.
1971	"Tan Territory" issue.
1972	Minority Advisory Committee (MAC) established.
1971–1974	Black leadership emerging.
1973	Corporate Few's Philadelphia conference. First caucus conference.
1973	Caucus leadership met in Cleveland and Chicago.
1974	Regional advisory panels established.
Fall 1974	Toronto meeting.

EXHIBIT 4   Wilson and McColough's 1968 Letter

May 2, 1968

To All Xerox Managers:

We at Xerox are among those who are compelled to accept the indictment of the National Advisory Commission on Civil Disorders: "What white Americans have never fully understood—but what the Negro can never forget—is that white society is deeply implicated in the ghetto. *White institutions created it, white institutions maintain it, and white society condones it.*"

We, like all other Americans, share the responsibility for a color-divided nation; and in all honesty, we need not look beyond our own doorstep to find out why.

In Rochester, one of the first American cities scarred by racial strife, Xerox continues to employ only a very small percentage of Negroes. In other major cities, including some that have suffered even greater violence, we employ no Negroes at all.

Thus, despite a stated policy that seeks to fulfill our obligations to society—and even though the significant steps we *have* taken have been publicly praised—our performance is still far from a shining beacon of corporate responsibility.

We know, of course, that many Negroes—fearing rejection—simply don't apply to Xerox for jobs. And of those who do apply, many fail to meet our usual standards of qualification. But those factors obviously cannot be used as excuses. They are, rather, the very problems which Xerox must and will attack in the future.

In order to respond with concerted action to the Advisory Commission's recommendations that American industry hire, train, and suitably employ one million Negroes within the next three years, we are therefore going to adopt these immediate courses of action:

First, *we will heavily intensity our recruiting of Negroes* and other minorities. If, as our past experience indicates, they are reluctant to come to us, then we will go to them. A special recruiting effort as University Microfilms in Ann Arbor, Michigan, has proved the validity of this approach by substantially increasing minority employment in the space of a few months. We will now extend that effort throughout all the departments, divisions, and subsidiaries of Xerox.

Secondly, *all managers responsible for hiring—regardless of geographical location—will reexamine their selection standards and training programs.* Our past efforts, by and large, have sought to find only the "best qualified" people for Xerox, regardless of age, race, or religion. But that goal, however valid, has inadvertently excluded many good people from productive employment.

We are, accordingly, going to change the selection standards that screen out all but the most qualified people. We will also begin devoting special attention to minority employees of limited qualifications to make them genuinely productive in the shortest possible time. Hopefully we can maintain standards of performance throughout.

(continued)

EXHIBIT 4   *(concluded)*

Effective immediately, therefore, all Xerox managers are directed, on an individual basis, to begin this effort, pending a more systematic companywide revision of standards.

Thirdly, *we are planning to increase substantially our training of unqualified Negroes, and other minority members.*

Although the Project Step Up Program to qualify people for "entry level" jobs has been successful in the Rochester area, we feel that its scope must be considerably broadened and the entry requirements modified. We are presently planning to incorporate the program into our present hiring process, and to extend it to major Xerox facilities outside Rochester.

The full and unqualified cooperation of all Xerox managers is expected in reaching our minority hiring goals. Corporate Personnel has been given the responsibility for implementing our plans, and for establishing an accountability system through which top management—beginning immediately—can regularly assess progress in all divisions, departments, and subsidiaries of the corporation.

Today there are 22 million Negroes in the United States. The exclusion of many of them from our society is a malignancy that the nation cannot endure. To include them as integral to the nation, however, will mean even more than the correction of an intolerable injustice. It will also mean the creation of an enormous and affluent market for new products and services, and of an equally enormous pool of manpower to help meet the critical shortages predicted for the future.
We are fully aware, of course, of the progress that Xerox has already made in assisting the civil rights movement.

But it simply has not gone far enough.

We must do more because Xerox will not add to the misery of the present condition of most Negores. It will not condone the waste of a great national resource. It will not compromise the conviction on which the success of this enterprise and of the nation depends.

Joseph C. Wilson   C. Peter McColough

---

for blacks once they were working in the company. There were numerous instances of inequitable treatment of black employees in the San Francisco area—the most dramatic of which culminated in what became known within Xerox as the "tan territory issue."

In 1969, the black employees started meeting together at one another's homes in an informal support group they called BABE (Bay Area Black Employees). The first leaders of the group were Richard Kier and Gene Ruffin, who were sales representatives at the time, and John Lewis, who later became the regional affirmative action manager. Once their own group was organized, BABE members drove down the coast on several weekends to help the black Xerox employees in Los Angeles form their own caucus group, LABE (Los Angeles Black Employees). The group's primary desire and strategy in this early stage was to increase the number of blacks working at Xerox and to ensure that only the best possible black employees were hired.

In 1970 BABE met with the regional management and convinced them to give black employees a major role in the recruiting and hiring of new black employees. A system was developed under which a black Xerox employee was present whenever white managers interviewed a black candidate. In instances where the hiring decision was not clear-cut, the black employee's recommendation was followed. As a result of this policy and of the personal recruitment of friends and colleagues by black employees, the number of black Xerox employees in the San Francisco area increased from 10 to 30 between 1970 and 1971.

While the number of blacks in entry-level jobs was increasing, the black sales representatives felt they still faced inequities within Xerox that limited their opportunity for fair compensation and advancement. They were especially disturbed because the company's managers, all of whom were white, consistently assigned inferior sales territories to the black sales representatives. In response, 30 black Xerox sales representatives in the San Francisco area filed a class-action suit against the company in the fall of 1971. All 30 sales representatives were members of BABE, but, for legal reasons, they filed it as private individuals.

Xerox's San Francisco district had two types of sales territories: "grey" and "tan." The "grey territories" were the geographical areas of the accounts that leased the more expensive, large-volume copiers—downtown San Francisco, for example. The smaller companies that leased the smaller, cheaper copiers were in the "tan territories." The names referred to the color of the copy machines; the expensive copiers were grey, and the low-end copiers were tan.

This distinction was important because the commissions in the two territories were different. The tan copiers paid from $50 to $125 for upgrades or new accounts; the grey copiers paid from $250 to $400. If an account in a sales representative's territory stopped leasing a copier or downgraded to a cheaper model, the company debited the representative's incentive commission account. Because many of the smaller accounts were less established, they were more likely to fail and stop leasing copiers. Also, some experienced sales representatives were able to

gerrymander territory configurations so that the accounts they knew were about to cancel were shifted to the tan territories. As a result, the tan territories were overloaded with poor accounts.

It was clear to the Bay area black sales representatives that they were all working in the "tan territories," regardless of their performance records, and the "grey territories" were assigned to white sales representatives. Their earnings were consistently lower than those of white sales representatives, and a greater number of black sales representatives went into "debt" to Xerox than white sales representatives.

To make matters worse, the regional management did not promote black employees to management positions. One man in particular, Axel Henri, a former Army major, had the top performance record in his district and was at the top of the promotion list for district manager. But the regional operating manager passed over him for the job and instead hired a white man from a southern California district. Although the Henri example was the most flagrant case of inequitable treatment, there were other successful black employees who deserved promotion and were consistently disregarded.

When the class-action suit over territory assignments and Henri's promotion was filed, corporate headquarters immediately sent a manager to San Francisco to internally investigate the black employees' claims. He reported to senior corporate management that the suit was valid and would almost certainly be won. Peter McColough (CEO by 1971) responded by sending David Kearns, who had recently been hired and would become president of ISG, and Archie McCardle, the president of Xerox, to San Francisco on the company's private jet the next day. He told Kearns to do whatever was necessary to solve the problem.

Bernard Kinsey, a black sales representative who had just started at Xerox, described the tension among the black employees when they heard that Kearns was flying to San Francisco. No one had any idea what this new man from the top echelon of Xerox would do. Kinsey would later become a leader of BABE and the Vice President of Advance Marketing.[1] He recalled:

> The caucus movement wasn't all nice and clean and everybody saying we agree with you. The law suit wasn't popular with management—we took a tremendous risk. There was a lot of hostility toward us from white Xerox and because many of us came from black colleges during the civil rights movement, nobody was interested any more in just waiting and saying 'we shall overcome.'

When he arrived in San Francisco, Kearns went to two meetings: first, one with regional management, and then one with the leaders of the black employees. After hearing the facts from both sides, Kearns announced his solution at a large joint meeting. He ordered an immediate change of policy to remedy the inequities in sales territory assignments. He promoted four blacks, including Henri, to managerial positions, right there at the meeting. Then Kearns canceled all the "debts" to Xerox that the black sales representatives had accumulated, ordered that the territories of all black sales representatives be reconfigured, and announced that the checks to equalize past earnings would be written and paid that afternoon.

Washington, D.C.: What Happened to Algy Guy?

Inequitable treatment was not the only difficulty faced by young blacks who joined Xerox in the early 1970s. There were also the less tangible, subtle disadvantages that came from not being part of the informal network of support, information, and mentoring shared by the other sales representatives.

In 1971, Gil Scott was recruited and hired by Xerox's Washington, D.C., district as an entry-level sales representative. A 25-year-old black man who had graduated from Hampton University in Virginia in 1968, Scott was attracted to

Xerox because it was a sales-focused business. Sales, with its stack rankings, performance ratings, and commissions, provided objective measures of success. He described his reasoning:

> I was looking for a job where if I put forth X amount of effort, it would be rewarded—with compensation, with potential for promotion. It was very much like the athletic field, where, if you had the talent, if you were faster, stronger, tougher, worked harder, practiced more, were more committed, then you could get results. It did not depend on who you knew or who your dad was or what school you graduated from. There was a level playing field where we could compete evenly. If you had outstanding performance, you could accelerate your career movement.

Scott was also attracted by Xerox's corporate culture, which seemed open to blacks. Xerox was a very young company and had an unusually relaxed environment. As Scott saw it, IBM, another marketing-focused business that he considered at the time, was "very stoic, or at least it was then. You did it only the IBM way and you could never not do what IBM said. Xerox was a lot looser, not as regimented." People wore traditional business suits, but long hair, colored shirts, and wide ties were also common. There was no insistence on conformity to one uniform culture. Scott did not feel that he would have to stop looking and acting like a black person to succeed at Xerox.

> What I liked about the company was that as I sat in the lobby I saw people . . . they were walking fast; they had long hair, dressed nicely; they were young people I could relate to. That's what attracted me. I said to myself, this is a place where I can feel comfortable. Xerox was teen-aged: it was not like an insurance company, where you could see a massive structure. It was not limiting to me; you had to wear a suit, but not 'you can only wear a white shirt and wing-tip shoes.' It was unique in corporate America.

Ten other black sales representatives were hired at the same time as Scott. Before their group was hired, there had been only three black sales representatives in the Washington district:

---

1. Special thanks should also be extended to Mr. Kinsey for having brought the events documented in this case to the attention of Harvard Business School.

Kent Amos, Barry Rand, and Bill Robinson. One day, after about three months at Xerox, the new recruits suddenly realized that Algy Guy, one of their cohort, was missing. No one had seen him for several weeks. They did not know if he had gone on vacation, quit, or been fired. After several weeks of wondering and worrying about Algy Guy's fate, they found out that he had quit. After that, the group of recruits decided to meet together regularly to stay in contact. Scott remembered why the meetings started:

> That rallying cry—'Whatever happened to Algy Guy?'—was the catalyst that brought us together. What sustained us was a mutual understanding that we needed one another to exist in this friendly but sometimes hostile environment called Xerox—friendly in its attitudes and in its structure, but unfriendly in the sharing of the information and nuances necessary to be successful in the competitive situation of corporate America.

With the help and support of Amos, Rand, and Robinson, the young sales representatives began holding meetings informally at night in their apartments and houses. They studied Xerox's pricing structure, learned how the copiers actually worked, and practiced giving presentations. The group also helped the people who were right out of college or the army to adjust to the corporate world. They knew that success in the corporate world—even in sales, which had objective measures of success—depended on intangible factors like a handshake or eye contact. Scott reminisced about some advice he received:

> As I was sitting in the lobby . . . Kent Amos pulled me aside and said (he didn't know me at all, I hadn't seen him before in my life), 'Let me tell you, don't come in here unless you have a suit on.' I only owned one suit at that time, and wearing a sport coat and tie was enough for me in most cases, but when I came back I had on a suit. And I wore that suit virtually every day until I was able to buy another one because I would not violate what he told me.

The group provided blacks with a support network. Although the black sales representatives were Xerox employees and were part of the formal organization at Xerox Corporation, in the early 1970s, this affiliation did not make them a part of the informal network that existed among the white employees. The black employees did not have access to the relationships that come from having a beer together after work, living in the same neighborhood, or belonging to the same country club. Informal networks were a source of useful information about corporate politics, policy changes, and career opportunities. A mentoring relationship was most likely to occur between people who interacted informally and felt comfortable together. The black support group compensated for this disadvantage. It provided black role models and mentors, as well as an informal network for information. It was an atmosphere in which black sales representatives felt comfortable asking questions they felt might make them look uninformed with white managers. Their goal was to be the best Xerox sales representatives possible, and by helping the company do well, they hoped they would achieve personal success.

Fortunately, the openness of Xerox's culture helped them; they felt free to meet as a group of blacks without generating an immediate backlash. In 1972, they decided to formalize the support group. They named themselves the "Corporate Few" because they felt that the name was literally true—they were the few blacks in corporate America. The black caucus in Xerox's Mid-Atlantic region was established.

In 1973, as one of its first acts as a formal organization, Corporate Few sponsored a conference in Philadelphia for all black Xerox employees. The conference was billed as nationwide, but it turned out to be regional because the Washington caucus members had limited contact with black Xerox employees in other areas of the country. It was held at a Holiday Inn on a weekend and was paid for by the attending black employees. Between 75 and 100 people attended, more than anyone in Corporate Few had expected. Amos, Rand, Robinson, Scott, and the other leaders wrote the conference agenda on the Amtrak train from Washington to Philadelphia; it was typed up that night by a sympathetic black secretary in Xerox's Philadelphia office.

Most of the conference consisted of information sessions and self-help workshops: sales, finance, and administrative training; self-motivation seminars; information about Xerox's corporate structure; and the best promotional path to follow for success. The guest speaker and "star of the show" was Art Crawford, a branch manager (supervising about 300 people) from New York City and the first black person to hold this position at Xerox.

Corporate Few members deliberately informed Xerox that they would be holding the conference. Some corporate executives reacted with suspicion and disbelief. They could not understand why the black employees needed to meet formally as a large group; any concerns they had could always be handled within the corporate structure. These executives did not find the caucus's explanation believable. People did not spend their own money to attend a conference on their own time just to learn how to do their jobs better. To them, the situation looked and smelled like the beginning of a labor union. Veiled threats of retaliation were made to the top figures in the black caucus group; they were told it was not good for a person's career to get involved in this kind of suspicious meeting.

Corporate Few held the conference despite the reaction of these managers, and it was a success. Gil Scott explained why they had told Xerox about the conference:

> We knew that we were a pressure group. We wanted to have a show of force and demonstrate our unity as black employees. We wanted to say, 'Hey, we're somebody you need to reckon with. Our goal is self-help and helping the company be better and helping us be better, but you'd better deal with us.'

Rochester, N.Y.: Challenging Corporate Management

In the early 1970s, a group of black Xerox employees in Rochester, New York, started meeting together to talk about the issues facing blacks at Xerox. Because Rochester was headquarters for the copier/duplicator group, Xerox's largest and most profitable division (and had been corporate headquarters until 1969), the people in this informal group were from many different areas: manufacturing, research and development, law, corporate marketing. But they all felt that there was a sharp dichotomy between the progressive image Xerox presented to the outside world and the actual situation for blacks inside the company.

The next year the group asked for and eventually had a meeting with McColough. At that time, just meeting with McColough was a major accomplishment, especially because most of the employees in the group were not managers. (McColough's meeting with the group followed Xerox's open door policy normally used by individual employees to raise issues to senior management.) The group prepared exhaustively for this first crucial meeting. Bill Hamilton, a black manager from Xerox's manufacturing division, recalled:

> The advantage we always had on management was preparation. I remember we would spend from 8:00 in the evening until 2:00 in the morning just compiling our data and getting our facts straight—and then we would come back the next night and spend the same amount of time getting the strategy together. We knew who was going to speak at the meeting; when they responded, whatever they responded, we knew what we would say. The whole meeting would be mapped out. We knew they weren't spending as much time on us as we were on them and that was the key.

After that first meeting, at the suggestion of Richard Kier, the group met with Kearns instead of McColough. Kier, one of BABE's original leaders, had been promoted to a headquarters job in Rochester in 1971 as a direct result of Kearns's handling of the "tan territory" issue. He knew Kearns from that meeting and trusted him. Also, while McColough was in Stamford, Connecticut (the new corporate headquarters), Kearns was located right in Rochester; this closeness was more conducive to the ongoing working relationship the group wanted. Once McColough had given corporate approval, it was more useful to work with Kearns because he was in charge of the areas (sales, marketing, and distribution) with the most employees.

At their first meeting with Kearns, the group got his attention by providing information about the actual number of black employees in his operation, including each one's location, salary, and position. Kearns had received similar information from his own staff, but these black employees suspected that much of it was inaccurate. Bill Hamilton explained, "Management was relying on data to analyze what was going on. We *knew* how many black people there were at every level; we knew them by name. In those days, there were so darn few of them."

The group's strategy in those crucial early meetings and throughout their working relationship with Xerox management was to always maintain a professional attitude about a topic that was potentially very emotional. In their first few meetings with Kearns, the group reminded him that Xerox had publicly and explicitly made it a business objective to increase the number of black employees and improve their work conditions. The company had made a public commitment to affirmative action and received very favorable publicity as a result. With this understood, the group members challenged Kearns to show them a business plan to achieve this stated objective. As business people, the group knew that if an objective was really important to the company, it would always have an official business plan to achieve it. Kearns saw this as a reasonable argument and agreed that a business plan was the logical way to approach the problem and told his HR subordinates to develop one. Hamilton explained their strategy: "It was a success because we came at it in a corporate way. We did it all by numbers, not personality. Management was comfortable looking at it in that light, and we were able to have a significant impact on the development of those numbers."

The group also planned how to manage the less tangible aspects of the meetings. For example, for their first meeting with Kearns, not wanting to seem adversarial, they decided not to go up to his office together. They knew that people would notice and talk if a group of black employees all took the elevator together to the president's floor, and they did not want that kind of publicity. Instead, the group planned to have each individual get on separate elevators throughout the building and all arrive at the executive floor at exactly the right time.

The success of the meetings with McColough and Kearns solidified the group, which until then had been informal. The leaders organized the Rochester black employees into the Concerned Association of Rochester, Inc. (CARI). Initially, CARI included only blacks in exempt positions, but Kier and Hamilton pushed to include all black Xerox employees—including secretaries, janitors, and cafeteria workers—and the group soon expanded. CARI's leaders continued to meet with Kearns every few months. The first president of the group was David Robinson, a corporate lawyer; it was his idea to incorporate CARI formally, a move none of the other caucus groups ever made. Hamilton described their reasoning:

> Primarily, it was to show that we were a professional entity, not just some disgruntled people loosely put together. This was a corporation, well thought-out, with bylaws. It was to give ourselves a tight structure to govern the organization. We wanted something that would exist when we, the individuals, left.

Xerox's Response

In February 1972, McColough created a Minority Advisory Committee (MAC) to study the issues of black Xerox employees throughout the company. This committee (later renamed the Employee Resource Advisory Committee, or ERAC) was made up of black employees from around the country; most were at the branch manager level or lower, because there were no blacks in upper management. The members were given access to virtually any information they needed for their research. The committee would meet with top managers throughout the corporation to report the results of its research and interviews. Xerox wanted to gather information so that nothing like the blowup in San Francisco could happen again. Kearns established a similar group for the ISG division, the Advisory Council on Affirmative Action.

These two committees brought black employees from around the country together for the first time. Leaders of local caucus groups—like Gene Ruffin from San Francisco, Art Crawford from New York, Bill Sykes from Chicago, and Kent Amos and Barry Rand from Washington—met and developed close friendships. They discovered that, although each group had formed in response to its own local problems, they shared very similar strategies and goals. They also had similar backgrounds; most were from middle-class families, had studied at black colleges, and had participated in the civil rights movement. Rand recalled:

> Most of us were all about the same age. And that meant that we graduated from high school in the era of civil rights activism, when no matter who you were in the black community—a doctor, a lawyer, or from the streets—everyone was geared to moving the black race forward. If you came out of that era and all of a sudden you had a new avenue that happened to be corporate America, then you changed your activism from the campuses, the courtrooms, and the lunch counters into the corporate boardroom.

Meanwhile, regional management also was changing in response to pressure from the black caucus groups. In Washington, D.C., for example, regional management responded to Corporate Few by establishing an advisory panel in early 1974 to address the concerns of black employees in the Mid-Atlantic Region. The panel's chairman was Gil Scott, who had become the manager of the regional affirmative action program. There were 17 black employees on the panel, one from each of the region's districts.

The all-black panel would be able to meet regularly with the region's top management, and address concerns before they became problems. Xerox was committed to take action if the panel made a formal recommendation. Similar panels were established at the same time in several other regions.

One of the earliest and most important issues the panel dealt with was the promotion system. At that time, in 1974, Xerox relied on a Management Resource Plan (MRP) as the information source for promotions. The MRP was a confidential list of promotable people; individual employees were not officially told if they were on the list. Many black employees, isolated from the informal networks, did not even know that such a list existed. Often, they would not know that jobs had been open until the position was filled and the new manager's name announced. The panel recommended that the MRP be made a public document and each employee be notified whether he or she was on the list. This would help compensate black employees for their isolation from the informal "grapevine" of information about status and promotion. In addition, the panel argued that all employees should know their status so that they could develop individual action plans, either to be promoted if they were on the MRP or to be placed on the MRP if they were not already.

The most innovative change the panel recommended was the institution of a job-posting system to supplement the traditional managerial promotional system (the MRP). Job posting was a simple process: when a position opened up, a notice describing the job and necessary qualifications was sent to each company location. All qualified candidates could then apply for the open job. But job posting had always been strictly a manufacturing procedure; it had never been used in Xerox's marketing organization. After the panel's recommendation, Xerox agreed to test job posting in the Mid-Atlantic region.

The panel studied the job-posting system used in Xerox's factories and adapted it to marketing.

The panel members built in restrictions to prevent excessive mobility. Unlike manufacturing, not all open positions were posted. Most jobs continued to be filled through the traditional system. However, when there was no clear appropriate candidate, a notice announcing the opening was sent to each district and put on a central bulletin board. Any Xerox employee could apply for the position and, if qualified, was guaranteed an interview. Positions could be posted only in nearby districts so that taking the job would not require relocation. An employee could apply at any time, with his or her manager's consent. However, an employee had to have been at his or her current position for 18 to 24 months to apply without the manager's consent.

Job posting was such a success that Xerox eventually implemented it throughout the United States. It was a resource for all employees, although it was most vital to blacks, who could be "trapped" in entry-level jobs if their manager neglected to recommend them for promotion. In addition, as Scott explained, "It really works both ways. It gives managers access to candidates who are being pigeonholed by other managers who won't tell them how good their people are." Scott credited much of the panel's success to the open minds of the regional managers, "They were willing to take some risks and encouraged us to do some things that challenged the system."

Caucus Groups throughout the United States

By 1974, caucus groups had arisen independently in six separate regions throughout the country: California, Washington, D.C., Rochester, Dallas, New York, and Chicago. Because the regions were so large, most caucuses were divided into smaller units, usually around major cities. For example, although Washington was the center of Corporate Few, activities also occurred in Cincinnati, Atlanta, Philadelphia, and other cities.

Each group had a leader; most had been unofficial founders of the caucuses and then had been officially elected by their group. Frequently, the leaders were the most successful black employees, those who had reached managerial positions and were high performers. Their success at Xerox gave them authority in the eyes of other black employees and added to the credibility of the caucus groups when they talked with the still predominantly white management of Xerox.

These caucus leaders had met one another through the Minority Advisory Committee (MAC) and through more standard Xerox conferences and training programs. They formed an informal network, describing it as "a revolution by telephone," to exchange news and encouragement.

When possible, the leaders tried to attend the local caucus conferences that were beginning to occur around the United States. They gave seminars and speeches on self-improvement and described what was happening in the other caucus groups. Sometimes they were able to combine these conferences with business travel for Xerox, and sometimes they spent their own money for plane tickets and hotels. The presence of the leaders at each conference linked the caucus groups together informally and gave the local leaders greater credibility.

The leaders' central message at conferences was that the key to the success of blacks at Xerox, both individually and as a group, was performance. All black employees had to excel in their field. As sales representatives, they had to have selling skills, and then, as they moved up into managerial positions, they had to develop service and administration skills as well. The caucus groups could help people learn the skills and obtain the information necessary for success, but individuals had to put in the time and effort. Once a person had proved his or her ability, the caucuses would fight the system to give that person an equal chance at promotion. Hamilton, a leader of CARI, recalled:

One of the things the rank and file didn't like about us was that we preached as much about you getting your act together and meeting your sales targets as we did about blacks having a right to that upper-level job. The first thing we preached was that you've got to be performing before we can start any kind of discussion.

However, performance alone was not enough to guarantee mobility up the corporate ladder for black employees. Barry Rand, a Corporate Few leader, explained why the caucus groups were necessary for black success in the corporate world.

There will always be people who will say "I don't want to get involved because of the risk, and I will go it alone. I will try to make it alone without help." They can move through the system, but inevitably, all of a sudden, they will hit prejudice, they will hit biases, because the system has biases. Corporations are just a microcosm of what is happening in society in general, regardless of the principles of the corporation. Blacks will run into that situation at some point, and they will look for help. They will find there is no help, so they will come back to the caucus.

The leaders met privately in Cleveland and Chicago in 1973 to clarify their strategies and goals. They discussed what the new caucus groups' next organizational step should be. They knew from experience that the local groups were easily diverted into radicalism by frustration with local problems. The majority of black employees were at the sales representative level and were not tied into the long-term plans of upper management to provide for equal opportunity throughout the company. The leaders worried that individual actions by local groups could jeopardize the relationships between the informal black leadership and top management and their long-range plans for change. They felt that some kind of national organization would help to coordinate the local groups and to give them a more formalized control over events.

The leaders also decided to commit themselves to helping one another succeed. Individu-

als would be held accountable for their performance to their peers in the black caucus group. Together, they would all work toward a standard of excellence and try to help everyone reach their peak, instead of competing for the top position. As part of this strategy, the leaders also committed themselves to developing talented black subordinates. They made a pact: those who did not help their own black subordinates to succeed would not be helped by others in the group. The commitment would help create a pool of qualified, successful black employees who could rise up through management ranks. As these black employees succeeded, they in turn would hire and advise more blacks, and the number of blacks at Xerox would keep increasing.

The leaders agreed that, in addition to their commitment to blacks within Xerox, they had a responsibility to the larger black community. They wanted to succeed at Xerox because their success in corporate America would open doors for people trapped in the poor black inner-city communities. The caucus groups would work through organizations like local youth groups and the United Negro College Fund (UNCF) to help the black community. The group agreed that Xerox also had a corporate responsibility to the black community; they decided to push the company to expand its use of black vendors and to support black education and involvement with the black community.

David Kearns

David Kearns was hired by Xerox from IBM in 1971, eventually becoming president of the Information Systems Group. It was during his first month on the job that the "tan territory" issue flared up. "I remember it vividly," Kearns recalled, "Archie [McCardle] called one afternoon and said 'I'm coming in the corporate plane. I'm going to pick you up and we're going to the West Coast.' That was my initial involvement." Kearns also remembered the signals he received from top management regarding his response.

I knew then how people at the very senior levels of the business felt about how people were treated in this company. It was very clear to me that my superiors wanted me to fix the damn thing. I mean, they were mad; McColough was mad.

The very fact that he and McCardle, the president of the company, were sent to deal with the problem was itself a strong signal. It was because of this signal and because of his conviction that "it was the right thing to do" that he took such quick and decisive actions to end the problems uncovered by the tan territory suit.

The Issue of a National Caucus

At a 1974 ERAC meeting with senior management, Kent Amos casually mentioned that they were considering expanding the upcoming caucus conference in Chicago to include people from throughout the country. His comment exacerbated a number of worries about the caucus groups that corporate management had been having for some time. They feared that this national meeting would be just the first step toward a nationalized caucus, which might be able to achieve the status and power of a union.

Even though Xerox was known to have a progressive relationship with its manufacturing union, management did not want any part of its sales force to be organized. Xerox's management was uneasy at the prospect of such a powerful group. Doug Reid, the senior corporate Human Resource manager, recalled:

There was a lot of concern that they would go from making suggestions to demands. If we recognized the blacks, then women and Hispanics and Native Americans, every other group would [demand similar recognition] . . . and the managers would spend all of their time meeting with caucus groups. Things would get out of hand. People said if blacks and other protected classes had prob-

lems, they should talk to the affirmative action managers; that's what they're there for. We don't need another vehicle to address this.

Corporate managers communicated with Amos later that week and told him that they wanted to have a meeting to settle the future status of the caucus groups. They suggested holding the meeting in Rochester. After talking with other leaders, Amos replied that they would rather not meet at corporate headquarters and jokingly offered the Bahamas as an alternative— its people were black and it had a warm climate. The company suggested Toronto as a neutral territory and Amos agreed. Seven black caucus leaders from around the country flew to the meeting: Kent Amos and Barry Rand from Washington, Art Crawford from New York, Bill Hamilton from Rochester, Bill Sykes from Chicago, Gene Ruffin from San Francisco, and Kerney Laday from Dallas.

Conclusion

Kearns knew the caucus leaders and approved of their approach of self-help and success through performance. He believed that racial discrimination was morally wrong; yet he understood corporate management's desire to keep limits on the caucus groups. They feared the emergence of a powerful national group with its own agenda.

Xerox had benefited from its progressive black hiring policies and willingness to work with the caucus groups. Kearns had to decide whether it was time to let black employees try to succeed alone. Should Xerox continue supporting the caucus groups as they moved to the national level? Or did the dangers of such a powerful group outweigh its potential benefits for black employees?

SEXUAL HARASSMENT, FREE SPEECH OR . . . ?

Dairy Mart

In early 1992, officials at Dairy Mart's corporate headquarters in Connecticut faced a rapidly escalating problem, and one they thought had been resolved. Dolores Stanley, a 10-year veteran of Dairy Mart, had given the company an ultimatum: If they did not reinstate her as manager of the Toronto, Ohio, Dairy Mart and remove all "adult" magazines from the shelves of the store, Stanley would sue for sexual harassment.

In October 1990, Stanley had been promoted from assistant manager of the Wellsville, Ohio, Dairy Mart, to manager of the Toronto, Ohio, store. Stanley was 33, a mother of three, and a practicing Presbyterian. In her first few days as manager, she had removed all "adult" magazines from the store's shelves.

The third-largest convenience-store chain in the United States, after 7-Eleven and Circle K,[1] Dairy Mart operated about 1,200 stores nationwide. Most sold "adult" magazines, although the store next to corporate headquarters in Enfield, Connecticut, did not. The magazines, including *Playboy* and *Penthouse,* were typically covered in sleeves and stocked behind the counters.

After learning of Stanley's actions, Dairy Mart officials had put the magazines back on the shelves. Dairy Mart's spokesperson, Betty Yopko, explained the store's response: "We're in the retailing business, not the censorship business. If a customer wants to buy them, that's their choice. We don't make the choice for our customers."[2]

For Stanley, this was not about censorship, but about her right to a workplace free of sexual harassment: "It goes against everything I believe in as a Christian. There's no way I could participate in that. There's nothing more damaging to the image of women than pornography."[3]

Stanley also argued that her action had been good for business. Yopko confirmed that business had improved under Stanley, but attributed the turnaround to other factors, including a corporate decision to cut beer prices.

Shortly after Dairy Mart officials put the magazines back on the shelves of the Toronto, Ohio, store, Stanley left Dairy Mart. According to Stanley, she was fired, and according to Dairy Mart officials, she refused to return to work. Now Stanley was threatening to sue under Title VII for hostile work environment harassment.

Stroh Brewery Company

In November 1991, eight female employees of Stroh Brewery filed suit against the company for sexual harassment, claiming they had been subjected to verbal harassment, unwelcome physical contact, and displays of condoms and lewd pictures.[4]

A privately held company, Stroh's had approximately 2,600 employees and $680 million in an-

This case was prepared by Andrea L. Strimling under the supervision of Lynn Sharp Paine.

Copyright © 1992 by the President and Fellows of Harvard College.

Harvard Business School case 393-033 (Rev. December 15, 1994).

1. Chris Roush, "The Curdling of Dairy Mart," *Business Week,* October 10, 1994, p. 112.

2. Tom Puleo, "Former Dairy Mart Manager in Ohio May Sue for Return of Her Job; Market Mores: Who Should Censor?" *The Hartford Courant,* January 13, 1992, p. A1.

3. Ibid.

4. Tony Kennedy, "Judge Says Stroh's Ad Strategies Won't Be Part of Harassment Trial; Ads Not in Workplace to Be Excluded, Ruling States," *Star Tribune,* November 9, 1993, p. 1D.

nual sales[5] representing an 8 percent share of the U.S. beer market, after Coors, Miller, and Anheuser Busch. Together, the four accounted for 88 percent of the market.[6]

In addition to the legal and managerial issues, the sexual harassment allegations raised a marketing question. The women argued that Stroh's advertising campaigns, including both printed promotions and the "Swedish Bikini Team" television advertisements, directly contributed to a sexually hostile working environment. The Swedish Bikini Team had first appeared in May 1991 promotions of Stroh's Old Milwaukee brand and was scheduled to appear in the January 1992 issue of *Playboy*. The Old Milwaukee ads featured five women in identical blonde wigs and blue bikinis,[7] parachuting in on a group of men camping.

Stroh's advertising campaign also included printed promotions, some of which were posted in the workplace. One poster showed an apparently topless women holding a beer in one hand and covering her chest with a bouquet of flowers. Another poster, headlined "Home Grown in Minnestrohta," featured women in revealing baseball uniforms.

According to one of the women who filed the suit, "You walk into the lobby to punch in, and you see pictures of Stroh's ads with women who are half-naked . . . When they [the male employees] are getting feedback from the top of the company that women are bimbos and that's OK, that's why I'm getting treated the way I'm getting treated."[8]

Using female models to sell beer was common within the industry. According to a consultant to the beverage industry, "You still basically have one iron-clad attitude in the brewing industry, which is that you cannot sell beer effectively unless you sell it to young men, and you can't sell beer effectively to young men unless you use sex."[9]

At the time of the suit against Stroh's, however, competitors such as Budweiser and Miller Lite were moving away from sex-based ads. Budweiser's advertising campaign included an ad featuring a 68-year-old woman playing electric guitar, and another showing a father-son basketball game. According to Bud brand manager, "if you upset women in the process of trying to appeal to a 21- to 27-year-old male, I just don't think that's going to last for long."[10] Miller Lite's brand manager said that the "It's it and that's that" campaign was "a conscientious effort to make the people in our commercials seem like they are in regular settings . . . trying to make men and women equal in those commercials."

The news of the suit against Stroh's broke just weeks before Minneapolis hosted the 1992 Super Bowl. On game day, activists picketed the Metrodome, where Stroh's was a featured beer. According to Kevin Ryan of Mark VII Distributors, "There was no measurable effect on total market sales, but it [the protest] had an adverse impact on some customer perceptions."[11]

Stroh's admitted that some of the sexual harassment claims were "substantially true,"[12] but argued that the harassment was not linked to the television advertising. Stroh's General Counsel said the company would not consider eliminating the Swedish Bikini Team ads unless "we were to determine . . . that they were offensive to a significant segment of our consumer base. . . . We believe [the ad] is working."[13]

---

5. *Ward's Directory of Public and Private Companies* (Detroit: Gale Research, 1994.)

6. *Beverage World 1993–94 Databank* (Dayton, Ohio: Keller International Publishing Corporation.)

7. Rorie Sherman, "Stroh's Case Plaintiffs Take Case to Public," *National Law Journal* (December 30, 1991), p. 7.

8. Martha T. Moore, "Taste Test: Debate Brews over Selling Beer with Sex," *USA Today* November 15, 1991, p. 1B.

9. Ibid.

10. Ibid.

11. Jill Hodges and Tony Kennedy, "Stroh's Settles Harassment Suit by Women Employees," *Star Tribune*, December 2, 1993, p. 1A.

12. Rorie Sherman.

13. Ibid.

Los Angeles County Fire Department

Los Angeles County Fire Department officials thought they had done the right thing. In July 1992, as part of a broader sexual harassment policy implemented to comply with state and federal law, the Department had banned sexually explicit magazines, including *Playboy, Penthouse,* and *Playgirl,* from dormitories, restrooms, and lockers in its 127 firehouses. Four years earlier, public scandal about pornographic movies played in public areas of LA city fire stations had led to new city policies banning the display of sexually explicit materials.[14]

County attorneys said that the ban was intended to protect the rights of female firefighters, and to correct the "sexually hostile environment" that had kept women off the force.[15] Of the 2,328 uniformed firefighters in Los Angeles County, only 10 were women.[16] Bunkrooms and bathrooms were generally not segregated by sex. According to women firefighters, the men showed explicit photos openly at work, making comparisons between their female colleagues and the women in the photos.[17]

Captain Steven W. Johnson, a thirty-year veteran of the force, was unhappy with the magazine ban. After county officials rejected his grievance, he filed suit against the county in December of 1993. Supported by the American Civil Liberties Union, he argued that the ban violated his rights to free speech. "I think during your off-duty time you should be able to study, snooze, or read a magazine of your choice . . . I happen to enjoy *Playboy,*" said Johnson.[18] Fire-

fighters, who often worked 24-hour shifts, were generally allowed to read or watch television in the evening between calls.

Technological Equipment Corporation

Stefan Eisenfeld thought he had taken a major step in advancing his career when he accepted a position in 1992 as a project manager in the Software Products Division of Technological Equipment Corporation (TEC). TEC was one of the most prestigious firms in the field, and Eisenfeld had set his sights on moving quickly up the ranks to a top corporate position.

Eisenfeld had exceptional qualifications, having graduated from MIT in 1990 with an M.B.A. from the Sloan School and a Ph.D. in engineering. In addition, he held advanced degrees in computer science and law. After graduating from MIT, Eisenfeld had spent two years working for a top management consulting firm. Although he had enjoyed the work and exceled at it, he wanted to move from consulting to management. When TEC recruited him, Eisenfeld saw an important career opportunity.

Eisenfeld moved into his office at TEC in 1992. In his new position, Eisenfeld reported directly to Ed Williams, a senior division manager who had a long career with TEC. Williams' office, decorated with expensive oak furniture and photos of his wife and three children, seemed to reflect success in his business and personal life.

Eisenfeld was quiet, considerate, and hardworking. He had grown up in a separatist Mennonite community in rural Pennsylvania and continued to practice his religion, although he did not follow all of the mores of the community. A committed employee, Eisenfeld worked long hours.

Late one Wednesday evening, Eisenfeld was in his office when he heard scuffling, and a woman's voice, coming from the conference room down the hall. Concerned that someone was being hurt, Eisenfeld ran to investigate, but the confer-

14. Jessica Siegel, "LA Rule Barring Playboy Fought," *Chicago Tribune,* December 17, 1993, p. 10.

15. Gale Holland, "LA County Contends Playboy Is Too Hot for Firehouses," *San Diego Union-Tribune,* June 8, 1994, p. A3.

16. Shante Morgan, "Firefighter Seeks Right to Read Playboy: LA County Policy Cited in Suit as Violation of Speech, Privacy Rights," *San Diego Union-Tribune,* December 17, 1993, p. A3.

17. Gale Holland.

18. Shante Morgan.

ence room door was closed. After returning to his office to call Security, Eisenfeld ran back to the conference room, bursting in to find his boss, Ed Williams, alone by the conference table. Eisenfeld was stunned. He was explaining to Williams what he had heard when Security arrived. Williams laughed at Eisenfeld, telling the guards, "What this guy needs is a real woman."

It was clear to Eisenfeld, from the noises and from Williams' response, that Williams had been with a woman in the conference room. The next week, Eisenfeld heard that Williams was having an affair with Jackie Evans, another division manager. Although she held the same title as Eisenfeld, Evans had been with TEC for six years, having advanced rapidly from an entry-level position. Intelligent and hard-working, Evans had a reputation for pushing projects through and rising with their success. Early on, Eisenfeld had noticed and admired the ease with which Evans seemed to fit into the TEC culture.

After the incident in the conference room, Williams began to make off-color sexual comments to Eisenfeld. He would repeatedly ask Eisenfeld to come to his office to discuss business, and then lean close to him and ask, "How big is yours?" or say "I need to speak to you about your masturbating overtime." On several occasions, Eisenfeld returned to his desk after lunch and found pornographic materials on his chair. He assumed Williams had left them there.

It also seemed to Eisenfeld that Williams had told Evans about the incident in the conference room and that she, too, was taking pleasure in embarrassing him. She would wink at him suggestively in the halls and nudge him when they were alone in the elevator.

One evening, Eisenfeld was working late on a project to meet an important deadline. Evans, who was reviewing some aspects of the same project, called him to her office. The office, which had a wonderful east view, was lit by soft incandescent lighting. Eisenfeld noticed that Evans' lipstick was fresh.

Eisenfeld was surprised, and relieved, by Evans' business-like approach. "Let's move to my round table," she said. "I want to get this project out of the way." They spent over an hour working through several tables of data, completely focused on the work. Then, Evans began sliding the arch of her foot along his leg. Eisenfeld jumped up from his chair, but Evans grabbed his hand, pulling herself up to his chest. The two of them fell into a large potted plant.

Evans laughed. "You are too much!" She couldn't seem to stop laughing, and her speech came out in bursts. "Don't take things so seriously . . . this is just to have fun . . . nobody will know."

Eisenfeld got up and left. He went back to his office, shut the door, and sat there for about an hour trying to figure out what to do. Then he went home.

During the next few days, Eisenfeld managed to avoid Evans, but Williams' jokes seemed to increase, with repeated allusions to virginity and sexual organs. Eisenfeld began to question his future with the company, but he did not know what he would say if a prospective new employer asked why he wanted to leave TEC. He also wanted to find a way to handle the problem, rather than running away from it.

Jacksonville Shipyards, Inc.

In late January 1985, Lawrence Brown, vice president for Operations for Jacksonville Shipyards, Inc., received what he thought was a routine call from Elmer "Ossie" Ahlwardt, vice president of the company's Mayport Division. Ahlwardt had several issues to discuss with Brown, including a request from welder Lois Robinson that a "Playboy type" poster be removed from the walls of the shipfitting shop. Having agreed to meet with Robinson after receiving her call a few days earlier, Ahlwardt wanted some advice on how to handle the request.

Jacksonville Shipyards, Inc. (JSI), a private subsidiary of publicly held Terex Corporation, was based in Jacksonville, Florida. The company repaired commercial and Navy ships at several shipyards, including the Commercial Yard and the Mayport Yard. As described by its employees, JSI was "a boys' club," employing seven women and 1,010 men as skilled craftworkers in 1983.

When Robinson called Ahlwardt, she was frustrated and angry. For several weeks, she had been trying to get sexually explicit material removed from the toolroom trailer and the shipfitters' trailer in the Mayport Yard. Such material was not unusual at JSI. In fact, it was pervasive. Though employees were encouraged to request permission to post most kinds of materials—and permission for political and commercial material was sometimes denied—prior approval was not required for the pictures of nude and partially nude women that were displayed throughout the workplace. These included vendors' advertising calendars, pages torn from magazines and taped up on the walls, and varnished wooden plaques with photos showing naked women in explicit poses of sexually submissive behavior. One picture showed a woman's body with the words "USDA Choice" written across it. Hard core pornographic magazines could be found in various work areas available for casual reading, even though bringing magazines and newspapers to work was officially prohibited. The nipple of a woman's breast served as the bull's-eye of a dart board displayed in one area.

Robinson had worked as a welder at JSI since 1977, having been promoted from third-class welder to first-class welder during that period. During her years at JSI, she and the other women had endured harassing behavior. A policy statement posted in some of the shops declared, "Abusing the dignity of anyone through ethnic, sexist, or racial slurs, suggestive remarks, physical advances or intimidation, sexual or otherwise, is not the kind of conduct that can be tolerated." Despite the statement, women's complaints about harassment had been met with laughter or derision. When one woman complained to her supervisor, he put his arms around her in a gesture of mock comfort and repeated a sophomoric sexual joke.

Finally, Robinson had decided something had to be done. Initially, she complained about the pictures to John Kiedrowski, her leaderman. Although Robinson had been assigned to work with the shipfitters and needed to check out welding equipment from the toolroom trailer every morning, Kiedrowski had told her that she had no business in the shipfitters' office. Robinson then spoke to Fred Turner, the welding department foreman. Turner had taken limited action to remove "pin-up" pictures around the shops, but did nothing about the sexually explicit calendars.

Robinson had next taken her complaint to Ellis Lovett, the shipfitting foreman. Lovett had responded by having a calendar within the shipfitters' trailer moved to a wall that could not be easily seen from outside the trailer.

By this point, Robinson's complaints had become common knowledge around the shipyards, leading to increasing verbal sexual harassment not only of Robinson, but also of other female employees. One woman who worked at the Mayport Yard specifically asked Robinson to stop making complaints because of the responses around the Yard.

Several days after the calendar in the shipfitters' trailer was moved, a "Men Only" sign appeared on the trailer door. At this point, Robinson decided to make a formal complaint. On January 23, she met with Everette Owens, a superintendent at the Mayport Yard, and Chief Shop Steward Quentin McMillan. She told them that the pictures and the "Men Only" sign were degrading and humiliating and that they constituted discrimination and harassment.

Owens disagreed. He told Robinson that the shipyards were a man's world in which she had chosen to work and that the men had "constitutional rights" to post pictures. Owens specifically told the foreman to leave vendors' advertising calendars up on the walls, but he did instruct someone to paint over the "Men Only" sign.

It was at this point that Robinson took her complaint to Ahlwardt, Owens' superior and vice president of the Mayport Yard. Ahlwardt was the highest ranking official and principal supervisor at the Yard. Ahlwardt, who had a "pin-up" in his office, saw nothing wrong with "Playboy type" pictures. However, he agreed to meet with Robinson to discuss her concerns.

In preparation for this meeting, Ahlwardt called Brown to ask for his advice. Brown, a 16-year veteran of JSI who had risen from machinery superintendent to vice president for operations, was responsible for policy and regulations concerning JSI employees at the Commercial and Mayport Yards. Ahlwardt was looking to Brown for guidance on the Robinson matter.

A NOTE ON THE LAW OF SEXUAL HARASSMENT

In October 1991, the attention of the United States was forcefully turned to the issue of sexual harassment in the workplace when Anita Hill, a law school professor, accused Clarence Thomas, a nominee to the United States Supreme Court and her former boss, of sexual harassment. The U.S. Senate confirmed Thomas to the Supreme Court despite the allegations, but the issue was far from dead. A month after the Hill-Thomas hearings, the Civil Rights Act of 1991 was passed following two years of wrangling and negotiations between the U.S. Congress and then President Bush.[1] That Act amended the Civil Rights Act of 1964 and expanded the rights of victims of discrimination, including victims of sexual harassment, to sue and collect damages up to $300,000.

The publicity of the Hill–Thomas hearings and the new civil rights laws contributed to an explosion of sexual harassment complaints filed with the Equal Employment Opportunity Commission (EEOC). In the last quarter of 1991, the EEOC received 1,244 claims of sexual harassment compared to 728 in the last quarter of 1990.[2] For 1991, the total came to 3,300. By 1993, the number for the year was 7,300.[3]

Sexual harassment is an issue few companies can afford to ignore. One study of 160 major U.S. companies found that sexual harassment had cost an average of $6.7 million per year, not including legal expenses.[4] These costs reflected absenteeism, low productivity, and high turnover associated with sexual harassment. Firms that fail to prevent sexual harassment also face increasing legal expenses, penalties, and damage awards. In 1993, approximately 1,500 people won $25 million from employers in EEOC cases, up from $12.7 million awarded to 1,340 people in 1992.[5]

This note provides a summary of federal law on sexual harassment in the United States, the first nation to have such laws, as well as a brief

---

This note was prepared by Wilda White and Andrea I. Strimling under the supervision of Lynn Sharp Paine.

Copyright © 1992 by the President and Fellows of Harvard College.

Harvard Business School case 393-032 (Rev. December 9, 1994).

1. Pub. L. 102-166, 105 Stat. 1071 codified at 42 U.S.C. at 2000e-2(k).

2. Carol Kleinman, "Number of Sexual Harassment Charges Filed Rises by 71 Percent," *Chicago Sun-Times,* March 8, 1992, p. A-30.

3. "Sexual Harassment Cases Increase in Number and Complexity," *Director's Monthly,* April 1994, p. 13.

4. International Labour Office, "Combatting Sexual Harassment at Work," *Conditions of Work Digest* 11, no. 1 (1992), p. 51.

5. Study by the Center for Women in Government reprinted in *The Wall Street Journal,* May 24, 1994, p. A-1.

overview of laws and policies in other countries. Although many individual states in the United States have their own laws against sexual harassment, this note addresses only the federal level.

U.S. Law on Sexual Harassment

Sexual harassment in the workplace is prohibited by Title VII of the Civil Rights Act of 1964, which was enacted as the culmination of the 1960s civil rights movement in the United States.[6] Title VII explicitly prohibits discrimination in employment on the basis of race, sex, religion, and national origin. According to some, the word "sex" was added at the last minute in a move to defeat the Act.[7] Although the Act passed, the last-minute addition meant there would be very little legislative history to help courts interpret the law.[8]

It was not until 1986 that the United States Supreme Court interpreted Title VII to include a prohibition against sexual harassment.[9] At the end of 1991, the courts recognized that sexual harassment could be the subject of a class-action lawsuit. In a class-action lawsuit, all the victims of sexual harassment in one workplace join together to sue the employer as a group.[10]

Definition of Sexual Harassment

There are two types of sexual harassment recognized by the courts: "quid pro quo harassment," and "hostile work environment harassment."[11] Both men and women may sue for either or both types of sexual harassment.

Quid pro quo harassment. "Sleep with me or you're fired," is perhaps the clearest example of "quid pro quo harassment." It usually involves sexual demands made in exchange for employ-

ment benefits. For example, terminating or disciplining a worker for refusing a supervisor's sexual advances, is a clear case of quid pro quo harassment.

Hostile work environment harassment. Hostile work environment harassment usually involves conduct which has the effect of unreasonably interfering with an individual's work performance or creating an intimidating, hostile or offensive work atmosphere.[12] The behavior constituting hostile work environment harassment can be cumulative. For example, raunchy jokes, lewd graffiti, and repeated sexual advances or innuendo may add up to a hostile work environment. A single act may also constitute hostile work environment harassment if it is egregious.[13] Conduct may be unlawful sexual harassment even if harassers do not realize that their conduct creates a hostile working environment.[14]

Because Title VII does not prohibit all conduct of a sexual nature in the workplace, employers have often expressed difficulty in distinguishing between innocuous compliments and conduct creating a hostile environment. Indeed, the EEOC noted that because "sexual attraction may often play a role in the day-to-day social exchange between employees, the distinction between invited, uninvited-but-welcome, offensive-but-tolerated, and flatly rejected social advances may well be difficult to discern."[15]

The reasonable woman standard. In 1991, two federal courts articulated a new standard to determine whether particular conduct constituted hostile work environment harassment. Under the new standard, the test for sexual harassment against a female is whether a "reasonable woman," rather than a "reasonable man," would

---

6. 42 U.S.C. 2000e et seq.

7. *Ellison* v. *Brady,* 924 F.2d 872, 875 (9th Cir. 1991).

8. Ibid.

9. *Meritor Savings Bank* v. *Vinson,* 477 U.S. 57 (1986).

10. *Jensen et al.* v. *Eveleth Taconite Company et al.,* 139 F.R.D. 657, 663 (1991).

11. *Meritor,* 477 U.S. 57.

12. 29 C.F.R. at 1604.11(a)(3).

13. *King* v. *Board of Regents of University of Wisconsin System,* 898 F.2d 533, 537 (7th Cir. 1990)

14. *Ellison,* 924 F.2d at 879.

15. Ruth Marcus, "Courts Strain to Define Sex Harassment; Recent Cases on Misconduct in the Workplace Yield Varying Rulings," *The Washington Post,* February 19, 1991, p. A1.

be offended by the conduct in question.[16] This standard, which has been neither explicitly endorsed nor rejected by the U.S. Supreme Court,[17] is illustrated in the *Ellison* case.

As described in the *Ellison* case, Ms. Ellison worked within 20 feet of her co-worker Sterling Gray. Ms. Ellison lunched with Mr. Gray on one occasion. Co-workers often lunched together in the IRS office where they both worked. A few months later, Gray asked Ellison out for a drink and lunch. She declined both invitations.[18] He began to pester her with unnecessary questions and to hang around her desk. Then Gray started to write her letters.

"I cried over you last night, and I'm totally drained today. I have never been in such term oil [sic]," read one note. Ellison asked a co-worker to tell Gray to leave her alone.[19] A few days later he wrote to Ellison again—this time a typed, single-spaced, three-page letter: "I know that you are worth knowing with or without sex. . . . Don't you think it odd that two people who have never talked together, alone, are striking off such intense sparks."

Ellison said that she was "frightened" by Gray's attention and "frantic" about "what he would do next." She complained to her employer and Gray was transferred to another office. Within six months, the employer permitted Gray to return to the office where Ellison worked. After her efforts to prevent the transfer failed, she filed a sexual harassment lawsuit. She also obtained permission to transfer temporarily to another office when Gray returned.

The trial court judge dismissed Ellison's case, calling Gray's conduct "isolated and genuinely trivial."[20] But the Ninth Circuit Court of Appeals refused to view the conduct as isolated or trivial. Instead it announced the "reasonable woman" standard and reinstated the lawsuit.[21] The court said that while a man might look at Gray's conduct and see him as a "modern-day Cyrano de Bergerac wishing only to woo Ellison with his word . . . ,"[22] sexual harassment had to be viewed from the perspective of the victim—in Ellison's case, what a "reasonable woman," not a "reasonable man" would find offensive.[23]

In support of the reasonable woman standard, the influential Ninth Circuit Court of Appeals observed that "men tend to view some forms of sexual harassment as 'harmless social interactions to which only overly sensitive women would object.'" The court was also persuaded that "the characteristically male view depicts sexual harassment as comparatively harmless amusement." While the court acknowledged that there was a broad range of viewpoints among women, it nonetheless concluded that many women have common concerns that men do not necessarily share.

The court explained that if it examined only whether a "reasonable person" would find the conduct harassing, it would run the risk of reinforcing the prevailing level of discrimination. Harassers could continue to harass merely because a particular discriminatory practice was common, and their victims would have no remedy. The court also noted that a "sex-blind reasonable person standard" tended to be male-biased and to ignore systematically the experiences of women.[24] The court therefore concluded that the "reasonable woman" standard should be used to determine whether conduct was sufficiently severe or pervasive to create a hostile working environment.

16. *Ellison,* 924 F.2d 871; *Robinson* v. *Jacksonville Shipyards,* 760 F.Supp. 1486 (M.D. Fla. 1991).

17. Some commentators have suggested that the Supreme Court's continuing use of "reasonable person" terminology indicates that it would be unwilling to endorse a "reasonable woman" standard. *Harris* v. *Forklift Systems, Inc.,* 114 S.Ct. 367 (1993).

18. *Ellison,* 924 F.2d at 873.

19. Ibid.

20. Ibid., at 876.
21. Ibid., at 878.
22. Ibid., at 880.
23. Ibid., at 878.
24. Ibid., at 879.

Employer Liability for Sexual Harassment

Both individuals and their employers can be held liable for sexual harassment. Title VII applies to employers with 15 or more workers. In addition to domestic companies doing business in the United States, the law also covers non-U.S. companies doing business in the United States, as well as U.S. companies employing U.S. citizens outside the United States.[25] For example, American citizens working in the European office of a U.S. company can sue under Title VII for sexual harassment.

An employer is legally responsible for acts of sexual harassment in the workplace when the employer—or its agents or supervisory employees—knew or should have known of the conduct, unless the employer can show that it took immediate and appropriate corrective action on learning of it.[26] It is difficult for an employer to escape liability under Title VII by claiming lack of knowledge of the offensive conduct. If an employer has some knowledge about incidences of sexual harassment, it cannot bury its head in the sand to avoid learning more.[27] Indeed, courts have said that managers have a duty to conduct further investigations if reports suggest the "workplace may be charged in a sexually hostile manner."

In one case, the court said that constructive knowledge of the events could be imputed to the employer because such sexually harassing behaviors were "too pervasive to have escaped the notice of a reasonably alert management."[28] The judge ruled that management failed to appreciate the gravity of the conduct complained of and thereby condoned and encouraged further harassment.

In some jurisdictions, an individual occupying a supervisory position can be held personally liable for a subordinate's acts of sexual harassment. In general, only supervisors who "contribute meaningfully" to employment decisions and who acquiesce in, ratify, or participate in the harassing behavior can be held individually liable under Title VII.

The Equal Employment Opportunity Commission advises companies to have an explicit policy prohibiting harassment, to provide a confidential system for reporting harassment, and to establish a mechanism for investigation of complaints. Once employers are aware of a sexual harassment issue, they have a duty to investigate the matter and deal appropriately with the offending personnel.[29] The employer is obligated to remedy the conduct fully without adversely affecting the terms or conditions of the complaining worker's employment. For example, an employer cannot remedy sexual harassment by transferring the complaining worker to another office. Although it is not necessary to terminate the harasser, the remedy has to be reasonably calculated to end the harassment and should be consistent with the seriousness of the misconduct.

To establish a legal claim for sexual harassment, it is necessary to show that the work environment was reasonably perceived to be hostile or abusive. The claimant need not show actual psychological harm.[30] Workers who prove they have been sexually harassed are entitled to injunctive relief enjoining the conduct complained of, back pay and lost benefits, front pay[31] or reinstatement, and attorney's fees. Under the Civil Rights Act of 1991, they are also entitled to compensatory and punitive damages. Compensatory damages is a monetary award for, among other things, emotional distress, pain, suffering, mental anguish, and loss of enjoyment of life. Punitive damages are available in those cases where an employer acted "with malice or reckless indifference" to the workers' civil rights.

25. Civil Rights Act of 1991, 42 U.S.C. 1981, § 109.
26. *Jacksonville Shipyards,* 760 F. Supp. at 1528.
27. Ibid., at 1529.
28. Ibid., at 1530.

29. *Mumford* v. *James T. Barnes & Co.,* 441 F.Supp. 459 (E.D. Mich. 1977).
30. *Harris* v. *Forklift Systems, Inc.,* 114 S.Ct. 367 (1993).
31. Front pay is the money employees would have earned in the future had they not been unlawfully terminated.

Courts may also order the employer to implement a broad program to eliminate sexual harassment as part of the remedy.

Sexual Harassment and Free Speech

No court has ever ruled that Title VII denies employers or their employees the right to free speech. In several cases, however, employers or employees have argued that prohibitions on the posting of pornography and limitations on workers' speech violate the First Amendment. Many free speech advocates have agreed.

The First Amendment to the United States Constitution generally prevents *government* from outlawing speech or expressive conduct because of disapproval of the ideas expressed. Burning the American flag to protest government policies is an example of expressive conduct protected by the First Amendment. Not all speech, of course, is protected. The government may lawfully restrict speech which is "of such slight social value as a step to truth that any benefit that may be derived from [it] is clearly outweighed by the social interest in order and morality."[32] For example, an individual who falsely shouts "fire" in a crowded theater is not protected by the First Amendment. Obscenity, child pornography, defamation, blackmail, and "fighting words" are other examples of unprotected speech. "Fighting words," words whose very utterance inflicts injury or tends to incite immediate violence, are excluded from First Amendment protection because their content embodies an intolerable (and socially unnecessary) mode of expressing whatever idea the speaker wishes to convey.

While the government may not lawfully regulate the content of speech, it may regulate the "time, manner, and place" of speech. "Time, manner, and place" restrictions are permitted when there is a legitimate government interest at stake and the government has no other means to achieve that interest.[33] For example, a state may enact a law requiring a permit for demonstrations held in city parks in order to provide security and to maintain public safety. The permit acts as a restriction on the time, place, and manner of demonstrations, but it does not restrict the subject of the demonstration.

The U.S. Supreme Court has not directly addressed the question whether Title VII violates the First Amendment. However, in its June 1992 decision in the case of *R.A.V.* v. *City of St. Paul, Minnesota,* the Court, in an aside, referred to Title VII's prohibition of "sexually derogatory 'fighting words,' among other words" as an example of the lawful regulation of conduct despite its speech component.[34] The court seemed to say that because the purpose of Title VII is to regulate employment practices, and not the content of speech, the incidental regulation of speech did not violate the First Amendment. While the Court's reference in *R.A.V.* does not constitute the law of the land, it does suggest how the Supreme Court might rule if presented with the question whether Title VII violates the First Amendment.

Sexual Harassment Laws and Policies outside the United States

Although the legal concept of sexual harassment originated in the United States, the issue of sexual harassment has become a topic of concern and debate in a number of other countries. As of 1994, researchers had identified twenty countries outside the United States that recognized legal claims of sexual harassment in the workplace, based either on specific statutes prohibiting sexual harassment or on general principles of labor, employment, criminal or tort law. (See Exhibit 1.)

This section provides a snapshot of sexual ha-

---

32. *Chaplinsky* v. *New Hampshire,* 315 U.S. 568, 572 (1942).

33. See, e.g., *Breard* v. *Alexandria,* 341 U.S. 622, 641 ff. (1951).

34. *R.A.V., Petitioner* v. *City of St. Paul, Minnesota,* 60 U.S.L.W. 4667 (June 22, 1992).

EXHIBIT 1   Countries with Penalties for Sexual Harassment*

Argentina	Japan
Australia	Netherlands
Austria	New Zealand
Belgium	Norway
Brazil	Russia
Canada	Spain
Denmark	Sweden
France	Switzerland
Germany	United Kingdom
Greece	United States
Ireland	

Source: Compiled by casewriter from Robert Husbands, "Sexual Harassment Law in Employment: An International Perspective," *International Labour Review* 131, no. 6 (1992): 543, and from other secondary sources cited in the text. Note: This list should not be regarded as comprehensive.

*The lists include countries with legal prohibitions at the state and/or federal levels, with the exception of Argentina where the law applies only to government offices.

rassment laws and policies in several countries. It is based on information available in English as of 1994 and does not attempt to be comprehensive or to place these developments in their full cultural contexts. Although sexual harassment is increasingly recognized as an issue in the countries discussed, the concept appears to play no role in public discourse in the vast majority of countries.

The European Union

In 1990, the Council of Ministers, the primary legislative body within the European Union, passed the Resolution on the Protection of the Dignity of Men and Women at Work. The Resolution defined sexual harassment as both quid pro quo and hostile working environment situations, and called on the European Commission[35]

to develop a code of practice on sexual harassment.[36]

In 1991, the European Commission prepared a Code of Practice and an official recommendation on sexual harassment. Focused on prevention and in-house resolution of complaints, the Code does not mention sanctions. The Code and recommendation are non-binding, but national courts of member states are required to take recommendations into account when deciding cases.[37]

Although the European Union and the United States share a common definition of sexual harassment, there are significant legal differences. According to one analyst, "the idea that sexual harassment constitutes a legal wrong is not widely shared in Europe."[38] In most countries in the European Union, sexual harassment "cannot be the basis for criminal prosecution or private civil actions for damages."[39] There are

---

35. The role of the Commission is "to act as the guardian of the Treaties, to serve as the executive arm of the Communities, to initiate Community policy, and to defend the Community interest in the Council." Emile Noël, "Working Together—The Institutions of the European Community," Office for Official Publications of the European Communities, Luxembourg, 1988, p. 13.

36. Anita Bernstein, "Law, Culture and Harassment," *University of Pennsylvania Law Review* 142 (April 1994): 1238.

37. Bernstein, p. 1239.

38. Ibid.

39. Ibid.

several exceptions. For example, in 1992, France passed a law that makes quid pro quo sexual harassment a criminal offense, and provides for "penalties of up to one year in prison and up to approximately $20,000 in fines."[40] Austria, Denmark, Germany, Greece, the Netherlands, Norway, and Sweden have provided protection against quid pro quo harassment without explicitly defining the term, principally through unfair dismissal cases.[41]

There are also important cultural differences that bear on issues of sexual harassment. According to one writer, "A widely held view in the [European] Community[42] is that sexual harassment amounts to less of a problem than Americans make of it [and that] . . . American devices, including legal doctrine, designed to respond to claims of sexual harassment may be inappropriate for Europe."[43]

Russia

In Russia, as in the former Soviet Union, quid pro quo sexual harassment is a criminal offense. However, the law has rarely been enforced.[44] The first known case went to court in 1994. A 35-year-old physician accused her boss, the chief physician, of repeatedly groping her and threatening to dismiss her if she resisted. Russian newspapers did not cover the story, and most people in the community told the complaining physician she was "crazy." The case was dropped under a general amnesty of February 1994.[45]

Sexual harassment appears to have increased as a result of economic and social change associated with the collapse of communism. According to one analyst, "the new Russia has a heady sense of permissiveness [that] has helped spawn a workplace climate of sexual swaggering and bullying that is no longer imaginable in the United States. . . . The demeaning jokes and salacious remarks that are increasingly considered a form of harassment in the United States are so commonplace in Russia that they do not register as harassment."[46] A typical advertisement for a secretary in Moscow requires applicants to be "18 to 25 years old and 5'7" with long hair." Some advertisements include "bez kompleksov" which means "without inhibitions." Women looking for jobs, who do not want to sleep with their employers, specify "intim nye predlagat" or "no intimate relations" in their advertisements.[47]

Although the feminist movement in Russia is small, awareness about sexual harassment is increasing. A Russian man who founded an organization to help women who have lost their jobs due to sexual harassment said he has heard of some U.S. businessmen who "behaved toward Russian employees in a way they dared not treat their American employees. 'The pay at Western companies is so much higher that most women just smile and bear it.'"[48]

Japan

Japan has no statutes that specifically prohibit sexual harassment, and the country's 1985 Equal Opportunity Law for Women does not mention the term.[49] Nevertheless, Japanese women have begun to file sexual harassment complaints under a general civil law that awards compensation for illegal acts. Successful litigation depends on the courts' interpretations of the general law, and women who win sexual harassment cases

40. U.S. Department of State Dispatch, February 1994, "France Human Rights Practices, 1993."

41. Robert Husbands, "Sexual Harassment Law in Employment: An International Perspective," *International Labour Review* 131, no. 6 (1992): 541.

42. The European Community was renamed the European Union, as a result of the Maastricht Treaty which went into effect November 1, 1993.

43. Bernstein, p. 1251.

44. Alessandra Stanley, "Sexual Harassment Thrives in the New Russian Climate," *The New York Times,* April 17, 1994, p. 8.

45. Stanley, p. 8.

46. Stanley, pp. 1, 8.

47. Stanley, p. 8.

48. Ibid.

49. *Chicago Tribune,* October 24, 1993, p. 12.

often lose their jobs, without back pay, front pay, or other damages.[50]

In 1993, the two sexual harassment claims brought to court were successful, with awards totaling $56,959.[51] As of 1993, two more cases were pending, and 355 complaints had been filed with the Tokyo Metropolitan Government.[52] A 1993 government survey found that 26 percent of working women in Tokyo had experienced at least one incident of sexual harassment in the preceding two years. Of those, 19 percent had been asked to have sex with their bosses and 30 percent had been shown pornographic pictures.[53] A survey of workers employed by Japanese firms in Singapore found that nearly half the women who responded had experienced sexual harassment.[54]

According to one of Japan's top lawyers, "Sexual harassment has been a problem . . . for a while. What we're seeing is a change in the women. They used to keep quiet, but now more are suing."[55] The chief of labor relations at the Tokyo Metropolitan Government attributed this in part to developments in the United States: "They see American women sue and realize they can do it too."[56]

In response to increasing public concern, the Japanese Labor Ministry recognized the concept of "seku hara," which it defined as "unpleasant speech or conduct with sexual references that creates a difficult work environment."[57] Japanese companies have begun to address the problem by writing new policies.

China

China has no laws that specifically define or prohibit sexual harassment in the workplace. However, in part due to coverage of the Hill-Thomas hearings, awareness of the issue has begun to increase.[58]

As in Russia, sexual harassment in the Chinese workplace appears to have increased as a result of social and economic change. According to one writer, "Among China's growing class of entrepreneurs, it is fashionable to hire a pretty 'secretary'—a mistress by another name. Armed with the power of [sic] hire and fire, male managers are more likely to abuse their female staff."[59] Millions of young women from poor provinces have moved to the coast for jobs in factories, hotels, and bars. Many of these women see sexual harassment as a necessary cost of employment. According to one seventeen-year-old woman, sleeping with her boss was the only way to get a decent job. "I wanted to get ahead . . . so I took the road that many girls have followed."[60]

Women who have been sexually harassed have little legal or societal support. Complaints must often be filed directly with those who are guilty. There is also a social stigma associated with being harassed, and women usually remain silent out of fear of "losing face." The Women's Federation, a governmental organization described by one scholar as a "last resort" for women who have been sexually harassed, has been able to get some harassers arrested by heavily publicizing the most egregious cases.[61]

Taiwan

As of March 1994, the Council of Labor Affairs was drafting an "equality working law for both

---

50. Ibid.

51. Ibid.

52. "Harassed Japanese Women Fight Back; More Businessmen Getting Caught in Act, Taken to Court," *Chicago Tribune,* October 24, 1993, p. 12.

53. Joanna Pitman, "Action Over Office Sex Pest Problem," *South China Morning Post,* October 21, 1993, p. 17.

54. Ian Stewart, "Singapore," *South China Morning Post,* March 26, 1994, p. 12.

55. *Chicago Tribune,* October 24, 1993, p. 12.

56. Ibid.

57. Pitman, p. 17.

58. Professor Stanley Rosen, University of Southern California, telephone conversation with author, September 12, 1994.

59. Andrew Browne, "China Wakes Up to Sexual Harassment," *Reuter Library Report,* March 17, 1993, BC Cycle.

60. Ibid.

61. Professor Stanley Rosen, University of Southern California, conversation with author, September 12, 1994.

sexes" which would fine employers who discriminate on the basis of sex and specify penalties for sexual harassment.[62] In addition, the Council publicly vowed to "crack down on the sexual harassment of foreign workers in Taiwan by their employers or company executives" in response to a complaint by a Thai woman about her supervisor's sexual advances.[63]

Australia

In 1984, Australia passed the Sex Discrimination Act, giving Australians the right to seek compensation for discrimination and harassment because of gender, pregnancy, sexual preferences, or family circumstances.[64] According to one of the authors of the Act, "there has been a big shift in how employers view the matter" since the bill was passed.[65] Approximately 10,000 people have used the new law to make complaints to the Human Rights and Equal Opportunity Commission, and more than 30,000 have made complaints to associated state bodies. The largest payout was a class-action suit of $1 million, but awards are usually between $1,000 and $5,000.[66]

As a result of increased public awareness and stronger legislation, many large employers have developed official policies on sexual harassment and established procedures for handling complaints. Smaller employers have been less proactive.[67]

Brazil

The Hill/Thomas hearings sparked debate about sexual harassment throughout Brazil, the country with the "largest and best-organized women's movement" in Latin America, according to one analyst.[68] Maria do Carmo (Tatau) Godhino, a feminist and leader of the opposition Workers' Party, said that the issue "was in all the papers, and some unions and journalists began making surveys to see if sexual harassment in the workplace exists in Brazil and what women thought about it."[69]

In response to the public debate, the Rio de Janeiro state legislature passed a law in 1991 that made the "cantada," a gross sexual proposition by a boss to a subordinate, illegal, and provided for fines of up to $17,000.[70] Lawmakers throughout Brazil have followed the Rio example, presenting legislatures with similar bills.

There is evidence of change in other Latin American countries, as well. Argentina passed a law against sexual harassment in government offices. Paraguay rescinded a law that had given husbands the right to prevent their wives from working outside the home, and Chile passed a law allowing women to work at night. As of February 1994, the Columbian Congress was considering a bill that would "make sexual harassment on the job a crime punishable by up to a year in prison, and would prohibit the firing of an employee for resisting sexual advances."[71] According to one analyst, sexual harassment is usually understood by Latin American women to

62. "Taiwan: Firms Required to Grant Males Leave When Wives Have Babies," *China Economic News Service,* Reuter Textline, March 23, 1994.

63. "Taiwan: CLA Vows Crackdown on Sexual Harassment of Foreign Workers," *China Economic News Service,* Reuter Textline, April 21, 1994.

64. Sue Neales, "Australia: A Decade Further Down the Road—Women," *The Age (Melbourne),* Reuter Textline, July 20, 1994.

65. Glenda Korporaal, "Australia: Sexual Harassment—Where Business Draws the Line," *Australian Financial Review,* Reuter Textline, May 17, 1994.

66. Neales, July 20, 1994.

67. Korporaal, May 17, 1994.

68. Jack Epstein, "Brazilian Women Leaders in Fight for Equal Rights," *National Catholic Reporter,* May 20, 1994, Vol. 30, No. 29, p. 6.

69. "New Laws on Rape and Sexual Harassment Favor Brazilian Women," *Notimex Mexican News Service,* April 22, 1992.

70. Daniel Drosdoff, United Press International, International Section, December 13, 1991.

71. "Latin America Awakens to Sex Harassment: In Countries Where Machismo Has Reigned for Centuries, Women Begin to Assert Rights," Associated Press, *Rocky Mountain News,* Denver Publishing Company, February 20, 1994.

mean "pressure to engage in sex to either get or keep a job ... Women's groups are not taking issue with the daily barrage of compliments ... called "gracejos' in Brazil ... that they receive when walking the streets of a city."[72]

Conclusion

Sexual harassment in the workplace is a complex legal as well as managerial problem. At a mini-

---

72. Daniel Drosdoff, United Press International, International Section, December 16, 1991.

mum, managers need to understand the legal framework governing sexual harassment, while recognizing that the legal definitions of hostile or harassing conduct are far from settled. What constitutes unlawful harassment depends on the perceptions and sensitivities of reasonable people. Managers who wish to avoid liability and provide a friendly, supportive workplace for both women and men will want to take claims of sexual harassment seriously. They will want to educate themselves and their employees about the types of conduct regarded as hostile by "reasonable men and women" and take steps to prevent such conduct from occurring.

MOD IV PRODUCT DEVELOPMENT TEAM

It was April 1989. Just four months remained until the Honeywell Building Controls Division (BCD) planned to introduce the Mod IV, and the product development team was fighting to stay on schedule. Mod IV, a motor used in heating, ventilating, and air-conditioning (HVAC) applications, represented the most ambitious project in the division's history, and the product's development reflected many of the changes the division had experienced in recent years. For three people in particular, Mod IV also typified the challenges of working amid new pressures and demands.

As director of HVAC Controls, one of the Building Controls Division's four product areas, Linda Whitman was the senior marketing person for the Mod IV product line and had pri-

---

This case was prepared by Joshua D. Margolis under the supervision of Anne Donnellon.

Copyright © 1990 by the President and Fellows of Harvard College.

Harvard Business School case 491-030 (Rev. March 5, 1991).

mary profit and loss responsibility for Mod IV. She could see the impact a delay would have on her area's performance, and she understood the pressing market need to have Mod IV contain attractive features. When she first became director of HVAC Controls in 1986, she realized that marketing had to play a more active role in development of Mod IV. Since then she had watched her fellow marketers on the Mod IV team work through problems and conflicts with engineers, and she knew some of the most difficult issues still had to be resolved. But addressing any issue required patience, persistence, and tact, and even then Linda often found herself torn. She had to make sure HVAC Controls met its projections, which required collaborating with engineering and manufacturing, both of which seemed at times overburdened and at times unresponsive.

Larry Rodgers, lead design engineer on Mod IV, had been involved in the Mod IV project for five years. He could sense the pressure mounting both on the team and on the division as Mod IV encountered difficulties entering the final months of the project. Larry and six of the engineers he supervised had their hands full trying to reduce the noise the Mod IV motor was generating. He knew the marketers had concerns about Mod IV's appeal to customers, but with BCD's limited resources and its stress on fast development, he wondered how he could address himself to marketing's concerns at this time. Like many engineers at BCD, Larry understood the competitive and financial challenges BCD faced, but he wondered if others appreciated the depth and complexity of design work and engineering problems.

John Bailey, general manager of BCD, could all but hear the footsteps of competitors eager to grab business from his division. Although he bristled at the thought of a delay and its effect on BCD's ability to meet corporate financial targets,[1] he wanted to respect the team's autonomy. John knew the team was grappling with several troublesome issues, and though he focused his attention on making sure the division met its objectives, he wanted to find ways to support the team as it addressed the problems before it.

Building Controls Division

Honeywell Building Controls Division (BCD) produced climate controls and systems for four market areas: HVAC, burners and boilers, lighting, and water products. BCD employed 1,250 people and recorded 1988 sales of more than $150 million. The division dealt with two types of customers, original equipment manufacturers (OEMs) and trade customers. The OEMs incorporated Honeywell products into their own

---

1. A widely cited economic model developed by McKinsey and Company "calculates that going 50 percent over budget during development to get a product out on time reduces . . . profits by only 4 percent. But staying on budget and getting to market six months late reduces profits by a third." (David Woodruff and Stephen Phillips, "A Smarter Way to Manufacture," *Business Week,* April 30, 1990, p. 111. See also Brian Dumaine, "How Managers Can Succeed through Speed," *Fortune,* February 13, 1989.)

products, which they in turn sold to the market. Trade customers sold Honeywell products directly to the market. BCD placed highest priority on the quality of its products, on the division's flexibility, and on its response to customers. The division's profitability and return on investment—both well above industry averages—were points of pride.

1981 marked the first and only year in Honeywell's history that its Residential and Building Controls Division lost money. Controls were Honeywell's original business, and the shock of 1981 brought new management to this division, management determined to regain Honeywell's competitive edge. As part of the recovery process, Honeywell split residential and building controls into two separate divisions, thus creating the Building Controls Division. To end the days when people from engineering, manufacturing, and marketing/sales worked in different locations, a new building was constructed with enough room to house everyone. To integrate the three major functional areas, BCD introduced a series of changes that intertwined to create a new form of product development. BCD hoped to transform itself into an agile organization capable of outmaneuvering competitors through faster development.

Product Development and the Controls Business

In the old system of product development, the product passed through each functional area in a sequence of discrete steps: marketers conceived of a product idea and passed it along to design engineers, who would design the product and pass the design to process engineers; process engineers determined how to make the product and then dropped the plans into the laps of the manufacturing engineers and the plants. At each stage in the sequence, people encountered problems created by work done at earlier stages. Process engineers, for example, would discover they could not make what the design engineers had crafted. Product development thus became a

game of "tossing the bear over the wall." When
you completed your particular piece of the project, you tossed it over the wall to the next group,
not caring what took place on the other side. If
you had problems with work done at previous
stages, you made your changes and tossed the
design back to the previous group for them to
adjust their work. The process was slow and
costly. Every change meant more time, higher
cost, and heightened animosity between functional areas.

But rapid changes in the controls business inspired the division to look for new approaches.
John Bailey explained:

> In the early 1980s the move to electronics and
> microelectronics was accelerating, and we were
> having a hard time dealing with that by using engi-
> neering and manufacturing techniques that had
> evolved over one-hundred years and were slighted
> toward a really slow-moving industry and slow-
> moving technology. To suddenly get into a cycle
> going from products that you could design and
> have on the line for thirty years, to three years'
> life expectancy—well, we couldn't do a *develop-
> ment* in three years. So there was a big need for
> change imposed on us by technology and by the
> new competitors that technology brought into the
> market.
>
> We went from a period of a really stable com-
> petitive environment, with two or three players,
> to at one point in the early 1980s we counted 160
> competitors—150 of them were little electric as-
> sembly shops, where a couple of engineers would
> get together, lay out a circuit board, stuff it, and
> start selling. A few of those competitors grew up,
> prospered, and became viable. They grew out of
> that change in technology. But it meant we had to
> change.
>
> We had to change for many reasons. We were
> coming out of a period when we weren't profitable
> enough. We were changing because we were going
> from part of a division to a stand-alone division.
> Our competitive environment was changing, tech-
> nology was changing, and our customers were de-
> manding a different set of requirements from us.
> So there was no alternative but to change.

Parallel Development and Teams

When BCD abandoned sequential development
in the mid-1980s, it embraced a new process
called "parallel development." In this system, a
core team of people assembled from the three
critical functions—manufacturing, marketing/
sales, and engineering[2]—worked together to
guide a project from the conceptual stage all the
way through final production. People still reported to their functional managers, who continued to supervise and evaluate all employees,
and each functional area continued to perform
its specialized role on the project; yet all areas
now worked on the same project simultaneously.
The core team guided and tracked the development, coordinating efforts across functions and
addressing issues of mutual concern. A program
manager secured resources for the team, orches-
trated its work, kept an eye on the complete project, and served as a liaison to senior managers.
One BCD employee described the personal
effect the new approach had:

> The team system does not allow people to single-
> mindedly defend the position of their functional
> area, of what's easiest, or best, or cheapest for
> their own functional area. It forces people to look
> at a bigger picture.

As BCD made the transition to parallel development, it had to confront its history and dis-
card old habits. Marketing had always enjoyed
a sacred position at BCD, as John Bailey explained: "Marketing called all the shots, controlled the purse strings. Engineering felt it
worked for marketing." To make the team-
system work, Bailey and his senior staff felt they
would have to create parity among the functional groups. Each area had to see itself as an
equal partner and contributor. People had to accept additional responsibility—responsibility
for the success of the entire project, not just for

---

2. "Engineering," when used alone, refers to both product
and process engineering.

their functional role. Team members now had to attend team meetings whether relevant to their functional area or not. A manufacturing engineer, for example, had to attend team meetings even if the project was only at a design stage. Since people were accustomed simply to completing a task and passing the project on, they felt team meetings stole time from doing actual work and added to total workload. As people gradually adapted to parallel development and teams, they continued to struggle with their expanded roles and responsibilities.

Many people at BCD felt the new product development system exerted too much pressure on them. Because people now worked on projects from beginning to end, not just when their piece had to be done, they had multiple projects to juggle at once. Combined with the emphasis on fast development, this at times overwhelmed BCD employees. Several people described the pressures they felt and what they perceived to be their sources:

> We have to make a decision on the deployment of resources. When it comes to choosing between things to do, the answer from above is, 'Do both'—with no added resources. Or if we get additional resources, we're just stealing them from another project.
>
> The system is heavily loaded, especially since we're learning a new way of working. There are many things to do with little headcount and no relief with the project schedule. Engineering doesn't have a realistic schedule. This puts stress on the system.
>
> Teams could help but there are obstacles to having a team work on a project. You need true support from management. If somebody's supposed to be dedicated to a team, management has to be willing to let that person spend all of his or her time on the project. Logistics also need work. You have to be able to work out the fractions of people's time. You need one fully dedicated person from each function, but you also rely on the entire functional group. So people working on multiple projects have to know how to split their

time. How do you prioritize projects? *All* work is high priority. And how do you reward people?

Even John Bailey recognized he would have to alter his management style.

> The tone of the way the division is managed comes right from the top. If I want teams, and I promote 'em and cultivate them, then there will be teams. If I'm going to dictate orders, then that's the way my staff will act—dictate orders. I mean those things get reflected right through an organization because I think people look up to see what's happening, and if you don't lead by example, then you're not going to get what you want. People watch actions more than words.
>
> I can't be autocratic and dictatorial to my people, as I tended to be when I was vice president of marketing with Honeywell Europe. All other things being equal, I'm a pretty good dictator. I'm very comfortable with that style. Part of the problem is, I grew up in this business. I understand HVAC. It's real easy for me to tell people what I think they have to do on almost any issue. But if I do that, and my staff does that, it goes right down the line, and we don't have teamwork. We also don't benefit from the ideas and perspectives of the whole workforce.
>
> So I've tried to learn to have patience, change my style, look for consensus, have involvement of my staff as a team, share more information, be more open. I've had to learn that you take a risk with this and not everything comes out the way you want it, but the potential payoffs far outweigh the risks.
>
> I don't know how you legislate dedication, creativity, or motivation into people. I don't think you can. You can't tell people they have to do it a certain way. What you do is create the environment and the responsibility and be flexible.
>
> But those are all new things for me. I didn't come to this as a natural team player. I got into this because it looked like the way this business could run best.

People throughout BCD spoke highly of John Bailey, crediting him with creating a vibrant climate, but they perceived remnants of an autocratic style. Two stories circulated widely through BCD, highlighting both John's own struggle to change and the two sides to communication within the division. One story detailed the way John and his staff calmly received a team's decision to cancel a project and start anew after the team determined the initial plan to be unfeasible. The other told of John's visit to a team meeting—to show his support—where he learned of a time delay. Although John made sure not to criticize the team, he was visibly upset and subsequently castigated his senior managers for not informing him of the delay. Some of those managers were themselves unaware of the delay, and the team both sensed and learned of John's displeasure with the news.

Using parallel development, BCD management believed the division was now in a position to make better products—and in less time. Because all functional areas participated in the entire development, team members could understand the needs of their teammates and could work on their pieces of the project with those requirements in mind. Engineers could design a product with a better grasp of customer needs and manufacturing requirements, while manufacturing and marketing people would understand the limits of what the engineers could do. Instead of tossing the product and problems back and forth over walls, teams could identify potential problems and prevent them. The walls could come down as people from different functions talked with one another more frequently. Fewer problems and overlapping work would deliver what John Bailey coveted most: reduced development time. According to the division's estimates, the new product development system had reduced development time from an average of 38 months to an average of 14 months. John saw speed as BCD's weapon for reclaiming competitive prominence, and he campaigned tenaciously to cut the time it took to get products from "concept to carton."

Although people attributed much of the divi-

sion's resurgence in the 1980s to the close working relationships that now existed between different functional groups, there was some feeling that antagonism had not evaporated entirely and that finger-pointing still occurred. A marketer and an engineer gave separate examples:

> From a schedule standpoint, engineering's credibility was no good. They were telling us dates that just weren't getting met. We tried to arrange shared goals and objectives, and it was like pulling teeth from engineering. They said they had their own milestones. The first shared deadline they suggested wasn't valid since we needed things from them well before that.
>
> We in engineering thought we had a minor design problem that we could solve as we worked on other problems. However, the problem didn't go away, so we moved it up on our list of priorities. Finally, we had to blow the whistle on ourselves because we felt the changes would require more time than the schedule allowed. We went to the head of marketing with our position. We said we were making progress but did not feel we would make our introduction date and needed more time. He said we had to stick to the dates we had. It's his prerogative to demand that the target dates be met, so the target dates were not changed, even though the team knew we weren't going to make it. Insisting that a date not change, though, can lead to a project problem. I'm not sure what's accomplished by insisting on unrealistic dates.

Mod IV

With its new strategy for product development, BCD approached the Mod IV project intent on "making the dates happen." John Bailey explained the urgency behind the project: "Two competitors have introduced new products and retooled. They have overcapacity and are just waiting to steal market share. We cannot make a mistake." BCD was spending $19 million to develop Mod IV and planned to have it replace products accounting for over 30 percent of the division's profit. These figures led one senior manager to call Mod IV "our golden egg." Although the golden egg was about to hatch, Mod IV had had a long gestation.

History of Mod IV

In 1981 Jay Elander, process engineer on the current Mod IV team, was asked to examine how the company could improve the quality of its motors and reduce their cost. His study turned into a cost-reduction, quality-improvement initiative executed in three phases. Mod IV represented the final and most ambitious phase. Although inspired by engineering, Mod IV promised the most dramatic innovations in manufacturing and therefore was deemed a "flexible manufacturing project." With the one Mod IV motor line, BCD planned to *automate* its entire assembly process and replace four families of motors—a total, per year, of more than 200,000 motors and over $20 million in revenue. The project promised to reduce costs and improve profit margins, making it attractive to the manufacturing people. But some marketers were concerned that customers would not accept this new motor and BCD would lose market share. That would reduce revenues, the primary index of marketing's contribution to the organization. The team, however, intended to offer a product replete with features and enhancements attractive to customers. The team would then use price incentives to encourage customers to convert to the Mod IV.

BCD began work on Mod IV in 1984, prior to the introduction of teams and parallel development, but the same design and process engineers had worked together on Mod IV from the beginning. They had even carved out an open office area, nicknamed "the bullpen," by removing partitions between cubicles and setting up a central conference table. Manufacturing engineers were frequent visitors to the bullpen and initiated many of the impromptu meetings. Design, process, and manufacturing, however, did not collaborate closely with marketing until 1986, when the current Mod IV marketing people began replacing their predecessors on the project. One engineer spoke about marketing's involvement:

> The marketing people have changed since the project began while the engineers have been the same since the beginning. Marketing decisions changed each time the marketing people changed. We had to do two rounds of market research. This has had a negative psychological effect. It leaves the impression that the rationale developed in marketing is only as good as the people who developed it. So we lived through a change of direction. Not one marketing person is the same as when the project began.
>
> For a long time, marketing didn't buy into Mod IV. They were force-fed enthusiastic. Now they're enthusiastic because it's a better product, but it's been a lot of extra work for them. They would have been better off with the combination of the old product and the absence of this extra work.

From the time Linda Whitman became director of HVAC Controls in 1986, she had collaborated closely with her peers in other functional areas. As she put it in terms of Mod IV, "Manufacturing and engineering were a whole lot further ahead in the project. And if it was going to be successful, there had to be a balance in terms of expertise and authority." Linda stressed equal participation, but her role as director gave her unique responsibilities.

> I feel that it's a mini general-manager position. I think that's the way business-unit directors are expected to perform. Of all the players, we have ultimate responsibility for the P&L [Profit and Loss]. And I am responsible for my engineering deliverables. The engineers do not report to me, but I am accountable for telling them what projects to work on and in what order. Likewise, sales does not report to me, but my marketing group controls the revenue plan and unit-sales targets they must achieve to earn bonuses. We're also responsible for developing their programs for customers and for authorizing special deals.
>
> We're responsible for defining the product road-maps and introducing the products. We

provide the technical support to customers—the training, the hotline, the technical support for the field reps. We're in charge of pricing, advertising, and sales promotion activities. We're also responsible for arbitrating unresolved delivery problems and for determining delivery codes and lead times. It runs the gamut.

Linda explained how marketing had to make up for lost time on Mod IV:

> Marketing was uninvolved for a long time—for two reasons. First, it was never a marketing-driven development, which is highly unusual. Second, marketing was so Johnny-come-lately. By the time we had a solid marketing team established, engineering and manufacturing were entrenched in the way they believed it should be done. That made it much harder when we did come along.

The new marketers' concern led the team to revise the project's scope, but marketers still had some lingering uneasiness. A marketer explained:

> Mod IV is replacing our bread and butter for no market-driven reason. Sure, it's a cost reduction and a quality improvement, but our motors already are very high quality and provide high margins, so from a marketing standpoint, it didn't have to be done. The customer-benefits derived from Mod IV, including modules, could be developed for our present motor lines.

Team Members

Linda Whitman—Director, HVAC Controls. Linda became the head of marketing for HVAC Controls, one of BCD's four market areas, in early 1986. In nine years with Honeywell, Linda had progressed through five positions, each time dramatically improving the department she supervised. Although Linda succeeded in each of her new positions, with three of her job changes she replaced an incumbent man who had been relegated to another position; as she acknowledged, "This was not the easiest thing for me."

Linda described herself as "results-oriented, hard-driving, intense, and compassionate." Organization, discipline, and strong strategic planning were Linda's hallmarks, but she insisted on letting her marketers work autonomously. She enjoyed working at BCD and praised its comfortable, diverse environment. Her management style, though, had caused her to think about "being female in an engineering-dominated, Midwestern manufacturing company."

> It's extremely difficult for many people to accept a woman who's hard-driving and results-oriented the same way they can accept a man in that role. It's the old classic. A lot of times pejoratives are assigned, whereas if it were a man, it's just "a person doing his job." I think there's much more forgiveness for men to have quirks than there is for women.

Linda was in her mid-thirties.

Jack Scott—Program Manager, Manufacturing. Jack served as Program Manager while also supervising the project's manufacturing efforts. He also supervised several other manufacturing activities. Jack had joined the Mod IV team a year-and-a-half earlier, and though he had known all of the project's engineers for ten years, he called himself "the new kid on the block." Jack described his role:

> I try to keep all ends tied together for the net result. Where are we on tooling dollars, engineering design, order and delivery of the production machines? I tie all the pieces together to make sure they hit the floor at the same time. I make sure communication is happening so that all things are getting done. I make sure we don't get one of these things where we get all done and someone says, "You didn't tell us about that."

Jack was in his forties.

Jay Elander—Senior Principal Process Engineer. "Father" of the Mod IV. Jay's 1981 study led to development of Mod IV, which he now worked on. Jay was in his sixties.

Larry Rodgers—Mechanical Design Manager. In charge of all engineering efforts on Mod IV, Larry supervised all seven design engineers working on HVAC Controls products. Six of those engineers were working on Mod IV, and Larry himself had worked on Mod IV since it began in 1984. Larry displayed constant equanimity, rarely letting the pressure of a situation disturb his demeanor, which some considered aloof. However, he readily acknowledged the history of tension on the project:

> The impetus for the program was increased profit. The project is attractive to manufacturing because they're profit-driven. Marketing is revenue-driven, and this product may reduce revenue. Since it will cost less to make the Mod IV, customers will want it for less, and that will reduce revenue. Engineering's objectives are to deliver at cost, on time, and with the specified features. Dates are our driver. Engineering is neither revenue nor profit driven. We're market driven, but we respond to manufacturing as well.
>
> To bring the product to market, engineering has to do certain things and marketing has to do certain things. What marketing has to do is often dependent upon engineering support. But what marketing needs engineering to do is not necessarily the next thing on the list of priorities for engineering.

Larry was in his forties.

Phil Bohrer—Mod IV Project Manager, Marketing. Phil spent the first part of his career as a research engineer, and after receiving an M.B.A., took this marketing position in June 1988. As the only marketer working full-time on Mod IV, Phil was marketing's field marshall on the project, responsible for the product's smooth introduction to the marketplace. But Phil was not always comfortable with this task because, as he saw Mod IV, "It's replacing our bread and butter. It's kind of scary. I'm feeling reasonably comfortable, but there are some things that make me feel uncomfortable." He attributed the tension between marketers and engineers to

the project's history: "It's somewhat a power struggle because this has been engineering's baby. Engineering saw marketing as just getting in the way." Phil was in his thirties.

Dick Bahn—Product Manager, HVAC Controls. As Product Manager, Dick supervised all technical content of HVAC Controls products, serving as the liaison between field sales and engineering. Dick spent the first 15 years of his career in engineering, where he had become friendly with Larry Rodgers when they both designed industrial air quality products. Dick joined marketing in 1986 and had worked on Mod IV since. Although his responsibilities spanned all HVAC products, Mod IV was the most important, so Dick attended the regular meetings and occasionally discussed the project with Larry. Dick also served as a mentor to Phil, who kept Dick apprised of Mod IV news. Dick's engineering background, friendship with Larry, and personal style made him a vital member of the Mod IV team. He understood the technical difficulties confronting product engineers, and his friendship with Larry helped ease tension when marketers had to push certain issues. Dick was in his forties.

Gordon Frayne—Market Manager, HVAC Controls. Gordon supervised marketing efforts directed at OEMs, customers who incorporated BCD products into units they in turn sold. He maintained a focus on customers, whereas Dick focused on products. Gordon started at Honeywell in sales. He had been the product manager for Burner and Boiler Controls just prior to joining HVAC Controls in 1987. Although Gordon devoted his time to many projects during the week, Mod IV was the most important product he had to introduce, and the weekly team meeting gave him an opportunity to learn about the project's progress, provide input, and voice his concerns. He described the role marketers played on the team:

Marketers with an engineering background have a tendency to tell engineering how to do things. People on our team are getting better at not doing that.

Marketers are forced to be confrontational to make things right for the customer. We've all had to play the bad guy at times. But Phil has had to make sure that the product can be introduced. That has put him in the role of "lead bad guy."

Gordon was in his thirties.

Team Meetings

Since autumn of 1988, the Mod IV team had been meeting Friday afternoons to discuss major issues and to resolve crossfunctional disputes. Although team members interacted almost every day, the meeting guaranteed joint discussion and allowed the team to delve into issues, address all concerns, and come to a resolution with all parties present. Team members explained why they often tumbled into conflict:

• "The risk at stake here is very high. Conflict on our team results from a desire to reduce risk. This product accounts for 30 percent of BCD's profit."

• "We've had a lot of problems with language on this project. We've had a lot of semantic issues with the differences between what's literally required in the application versus what's required in order to position the product in our distribution channel. What's been hard about that is we haven't known we've disagreed.

"For example, we asked distributors whether they would need more single-shaft or more double-shaft motors. The distributors said, 'The majority of applications will be single-shaft.' Engineers and marketers were sitting in the same room, listening to the same distributors say that. Engineers took that information and prepared to make primarily single-shaft motors. When marketers found out, they felt it was a disaster. Regardless of where the majority of applications

fall, the distributor always wants to make sure either case can be handled, so the distributor will stock double-shaft motors, which can also be used for single-shaft applications. We all heard the same piece of information in the same setting. Engineering was listening for the literal application. Marketing was listening for the customer's buying preferences."

• "I worked on the biggest 'It will happen' project in the history of the United States—the Apollo project. They said, 'You will get to the moon.' But we couldn't go until we were ready. And Apollo had unlimited funds. If management thought someone or something could help, the project got it. Mod IV doesn't have that luxury. I can understand why BCD management can't run over on cost or schedule. They can't go to corporate, whatever the justification, and say there's been an overrun on the motor. Honeywell can't accommodate that right now. It's blind, though, to think that just by saying something's going to get done by a certain date, it's going to get done."

• "Because we do many things at the same time in crossfunctional teams, the discrete checkpoints get lost. Definite meanings don't exist."

• "Larry [engineering] and Phil [marketing] are the two most prone to clash. It's because of their roles. The two roles are adversarial. Larry and Phil have to represent different interests. Larry's is what's fastest and least expensive. Phil's is what's best for the customer."

April 1989

Mod IV was behind on both design schedule and production schedule. Still, the team was fighting to meet the August 1989 date for introducing Mod IV to the marketplace. The marketers were busy preparing a training video for

Mod IV users. The engineers had their hands full with a noise problem. And the manufacturing engineers were ordering parts and arranging the assembly lines. The team as a whole still had to decide about control modules.[3]

John Bailey was aware of the difficulties confronting Mod IV.

We have several problems going on right now, and I'm not really happy about them, but no one expects me to be happy about them. But I know all those people are really working hard to resolve the problems. Now if you jump in there and shout, or accuse, then what you're basically saying is you don't have faith in the people you've assembled to get the job done, or you don't think that they're giving it their best effort. We may lack some skills in the technology we're in, but basically I think we have a good set of people, and I think they're working really hard. My job is to support them rather than shout at them.

My highest priority on this project is quality. I know it's $19 million and the clock's ticking on the cash-flow and all that, but our bread and butter is the motor line. This new motor has to be equal to the performance of the old one, has to be, because we have such a good reputation, and we have two competitors out there just waiting to take our market share. So I can't risk performance problems on the new motor, even if we have to say we'll never run the $19 million investment. It would be better to do that than to risk our share.

Yeah it bothers me that the machines are sitting there and we're slipping. But I'm comfortable that we really are making it right, and we're not going to go forward until we have confidence that we can make it.

We sometimes hasten to assume that people want to be directed. I try to listen to a team's problems, make them feel empowered, and suddenly they feel they can climb mountains. It gives them an emotional lift.

If I think they're giving it their best shot, and problems are occurring because of the technology, or because of resources, or because of vendors, then let's go work those problems. Work the things, the issues. Don't blame the people. I think we have good people. They're working hard, doing the best they can. If there's a problem, maybe we didn't select the right ones for the team, maybe we haven't trained them right, maybe we haven't given them the right resources. Let's go work those issues.

John wanted to respect the integrity of the team, but he also had to consider Honeywell's posture toward Wall Street. To make itself a less desirable takeover target, Honeywell had adopted a plan requiring each division to cut costs and improve financial performance. A *Fortune* article described how Honeywell CEO James Renier planned to handle the challenges:

How will Honeywell fend off the poachers? Says Renier: "Get the share price up. There is no other answer." To do that, he must boost performance in the core businesses, which may require a less-than-gentle touch. Asked if he is, as one analyst described him, more of a "butt kicker" than his predecessor, Renier cracks a rare smile and says, "Sometimes it's necessary. It's been necessary with my kids. I have eight, so I know something about it."[4]

Since BCD had started using teams, John had grown accustomed to serving as a buffer, and the financial requirements only added to the pressures he had to absorb.

We're running at the best return rate of any manufacturing division in the company, and we're being asked to do more. What I'm being told is, "Perform better in the short term." But my people here have talked for years about working toward the long term—this is our strategic direction.

Everybody sees the task we have in front of us

---

3. A control module would allow users to tailor the motor for different applications. It is discussed further in the text.

4. Ronald Henkoff, "Butt Kicking at Honeywell," *Fortune*, 22 May 1989, p. 141.

and is asking how we can do it. I'm saying I don't have all the answers. Let's just prioritize what's most important. Let's look at as big a picture as we have responsibility for. I can't look at all of Honeywell, but I can look at all of BCD, and Larry Rodgers can look at all motor projects. Let's prioritize within our respective areas and see where we're going to get the best bang for our bucks.

As John reviewed the history of Mod IV, he put it in the larger context of the division's current challenges.

In hindsight, if I had it to do all over, I wouldn't try to implement a new design and a new line simultaneously. I thought we had laid out sufficient time between phases that we could manage it. But it's too much to ask. It's too many variables for one team to manage. We should have developed the design and made it off-shore or somewhere else or even here, hand-assemble it, even if it was going to be a cost-penalty until we understood how to make it, and then automate it, instead of trying to take a new design straight into automation. That's what I've learned. I'll never make that mistake again. I take that as my fault. That's not the team's fault. I never had a project this big before.

Now to maintain our level of performance in an environment where some of our historical competitive advantages are going away says that we've got to redefine the way we're going to compete. Just being the biggest isn't going to do it anymore, and so speed of response is one of the things we've nailed to the ground. We're going to learn to be a faster-response competitor, not just in product development but in order-processing, production, and shipping. It is a huge challenge to learn to do that, produce better financial results than 15 percent operating profit and 25 percent ROI, continuously, and grow. When I wrap that together, that is my challenge—to get all that done simultaneously. Use timing, instead of just manufacturing or global distribution, as a competitive weapon.

Learning to do that is a challenge, and maintaining all of those good ratios simultaneously with fewer resources to invest than we've ever had before—that's big.

Control Modules and Mounting Pressure

The team would have to gather soon to discuss control modules, a volatile issue that had inspired heated debate. A module could be added to a standard motor to change its function, thereby providing increased flexibility and eliminating the need to have distributors stock separate motors for different applications. The motor's flexibility would appeal to customers, and distributors would welcome the reduction in stock. Inventory management was a major concern for distributors, but with modules and a base motor, distributors would now be able to configure their own special units and avoid carrying hundreds of different motors.

One competitor had introduced control modules in its new motor, and another competitor had followed with an even better modular system. Phil Bohrer, marketing project manager for Mod IV, concluded, "Motor customers expect Honeywell to come out with a better module provision." The Mod IV business plan did mention modules, but marketing and engineering interpreted the commitment to modules differently. Phil explained:

Engineering did not have a module provision and intended to solve the problem by having the distributor stock a large number of different circuit boards. We can't give distributors—our customers in this case—the impression that they have to stock extra components because it saves us money.

Engineering doesn't consider modules important. They see modules as peripheral. They say that only the most sophisticated units need them, and that's only 10 percent of volume. But the varieties within that 10 percent account for over half of the total varieties of Mod IV motors. That's why the distributors don't want to stock extra motors or circuit boards.

Phil believed the Mod IV had to include a module to provide a feature customers desired. Although a module did not have to be available for the initial product introduction, Phil did not want to make this suggestion. Engineering, he

EXHIBIT 1   Events

	Division History	People	Mod IV
1981	Honeywell Residential and Building Controls Division loses money.	John Bailey returns from Europe to become Vice President of Marketing for Residential and Building Controls Division.	
1984			First Mod IV business plan. First round of market research.
1985	Building Controls and Residential Controls begin operating separately. Marketing departments for the two are split. First project using teams.	John Bailey is head of Building Controls.	
1986	Building Controls Division officially formed. Engineering and manufacturing departments are now split between BCD and Residential Division.	Linda Whitman becomes director of HVAC Controls.	New round of market research.
1988	*Project Development Process Guide* released.	Phil Bohrer hired as full-time marketing person for Mod IV.	Weekly team meetings begin.
1989	May: Production start-up for Mod IV (projected) August: Delivery of Mod IV (projected)		

felt, had dismissed the importance of modules for too long and might be tempted to use the offer as yet another way to postpone work on them. Phil wanted to get the engineers' commitment to develop modules.

Larry Rodgers understood the marketers' interest in modules, but with limited resources at his disposal, not to mention other design problems confronting him and his staff, he felt he could not actively develop them at this time. He outlined his concern with modules:

> As we wrote the Mod IV Business Plan, modules were defined in concept but not in detail. The number of modules and their specific functions weren't detailed in the Business Plan.

At times, marketing establishes criteria that are very difficult for engineering to meet. Marketing defined a Mod IV case that is small enough to fit the product strategy but not big enough to fit the module, as we normally produce it, and everything else that has to go into the unit.

With regard to space inside the unit, we might be able to split the module into two parts, which would make it fit into the unit. That's not how we normally produce a module. It means additional plastic parts and therefore added cost, so I haven't entertained it as an option.

Larry and his staff were concentrating their efforts on solving a noise problem with Mod IV. The motor was producing excessive noise, and the engineers were trying to determine the

EXHIBIT 2   Organization Chart: Honeywell Building Controls Division

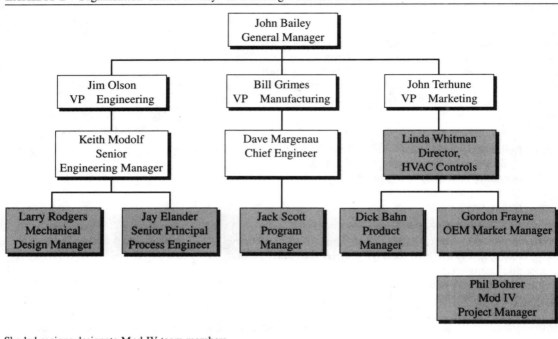

Shaded regions designate Mod IV team members.

source of the noise and correct the problem. Larry was confronting a classic engineering dilemma.

If there are design changes that involve a manufacturing tool, there is no way to test that change until the tool is completed, and that's a long lead-time proposition. Final testing of the change cannot be done until final production parts are available, and that happens precisely when we're also trying to move the product into production. So pressure mounts at that one time. There's also pressure up front when a designer suggests a change of this sort. There's simply no way an engineer can be sure a proposal will work when it's being suggested without giving adequate time to test it.

Linda Whitman also found herself in a typical predicament:

It's sometimes really hard for me to figure out what is the right thing to do. Getting new products out when we do requires prodding and nagging and pushing and cajoling and pleading. I'd prefer not to do all that because I see the tremendous loads engineering and manufacturing have, and I feel bad about bothering them. But if I don't keep after them, my revenue plan suffers. I understand the pressures they face, and if I push too much, I'll only alienate my colleagues in the other functional areas, and things will get worse. As it is, they're beleaguered. They're just stressed to the max. Putting more stress on people doesn't get any results.

When I'm feeling frustrated, it feels like there are two extreme courses, and it's hard to keep perspective on other courses of action. Is it best just to be real nice with them, be patient, and take the heat because I'm seen as not being able to get the deliverables out of engineering and manufacturing? Or should I be a jerk and say 'the heck with it, they never deliver,' and then they'll do even *less.* So it's really hard.

Surveying the challenge facing the team, one team member concluded:

> Pressure on schedule originates with Return on Investment (ROI). If the schedule is strung out, ROI decreases. That's a good reason to have milestones chiseled in stone—leverage, since things

must be done by certain dates to achieve that ROI. It also lets customers know when things will be ready. But it's not good to insist on a chiseled date when it's clear you're not going to meet the date.

Production would have to start soon to assure punctual market introduction; any additions or changes to Mod IV would threaten a delay in production. Still, Mod IV had to meet strict quality standards and satisfy market needs.

LOTUS DEVELOPMENT CORPORATION: SPOUSAL EQUIVALENTS (A)

As the meeting drew to a close, Russ Campanello could not help but think, "Oh, my God, I've been in the job only for a few months. I can't believe this is the first policy decision I'm facing."

Soon after being named vice president of Human Resources (HR) in June 1989 at Lotus Development Corporation, headquartered in Cambridge, Massachusetts, three women came to Campanello with a proposal to radically change Lotus's benefits package. The proposal extended all corporate benefits given to the spouses of married, heterosexual employees to the domestic partners, or "spousal equivalents," of lesbian and gay employees.

If adopted, Lotus would be the only publicly traded corporation to offer such benefits. Margie Bleichman, AnnD Canavan, and Polly Laurelchild-Hertig, calling themselves the Extended Benefits Task Force, met with Campanello to tell him their stories. They were "educat-

ing, as well as proposing," according to Campanello. Canavan argued that benefits could be as much as 40 percent of an employee's total compensation, Lotus was committed to benefit equity, yet Lotus denied her the company-subsidized compensation of dependent care benefits. Various Lotus policy statements did outline the company's commitment to both equity and diversity. Further, because employee turnover in the software industry was rapid, software executives considered the recruitment and retention of employees through highly competitive compensation and benefits packages critical to financial success.

But when Campanello took over Lotus Human Resources, he found widespread pay and benefits inequities between company divisions, a lack of structural integrity between grade levels, as well as a department in disarray. Company efforts to hire and retain women and minorities were also proving to be a challenge, attracting government attention. These concerns came to Campanello's desk in the worst year of Lotus's until-then, extraordinarily successful business history.

Campanello was under pressure to resuscitate his department quickly. He needed to hire for some critical positions and reinvigorate sagging

This case was prepared by Sarah B. Gant under the supervision of Mary C. Gentile.

Copyright © 1994 by the President and Fellows of Harvard College.

Harvard Business School case 394-197 (Rev. March 13, 1995).

EXHIBIT 1   Five-Year Summary of Selected Financial Data (unaudited; in thousands, except per share data)

	1988	1987	1986	1985	1984
Net sales	$468,547	$395,595	$282,864	$225,526	$156,978
Operating income	69,011	95,105	63,856	60,931	58,687
Net income	58,925	72,043	48,300	38,150	36,046
Net income per share	1.29	1.58	1.03	0.77	0.75
Total assets	422,122	317,653	209,009	185,803	122,211
Working capital	225,460	139,718	81,331	93,621	72,181
Long-term debt	95,000	30,000	30,000	–	–
Stockholders' equity	232,196	202,046	114,593	138,542	96,229

Source: Lotus Development Corporation, 1988 Annual Report.

employee morale. Additionally, the integration of HR into Lotus's overall business strategy was what drew Campanello to the company in the first place, but with increasing competition there was increasing pressure to shift away from some of Lotus's distinctive HR policies of the past.

Campanello wanted to begin his tenure with a morale-building policy "win." Yet he now faced the possibility that his first major decision might be about a controversial policy not of his own design. Given the issues on his desk, and the possible repercussions of discussing the extension of benefits to lesbian and gay employees, he could think of many more reasons to ignore the proposed policy than reasons to consider it.

Lotus Background: Business Climate

It was unclear whether personal computers would ever extend beyond the hobbyist market when Dan Bricklin and Bob Frankston of Software Arts Products, Inc., introduced the first computer spreadsheet, VisiCalc, in 1979. Ten years later, however, there were over 15 million business users of PCs[1] and sales in spreadsheets had grown to $444.2 million annually.[2]

Business users accounted for 65 percent of the PC software sales within the $9 billion industry.[3]

Lotus's first product, designed specifically for the IBM PC, the Lotus 1-2-3 spreadsheet co-written by "techie" entrepreneur Mitchell Kapor, entered the marketplace in January 1983. Lotus spent nearly $1 million to market 1-2-3 in its first year. The program quickly gained market dominance among business applications software and rose to become the virtual corporate standard for personal computer spreadsheet software.[4] On average, Lotus shipped one copy of 1-2-3 for every five IBM PCs sold from the mid- to the late-1980s.[5] Lotus introduced its second product, Symphony, in June 1984. Symphony integrated 1-2-3 spreadsheet technology with other common business functions, including graphics, word processing, and communications.

By the end of 1988, Lotus had shipped 4.8 million units of 1-2-3 and Symphony and had 1988 net sales of $470 million (see Exhibit 1). It had developed and introduced a number of other software products and marketed several information services, but remained largely a one

1. Paul Saffo, "Looking at VisiCalc 10 Years Later," *Personal Computing,* November 1989.

2. Deidre A. Depke, "The Software Market Is Downright Mushy," *Business Week,* October 2, 1989.

3. Depke.

4. Ed Scannell, "The Once and Future King?" *InfoWorld,* January 23, 1989.

5. Scannell.

EXHIBIT 2   Cost of Sales

	1988	Percent Change	1987	Percent Change	1986
Cost of sales	$90.8	32%	$68.7	25%	$54.7
As a percent of sales	19.4%		17.4%		19.3%
Nonoperating income	$10.9	39%	$7.8	9%	$7.2
As a percent of sales	2.3%		2.0%		2.5%
Net income	$58.9	−18%	$72.0	49%	$48.3
As a percent of sales	12.6%		18.2%		17.1%
Net income per share	$1.29	−18%	$1.58	53%	$1.03
Weighted average shares outstanding	45.6		45.7		46.8

Source: Lotus Development Corporation, 1988 Annual Report.

product company. The success of its first five years rested solely on its 66 percent share of the spreadsheet market.[6]

In the late 1980s, when the PC market hit a downturn, software sales sagged. Revenue growth was about 18 percent at Lotus in 1988, only a bit slower than the industry average, but a poor comparison to the 40 percent growth of the previous year.

Lotus executives called 1988 a "miserable year". Sales of 1-2-3 slowed as customers put off purchases in expectation of a long-promised, upgrade, Release 3.0. Customers were also confused when Lotus decided to release version 2.2, a compromise upgrade that could run on older, less powerful PCs, alongside Release 3.0 which required newer, more expensive hardware. Delays in getting Release 3.0 to market also created an opportunity for spreadsheet competitors to slice into Lotus's dominant market share.

Competition

By 1989 Microsoft and Borland were selling 40,000 spreadsheet programs a month between them, compared with Lotus's 100,000.[7] A year earlier Microsoft, Lotus's main competitor, had surpassed Lotus as the PC software market leader. Microsoft was far larger than Lotus and better positioned with its broad spectrum of products.

According to one Lotus executive, "All of a sudden [Lotus] realized that they were going to have to start acting like a business . . . that margins were going to shrink, that you could not be a one product company, that you had to diversify in the marketplace." Lotus management spent much of 1988 defending the company's market position with promotional programs and distribution channel incentive programs. The cost of 1988 sales increased 32 percent over the previous year; cost of sales as a percent of sales increased from 17.4 percent in 1987 to 19.4 percent in 1988 (see Exhibit 2). Defensive strategies came at the expense of new-product development and release; Lotus spent about twice as much on marketing and sales as it did on research and development in 1989.[8]

Sales

Lotus sold its products principally in North America through two distribution channels:

6. John McMullen, "Spreadsheet Consolidation," *Datamation,* December 1, 1989.

7. Keith H. Hammonds, "The Underdog Nipping at Lotus's Heels," *Business Week,* January 23, 1989.

8. John Gantz, "Lotus the Cash Machine Counts Its Money and Waits to Grow Up," *InfoWorld,* July 10, 1989.

direct sales to major Lotus resellers representing 2,500 sales locations, and sales to distributors which in turn sold to 4,500 Lotus authorized resellers. Lotus maintained 19 North American field sales offices staffed by 280 representatives who provided sales support to resellers and corporate accounts. Lotus also sold directly to 11 European countries, Japan, Australia, Mexico, and Brazil. Where the company did not have a direct presence it sold through an international network of distributors.

As Lotus tried to retain market share, several factors stood in the company's favor. Many corporations limited the types of PC spreadsheet packages used internally in order to improve user support and training, and to simplify upgrade administration. Change was costly. In addition to retraining costs, newer packages often required expensive hardware upgrades.

Lotus Background: Internal Climate

Lotus had more than 2,500 employees in 1989. About 1,800 worked in the liberal environs of Cambridge; 400 worked outside of the United States. The average age of employees was 32, and the average length of service was under three years.

Lotus management did not consider the youth of their employees and the rapidity of turnover a problem. Lotus's demographics were consistent with those of industry competitors; attrition and migration were viewed as ways to retain the most creative workers while having a pipeline to diverse technological experiences. Employment in the software industry as a whole had risen every year since 1988, the first year that data were available from the U.S. Bureau of Labor Statistics. Between 1989 and 1992 employment at Microsoft and Borland, Lotus's main competitors, grew by 104 percent and 128 percent, respectively. The nature of writing software had also changed significantly since Lotus's founding. Two people created Lotus 1-2-3; 150 people were responsible for the development of 1-2-3 Release 3.0.

Even in an industry known for high employee turnover however, management changes at Lotus in the late 1980s were notable. Eleven top executives left Lotus between 1987 and 1989.[9] Industry observers attributed delays in Release 3.0, in part, to high turnover and changing management style. The 35 programmers who worked on Release 3.0 "worked on their own, without detailed schedules or goals and little sense of what others on the team were doing or how their part fit into the whole."[10]

In response to stiffening competition in the late 1980s, management tightened its watch over expenses, removed long-held perks like picking up the tab for "take-out" ordered for working lunch meetings, and lowered subsidies for some employee benefits. According to one software engineer, "budgets were being reviewed incredibly strictly." Once wholly-subsidized health care benefits now required 15 percent employee participation.

Even though Lotus avoided all but the most limited layoffs, and other software companies typically required as much as 30 percent employee participation in benefits costs, these changes were a psychological blow to a company used to dramatic profit margins and generous employee policies.

Lotus Culture

Like many entrepreneurial start-ups, Lotus was strongly defined by the personalities of its founders. Mitch Kapor incorporated Lotus Development Corporation in 1982. The company really began about a year before that, however, in Kapor's house when Kapor hired his first employee, Janet Axelrod, a friend of a friend, to "take care of anything that came along that wasn't related to technology."

Axelrod was 29 in 1981 and had been unemployed for about a year. Prior to that she worked

9. Keith H. Hammonds, "The Spreadsheet That Nearly Wore Lotus Out," *Business Week,* July 3, 1989.

10. Hammonds, "The Spreadsheet That Nearly Wore Lotus Out."

EXHIBIT 3   Lotus Operating Principles

Lotus Operating Principles

These Operating Principles are intended to serve as guidelines for interaction between all employees. Their purpose is to foster and preserve the spirit of our enterprise and to promote the well-being of all concerned.

Commit to excellence

Insist on integrity

Take responsibility; lead by example

Communicate openly, honestly, and directly

Treat people fairly; value diversity

Listen with an open mind; learn from everything

Establish purpose before action

Respect, trust, and encourage others

Work as a team

Encourage risk-taking and innovation

Have fun

Source: Lotus Development Corporation.

---

for the Haymarket People's Fund, an "activist-controlled foundation committed to radical social change."[11] Kapor gave Axelrod free reign; she hired, fired, and set the tone of the rapidly growing Lotus. Axelrod recalled:

> It got clearer and clearer to me that being [at Lotus] I was going to have the opportunity to test some of the things that I believed in. . . . And that is what I set out to do as Lotus was growing.

Axelrod was largely responsible for Lotus's early corporate culture. She established the company's broadly integrated HR function, championed workplace diversity, encouraged Lotus's philanthropy, and got the company to sponsor events such as an annual fundraising walk organized by the AIDS Action Committee. She also worked to establish Lotus's "Operating Principles" (see Exhibit 3). Some even said Axelrod named the company.

Axelrod left the vice presidency of Human Resources in 1987, but continued on as a part-time consultant. She oversaw projects like the establishment of Lotus's day care center, and continued to steer the company's philanthropic giving. Axelrod still carried a lot of weight with senior management from Lotus's early years; Campanello called her "an incredible person" and considered her to be his mentor.

The rapid success and growth of Lotus, as well as management changes, eventually began to move the company away from its personality-driven culture. Jim Manzi, a McKinsey and Co. consultant, joined Lotus in May 1983 as director of Corporate Marketing and became vice president of Marketing and Sales in September of that year. He became president of Lotus in October 1984, CEO in April 1986, and chairman in July 1986 when Kapor stepped down. In Axelrod's view,

> It gets more and more difficult the more successful a business becomes . . . to pull people kicking and screaming into the twenty-first century on

---

11. Haymarket People's Fund, "Annual Report," 1990–1991.

some . . . issues. Most people go into business because they really don't [care] about anything that has to do with human beings. So that was sort of the opposite of where I was coming from. And everything stems from that.

Russ Campanello

Campanello took a circuitous route to HR. He entered the Lowell Technological Institute, what he called "the poor man's MIT," as an engineering major but quickly decided to try liberal arts and eventually marketing. He nearly dropped out several times. When he confessed to a finance professor that "nothing made sense" except maybe psychology, the professor suggested Human Resources. There, Campanello found a combination of traditional business concepts and theory about human behavior and motivations. According to Campanello, at Lotus HR was

> a very powerful force within the organization . . . that was very different from the five or six other firms that I had gotten interviews and offers from . . . [at Lotus] they were talking about the cultures, and the values, and the people in the business. That's why I joined. It was a Human Resource organization positioned differently in the business and it was a Human Resource organization that stood for some values. It was started by a very powerful person who still had a very powerful presence in the business. It was looking to position itself more closely to the business.

At Lotus, Campanello was "looking for a place where the Human Resources function wasn't carried outside the center of the business, [but] where there was an affiliation [between] . . . the values of the organization and how they got played out inside the company." Campanello believed in the "gains to be made in productivity if you get the human equation right." To him, HR was central and critical to an organization's long-term success.

Lotus Human Resources

Campanello left Wang Laboratories in 1987 to join Lotus as the HR manager of the sales divi-

sion. Campanello was at Lotus just over a year when his boss left. He became the interim head of HR in November of 1988 while Lotus conducted a nation-wide search for a new HR vice president. After the company interviewed outside candidates for nine months, Campanello was asked to be vice president for Human Resources.

According to Campanello, "There was a tremendous amount of change internally . . . getting organized to contribute to the business . . . there was a lot of stuff to be addressed." For example, despite Lotus's stated commitment to recruit, hire, and develop a diverse workforce, by 1989 its limited success in doing so came to light and attracted government attention. To help address the problems, Lotus founded a Diversity Advisory Group (DAG) "to provide independent and objective input to top management about issues regarding diversity in the company."[12] DAG was mandated to design Lotus's response to changing demographics in the workforce and to write an annual "Lotus Diversity Report" summarizing the company's diversity efforts and assessing their statistical results within the organization. Human Resources was particularly concerned with improving the company's ability to attract and retain women and minorities, both to prevent government intervention in the company and because competition for employees within the software industry was so keen.

In addition, Campanello needed to fill some key positions. Among Campanello's early hires as vice president was a new director of Compensation and Benefits, Keith Peden, and a new manager of Benefits, Diane Duval. Campanello hired Peden away from Alexander & Alexander Consulting Group, a benefits consulting firm located in Boston, because he was "a builder . . . [who] likes to push limits." Peden remembered being promised, "the ultimate consulting engagement."

What Peden found when he joined was that

---

12. *The Lotus Diversity Report,* December 27, 1990, p. 1.

Lotus Human Resources had "no infrastructure, literally, for decision making . . . there was no context for . . . our benefits philosophy. Lotus led, but led out of a position of not understanding what leading cost."

Peden understood his first challenge to be to establish a clear benefits philosophy and an integrated compensation and benefits policy that corrected the "tremendous inequities" that existed across the company (see Exhibit 4). Peden was committed to offering "as much choice as possible to give flexibility" to employees and to making the whole organization aware of the "dollar value" of benefits received (see Exhibit 5). Peden worked to define what Lotus wanted to accomplish through its compensation and benefits programs, and what type of workers the company wanted to attract.

Lotus wanted to be an "upper quartile provider" of compensation and benefits when compared with packages offered by competitors in order to recruit and retain the best employees in the industry. Peden developed compensation and benefits profiles on every company in the software industry to better understand what Lotus was up against in meeting that goal.

The Extended Benefits Task Force

Nearly since the founding of Lotus, lesbians and gay men at the company connected through two electronic mail networks, "lambda" and "@gala". "lambda" was open and interactive; gays, lesbians, bisexuals, and heterosexuals used the network to discuss a wide variety of gay and lesbian issues. "@gala," "lambda's" predecessor, began as a confidential mailing list. AnnD Canavan, a quality assurance manager, maintained the mailing list of 50–65 people and controlled access in order to protect confidentiality. "@gala" was largely social until the spring of 1989 when (according to Polly Laurelchild-Hertig, a senior international communications assistant), Canavan began to think

maybe [the network] should do something a little bit more. Maybe there's some potential here. So

she called a meeting and said bring ideas of what you would like "@gala" to be . . . the one that got the most attention . . . was the idea of benefits.

Canavan and Laurelchild-Hertig soon became the core of the group to create a working extended-benefits proposal along with Margie Bleichman, a principal software engineer. The three women named themselves the Extended Benefits Task Force and began to work on a proposal to "extend Lotus employee benefits to non-married 'spouse equivalents' of Lotus employees in the same manner as benefits are routinely extended to legal spouses now."[13]

The members of the Task Force were "under the impression that other companies already offered this and [they] just had to call them up and get their models." Laurelchild-Hertig's experience of calling someone in the HR department of one corporation that the group thought offered benefits to lesbians and gays was typical:

They started chuckling and said something to the effect of "not in my lifetime" . . . it was kind of a rude awakening. They weren't rude about it. I took them so completely by surprise . . . that they just had to laugh.

The Task Force did find a few models, but they were not of publicly traded companies. Ben & Jerry's Homemade, the *Village Voice,* The American Friends Service Committee, the ACLU/San Francisco, Montefiore Medical Center, a few other nonprofits, and several West Coast cities offered spousal equivalency benefits (see Exhibit 6).

Bleichman, Canavan, and Laurelchild-Hertig developed their working proposal based on these models and their casual conversations with Lotus's unmarried population living in committed relationships. Other than occasional questions put out on "@gala," input was consciously limited. According to Laurelchild-Hertig, the Task Force

---

13. "Benefits Proposal," unpublished document, May 23, 1989.

EXHIBIT 4   Mission Statement

Mission Statement
Compensation, Benefits, and Human Resource Systems

Lotus intends to be a market leader in total compensation, delivered through a flexible, innovative, and well-managed pay-for-performance system. The process must equitably recognize the different contributions of employees, business units, and work teams throughout the company. In addition, the department and Human Resources will showcase the capabilities of Lotus and its products in the area of work group computing. This will be done by modeling the use and management of an integrated system on the desktop to empower human resource and management decision making. All programs or processes developed by the group will be done in a collaborative process that involves input from our clients—employees, managers, and Human Resource Consultants.

Key Tenets

1. To provide compensation programs that are in the *upper quartile of the industry* when compared to representative programs of our competitors.

2. To integrate all programs into a *total compensation package* that is understood by management and employees alike.

3. To provide our clients with *knowledgeable, accountable, and timely service.*

4. To ensure *sound financial management* and vendor accountability in the design, implementation and maintenance of the Compensation, Benefits and HRIS* process' at Lotus.

5. To provide Lotus with an integrated Compensation and Benefit program, offering *flexible delivery systems* that acknowledge pay *for performance.*

6. To ensure the candid *forthright communication* of all Lotus programs to all client bases, stating purpose, criteria, guidelines, and the objectives of all plans.

7. To offer a *cost-effective mix* of short-term, long-term, and deferred compensation and benefit plans.

8. To ensure a *strategic approach* to compensation and Benefits plan design, integrating cost utilization and funding with the *corporate business plan.*

9. To maximize the *cost-effective administration* of plans by creating vendor accountability, growing in-house capabilities, *maximizing work group computing* capabilities, and Human Resource systems integration.

10. To take advantage of the company's ability to *provide tax effective* compensation and benefit plans to its employees.

11. To *integrate* all worldwide compensation, benefits, and HRIS programs to support *Lotus' philosophy.*

12. To provide an example of the *Human Resouce consulting model* in action for all clients to experience and interact with.

*Human Resource Information Systems.

Source: Lotus Development Corporation.

EXHIBIT 5   Cost of Benefits to Lotus*

	Employee Only	Employee Plus One Dependent	Employee Plus Two or More Dependents
Medical			
Option 1	$2,147	$4,272	$5,753
Option 2	1,889	3,778	5,087
Option 3	1,760	3,499	4,744
Option 4	2,147	4,272	5,753
Dental			
Option 1	232	465	697
Option 2	186	372	588
Vision			
Option 1	37	73	110

*Lotus first looked at cost of benefits as negotiations with insurers around the spousal equivalents decision were under way in 1991. The different option packages gave employees flexibility regarding what was covered, how much of costs were wholly covered, where services were performed, etc.

Source: Lotus Development Corporation.

EXHIBIT 6   Models Looked at by The Extended Benefits Task Force

Private Sector

The Village Voice (since 1982)
American Civil Liberties Union/San Francisco (1983)
The American Friends Service Committee (1987)
The American Psychological Association (1983)
Ben & Jerry's Homemade (1989)
Montefiore Medical Center (1991)*

Public Sector

Berkeley, California (1985)
Laguna Beach, California (1990)
Santa Cruz, California (1987)
Seattle, Washington (1990)
San Francisco, California (1991)
West Hollywood, California (1985)

*Of the models, only Montefiore Medical Center did not offer the extended benefits to unmarried, heterosexual couples as well as lesbian and gay couples.

Really didn't want to become this mass committee of the entire company . . . we felt we would be much more effective if the people that were working on it knew about it and everybody else learned about it once it was further along. Projects get done more effectively if you have a limited number of people . . . and because if there was going to be any opposition, we wanted [the proposal] to get really far along before it ran into that.

Bleichman also got strategic advice from Axelrod, who promised to get Campanello to focus on it and to help it move through the company in any way she could.

Implementation Concerns

Benefits Issues

Most of the models that the Extended Benefits Task Force found covered unmarried, heterosexual as well as lesbian and gay couples. According to one actuarial and benefits consultant, in any given population, the number of unmarried, heterosexual couples living together in committed, long-term relationships would outnumber lesbian and gay couples in similar relationships three to one.[14] According to 1990 Census data, 27 percent of the 91 million U.S. households defined themselves as "traditional families" with children living with two opposite-gender parents—down from 40 percent in 1970. Almost 2.6 million households were made up of unmarried, heterosexual couples, and 1.6 million of lesbian or gay couples, according to the same Census data.

From the outset, Campanello chose to consider extending spousal equivalency benefits only to lesbian and gay couples in committed, long-term relationships. Heterosexuals had the option to marry legally and get the benefits that lesbians and gays sought.

The working proposal of the Task Force presented Peden with a "challenge." Given his commitment to developing benefits equity, he was concerned that any changes to Lotus's benefits program provided "no more or no less risk for the company to insure" the proposed group than any other group. Benefits accounted for about 26 percent of Lotus's payroll expenses, about the 50th percentile in terms of cost industrywide. The youth of the Lotus workforce, and its relative health, lowered benefits costs in relation to many other industries.

Peden "really struggled" to clarify the issues Lotus needed to address in instituting a spousal equivalency policy. The model organizations that the Extended Benefits Task Force discovered "weren't in a data sharing mode." Statistics were difficult to find since few insurance companies and other benefits providers had followed lesbian and gay couples either at all or for a statistically significant period of time. The organizations that were conducting such research were reticent to share information other than in off-the-record conversations; documentation would not be available for years. Peden did cost modeling for the proposed extended benefits program based on what little actuarial information he could find.

Several studies estimated the number of lesbians and gays within various population groups. The most commonly used statistic, however, came from a Kinsey Institute for Human Sexuality study conducted in 1948 which indicated that 10 percent of any given male population was gay. A Task Force survey verified the statistic as accurate for lesbians as well as gays at Lotus. Peden's inquiries with municipalities that offered spousal equivalents benefits also revealed that lesbian and gay committed relationships "were every bit as committed, and statistically more so, than heterosexual married relationships" in regard to monogamy, as well as longevity of relationship.

Despite the fact that Acquired Immune Deficiency Syndrome (AIDS) was not limited to the gay community and lesbians were among the lowest risk populations for AIDS—at less risk,

---

14. Andrew Sherman, interview, March 4, 1993.

EXHIBIT 7A   Cumulative Total of U.S. Acquired Immune Deficiency Syndrome (AIDS)
Cases as of 12/31/89, Broken Down by Exposure Category Among Adults

		Cases
Male homosexual or bisexual sexual contact	61%	70,093
Intravenous (IV) drug use (among females and heterosexuals)	21	24,212
IV drug use (among homosexual and bisexual males)	7	8,117
Heterosexual sexual contact	5	5,630
Sex with IV drug user		2,871
Born in Pattern II country*		353
HIV heterosexual exposure category not specified		559
Sex with bisexual male		353
Sex with person born in a Pattern II country		82
Sex with person who received contaminated blood during a transfusion		81
Sex with hemophiliac		52
Undetermined	3	3,842
Blood transfusion	2	2,830
Hemophiliac use of blood products	1	1,062
Total		115,786

*A Pattern II country is where exposure to the Human Immunodeficiency Virus (HIV) is commonly transferred through heterosexual intercourse.

Source: Centers for Disease Control.

in fact, than heterosexuals—Peden found that many people's first concern was the cost of AIDS-related health care. The cost of other catastrophic illnesses was frequently greater than that for AIDS however (see Exhibit 7).

And, while large industries typically find 65 percent–70 percent family participation in health care benefits, only 40 percent of Lotus employees carried family coverage. The lesbian and gay population was less likely to require maternity-related care and, similarly, were less likely to require dependent care for minor children than were heterosexual couples.[15]

---

15. David J. Jefferson, "Gay Employees Win Benefits for Partners at More Corporations," *The Wall Street Journal*, March 18, 1994.

Insurance Issues

In 1989 Lotus was partially self-insured. The company did purchase reinsurance, or stop-loss coverage, from an outside carrier. At the time Lotus was self-insured to $140,000 per claim; in the event of a catastrophic claim, Lotus was responsible for costs up to $140,000 and the reinsurance company covered costs from $140,000 to a one-million-dollar cap. The plan document that governed Lotus's medical coverage could not be altered without the authorization of the reinsurer.

Lotus also offered employees the option of participating in a health maintenance organization (HMO). Fifteen percent of Lotus employees opted for that plan over Lotus's partially self-insured program. The HMO was reticent to accept the lesbian and gay couples that Lotus

EXHIBIT 7B Typical Catastrophic Health Care Costs in 1988

Stroke	$50–100,000
AIDS	40–70,000
Cancer	20–300,000
Cesarean section	5–10,000
Premature birth	1–500,000

was proposing into its covered pool without statistical information on the potential risks it might encounter in doing so. The carriers faced the same information vacuum that Peden did when he attempted his cost modeling.

Lotus began to explore extending its benefits programs with its own insurance carriers, as well as with other companies. Diane Duval led Lotus's effort to negotiate whether extended coverage was a possibility with insurance carriers, including life and dependent life insurance carriers, and what additional costs Lotus might face in renegotiating current contracts.

Tax Issues
Lotus's tax-qualified flexible benefits program was covered under section 125 of the Internal Revenue Service (IRS) Code. Because the IRS Code did not recognize spousal equivalents as fitting the definition of an eligible, dependent spouse, Lotus was advised that a conservative reading of the Code indicated that extending benefits to noneligible dependents could disqualify the company's entire plan. Disqualification would mean, among other things, that employee premium payments would come from earnings after taxes, not pre-tax earnings. Duval began to explore holding employees participating in the proposed extended benefits program outside of the qualified program so as not to jeopardize it.

If Lotus decided to go ahead with the extended benefits program, the company would have to impute as income the fair market value of any company-subsidized portion of coverage

for the spousal equivalent and any dependent children not under the legal guardianship of the employee. Duval estimated that Lotus would need to impute the salary of such employees by about $200 a month, resulting in an increased tax obligation.

But Duval and Lotus corporate counsel Chris Ciotti also were concerned that Lotus's benefits offerings be consistent between married employees and lesbian or gay employees and their spousal equivalents. An outside benefits consultant suggested that Lotus might consider "grossing up" the salaries of lesbian or gay employees participating in the proposed program to cover any additional tax and imputed income liabilities.

Legal Issues
Ciotti spoke with corporate counsel at the public and private organizations that offered spousal equivalency benefits to discover what legal liabilities Lotus might face in extending its benefits. She heard of only one related suit, against a city, having to do with lack of due process.

Ciotti "picked the brains" of her peers at other corporations about the potential impact the revised benefits package might have on unmarried, heterosexual couples, customers, and investors. The response was a "mixed bag . . . someone could always sue us," according to Ciotti. Although there was the possibility of legal action, no precedent existed, however.

Ciotti also focused her attention on how Lotus might prevent abuse of the proposed extended benefits program. Several model organizations used affidavits, signed either by the employee, or by both the employee and his or her spousal equivalent, attesting to the committed, long-term status of the relationship. Lotus was concerned that in creating compensation and benefit equity for lesbian and gay employees, it parallel requirements for married, heterosexual employees as closely as possible.

In Ciotti's mind the most likely legal action would be a reverse discrimination suit filed by a heterosexual employee living in a committed,

---

EXHIBIT 8   Lotus Corporate Policy

Lotus Corporate Policy
Lotus's Philosophy on Discrimination-Free Work Environment
Policy Number-LOTUS 4.0
Policy Dated 07/01/85

Policy

Lotus Development Corporation strives to create and maintain a work environment characterized by fair treatment, diversity, and respect for the individual.

Lotus is committed to offering equal opportunity for employment, advancement, and benefits to all employees. Lotus' policy is to stand against discrimination in all areas, including recruiting, hiring, job assignments, supervision, training, promotions, rates of pay, and benefits because of sex, race, religion, national origin, age, veteran status, disability, or sexual preference.

Discrimination generally takes three basic forms: differential treatment, differential impact, or the presence of a hostle/offensive/discriminatory work climate.

- Different treatment refers to instances where the employer, through its policies or managers, treats some similarly situated employees differently than others because of their race, religion, sex, national origin, age, veteran status, disability, or sexual preference.
- Differential impact involves employment practices that seem neutral, but in fact they affect one group more adversely than another. The brunt is often borne by groups of individuals with a shared characteristic such as gender, race, religion, age, national origin, disability, or sexual preference. Differential impact cannot be justified by any business necessity.
- Discriminatory work climates are those characterized by subtle, yet repeated offensive practices and behaviors that have the effect of making certain groups of individuals feel excluded. Racial and sexist comments engaged in by managers during work meetings or events are examples of behaviors which contribute to a discriminatory work environment.

Lotus's preference for a diverse work environment comes out of a recognition that difference enriches our individual lives and the life of our company.

Since prejudice and discrimination are widespread in our culture, it is generally an uphill battle to create a workplace that is universally respectful of and responsive to individuals of diverse backgrounds. Our goal, therefore, is to build a company which nurtures, supports, sustains, and draws from all its members, with regard only to merit.

Source: Lotus Development Corporation.

---

long-term relationship who was denied spousal equivalency coverage. There was also the possibility that if Lotus required some sort of affidavit from a lesbian or gay employee, that employee could file a discrimination suit based on the fact that married, heterosexual couples did not need to provide any documentation verifying the legality or status of their marriages or claimed dependents. Lotus did have a non-discrimination policy which included sexual orientation, but it did not mention marital status (see Exhibit 8).

Reactions

Typically, Human Resources changed benefits policy without any formal comment period or roll-out strategy. Campanello began to consider whether employee input would be useful in this instance and whether a public relations strategy would be necessary. In addition to the lesbian and gay only limitation, Campanello was considering other limits as well; namely that the policy be domestic only. Some countries where Lotus operated had national health care which made such an extended benefits policy unnecessary, but Campanello was also concerned about inflaming cultural biases at the cost of business.

Facing a Decision

Campanello could not get the initial meeting with the Extended Benefits Task Force off his mind. When the three women left his office, Campanello was most surprised by how moved he was. After all, he was jokingly known around the free-wheeling Lotus offices as, "the guy in the suit."

What really gave him pause to reflect, was the issue of lesbian and gay partners. Bleichman had told him that when she joined Lotus in July of 1987, she thought the company "was like nirvana for being out as a gay person . . . it was just an incredible place to be. A lot of gay people were out and [she] was really excited about it." Knowing that the company had a nondiscrimination policy based on sexual preference, on her first day she filled out benefits forms to include the name of her female partner on lines asking for information about her spouse. They had been together for more than 10 years and were raising two children. It was, according to her, "naive." A few days later someone processing her medical benefits called to tell her that Lotus's insurance company could not support her request to cover her partner. Bleichman remembered it as "not a bad conversation."

During the meeting Campanello thought:

She's been with her partner 10 years and I got divorced after three. And look at the stresses that a lesbian couple has to face in the world . . . I was asking a lot of questions and they were helping me [to understand]. I was impressed by their willingness to share. . . . It was a frank conversation and the more they talked, the more I got it—the more I began to understand that this was about creating equity. . . . There was something inherently wrong with the system [currently in place] that didn't acknowledge the partners of this community.

Moved as he was by the women and their experiences, Campanello still had a number of questions. He wondered whether this should be the first major policy issue for him to champion. He had a number of changes within his division to think about. He had to overhaul the compensation and benefits system to reflect Louts's commitment to equity, and there was company-wide morale to consider. These were difficult financial times for Lotus. The company needed to pay more attention to the "bottom line." Campanello had the issues raised by the Diversity Advisory Group to think about, as well.

Even if Lotus was committed to leadership on compensation and benefits issues, there were many conflicting attitudes and values about lesbians and gays among Lotus employees. Campanello wondered whether it was the role of business to challenge those ideas. What would extending benefits coverage to "spousal equivalents" say about Lotus, and how would it play out in the marketplace?

QUANTUM SEMICONDUCTOR, INC.

At 10:00 A.M. on April 4, 1989, Peter Chanson headed for a special meeting of Quantum Semiconductor's Executive Committee. Chanson, Manager of Health and Safety had been asked by Quantum's CEO to discuss the reproductive health studies that suggested that female workers in semiconductor fabrication areas suffer a high rate of miscarriages. Since a majority of Quantum's production workers were women in their child-bearing years, these findings had important implications. This meeting had been called to discuss what course of action the company might take in response to past findings and in anticipation of the outcome of current studies.

As Chanson looked around the conference table, he saw that all invited were there: CEO and President, James Atherton; all the vice presidents; Director of Public Relations, Karen Kiner; Quantum's legal adviser, Roger Loveless; and physician and occupational health consultant, Dr. Susan Newman. (See Exhibit 1.)

Atherton called for everyone's attention. "I've called this meeting because Peter here has been after me about it for the last two months," he smiled ruefully at Chanson.

> You're all familiar with the publicity surrounding reproductive health hazards to women in semiconductor fab [fabrication] areas. Peter has approached me, and probably many of you as well, about our need to address this. We need to understand what's going on in the industry and how it might affect us. Should we take action now or wait three years for the SIA[1] study results to appear? Unfortunately, at this point, we still have more questions than answers.

He turned to Chanson.

"First, I'd like to refresh your memory about the Digital Equipment Corporation (DEC) study,"[2] Chanson began:

> In 1986, DEC sponsored an epidemiological study to investigate reproductive health risks at its semiconductor production facility. The study's results indicated that women in fab areas suffered a miscarriage rate of about twice that of the national average. We all remember the nationwide media attention and the pressures from public and government to respond. The SIA appointed a panel of experts to review the DEC study in detail, but it's still unclear to what extent the study's conclusions should be applied to the rest of the industry. After nearly two years, the SIA, with participation and contribution from more than 17 semiconductor companies, has begun its own $3.5 million study. IBM and Motorola have initiated their own independent studies. All three studies began early this year and will take about three more years to complete.
>
> This is a difficult issue—a large majority of the industry workforce is female. It's particularly serious for us because 90 percent of our fab workers are women. If the studies confirm reproductive health hazards to women, then all women of child-bearing potential are theoretically susceptible. We might have to face the possibility of banning women from fab areas, which could create a catastrophic labor shortage. In addition, we might then expect a surge of worker compensation and third-party liability lawsuits.
>
> Our current safety practices don't address the issue apart from informing female fab workers about possible reproductive health hazards. We don't offer any protective measures for pregnant workers, such as temporary transfer, nor do we

1. Headquartered in Cupertino, California, the Semiconductor Industry Association (SIA) represented American semiconductor manufacturers.

2. See Appendix A for a detailed description of the DEC study and subsequent public and industry reactions.

EXHIBIT 1   Organizational Structure of Quantum Semiconductor, Inc.

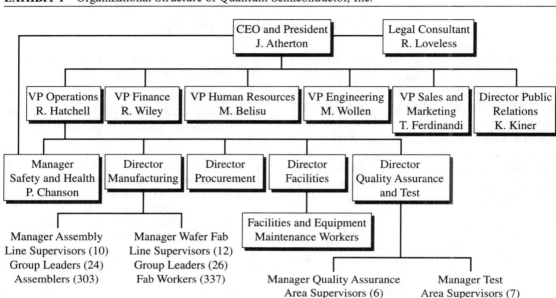

guarantee the same jobs when they return from temporary leave. The fact that we are not actively protecting pregnant employees or engaging in related health and safety projects might place us at a disadvantage in a legal defense. We need to take a proactive approach—I think we should determine a plan of action that can prepare us for the worst case.

Karen Kiner, Director of Public Relations, nodded in approval.

I would like to point out some advantages to Peter's suggestion: The fact that we are confronting this occupational health issue rather than ignoring it, and the possibility that we will do something to protect our employees can greatly enhance our image. The public, media, and government will see us as a concerned, proactive and safety-conscious employer. Even if we can't protect our employees 100 percent, our efforts will definitely improve our reputation and labor relations.

Ralph Hatchell, Vice President of Operations, shook his head. "From what I've heard, even if these studies confirm reproductive risks, they may not be able to prove that it's due to work exposure, or to point to any particular chemicals or processes as the cause."

· Dr. Susan Newman explained, "That's typical of epidemiological studies. It might be a single agent that's the cause or it might be a combination of factors. From these kinds of studies and for these kinds of problems, it's hard to ever be sure."

"The easiest option is to bar pregnant women from the fab," said Mark Wollen, Vice President of Engineering. "We should make it a requirement for women to notify the company as soon as they become pregnant. Since only a small percentage of women would be pregnant at any time, it shouldn't have a big impact on production."

"How do you propose to bar pregnant women?" legal consultant Roger Loveless interjected.

You can't fire a woman just because she's pregnant without expecting to be sued for sex discrimination. Even if your justification is to protect her or the fetus, such "protective exclusion" has gotten quite a number of companies into trouble. Worse yet, some women may feel pressured to get sterilized to keep their jobs and later sue the company. This happened at American Cyanamid a few years ago. AT&T received criticism when a plant manager transferred pregnant women from fab areas to other jobs within the company after the DEC study results were announced.[3]

Dr. Newman remarked,

What's worse, removing a pregnant woman from a hazardous environment does not necessarily mean full protection to her fetus. Fetal development is most affected by toxic chemical exposure in the first few weeks of pregnancy; spontaneous abortion often results. So if protection is granted to pregnant women, the same consideration should be given to fertile women as well. By the time the pregnancy is detected, the fetus may already be affected.

But let's go with your idea for the moment—pregnant workers are to be removed from fab areas. The problem then is to find out who's pregnant as soon as possible; we could give free monthly pregnancy tests to all fab employees. But, unless we're willing to guarantee job security (and wages) for pregnant employees, many may be unwilling to take the free pregnancy test. Experience in cases like this show that some workers do not want to endanger their jobs by letting the company know ahead of time about their pregnancies. I've seen cases in which women continue to work until their pregnancies became obvious and then have had to take lower-paid jobs or temporary leave without any guarantee of returning to their former positions.

Ralph Hatchell frowned.

You talk as if reproductive hazards are proven to exist. Our plant has high safety and health standards. The measured chemical levels in the fab rooms are an order of magnitude below the OSHA standards. Most plants pose risks in one form or another; our workers are probably safer in the fab than at home using cleaning chemicals or simply breathing the smog in Los Angeles. We are doing the best we can to keep our workers healthy and happy. In addition, we have an open door policy, so if any of them has a problem, he or she can always talk to the responsible manager.

Chanson bit his lip.

I agree with you to some extent. I don't think anybody can *prove* that semiconductor manufacturing is hazardous to workers' health, or, for that matter, that it's perfectly safe. Because of the high tolerances our processes require, we have to keep airborne particulates and chemical contamination at very low levels. But, even with very low concentrations of chemicals in the air, are there adverse health effects to workers over years of exposure? Meeting government standards cannot guarantee a healthy work environment. The regulatory agencies are also learning, and often look to the industry for guidance. Our industry is fairly new, our technology is highly advanced and dynamic, and our processes are complicated. It might take another decade to get some definitive answers to these concerns.

Having worked closely with workers, supervisors, and regulatory agencies, I think we can improve our safety and health practices. Workers do complain to their supervisors, as in any industry, but many of these complaints never come to our attention. I've spent some time talking to the people on the floor and some of what I've heard makes me nervous. For example:

• Several of our female employees expressed their fears of losing their jobs or having to take a pay cut should they become pregnant.

• Some of our supervisors feel that we don't put sufficient effort into educating the workers about suspected hazards. The information in the Material Safety Data Sheets or manufacturing specifications are often insufficient and incomprehensible to lay people. Non-English speaking workers

---

3. *The Wall Street Journal,* February 5, 1987.

tend to understand the information we dissemi-
nate about these hazards even less. We have a general tendency to be vague about hazards. Very
likely, the employees will find out sooner or later.
And it's best if they hear it from us, rather than
from a newspaper, a union organizing group, or a
labor law office.
• A process engineer pointed out to me that we
don't monitor hazardous gases other than arsine,
phosphine, and diborane. There've been complaints about headaches and nausea. The solvents,
metals, etc. may be checked once or twice a year
by OSHA inspections. Giving visible attention to
reproductive health issues indicates to our workers that we do care about their safety and health.

Mimi Belisu, Vice President of Human Resources, suggested,

We can offer both free pregnancy tests to all fab
workers and transfer any who are pregnant. With
a small percentage of women pregnant at any
given time, reshuffling people to accommodate the
temporary transfers won't be a big problem. On
the other hand, offering to transfer all women
with child-bearing potential might create problems that we just couldn't handle.

Karen Kiner said, "It seems like our only sure
way is complete automation."
"Come on, Karen, that's just not realistic. Total automation has been contemplated by some
of the big companies in our industry, but, to
date, it hasn't been implemented by any American company," Ralph Hatchell remarked.

A Japanese plant built in 1985 was equipped with
a completely automated processing line, and the
total cost was around $250 million. But for a
price that we can afford, I don't think we can get
there within the next ten years. Partial automation is increasingly popular in the industry; that'll
cut 10 to 20 percent of the labor and reduce some
hazards. Realistically, there's a limit to how much
we can spend.

Tom Ferdinandi, Vice President of Sales and
Marketing, made another suggestion,

From what Sue said, all fab workers with child
bearing potential are theoretically at risk. We

could hire "selectively" to avoid putting new female workers into the fab rooms. Start a gradual
layoff of the current female fab workforce and replace them with men. By the time the crisis hits
three years from now, we should have a male-
dominated fab workforce—no impact on operations and no added cost.

"A gradual phase-out of women in the fab
workforce would be considered sex discrimination," Mimi Belisu interrupted.

As I'm sure Roger will confirm, there are legal
precedents that stipulate that employers may not
fire women or refuse to hire them because of suspicions that their exposure to chemicals or radiation on the job may some day cause reproductive
or fetal damage. To justify such exclusions, employers must have proven evidence that the reproductive hazards affect only females and not males.
Existing evidence simply isn't conclusive enough
to justify that.

Bob Wiley asked, "Mimi, what's the common
practice regarding pregnant employees at other
companies?"
Belisu replied,

I don't know how small companies handle it.
Most larger companies, like Advanced Micro Devices and Intel, require employees to notify their
supervisors as soon as they become aware that
they're pregnant or if they plan to get pregnant.
When a supervisor is informed, he or she issues
the employee a list of chemicals, including their
airborne concentrations, to which she is exposed
in her normal working environment. The employee is supposed to check with her personal physician about whether she should continue working
in the environment during her pregnancy. The physician must sign the form in order for the employee to continue working in the same area. The
employee can also request a normal disability
leave at, for example, 60 percent of her gross
wages, or be transferred out of the fab area for
the term of her pregnancy. Some companies, DEC
for example, promise equal pay and status, and
guarantee the former job after pregnancy, but
most don't. Others have no mandatory restrictions
but allow women to voluntarily transfer out of
jobs with possible reproductive hazards.

Chanson added, "Health and safety standards can differ quite a bit, in general, among companies in the semiconductor industry."

"What about seeking alternative processes and materials to those which pose reproductive health hazards?" asked Karen Kiner.

Dr. Newman spoke deliberately,

There is no unequivocally safer option. First, we're not really sure which chemicals or processes pose reproductive hazards. There are many suspected chemical agents in semiconductor manufacturing that are constantly changing. Hence, their toxicities and adverse effects to humans are usually determined by unreliable methods like extrapolation from similar known chemicals, reference to past industrial medical data, or extrapolation from animal studies. Second, the new replacement chemicals or processes are not necessarily better; they may pose other health hazards that can take another five to ten years to be detected.

For example, xylene, a solvent used a decade ago and regarded as acutely toxic in high dosages, has today been largely replaced by glycol ethers. Recent studies indicated glycol ether may cause sterilization in males and is a suspected reproductive toxin to females as well. On the process side, an example is the wet etch process with its dangers of either inhalation of fumes or accidental skin contact. Many of these processes have been replaced with plasma or dry etch processes, which supposedly offer better quality as well as safety. However, the reactive plasma and its emission of radio frequency radiation pose another potential hazard, particularly in cases of leakage or equipment malfunction.

I don't mean to say that you shouldn't consider finding alternative materials. Chemicals like arsenic and its compounds are extremely toxic and must be eliminated where possible. They cause various systemic degeneracies with long-term exposure, even at very low dosages.

Mark Wollen replied,

Unfortunately, finding replacements for chemicals like arsenic is difficult and, in many instances, not technically feasible. Besides, finding alternative materials and processes is something we should leave to material vendors and equipment producers, or large semiconductor manufacturers who have lots of money to spend on such "vague" projects. One thing for sure, whoever can come up with safer replacements for chemicals like arsine or phosphine is guaranteed to make a lot of money.

"Another option is to make real improvements in our health and safety programs," Chanson countered. "Although we have a good safety control and training programs that meet all federal, state, and local regulations, there is always room for improvement." He listed some examples:

Add detectors or perform more frequent air sampling for chemicals other than those required by law; that'll cost about $20,000 per year . . . retrofit the cleanroom air flow system to increase fresh make-up air, or add air scrubbers to remove gases that exist at very low concentrations; that'll probably cost at least $3 million . . . offer better training to employees, make sure that they understand the potential hazards and the care required in processing, provide instructions in foreign languages for the groups that need it, and perform more frequent safety checks; maybe $200,000 per year. Start an "Occupational Health Monitoring Program" on a quarterly or bi-yearly basis. We'd systematically monitor the levels of suspected toxins in workers' blood or urine samples. Only a representative group of 10 percent to 20 percent of workers would need to be tested; maybe $300 per worker for each analysis.

"I think that's an excellent idea," said Dr. Newman.

In improving your health and safety programs, you're protecting all employees, pregnant and nonpregnant, male and female. This option addresses the legal discrimination issue as well as the suggestion—from animal tests and past health reports—that men are as much at risk as women. Although the DEC study indicated that men might not be affected, that's still to be answered by the current studies.

Bob Wiley, VP of Finance, shook his head.

Such improvements won't necessarily keep us from being sued three years from now, or convince outsiders that it is safe while we still have the toxic chemicals around. Maybe we're now at a 90 percent safety level. We can never reach 100 percent, but to get to 99 percent, there's no end to all the improvements we'd have to make. Besides, have you come up with a total estimate? The changes you've suggested sound expensive and might significantly delay planned production. The costs of new equipment and retrofitting facilities will definitely raise unit costs. We need to put whatever money we can spare into R&D or new production facilities. If we expect to remain competitive, we simply can't afford such extravagance.

Roger Loveless, the attorney, interrupted,

I'm not sure I see the need to take any major step at this time. You have a lot to lose and little to gain no matter what you decide. All semiconductor producers, equipment manufacturers, and materials vendors are facing the same risk. If current studies confirm reproductive health hazards, the government might enact stricter controls or enforce new labor and safety regulations that are at odds with whatever you decide to do. I agree that there might be liability suits, but that doesn't necessarily mean we'll lose. Don't quote me on this, but I think that an industrywide move to ban women altogether from chip production is unlikely to happen. My suggestion is to wait for the industry consortia and leaders like the SIA and IBM to take the initiative and avoid the costs associated with immediate action.

Tom Ferdinandi cautioned,

Whatever choice we make, we have to make sure that it will not impact our ability to be competitive down the line. We can't afford to miss delivery schedules or raise our product prices because of labor shortages or big investments in safety. On the other hand, if we can anticipate the problems that will afflict the industry when the SIA study results are in, and prepare ourselves while our competitors are doing nothing, that might give us a competitive advantage.

If these occupational health issues force us to incur higher production costs, that would put us at a disadvantage vis-à-vis our Japanese competitors, who aren't plagued with all these costs of minimizing health and safety risks. And, it's not because their processes and chemicals are any safer than ours. They operate in a completely different arena. Japanese industry doesn't have as much governmental regulation or public pressure as we do in the United States. As far as I know, they don't have any regulatory agency equivalent to OSHA. If there is any concern, it's about environmental health issues in communities near semiconductor plants.

Atherton was frustrated. More than two hours had gone by, and he knew this discussion could go on forever. He tapped the table.

We can't solve this problem in a day or two. Sometimes I think it's a "damned if we do, and damned if we don't" situation. We need to put more thought into this issue and examine each option in more detail.

He turned to Peter,

I want a summary of all viable options, many of which we have discussed here and others that I'm sure you will think of later. Include implications, tangible or intangible costs and benefits for each option, and give me a recommendation. You need to get feedback from the VPs and Roger and Sue in making the recommendation. I'd like your report in two weeks.

Quantum Semiconductor, Inc.

Quantum Semiconductor, Inc., was founded by James Atherton and a group of associates in 1983. The company's revenue had grown from $5 million in the first year of operation to more than $100 million in 1988, and was projected to exceed $200 million by 1993. Quantum designed, developed, manufactured, and marketed a variety of digital integrated circuits using proprietary 1.0- and 1.2-micron NMOS (N-channel Metal-Oxide-Silicon) and CMOS (Complementary Metal-Oxide-Silicon) technologies. Its line of products included Dynamic and Static RAM (Random Access Memory), PROM (Programmable Read-Only-Memory), EPROM (Erasable Programmable Read-Only-Memory), and Logic.

These products were generally used in four market sectors: military and aerospace, computers, communications, and instrumentation. About 60 percent of Quantum's products were customized to specific design and performance requirements of customers. (Exhibit 2 gives a summary of Quantum's financial statements.) Quantum marketed its products from its headquarters, regional, domestic, and foreign sales offices. The company's foreign sales were made in nine countries and constituted 20 percent of the total revenue in 1988 (up from 10 percent in 1986). Quantum's headquarters and production facilities were co-located in Santa Clara, California, the heart of Silicon Valley.

Competition

Throughout the 1980s, the increasingly global semiconductor industry was intensely competitive and characterized by steady price erosion and rapid technological change. The industry consisted of several major domestic and international semiconductor companies, many of which had substantially greater financial, technical, and marketing resources than Quantum, as well as smaller emerging companies vying for a share of the existing market (Exhibit 3). Customers were extremely price-sensitive and competitors frequently lowered prices to gain market share, causing responsive price reduction by other manufacturers, often resulting in industrywide reductions in profitability. In addition to price, important elements of competition included product performance, quality and reliability, on-time delivery capability, diversity of product line, application support, financial strength, and the ability to respond rapidly to technological innovation. To maintain its competitive position, Quantum recognized the need to continually develop new and improved products as well as to strive for more cost-effective operations.

Japanese competition had proven to be particularly tough for Quantum since the mid-1980s. Although a relative latecomer to the semiconductor industry, Japan had emerged as the major competitor by the early 1980s. Japanese firms had become the global sales leaders and low cost producers, dominating the commodity segments of the business. There were many factors which contributed to the success of these Japanese companies. In manufacturing, for instance, U.S. firms historically emphasized pushing products to their technological frontiers while Japanese companies had focused more heavily on raising yields and reducing costs.

Employees

Data on Quantum's employees, as of December 31, 1988, are shown in Exhibit 4. Like most of the industry's workforce, Quantum's employees were not represented by a labor union or a collective bargaining agreement. Almost 80 percent of the workers had at least two years of experience prior to coming to Quantum. Quantum management believed that its ability to attract and retain qualified personnel was essential to its continued success. To achieve that goal, Quantum offered competitive wages and good employee benefits. Like many companies in the industry, Quantum also offered a variety of bonus and profit-sharing plans.

Mimi Belisu, Vice President of Human Resources, explained the many incentives for working in the semiconductor industry:

> This industry has a large job market, especially here in Silicon Valley. Quantum, like most companies its size, offers relatively high wages and rapid pay increases, high overtime rates and hours (in good times), good employee benefits, a clean working environment, and little heavy-duty work. It does, however, require care and precision. Manual dexterity, particularly in wafer handling, is a must.

Belisu admitted that there were also some risks to balance those benefits:

> Because semiconductor sales have fluctuated dramatically, there have been as many small start-up companies springing up as companies going out of business. In prosperous times, companies offer higher wages and benefits to snatch skilled

EXHIBIT 2   Financial Summary of Quantum Semiconductor, Inc.

CONSOLIDATED STATEMENTS OF OPERATIONS

	Year Ended December 31 of		
	1986	*1987*	*1988*
Revenues:			
Net sales	$ 45,829,000	$ 71,362,000	$ 101,405,000
Development contracts	3,984,000	1,410,000	—
	49,813,000	72,772,000	101,405,000
Cost and expenses:			
Cost of sales	31,658,000	45,850,000	68,316,000
Research and development	9,922,000	12,352,000	14,210,000
Selling, general & administrative	10,470,000	12,921,000	17,201,000
	52,050,000	71,123,000	99,727,000
Income (loss) from operations	(2,237,000)	1,649,000	1,678,000
Interest expense	(2,991,000)	(2,991,000)	(1,464,000)
Income (loss) before income taxes	(5,228,000)	(1,342,000)	214,000
Provision for income taxes	—	—	69,000
Net income (loss)	$ (5,228,000)	$ (1,342,000)	$ 145,000

CONSOLIDATED BALANCE SHEETS

	December 31 of	
	1987	*1988*
ASSETS		
Current Assets:		
Cash and cash equivalents	$ 2,243,000	$ 2,562,000
Accounts receivable	14,331,000	15,682,000
Inventories	10,310,000	15,203,000
Prepaid expenses and other current assets	1,283,000	396,000
Total current assets	28,167,000	33,843,000
Property, plant and equipment	29,863,000	42,130,000
Other assets	3,468,000	2,859,000
	$ 61,498,000	$ 78,832,000
LIABILITIES AND SHAREHOLDERS' EQUITY		
Current liabilities:		
Accounts payable	$ 6,586,000	$ 13,623,000
Accrued expenses	4,407,000	6,582,000
Deferred income on shipments to distributors	5,690,000	5,529,000
Current portion of obligations under capital leases	6,627,000	4,512,000
Total liabilities	23,310,000	30,246,000
Long-term debt	3,061,000	12,121,000
Shareholders' equity:		
Preferred and common stocks	84,304,000	85,497,000
Accumulated deficit	(49,177,000)	(49,032,000)
Total shareholders' equity	35,127,000	36,465,000
	$ 61,498,000	$ 78,832,000

EXHIBIT 3 1988 and Preliminary Estimated 1989 Global Semiconductor Market Share Rankings for Top 20 Manufacturers

Company	1989 Rank	1988 Rank	1988 Revenue (millions of dollars)	1989 Revenue (millions of dollars)	% Change	1989 Market Share
NEC	1	1	4,543	4,964	9%	8.9%
Toshiba	2	2	4,395	4,889	11%	8.8%
Hitachi	3	3	3,506	3,930	12%	7.0%
Motorola	4	4	3,035	3,322	9%	5.9%
Fujitsu	5	6	2,607	2,941	13%	5.3%
Texas Instruments	6	5	2,741	2,787	2%	5.0%
Mitshubishi	7	8	2,312	2,629	14%	4.7%
Intel	8	7	2,350	2,440	4%	4.4%
Matsushita	9	9	1,883	1,871	(1%)	3.4%
Philips	10	10	1,738	1,690	(3%)	3.0%
National Semiconductor	11	11	1,650	1,618	(2%)	2.9%
SGS-Thomson	12	12	1,087	1,301	20%	2.3%
Samsung	13	18	905	1,284	42%	2.3%
Sharp	14	15	1,036	1,230	19%	2.2%
Siemens	15	20	784	1,194	52%	2.1%
Sanyo	16	14	1,083	1,132	5%	2.0%
Oki	17	17	947	1,125	19%	2.0%
Advanced Micro Devices	18	13	1,084	1,082	0%	1.9%
Sony	19	16	950	1,077	13%	1.9%
AT&T	20	19	859	873	2%	1.6%

Source: Dataquest, January 1990.

employees from each other. On the other hand, in recessionary times there are apt to be massive lay-offs—of both workers and engineers.

Employee training was conducted by the Human Resources Department in conjunction with safety and manufacturing personnel. A general training session for new hourly employees took more than a day (see Exhibit 5 for training agenda) and covered: company policies and employee benefits; employee rights and regulations established by government; emergency and accidents response; chemical handling and personnel safety; and hands-on process training conducted on an individual basis by a production supervisor. Safety training was mandatory for all workers and was repeated once a year. At the end of safety training sessions, employees were given a test; at least 80 percent correct was required. Some employees retook tests often; this was at the discretion of supervisors.

Quantum had informed employees about the DEC study results, telling them that the results were viewed as inconclusive and could not confirm reproductive health hazards in fab areas. Employees in fab areas who became pregnant could request a leave of absence, receiving temporary disability status with 60 percent of gross pay, as well as the usual six-week of maternity leave before and after the birth with full pay. A new fab worker typically required six months of training to reach full productivity; in other areas (except maintenance), six weeks was all that was needed. Female fab workers who took maternity

EXHIBIT 4   Employee Data of Quantum Semiconductor, Inc. (as of December 31, 1988)

Function	Male	Female	Total Employees	Avg Work Hrs/Week	Avg Gross Wage ($/Hr)
Administrative			52		
Technical Professionals			348		
Nonprofessionals					
Wafer Fab	29	308	337	44.1	13.50
Assembly	17	286	303	43.8	11.20
Maintenance	18	0	18	52.2	18.20
Test	33	14	47	44.7	13.60
Quality	36	15	51	42.9	11.10
Others	26	12	38	42.5	10.60
Total			1,194		

Nonprofessional Employees Age Distribution by Work Areas (December 31, 1988)

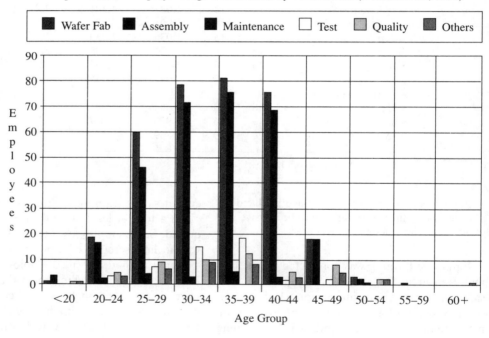

leave were guaranteed their former jobs. A woman who left when she became aware of her pregnancy, however, vacated the position long enough so that her replacement would be fully skilled when the original employee was ready to return. Hence, there was no guarantee that employees who left at the beginning of their pregnancies could return to former jobs after their pregnancies—although they would be granted priority for any positions that became available in their previous functions. Since mid-1986, half of these employees (who returned to the com-

---

EXHIBIT 5   Training Agenda for New Employees at Quantum Semiconductor, Inc.

FAB ORIENTATION (Interactive discussion conducted by safety & manufacturing)
Gowning for Fab rooms
   Demonstration of proper gowning, personal safety equipment, & entering fab room
Safety
   Chemical handling
   Emergency alarms
   Odors
   Chemical spills
   Accidents
   Evacuations
   Earthquakes
   Power outages
   Fire
   First aid
Manufacturing Travelers (Run Cards) and Logsheets
   Entries & related documents
   Error correction
Wafer Handling
   Demonstration of wafer handling techniques
Microscope Use
Computer Terminals
Fab Policy
Fab Tour
   Emergency exits, showers, eye wash, etc.
   Outside relocation sites
Read all specifications and take written tests covering all above subjects

WORK STATION TRAINING (on the job training by group leader)
Trainee read station specifications which include safety precautions and hazards specific to
work station
Trainer runs station while trainee observes
Trainee runs station under immediate control of *trainer*
Trainee runs station while *trainer* observes & does spot checks
Trainee reviews station specifications
Trainer audits trainee
Trainee takes written tests, given by Quality/Process Engineering
Trainee certified, if passed

---

pany) had been able to move back into their former jobs. These women usually were more experienced and handled the particularly critical processes.

Cleanrooms
Because of the microscopic dimensions of circuitry on semiconductor chips, with one micron (one thousandth of a millimeter) the typical width of an individual circuit, a dust speck could easily render an entire integrated circuit inoperative. In addition, chemical impurities could degrade or destroy the electrical properties of a chip. Therefore, it was imperative that

wafer processing[4] be carried out in an environment that was meticulously controlled with respect to cleanliness, temperature, and humidity. Human beings were the main source of contaminants which threatened product quality and yields. All personnel entering the fab cleanroom wore white "bunny suits" covering them from head to toe, face masks, protective eye glasses, and were allowed to wear neither make-up nor contact lenses.

Air in the cleanroom was recycled with a steady make-up stream entering from outside to provide fresh oxygen as shown in Exhibit 8a. Clean and conditioned air flowed in uniform laminar currents from ceiling to floor, limiting the stirring and spreading of any existing contaminants. The air was checked continuously for airborne particles to ensure that the particle count and size were within limits. Gas monitors measured arsine, phosphine, and diborane concentrations; an alarm sounded whenever the concentration of any of these chemicals exceeded the threshold limit values (see *Appendix C* for details about exposure standards). Air samples of other chemicals, typically solvents and metals, were taken once or twice a year in anticipation of OSHA inspection.

Around stations with wet processes, where baths of strong acids and caustics were located under hoods, laminar air streams flowed from tops of the hoods to the surface of baths and then into slits on the side of bench sinks, above the surfaces of the corrosive liquids (Exhibit 8b). Hazardous exhausts went to a "scrubber" to reduce their concentrations before being released into the atmosphere. These exhaust streams were sampled to ensure that the concentrations of any airborne chemicals were below EPA limits.

Airborne toxic gases in the cleanroom could be caused by the following: leakage in reactors or furnaces; leakage in equipment exhaust lines; open-air manual operations with chemical baths or photoresists; and the release of substances such as arsenic from the wafers. The concentrations of these chemicals in the air, which were normally very low, could accumulate with time, since 90 to 95 percent of the room's air was recirculated.

Chanson's Quandary

Peter Chanson had been with Quantum for five years. His first four years had been spent on the production floor where, as a manufacturing engineer, his duties included safety-related responsibilities such as training workers, writing manufacturing standards, and buying safety equipment. He became the contact point for any safety-related problems, from employee complaints to OSHA inspections. In 1988, when the company had grown to more than 1,000 employees, a formal safety department was established; Chanson was offered the position as Manager of Health and Safety. (Exhibit 9 shows the various regulatory agencies with whom he communicated.) He reported to the Vice President of Operations, Ralph Hatchell, although he could go directly to the CEO and President if special problems arose. For support, Chanson was assigned an engineer on an as-needed basis and a full-time administrator. In September of 1988, Chanson began part-time study toward a master's degree in public health.

As Chanson reflected on all the options discussed in the meeting, he felt that more research and analysis would be necessary to generate more viable options and explore the full implications of each. The complexity of it all was daunting. He needed to pull together the relevant background information related to the company, its manufacturing processes and the hazards therein, competition, the industry, views of labor, standards and regulations, legal precedent, and health studies.[5]

---

4. A detailed description of the fabrication of semiconductors onto silicon substrates is given in *Appendix B*. Exhibit 6 depicts the process flow diagram. Exhibit 7 details the primary chemical and radiation hazards associated with these processes.

---

5. A summary of recent industry, regulatory, and legal events are given in *Appendix D.*

EXHIBIT 6   A General Process Flow for CMOS Wafer Fabrication at Quantum Semiconductor, Inc.

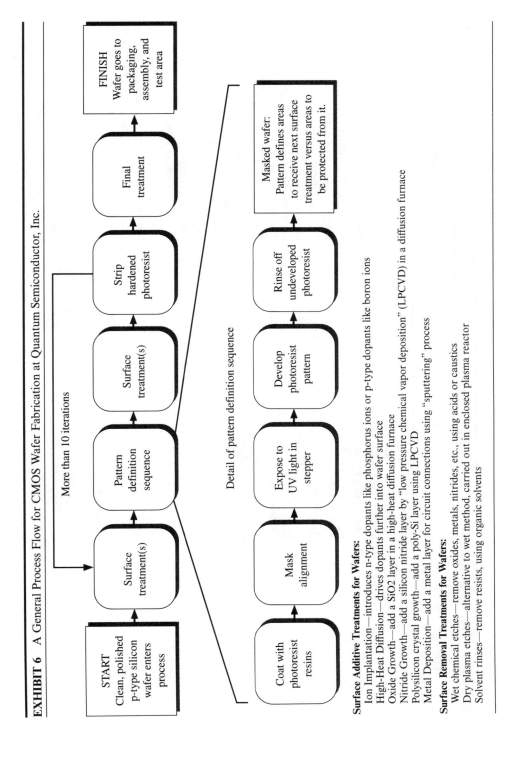

Surface Additive Treatments for Wafers:

Ion Implantation—introduces n-type dopants like phosphorus ions or p-type dopants like boron ions
High-Heat Diffusion—drives dopants further into wafer surface
Oxide Growth—add a SiO2 layer in a high-heat diffusion furnace
Nitride Growth—add a silicon nitride layer by "low pressure chemical vapor deposition" (LPCVD) in a diffusion furnace
Polysilicon crystal growth—add a poly-Si layer using LPCVD
Metal Deposition—add a metal layer for circuit connections using "sputtering" process

Surface Removal Treatments for Wafers:

Wet chemical etches—remove oxides, metals, nitrides, etc., using acids or caustics
Dry plasma etches—alternative to wet method, carried out in enclosed plasma reactor
Solvent rinses—remove resists, using organic solvents

EXHIBIT 7 Primary Health Hazards of Chemicals and Radiations Associated with Wafer Fabrication at Quantum

Process	Substance	TLV–TWA* (ppm)	Primary Hazards & Health Effects	Note
Wafer Cleaning	Sulfuric Acid	1 mg/m3	Chemical Burns	
	Hydrogen Peroxide		Respiratory Irritation	
	Hydrochloric Acid	5	Chemical Burns	
	Ammonium Hydroxide		Chemical Burn	
Wet Etching	Hydrofluoric Acid	3	Severe Chemical Burns	
	Acetic Acid	10	Eye & Respiratory Irritation	
	Phosphoric Acid	1 mg/m3	Chemical Burns	
	Ammonium Fluoride		Chemical Burns	
	Nitric Acid	2	Chemical Burns	
Plasma Etching	Carbon Tetrachloride	30 mg/m3	Liver & Kidney Damage	1,2
	Carbon Tetrafluoride		Anesthesia	3
	Boron Trichloride		Respiratory Irritation	
	Silicon Tetrachloride		Respiratory Irritation	
	Chlorine	1	Eye & Respiratory Irritation	4
	Sulfur Hexafluoride		Asphyxiation	3
	Radio Frequency Radiation	4.9mW/cm2 @13.56MHz	Thermal Damage	
Photolithography	2-Ethoxyethyl Acetate		Miscarriages/Birth Defects/ Testicular Atrophy	2
	Xylene	100	Narcosis (acute)/Liver & Kidney Damage (chronic)	2
	n-Butyl Acetate	150	Eye & Respiratory Irritation	
	Glycol Ethers	5	Male & Female Reproductive Hazards/Pancytopenia	6
	Freons or CFCs	1000	Cardiac Arrythmias	
	1,1,1-Trichloroethane	350	Cardiac Arrythmias	
	Dichloromethane	100	Cardiac Arrythmias/metabolized to carbon monoxide	1

Process	Chemical / Radiation	TLV*	Adverse Health Effect	Notes
	Methanol	200	Visual Field Disturbances	
	Trichloroethylene	50	Cardiac Arrythmias	
	Ultraviolet Radiation	0.1 µW/cm2	Erythma (acute)/Skin Cancer (chronic)	
Photoresist Stripping	Organic Acids		Chemical Burns	
	Phenol		Respiratory Irritation/Liver & Kidney Damage	2,5
	Chromium Trioxide		Cancer/Liver & Kidney Damage	
	Alkyl Benzenes		Narcosis (acute)/Liver & Kidney Damage (chronic)	2
	Radio Frequency Radiation	4.9mW/cm2 @13.56MHz	Thermal Damage	
Doping	Arsenic Trioxide		Cancer/Liver & Nasal Septum Damage	
(Diffusion/Ion-Implantation)	Arsine	0.05	Anemia/Kidney Damage/Death	1,4,(6)
	Diborane	0.1	Respiratory Irritation	4
	Phosphine	0.3	Respiratory Irritation	4
	Phosphorus Oxychloride		Respiratory Irritation	4
	Boron Tribromide		Respiratory Irritation	
	Boron Trichloride		Respiratory Irritation	
	X-Ray Radiation	~0.5 mRem/hr	Cancer/Cumulative Tissue Damage	
Metalization	Radio Frequency Radiation	4.9mW/cm2 @13.56MHz	Thermal Damage	

*Threshold Limit Values—Time Weighted Average. 8 hours/day and 40hrs/week exposure without adverse effects (from ACGIH).

Note: (1) Suspected carcinogens   (4) Highly toxic
(2) Can be readily absorbed through the skin   (5) Skin absorption can cause death
(3) Practically non-toxic   (6) Suspected reproductive toxins

Sources: D. Baldwin & J. Stewart, "Chemical & Radiation Hazards in Semiconductor Manufacturing", *Solid State Technology*, August 1989; P. Wald & J. Jones, "Semiconductor Manufacturing: An Introduction to Processes & Hazards", *American Journal of Industrial Medicine*, 11:203–221, 1987

EXHIBIT 8a   Cross-Sectional Schematic of Quantum's Cleanroom Air Recycling System

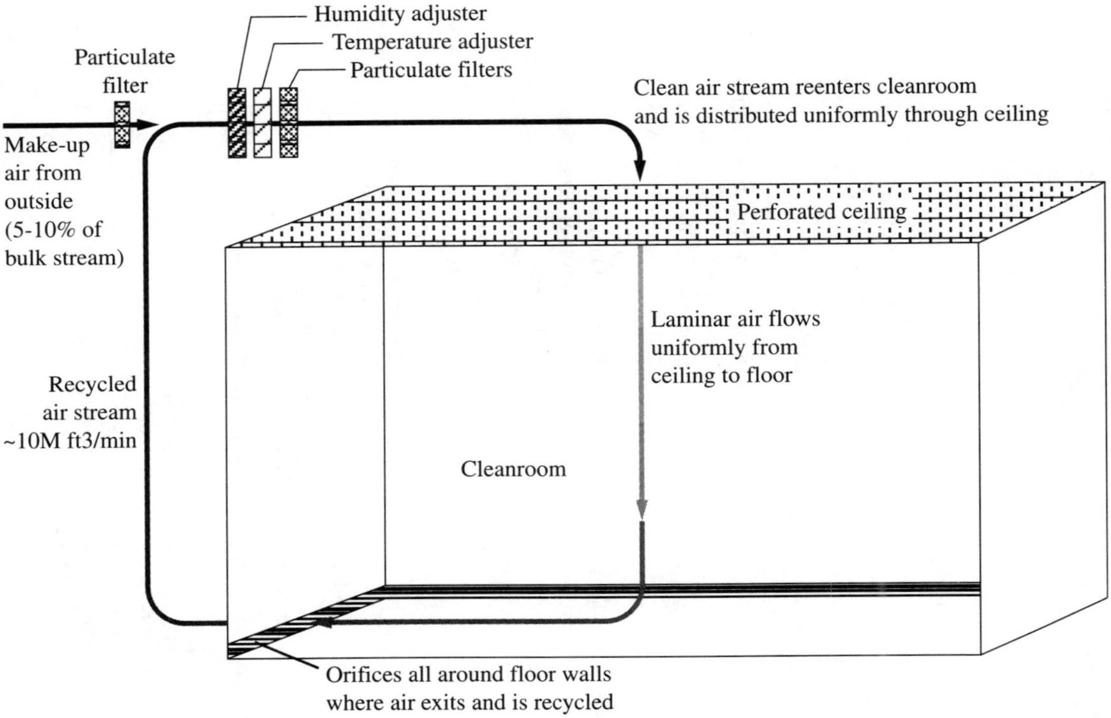

APPENDIX A
THE DIGITAL EQUIPMENT CORPORATION STUDY AND SUBSEQUENT REACTIONS

Digital Equipment Corporation (DEC) initiated a study in 1983, after workers at its Hudson, Massachusetts, plant expressed their alarm about what seemed to them to be a high incidence of miscarriages among fab workers. The company examined its medical and insurance data and found nothing out of the ordinary, according to Jeff Gibson, DEC's spokesman. In early 1984, it called in Harris Pastides, an epidemiologist, and Edward Calabrese, a toxicologist, both from the University of Massachusetts at Amherst.[6] The company said it spent several hundred thousand dollars on the study.[7]

On February 16, 1986, *The Wall Street Journal* reported:

The DEC study is the largest examination yet of occupational effects on the health of production workers in the semiconductor industry, where a majority of the 55,000 work-

---

6. *The New York Times,* January 14, 1987.
7. *The Wall Street Journal,* December 16, 1986.

EXHIBIT 8b   Cross-Sectional Schematic of Air Flows in a Wet Etch Station at Quantum

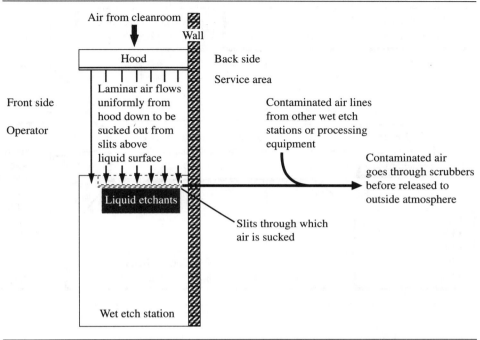

ers are women. University of Massachusetts researchers surveyed 744 of the 2,000 workers at DEC's Hudson, Mass., semiconductor plant.

In one phase of production (diffusion areas) where many acids were used for etching, the study found a 39% miscarriage rate, more than twice the 18% rate found in the rest of the plant. Among the general public nationally, a 10% to 20% miscarriage rate is typical, said Harris Pastides.

The study also reported a higher rate of general malaise, including headaches, nausea, dizziness, etc. However, there was no evidence that babies born to fab workers suffered a higher than normal rate of birth defects, nor that fab workers had abnormal infertility rates; wives of male fab workers showed no abnormal reproductive health effects.[8] The study was based on statistical data gathered by personal interviews with manufacturing workers, wives of male manufacturing workers, and nonmanufacturing workers who had worked at the plant for the last five years.[9]

The researchers and DEC agreed that the study did not prove a cause-effect relationship between chip production and miscarriage.[10] "We feel rather strongly about the need for a follow-up study," Pastides said. "This type of study design at best can indicate an association

8. *San Jose Mercury News*, December 5, 1986.

9. H. Pastides et al., "Spontaneous Abortion and General Illness Symptoms Among Semiconductor Manufacturers," *Journal of Occupational Medicine* 30, no. 7 (July 1988).

10. *Science News,* January 31, 1987.

EXHIBIT 9   Major Safety and Health Regulatory Agencies Interacting with Quantum

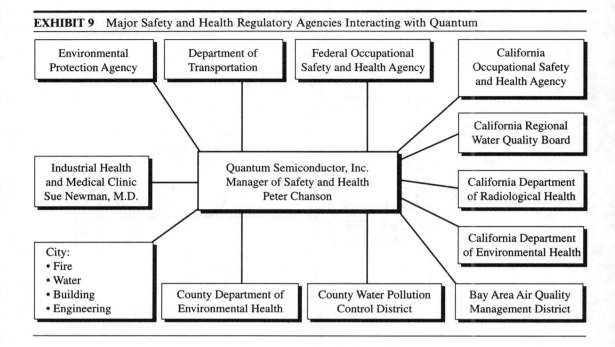

between occupation and outcome. It really needs to be followed up by a much, much more detailed analysis of the actual chemicals that were worked with."[11]

"Obviously these findings present a concern in the industry," said John Greenagel, public relations manager of Advanced Micro Devices (AMD) Inc. in Sunnyvale, California. "We think we should do a similar type of study, expanded on a nationwide basis, first of all to confirm or deny the results of that study. If it indicates that there is a problem, then obviously we want to identify what the causes are and solve that problem." The results of the study could "accelerate an already developing trend to get the wafer away from the person," said Jerry Hutcheson, chief executive officer of VLSI Research Inc. in San Jose, a leading semiconductor manufacturer. Hutcheson, one of the two experts who visited the Digital Equipment plant, said companies were using sophisticated monitoring devices to detect leaks and were installing more double-lined pipes to lessen the chance of gas leaks.[12]

Even before the study was completed, DEC established a policy of encouraging pregnant production workers to transfer to other jobs with equal pay and status. After the study, the company offered free pregnancy testing to all employees. Any woman of child-bearing age was also given the option to transfer to another job with equal pay and status.[13] Few women had requested such moves.[14] In addition, DEC promised to "consider" transfer for men as well and was proceeding to revamp employment procedures and improve chemical monitoring.

After the DEC study results were announced, other companies briefed their employees

11. *San Jose Mercury News,* December 5, 1986.
12. Ibid.
13. *Boston Globe,* January 27, 1987.
14. *Electronics Chemical News,* January 11, 1987.

about its findings. Greenagel (AMD) said, "We don't want to alarm anybody, but we did want people to be aware of it. We want people to know what we know, and we want them to hear it from us." Gray Allen, a spokesman for National Semiconductor, said the reaction of employees was "sort of ho-hum—'thanks for telling us'—but business as usual as far as they were concerned." At Intel, employees "showed no expression of alarm," spokeswoman Glynnis Kaye said. "But they're obviously curious to get more information on it, as are the rest of us."[15]

Several of the local (Silicon Valley) companies, including AMD and Intel, had policies that either required or recommended that pregnant employees notify their supervisors of their pregnancies. The employees were also asked to consult their doctors about whether to continue to work in the same environment. But, unlike DEC, these companies did not guarantee that other jobs would be available. "As you know, we are running on a very lean basis," Greenagel (AMD) said. "And we know it is going to be more difficult to accommodate [transfer] if we get big numbers."[16]

In January 1987, AT&T disclosed that 15 pregnant employees in fab areas were warned about the possible high risk of miscarriage. When the company "strongly recommended" that these employees transfer to new jobs, at least until they had given birth, all complied.[17] The company also guaranteed them comparable pay and benefits with the new jobs.[18] At IBM, the world's largest semiconductor manufacturer, employees were reminded that they could request to be transferred if they were concerned about their health.[19] "We have no reasons to change our work practices." said Rich Coyle, spokesman from IBM's corporate headquarters. "We believe they are safe."[20] Other semiconductor manufacturers, such as Intel, National Semiconductor, Texas Instruments, and Advanced Micro Devices, encouraged mothers-to-be to remove themselves from chip production areas.[21]

"The question we don't know is how far the implications go," said Dr. Joseph LaDou, a medical professor at the University of California, San Francisco, who had studied semiconductor worker health for several years. "There is a concern about women of child-bearing age who are not pregnant. It's not inconceivable that there could be damage to the reproductive cells of men as well." Dr. LaDou added that there was still "little understanding" of how some of the materials and processes in semiconductor fabrication may affect the fetus.[22]

One executive of a major California firm, who asked not to be identified, said that in addition to problems of Japanese competition, companies might now be subjected to lawsuits and workers' compensation claims.

APPENDIX B
THE SEMICONDUCTOR FABRICATION PROCESS

In the fabrication of semiconductor devices, Quantum used silicon as the base or "substrate" for building integrated circuits. The silicon substrates, in the form of thin round wafers either four or six inches in diameter, had one well-polished side on which circuits would be built. Like

15. *San Jose Mercury News*, December 5, 1986.
16. Ibid.
17. *Time,* January 26, 1987.
18. *Los Angeles Times,* January 19, 1987.
19. *The New York Times.*
20. *Burlington Free Press,* January 1, 1987.
21. *Time.*
22. *The New York Times.*

most semiconductor manufacturers, Quantum bought wafers from various external material suppliers. Wafers were processed in batches of up to 50 wafers that were loaded onto a quartz cassette.

The process of making semiconductor chips was to build circuit patterns, layer upon layer, onto the polished wafer surface—a process often involving several hundred operations. A generic process flow diagram for producing CMOS integrated circuits is shown in Exhibit 6. The eight fundamental steps of wafer fabrication were:

1. *Oxide formation.* After the wafer was cleaned to remove impurities from its surface, a layer of silicon dioxide, which served as electrical insulation, was formed on the surface of the wafer by exposing the wafer to oxygen at high temperature.
2. *Photoresist deposition.* The oxidized wafer surface was coated with a thin film of photoresist, an ultraviolet (UV) light-sensitive material.
3. *Photoresist exposure.* The wafer with photoresist coating was then exposed to UV light through a circuit pattern or "mask." The pattern areas exposed to UV light would be polymerized or hardened. For each successive layer of circuitry, precise alignment of the mask relative to the previous layer's pattern was critical.
4. *Photoresist development.* The unexposed areas of the photoresist pattern were removed by washing the wafer in a chemical solvent or "developer." The developer was then rinsed away by another solvent. Finally, the wafer was baked to harden the remaining exposed photoresist patterns.
5. *Oxide etching.* The oxide layer was etched away wherever it was left unprotected by the hardened photoresist layer, leaving open areas on the surface of the silicon. Two methods were employed in this process: on the 4-inch line, wet etch where the wafer was immersed in heated hydrofluoric acid; and, on the newer 6-inch line, the more expensive plasma (dry) etch which offered superior results and was done in a closed reaction chamber, using very high temperature reactive gases.
6. *Photoresist stripping.* The remaining polymerized photoresist pattern was stripped away by strong organic solvents, leaving a patterned layer of silicon oxide on the silicon wafer.
7a. *Diffusion.* The wafer was exposed to a source of "dopant" atoms in a closed furnace. The dopants diffused into the open areas of the silicon and altered their electrical characteristics, converting these silicon regions to an n-type (if n-type dopants like boron and phosphorus were used) or a p-type (if p-type dopants like arsenic and antimony were used). This process was also referred to as "junction formation."
7b. *Ion Implantation.* This was an alternative method to diffusion. This process involved a small accelerator propeling a beam of dopant atoms directly onto the desired regions of the wafer.
8. *Metallization.* When all layers had been fabricated, metals were deposited on the selected regions of the circuit, providing electrical interconnections in circuitry and contacts for wiring in later assembly operations.

After a wafer had gone through all fabrication processes, the individual chips or "dice," as they were called, were inspected and tested, and bad dice were marked. The dice on the wafer were then separated using a pulsed laser beam or diamond-impregnated saw blade.

In the next operations, called "assembly," dice were assembled into specific packages. Each chip had to be attached to a carrier package and metal lead frame using epoxy or other bonding. Carriers were usually made of insulating materials—typically ceramic or plastic. Once the die was physically attached to the carrier, electrical connections were provided between the chip and the package leads or pins by means of "wire bonding." The package was then sealed and tested for leaks, temperature and electrical stress endurance (burn-in), and electrical performance (final test). The last steps were marking, packing, and shipping.

Assembly operations posed relatively lower health hazards than wafer fab operations. The chemicals often used in assembly processes were alcohols, freons (CFCs), epoxy, weaker acids, and plating solutions. The health risks in assembly operations were associated more with ergonomic stress factors, such as repetitive motion and eye strain, rather than chemical or radiation hazards characteristic of wafer fab.

Although semiconductor fabrication was highly controlled, minute impurities, difficulties in the process or defects in the masks caused a substantial percentage of wafers to be rejected or the individual dice on each wafer to be nonfunctional, resulting in the yield problems indigenous to the industry. To minimize the yield and quality problems, Quantum tested its products at numerous stages in the fabrication process, performed high temperature burn-in qualification as well as continuous reliability monitoring on all products, and conducted numerous quality control inspections throughout the entire production flow. Even so, Quantum had periodically experienced technical problems in its manufacturing processes, resulting in lower than acceptable yields and causing reduced operating margins and delayed product shipments.

Quantum planned to install a new 8-inch processing line within the next five years, depending upon state-of-the-art technical feasibility, sales, and profit margins. The goals for the 8-inch wafer line were to increase yield, improve product quality, handle high performance designs and large lots, and reduce labor and turnaround time. Because of increasing fragility and risk in handling the large 8-inch wafer, automated processing equipment would be required and operators would only be needed to transfer loaded wafer cassettes between certain operations, and perform process controls. Safety features would likely be improved with new automated equipment, although some retrofitting would be possible to accommodate specific requirements. For the new 8-inch wafer fab line, a new Class 1 (no more than 1 airborne particle larger than 0.5 micron in diameter per cubic foot of air) 15,000 square-feet fab cleanroom would be built. The new facility would be located next to the current fab facility, and stricter fire and safety standards and gas monitoring systems would be incorporated. The total cost for facilities and capital equipment was estimated to be in the $50–75 million range.

APPENDIX C
STANDARDS

In the 1970s, there were very few regulations specifically addressing chemicals used in semiconductor manufacturing. Chemical exposures to workers were limited by standards that were set by governmental and sometimes nongovernmental professional agencies:[23]

1. Occupational Health and Safety Administration (OSHA) set and regulated the standards, called Permissible Exposure Limit (PEL), equivalent to Time Weighted Average (TWA). There were about 400 substances on the OSHA list.

2. National Institute of Occupational Safety and Health (NIOSH), in the course of developing criteria for standards, sometimes made recommendations for occupational exposure

---

23. S. Lipton and J. Lynch, *Health Hazard Control in the Chemical Process Industry* (New York: John Wiley & Sons, 1987), pp. 7–13.

limits to OSHA. Despite the fact that NIOSH was a U.S. government agency, these recommendations could not be enforced unless adopted by OSHA.

3. American Congress of Governmental Industrial Hygienists (ACGIH) which was a private professional society made up mainly of industrial hygienists employed by government agencies. A committee of this group, Chemical Substances Threshold Limit Value Committee, published an annual list of Threshold Limit Values (TLV) for about 600 substances. While this list had no regulatory authority, it was often used voluntarily by employers, since it was the most up-to-date list. It had been incorporated into laws and regulations of many foreign countries.

4. American Industrial Hygiene Association (AIHA) was the largest industrial hygiene society. Its Workplace Environmental Exposure Limit (WEEL) Committee set limits for about 100 substances, and their list did not, in general, overlap with the TLV list.

The exposure standards widely used in the semiconductor industry were the TLVs. The TLVs were divided into three categories: Time Weighted Average (TWA), Short Term Exposure Limit (STEL), and Ceiling (C) limit. The most commonly imposed exposure limit was the TWA, which was the maximum permissible concentration for a normal forty-hour workweek. Theoretically, during this period nearly all workers could be exposed repeatedly, at this level, day after day, without adverse effects. The STEL was defined to be the level that should not be exceeded during any fifteen-minute time interval. The STEL was the maximum concentration to which workers could be exposed continuously for a short period of time without suffering from: (1) irritation; (2) chronic or irreversible tissue damage; or (3) narcosis of sufficient degree to increase the likelihood of accidental injury, impair self-rescue, or materially reduce work efficiency. The C limit was the concentration that should not be exceeded even instantaneously.[24]

A 1977 report published by ACGIH noted that "because of wide variation in individual susceptibility . . . a small percentage of workers may experience discomfort from some substances at concentration at or below the threshold limit; a smaller percentage may be affected more seriously by aggravation of a preexisting condition or development of an occupational illness" and the TWAs were to be used "as guides in the control of health hazards, and [not] as fine lines between safe and dangerous concentrations."

Some health experts felt that the setting of standards was difficult in the semiconductor industry because of the high number of "exotic" chemicals, the many different ways which they were used in processes, and the constant changes in chemicals and processes that were trademarks of the industry. The TLVs did not necessarily offer full protection since they could not account for the effects of a combination of chemicals, their reactivity with one another, and their cumulative amounts over a long exposure period.[25] It was also difficult to determine the levels safe enough to avoid adverse health effects from long-term exposure, (e.g., reproductive, respiratory, and nervous system effects; cancer).

Many semiconductor manufacturers, however, maintained that the chemical exposure levels in their plants were much below the TLV standards. For example, IBM set an internal standard which was 25 percent of the TLV.[26] Some installed sophisticated monitoring equipment that could detect a toxic gas in concentrations as small as 20 parts per billion.[27]

---

24. J. Ohlson, "Dry Etch Chemical Safety," *Solid State Technology,* July 1986.
25. *San Jose Mercury News,* November 9, 1987.
26. J. Ohlson.
27. R. Erlich, "Too Clean for Comfort," This World, *San Francisco Chronicle,* June 4, 1989.

APPENDIX D
INDUSTRY, REGULATORY, AND LEGAL BACKGROUND

In February of 1987, *The Wall Street Journal* reported:

> Only 15 of the 500 largest U.S. companies have comprehensive policies covering reproductive hazards, according to a recent report by the Congressional Office of Technology Assessment. One problem in establishing such policies is a lack of conclusive data. Few industrial compounds have been satisfactorily approved [as posing no] reproductive hazards to men, women, or unborn children. And the federal government regulates only four identified threats to reproductive health: ionizing radiation, lead, the sterilant ethylene oxide, and the pesticide dibromochloropropane.[28]

At a June 28, 1989, hearing, labor and government officials told a House oversight panel that government (OSHA) should "focus heightened attention" on working conditions in the semiconductor industry. Barbara Easterling, executive vice president of the Communications Workers of America, recommended that the House Education and Labor subcommittee prompt OSHA to hire more inspectors, and NIOSH to conduct more research to regulate the potential problems of rapidly changing technologies and the use of new untested chemicals. Philip Bierbaum, NIOSH Division Director of Physical Sciences and Engineering, stressed the importance of acting early while processes and chemicals were still being developed and adopted by the industry. While acknowledging certain "questions" about health hazards in the semiconductor industry, Lee Neal, SIA director of health and safety, testified that the industry was safe and that "every effort had been made to analyze and prevent potential problems."[29]

GOVERNMENT REGULATIONS

The Occupational Safety and Health Act was the basic legislation that held company owners and managers legally responsible for employee safety and health. It required employers to maintain and document effective safety and health programs. A general statement of policy, signed by the company president or CEO, served as a starting point for the management's commitment to provide a safe and healthy work environment.[30]

The U.S. Department of Labor's Occupational Safety and Health Administration (OSHA) assumed the responsibility for enforcing regulations, except in states where a state OSHA had been established. OSHA inspectors were authorized to enter company premises at any time, without prior notice, and could issue citations for violations of OSHA regulations. Violations of regulations had to be corrected within a certain time frame, and a company could be fined for serious violations. Repeated violations, failure to take corrective action, or intentional negligence could lead to the forced shutdown of operations; legal action ensued if violations were not corrected. In the worst cases, company executives could be charged with criminal negligence.

---

28. *The Wall Street Journal,* February 5, 1987.

29. *Occupational Safety & Health Reporter,* July 5, 1989, pp. 172–173. *The Bureau of National Affairs, Inc.,* 1989.

30. *Occupational Safety & Health Programs: A Manager's Guide,* American Electronics Association, 1985.

REPRODUCTIVE HEALTH LEGAL ISSUES

The Equal Employment Opportunity Commission indicated that "A policy that expressly excludes women on the basis of pregnancy or capacity to become pregnant is discriminatory and is in violation of a 1982 amendment to the Civil Rights Act." Employers were expected to support such "protective exclusion" with "reputable, objective, scientific evidence" that a hazard adversely affect the potential offspring only through the female parent and not the male. "This approach prevents unnecessary limitations on women's employment opportunities, while preserving the employers'—and society's—legitimate interest in protecting the health of offspring," the Commission said. The "same impulse that has led some employers to exaggerate the risks of employing handicapped workers can also lead to exaggeration of risks to offspring."[31]

"At the same time, many women who had become pregnant were beginning to demand the right to transfer out of jobs they believed to be hazardous, even when there was only sketchy evidence of any hazard," the *New York Times* reported. "Many cases emerging from similar conflicts provoked fears that the issue of fetal health could be misused both by workers seeking to avoid unpleasant work and by employers who hope to keep women from desirable jobs."

> Lawyers have grappled with the issue of when employers may exclude fertile women from potentially hazardous jobs and when pregnant women may request transfer ever since five women at the American Cyanamid Co. disclosed 10 years ago that they had undergone sterilization to keep their high-paying jobs at the company's West Virginia lead pigment plant. Those women subsequently sued, contending that the company had violated their civil rights, and in 1983 they settled their claims for a total of $200,000."[32]

In 1987, United Auto Workers sued Johnson Controls Inc., a Milwaukee-based company, over its policy of excluding women from battery-making jobs involving exposure to lead. The lawsuit was based on discrimination over the so-called fetal-protection policy, implicitly assuming that only women would be adversely affected. Johnson representatives maintained that its plan was solely to protect unborn children and did not discriminate against women. While some battery producers barred only pregnant women, Johnson's policy included all women of child-bearing age. In limited legal tests, courts had ruled that fetal-protection policies were discriminatory unless a company presented clear scientific evidence that workplace hazards posed a particular risk to unborn children.[33]

A 1988 study, which surveyed 198 large chemical and electronics companies in Massachusetts, found that nearly one in five companies restricted women on the basis of potential reproductive health risk. Their job exclusion practices varied widely, from banning only pregnant women to all women of child-bearing age, from mandatory transfer to voluntary transfer. Some companies, in taking health histories of new employees, asked women whether they were pregnant at the time of hiring as well as asking for detailed histories of earlier pregnancies. Two firms conducted pregnancy tests at the time they were hiring women. Of the 198 companies, 43 percent asked women to report when they became pregnant.[34]

---

31. *The Wall Street Journal,* October 3, 1988.
32. *The New York Times,* August 2, 1988.
33. *The Wall Street Journal,* February 5, 1987.
34. *The New York Times,* December 25, 1988.

EXHIBIT 10a Occupational Injury and Illness Rates (cases per 100 workers)

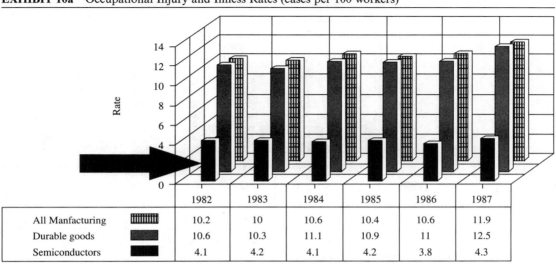

	1982	1983	1984	1985	1986	1987
All Manfacturing	10.2	10	10.6	10.4	10.6	11.9
Durable goods	10.6	10.3	11.1	10.9	11	12.5
Semiconductors	4.1	4.2	4.1	4.2	3.8	4.3

Annual Incidence Rates

Source: U.S. Bureau of Labor Statistics (Annual Survey—1982–1987)

Health indicators for the semiconductor industry were often confusing and conflicting. According to data taken from U.S. Bureau of Labor Statistics' (BLS) Annual Survey through companies' reported injuries and illnesses to OSHA, the semiconductor industry had one of the lowest rates of worker injuries and illnesses of all U.S. manufacturing industries (see Exhibit 10a).[35] Other evidence (shown in Exhibit 10b) derived from Doctors' First Report of Injury forms, indicated that the rate of illness caused by systemic poisoning in the semiconductor industry was the highest among all manufacturing industries.[36] Safety and health practices among semiconductor companies also varied. Some firms placed a high priority on workplace health and safety; others displayed serious shortcomings.[37] The controversy over long-term chemical exposures in semiconductor manufacturing would probably continue for many years.

35. D. Lassiter, *Solid State Technology,* July 1989.

36. P. Robbins, C. Butler, and K. Mahaffey, "Occupational Injury and Illness in the Semiconductor Industry for 1980–1985," National Institute for Occupational Safety and Health, Division of Standards Development and Technology Transfer, Cincinnati, Ohio.

37. R. Erlich, "Too Clean for Comfort," This World, *San Francisco Chronicle,* June 4, 1989.

EXHIBIT 10b   Systemic Poisoning in Work Loss Cases to the Total Work Force

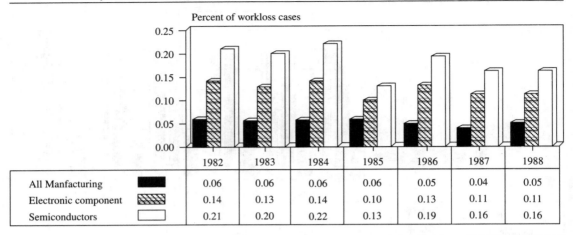

Percent of workloss cases

		1982	1983	1984	1985	1986	1987	1988
All Manfacturing	■	0.06	0.06	0.06	0.06	0.05	0.04	0.05
Electronic component	▨	0.14	0.13	0.14	0.10	0.13	0.11	0.11
Semiconductors	☐	0.21	0.20	0.22	0.13	0.19	0.16	0.16

Source: California Workers Compensation records (Joseph Ladou, M.D.)

THE MIAMI HERALD PUBLISHING COMPANY

We have some very important public obligations that go beyond the return to the share-holder. . . . We have an obligation to have a fair return to the people who own the paper and in my view you would not have a free or a safe press if you didn't make a profit. But, having said that, there are twin obligations here and the obligations are not solely to make money, but to make a difference in the community.

David Lawrence, Jr.
Publisher, *The Miami Herald*

On April 6, 1994, David Lawrence Jr., publisher of *The Miami Herald* and chairman of The Miami Herald Publishing Company, left the unceasing blinking lights and buzzes of his telephone system to themselves briefly as he glanced

This case was prepared by Sarah B. Gant under the supervision of Mary C. Gentile and Jeffrey F. Rayport.
Copyright © 1994 by the President and Fellows of Harvard College.
Harvard Business School case 395-022 (Rev. February 23, 1995).

out of his windows at Biscayne Bay five floors below. He had just returned to his office from a meeting with Buddy MacKay, Florida's lieutenant governor, having agreed to co-host local arrangements for 34 heads of state who would meet in December 1994 for "Summit of the Americas" in Miami. The event would provide Lawrence and Miami with a once-in-a-lifetime opportunity to showcase the community, the "crossroads of the Americas," as a model of multiculturalism and multilingualism. Lawrence saw his paper as "a very powerful institution" that played a critical role in making that image of Miami a reality.

But there were other issues on Lawrence's mind. The date of his annual budget and strategy presentation to Knight-Ridder executives was coming up. The Miami Herald Publishing Company was wholly-owned by Knight-Ridder, Inc., and was its most profitable newspaper within a $2.5 billion publishing empire. These were not the best of times for the U.S. newspaper industry, and Lawrence, the son of a newspaperman and a 30-year industry veteran, was committed to strengthening his paper despite intensifying industry woes.

The facts were sobering. Eight of the nation's 10 largest U.S. newspapers were struggling with the impact of "an irrevocable shrinkage of national readership."[1] Advertising revenues, generally accounting for three-quarters of a major newspaper's total revenues, had declined in the mid-1980s and then plummeted during the recessionary late 1980s and early 1990s. Electronic, interactive, and on-line media formats for delivering information were proving to be stiff competition, along with traditional electronic media such as radio and television.

Television, the major threat, was fragmented into network broadcast affiliates, cable-TV operators, and independent broadcast stations. For most consumers, these had become the information sources of choice. In response, the editorial content and style of many newspapers were changing to meet the demands of "television age" readers—as could be seen by increasing use of color, and prose designed to grab the attention of a busy society used to sound bites and computer bytes. *USA Today,* with its street vending boxes that resembled television sets, was a dramatic example of a print-imitating-TV strategy, and one that even traditional, mainstream newspapers followed closely.

1. William Glaberson, "8 of 10 Largest U.S. Papers Have Declines in Circulation," *The New York Times,* April 30, 1994.

Industry analysts believed the best way for newspapers to remain competitive was to target segments of their markets with niche products. Niche products, marketed to specific customer segments, were more responsive to the information needs of targeted groups than were mass media forms. They delivered a more concise product (typically less expensive to produce) and a higher-quality circulation to advertisers. Circulation quality, or readership "purity," was defined as the paper's ability to deliver a targeted or specific audience which was a likely market for an advertiser's products or services. Nevertheless, Lawrence believed,

as the world and the media fragment more and more and more, there is a big-league opportunity for free-standing, fully competitive newspapers and the key to that is for us to be increasingly authoritative. We live in a world where you are blizzarded by ever more information. The problem . . . is not can I get enough information, but what does the information mean? What's the "sorting out"? Our opportunity in many ways is in the "sorting out" business.

The particularities of being in the information "sorting out" business were unique in Miami, the third largest Hispanic market in the United States. Lawrence questioned how any marketing strategy that segmented Miami, "a community deeply fragmented" by racial, ethnic, and political differences, would serve the city and ultimately his business. Nevertheless the Herald already marketed several niche products in what it called its "augmentation" strategy, and was exploring several new ventures. Lawrence's concern for the Miami community notwithstanding, he believed his company needed "to look at a lot of different opportunities" in national and international markets, including nonprint products and interactive media.

One of the significant existing niche products was *El Nuevo Herald,* a Spanish-language daily delivered as a supplement to the *Miami Herald.* For years, Lawrence and others had discussed the optimal relationship between *El Nuevo* and the *Herald*—possible scenarios ranged from promoting the Spanish-language paper more heavily to marketing it as a fully stand-alone product. Managers debated what such change would do to the social fabric and politics of Miami, what it would do economically for the company and for Knight-Ridder. It was a complex discussion that involved potential added costs as well as added revenues, and involved significant changes in current systems of promotion, distribution, and sales. Lawrence's short answer to the relationship question was: "In the short-term we could make a good deal more money [by separating the papers into two distinct products] . . . millions more would flow in here is the top-of-the-head answer . . . but we have to think about whether this would just subdivide and fragment this community further. And what would the long-term impact be on circulation and advertising?"

The future of the Herald depended in large part on how it defined its market. But given the role of a major metropolitan daily newspaper in reflecting and shaping its community, what should that market be? Was there one market or several? How would the Herald best serve its market(s)?

Newspaper Industry Overview

In 1980 the revenue mix of a typical metropolitan daily newspaper was derived 84 percent from advertising, 15 percent from circulation, and 1 percent from other newspaper sources. By 1992, the mix had changed: 73 percent of revenues came from advertisers, 24 percent from circulation, 1 percent from other newspaper sources, and 2 percent from nonnewspaper sources. Those trends were continuing (see Exhibit 1). In 1994 newspapers were facing three advertising revenue dilemmas: their advertisers' budgets were, in many cases, shrinking; the sources of advertising dollars were shifting; and the competition for advertising dollars was growing.

Newspaper advertising spending had plummeted between 1987 and 1992, when a recovery

EXHIBIT 1 Newspaper Revenue Mix and Growth

	Metros	
	1980	*1992*
Mix:		
Advertising	84%	73%
Circulation	15	24
Other	1	1
Total Newspaper	100%	98%
Non-newspaper	0	2
TOTAL	100%	100%
	1980–92	*1989–92*
Growth		
Advertising	5%	(6)%
Circulation	11	11
Other	5	6
Total Newspaper	6%	(3%)

Sources: Inland Press Association and Bernstein estimates.

(which analysts believed would be short-lived) began (see Exhibit 2). Not only did advertising revenue represent a declining percentage of a metro daily's total revenues, but the mix of advertising sales was also changing dramatically (see Exhibit 3). Within the core business of run-of-press (ROP) advertisements, retail and national ad sales were declining while only classified ad sales grew—the segment most targeted by electronic marketing media.[2] Between 1980 and 1992, the most significant area of ad revenue growth was pre-printed inserts or "pre-prints."[3]

Retail had traditionally been the backbone of newspaper ad revenues. There were few alternatives to newspapers' ROP display ads for affordable, mass-distribution advertising prior to the 1970s; rates could increase annually with

2. Run-of-press (ROP) advertisements were retail, national, or classified display advertisements printed directly in the pages of a newspaper, in contrast to pre-printed inserts.

3. Pre-prints were advertisements, often of multiple pages, printed separately from the newspapers that carried them. They were typically inserted into the folds of newspapers for delivery, or delivered through other vehicles such as "shoppers" and other wholly commercial publications.

EXHIBIT 2   Newspaper Advertising Spending

Sources: U.S. Department of Commerce, Newspaper Association of America, and Bernstein estimates.

little fear of accounts walking away. By the recessionary late 1980s, however, advertising budgets became retailers' most discretionary expense. Alternatively, if they had the budgets, advertisers were as likely to turn to increasingly competitive local TV spots as newspaper display ads.

The nature of retailing was also changing. Discounters like Wal-Mart and "category-killers" like Home Depot relied on pre-prints more than ROP ads and, according to industry analysts, fueled the trend away from ROP advertising to pre-prints. According to one industry analyst, "Wal-Mart alone costs the traditional advertising media about $1 billion a year in foregone revenue, and newspapers lose the most. We expect Wal-Mart to make up a third of the department-store industry by 1997."[4] Studies suggested that ROP advertising carried a more

upscale image and was more believable than pre-prints (see Exhibit 4), but pre-prints could present more products more economically (sales returns on spending could be five times that of ROP ads) and often in a more graphically compelling format.

Discounters and category killers were largely indifferent to pre-prints' method of delivery—whether they got to consumers' homes via a direct mail service (which could also reach non-newspaper subscribers) or bundled inside the daily paper. To compete for pre-print business, more than 80 percent of U.S. newspapers by 1994 had developed "total market coverage" (TMC) vehicles to get pre-prints to nonsubscribers and "alternate delivery systems" to distribute periodicals and marketing materials to targeted neighborhoods.[5] Pre-prints were highly profitable to newspapers but represented "cannibalization of a serious order," since they took sales

4. "Red Sky at Morning: The Newspaper Industry," Bernstein Research, p. 32.

5. "Red Sky," p. 40.

EXHIBIT 3   Newspaper Advertising Revenue Mix

	Metros	
	1980	*1992*
Retail	53%	42%
Classified	30	35
National	9	7
Total ROP	92%	83%
Retail	7	12
National	1	3
Other	0	3
Total Pre-print	8%	17%
TOTAL	100%	100%
Memo: Pre-print % category		
Retail	12	22
National	10	29

Sources: Inland Press Association and Bernstein estimates.

from more expensive ROP ads and had lower margins than traditional ROP advertising.[6] Newspapers, now in competition with direct mailers, local TV, and radio for retail advertising dollars, had lost their advertising pricing power.

Aggressive pricing wars between media to attract national advertisers during the late 1980s and early 1990s had also "pushed all but the most captive [national] newspaper advertisers into other media. Those forced to remain, such as airlines and car companies, whose fare wars and leasing deals are too information-heavy for TV, and often too time-sensitive for magazines," remained the core of newspapers' national accounts.[7] Analysts predicted that newspapers would "slash" rates for national advertisers throughout the 1990s in order to retain the accounts they had, attract new national advertisers, and win back accounts from TV, radio, and other print media.

Classified advertising, having grown from a quarter to a third of total ROP spending be-

6. "Red Sky," p. 14.
7. "Red Sky," p. 12.

tween 1975 and 1992, had been the only area of ROP ad growth for newspapers. As with retail advertisers, there were few vehicles prior to 1980 to compete for classified ad dollars. By the early 1990s, however, analysts recognized the exponential growth of electronic, interactive formats that allowed consumers to sort such information. As one analyst queried, "Given that untold numbers of electronic competitors—from tiny start-ups to on-line services, [regional Bell operating companies] and cable companies—are attempting to cherry-pick newspaperdom's most lucrative franchise, the question is: Is the denouement at hand, or will we get a good recovery out of classified before the (micro)chip hits the fan?"[8]

Miami

In 1950 there were 2.7 million Floridians; by 1990 Florida, with nearly 13 million inhabitants, was the fourth most populous state in the United States. Miami was a small city in 1950—but growing as winter vacationers to Miami Beach began to establish longer-term roots. The advent of widely available air-conditioning played a big part in Northerners' willingness to see South Florida as a year-round home.

The total population of the Miami/Fort Lauderdale ADI comprising Dade, Broward, and Monroe counties—the area that *The Miami Herald* served—had grown 69 percent, from 1,940,478 to 3,270,606, between 1970 and 1990 alone (see Exhibit 5).[9] Over the same period, the Hispanic population had increased 232 percent, from 322,554 to 1,071,531, making the area the

8. "Red Sky," p. 15.
9. ADI (area of dominant influence) was the geographic area roughly corresponding to the reach of the dominant broadcast signal of TV networks and affiliates within a metropolitan area. The term was created by the now-defunct Arbitron Ratings Company, and its meaning was similar to A. C. Nielsen's DMA (designated market area). Census information referred to the Miami/Ft. Lauderdale CMSA (consolidated metropolitan statistical area).

EXHIBIT 4   Attitudes Toward Advertising Media

More people look forward to newspaper advertising than any other media advertising.

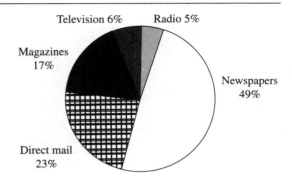

Newspapers are the most believable advertising medium

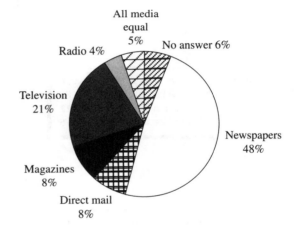

Newspapers are the dominant advertising influence on unplanned purchases

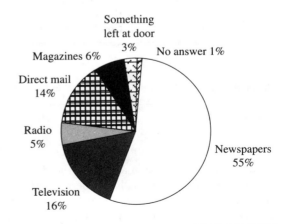

Source: NAB Key Facts 1989 & 1991.

EXHIBIT 5   The Miami/Ft. Lauderdale ADI*

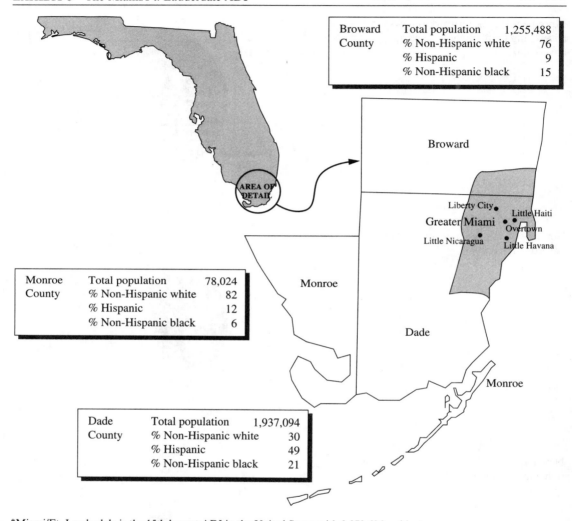

Broward County	Total population	1,255,488
	% Non-Hispanic white	76
	% Hispanic	9
	% Non-Hispanic black	15

Monroe County	Total population	78,024
	% Non-Hispanic white	82
	% Hispanic	12
	% Non-Hispanic black	6

Dade County	Total population	1,937,094
	% Non-Hispanic white	30
	% Hispanic	49
	% Non-Hispanic black	21

*Miami/Ft. Lauderdale is the 15th largest ADI in the United States with 3,270,606 residents.

Source: 1990 Census.

third largest Hispanic market in the United States (see Exhibit 6). Fully 90 percent of the Hispanic population lived in Dade County itself. Between 1970 and 1990 the Hispanic population of Dade grew 219 percent while the non-Hispanic population grew 2 percent. Of Dade's 1,937,094 residents, 949,176 were Hispanic in 1990.

The changing demographics of Miami, what *Newsweek* called in 1988 "the most abrupt demographic upheaval [faced by] any city on the North American continent," did not occur with-

EXHIBIT 6   Top 10 Hispanic Metropolitan Areas in the United States*

Metropolitan Area	Total Hispanic population
Los Angeles	4,779,118
New York	2,777,951
Miami/Ft. Lauderdale	1,061,846
San Francisco	970,403
Chicago	893,422
Houston	772,295
San Antonio	620,290
Dallas	518,917
San Diego	510,781
El Paso	411,619

*67% of Florida's Hispanics reside in South Florida making Miami/Ft. Lauderdale the 3rd largest Hispanic metropolitan area in the United States.

Source: Market Segment Research 1993.

out creating tensions among both existing Hispanic and non-Hispanic demographic groups.[10] Greater Miami's "Little Havana," "Little Nicaragua," and "Little Haiti" neighborhoods, along with the African-American enclaves of "Overtown" and "Liberty City," each had its established social, political, and economic flavor.

The Hispanic population itself was changing. In 1980, nearly 80 percent of Dade's Hispanics were of Cuban origin, but a steady influx of Nicaraguans, Puerto Ricans, Colombians, and others were altering the social, political, and economic climate of the city (see Exhibit 7). Many of Miami's Cubans came to the city soon after Fidel Castro came to power in 1959. Many were

10. Tom Morganthau et al., "Miami," *Newsweek,* January 25, 1988, p. 22.

EXHIBIT 7   Country of Origin: 1990

Dade County
(Hispanic Population 949,176)

Cuba	54%
Nicaragua	8
Puerto Rico	7
Colombia	6
Dominican Republic	2
Mexico	2
Honduras	2
Peru	2
Guatemala	1
Ecuador	1
El Salvador	1
Panama	1
Other*	8

*Represents the 13 Hispanic countries not listed above.

Source: 1990 Census.

well-educated and had established businesses or professional careers in Cuba. Newer waves of Hispanic immigrants often did not share the educational and economic strengths of the early Cuban exiles, and faced the added difficulty of having to wrest social, political, and economic rewards from established Cubans.

The growth and business development of southern Florida, particularly Miami, was inseparable from its Hispanic, particularly Cuban, population. About a quarter of a million Cubans came to the United States during each decade between 1960 and 1980, and 150,000 during the 1980s. Many settled in Miami. As one Cuban-born executive of the Herald put it, "If I wanted to have a high school reunion and actually see most of my classmates, I wouldn't do it in Havana. I'd do it in Miami."

Cubans came to the United States for political rather than economic reasons. Most did not see themselves as immigrants but exiles who planned to return to Cuba as soon as Castro's government fell. Many were highly patriotic (both on behalf of their native country and of the United States), did not intend to assimilate into U.S. culture, and tended to be conservative, well-educated, and middle-class. In parts of Greater Miami, residents could pass from childhood to old age speaking only Spanish, shopping only in Cuban-owned stores, eating in Cuban-owned restaurants, going to Cuban-dominated churches and schools. A group of Cuban exiles, supported by the Central Intelligence Agency, invaded Cuba at the Bay of Pigs in April 1961. In the 1990s, Alpha 66, a Cuban paramilitary group based in Miami, was still conducting exercises to hasten Castro's downfall.

In addition to Cubans, Miami was home to similarly patriotic Nicaraguans displaced by the Sandinista revolution, as well as dissidents, exiles, and immigrants from other Central and South American nations. Because the Caribbean, Latin, and South American nations of origin of Miami's Hispanics were not far away,

there was frequent travel back and forth. According to one Herald executive, Miami seemed more the northernmost reach of Latin America than the southernmost reach of the United States.

Roberto Suarez, himself an exile from Castro's Cuba, publisher of *El Nuevo Herald* and former president of The Miami Herald Publishing Company, believed that as Greater Miami was growing and the city's demographics were changing,

> local businesses, and that included *The Miami Herald,* did not recognize what was really happening until an Hispanic was elected mayor in [1973]. And then they said, "There has been a shift here." The thought process had been that [the Cubans] were just one more immigration . . . in a few years everyone would have been assimilated, the old melting pot principle would have taken place, and everybody would be happy. Well, that did not happen. It did not happen because the immigration did not stop . . . the [Cuban population of Miami] became so massive that people did not feel the need to become integrated—ever.

In 1994, 47,000 (74 percent) of Dade County's businesses were Hispanic-owned and the county's 320,000 Hispanic households spent $10.2 billion annually. South Florida Hispanics were more affluent, better educated, and more likely to have white-collar jobs than other U.S. Hispanics (see Exhibit 8). In comparison with the total population of the Miami/Fort Lauderdale ADI, ADI Hispanics were in most demographic respects barely distinguishable from their non-Hispanic neighbors (see Exhibit 9).

It was not just residents that contributed to the heavily Latin flavor of Miami. Better than a quarter of Miami's economy was dependent on international commerce and tourism. Miami, "a thriving and sophisticated mecca for international trade," according to *Business Week,* was "building on its deep Hispanic roots and proximity to promising markets in Mexico, the Caribbean, and South America . . . attracting a surprising new wave of blue-chip investors and

EXHIBIT 8   South Florida Hispanics Compared with Other U.S. Hispanics

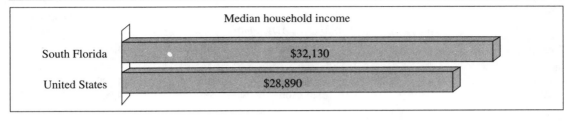

Median household income

South Florida	$32,130
United States	$28,890

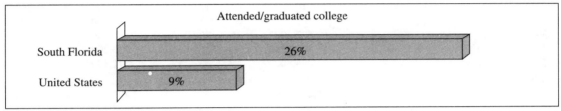

Attended/graduated college

South Florida	26%
United States	9%

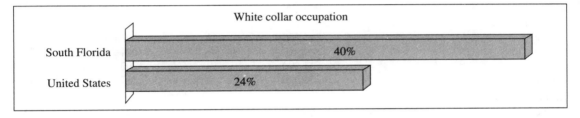

White collar occupation

South Florida	40%
United States	24%

Source: 1991 U.S. Hispanic Market

traders from the United States, Europe, and Asia."[11] In addition, in 1991 nearly a third of Miami's eight million visitors (who, in total, spent a little over $7 billion) came from Latin America (see Exhibit 10).

Despite Hispanics' long presence in southern Florida, relations with the non-Hispanic population were not always good. Poor or nonexistent relationships between Hispanics, non-Hispanic whites, and African-Americans contributed to tensions that fueled riots in Liberty City in 1980 and 1982.[12] By 1990 there were fewer than 400,000 African-Americans in Dade County

and, according to Lawrence, a "very small black middle class"—the 6,700 businesses in Dade County owned by African-Americans tended to have only a handful of employees (see Exhibit 11). There was one independent African-American newspaper in Dade, the weekly *Miami Times,* with a circulation of under 20,000. According to Lawrence, African-Americans frequently felt themselves to be "third-class" citizens.

The recessionary late 1980s and early 1990s had hit Miami hard. And even by 1994, many had still not recovered from the devastation wrought by Hurricane Andrew in 1992. The deep anger of Miami's African-American com-

11. Gail De George and Antonio N. Fins with Irene Recio, "Latin America's Newest Capital City: Miami," *Business Week,* September 30, 1991, p. 120.

12. Morganthau, p. 29.

EXHIBIT 9   Demographic Profile of ADI Hispanics, Compared with Total ADI Population

	Miami/Ft. Lauderdale ADI Adults		*Miami/Ft. Lauderdale ADI Hispanic Adults*	
Total	2,670,000	100%	903,500	100%
Sex:				
Men	1,260,500	47	424,500	47
Women	1,409,500	53	479,000	53
Age:				
18–24	310,700	12	122,100	14
25–34	567,300	21	213,100	24
35–44	527,600	20	166,800	18
45–54	389,600	15	130,200	14
55+	874,800	33	271,300	30
Marital status:				
Married	1,423,000	53	492,100	54
Single	602,800	23	204,100	23
Widow/separated/divorced	644,200	24	207,300	23
Household size:				
One	384,400	14	101,600	11
Two	930,900	35	244,200	27
Three	518,400	19	200,000	22
Four+	836,300	31	357,700	40
Adults in household:				
One	464,200	17	124,900	14
Two	1,466,400	55	433,800	49
Three+	739,400	28	334,800	37
Children in household:				
None	1,715,400	64	531,000	59
One	421,100	16	164,300	18
Two	348,700	13	151,900	17
Three+	184,800	7	56,300	6
Ages of children:				
Under 2	169,200	6	71,600	8
Ages 2–5	327,100	12	126,200	14
Ages 6–11	448,400	17	170,300	19
Ages 12–17	450,300	17	160,100	18
Education:				
College graduate+	753,000	28	199,000	22
Some college	606,700	23	188,100	21
High school graduate	890,900	38	276,800	31
Some high school or less	419,400	16	239,600	27
Employment status:				
Employed full-time	1,291,900	48	435,700	48
Employed part-time	272,100	10	98,800	11
Not employed	1,106,000	41	369,000	41

(continues)

EXHIBIT 9 *(concluded)*

	Miami/Ft. Lauderdale ADI Adults		Miami/Ft. Lauderdale ADI Hispanic Adults	
Industry of employment:				
Services	648,500	24	201,000	22
Wholesale/retail trade	290,300	11	105,300	12
Manufacturing	151,900	6	76,700	8
Finance/insurance/real estate	130,400	5	40,000	4
Transportation/commun/utilities	124,100	5	43,100	5
Construction	106,000	4	43,200	5
Other	112,800	4	25,200	3
Occupation:				
Prof/manager/tech	576,000	22	154,000	17
Clerical/sales	490,300	18	171,200	19
Service/other	497,700	19	209,300	23
Retired	439,900	16	101,500	11
Other/not employed	666,100	25	267,500	30
Household income:				
$50,000+	773,500	29	211,800	23
$35,000+	1,328,300	50	365,900	40
$25,000–$34,999	507,700	19	152,500	17
Less than $25,000	834,000	31	385,100	43

Source: Scarborough Multi-Media Study 1993.

munity, feeling ever more disenfranchised in an increasingly Hispanic city, in the opinion of one Herald executive, also surfaced during widely publicized robberies and murders of tourists lost in predominantly African-American neighborhoods in 1993 and 1994.

In 1980, the same year as the first of the Liberty City riots, 125,000 Cubans, a few thousand of whom were later found to be career criminals or mentally ill, came to Miami over a three-month period in the Mariel boatlifts. In response to changing demographics and urban tensions, between 1980 and 1985 an estimated 115,000 non-Hispanic whites left Dade. In November 1987 such "white flight" had mostly ended, but a statewide poll reported that 69 percent of all Floridians (and 62 percent of southern Floridians) thought "Cuban immigration, overall, had hurt the state's 'quality of life.'"[13] In

November 1988 apprehensions about the "Hispanicization" of Florida reached such an emotionally charged level that a ballot initiative to make English the "official language" of the state passed with 83 percent of the vote, and a 3 to 2 margin in Dade. Many of Dade's Hispanics believed the ballot question was motivated by racism.[14]

Lawrence was widely commended for his Spanish-language efforts and appeared frequently on Spanish-language radio and TV programs. Nevertheless, while encouraging his own executives to learn Spanish as a sign of respect for others, he was sanguine about the primary place of English and of English-language jour-

---

13. Morganthau, p. 29.

14. Pamela Varley, "Language and the Melting Pot: Florida's 1988 'Official English' Referendum." Kennedy School of Government Case Studies C16-90-990.0 and C16-90-990.1. President and Fellows of Harvard College, 1990.

EXHIBIT 10 Distribution of Overnight Visitors to Greater Miami

Origin	1989 Number (000s)	1989 Percent Share	1990 Number (000s)	1990 Percent Share	1991 Number (000s)	1991 Percent Share
Total Domestic	4,823.4	62.5%	4,617.5	57.2%	4,377.4	52.1%
International:						
South America	680.0	8.8	825.7	10.2	1,054.4	12.5
Central America	251.8	3.3	556.3	6.9	656.0	7.8
Caribbean	358.9	4.7	604.6	7.5	583.6	6.9
Total Latin America	1,290.7	16.7	1,986.6	24.6	2,294.0	27.3
Europe*	1,241.5	16.1	1,081.4	13.4	1,275.8	15.2
Canada	211.3	2.7	248.8	3.1	221.4	2.6
Japan and Far East	63.7	0.8	55.3	0.7	88.5	1.1
Others	86.8	1.1	82.9	1.0	144.9	1.7
Total International	2,894.0	37.5	3,455.0	42.8	4,024.6	47.9
Total Visitors	7,717.4	100.0%	8,072.5	100.0%	8,402.0	100.0%

*Major contributing countries.

Origin	Economic Impact ($ millions) 1989	1990	1991
Domestic	$3,562.5	$3,489.2	$3,751.2
International	$2,137.5	$2,610.8	$3,441.4
Total	$5,700.0	$6,100.0	$7,192.6

Source: Strategy Research Corporation.

nalism in Dade County, no matter the area's demographic and assimilation trends:

There are hundreds of thousands of people in this community who do not speak Spanish so could not read *El Nuevo Herald.* You could not graduate from school in Dade County, Florida, without knowing English. If you had an ounce of wisdom about you, you would say, "I need to learn English in the United States of America." So there is some chance that everybody here could learn English. I believe that the definition of *The Miami Herald* is, and should be, to try and reach everybody. I believe that is a different definition than *El Nuevo Herald.*

The Miami Herald

The Miami Herald was founded on December 1, 1910. It was acquired from Frank B. Shutts by John S. and James L. Knight in 1937. In 1994 the paper employed 2,552 people, including 100 editors and department heads, 163 reporters, 80 copy editors, and 28 photographers. It had foreign bureaus in Bogota, Jerusalem, Managua, Mexico City, and Rio de Janeiro. The paper, generally regarded as one of the 10 best in the United States, had won 14 Pulitzer prizes between 1951 and 1993 (see Exhibit 12).

As the only metropolitan morning paper in Dade County and the largest circulation paper in the southeastern United States, the *Herald* circulated primarily in Dade and in neighboring

EXHIBIT 11   Demographic Profile of Dade County African-Americans, Compared with Total ADI Population

	Total Dade County Adults		Dade County African-American Adults	
Total	1,540,000	100%	257,800	100%
Sex:				
Men	721,200	47	116,600	45
Women	818,800	53	141,200	55
Age:				
18–24	190,100	12	47,200	18
25–34	337,800	22	68,400	27
35–44	308,800	20	67,200	26
45–54	236,500	15	33,600	13
55+	466,800	30	41,400	16
Marital status:				
Married	800,500	52	112,800	44
Single	368,300	24	88,200	34
Widow/separated/divorced	371,200	24	56,800	22
Household size:				
One	195,800	13	18,800	7
Two	453,400	29	45,900	18
Three	326,100	21	60,300	23
Four+	564,700	37	132,800	52
Adults in household:				
One	245,600	16	37,700	15
Two	783,500	51	126,200	49
Three+	510,900	33	93,900	36
Children in household:				
None	927,500	60	105,300	41
One	263,400	17	51,700	20
Two	222,000	14	43,800	17
Three+	127,100	8	57,000	22
Ages of children:				
Under 2	104,100	7	27,000	10
Ages 2–5	209,200	14	60,000	23
Ages 6–11	294,700	19	82,000	32
Ages 12–17	302,700	20	90,600	35
Education:				
College graduate+	419,800	27	48,000	19
Some college	347,300	23	58,500	23
High school graduate	469,900	31	96,900	38
Some high school or less	303,000	20	54,400	21
Employment status:				
Employed full-time	751,200	49	134,200	52
Employed part-time	162,600	11	25,800	10
Not employed	626,200	41	97,800	38

(continues)

EXHIBIT 11   *(concluded)*

	Total Dade County Adults		Dade County African-American Adults	
Industry of employment:				
Services	388,500	25	82,300	32
Wholesale/retail trade	166,500	11	26,500	10
Manufacturing	92,300	6	6,200	2
Finance/insurance/real estate	79,400	5	9,800	4
Transportation/commun/utilities	73,300	5	13,100	5
Construction	61,100	4	11,400	4
Other	52,700	3	10,700	4
Occupation:				
Prof/manager/tech	314,400	20	35,900	14
Clerical/sales	301,200	20	57,100	22
Service/other	298,200	19	67,000	26
Retired	201,900	13	20,300	8
Other/not employed	424,300	28	77,500	30
Household income:				
$50,000+	436,300	28	45,200	18
$35,000+	715,400	46	96,700	38
$25,000–$34,999	279,900	18	70,500	27
Less than $25,000	544,700	35	90,600	35

Source: Scarborough Multi-Media Study 1993.

Broward county (see Exhibit 13) with some circulation elsewhere in Florida. By 1993 the company estimated that the *Herald* had a circulation of about 400,000 daily and 525,000 Sundays with more than a million readers daily and 1.3 million on Sundays.[15] The *Herald* had the 10th greatest penetration rate of all U.S. daily newspapers (see Exhibit 14). In Dade County, the *Herald's* 1993 household penetration rate was 37 percent daily and 48 percent Sundays. In Broward County it was 18 percent daily and 22 percent Sundays and in Monroe County (the Keys) it was 29 percent daily and 47 percent Sundays. Home-delivery sales were typically 73 percent of total sales daily and 64 percent on Sundays.

---

15. Readership figures were determined through a Scarborough Market Research telephone poll which found that approximately 2.5 individuals read each copy of *The Miami Herald* sold.

Even though circulation figures improved for the *Herald* during the late 1980s through 1990, they had declined every year since. Arden Dickey, vice president of circulation, attributed the circulation increases to the launch of *El Nuevo Herald* in 1987, the creation of an aggressive street hawker program, and the closing in 1988 of Cox Enterprises, Inc.'s *The Miami News* (circulation 53,000). Decline began significantly in March 1991 when the *Herald* raised its daily single-copy price from $.25 to $.35. According to Dickey, "we lost 9,000 copies and still have not recovered that. . . . The theory used to be, if you have a price increase a lot of people stop [buying the paper] but within nine months to a year, you get them all back. . . . That does not hold any more."

In 1993 the *Herald* produced six daily and eight Sunday editions. It also carried four daily local zoned news sections serving Dade, Bro-

---

EXHIBIT 12   Pulitzer Prizes: *The Miami Herald*

1951   Meritorious Public Service for crime reporting during the year.

1967   Local Investigative Specialized Reporting for reporting that helped to free two persons wrongfully convicted of murder.

1976   Local General Spot News Reporting for reporting over eight and one-half years that led to the exoneration and release of two men who had twice been tried for murder and wrongfully convicted and sentenced to death in Florida.

1980   Feature Writing for "Zepp's Last Stand."

1981   International Reporting for dispatches from Central America.

1983   Editorial Writing for a campaign against the detention of illegal Haitian immigrants by federal officials.

1986   Spot News Photography for photographs of the devastation caused by the eruption of the Nevado del Ruiz volcano in Columbia.

1986   General News Reporting for police beat reporting.

1987   National Reporting for coverage of the U.S.-Iran-Contra connection.

1988   Commentary for effective use of humor as a device for presenting fresh insights into serious concerns.

1988   Feature Photography for portraying the decay and subsequent rehabilitation of a housing project overrun by the drug crack.

1991   Spot News Reporting for stories profiling a cult leader, his followers, and their links to several area murders.

1993   Meritorious Public Services for coverages that not only helped readers cope with Hurricane Andrew's devastation but also showed how lax zoning and building codes had contributed to the destruction.

1993   Commentary for coverage of political and social conditions in Haiti and columns on Cuban-Americans in Miami.

---

ward, Monroe, and Palm Beach counties. On average, it had 75 pages on weekdays and 227 pages on Sundays. It also produced six zoned "Neighbors" editions (including one that included some content in Creole for the Haitian community) and five zoned "Hometown *Herald*" editions twice weekly. "Neighbors" and "Hometowns" were oriented toward local news and advertising. "Neighbors" were tabloid-style inserts, and "Hometowns," a new product using more color and circulated only in upscale Broward County, were broadsheets. The *Herald*'s International edition, founded in 1946 and printed in English, circulated daily (circulation 5,000) and Sunday (circulation 9,000) in 30 cities throughout the Caribbean and Latin America. Upper-income professionals, executives, and

EXHIBIT 13   *The Miami Herald* Circulation and Penetration by County

	Circulation	Penetration
Dade County		
Daily	258,521	37%
Sunday	337,640	48
Broward County		
Daily	99,850	18
Sunday	124,283	22
Monroe County		
Daily	10,214	29
Sunday	16,547	47
Total		
Daily	368,585	28
Sunday	478,470	37

Source: ABC Audit, June 1993.

EXHIBIT 14   Circulation/Penetration of 25 Largest Daily U.S. Newspapers

	By Daily Penetration	Daily		Sunday	
		(1)	*(2)*	*(1)*	*(2)*
	Newspaper	*Circulation*	*Penetration*	*Circulation*	*Penetration*
1	Newsday	747,890	55.43%	825,674	66.46%
2	Cleveland Plain Dealer	395,791	53.05	543,050	72.44
3	Washington Post	813,908	49.98	1,138,877	65.33
4	Portland Oregonian	332,652	49.22	441,244	62.12
5	San Diego Union-Tribune	383,827	46.13	455,128	54.37
6	Newark Star-Ledger	473,558	45.98	704,247	59.57
7	Dallas Morning News	517,850	38.66	814,404	62.82
8	San Francisco Chronicle	544,253	37.70	None	0.00
9	Orange County Register	343,906	36.38	407,692	42.54
10	Miami Herald	386,664	38.11	509,443	47.29
11	St. Louis Post-Dispatch	342,340	34.78	559,223	55.84
12	Arizona Republic	347,839	34.62	547,995	55.28
13	Minneapolis-St. Paul Star	410,754	34.38	696,439	55.98
14	Boston Globe	507,647	33.93	814,036	48.38
15	Rocky Mountain News	342,885	30.56	453,342	52.55
16	Houston Chronicle	413,448	28.72	606,525	41.46
17	Chicago Sun-Times	535,793	25.74	524,475	22.71
18	Detroit Free Press	556,116	25.25	None	0.00
19	Philadelphia Inquirer	486,568	24.37	943,657	46.60
20	Los Angeles Times	1,089,690	23.00	1,488,484	30.85
21	Detroit News	366,988	21.27	1,186,116	53.61
22	Chicago Tribune	690,842	17.06	1,101,863	24.17
23	New York Daily News	764,070	10.07	927,255	11.93
24	New York Times	1,141,366	10.03	1,756,635	15.26
25	New York Post	394,431	4.76	None	0.00

Notes: 1. Circulation figures are total for the newspaper.
2. Penetration figures are only for the City Zone or Newspaper-Designated Market of each paper.

Source: FAS-FAX (September 30, 1993).

government officials were the principal readers of the international edition.

Circulation revenue was $48,603,000 in 1993 and advertising revenue was $249,272,000 (see Exhibit 15). Hurricane Andrew, while devastating southern Florida and causing additional circulation declines between 1992 and 1993, fueled retail and classified revenue growth for the *Herald* as businesses reopened and rebuilding spurred the local economy and job market.

The *Herald's* major competitors were the *Fort Lauderdale Sun-Sentinel* (circulation 255,000 daily/344,000 Sundays), the Spanish-language daily *Diario Las Americas,* eight major broadcast-TV stations, numerous radio stations, cable TV stations, and weekly shoppers and community papers.

El Nuevo Herald

In 1976, three years after Miami elected its first Hispanic mayor, the Herald created *El Miami*

EXHIBIT 15 *The Miami Herald* Circulation and Financial Information

	1993	1992	1991
Average Circulation			
Daily	401,733	405,779	425,304
Sunday	526,231	527,658	532,158
Average Linage (in 000s of six-column inches)			
ROP Full-Run			
Retail	1,100.7	1,022.6	1,046.4
General	225.4	257.7	261.8
Classified	999.7	914.1	868.2
Total	2,325.8	2,194.4	2,176.4
ROP Factored			
Part-Run	675.3	566.4	517.6
Pre-prints—Full-Run	667.7	669.7	592.7
Part-Run	1,265.3	987.6	984.9
Total Pre-prints Inserted (in 000s)	571,914	520,200	457,549
Advertising Revenue (in 000s)			
Retail	$112,878	$110,665	$109,519
General	38,911	43,154	39,945
Classified	97,483	85,618	80,298
Total	$249,272	$239,437	$229,762
Circulation Revenue (in 000s)	$ 48,603	$ 48,473	$ 49,071

Source: 1993 Annual Report, Knight-Ridder, Inc.

Herald. According to Roymi Membiela-Cordoba, an employee of the Herald at the time and in 1994 the director of new business and Hispanic market development, it was "very poorly done." It was a small section of the *Herald,* had a small staff, and carried mostly translated copy from the English-language paper. Periodically, Herald executives would talk about doing away with it altogether.

According to Membiela-Cordoba, many Herald executives had always "assum[ed] that the Hispanic community was going to assimilate . . . and we would dismantle [*El Miami Herald*]. There was not enough commitment to the market and what we interpreted as a way to make the Hispanic community happy was perceived totally in the opposite way. We alienated a lot of people, and created a lot of enemies instead of allies because of the lack of follow-through we had and lack of sensitivity to the Hispanic community." Membiela-Cordoba was in sales at the time; she remembered being thrown out of the stores of potential advertisers, physically threatened, and told "she should be ashamed" to be a Cuban who worked for a pro-Castro company that did not represent the Hispanics of Miami.

By 1985 relations between the Herald and the Hispanic community were tense, punctuated by the periodic bomb threats. Some anti-Castro Cubans perceived the *Herald* to be pro-Castro and pro-Communist. Miami's Hispanic community wanted a paper that published articles that were important to them and their businesses—and they wanted it in decent Spanish.

EXHIBIT 16   Top U.S. Spanish-Language Daily Newspapers

		Circulation	
Newspaper	*Base*	*Daily*	*Sunday*
El Nuevo Herald	Miami	101,389	126,614
La Opinion	Los Angeles	97,864	63,395
Diario Las Americas	Miami	66,611	70,506
El Diario/La Prensa	New York	48,198	35,687
Noticias En Espanol/Times	Laredo, Texas	22,170	23,869

Source: VAC Audit, June 30, 1993; SRDS Hispanic Media and Markets, March 1993 and June 1993.

According to Membiela-Cordoba, "it took us longer than a lot of us would have wanted. It was close to 10 years before the Herald figured it out. . . . [The Hispanics] were not assimilating, and not only were the ones here not assimilating, but they were gaining new members of different nationalities by the day. . . . Aside from the fact that it was becoming very difficult to operate in this community . . . I think Knight-Ridder recognized that in many ways they were missing [Hispanic advertising and circulation] dollars."

In early 1986 the Herald began 18 months of research into Dade's Hispanic population. The research found, among other things, that 27.1 percent of Dade's Hispanics read English fairly well, 11 percent read English poorly, and 21.2 percent did not read English at all. Some of the 40.7 percent who said they read English well, still preferred to read in Spanish. On November 21, 1987, the Herald relaunched its Spanish-language paper as *El Nuevo Herald.* According to then-publisher of *The Miami Herald,* Richard G. Capen, Jr., "In developing the content of our expanded Spanish-language daily, we have relied heavily on what Hispanics tell us they want in their newspaper."[16] According to the *Herald* article that announced the new edition, the "expansion of *El [Nuevo] Herald* comes at a

difficult moment in the newspaper's relationship with some leading Cuban-Americans."[17]

By 1994, *El Nuevo Herald* accounted for somewhat less than 10 percent of the total annual revenues of The Miami Herald Publishing Company. Its newsroom employed more than 100 people, including 35 editors, 21 reporters, and 5 photographers. The National Association of Hispanic Publications had named *El Nuevo* the best Spanish-language newspaper in the United States each year since 1989. With a daily circulation of 101,389 (a 42 percent increase since 1987) and 126,614 on Sundays, (a 54 percent increase since 1987) it was also the highest circulation Spanish-language newspaper in the United States (see Exhibit 16). The company estimated that *El Nuevo* was read by 200,000 people daily and 300,000 on Sundays. It was typically 42 pages daily and 70 on Sundays.

The paper was available on request to home delivery customers of *The Miami Herald* for a $.10 daily delivery charge. It could also be purchased, with no additional charge, together with the *Herald* in newspaper racks and from vendors in Hispanic neighborhoods. *El Nuevo* also circulated, either with or without the English-language paper, to a limited extent in other cities in southern Florida and some places in the Caribbean and Latin America.

---

16. Celia W. Dugger, "Herald Expands Spanish Edition," *The Miami Herald,* October 27, 1987.

17. Dugger.

EXHIBIT 17 Miami's Spanish-Language Community Publications

Newspaper	Week Day	Circulation
El Nuevo's Vida Social*	Tuesday	101,389
Exito†	Wednesday	59,916
Mi Casa†	Thursday	50,000
El Nuevo Patria	Thursday	20,340
El Heraldo De Broward Y Palm Beach	Tuesday	15,000

*Distribution of 101,389 is included with *El Nuevo*. An additional 120,000 are distributed to nonsubscribers.
†Free publication.

Source: VAC Audit, June 30, 1993; SRDS Hispanic Media and Markets, March 1993.

El Nuevo had several local competitors: *Diario Las Americas* and several community papers (see Exhibit 17); television stations with Spanish-language programming (Univision/Channel 23 and Telemundo/Channel 51); and several radio stations.

Growing *El Nuevo Herald*

By 1994 the Herald's relationship with Dade's Hispanic community had improved. *El Nuevo* had grown into a newspaper that any Spanish reader could "be proud of," according to Suarez. And, contrary to what some had expected, several of the statistics of the 1987 research remained virtually unchanged—particularly regarding the English-reading ability and preferences of South Florida's Hispanics (see Exhibit 18).

According to Membiela-Cordoba, *El Nuevo* had a 36 percent penetration rate in Dade's Hispanic households by 1994. She believed the paper had not "yet touched the tip of the iceberg [in terms of circulation, and would] not penetrate a bit more until we separate the newspapers." She also believed *El Nuevo* lost ad sales by being bundled with the English-language *Herald*.

In mid-1994, 80 percent of all the ads appearing in *El Nuevo* were sold as a combination buy with the English-only *Herald*, while 20 percent ran in *El Nuevo* only. According to Membiela-Cordoba, 20 percent of the ads that ran in *El Nuevo* were national ROP ads; she expected to hold these advertisers and attract new ones as more companies discovered the potential of the Hispanic market (see Exhibit 19). The Herald's market research division maintained significant databases on merchandise and services purchased by southern Florida's Hispanics, and periodically polled the Hispanic population for information regarding brand loyalty and

EXHIBIT 18 Miami ADI Hispanics Read and Speak Mostly in Spanish

Reading Ability	Spanish	English
Read well/very well	97%	40%
Fair	2	22
Poor/very poor	1	10
Cannot read	0	29

Language Spoken Most Frequently

	At Home	At Work	On Social Occasions
Spanish	74%	49%	69%
English	7	16	5
Both	18	35	26

Source: The 1991 South Florida Latin Market—Strategy Research Corporation.

400 *The Miami Herald Publishing Company*

EXHIBIT 19 Hispanic Market Purchases

Category	Dade County Total Household ($ millions)	Hispanic Spending (% of Total Market Spending)		
		Dade	Los Angeles	New York
Food At Home	$1,126	59%	29%	17%
Food Away from Home	644	52	24	13
Alcoholic Beverages	105	52	25	14
Apparel and Services	6,682	56	27	15
Clothing	458	55	27	15
Men and Boys	164	56	27	15
Women and Girls	245	52	25	14
Children under 2	49	70	39	23
Footwear	104	61	31	18
Other Apparel Products and Services	106	55	27	15
Transportation	1,693	49	23	12
Vehicle Purchases	716	49	22	12
Cars and Trucks, new	283	40	17	9
Cars and Trucks, used	430	57	28	16
Gasoline and Motor Oil	360	51	24	13
Other Vehicle Expenses	499	47	21	12
Public Transportation	118	55	27	15
Electricity 228	47	21	12	
Telephone	256	57	28	16
Personal Services	94	57	28	16
Laundry and Cleaning Supplies	52	60	30	17
Household Furnishings	291	43	19	10
TVs, Radios, and Sound Equipment	164	53	25	14
Health Care	341	40	17	9
Tobacco Products	61	39	17	9
Life and Other Personal Insurance	58	32	13	7
Cash Contributions	147	32	13	7
Total Consumer Expenditures	$9,659	46%	23%	13%

Source: DRI/McGraw-Hill, June 1992.

other issues related to consumer spending patterns.

It was difficult, however, to convince some advertisers who were already placing English-language ads to run ads in the Spanish-language paper when both papers were sold together. And, according to Membiela-Cordoba, "there were some lines of business we have really not been able to tackle in Spanish . . . like the pre-print business. It's impossible to justify to [advertisers] the additional cost of giving you two copies of their pre-print to insert in the same

newspaper." If the papers were separated, Membiela-Cordoba believed, her sales force could take advantage of both the growing interest in "buying" into the Hispanic market, and the ad rate differentials between the two newspapers (see Exhibit 20). An independent *El Nuevo,* she believed, would deliver a high-quality Hispanic circulation to advertisers at highly competitive rates.

Joe Natoli, president of the Herald, also believed in the potential of the Hispanic market, both in Miami and nationally. He wanted the

EXHIBIT 20   *Miami/Herald/El Nuevo Herald* General Ad Rates

Contract Size in Column Inches	Herald*/El Nuevo Herald Combo		Herald*		El Nuevo Herald	
	Daily	Sunday	Daily	Sunday	Daily	Sunday
Open Rate	$289.50	$339.75	$259.50	$305.75	$40.00	$45.25
31.5″	281.25	329.75	252.25	297.00	38.50	43.75
63″	278.75	326.75	250.50	294.50	37.75	43.00
126″	277.00	325.00	249.25	293.50	37.00	42.00
250″	275.00	322.50	248.00	291.75	36.00	41.00
500″	264.75	310.25	238.00	280.25	35.50	40.00
750″	256.50	301.50	230.50	272.25	34.75	39.00
1,200″	245.50	288.50	220.25	259.75	33.50	38.25
1,600″	239.50	281.25	215.00	253.00	32.75	37.50
3,510″	229.75	270.00	205.50	242.50	32.25	36.75
5,265″	213.75	250.50	190.00	223.75	31.50	35.50
6,500″	201.50	235.50	178.50	209.50	30.50	34.75
7,020″	194.50	227.75	172.25	202.50	29.75	33.75
9,000″	178.75	210.75	157.00	186.25	29.00	32.75
10,530″	162.00	189.00	141.00	165.00	28.00	32.00
12,500″	143.75	169.00	123.25	145.75	27.25	31.00
14,040″	132.75	166.75	112.75	144.25	26.50	30.00
18,000″	127.25	164.75	108.00	143.00	25.75	29.00
25,000″	124.75	161.00	106.00	140.00	25.00	28.00

*All General ads run in *The Miami Herald* will be automatically picked up into Boca News.

Color Rates—National Page Rates

Product	One Color	Two Color	Full Color
Herald/Boca News			
Daily	$2,325.00	$3,125.00	$3,930.00
Sunday	2,535.00	3,335.00	4,140.00
El Nuevo			
Daily & Sunday	$540.00	$720.00	$890.00
International Edition	$160.00	$200.00	$250.00
Neighbors & Hometown Heralds			
One zone	$315.00	$420.00	$630.00
Two zones	263.00	342.00	525.00
Three or more zones	210.00	263.00	420.00

Herald "to focus on companies trying to reach the Hispanic market. There's more and more focus on that around the country. We have a strategic advantage in having the best Spanish-language newspaper in town, or in the country, in *El Nuevo Herald.*" Natoli believed the Herald's Hispanic market research and sales strategy expertise, both for Miami and the national Hispanic market, represented marketable information and services. The Herald was experimenting with seminar formats to introduce advertisers to ways to reach the Hispanic market.

EXHIBIT 20 *(concluded)*   Pre-print Cost per Thousand: *The Miami Herald/El Nuevo Herald*

Pages/Size	Full Run	Part Run*
2 Tabloid	$44.75	$51.50
4 Tabloid	47.00	53.50
6 Tabloid	49.25	55.75
4 Standard/8 Tabloid	51.50	57.75
6 Standard/12 Tabloid	54.50	61.00
8 Standard/16 Tabloid	64.50	70.50
10 Standard/20 Tabloid	69.00	74.50
12 Standard/24 Tabloid	72.25	77.75
14 Standard/28 Tabloid	80.75	87.25
16 Standard/32 Tabloid	86.25	91.50
18 Standard/36 Tabloid	90.75	95.50
20 Standard/40 Tabloid	95.25	99.75
22 Standard/44 Tabloid	99.25	103.00
24 Standard/48 Tabloid	103.75	108.25
26 Standard/52 Tabloid	108.25	112.50
28 Standard/56 Tabloid	112.50	116.50
30 Standard/60 Tabloid	117.00	120.75
32 Standard/64 Tabloid	121.25	125.00
34 Standard/68 Tabloid	124.50	128.25
10 Tabloid	53.00	59.25
14 Tabloid	59.50	65.75
18 Tabloid	66.75	75.00
22 Tabloid	70.50	76.00
26 Tabloid	76.75	82.50
30 Tabloid	83.50	89.50
34 Tabloid	88.75	93.50
38 Tabloid	93.00	97.75
42 Tabloid	97.25	101.25
46 Tabloid	101.75	105.50
50 Tabloid	106.00	110.50
54 Tabloid	110.50	114.50
58 Tabloid	115.00	118.75
62 Tabloid	119.00	123.00
66 Tabloid	122.75	126.75

*The minimum quantity for part run pre-prints is 20,000.

Source: The *Miami/Herald* Publishing Company.

Suarez felt the Herald could make money and grow *El Nuevo* by selling the Spanish-language edition as a separate product locally. He also believed that the "biggest opportunity [for *El Nuevo*] was to expand the [paper's] geography" by selling it nationally in the 10 significant Hispanic markets of the United States. Other Herald executives also saw a growth opportunity for *El Nuevo* in the United States—particularly by entering into partnerships with newspapers in significant Hispanic communities which would carry *El Nuevo* inside their English-language dailies just as *The Miami Herald* did in Miami. The Herald could create a satellite-transmittable core product in Miami, leaving spaces for the partnership paper to drop in local news, TV, and sports listings. But, Suarez admitted, that plan had not been "a top priority because the priority up to now has been to strengthen the newspaper. And we have put a lot of effort into strengthening our commitment to the community."

Circulation Issues

In 1994, *The Miami Herald* and *El Nuevo Herald* together cost $.35 on newsstands or $3.25 per week by home delivery. For the first 14 years *El Miami Herald* and then *El Nuevo Herald* went to any home delivery customer who asked for it for free. In 1991 a $.05 daily delivery surcharge was added and in 1993 the surcharge was increased to $.10. Notably, when the *El Nuevo*'s delivery surcharge doubled, only 3,500 copies were lost, according to Dickey.

If the papers were sold separately, Dickey believed 20,000–30,000 people who wanted only the Spanish-language daily would drop the *Herald* immediately. He also believed that *El Nuevo* would lose 20,000 copies, because people who got the two papers for $.35 would not pay the talked-about $.35 for the English-language paper and an additional $.25 for the Spanish-language paper; they would buy just the English-language paper.

Suarez believed the Spanish-language paper would recover as the market grew, as the paper strengthened, and as people who previously did not want to pay $.35 for two papers together could now pick up the Spanish-language paper alone for $.25—in effect, getting a newspaper for a dime less than they could before.

The *Herald,* like most major newspapers, was a member of the Audit Bureau of Circulation (ABC) and had to abide by ABC rules to maintain its membership. The ABC was an independent, not-for-profit organization that monitored the circulations of newspapers and magazines. Because advertising rates were linked to circulation figures, the ABC's imprimatur on circulation figures was a critical data point to advertisers. Publications crossed ABC rules at their peril.

According to Dickey, the Herald would lose

significant marketing opportunities if the papers were separated. The ABC required that whenever two newspapers were published and jointly distributed by the same company, to count as paid circulation the minimum charge for the two products must be 130 percent (100 percent for the higher-priced product and 30 percent for the lower-priced product). However, so long as *El Nuevo* did not carry a masthead price and was not sold independently within the *Herald*'s primary distribution area, the *Herald* and *El Nuevo* were considered a newspaper and its supplement. According to ABC rules, a newspaper company could discount a newspaper (or a newspaper and its supplement) by as much as 50 percent and still consider all such subscriptions paid circulation. According to the Newspaper Association of America, 1994 median churn rates, or subscriber turnover, for newspapers with a circulation of 300,000 to 400,000 was over 65 percent. Like most major newspapers, the *Herald* discounted nearly 50 percent of all new subscriptions by 50 percent in order to attract new subscribers.

If the *Herald* and *El Nuevo* were considered two separate products, the Herald's 50 percent start-up discount would be eliminated. According to Dickey,

> In addition to this initial loss that we would be taking in circulation [if there is a separation] . . . it's going to be harder to sell newspapers . . . I can pretty much assure you that *The Miami Herald* will find it increasingly more difficult to grow in circulation. Some people would argue, well that is not so bad because *El Nuevo*'s going to grow and grow and grow. But what is the real growth potential? . . . How many cities in this country support two newspapers? . . . There are only so many advertising dollars out there.

Dickey was unpersuaded by arguments that revenues brought in by delivering a "pure" readership to advertisers would compensate for any potential shifts in circulation quantity.

Editorial Issues

Barbara Gutierrez, the managing editor of *El Nuevo Herald,* thought the first step for growing her publication beyond its current penetration rate lay in strengthening its editorial content. *El Nuevo* needed to cover local stories better and be more inclusive of non-Cuban Hispanics, it needed to have its own editorial voice, and it needed a stronger business page.

Thirteen Hispanic nationalities worked in Gutierrez's newsroom and in 1993 *El Nuevo* had added a Sunday Portuguese news page for the growing Brazilian community. Nevertheless, she thought, "we're going through restructuring and revision because this paper used to mostly cover the needs of Cuban-Americans. In the last two to three years, we have realized that this town has changed. A lot of people who live here, who visit here on a regular basis . . . are other Latin Americans. And we're trying to balance that . . . [but it is] difficult because certain groups are not as vocal and not as savvy as to how to get the media's attention as Cubans because Cubans have been here for a long time. They've adapted to the system; they're very much the shakers and the movers of this town."

Hispanic news was not covered exclusively in *El Nuevo,* Gutierrez explained. The *Herald* also had Hispanic reporters in Miami and covered events in Latin America and the Caribbean. There was more Hispanic-focused reporting in the Spanish-language paper, however, and it was often more detailed or carried a different slant than that in the English-language paper; the papers responded to the needs of largely different readerships. For example, on a day when Fidel Castro held a news conference and discussed both a crackdown on Havana's black market and further restrictions on the use of U.S. dollars in Cuba, the *Herald* focused on black market issues while *El Nuevo* focused on the dollar restrictions. According to Gutierrez, her readers had relatives in Cuba and sent U.S. dollars to them so currency restrictions were more important to her readers than black market issues. The English-language paper focused on the black market, however, because that was of more importance to English-speaking businesspeople and politicians who followed Cuban news. As *El Nuevo* became a stronger paper, she believed, some Hispanics who read English as easily as they did Spanish turned to the Spanish paper first because it presented news in a format and with a focus that was more valuable to them.

Suarez pointed to the hiring at the end of 1993 of Alvaro Vargas Llosa, the son of the Peruvian novelist and one-time presidential candidate, as a clear signal of the Herald's commitment to growing *El Nuevo* into a paper with an independent editorial voice. Vargas Llosa, the first opinion page editor of *El Nuevo Herald,* believed that an editorial page that balanced the demands of the multifaceted Hispanic community of Miami would help the circulation of *El Nuevo* grow. Key to that growth, he believed, would be developing an authoritative voice for *El Nuevo* that helped Cubans adjust to the changing demographics of Miami and helped other Hispanic nationalities build a stronger relationship with the city's newspaper.

El Nuevo had never carried its own editorials. It carried signed opinions, but had never had an independent editorial voice. With Vargas Llosa, *El Nuevo* was moving closer to that independent voice.

An International *El Nuevo Herald*

Another way to grow *El Nuevo,* in the opinion of some Herald executives, was to market it internationally. Suarez saw a significant opportunity in Cuba, a nation about 100 miles away, the size of Florida, with 11 million people, and no free press. *El Nuevo* already had a limited distribution there. Suarez believed Castro would fall and Cuba would open up in the near future. Herald executives actively discussed the "Cuba Plan," as Suarez called it, and adjusted it for potentially immediate implementation as the political situation changed. Suarez believed that Cubans still in Cuba would be starved for unbiased journalism and the Cuban exiles of Miami would "not be exiles anymore . . . a lot of traffic will be established between south Florida and Cuba. A lot of people are going to start businesses there, but they're going to keep their homes here and their businesses here."

Mark Seibel, the Herald's director of international operations, believed a Cuban edition of *El Nuevo* would need to happen in partnership with island Cubans:

> People in Miami think that they are Cuban, but they're not any more. . . . The way we approach what is going on on the island will not be useful to those people . . . we'll come in and there will be certain things, code words and events and developments that an island Cuban will know instinctively what's going on and how it's happening. And our writers won't. Our phrases will be wrong. Our perspective will be incorrect. My own belief about *El Nuevo* . . . is that its future lies in providing the base for something else . . . you might be able to take *El Nuevo* as a base product in terms of U.S. coverage and international coverage . . . but you would have to have local Cubans editing and writing the local content.

Seibel saw little opportunity for *El Nuevo* in Central and South America. He argued against several Herald executives who believed a U.S.-based newspaper would fill the need for a free press in the region: "There are a lot of Spanish-language newspapers in Latin America . . . [the free press argument] is a slap at the quality of the Latin American press." Besides, he argued, *El Nuevo Herald* was Cuban-, Caribbean-, and Central American-focused. It would need a far stronger South American focus to succeed.

Other International Products

According to Seibel, the Herald historically, "as an institution, did not understand our position in Latin America and did not take advantage of it. It was really just inattention, failure, I think, on the part of this institution, to see what was going on in Latin America, to see that the [Herald] already had a stake . . . it's foolish for us to ignore Latin America as a major market for us."

The international edition of *The Miami Herald* had languished in circulation and advertising for many years until Seibel was assigned to international operations in 1992. And, in September 1993, the Herald launched its first international niche publication in decades. "Florida Marketplace," a Spanish and Portuguese weekly shopper inserted into the international edition and newspapers in Brazil, Colombia, and Venezuela. It had been a modest revenue generator—making about $1 million annually—from the outset. Seibel wanted to add editorial content.

The same month "Florida Marketplace" began, the Herald also launched "CubaNews," an English-language monthly newsletter reporting on economic, political, and commercial trends in Cuba. According to Seibel, "the Herald collects an awful lot of information that we don't put in the newspaper and we ought to resell or find a way to package it. A good way of doing that is newsletters. . . . With a newspaper, every time you add a reader, you have to spend $.25 on materials. With a newsletter, you spend maybe a couple of pennies. And newsletters tend to be very high-priced items." A subscription to "CubaNews" was $350 a year. In its first year, academics and government officials were the primary subscribers to "CubaNews," as well as a few businesspeople, but Seibel expected subscriptions to increase as political and economic changes occurred in U.S.–Cuba relations.

Other "Augmentation" Products of the Herald

By 1994, The Miami Herald Publishing Company had launched a number of "augmentation" products (see Exhibit 21). Some of the new ventures just broke even or made only small profits, but in each case they were "information sorting" experiments in an attempt to understand how to keep the Herald profitable in the next decade. According to Lawrence, "the preponderance of money that comes in here comes from the basic, solid, good-old newspaper business. There is only one thing we have done so far, besides *El Nuevo,* that has a large amount of revenue attached to it—$15 million or so—and that's alternate delivery"—the Herald's zip code-and-date-specific delivery system for direct marketing materials and magazines.

EXHIBIT 21   The Miami Herald Publishing Company—Augmentation Initiatives

El Nuevo Herald

Database
marketing

Consumer events
marketing

International Women's Show •
Tropic Hunt • Copa Latina

Audio text
voice services

Voice Personals •
TeleHerald • Tell 'N' Sell •
Autoline/El Automatico

Advertiser-sponsored
local print products

Video text

**Newspaper
Core
Business**

Book publishing

Political Almanac • The Big One •
La Ira De Los Vientos • Hurricane
Preparedness • Outdoor Guide

Alternate delivery

Herald Express/Herald Direct •
Diversions

FAX newspaper
Satellite Edition

Print and deliver

Newsletters

CubaNews

Niche
Publications

Book Fair • South Florida Golf •
MVP • Florida Marketplace •
Health Beat • Vida Social

Factline

Info Store

Customized research
and data services

Property Line

Lawrence considered several of the augmentation products, such as Voice Personals and Autoline/El Automatico, "synergistic" with the core newspaper. Voice Personals, a purchased audio text voice "meeting and dating" service came with complimentary classified print advertisements. Autoline/El Automatico, another audio text voice service, was described as a database "parking lot." It too was sold in conjunction with print classifieds. It listed used cars according to make, year, price, and location for audio retrieval. Audio text services made traditional classified advertising "far more effective," according to Lawrence.

The Herald's involvement in events marketing, such as the International Women's Show or the *Copa Latina* soccer tournament, both begun in 1993, brought advertising revenues to *The Miami Herald* and *El Nuevo Herald* from vendors and sponsors. According to Lawrence, there was

> going to continue to be a big appetite for trying new things . . . all sorts of things we haven't even thought of yet, but I don't see any picture that says in the aggregate that those would come close in this generation to touching what the revenues are from basic newspapering. . . . We're interested in exploring a daily television show. . . . There is no larger news gathering organization in any community than the local newspaper. A big TV news operation would have 80 people in it. In the English [*Herald*] alone we have 437 people. . . . Then we have 100 more people who work in the Spanish [*Herald*], that's 500-plus people . . . in the process of gathering news, editing it, packaging it, and so forth. So are we willing to consider all sorts of things? Absolutely.

Decisions

When executives at the Herald spoke about future growth, there seemed to be a consensus that it would have something to do with the Hispanic market. When talk turned to what a growth product would look like and where it would sell, discussion became animated. Lawrence believed that "there are some special opportunities in the international markets. . . . The *Herald* has an extraordinary name in Latin America . . . there are

things that we could be doing in up to three languages—Portuguese, Spanish, and English." What Lawrence did not want was

> one newspaper in one language to seek to reach one segment of the community and another newspaper in another language to reach another segment of the community . . . our basic obligation is as a newspaper that goes to hundreds and thousands of homes in the morning. I have no doubt whatsoever that there's a future for a mass circulation newspaper. . . . The reality is there's a great relationship between newspaper reading and people who participate in the community, people of a certain education level, people of a certain income level, and so forth. We need to be writing about people who might never take the newspaper. We need to write about neighborhoods that feel relatively disenfranchised in this world . . . I'm not interested in only giving you what you want, because I think that is very unhealthy. . . . There is something very healthy in your skimming the paper and seeing some things from time to time that you never would have thought of [asking about] . . . I do believe my obligation as long as I'm in this business is to begin by worrying about the core, what I give everybody.

Lawrence faced a dilemma. He believed his core product played a significant role in keeping Miami together as a community and that segmenting the Herald's product offerings by consumer preferences would damage the community. But he needed to fulfill his obligation to his shareholders—and no one was telling him that circulation or ad revenues for his English-language core product were going to grow significantly in the future. Lawrence believed his company's participation in a number of augmentation ventures in international markets and nonprint media could secure a healthy future for the Herald. But none of these products were moneymakers now—nor would they be anytime soon, he thought.

Lawrence realized he was weighing his sense of obligation to shareholders against his vision for the community of Miami. Lawrence also realized that his vision was not the only one for that community.

BAYBANK BOSTON

As Richard Pollard, chairman of BayBank Boston, got off the phone with Richard Syron, president of the Boston Federal Reserve Bank (the Fed), he could not help but feel a mixture of concern and satisfaction about the results of the Fed's new study of mortgage lending. A bomb was dropped on the Boston banking industry in 1989 when a Fed study of neighborhood lending patterns provided evidence of discrimination. A 1990 analysis of home mortgage lending data seemed to confirm the earlier study. Local bankers had been quick to point out that neither of these studies reflected all the variables that go into a lending decision. The bankers argued that the patterns discovered by the Fed could simply reflect differences in the quality of loan applications rather than racial discrimination.

The 1992 study was designed to meet this objection, thanks in large part to the participation of Boston bankers, who voluntarily opened up their mortgage files to the Fed researchers. As Syron explained it, the researchers confirmed Pollard's belief that the banks were not turning down qualified black applicants. Rather, the study detected a more subtle source of bias in the mortgage lending process. (See Exhibit 1 for BayBank's mortgage loan process.) According to the new study, applicants who met the credit criteria on the first cut were given loans without regard to race. However, a large number of applicants (80 percent) initially failed to meet standard credit criteria. In most of these cases, the problems were eventually overcome and a mortgage was approved. It was in this discretionary process of working the application that racial

differences were found, even after all credit factors were considered. Black and Hispanic applicants were more likely to be denied a mortgage. The racial disparity found in this study was much lower than that implied by the previous studies, but it was significant nonetheless. (See Exhibit 2 for excerpts from the 1992 study.)

During the last three years, Pollard had spent a tremendous amount of time and energy both as the chairman of BayBank Boston and of the Massachusetts Bankers Association (MBA) dealing with the issues raised by the earlier studies. The new study forced Pollard to ask himself: Would existing programs adequately address the problem? If not, what else needed to be done to provide equal access to banking services and resources? Was BayBank Boston doing enough?

The Evolution of BayBanks, Inc.[1]

Once called Baystate Corporation, BayBanks had always had a strong regional presence in the suburbs around Boston. Until the mid-1970s, Baystate was made up of 11 banks, each with its own name, identity, and customer base. Baystate was a substantial player in the state, holding 11 percent of Massachusetts' deposit base throughout the late 1970s. By 1976, its eight banks in the Boston suburbs had 144 branches. Its hallmark was a commitment to customer service and an appeal to local bank loyalty.

William Crozier's plan. In the mid-1970s, Baystate began to reevaluate its decentralized structure and local marketing strategy. William Crozier, then newly appointed chief executive officer and chairman, proposed a common corporate identity, to improve marketing and advertising impact, and to increase operating efficiency by centralizing data processing. With the approval of the Baystate shareholders in the spring of 1976, Crozier's proposal became a reality and BayBanks, Inc., was born. The local

This case was prepared by Christine C. Remey under the supervision of J. Gregory Dees.

Copyright © 1993 by the President and Fellows of Harvard College.

Harvard Business School case 393-095 (Rev. June 21, 1993).

EXHIBIT 1   BayBank Mortgage Loan Approval Process

STEP 1: Preliminaries
 a. A potential applicant identified a property to purchase and negotiated a price.
 b. The applicant decided to approach BayBank for a mortgage.

STEP 2: The Applicant Inquired at Branch Office
 a. A mortgage specialist conducted the preliminary interview focusing on the applicant's ability to service the debt, based on gross income.
 b. If the applicant was interested in applying for one of the mortgage products offered, he/she was given a BayBank Mortgage Application Package.

STEP 3: Branch Review of Completed Application
 a. After the mortgage specialist received the application, an appointment was made to review the application process with the applicant.
 b. At the appointment, the application was reviewed for completeness and for any obvious obstacles to making the loan. If there were any missing forms or problems, the applicant may be asked to supply additional information.
 c. The applicant paid an application fee and one point (1% of the loan).

STEP 4: Bank Underwriting Process at BayBank Mortgage Corporation
 a. An underwriter and loan processor reviewed the application using secondary market criteria. Credit reports were ordered, income and bank accounts were verified, and the property was assessed.
 b. A senior underwriter reviewed the work of the underwriter and loan processor. The file was passed through a quality control process. The senior underwriter finalized the decision and sometimes recommended an alternative method for making the loan.
 c. If the underwriter recommended the loan be denied, the senior underwriter must review the loan to assure that all possibilities for approving the loan have been exhausted. If the senior underwriter agreed with the recommendation, the loan was given to the CRA manager for review. If the CRA manager did not find an alternative program to grant the loan, the loan was reviewed by senior staff at BayBank Mortgage Corporation. If senior staff agreed with the decision, a denial letter was written that explained the reasons for denial.
 d. The bank's closing department prepared instructions and closing documents for the bank's attorney. The attorney made an appointment with the applicant for the closing.

---

banks took on the new BayBank name and retained their regional identity as a surname. For instance, Harvard Trust in Cambridge became BayBank/Harvard Trust.

Crozier also made a decision to strengthen the corporate side of the business. A presence in Boston's financial district was essential to corporate banking in Massachusetts. Richard Pollard, a commercial banker from the Chase Manhattan Bank, was hired and a new bank, BayBank Boston, was created to house the corporate banking function. The bank eventually became

---

EXHIBIT 2 Excerpts from "Mortgage Lending in Boston: Interpreting HMDA Data" (1992)

The Home Mortgage Disclosure Act (HMDA) data for 1990, which were released in October 1991, showed substantially higher denial rates for black and Hispanic applicants. These minorities were two to three times as likely to be denied mortgage loans as white applicants were. In fact, high-income minorities in Boston were more likely to be turned down than low-income whites. The 1991 HMDA data, which are being released currently, show a similar pattern.

This pattern has triggered a resurgence of the debate on whether discrimination exists in home mortgage lending. Some people believe that the disparities in denial rates are evidence of discrimination on the part of banks and other lending institutions. Others, including lenders, argue that such conclusions are unwarranted, because the HMDA data do not include information on credit histories, loan-to-value ratios, and other factors considered in making mortgage decisions. These missing pieces of information, they argue, explain the high denial rates for minorities.

The results of this study indicate that minority applicants, on average, do have greater debt burdens, higher loan-to-value ratios, and weaker credit histories and are less likely to buy single-family homes than white applicants, and that those disadvantages do account for a large portion of the difference in denial rates. Including additional information on applicant and property characteristics reduces the disparity between minority and white denials from the originally reported ratio of 2.7 to 1 to roughly 1.6 to 1. But these factors do not wholly eliminate the disparity, since the adjusted ratio implies that even after controlling for financial, employment, and neighborhood characteristics, black and Hispanic mortgage applicants in the Boston metropolitan area are roughly 60 percent more likely to be turned down than whites. This discrepancy means that minority applicants with the same economic and property characteristics as white applicants would experience a denial rate of 17 percent rather than the actual white denial rate of 11 percent. Thus, in the end, a statistically significant gap remains, which is associated with race.

Estimating an equation that includes an explicit measure for race is not the only way to test whether race is an important factor in the mortgage lending decision. An equally good alternative is to estimate an equation for white applicants and then plug in the obligation ratios, loan-to-value ratio, credit history, and other values for each black/Hispanic applicant to calculate that applicant's probability of denial. The resulting discrepancy between the actual minority denial rate and the estimated minority denial rate based on the white equation can be interpreted as the effect of race on the mortgage lending decision.

Probability of Black/Hispanic Denials Based on White Experience

Characteristics and Experience	Denial Rates (%)
Actual denial rate for blacks/Hispanics in sample	28.1%
Denial rate for blacks/Hispanics with black/hispanic characteristics but white experience	20.2
Denial rate for blacks/Hispanics with white characteristics but black/Hispanic experience	18.2
Actual denial rate for whites in sample	10.3

If blacks/Hispanics had their own characteristics, that is, high obligation ratios, weaker credit histories, higher loan-to-value ratios, and less likely to buy a single-family home, but were treated by lenders like whites, their average denial rate would be 20.2 percent rather than the actual 28.1 percent experienced by minority applicants. In other words, economic, property, and neighborhood characteristics explain much of the higher minority denial rate, but 7.9 percentage points remain unexplained.

If the 7.9 percentage point discrepancy is attributed to the effect of race on the lending decision, this amount can be added to the white denial rate to estimate the racial impact starting from the white base. That is, the third line [in the above table] shows what the denial rate would have been for black and Hispanic applicants,

---

(continued)

EXHIBIT 2 *(concluded)*

if they had white obligation ratios, loan-to-value ratios, credit histories, and other characteritsics but were treated by lenders like minorities. Thus, even if minorities had all the economic and property characteristics of whites, they would have experienced a denial rate of 18.2 percent, 7.9 percentage points more than the actual white denial rate of 10.3.

This study has examined one avenue through which differential treatment could affect minorities' access to credit and opportunities for homeownership. It found that black and Hispanic mortgage applicants in the Boston area were more likely to be turned down than white applicants with similar characteristics.

It is important to clarify the limited focus of this analysis; it abstracts from discrimination that may occur elsewhere in the economy. For example, if minorities are subject to discrimination in education or labor markets, they will have lower incomes and their applications may reflect higher obligation ratios, greater loan-to-value ratios, or poorer credit histories. Similarly, if blacks and Hispanics are discouraged from moving into predominantly white areas, they will limit their search to neighborhoods sanctioned for minorities. They tend to be older central cities with high-density housing, such as two- to four-family homes. Denial of a mortgage loan application on the basis of either these economic or property characteristics would not be considered discriminatory for the purpose of this study.

Even within the specific focus of conventional lenders, the reported measure of the hurdles faced by minorities should be placed in perspective; differential treatment can occur at many stages in the lending process. For example, minorities may be discouraged from even applying for a mortgage loan as a result of a prescreening process. Similarly, if white applicants are more likely than minority applicants to be "coached" when filling out the application, they will have stronger applications than similarly situated minorities. In this case, the ratios and other financial information in the *final* applications, which were the focus of this analysis, may themselves be the product of differential treatment. This study does not explore the extent to which coaching occurs, but rather focuses on the impact of race on lenders' decisions regarding the final applications received from potential borrowers.

Source: Alicia H. Munnell, Lynn E. Browne, James McEneaney, and Geoffrey M.B. Tootell, "Mortgage Lending in Boston," Federal Reserve Bank of Boston, Working Paper No. 92-7, October 1992.

a base for retail expansion in Boston with subsequent expansion into the so-called streetcar suburbs of Boston.

Electronic banking. In a preemptive strike, Crozier bet early and heavily on technology, particularly automatic teller machines (ATMs) and electronic funds transfer capabilities. Crozier's bet turned out to be a good one.

> As the growth of the 1980s erupted on all fronts, BayBanks met market needs by launching an expansion program unparalleled in the company's history. The stars of that expansion were the Bay-Bank Card and the X-Press 24™ network, one of the most successful electronic banking programs ever executed in the United States.[2]

By the middle of 1989, BayBank ATMs had 39 percent of Suffolk county's ATM market share.

BayBanks, Inc., profited financially due to a boost in individual accounts and service charges. By the end of the 1980s, BayBanks, Inc., was approaching $10 billion in total assets.

Adjusting to life in the city. Over the course of a decade, BayBanks, Inc., had created an organization that incorporated the strengths of the suburban community banks, aggressive corporate marketing, an extended ATM network, and a growing corporate business. As the rapid growth of the 1980s subsided, BayBanks management decided to expand the Boston branch network beyond the downtown business district and the airport into some of the residential neighborhoods:

> The prospect of slower economic growth requires a modification of the rapid expansion strategies that worked to our great advantage during the

1980s. . . . To be sure, growth opportunities continue to present themselves. For example, we are now engaged in a major program of service to residential communities of the City of Boston where we have not had a presence.[3]

BayBank Boston planned to capitalize on the retail banking skills developed by its parent. However, just as this expansion strategy was being developed in 1988, events began to unfold that made it all too clear that doing business in the city was quite different from serving the suburbs. Not only were the economics and competitive dynamics of city banking different, but city banks had to deal with a much more complex set of social and political issues.

The Challenges of Inner-city Banking

Over several decades, the living conditions in U.S. urban centers had steadily deteriorated. "Crime rates were soaring, riots were erupting in black neighborhoods, city treasuries were empty, city streets were clogged with traffic, and signs of continued decline were pervasive."[4] According to many community activists, banks had facilitated the decline through "redlining" and "disinvestment." Redlining referred to "a practice by which local lenders draw a red line around sections of a city, literally or figuratively, to delineate areas within which they will not lend."[5] Disinvestment was defined as taking deposits from an inner-city community and using them to make loans elsewhere. Critics argued that restricted access to bank credit had several negative effects on inner-city neighborhoods: constraining opportunities for home ownership, discouraging rehabilitation and maintenance of residential and commercial property, and undermining local business development efforts. The credit gap had been filled in part by higher priced, less carefully regulated sources: rent-to-own programs, consumer credit companies, second-mortgage companies, even loan sharking.

The bankers' response stated simply was: If

fewer loans have been made in inner cities, it has largely been because inner cities present fewer prudent and profitable loan opportunities. Banks had an obligation to their depositors (including inner-city depositors) and to their shareholders to allocate loan funds to their most profitable use within the constraints of prudent lending practices. Because banks operated on rather thin margins, it took only a small increase in loan default rates to eliminate the profit on a large loan portfolio. Concerns about prudence were enforced by banking regulators and by secondary markets. By the 1980s, it had become common practice for banks to sell the mortgages they originate to organizations (such as Federal National Mortgage Association) that package them as mortgage-backed securities. These organizations have criteria for the kinds of mortgage loans they will purchase. Banks that did not comply limited their capacity to originate new loans. Accordingly, bankers argued that the lack of bank credit should be seen more as a symptom, rather than a cause, of urban decline.

Trying to be part of the solution. In the early 1960s, in response to public criticism, a number of Boston savings banks formed the Boston Banks Urban Renewal Group (B-BURG).[6] Working with Mayor Collins, the group committed $2.5 million to rehabilitate affordable housing and to provide home ownership loans insured by the Federal Housing Administration (FHA). By 1968, with inner-city tensions at new heights, newly elected Mayor Kevin White attempted to reinvigorate and to expand B-BURG by arranging a $29 million low-income, minority loan pool funded by large financial institutions and insured by the FHA. The results of this expanded effort were tragic.

In the early 1970s, more than 70 percent of B-BURG-assisted homeowners were unable to keep up their mortgage payments. . . . The banks foreclosed on more than a thousand single-family homes and multiunit dwellings in the area. The local HUD [Housing and Urban Development] office took over these houses after paying the banks full compensation for their lost loan moneys. . . . The solution for beleaguered bureaucrats became condemnation.[7]

Shoddy underwriting practices and drive-by inspections contributed to the extraordinary default rate. "It was simple human nature. With the government assuming the risk, screening standards always seemed to diminish."[8] Because the target area for B-BURG loans was limited to the Jewish communities of Dorchester and Mattapan, B-BURG has also been criticized for indirectly destroying those communities. With B-BURG money readily available to black applicants, "opportunistic real estate brokers fueled white flight by engaging in unscrupulous blockbusting practices, resorting to threats and even break-ins and arson to encourage Jews to sell their homes at below-market prices."[9]

Increasing federal regulations. Lobbying by community groups generated enough political awareness that inner-city residents were starting to demand legal recourse for lending injustices. In response to the public outcry, the Home Mortgage Disclosure Act of 1974 (HMDA) required that banks submit information on mortgage application denial and acceptance percentages to the federal regulators. The idea was that this data could identify patterns of discrimination.

Three years later, Senator William Proxmire (D, Wisconsin) introduced the Community Reinvestment Act (CRA) to reinforce the idea that "a bank charter carries with it an obligation to serve the credit needs of the area the bank is chartered to service, consistent with prudent lending practices."[10] A supporter of the CRA, Ralph Nader, urged that the CRA "would, in effect interject the community service factor into the market calculations of depository institutions."[11] Bankers rejected the need for regulation and claimed that if good business were present, the bankers would find it, as A. A. Milligan of the American Bankers Association articulated:

We do not deny that there is a problem . . . we believe that competitive pressures will in the future, as they have in the past, force [any offending] banks to change their policies. Their competitors within their communities will take advantage of these local loan opportunities and will advertise the fact that they are concerned about community development, whereas the other institutions are not.[12]

Nader pushed the Senate Committee to put some "teeth" in the CRA, while others, like Senator Jake Garn (R, Utah), objected,

The answer isn't more rules and regulations. Piecemeal, we are heading for credit allocation and government bureaucrats back here interfering with the private sector. I'm sick and tired of the anti-business attitude of this committee . . . the Ralph Nader's have their asses kissed every day and are told how wonderful their testimony is over and over again, while we are building up a regulatory burden that is going to destroy the housing industry in this country.[13]

Despite Garn's objections, the CRA was passed in 1977. (See Exhibit 3.) It would be enforced by the banking regulators, such as the Federal Reserve Board and the Comptroller of the Currency. Banks reported on their community activities and were given a rating by their federal supervisory agency. Furthermore, bank regulators considered CRA compliance in approving or denying bank requests for branch expansion, merger, or acquisition. It was in this process that community groups had their leverage.

The Boston Banking Controversies, 1989–92

For a decade, the passage of the CRA appeared to many community groups as merely a symbolic victory. As Nader feared, the CRA seemed to lack "teeth." Bank credit was still perceived as a major problem in inner-city communities. CRA reports seemed superficial and few banks got unsatisfactory ratings. By 1988, "of more than 50,000 applications for merger or

---

EXHIBIT 3   Excerpts from the Community Reinvestment Act of 1977

Findings and Purpose

SECTION 2. (a) The Congress finds that—

(1) regulated financial institutions are required by law to demonstrate that their deposit facilities serve the convenience and needs of the communities in which they are chartered to do business;

(2) the convenience and needs of the communities include the need for credit services as well as deposit services; and

(3) regulated financial institutions have continuing and affirmative obligation to help meet the credit needs of the local communities in which they are chartered.

(b) It is the purpose of this Act to require each appropriate Federal financial supervisory agency to use its authority when chartering, examining, supervising, and regulating financial institutions, to encourage such institutions to help meet the credit needs of the local communities in which they are chartered consistent with the safe and sound operation of such institutions.

Community Reinvestment Programs and Procedures

SECTION 4. Each appropriate Federal financial supervisory agency shall develop programs and procedures for carrying out the purposes of this Act. Such programs and procedures shall include—

(1) requiring that in connection with an application for a deposit facility, the applicant
   (A) delineate the primary savings service area for the deposit facility;
   (B) analyze the deposit and credit needs of such area and how the applicant proposes to meet those needs;
   (C) indicate the proportion of consumer deposits obtained from individuals residing in the primary savings service area by the deposit facility that will be reinvested in that area; and
   (D) demonstrate how that applicant is meeting the credit needs of the primary savings service areas in which it or its subsidiaries have already been chartered to do business;

(2) using, as factors to be considered in approving applications for deposit facilities, the applicant's record in meeting the credit needs of the primary savings service areas in which it or its subsidiaries have already been chartered to do business, and its proposal for meeting the credit needs of the primary savings service area associated with the pending application;

(3) permitting and encouraging community, consumer, or similar organizations to present testimony at hearings on applications for deposit facilities on how the applicant has met or is proposing to meet the credit needs of the communities served by or to be served by the applicant or its subsidiaries; and

(4) requiring periodic reports from regulated financial institutions concerning the amount of credit extended in the institutions' primary savings service areas and making such reports available to the public.

Annual Report

SECTION 5. Each appropriate Federal financial supervisory agency shall include in its annual report to the Congress a section outlining the actions it has taken to carry out its responsibilities under this Act.

---

expansion by banks made since the act took effect, only eight have been denied on grounds that banks were not complying."[14]

Leak of the Fed Study
In 1988, a group of researchers at the Boston Federal Reserve Bank began working with 1982–87 real estate transaction data to explore "how the Community Reinvestment Act (CRA) could be used more effectively to promote the creation of affordable housing."[15] Just as BayBank Boston began to establish a presence in city neighborhoods, news began to leak about the Boston Fed's research. January 11, 1989, was

a day that would change the next three years for Pollard, BayBanks, and the Boston banking industry, because of the following headline,

**Inequities Are Cited in Hub Mortgages
Preliminary Fed Finding Is "Racial Bias"[16]**

The Boston newspapers had received a copy of a preliminary draft of the study. The article stated that the study

> Concludes from statistical analysis that if banks and thrifts competed with equal aggressiveness in white and minority neighborhoods, they would have made "far fewer loans in predominantly white neighborhoods . . . and would have more than doubled their actual number of mortgage loans in the predominantly black areas of Mattapan/Franklin Park and Roxbury." . . . "Long after the passage of the CRA, banks and thrifts continue to compete more aggressively in white neighborhoods and leave minority neighborhoods to mortgage companies," the study says. "Boston has become a city with significant unmet credit needs for affordable housing and continues as a city with significant racial lending bias."[17]

This story started an avalanche of media attention. One banking expert claimed that in the 90 days after January 11, the Boston media did not miss a single day of coverage. Racial bias, redlining, disinvestment—none of these charges were new; so, how could this headline capture the attention of journalists, readers, viewers, and bankers? James Campen, a professor at the University of Massachusetts, suggested that

> What mattered even more than the study's findings . . . was its sponsorship. This was the first study ever by any of the four federal bank regulatory agencies that had contained such conclusions. The fact that the study was done at the Fed gave it and its findings a respectability and credibility that no study sponsored by community advocates or the media could hope to achieve.[18]

Richard Syron, the week-old president of the Boston Fed, called the conclusions of the study "premature" and stated that his staff "had a responsibility to pursue them and make some determination whether the Boston-area banks were discriminating."[19] More research into lending practices was planned.

The banking industry response. Bankers were convinced that they were being falsely accused. Pollard remembered his own reaction,

> Banks wanted to make mortgages. In the late 1980s, the competition was fierce. The banks were booming and mortgage companies were stealing our business. We wanted all the mortgages we could get—black or white—it did not matter. If anything, we were willing to stretch to make a mortgage to a minority applicant just because we needed the volume. It was inconceivable to us that we could be discriminating.

Other industry executives echoed this response. The Massachusetts Bankers Association's (MBA) president, Robert Sheridan, encouraged further study, stating that "I think the record of the industry is impeccable, and we would welcome any intensive scrutiny. . . . A thorough, complete analysis will show no bias."[20]

Falsely accused or not, Pollard suspected that this issue would dominate his professional life for a while. Not only was he chairman of a Boston bank, but he was to become chairman of the MBA in June. The MBA represented more than 200 financial institutions. Edward P. Shea,[21] a vice president of the MBA, recalled "our pitch was that we, as the trade association, could represent their combined interests, or they [the banks] could take a chance on their own." As the media, the politicians, and the community groups probed into the allegations of the leaked study, the banks opted for a collaborative effort. Though it put pressure on Pollard as in-coming MBA chairman, collaboration was welcomed by BayBank Boston. As the newcomer to city banking, BayBank Boston did not have much experience to draw on and its record of lending in inner-city neighborhoods was nearly nonexistent. There was strength in numbers.

Given its expansion plans, BayBanks, Inc., was vulnerable to attentive CRA scrutiny. BayBank Harvard Trust had made a formal request to open a new branch in Allston, a working-class neighborhood on the west end of Boston.

Community groups were aware of BayBank's request and used the opportunity to express their concerns. They picketed an existing branch to fuel opposition to the Allston request. Community activists felt that BayBank should not be allowed to expand until it addressed CRA issues. Pollard remembered that day well, "because once they finished picketing at the branch, the community activists walked a few blocks to my house, where they demonstrated and left messages in my mailbox."

Fortunately, Crozier, chairman of BayBanks, Inc., had anticipated the need for expertise in community relations. After a lengthy "courtship," Crozier hired Thomas Kennedy. Kennedy was well versed in the issues of inner-city life. While studying at the Episcopal Theological School, Kennedy had volunteered for an internship program in New York City, working as a retail salesman and living in East Harlem. Kennedy reflected on his experience as "formative and pivotal, exposing me to urban living and poverty." Upon returning to Boston and being ordained as an Episcopal priest, Kennedy spent a number of years in Church-sponsored outreach activities that he referred to as "street ministry," including a period as dean of the Cathedral Church of St. Paul. He first met Crozier serving on a private school board in 1971. Kennedy remembered a conversation they had in 1987:

> Crozier was talking stream of consciousness, saying that his bank needed to reach out to the community and understand its needs. As he described the role of an individual helping the bank in that capacity, I looked at him and said, "Are you talking about having a clergyman come to your bank?" This was the craziest idea I had ever heard. However, he was persistent. By May of 1989, I was community affairs officer at Bay-Banks, reporting directly to Pollard and indirectly to Crozier.

Kennedy worked with Pollard, tackling the sensitive issues of discrimination and inner-city lending.

As BayBanks dealt with the Allston branch challenge, members of the MBA met weekly for breakfast to discuss the scope of the problem, possible explanations, and an industry response. Pollard analyzed the discussions,

> The key was to break the issue into its elements. We decided that the mortgage lending issue was the tail wagging the dog. It was the symptom of the disease—not the disease. The inability of a minority applicant to get a mortgage is caused by disinvestment in that community, lack of economic growth, poor income level—all of which needed to be dealt with differently.

This realization led to the identification of four problem areas: mortgage lending, affordable housing, access to bank services, and small-business loans. Each problem was addressed by the MBA by setting up task forces chaired by bankers. Clark Miller, executive vice president of the Bank of Boston, offered to lead the effort on mortgage lending. Richard Driscoll, chairman of The Bank of New England, who had been active in the housing issues, volunteered to work on affordable housing. Pollard assumed responsibility for banking services. Finally, Shawmut Bank's president, John P. Hamill, took the lead on small-business lending.

Further government pressure. On several fronts, regulatory pressures concerning community banking practices were mounting. While the Boston Fed continued its research, Boston Mayor Ray Flynn, working through the Boston Redevelopment Agency (BRA), decided to hire Charles B. Finn of the Hubert H. Humphrey Institute of Public Affairs at the University of Minnesota. Finn's 1988 studies of home mortgage lending in Detroit[22] and Atlanta[23] heightened public awareness of discrimination in lending. Ultimately, Detroit and Atlanta financial institutions donated funds for a below-market-rate mortgage loan pool similar to B-BURG.

1989 saw significant activity on a national level as well. In a highly visible case, the Federal Reserve Bank of Chicago employed the CRA to halt an acquisition by Continental Bank.[24] By

---

EXHIBIT 4 Amendments to the Financial Institutions Reform, Recovery, and Enforcement Act of 1989

As of July 1, 1990, CRA ratings are no longer on a numerical basis; rather they are written evaluations using a four-tier descriptive system:

Outstanding record of meeting community credit needs.
Satisfactory record of meeting community credit needs.
Needs to improve record of meeting community credit needs.
Substantial noncompliance in meeting community credit needs.

Each institution will have its performance reviewed in five major categories:

1. Ascertainment of community credit needs.
2. Marketing and types of credit extended.
3. Geographical distribution and record of opening and closing offices.
4. Discrimination and other illegal credit practices.
5. Community development.

An "outstanding" rating will be achieved only by financial institutions that demonstrate certain qualities, including leadership in ascertaining community needs, participation in community revitalization, and affirmative involvement in planning, implementing, and monitoring their CRA-related performance. Most CRA observers agree that "outstanding" ratings will be difficult to achieve.

CRA evaluations can be found at an institution's main office and designated branch in each of its local communities. They are not, however, required to provide free copies.

Source: Virginia M. Mayer, Marina Sampanes, and James Carras, *Local Officials Guide to the Community Reinvestment Act,* Washington, D.C.: National League of Cities, 1991, p. 15.

March, the federal financial supervisory agencies completed a review of the CRA and its enforcement. The agencies stated that:

> The CRA and the implementing regulations place upon all financial institutions an affirmative responsibility to treat the credit needs of low- and moderate-income members of their community as they would any other market for services that the institution has decided to serve. As with any other targeted market, financial institutions are expected to ascertain needs and demonstrate their responses to those needs.[25]

Specific suggestions for effective programs included: more flexible lending criteria, participation in government-insured lending programs, improved advertising and marketing efforts, involvement at all levels of management, improved customer assistance, adoption of a branch closing policy (specifically appropriate notice), assistance in community development programs, establishment of a community development corporation, the funding of a small-business investment corporation, and investments in state or municipal bonds. Finally, amendments to the Financial Institutions Reform, Recovery, and Enforcement Act of 1989, clarified and strengthened the CRA reporting and evaluation process. CRA evaluations would be more detailed and publicly available. (See Exhibit 4.) Lenders would be required to provide information on the sex, race, and income of mortgage applicants, as part of their HMDA reporting. These additions permitted more thorough analysis of mortgage lending practices.

Community groups response. The news of the Fed study energized a number of community groups. It was just the sort of credible evidence that they needed to press their case for more community banking. There were many local community groups interested in the CRA and its interpretation. The Massachusetts Urban

Reinvestment Advisory Group (MURAG) had been formed nearly 20 years earlier to focus attention on the disinvestment problem. The Dudley Street Neighborhood Initiative, a Roxbury community group, was involved in "a grassroots effort to preserve and redevelop our neighborhood for the people who live and work in it."[26] The Greater Roxbury Neighborhood Authority, Nuestra Communidad Community Development Corporation, and Urban Edge Community Development Corporation were also active. Another participant was the statewide affordable housing coalition, the Massachusetts Affordable Housing Alliance. A Boston union of hotel workers, Local 26, through their subsidiary, Union Neighborhood Assistance Corporation (UNAC), was involved because of a housing trust fund benefit that had recently been granted. These community groups threatened class-action suits, organized demonstrations, and submitted information to the media. Also active nationally but sited in Boston, the Reverend Charles Stith and his group, the Organization of a New Equality (O.N.E.), encouraged the efforts. No one organization or individual emerged as the leader. In addition, representing the business interests of the minority community, the Minority Developers Association took an active interest. The groups shared a common concern about the problem, while representing a diversity of interests and political perspectives.

Working toward a Solution

During the spring of 1989, industry, community groups, and government agencies worked separately. The MBA needed time to analyze the problem from the perspective of the industry as a whole and individually within each financial institution. Several of the community groups united as the Community Investment Coalition (CIC) and insisted on representation in the bankers' meetings. By early June, three forums were scheduled by the MBA, each one dealing with a facet of the problem. The Boston Fed agreed to host the forums, so that all parties would feel comfortable. The MBA made an effort to be inclusive and thereby opened the forums to everyone. Of course, not all of the participants agreed with this collaborative approach. Bruce Marks of UNAC refused to attend the forums. Instead his group organized a sit-in at the Bank of Boston.

The forums. As Pollard entered the first forum on small-business lending, a reporter inquired, "Do you think that the banks have caused these problems?" He responded, "I do not know if the banks are part of the problem, but we are certainly part of the solution." This was the tone the MBA tried to set. The bankers and the community representatives were addressing the issues and designing solutions together. Shea of the MBA explained that the emphasis of this first forum was to explore ways "to develop jobs, incomes, stability, and savings, so that residents will be able to afford housing on truly market standards."

The second forum addressed affordable housing. Richard D. Driscoll's comments reenforced the emphasis on problem solving.

> The problem of affordable housing in our community is critical and needs more involvement by everybody, certainly by banks. . . . Everybody has to abandon old ideas about how this problem will be solved. Certainly banks have to stop saying "we've never done it this way before" or "our current policies prevent us from doing that" or "it's not my problem, let's give it to the government."[27]

In July, the third session, addressing bank services, was held. The concerns raised ranged from branch openings and closing to cashing welfare checks.

With over 90 bankers and over 100 community representatives at each of the forums, recognition of the needs of the community, as well as the limitations on private organizations were acknowledged by participants. After the forums, the bankers' task forces continued to work on solutions. Yet, there were some skeptics. Peter Dreir of the Boston Redevelopment Authority (BRA) commented, "This could be a window of opportunity or it could simply be a window dressing."[28] Another doubter, Representative Joseph P. Kennedy (D, Massachusetts) stated that "While it's encouraging to see the formation of task forces, and forums . . . I still am unclear at what specific measures came out of them."[29] The MBA promised to reveal their plan and the banks' commitments to the reinvestment efforts in late September.

Negotiating a Settlement

While the bankers were drafting a plan, pressure continued to mount from the media, community groups, and politicians. The Greater Roxbury Neighborhood Authority printed and circulated their study on patterns of mortgage discrimination. Peter Dreir of the BRA continually made reference to the Finn study, but failed to state when the study would be released to the public. On August 24, the Community Investment Coalition (CIC) took a stand "calling for the infusion of $2.1 billion in private bank loans and the reopening of closed bank branches to redress years of lending bias and neglect."[30] As reported, the CIC groups "want the city's largest banks to finance the construction and rehabilitation of 12,000 housing units. They want a program of discounted mortgage rates at 5 percent and 15 more bank branches and ATMs for the minority communities."[31] The CIC sent their 29-page analysis and plan to all of the banks in Boston. Pollard reported that in the enclosed letter the CIC stated, "While the details of the plan are open for discussion, its scope is nonnegotiable." The CIC insisted on a response by September 11 and urged that the bankers open their discussions up to CIC representatives.

Official release of the Federal Reserve study. On August 31, 1989, the final version of the Fed study was released. The study had compared mortgage origination patterns in predominantly black and predominantly white neighborhoods. The researchers found significantly lower mortgage activity in predominantly black neighborhoods, even controlling for income and wealth levels. The central findings were:

> Controlling for all the economic and other non-racial factors, the results suggest that neighborhoods with over 80 percent black residents would still have 24 percent fewer mortgage loans relative to the housing stock than neighborhoods with less than 5 percent black residents.[32]

> While realtors, developers, lenders, and others probably all share some responsibility for the racial pattern of mortgage activity, one group stands out as having a special role to play in correcting this situation. Not only are banks and thrift institutions central to the home ownership process, but unlike other lenders they have an affirmative obligation under the Community Reinvestment Act to help meet the credit needs of their entire community.[33]

In response to the official release of the study, Pollard maintained his early position that "if people think that somehow banks don't want to make mortgages in black areas, that couldn't be further from the truth."[34] Many bankers concurred. Some privately expressed skepticism regarding whether there was even enough good business in the urban centers for all the banks to fulfill their CRA obligations.

The conclusions of the Fed study further verified the allegations the CIC had been making over the summer. The local newspaper and television coverage continued to push the discrimination theme, as is evident in this cartoon.[35]

In lieu of a specific counteroffer to the CIC proposal, the MBA scheduled an open meeting on September 8. Following the meeting, the community groups hosted a meeting of their own to discuss their proposal and to negotiate the specifics of a plan. At this meeting in Roxbury, Pollard commented that "It is clear at this point that there is no single answer. . . . The possible solutions we have identified all depend on cooperation among bankers, government officials, and community leaders. We think we have already gone a long way and we expect more progress in the months to come."[36] Pollard went on to commit $150,000 of the MBA funds to establish a community banking council. Throughout the fall, the MBA task force meetings were open to all interested parties.

Struggling to reach an agreement. As the MBA worked on a four-pronged plan for community investment, BayBank Boston announced its intention to locate branches and install new ATM machines in minority neighborhoods. Thomas Kennedy of BayBank Boston explained,

> We were already committed to doing something in the neighborhoods of Boston. In fact we applied to open a branch in Allston and already had approval for a branch in Jamaica Plain, which are both low- to moderate-income neighborhoods. The preliminary work had already been done. In response to the pressure, we analyzed our customers by residential zip codes. It turned out we had over 16,000 BayBank customers in the neighborhoods of Roxbury, Mattapan, and Dorchester—and they had no place to bank in their community.

Other Boston banks were developing plans to commit their personnel, funds, and branches to the MBA plan. The atmosphere was generally positive.

However, the negotiations stalled due to disagreement on the mortgage lending issue. The community groups and the bankers could not

Boston's Largest Banks (1981–1987)

Bank	Total Deposits ($000)	Mortgage Loans White/Minority
The First National Bank of Boston	$7,482,003	2.1 : 1
Bank of New England	6,029,462	1.9 : 1
State Street Bank	3,983,204	*
Shawmut Bank	3,131,746	2.3 : 1
Boston Five	1,466,343	0.9 : 1
The Provident	1,146,728	4.2 : 1
Home Owners	1,105,742	2.6 : 1
United States Trust Company	886,691	1.8 : 1
South Boston Savings Bank	766,185	7.4 : 1
Neworld Bank for Savings	754,818	1.9 : 1
First Mutual of Boston	563,696	2.5 : 1
BayBank Boston, Harvard Trust, Norfolk	433,230	11.7 : 1
First American Bank	386,451	0.6 : 1
Capital Bank and Trust	328,718	10.2 : 1
Haymarket Co-Operative Bank	325,606	no mortgage loans to minority neighborhoods

*Too few mortgages to calculate ratio.

Source: Adapted from Charles Finn, "Mortgage Lending in Boston's Neighborhoods 1981–1987," December 1989.

reach resolution over the mortgage rates. The CIC, with political support in the mayor's office, demanded rates 2 percent below standard rates with no up-front point charges, but the bankers criticized the proposal as unsustainable in the long term. The bankers offered standard rates with two points. John Hamill of Shawmut vowed that "[w]e're 90 percent there. . . . We're going to keep working until we have something everybody is happy with."[37] Ultimately, the bankers were able to sell the community groups on market rate mortgages. They did this by addressing inequities in the loan underwriting criteria and by arranging a program to assist with down payments. For instance, in the past, rent payments did not have the same weight as prior mortgage payments in demonstrating creditworthiness. This would be changed in the new program.

In December of 1989, just as the final details of an agreement between the banks and the community groups were being worked out, the BRA finally released the study by Charles Finn (See table on page 420). It again hit hard at the theme of discrimination and the special role of banks in exacerbating the problems of inner-city neighborhoods. The Finn study went beyond the Federal Reserve study in its evaluation of individual banks and BayBank stood out because of its history as a suburban bank.

The mayor and BRA officials wanted to use the Finn study to pressure the banks into a below-market-rate mortgage program. However, many observers of the summer forums and participants in the fall meetings felt that the release of the Finn study by the BRA did more harm than good, a sentiment that was captured in this cartoon.[38]

Pollard, speaking on behalf of the MBA, admitted, "We have to pause a minute to see what's happening here . . . the BRA study has thrown everything into confusion. . . . You do not want to look reactive, you want to look positive. If we don't come out with something this week it's not because we don't have it."[39] A local editorial writer wondered,

Who figures to be hurt most by this? Who else but the people whom the program would benefit the most? As one activist put it: "The bottom line is that if this process goes by the wayside it's the black community—not some of those people who are part of the negotiations—that will suffer." Neither Mayor Flynn nor the BRA want this, we're sure—but what are they going to do to prevent it?[40]

Breaking the stalemate. It was in this atmosphere of urgency and confusion that racial tensions were dramatically heightened in the city of Boston. In October, the police reported that Carol Stuart, a pregnant white female, had been shot and killed while driving through Mission Hill with her husband, Charles. Since the horror of that day, an investigation had begun to find the assailant, as described by Charles Stuart, "a black, with a raspy voice, high strung, wearing a black jogging suit."[41] Police were very aggressive in their tactics and incurred the anger and frustration of the black community. By early January 1990, the investigation began to focus on Charles Stuart as the murderer of his wife as a result of his leap to death off the Mystic River Bridge. Members of the city's black community demanded a public apology from Flynn for the aggressive police tactics. Flynn refused to apologize.

Revived racial tensions made it hard for Flynn's administration to take further steps to threaten the carefully negotiated MBA reinvestment plan, a plan in which many community leaders had invested a great deal of time and energy. The reinvestment plan was announced, in January 1990, at the annual Martin Luther King Day Breakfast, co-sponsored by Union United Methodist Church and St. Cyprian's Episcopal Church. The MBA plan called for concerted activity on all four fronts of mortgage lending, affordable housing, economic development, and access to banking services. (See Exhibit 5 for an overview of The Massachusetts Bankers Association Community Investment Program.) Many of the programs were innovative. General Elec-

tric Credit and Fannie Mae had agreed to insure and purchase loans made with underwriting criteria more appropriate for low- to moderate-income home buyers. The Minority Enterprise Investment Corporation (MEIC) planned to work closely with minority loan applicants to help make their businesses viable candidates for financing, blending business consultation with traditional, hard-nosed underwriting. Nearly all Massachusetts banks agreed to cash government checks even for individuals who did not have accounts at the bank. And the Massachusetts Community and Banking Council (MCBC) planned to keep alive an ongoing dialogue between the community groups and the bankers.

Reactions to the MBA Plan

The community representatives were pleased with the MBA plan. Willie Jones of the CIC commented that the MBA program "should provide for the level of affordability we've been striving for."[42] At the announcement of the program, the Reverend Charles Stith, pastor of the United Methodist Church and head of Organization for a New Equality (O.N.E.), was ecstatic, exclaiming "I have never been more proud to be a citizen of this city than I am today."[43] The new year was devoted to establishing the new corporations, getting the products to the public, locating affordable housing projects, and finding sites for branch openings. Many of these activities were followed up on by the task forces, while others were up to individual banks.

BayBank Boston was satisfied with the MBA plan and its opportunity for participation. Pollard viewed it as "a permanent thing in which the funds will be replenished over and over. In the long run, it will have a more significant impact."[44] The BayBanks' board had been following the progress throughout 1989; therefore, the board quickly approved multiple commitments. BayBanks' contributions were:

- $5 million for mortgage lending at a discounted rate.

EXHIBIT 5   The Massachusetts Bankers Association (MBA) Community Investment Program

The Massachusetts Bankers Association Community Investment Program

---

NEED: Mortgage lending to overcome obstacles in providing mortgages to low- and moderate-income individuals

Community Home Buyer's Program

A more flexible mortgage product insured by GE Mortgage Insurance that would be sold to Fannie Mae.

All participating banks would allocate a specific amount of funds for this program.

Estimated amount to be allocated by the banks $100 million.

Soft Second Product

To assist homebuyers with down payment requirements

The first mortgage would be purchased by Fannie Mae; the "soft second" mortgage would be held in the bank's portfolio.

NEED: Affordable housing to develop affordable housing units in low- and moderate-income communities

Massachusetts Housing Investment Corporation (MHIC)

A multibank loan consortium that would provide debt to nonprofit and for-profit affordable housing developers

Established programs:
• Construction Loan Program (for construction and preservation of housing)
• Permanent Financing Program (to finance affordable rental housing)

$100 million investment by banks

Massachusetts Bankers Equity Fund

To pool the investments of the banks to provide equity to affordable housing developers

To encourage banks to make equity investments in low income housing tax credit projects

Estimated investment $100 million

NEED: Economic development to meet the credit needs of minority-owned businesses in order to further economic development in minority communities

Massachusetts Minority Enterprise Investment Corporation (MEIC)

A multibank community development corporation

To make equity investments or loans available to start-up or existing minority-owned businesses

Estimated investment from the banks:
• $10 million in equity capital
• $50 million in lines of credit

The Commonwealth Enterprise Fund

An SBA-licensed subsidiary to establish an equity pool for minority enterprise

To establish a vehicle within which banks can invest in minority-owned businesses

---

NEED: Bank services to deliver bank services and products to minority, low-, and moderate-income communities

Massachusetts Community and Banking Council (MCBC)

A research and policy advisory center

To promote community investment in minority, and low- and moderate-income communities

Activities include:
• fact finding
• community liaison
• community outreach
• education
• dispute resolution

New branches and ATMs in minority, low-, and moderate-income communities

All banks agreed to provide check cashing services for government checks (including welfare checks)

- $10 million in equity participation for the development of affordable housing for which the bank received tax credits).
- $2 million to Massachusetts Minority Enterprise Investment Corporation ($.5 million in equity investments and $1.5 million in loans).
- 5 branches and 25 ATMs in low- and moderate-income areas.
- Pollard would chair the Massachusetts Community and Banking Council.

As the new player in the city and in keeping with its ATM strategy, BayBank Boston had decided to take the lion's share of the MBA's promised total of 9 new branches and 30 ATMs.

Members of the MBA were particularly delighted that they had avoided the temporary and potentially disastrous remedy of a below-market minority loan pool. They believed that they would avoid another B-BURG and they had not repeated what they perceived to be the mistakes made in Atlanta and Detroit. As Sheridan of the MBA commented,

> Without question, the "big bang" approach of a one-shot loan pool would have put money out on the street sooner. However, the Association is convinced that if the mandate of the Community Reinvestment Act is to be taken seriously, it must be seen as a coherent, financially sound enterprise that will live on after media and even advocate attention has moved on to other things.[45]

The financial soundness of the MBA plan was crucial to the Massachusetts banks and to banking regulators. The turn of the decade brought with it a recession that hit the Northeastern states particularly hard. After several years of boom, Massachusetts experienced high unemployment and a major decline in real estate values. These economic strains took their tolls on the banks. The most dramatic evidence of this was the failure of the Bank of New England, as well as many smaller banks. The Bank of New England's chairman, Richard Driscoll, who had headed the MBA task force on affordable housing, resigned from the bank while the MBA process was unfolding. Many banks were reporting losses and cutting dividends. In this environment, BayBanks, Inc., reported its first loss ever. It lost nearly $70 million in 1990. Following a rash of failures in the savings and loan industry, both banks and their regulators had a special interest in assuring that a community investment program be consistent with the safety and soundness of the financial institutions.

Second Mortgage and Home Improvement Loans

Media and advocacy attention did subside for close to a year—until the Bank of New England was to be purchased by Fleet/Norstar Financial Group. Bruce Marks of UNAC assembled documents showing that Fleet as well as other banks had financed private mortgage companies which in turn charged customers interest rates well above the typical bank market rate. He alleged that Fleet was indirectly "lending at loanshark rates."[46] Not only was this usurious, according to Marks, but it led to an unfortunately high number of foreclosures.

After a 90-day moratorium on foreclosures in Suffolk and Hampden counties, the allegations had been reviewed by the federal regulators. Fleet's purchase of the Bank of New England was approved. However, this issue did not end there. Community groups demanded a more thorough investigation. Despite an aggressive advertising program, called "Setting the Record Straight,"[47] Fleet continued to be featured in the Boston press as the financier of "loanshark" loans to elderly and minority communities. Once again the Boston Fed was called upon—this time to study second-mortgage and home improvement lending. Their August 1991 study concluded that:

> Certain individuals have suffered great hardship, including the loss of their homes, because of burdensome second mortgages. High rates are only one dimension of the second-mortgage problem, but it is one that permits quantification. We estimate that loans with interest rates of 18 percent

Estimates of Nonacquisition Loans in Suffolk County

Interest Rate	Total Suffolk County	Roxbury and Mattapan
18% or greater	698	207
15% to 18%	1,630	298
Less than 15%	39,581	2,147
Unidentified	9,314	1,370
Total	51,223	4,022

Source: Adapted from Table 1 of Alicia Munnell and Lynne Browne, "Second Mortgages in Suffolk County," The Federal Reserve Bank of Boston, August 14, 1991, p. 12.

or more account for 1.4 percent of the nonacquisition[48] mortgages made in Suffolk county from 1987 to 1990. In the [predominantly black] neighborhoods of Roxbury and Mattapan, 5.1 percent of nonacquisition mortgages carried rates of 18 percent or more. These mortgages are supplied by a relatively small number of specialized lenders. Banks are not providers of high-rate second mortgages, although they are important suppliers of nonacquisition mortgages throughout Suffolk county. The major Boston banks have at times provided financing to some of the high-rate lenders or purchased loans from these lenders; but most of the larger high-rate lenders have many other funding sources. Finally, our survey revealed that many different lenders—banks, mortgages companies, finance companies, contractors, and individuals—operate throughout Suffolk county, offering borrowers a spectrum of rates.[49]

Media coverage expanded to cover loans made by home improvement companies as well. Several of the major Boston banks, including BayBanks, were named as financiers of questionable lenders. One television station ran a hard-hitting investigative report on the tragedies that sometimes resulted from questionable lending practices. The Massachusetts attorney general initiated a probe of the banks and their relationships with private mortgage and home improvement companies.

In October 1991, an analysis of 1990 HMDA data was released. Nineteen-ninety was the first year that race, sex, and income data were reported. The data once again showed racial differences, even when income level was held constant. The release of this data made national news with lead stories in major newspapers. Though it was unrelated to Boston's second-mortgage problem, this information simply fueled the fire.

Accused of forcing as many as 1,000 people out of their homes by "strip-mining the equity from minority communities,"[50] Fleet terminated business with 38 private mortgage companies. In defending Fleet Finance, the subsidiary involved, a spokesperson explained, "The higher the risk, the higher the rate. It's not illegal to make a profit."[51] Nonetheless, working with Mayor Flynn, Fleet agreed to establish an $11 million fund to refinance 550 cases on more favorable terms.

Employing the concept of lender liability, the attorney general threatened to investigate the banks individually. BayBanks was the major provider of financing to home improvement companies in Massachusetts. BayBanks managers felt that they had been careful in selecting the home improvement companies with which they dealt. As Pollard explained,

The only way to control this business is on a complaint basis. BayBanks was legally bound to repair anything that broke down, to replace poor workmanship, or to complete an incomplete project. When a home improvement salesman carried BayBanks' paper, the consumer was protected. In general, there were no complaints. When we did receive two or three complaints from the same company, we dropped them. We policed that part of our business.

He felt that the media and community activists had overestimated the problem, at least as it related to companies funded by the banks. He also wondered why banks were being held responsible for their customers' behavior. Nonetheless, Pollard wanted to resolve this issue quickly. Bay-Banks entered into discussions with the community and the attorney general.

On February 19, 1992, the attorney general announced an agreement with BayBanks. The agreement drew on the organizations created by the MBA reinvestment plan. BayBanks created a Victim Resolution Program to be run through the recently created MCBC, improved procedures for indirect home improvement lending by offering a product directly to the consumer, committed at least $5 million to a home improvement loan program, and committed $6 million in loans to another MBA-created entity, MHIC. In addition to the commitments made to the attorney general, BayBanks got out of the business of funding home improvement companies. The results were immediate: "[e]ven before hearing a word of the settlement, activists said BayBanks' combination of financial aid and corporate responsibility set a new standard for other banks in Massachusetts and across the country."[52] Shortly after BayBanks announced their agreement, Shawmut Bank agreed to a similar resolution plan, facilitated by the MBA corporations and council. Fleet's earlier plan was characterized by community activists as "totally inadequate . . . purely political and it flies in the face of justice and fair play."[53] In response to these comments and upon further investigation, Fleet also settled with the attorney general two months later.

Continuing National Attention
In May 1992, the nation focused on urban poverty as South Central Los Angeles erupted in riots after the Rodney King verdict was an-nounced. Despite a videotape depicting several white police officers severely beating Rodney King, a black male motorist whom they had stopped, the officers were found not guilty of criminal wrongdoing. The verdict fueled a sense of injustice. After the riots, the federal government began to talk more seriously about improving urban conditions. And racial discrimination became an even more prominent topic of discussion.

At the same time, the Office of the Comptroller of the Currency began an investigation of 266 banks, all of which had shown a disparity in their lending patterns, according to the HMDA data. Bankers and industry experts hoped that the result would not be further regulations. Banks, it was felt, cannot bail out the nation's inner cities. In a *New York Times* editorial, Lawrence White, finance professor at New York University, argued that enough was enough in terms of regulations,

> The Community Reinvestment Act is at best obsolete . . . [I]n today's competitive environment, banks need no assistance in discovering good customers. If serving the local community is profitable, the law is unnecessary. If it is not profitable, a bank must earn extra profits from other activities to subsidize those losses. But banks and nonbank rivals have competed so fiercely in other financial services that extra profits are scarce—leaving banks with a choice of shirking their community reinvestment requirements or suffering losses. . . . If supplying unprofitable financial services to local companies and households serves a public purpose, that case should be made explicitly, and *public* resources should support those services.[54]

These concerns were raised at a time when banking regulators were described as "schizophrenic" because "[t]he Bush Administration, fretting that tight-fisted bankers are hobbling economic recovery, wants more aggressive lending. Congress, worried that another savings and loan mess is about to land on it, has ordered tighter regulation to cut risk."[55]

When Racial Disparity Persisted

Pollard was concerned about the regulatory issues, but for the moment he had to focus specifically on Boston. The Federal Reserve Bank of Boston had just completed the "end all-be all" study of mortgage lending patterns. The researchers at the Fed had worked with the bankers to understand the practical criteria for evaluating a loan and they had complete access to loan files. The methodology was thorough. Because of their cooperation in the study, it would be hard for the banks to ignore the results.

Richard Syron, president of the Fed had called to tell Pollard that even with all this information, evidence of racial disparity remained. The results reflected aggregate patterns; individual bank performance was not studied. But there was no reason to think that BayBank would be an exception. What held in the aggregate probably held for BayBank Boston. The question was: What, if anything, should he do about it?

NOTES

1. Unless otherwise noted, facts and figures from this section were drawn from Professor Walter J. Salmon's "Baystate Corporation" cases (HBS cases (A) No. 579–117, (B) No. 579–118, and (C) No. 579–119).
2. BayBanks, Inc. Annual Report, April 1990, p. 6.
3. Ibid., p. 7.
4. Jon C. Teaford, *The Rough Road to Renaissance: Urban Revitalization in America, 1940–1985* (Baltimore, Maryland: The Johns Hopkins University Press, 1990), p. 168.
5. Katharine L. Bradbury, Karl E. Case, and Constance R. Dunham, "Geographic Patterns of Mortgage Lending in Boston, 1982–1987," *New England Economic Review* (September/October 1989), p. 3.
6. See *The Death of an American Jewish Community* (The Free Press, 1990), for details about B-BURG.
7. Ibid., p. 332.

8. Ibid., p. 175.
9. Ibid.
10. Congressional Record S. 406, January 24, 1977, p. 1.
11. Ibid., p. 20.
12. Ibid., p. 315.
13. Ibid., p. 324.
14. Teresa M. Hanafin, "Lending law is faulted as largely ineffective," *The Boston Globe,* January 11, 1989, p. 13.
15. James T. Campen, "The Struggle for Community Investment in Boston, 1989–1991," in Gregory D. Squires (ed.), *From Redlining to Reinvestment: Community Responses to Urban Disinvestment* (Philadelphia: Temple University Press, 1992), p. 38.
16. Steven Marantz, "Inequities Are Cited in Hub Mortgages," *The Boston Globe,* January 11, 1989, p. 1.
17. Ibid.
18. James T. Campen, "The Struggle for Community Investment in Boston," in Gregory D. Squires (ed.), *From Redlining to Reinvestment: Community Responses to Urban Disinvestment* (Philadelphia: Temple University Press, 1992), p. 41.
19. Peter G. Gosselin, "Boston Fed Chief Promises Further Study," *The Boston Globe,* January 11, 1989, p. 13.
20. Steven Marantz and Teresa Hanafin, "Report of Lending Bias Draws Mix of Reactions," *The Boston Globe,* January 12, 1989, p. 1.
21. The author would like to thank Ed Shea for his time and counsel in preparing this case. Special thanks also goes to the staff of the MBA for sharing information on this subject.
22. "The Race for Money," a newspaper series printed in *The Detroit Free Press,* July 24–27, 1988.
23. The series, "The Color of Money," was written by Bill Dedman of *The Atlanta Journal & Constitution,* May 1 through November 3, 1988.
24. Bill Barnhart, "Fed Hits Continental's Civic Investment," *The Chicago Tribune,* February 16, 1989, Sec. 3, p. 1.
25. Joint Statement of the Federal Financial Supervisory Agencies Regarding the Community Reinvestment Act, March 21, 1989.
26. Dudley Street Neighborhood Initiative, *A Neighborhood Building Its Future,* 1991.

27. Steven Marantz, "Bank of N.E. Official Urges More Community Lending," *The Boston Globe,* June 23, 1989, p. 21.
28. James T. Campen, "The Struggle for Community Investment in Boston," in Gregory D. Squires, (ed.), *From Redlining to Reinvestment: Community Responses to Urban Disinvestment* (Philadelphia: Temple University Press, 1992), p. 48.
29. Steve Marantz, "Banks Eye Kennedy-amended Bailout Bill," *The Boston Globe,* August 2, 1989, p. 25.
30. Roxbury Leaders Ask $2.1-B in'Bias Loan,'" *The Milford Daily News,* August 25, 1989, p. 20.
31. Mary Anne Kane, *Channel 7 WNEV TV,* August 24, 1989, transcript published by New England Newswatch (Framingham, Mass.).
32. Katherine L. Bradbury, Karl E. Case, and Constance R. Dunham, "Geographic Patterns of Mortgage Lending in Boston, 1982–1987," *New England Economic Review* (September/October 1989): 21.
33. Ibid., p. 26.
34. Allan R. Gold, "Racial Pattern Is Found in Boston Mortgages," *The New York Times,* September 1, 1989, p. A20.
35. Dan Wasserman, *The Boston Globe,* September 5, 1989, p. 14. Copyright, 1989, Boston Globe. Distributed by the Los Angeles Times Syndicate. Reprinted with permission.
36. Media Advisory, "Massachusetts Bankers Association Testifies on Community Reinvestment Issues," September 29, 1989.
37. Steve Marantz, "No Agreement on Neighborhood Lending," *The Boston Globe,* December 15, 1989, p. 80.
38. Reprinted with permission from *The Boston Herald,* December 26, 1989.
30. Steve Marantz, "AFTERMATH OF THE BRA'S MORTGAGE LENDING REPORT: Hub Bankers Postpone Unveiling of $1 Billion Reinvestment Plan," *The Boston Globe,* December 21, 1989, p. 41.
40. "The Timing Was Terrible," *The Boston Herald,* December 22, 1989, p. 34.

41. Peggy Hernandez, "Minority Leaders in City Demand an Apology," *The Boston Globe,* January 5, 1990, p. 21.
42. Steve Marantz, "$400m Investment Plan for Hub," *The Boston Globe,* January 11, 1990, p. 51.
43. Ibid.
44. Steve Marantz, "Banks' $1 Billion Reinvestment Plan Called National Model," *The Boston Globe,* January 15, 1990, p. 22.
45. Statement issued by Robert K. Sheridan, President of the Massachusetts Bankers Association, August 1990.
46. Peter Canellos and Gary Chafetz, "Mortgage Companies Got Credit from Fleet," *The Boston Globe,* May 8, 1991, p. 18.
47. Doug Bailey, "Ad Campaign Responds to Critics," *The Boston Globe,* June 18, 1991, p. 1.
48. The Boston Fed defined nonacquisition mortgages as "second mortgage loans, refinancings of first mortgages, and first mortgages on properties with no existing mortgage." (Alicia Munnell and Lynn Browne, "Second Mortgages in Suffolk County: 1987–1990," The Federal Reserve Bank of Boston, August 14, 1991, p. 1.)
49. Alicia Munnell and Lynn Browne, "Second Mortgages in Suffolk County: 1987–1990," The Federal Reserve Bank of Boston, August 14, 1991, pp. 10–11.
50. John R. Wilke, "Back Door Loans: Some Banks' Money Flows Into Poor Areas—And Causes Anguish," *The Wall Street Journal,* October 21, 1991, p. A1.
51. Ibid.
52. Mitchell Zuckoff, "Shawmut Is Said to Settle Over Loan Scams," *The Boston Globe,* February 22, 1992, p. 1.
53. Ibid.
54. Lawrence J. White, "Don't Handcuff the Healthy Banks," *The New York Times,* May 17, 1992, p. F13.
55. Mike McNamee and Tim Smart, "The Head-Spinning Split Over Banking," *Business Week,* June 8, 1992, p. 43.

G. HEILEMAN BREWING COMPANY (A): POWER FAILURE AT POWERMASTER

In early June 1991, the G. Heileman Brewing Company announced plans to introduce Colt 45 PowerMaster, a higher alcohol version of its number-two malt brand Colt 45. The brewer, which had received initial approval for its product's label from the Bureau of Alcohol, Tobacco, and Firearms (BATF), planned to launch PowerMaster in mid-July with a radio and billboard campaign from Lockhart and Pettus, a black-owned advertising agency in New York City. The slogan for the beer, which Heileman planned to market on the basis of superior taste, would be "Bold Not Harsh." Point-of-sale material would feature the brand name with a bold horse image surrounded by lightning. Colt 45 PowerMaster would retail for the same price as the lower-alcohol Colt 45 brand.

On June 21, 1991, however, Heileman received a letter from BATF which revoked its approval and which requested that the brewer remove the word "power" from the product's label. BATF said that it had made a mistake in approving the label in the first place and claimed that it now believed Heileman was violating a federal law—dating back to the 1930s—which forbade brewers from stating, or even implying, the alcohol content of their product in advertisements or on the label. The law was passed to discourage competition on the basis of alcohol content. "Power," the agency now realized, could be viewed as an implied reference to the malt product's higher alcohol content.

The United States Brewing Industry in 1990

Americans consumed 193.2 million barrels[1] of beer in 1990, or 23.4 gallons per capita for all Americans, regardless of age. That was seventeen times the amount of spirits or "hard" alcohol consumed, but only about one-half the per capita consumption of soft drinks.[2] Although there were over 200 registered breweries and microbreweries in the United States in 1990, the market share of three companies—Anheuser-Busch, Miller, and Coors—represented over 75 percent of the total sales volume. The market share of the top five brewers, including Stroh and Heileman, represented over 90 percent of total sales volume.[3] See Exhibit 1 for a historical summary of industry activity.

The industry was subdivided into numerous segments, including Premium, Light, Popular, Superpremium, Imported, Malt Liquor, Dry, Ale, and Non-Alcoholic. The Premium beers, which included such brands as Budweiser, Miller High Life, and Coors, led the category with 38 percent market share. However, Premium beer's share of market had been declining for nearly a decade. Fierce price wars within the industry had lured many premium brand drinkers to both new brands and new brewers, particularly in the light and dry segments.[4]

The Light segment captured 31 percent market share and was considered by many experts to be the industry's most viable growth segment.

This case was prepared by Wendy S. Schille, under the supervision of Stephen A. Greyser.

Copyright © 1991 by the President and Fellows of Harvard College.

Harvard Business School case 592-017 (Rev. December 11, 1991).

1. A barrel is the equivalent of 31 gallons of beer.
2. *Beverage Industry,* "Per Caps: Some Changes Brewing?" February 1991, p. 21.
3. *Modern Brewery Age,* "1990: The Year in Review," p. 8.
4. *The Price Book,* "The Beer Industry," by John J. Norton, July 1991, p. 3.

EXHIBIT 1 Selected Information on Production by Brewer and by Brand (millions of barrels)

	1981	SOM %	1982	SOM %	1983	SOM %	1984	SOM %	1985	SOM %	1986	SOM %	1987	SOM %	1988	SOM %	1989	SOM %	1990E	SOM %
ANHEUSER-BUSCH																				
Budweiser	39.1	21.5	40.6	22.2	42.7	23.2	44.4	24.3	45.4	24.8	48.0	25.6	49.4	26.4	50.6	27.0	50.5	26.9	49.2	25.7
Bud Light	—		3.3	1.8	3.7	2.0	4.0	2.2	5.7	3.1	6.8	3.6	8.2	4.4	9.5	5.1	10.5	5.6	11.5	6.0
Busch	3.1	1.7	3.4	1.9	3.4	1.8	4.4	2.4	6.0	3.3	7.3	3.9	8.2	4.4	8.9	4.7	9.2	4.9	9.5	5.0
Michelob	7.7	4.2	7.4	4.1	7.0	3.8	6.7	3.7	6.0	3.3	5.5	2.9	5.2	2.7	4.7	2.5	4.0	2.1	3.5	1.8
A-B Natural Light	1.9	1.1	1.5	0.8	1.0	0.6	1.2	0.6	1.2	0.7	1.6	0.9	1.9	1.0	2.0	1.1	2.6	1.4	3.3	1.7
Bud Dry	—		—		—		—		—		—		—		—		—		3.0	1.6
Michelob Light	2.7	1.5	2.9	1.6	2.7	1.5	2.8	1.5	2.8	1.5	2.6	1.4	2.7	1.4	2.5	1.3	2.1	1.1	2.0	1.0
Busch Light	—		—		—		—		—		—		—		—		1.5	0.8	1.9	1.0
Michelob Dry	—		—		—		—		—		—		—		—		—		1.2	0.6
Mich. Classic Dark	—		—		—		—		—		—		—		—		—		—	
LA	—		—		—		0.4	0.2	0.4	0.2	0.1	0.1	0.1	0.1	0.1	0.1	0.1	0.1	0.1	0.1
Others	—		—		—		0.1	0.1	0.2	0.1	0.2	0.2	0.2	0.2	0.1	0.1	0.1	0.1	0.3	0.2
TOTAL	54.5	30.0	59.1	32.4	60.5	32.9	64.0	35.0	68.0	37.1	72.3	38.6	76.1	40.6	78.5	41.9	80.7	43.0	85.5	44.6
MILLER																				
Miller Lite	16.3	9.0	17.2	9.4	17.9	9.8	18.0	9.9	18.5	10.1	18.9	10.1	19.3	10.3	19.5	10.4	20.0	10.6	20.3	10.6
Milwaukee's Best	—		—		—		1.9	1.0	3.0	1.6	4.3	2.3	5.8	3.1	6.6	3.5	7.3	3.9	8.0	4.2
Miller High Life	22.3	12.3	20.4	11.2	17.0	9.2	14.3	7.8	12.2	6.6	10.8	5.8	8.9	4.8	8.1	4.3	7.6	4.0	6.8	3.5
Genuine Draft	—		—		—		—		—		1.0	0.5	2.3	1.3	3.7	2.0	4.6	2.4	5.7	3.0
Meister Brau	—		—		0.6	0.3	1.9	1.0	2.0	1.1	2.0	1.1	1.2	0.6	1.1	0.6	1.1	0.6	1.1	0.6
Lowenbrau	1.5	0.8	1.4	0.8	1.5	0.8	1.2	0.7	1.2	0.7	1.3	0.7	1.2	0.7	1.0	0.5	0.9	0.5	0.9	0.5
Others	0.2	0.1	0.3	0.1	0.5	0.3	0.2	0.1	0.2	0.1	0.2	0.1	0.2	0.1	0.3	0.2	0.4	0.2	0.7	0.3
TOTAL	40.3	22.2	39.3	21.5	37.5	20.4	37.5	20.5	37.1	20.2	38.5	20.5	38.9	20.8	40.3	21.5	41.9	22.2	43.5	22.7
COORS																				
Coors Light	3.1	1.7	3.2	1.7	3.8	2.1	4.7	2.6	6.0	3.2	7.1	3.8	7.9	4.2	8.7	4.7	10.5	5.6	11.7	6.1
Coors	10.1	5.5	8.5	4.7	9.7	5.3	8.4	4.6	8.6	4.7	8.0	4.2	7.3	3.9	6.5	3.5	5.1	2.7	4.2	2.2
Keystone	—		—		—		—		—		—		—		—		1.1	0.6	2.2	1.1
Coors Extra Gold	—		—		—		—		—		—		0.3	0.2	1.0	0.5	0.9	0.5	0.7	0.4
Others	0.1	0.1	0.2	0.1	0.2	0.1	—		0.1	0.1	0.1	0.1	0.2	0.1	0.1	0.1	0.1	0.1	0.2	0.1
TOTAL	13.3	7.3	11.9	6.5	13.7	7.5	13.1	7.2	14.7	8.0	15.2	8.1	15.7	8.4	16.5	8.8	17.7	9.5	19.0	9.9
STROH																				
Old Milwaukee	5.1	2.8	6.0	3.3	7.6	4.1	7.1	3.9	7.5	4.1	7.5	4.0	7.2	3.8	7.2	3.8	7.0	3.7	6.6	3.4
Schaefer	3.0	1.7	2.5	1.4	3.0	1.6	4.0	2.2	4.1	2.2	4.3	2.3	4.1	2.2	3.9	2.1	3.5	1.9	3.0	1.6
Schlitz Malt	2.5	1.4	2.6	1.4	2.6	1.4	2.1	1.1	2.0	1.1	2.0	1.1	2.0	1.0	1.9	1.0	1.8	1.0	1.9	1.0

Beer market share data (SOM = Share of Market). Shipments in millions of barrels alternating with SOM percentages. Column headers (years) are not shown on this portion of the table.

Brand																				
Old Milwaukee Light	—	—	0.8	0.4	1.0	0.6	1.5	0.8	1.8	1.0	1.9	1.0	1.9	1.0	1.9	1.0	2.0	1.1	1.8	0.9
Stroh	5.5	3.0	5.4	3.0	5.5	3.0	5.3	2.9	4.9	2.7	4.0	2.1	3.6	1.9	3.1	1.7	2.0	1.1	1.5	0.8
Schlitz	5.7	3.1	4.1	2.2	3.2	1.8	1.7	0.9	1.4	0.7	1.0	0.5	0.8	0.4	0.7	0.3	0.7	0.4	0.7	0.4
Stroh Light	0.6	0.3	0.6	0.3	0.7	0.4	0.8	0.4	0.7	0.4	0.7	0.4	0.7	0.4	0.8	0.4	0.7	0.4	0.5	0.3
Piels	—	—	—	—	—	—	—	—	—	—	0.5	0.3	0.5	0.3	0.5	0.2	0.4	0.2	0.3	0.2
Goebel	—	—	0.3	0.2	0.3	0.2	0.6	0.3	0.4	0.2	0.4	0.2	0.3	0.2	0.2	0.1	0.1	0.1	0.1	—
White Mountain	—	0.2	—	—	—	—	0.1	0.1	—	—	—	—	0.3	0.2	—	—	0.2	0.1	—	—
Schlitz Light	0.3	—	0.4	0.2	0.3	0.2	—	0.1	0.1	—	0.4	—	—	—	—	—	—	—	—	—
Signature	—	0.3	—	—	—	—	—	—	0.1	—	—	—	—	—	—	—	—	—	—	—
Erlanger	0.5	0.1	0.1	0.1	—	—	—	—	—	0.1	0.1	—	—	—	—	0.1	—	—	—	—
Others	0.2	0.1	0.1	0.1	0.1	0.1	0.7	0.4	0.5	0.3	—	—	0.2	0.1	—	—	—	—	—	—
TOTAL	23.4	12.9	22.9	12.6	24.3	13.2	23.9	13.1	23.4	12.8	22.8	12.2	21.6	11.5	20.5	10.9	18.4	9.9	16.4	8.6
HEILEMAN	%		%		%		%		%		%		%		%		%		%	
Old Style, Light & Export	5.4	3.0	5.6	3.1	5.8	3.1	5.0	2.7	4.9	2.7	5.0	2.7	4.9	2.6	4.6	2.5	4.2	2.2	4.1	2.2
Colt 45	1.2	0.7	1.5	0.8	1.6	0.9	1.6	0.9	1.8	1.0	2.0	1.1	2.0	1.0	2.0	1.1	1.8	1.0	1.8	0.9
Joseph Schmidt & Rainier	1.7	0.9	2.0	1.1	2.3	1.3	2.4	1.3	2.2	1.2	2.0	1.1	1.8	1.0	1.8	1.0	1.8	1.0	1.7	1.0
Carling Black Label & Light	1.0	0.5	1.6	0.9	1.9	1.0	2.1	1.2	2.2	1.2	2.3	1.2	2.3	1.2	2.1	1.1	1.8	1.0	1.6	0.8
Carl Schmidt	—	—	—	—	—	—	—	—	—	—	—	—	—	—	1.0	0.5	0.7	0.4	0.6	0.3
Mickeys	0.4	0.2	0.5	0.3	0.5	0.3	0.4	0.2	0.4	0.2	0.4	0.2	0.3	0.2	0.4	0.2	0.5	0.3	0.5	0.3
Blatz & Light	1.5	0.8	1.7	0.9	1.8	1.0	1.6	0.9	1.3	0.7	1.2	0.6	1.0	0.5	0.8	0.4	0.6	0.3	0.4	0.2
Henry Weinhard	—	—	—	—	0.6	0.3	0.8	0.4	0.7	0.4	0.6	0.3	0.5	0.3	0.3	0.2	0.4	0.2	0.4	0.2
Lone Star	—	—	—	—	—	—	—	—	0.4	0.2	0.4	0.2	0.4	0.2	0.4	0.2	0.4	0.2	0.3	0.2
Red, White & Blue	—	—	—	—	0.9	0.5	1.1	0.6	0.9	0.5	0.8	0.4	0.7	0.4	0.5	0.2	0.3	0.2	0.2	0.1
Others	2.8	1.6	1.6	0.8	2.2	1.1	1.8	1.0	1.8	1.0	1.4	0.8	1.1	0.6	0.7	0.4	0.5	0.3	0.4	0.2
TOTAL	14.0	7.7	14.5	7.9	17.5	9.5	16.8	9.2	16.2	8.9	16.1	8.6	15.0	8.0	14.6	7.8	13.0	7.1	12.0	6.3
PABST	%		%		%		%		%		%		%		%		%		%	
Pabst	NA	NA	NA	NA	NA	NA	NA	NA	NA	NA	NA	NA	NA	NA	NA	NA	3.1	1.6	3.0	1.6
Hamms & Light	NA	NA	NA	NA	NA	NA	NA	NA	NA	NA	NA	NA	NA	NA	NA	NA	1.1	0.6	1.4	0.7
Olde English	NA	NA	NA	NA	NA	NA	NA	NA	NA	NA	NA	NA	NA	NA	NA	NA	0.9	0.5	1.2	0.6
Olympia	NA	NA	NA	NA	NA	NA	NA	NA	NA	NA	NA	NA	NA	NA	NA	NA	0.7	0.4	0.8	0.4
Others	NA	NA	NA	NA	NA	NA	NA	NA	NA	NA	NA	NA	NA	NA	NA	NA	0.8	0.4	0.2	0.1
TOTAL	19.2	10.6	17.5	9.6	12.8	7.0	11.8	6.5	9.1	5.0	6.7	3.6	6.5	3.5	6.1	3.2	6.6	3.5	6.6	3.4

SOM = Share of market.
NA = Not available.

Source: *Beverage Industry*, "Beer '91 Exclusive," by Gary A. Hemphill, January 1991, p. 24.

Some 25 new domestic light beers had been introduced between 1980 and 1989, which meant that by 1990 virtually every successful domestic brand carried a "light" extension. In fact, of the four top-selling brands in 1990, three—Miller Lite, Coors Light, and Bud Light—were light beers.[5]

Popular brews, including such brands as Busch, Milwaukee's Best, and Old Milwaukee garnered 18 percent market share. Much of the success of the popular-priced segment depended on the current economic condition. Coors Brewing Company took advantage of the depressed state of the American economy by introducing two new products into the popular segment in 1989. Keystone and Keystone Light quickly captured 15 percent of the segment to the detriment of some lesser-known Popular brands from Stroh and Heileman.[6]

Superpremium beers (which included brands such as Michelob and Lowenbrau, as well as microbrewery brands), Imports, and Malt Liquors each had 3 percent market share. Dry beers held 2 percent market share, and Ales and Non-Alcoholic beers held 1 percent each.

The distinction among Popular, Premium, and Superpremium beers was a matter of pricing. Popular beers generally retailed for about a dollar less per six-pack than Premium beers, while Superpremium beers sold for up to four dollars more per six-pack than Premium brews.

The distinction between Dry beers and Ales was a matter of flavor. In a Dry beer, the sweetening sugars and bittering hops were exactly balanced in brewing so that the resultant product offered a clean, smooth flavor that lacked any aftertaste. Dry beers were meant to appeal to Americans' "soda pop" taste and were also expected to draw a strong female following, either from the nonuser segment or away from Light beers. Ales, brewed with a special yeast, featured more body and a stronger flavor.

Light beers featured about one-third less alcohol and fewer calories than did regular beer, which had an alcohol content of 3.5 percent. Malt Liquors had an alcohol content of 4 percent or higher. (By way of comparison, wine typically had an alcohol content of 12 percent, while a "hard liquor" such as vodka had between 40 percent and 60 percent alcohol by weight.) See Exhibit 2 for a summary of changes in segment activity between 1980 and 1990.

Although industry growth had been flat for a decade, beer sales in 1990 increased 1.9 percent over 1989 sales, driven mainly by new product introductions in the dry, bottled draft, and non-alcoholic segments. Bottled draft was marketed as a nonpasteurized, and hence "fresher," version of standard bottled beer.

Until the introduction of Miller Genuine Draft in 1986, the term "draft" was generally reserved for on-premise sales of beer dispensed directly from a keg. In 1990, Anheuser-Busch introduced Bud Dry Draft and Busch Light Draft, further line extensions under the Budweiser and Busch brand names, respectively.

In the nonalcoholic beer segment, Miller and Anheuser-Busch both entered in a big way during 1990. Miller put $14 million into media to support its brand Sharps, which quickly attained market leadership in the category, knocking out Kingsbury, Heileman's thirty-year-old brand which had dominated this previously dormant category. Anheuser-Busch spent $7 million on its brand O'Doul's, which also overtook Kingsbury by year-end. Case sales in the nonalcoholic segment nearly doubled from 9.6 million cases in 1989 to 18.1 million cases in 1990.

Anheuser-Busch spent $70 million in advertising and promotion in 1990 for its Bud Dry brand, which was rolled out nationally in that year and quickly became the number one beer in the dry segment. Anheuser-Busch's Michelob Dry, introduced in 1989, held the number two position in the category.

The Malt Liquor Category

Although malt liquors made up only three percent of the beer category's volume in 1990—six

---

5. *The Price Book,* July 1991, p. 3.
6. Ibid.

EXHIBIT 2   Market Breakdown by Product Segment: 1980 and 1990

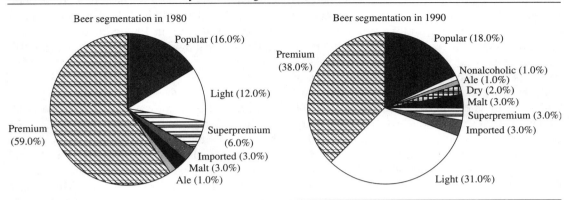

Source: *The New York Times,* July 21, 1991, p. D4.

million barrels out of a total of 193 million barrels—the segment represented over $500 million in retail sales. Some sources estimated the segment's dollar size as closer to $1 billion.

The segment was dominated by Stroh Brewing Company's Schlitz Malt Liquor and Heileman's Colt 45, which collectively accounted for over 60 percent of malt liquor sales volume. While Anheuser-Busch and Miller Brewing each had malt liquor entries, branded King Cobra and Magnum, respectively, neither brewer controlled more than a few share points in the category. These products all contained 4.5 percent alcohol. The demographics of the malt liquor segment were overwhelmingly concentrated among black, inner-city, and lower-income consumers. Although blacks represented approximately 11 percent of the United States adult population in 1989, this group accounted for 66 percent of malt liquor consumption. By contrast, blacks also accounted for nearly one-third of low-alcohol beer drinkers. Black consumers were proportionately represented among beer drinkers in other categories, including regular (premium, superpremium, and popular) beers, ales, and imported brews.

One-third of consumers in the malt liquor category had household incomes of less than $15,000 per year, while 75 percent had house-

hold incomes of less than $35,000. Of the total U.S. population in 1989, 56 percent had household incomes of less than $35,000 per year, while 20 percent had household incomes of less than $15, 000.[7]

Advertisements for the products typically featured virile black males and symbols of sexual prowess. Schlitz advertisements, for example, depicted a bull crashing through a brick wall, while Heileman had formerly employed actor Billy Dee Williams to pitch its Colt 45 amid snarling pit bulls, rearing stallions, and gyrating go-go dancers.[8]

In the past two years, a subsegment within malt liquor had begun to grow rapidly. Companies such as Pabst Brewing and Stroh's had introduced so-called "up-strength" products, malts which contained as much as 5.5 percent alcohol. In 1990, the McKenzie River Corporation introduced a new brand called St. Ides which boasted a 5.9 percent content, making it the most potent malt on the market.

While Colt and Schlitz had experienced flat

---

7. Mediamark Research Inc, "Beer, Wine and Liquor Report," Spring 1989.

8. *The Wall Street Journal,* "Malt Advertising That Touts Firepower Comes Under Attack by U.S. Officials," by Alix M. Freedman, July 1, 1991, p. B4.

or declining sales for the past decade, the new entrants saw growth of 25 percent to 30 percent per year. Pabst's Olde English 800, the number three malt liquor brand, and the number one up-strength brand, increased sales volume by a third in 1990 to 1.2 million barrels. Schlitz's sales were 1.9 million barrels in 1990, while sales of Colt 45 reached 1.8 million barrels.[9] Billboard and point-of-sale material for Olde English 800 proclaimed "It's the Power," while Stroh's entry, Schlitz Red Bull, which had been introduced in only four states, featured the slogan "The Real Power." Point-of-sale material for St. Ides told consumers "It will blow you away." St. Ides also intermittently placed stickers on its malt containers which blazoned "No. 1 Strongest Malt."

Olde English point-of-purchase posters additionally made reference to the term "eight ball," in the phrase "8 Ball Anyone?" The accompanying illustration depicted two particularly buxom women in a pool hall. However, according to both law enforcement officials and inner city consumers, "8 Ball" was hardly meant to conjure up images of billiards. The term was street slang, law enforcement officials said, for buying an eighth of an ounce of drugs, typically crack or cocaine. "What Olde English is trying to put over," said one denizen of Harlem quoted in *The Wall Street Journal,* "is that [Olde English] is a cheaper high than drugs."[10]

According to Heileman's director of marketing Hugh Nelson: "We want[ed] to participate in the growth of the up-strength malt liquor category, which is where the consumer is going . . . We have done extensive research in the category to find out what the consumer wants to drink."[11]

Heileman planned to use billboard advertisements featuring a rough- and rugged-looking

black model holding a bottle of Colt 45 PowerMaster, with the words "Bold Not Harsh" emblazoned across the board. Heileman had introduced Colt 45 Dry in 1990 with advertisements that featured a lightning bolt and the slogan "It's got more."

The G. Heileman Brewing Company

In 1990 G. Heileman was one of America's oldest and most venerable brewers, with a 132-year history of brewing fine regional beers. In the mid-eighties Heileman overtook Pabst and Coors to become the number four American brewer behind Anheuser-Busch, Miller, and Stroh. However, when the company was acquired by Australian entrepreneur Alan Bond in 1987, nearly $800 million in debt was piled onto the company's balance sheet, reducing Heileman's net worth from $1 billion to roughly $300 million. The company, which had slipped to the number five position among American brewers by 1990, had been struggling to keep its head above water ever since.[12] Heileman's brands included popular regional brews such as Old Style, Colt 45, Rainier, Carling Black Label, Henry Weinhard, and Red, White & Blue. In 1990, Heileman introduced an unprecedented five dry beer line extensions for brands including Old Style, Rainier, and Colt 45.

On January 24, 1991, Heileman, unable to meet its payment schedule, filed for protection from its creditors under Chapter 11 of the Federal Bankruptcy Code. While Heileman executives remained upbeat, predicting they would emerge from bankruptcy within six to eight months, beer industry analysts were not nearly as optimistic. Analysts cited Anheuser-Busch and Miller's huge advertising and promotion muscle vis-à-vis Heileman and the other brewing companies, as well as Heileman's lack of any national premium or light segment brands. Heile-

9. *Beverage Industry,* "Brewers fight back, boost sales 1.9%," by Gary A. Hemphill, January 1991, p. 25.

10. *The Wall Street Journal,* July 1, 1991, p. B1.

11. *The Wall Street Journal,* "New Heileman Malt Attracts Fierce Industry and Social Criticism," by Alix M. Freedman, June 17, 1991, p. B1.

12. *The New York Times,* "Heileman in Chapter 11, but Upbeat," by Eric N. Berg, January 25, 1991, p. D1.

man dropped from 7.1 percent of the category in 1989 to 6.3 percent in 1990. The company had been steadily losing share since 1985.

PowerMaster and Community Reaction

Although PowerMaster was touted in its pre-launch publicity material as "an upscale product which will be marketed on the basis of its taste," news of its imminent introduction stirred up a storm of controversy among minority advocates and alcohol foes. Clergymen in New York City and Chicago threatened to whitewash over billboard advertisements if the product was launched as scheduled.

Protesters assailed the company for targeting its products at lower-income, inner-city blacks. They claimed that this population group suffered disproportionately from alcohol-related disease.

The Reverend Calvin Butts of the Abyssinian Baptist Church in New York's Harlem, quoted in *The Wall Street Journal,* stated: "This is obviously a company that has no sense of moral or social responsibility." He vowed to continue his campaign, begun the previous year, to whitewash liquor and tobacco billboards. According to George Hacker, director of the National Coalition to Prevent Impaired Driving, quoted in the same article, "The real irony of marketing PowerMaster to inner-city blacks is that this population is among the most lacking in power in this society."[13]

By the third week in June, twenty-one consumer and health groups had publicly called on Heileman to halt the marketing of PowerMaster and for BATF to limit the alcohol content of malt liquor. United States Surgeon General Antonia Novello called on Heileman as well, asking the company to change the name of PowerMaster and scrap its marketing campaign.[14]

Even one of the bigger brewers got into the act. In a June 20 letter, Anheuser-Busch Inc. unit president Patrick Stokes asked Heileman chairman Thomas J. Rattigan to reconsider the strategy for PowerMaster, which, according to Stokes, "appears to be intentionally marketed to emphasize high alcohol content."[15] For several years, Anheuser-Busch had been running a series of advertisements entitled "Know When To Say When," which advocated safe driving and moderation in alcohol consumption.

Heileman responded by citing research which it claimed showed that consumers would opt for PowerMaster not on the basis of its alcoholic content but because of its flavor. Heileman believed it had been and remained a responsible citizen in the community.[16]

After clergymen George Clements and Mike Pfleger of the Holy Angels Church in Chicago were arrested for trespassing during a protest demonstration in Heileman's lobby, ABC-TV's Nightline decided to devote a segment to the PowerMaster controversy. Invited guests included Heileman president Thomas Rattigan, Reverend Clements, United States Surgeon General Antonia Novello, and the president of the Association of National Advertisers, DeWitt F. Helm, Jr. (The ANA was the national trade association of company advertising management.) It could be expected that Clements would defend his right to protect the safety and welfare of his neighborhood which he felt was threatened by the introduction of such a potent malt liquor product. However, it was unclear what the tenor of the rest of the conversation would be, or indeed, whether Rattigan would even accept the invitation to appear.

Precedents in Other Product Categories

Heileman was not the first manufacturer to attract the ire of minority and health activists. Two

13. *The Wall Street Journal,* June 17, 1991, p. B1.
14. *Advertising Age,* "Malt Liquor 'Power' Failure," by Steven W. Colford and Ira Teinowitz, July 1, 1991, p. 29.

15. *The Wall Street Journal,* July 1, 1991, p. B4.
16. *The Wall Street Journal,* June 17, 1991, p. B4.

recent occurrences demonstrated how powerful these groups could be when provoked.

R. J. Reynolds: A Cigarette Company Gets Burned

In December 1989, in a first for a cigarette maker, R. J. Reynolds, a division of RJR Nabisco Corporation, announced that it would begin test marketing, in Philadelphia, a cigarette called Uptown that was expected to appeal "most strongly" to black consumers.[17] The cigarette would feature a lower menthol content which research had shown black consumers favor. The marketing plan included advertising meant to associate the cigarette with glamorous, high fashion nightlife. The advertising copy would read: "Uptown. The place. The taste."[18]

Reynolds, like most cigarette companies, was faced with an increasingly shrinking customer base. It was generally acknowledged within the industry that the business had become a matter principally of stealing customers from other brands rather than attracting new smokers. As a result, new cigarette brands were targeted at increasingly narrow market segments. In 1990, for example, there were over 350 brands and styles of cigarettes on the market.[19]

In Philadelphia, thirty community organizations, including religious and minority groups, quickly organized to protest the cigarette's introduction. The planned introduction caused controversy in the black publishing community over whether to accept Uptown advertisements in black-run newspapers and magazines. Both types of publications depend heavily on advertising revenue from cigarette companies.[20]

By mid-January Secretary of Health and Human Services, Dr. Louis W. Sullivan had joined the opposition to Uptown. In a January 18th speech at the University of Pennsylvania, located in Philadelphia, Sullivan denounced R. J. Reynold's "slick and sinister advertising." He also expressed outrage at the company for "deliberately and cynically test-marketing a cigarette aimed at blacks," and for "promoting a culture of cancer."[21]

Aftermath. Faced with such intense opposition, Reynolds announced on January 19 that they would cancel plans to launch Uptown. The company claimed the scheduled test market could no longer be considered reliable because of the "unfair and biased attention the brand had received." There was bitterness within the company over the decision. Reynold's senior vice president of public relations, cited in *The New York Times,* said: "There's a feeling here that we were cheated on this one . . . Maybe, in retrospect, we would have been better off not saying we were marketing to blacks. But those were the smokers we were going after, so why shouldn't we be honest about it?"[22]

Six months later, in June 1990, Reynolds introduced two new varieties of its leading Salem brand, Salem Gold and Salem Box. Although neither brand was conspicuously targeted to blacks, the cigarettes were similar in concept to the ill-fated Uptown brand.[23]

Canandaigua Wine Company: Trouble Uncorked

In September 1990, activist groups, including the Center for Science in the Public Interest and the National Council on Alcoholism and Drug Dependence began criticizing the Canandaigua Wine Company for marketing Cisco, a high-alcohol "fortified" wine which the activist

17. *The New York Times,* "A Cigarette Campaign under Fire," by Anthony Ramirez, January 12, 1990, p. D1.

18. *The New York Times,* "Health Chief Assails a Tobacco Producer for Aiming at Blacks," by Philip J. Hilts, January 19, 1990, p. A1.

19. *The New York Times,* January 12, 1990, p. D4.

20. *The New York Times,* January 12, 1990, p. D4.

21. *The New York Times,* January 19, 1990, p. A1.

22. *The New York Times,* "Reynolds, after Protests, Cancels Cigarette Aimed at Black Smokers," by Anthony Ramirez, January 20, 1990, p. A1.

23. *Advertising Age,* "RJR's New Smokes Look Uptown," by Judann Dagnol, June 25, 1990, p. 6.

groups claimed was deceptively packaged to re-semble a much lower-alcohol wine cooler. Forti-fied wines are also known as Dessert wines.

Cisco came in a short-necked glass bottle, with a full-wrap pastel-colored shoulder label and a twist cap similar to traditional wine cooler packaging, and was available in a variety of fruity flavors. For these reasons, protesters com-plained that it was easy for consumers, particu-larly young consumers, to confuse the 20 percent alcohol Cisco with a wine cooler which typically has 5 percent or less alcohol by volume. Critics charged that the pastel-colored label was most appealing to young (often under-aged) consum-ers. Cisco, which was often sold side-by-side with wine coolers in a store's refrigerated sec-tion, featured point-of-purchase material which proclaimed Cisco "Takes You By Surprise!" The Cisco brand was purchased by Canandaigua in 1989 from a small western winery.[24] [25] Other for-tified products were typically sold in dark bottles and were often kept either behind the counter or on the back shelves at liquor stores.[26]

Canandaigua officials countered the criticism by pointing out that Cisco had always been clearly labeled "Alcohol 20 percent By Volume." In addition, since Cisco was only sold in single bottles rather than the four-packs favored by wine coolers and could cost up to 50 percent more than a wine cooler, the company felt it was unlikely that consumers would be confused. Ac-cording to company officials, all dessert wines have the same 20 percent alcohol content. Ca-nandaigua president Richard Sands said the company had received no complaints from con-sumers claiming they had mistaken Cisco for a wine cooler.[27]

Meanwhile, the Bureau of Alcohol, Tobacco, and Firearms, which said it had received com-plaints, began a reexamination of Cisco's pack-aging. In January, Surgeon General Antonia Novello, called a press conference to express her concern that consumers, particularly teenagers, were being endangered by high-alcohol drinks which looked like mild wine coolers but were as potent as five shots of vodka. Novello claimed that youths had begun calling Cisco "liquid crack" because of its strong effect, and added that [Cisco is] an incredibly potent, potentially lethal alcoholic beverage."[28] Earlier in the month ten Washington, D.C. area teenagers suffered acute ethanol poisoning after consuming an un-disclosed amount of Cisco wine, which the youths claimed they believed to be a wine cooler. Both NBC and local media had picked up the story, which led to charges that Cisco was "poi-son" and could "kill your child."

On January 9, 1991, Southland Corporation announced its more than 3,000 company-owned 7-Eleven stores would remove Cisco from store shelves in an effort to protect customers. Al-though the corporation had not received any complaints about Cisco, a spokesperson said Southland "shares concerns of consumer groups over the marketing and packaging of the prod-uct." A letter sent to over 3,000 7-Eleven fran-chises strongly urged these stores to stop selling Cisco as well.[29]

Although Canandaigua chairman Marvin Sands claimed the real problem was underage drinking and alcohol abuse, and not Cisco, he said company officials would meet with Dr. Novello on February 4, 1991, to discuss the issues.

Aftermath. On February 5, 1991, shortly after

24. *The Wall Street Journal,* "Groups Seek to Force Ca-nandaigua to Halt Sales of High-Alcohol Wine," by Thomas R. King, September 12, 1990, p. B6.

25. *Beverage Industry,* "Canandaigua Gives Cisco New Look after Complaints," by Tracey L. Walker, March 1991, p. 1.

26. *The New York Times,* "Surgeon General Calls Potent Wine a Threat," January 10, 1991, p. D21.

27. *Beverage Industry,* March 1991, p. 1.

28. *The New York Times,* January 10, 1991, p. D21.

29. *The Wall Street Journal,* "7-Eleven Stores to Remove Their Cisco Wine Supplies," January 9, 1991, p. B3.

meeting with Surgeon General Novello, Canandaigua company officials unveiled a new bottle and label design for Cisco. Cisco's new packaging would include a dark green, long-neck bottle with a front panel label and a neck band. The label had a black background with lettering that was color-coded by flavor. The company increased the size of the lettering on the content statement ("Alcohol 20 percent By Volume") to the maximum allowed by federal regulations. In addition, the words "This Is Not a Wine Cooler" were placed in two locations on the label and the statement "This Container Serves 4 Persons And Is Best Served Over Ice," was prominently displayed. Canandaigua also asked distributors and retailers to remove the "Takes You By Surprise!" point-of-purchase posters.

The Reaction of BATF to PowerMaster

The Bureau of Alcohol, Tobacco, and Firearms approved over eighty thousand labels for beer, wine, and distilled spirit products in 1990. In some instances, products were approved on the basis of the label alone, without regard to how the product would be marketed. If it came to the agency's attention later that a particular product was being marketed in violation of federal regulations, an investigation would be launched.

In the case of PowerMaster, a BATF spokesperson cited in *Advertising Age* claimed, "We got to review the [PowerMaster] labels in isolation and did not see them in the context of a full advertising campaign and its presentation to the public . . . It was only [in campaign context] that we could see that the company was going with the alcohol strength advertising." According to the spokesperson, the targeting of black or inner-city consumers was "not our concern."[30] When asked why wine and liquor did not fall under the same regulations as brewed beverages,

another agency spokesperson said: "It's the way the world was in those days. I'm told Congress was not as concerned about wine, certainly, nor about distilled spirits, because everyone recognized their strength. But they didn't want brewers competing on the basis of alcoholic strength."[31]

In the wake of their confrontation with Heileman, BATF also put Pabst, Stroh, and McKenzie malt advertising under review.

BATF claimed that because malt products were chiefly marketed via inner-city billboards and point-of-sale posters, advertising abuses were difficult to detect. In addition, BATF could enforce sanctions against brewers only by bringing criminal action through the Justice Department, which was said not to consider such action a high priority.

Tom Pirko, an industry analyst cited in *The Wall Street Journal* added, "The [malt liquor] products are so heavily identified with the [power] claims that these products *are* the claims . . . You take away the claims and the category becomes almost generic."[32]

Aftermath

In the face of overwhelming protest from community and health activists, as well as regulatory pressure, Heileman quietly announced in early July that it was canceling plans to introduce its Colt 45 PowerMaster brand. The company, while denying any wrongdoing, said it could not afford the expense of a court fight over the product's labeling. Because of the earlier approval of PowerMaster's label, BATF agreed that Heileman distributors would be allowed to sell what PowerMaster they had in stock over the next four months. However, during that time, Heileman would not be able to advertise the product.

---

30. *Advertising Age*, "Fighting the Power: Heileman's New Malt Liquor Draws Government Ire," by Ira Teinowitz, June 24, 1991, p. 61.

31. *Chicago Tribune*, "Brewer to Drop Controversial Malt Liquor," by Janet Cawley, July 4, 1991, sec. 1, p. 3.
32. *The Wall Street Journal*, July 1, 1991, p. B4.

THE FCC AND LICENSE AUCTIONS FOR EMERGING TECHNOLOGIES

In 1994 FCC (Federal Communications Commission) Chairman Reed Hundt, a political appointee of President Clinton, believed the much-touted "information superhighway" would be "the single most important development in our economy over the next couple of decades" and no less than "the most important factor in the formation of our national character in the next century.[1]

In speeches and in the press, Hundt likened spectrum, the electromagnetic waves of energy that would carry emerging technologies and for which the FCC would be auctioning off licenses, to a natural resource equivalent in economic potential to the 100 million acres of land—10 percent of the nation's total public domain—granted to 29 railroad companies in the mid-nineteenth century. Just as those land grants shaped patterns of personal wealth and public philanthropy for over a century, Hundt expected spectrum license assignments for the two classifications of emerging technologies, Personal Communications Services (PCS) and Interactive Video and Data Services (IVDS), to shape future patterns of wealth. These technologies promised new products and services such as two-way paging devices, hand-held computers and communicators, and interactive shopping and educational services. "Just imagine," Hundt said at a 1994 Urban League convention, "if American industries had sought to include African-Americans at the emergence of other industries, America would undoubtedly be a different and better place today."[2] Hundt was determined to "create opportunities for all Americans, so that the businesses [the FCC] create[s] look more like the people we serve.[3]

At the close of the 1993 legislative year, Congress had passed the Emerging Technologies Act, a rider to the Omnibus Budget Reconciliation Act of 1993. The legislation reallocated 220 megaHertz (MHz) of spectrum, some previously set aside for government use, for new commercial uses and established auctions as a format for assigning licenses. The legislation was cited by the press as "the most sweeping legislation to affect the wireless industry in 10 years."[4] Reassigning public spectrum for private use meant that emerging technologies would have the operating space they needed to develop. It also meant that congressional representatives would seek assurances that the public good was served through commercial uses. Moving from previous methods of assigning licenses—lotteries and comparative hearings—to apparently less egalitarian auctions, created challenges for the FCC as it strived to meet its congressional mandate to provide "meaningful opportunities" for new entrants into the emerging technologies marketplace.

Signed into law by President Clinton in the spring of 1994, the legislation stated that the FCC should further "the development and rapid deployment of new technologies while promot-

---

This case was prepared by Sarah B. Gant under the supervision of Mary C. Gentile.

Copyright © 1995 by the President and Fellows of Harvard College.

Harvard Business School case 395-139 (Rev. March 21, 1995).

1. Reed E. Hundt, Speech before the American Psychological Association's Annual Convention, Los Angeles, California, August 13, 1994.

---

2. Hundt, Speech, July 26, 1994.

3. Edmund L. Andrews, "FCC to Reserve Licenses in Affirmative-Action Move," *The New York Times,* June 30, 1994.

4. William J. Franklin, "Proposed Auction Rules for PCS," *Cellular Business,* December 1993.

ing economic opportunity . . . by disseminating licenses among a wide variety of applicants, including small businesses, rural telephone companies, . . . minority groups and women ("designated entities").[5] Thus, Congress mandated that the FCC ensure the involvement of minorities and women in rapidly emerging telecommunications technologies. The specifics of how the agency was to do this were largely left up to FCC commissioners and staff, however. "Nonremedial affirmative action" or preference policies not narrowly tailored to rectify discrimination against specific parties—the crux of past FCC preference programs—had been litigated up to the Supreme Court. The FCC had prevailed at the time, but the make-up of the high court had since changed. The FCC needed to weigh how to fulfill its congressional mandate to create meaningful opportunities for designated entities without running into insurmountable constitutional challenges.

The legislation contained economic and efficiency pressures for the FCC to plumb as well. One impetus behind competitive-bid auctions was the raising of revenues for the U.S. Treasury. FCC decision makers were concerned, however, that competitive-bid auctions not simply favor existing telecommunications giants. They believed that access to capital was the foremost barrier to the success of designated entities. One congressional representative clarified a related concern in a letter to Hundt when he stated his fear "that the Commission may abandon [designated entities] out of a belief that revenue maximization and economic efficiency take precedence . . . it was not Congress' intent that the auctions yield the maximum dollar figures possible per license."[6]

The FCC also faced time constraints. Con-

gress required auctions to have begun within nine months of the enabling legislation's becoming law; they were expected to take between one and three years to complete.[7] Greater efficiency in getting licenses awarded—in contrast with the highly criticized inefficiencies of comparative hearings and lotteries—could benefit U.S. consumers (both individual end-users and service firms under contract to license-holders), further America's competitive advantage in what promised to be the international economic driver of the century, and stanch the flow of global investment capital into spectrum technologies under development in other nations. Yet, FCC staff debated whether the speed of the auction process itself would raise barriers for designated entities.

Underlying all of this were organizational politics and pressures, as the make up of the Congress, the courts, and the presidency changed. Political appointees at the FCC, including commissioners and senior policymakers, headed a federal bureaucracy which had seen mandates and leadership come and go. Political appointees and career bureaucrats, lawyers, and policymakers sometimes came into conflict as they debated trade-offs between the "best" policies and their potential to foster time-consuming and costly implementation strategies and legal challenges.

In 1994, FCC staff faced writing auction rules that would uphold the congressional mandate to promote diversity, yet withstand constitutional challenges. The Commission needed to raise money for the U.S. Treasury, but needed also to be attentive to the broader public interest. The staff could shape, to some extent, the outcome of auctions, but they did not want to award licenses to ventures that could not succeed in the marketplace. Finally, no good would be served if any part of the process delayed the delivery of services to consumers.

5. Franklin.

6. Unattributed, "FCC Clears Way for Narrowband PCS Auctions This Summer," *Communications Daily,* April 21, 1994.

7. Franklin.

Building the Superhighway: Government and Industry

Hundt called the auctioning of spectrum "the largest sale of public property since the Oklahoma land rush."[8] A natural resource that, by congressional mandate, served the public good, spectrum was regulated in the United States both by the National Telecommunications Information Agency (NTIA) and the FCC. Federal agencies including the Central Intelligence Agency and the Federal Bureau of Investigation, as well as local government entities such as police and fire departments, used NTIA-regulated spectrum. The FCC regulated commercially used spectrum.

Electromagnetic spectrum, like radiowaves, was divided into bandwidths of energy. It was a limited resource but, as technologies advanced, the FCC could require license-holders to use increasingly smaller bandwidths. There was also the possibility that new technologies would be developed to utilize higher and lower frequencies of spectrum than were usable in 1994. The FCC could also free frequency by nonrenewal of licenses.[9]

According to Hundt, employment in the communications sector would soar from 3.6 million workers in 1994 to 5 million by 2003.[10] These workers would create the technology, equipment, and infrastructure necessary to handle— even before emerging technologies were in place—America's estimated annual 500 billion minutes of long-distance calls and fax transmis-

sions.[11] Industry analysts predicted that end-user costs for PCS would be half that for similar cellular services, and that a likely "100 million [PCS] subscribers could generate $50 billion a year in revenues for the providers of these advanced communications services" within 10 years.[12] Telecommunications hardware alone was a $40-billion industry in 1993.

Broadband and Narrowband Personal Communications Services; Interactive Video and Data Services

Of the spectrum freed up by The Emerging Technologies Act, the FCC planned to allocate 120 MHz—four times the amount originally designated for cellular services—to broadband PCS,[13] 3 MHz for narrowband PCS, and the remaining 77 MHz to IVDS.

The technologies that would utilize these radiowaves were still largely in development in

---

8. Unattributed, "Hundt: 'Oklahoma Land Rush'; FCC Adopts Spectrum Auction Procedures," *Communications Daily,* March 9, 1994.

9. The spectrum that the emerging technologies section of the budget bill established for new technologies was either unused by government entities, would be freed by compressing existing users onto narrower bandwidths, or would be freed by moving license-holders onto wholly different bandwidths.

10. Hundt, Speech, July 26, 1994.

11. Andrew Kupfer, "The Future of the Phone Companies," *Fortune,* October 3, 1993.

12. Bureau of National Affairs Management Briefing, "FCC Prepares for First-Ever Auction of Airwave Licenses," July 25, 1994; Ralph Vartabedian, "FCC Gives Minorities an Edge in Wireless Auction," *The Los Angeles Times,* June 30, 1994.

13. A total of 120 MHz of spectrum for broadband PCS was divided into bands of different widths. There were three larger 30 MHz blocks—A, B, and C; and three smaller 10 MHz blocks—D, E, and F. The FCC divided the country geographically into 51 major trading areas (MTAs) based on divisions in the *Rand McNally Commercial Atlas and Marketing Guide.* Each MTA contained about 10 smaller zones called basic trading areas (BTAs), of which there were a total of 493. Spectrum in blocks A and B was to be auctioned according to MTA zones, while spectrum in blocks C, D, E, and F was to be auctioned along BTA lines. This division provided for as many as six competing types of PCS systems in a given zone—considerably more competition than existed in the cellular industry, in which two competitors existed in most areas. Lygeia Ricciardi prepared this case under the supervision of Professor Richard S. Tedlow, "The Federal Communications Commission in 1994," The President and Fellows of Harvard College, Harvard Business School case no. 795-056, December 5, 1994.

1994, and the infrastructure to support them had yet to break ground. As one writer for *The Washington Times* commented, "every one's betting billions and billions of dollars on something that doesn't exist. No one has made a PCS 'phone' or handset yet. There isn't a national network for PCS users. No one even knows exactly what PCS will be used for. Yet no one wants to be left behind, and they're willing to pay a lot of money to be sure they aren't."[14] As great as the risks were to enter the PCS and IVDS market, revenue estimates for those who would succeed were staggering. The ticket to enter the race was an FCC-regulated license to operate. The press estimated that bids for IVDS licenses would begin at a few hundred thousand dollars and those for PCS broadband would start in the tens of millions. But, the $12 billion in annual revenue projected for PCS broadband license holders was one and one-half times more than the total revenue of the top 100 African-American-owned businesses in the United States.[15]

The FCC defined PCS broadly as a "family of mobile or portable radio services which can be used to provide service to individuals or businesses, and which may be integrated with a variety of competing networks."[16] PCS were essentially a digital version of cellular services, but PCS equipment could be far smaller and lighter than cellular equipment. Because PCS were digital, a greater variety of transmissions, including those integrating images were possible. Transmissions were also more likely to be reliable.

Broadband PCS in the 2 gigaHertz (GHz) range had the bandwidth to support data trans-

missions as well as voice services. Likely broadband PCS products included small, lightweight, multifunction portable telephones and multichannel cordless phones, wireless facsimile machines and other imaging devices, and paging devices with two-way data capabilities. The popular press waxed eloquent on the commercial likelihood of Dick Tracy-sized watch-phones and Star-Trek-style hand-held computers and communicators. As one newspaper saw it, "Newspapers will beam their articles to pocket devices over the airwaves. Homeowners will turn on their kitchen lights while riding the commuter train home. Vending machines will signal their owner by radio whenever they need a refill."[17] According to the FCC, PCS had "the potential to increase business productivity and enhance efficient delivery of important public services . . . [and could provide] more efficient and lower cost communications to the public at large."[18]

Narrowband PCS frequencies lay in the 900 MHz range and could support data transmissions only. Narrowband PCS was projected to be used for new services such as advanced voice paging, two-way acknowledgment paging, and other limited data services.

IVDS were transmitted in the 200 MHz range and would likely integrate television broadcast stations, cable television stations, wireless cable facilities, and direct broadcast satellite stations with interactive consumer technologies. IVDS was a short-distance communications service through which license-holders could provide information, products, or services—such as home banking and shopping services, as well as educational and pay-per-view services like home video rentals—to individual subscribers at fixed locations.

14. Jeff Nesbit, "Firms Pick Partners for Wireless Dance," *The Washington Times,* October 21, 1994.

15. Dave Schwab, "Women, Minorities Get Bid Preference for FCC Licenses," *San Diego Business Journal,* July 17, 1994.

16. FCC Fact Sheet, "Broadband PCS Fact Sheet," August 1994.

17. Aaron Zitner, "For Sale: A New World of Wireless," *The Boston Globe,* December 4, 1994.

18. FCC Fact Sheet, "Broadband PCS Fact Sheet," August 1994.

FCC Background

The FCC's mission was to regulate the communications industry to promote services to U.S. consumers and stimulate the economy. Its mission varied somewhat with the changing politics of Washington, emerging public needs, and technological innovations. According to William Kennard, FCC general counsel, in 1994:

The regulatory landscape [was] changing rapidly . . . mainly as a result of increased demands for technology by the public and the convergence of technologies. The [FCC had] a unique opportunity . . . to shape the creation of some new industries. The Commission [felt] that in order to fulfill its statutory mandate . . . it [was] important to create opportunities not only for consumers to get new services and technologies, but also to provide opportunities for new entrants into these businesses.

Created by the Communications Act of 1934, the FCC described itself as "an independent federal regulatory agency responsible directly to Congress."[19] The Act gave the agency the exclusive authority to grant broadcast licenses based on "public convenience, interest, or necessity."[20] The chairperson of the FCC, together with four commissioners, oversaw the agency and were its most senior decision makers. Each was appointed by the U.S. president and approved by Congress. Commissioners served a staggered five-year term, and no three of them could be of the same political party.[21]

The FCC carried out legislation passed by Congress. Legislation typically derived from FCC internal studies and recommendations to Congress, or was initiated by congressional representatives including those on the House and Senate Subcommittees on Telecommunications and Finance. Individuals, industry lobbyists, and activists could also initiate legislation. When a bill became law, the FCC was often solely responsible for its implementation. It had significant freedom to determine how to implement laws through rulemaking procedures after the public had the opportunity to comment on proposed rules.

In addition to Congress, the courts also had an impact on FCC regulations. The FCC would sometimes alter regulations in response to court rulings after a disgruntled regulated entity brought suit. In some cases, the courts had demanded remedies for specific constitutional challenges, including financial restitution for injured parties. The FCC was naturally adverse to inviting such court orders since they could delay the commercial use of regulated technologies for years.

The FCC, Minorities, and Women

According to FCC statistics, minorities owned 3.5 percent of the 4,950 AM radio stations in the United States, 2 percent of the 4,920 FM stations, and 2.3 percent of the 1,151 television stations.[22] A Supreme Court decision addressing what a lower court described as "the extreme underrepresentation of minorities in the broadcast media," also argued that the few minorities that held licenses had less valuable stations, which served smaller markets and smaller audiences, than majority-owned stations.[23] According to David Honig, executive director of the Minority

19. FCC, 1992 Annual Report, p. 5.

20. Kay A. Hoogland, "Metro Broadcasting, Inc. v. FCC: Non-remedial Affirmative Action Becomes an Exclusive Prerogative of Congress," *Employee Relations Law Journal,* December 22, 1990.

21. Lygeia Ricciardi prepared this case under the supervision of Professor Richard S. Tedlow, "The FCC Today and Tomorrow," The President and Fellows of Harvard College, Harvard Business School case study no. 794-076 (Rev. February 18, 1994).

22. Unattributed, "Meeting in Dispute: House Panel Quizzes Hundt on Minority Auction Goals," *Communications Daily,* May 23, 1994.

23. Hoogland.

Media Ownership and Employment Council, "In the past three years, minority ownership in broadcasting has been in steady decline; with other new technologies now emerging, we believe new and more aggressive approaches are needed to foster more minority ownership opportunities."[24]

The FCC's policy of automatically renewing, without significant review, most licenses—many of which were originally awarded in the 1930s and 1940s—limited the participation of designated entities in mature communications industries. Traditional broadcasting, a mature market, presented fewer immediate opportunities for the participation of minorities and women than did wholly new industries like PCS and IVDS. Even the relatively new cable and cellular industries were already maturing, and with little racial and gender diversity among license owners. Nine of 7,500 cable operators in the United States, for example, were minorities in 1994.[25]

FCC Preference Policies

On December 18, 1986, the Republican-dominated Commission of the FCC authorized staff members to conduct an inquiry into FCC preference policies that had helped minorities and women obtain radio and television licenses for nearly a decade. Through the preference policies, women and minority owners of broadcast stations had increased their ownership from fewer than 50 stations, or less than one percent of the total when the policies were adopted in 1978, to just over 300, or three percent 10 years later.

The FCC had adopted the policies, outlined in the May 1978 "Statement of Minority Ownership of Broadcasting Facilities," during the Carter Administration following the completion of a study which showed that efforts to promote diversity through employment and programming guidelines had failed. The policies provided that (1) broadcasters in danger of losing their licenses for failing to meet FCC qualifications could cut short proceedings against them by holding "distress sales"—selling their stations to minority-controlled or women-controlled interests for up to 75 percent of the fair market value of the station and the license, (2) the FCC could give women and minorities preference, or a "plus factor," over otherwise equally qualified white men in awarding licenses—meaning that the license applications of designated entities received greater weight, but were not assured of a license award, and (3) owners could receive tax breaks for selling their stations to members of minority and women's groups.

Believing the policies to be unconstitutional however, in 1986 the FCC announced that it would, pending the outcome of its inquiry, "delay action on any competitive license proceedings in which the policies relating to women and racial minorities might be a decisive factor." The press noted that the Commission, despite criticism, was "interested in shelving the preference policies . . . in line with the Reagan Administration's assaults on the use of racial preferences to redress past instances of discrimination in the workplace."[26] While all of the commissioners voted to go forward with the inquiry, attitudes toward the preferences were divided. One commissioner critical of the preferences noted that, "America is governed by a fundamental principle; that all Americans are entitled to be treated equally under the law, without regard to their race or gender," while another, a Democrat and the Commission's most senior member, felt, according to *The New York Times,* that the FCC had "broad discretion to maintain the preferences in the public interest."

Language inserted into a 1988 spending bill

---

24. Jube Shiver, Jr., "Plan to Auction Airwaves Raises Protest," *The Los Angeles Times,* May 20, 1994.

25. Hundt, Speech Before the National Urban League, July 26, 1994.

26. Reginald Stuart, "FCC to Hold Inquiry into Preference Policies," *The New York Times,* December 17, 1986.

passed just prior to the 1987 year-end holiday recess by a bi-partisan group of senators cut short the Commission's efforts to dismantle preference programs, however. Congress prohibited the FCC from using any appropriated funds to either conduct an inquiry or dismantle the programs in 1989 and 1990 as well. According to an aide to Senator Lowell P. Weiker Jr. (R-CT), one of the bi-partisan group, "The only way you have any kind of level playing field is to give minorities and women preferences."[27]

Court Challenges

According to the legal press, by 1994, court support for nonremedial affirmative action policies had been receding for several years, as ruling after ruling declared such measures unconstitutional.

On March 31, 1989, a three-judge panel of a federal appeals court had ruled 2–1 that "distress sales" were unconstitutional. The judge who wrote the majority opinion in the case, *Astroline Communications Co.* v. *Shurberg Broadcasting,* argued that a link between minority ownership and programming diversity—the stated FCC goal of the policy—had not been established, that the FCC had adopted a racial set-aside program before exploring neutral alternatives such as equal employment opportunity (EEO) options, and that the policy was discriminatory against non-minorities. He wrote, "The distress sale policy is not narrowly tailored to remedy past discrimination because its effect is unrelated to the need for such a remedy, and it provides no procedures for insuring that the policy's beneficiaries have actually suffered from the effects of past discrimination."[28]

At the time of the ruling, the FCC estimated that there were approximately six distress sales each year as about 800 radio stations and 80

television stations changed hands annually.[29] In the 10 years since the FCC had established the preference policy, minorities or women had bought a total of 38 stations through distress sales.[30] Twenty-two of those sales had occurred in 1980, the last year of the Carter Administration.[31]

On April 21, 1989, a different three-judge panel of the same federal appeals court had ruled 2-1 in *Metro Broadcasting, Inc.* v. *Federal Communications Commission* that the FCC's policy giving minorities and women preference in the awarding of new licenses was constitutional. The conflicting findings almost assured a hearing before the Supreme Court.

On January 9, 1990, the Supreme Court agreed to hear arguments on the constitutionality of the two federal programs. Several days later, a *New York Times* editorial argued that, "if these mild doses of affirmative action are too strong, it's hard to imagine what can survive. When the justices examine the programs they'll find no system of rigid racial quotas, no fixed percentage of franchises set aside for minorities, not even a goal or timetable based on population . . . [the FCC's] objective is more diverse ownership and, in time, more diverse programming."[32]

The FCC's brief to the Supreme Court argued that once the Commission adopted the policies, Congress had both endorsed and expanded them before ultimately forbidding the agency from extirpating them. According to the FCC, minority and women's ownership of stations was a congressionally mandated agency priority. According to the brief, when minorities were represented among station owners, "programming is more likely to reflect fairly the different perspec-

---

27. Associated Press, "FCC to Revive Minority-Help Policies," *The New York Times,* January 6, 1988.

28. Martin Tolchin, "FCC Policy Assisting Minorities Is Overturned," *The New York Times,* April 1, 1989.

29. Tolchin.

30. John Burgess, "Appeals Court Strikes Down FCC Program," *The Washington Post,* April 1, 1989.

31. Mary Lu Carnevale, "FCC Program On Minorities Dealt a Setback," *The Wall Street Journal,* April 3, 1989.

32. Editorial, "A Good Place to Act Affirmatively," *The New York Times,* January 13, 1990.

tives of minority groups, to the benefit of both the minority and non-minority community."[33]

The Bush Administration's Justice Department meanwhile wrote a separate brief arguing that the preference policies, designed as they were to increase programming diversity rather than as a remedy for past discrimination, were unconstitutional.

The high court would decide whether a federal agency could initiate a policy and later have it ratified by Congress, or whether Congress must initiate the policy. Further, the court would rule on whether preferences were allowable only when they were narrowly tailored to correct well-documented discrimination.

In June 1990 the Supreme Court held that the FCC's minority preferences in proceedings for new broadcast licenses and in distress sales did not violate the equal protection clause of the Fourteenth Amendment. The majority opinion stated that "benign race-conscious measures mandated by Congress—even if those measures are not remedial in the sense of being designed to compensate victims of past governmental or societal discrimination—are constitutionally permissible."[34] Commentators noted that the Court applied a "deferential standard of review" because it was Congress that had mandated the policies. They argued that the implications of the ruling would be limited to the broadcast industry and that, despite the ruling, nonremedial affirmative action would be greatly constrained in the future.

The decision, while regarded as a victory for proponents of affirmative action programs, was seen as an anomaly in the Court's steady retreat from support of nonremedial affirmative action programs and policies. Commentators empha-

sized that the high court upheld FCC preference policies primarily because of their congressional imprimatur. They noted that the Supreme Court's 1989 ruling in *Richmond* v. *J. A. Croson Co.*—a case which adopted a "strict scrutiny standard" of municipality-mandated minority set-aside programs—as more consistent with the court's retreat from nonremedial affirmative action. In the *Richmond* case, the Court had found that state and local governments did not have sufficient authority to enact preference policies that did not first establish a clear nexus between the subjects of the policy and past discrimination.

Commentators saw Justice Sandra Day O'Connor's dissenting opinion, stating that "the Constitution provides that the Government may not allocate benefits and burdens among individuals based upon the assumption that race or ethnicity determines how they act or think," as more consistent with high court opinions and a bellwether for future holdings.[35] Both the majority and dissenting opinions dealt specifically with racially motivated policies and did not address issues of gender-based preferences.

Programming Diversity

There was considerable debate in the press, as well as between the majority and dissenting Supreme Court opinions, as to what if any impact station ownership in fact had on programming diversity. A *Newsday* opinion attacked the Supreme Court decision, stating that "what the courts call 'benign' others call liberal condescension. Blacks are perfectly capable of achieving station ownership without training wheels courtesy of the FCC. But until the training wheels come off, no one, blacks included, will be 100 percent sure."[36] On the same day, a *New York Times* editorial declared, in reference to the Su-

33. Stephen Wermiel and Mary Lu Carnevale, "Supreme Court's Study of Affirmative Action Turns to Federal Plans Aiding Minority Firms," *The Wall Street Journal,* March 26, 1990.

34. Susan G. Strother, "Minorities Get Help from the Supreme Court," *The Orlando Sun Sentinel,* October 1, 1990.

35. Hoogland.

36. Mona Charen, "Court Misses the Mark on FCC 'Quotas'," *Newsday,* July 2, 1990.

preme Court's dissenting opinion, that "Americans know that declaring society should be colorblind is to pronounce victory in a war on racism that is far from over."[37]

The Court's majority decision argued that the FCC was mandated to promote programming diversity, that the viewing public suffered when programming was not diverse, and that there was a direct correlation, supported by empirical evidence, between diversity of ownership and diversity of programming. The FCC's Statement of Policy on Minority Ownership of Broadcasting Facilities in 1978 had concluded that

> The views of racial minorities continue to be inadequately represented in the broadcast media. This situation is detrimental not only to the minority audience but to all of the viewing and listening public. Adequate representation of minority viewpoints in programming serves not only the needs and interests of the minority community but also enriches and educates the non-minority audience. It enhances the diversified programming which is a key objective not only of the Communications Act of 1934 but also of the First Amendment.[38]

Nevertheless, the fact remained that the two largest broadcast stations of Latino programming in the nation—Telemundo Group and Univision—were owned by Wall Street financier Saul Steinberg and Hallmark Cards, respectively.

James S. Winston, executive director and general counsel to the National Association of Black-Owned Broadcasters (NABOB), was "not sure there [was] any special responsibility [imposed by the FCC] to do increased minority programming" if the FCC did award a license through a preference program.[39] Minority owners, according to an article in *The New York*

Times, "like their white colleagues, face the task of making their stations successful businesses."[40] Numerous articles published after the Supreme Court ruling quoted minority and women station owners who stated that their racial, ethnic, or gender status did—and did not—impact programming decisions. There seemed to be no clear consensus. One article even noted that the FCC's concern with programming diversity smacked of "content regulation" akin to censorship.[41]

Economic Diversity

Although content diversity had been a legal and policy justification for enhancing diversity in broadcasting (and later cable) ownership and management, the 1994 auctions addressed common carrier services where programming was not necessarily an issue. Beyond that, the nexus between diversity of ownership and diversity of programming, although upheld in the past, was often questioned. Broadcasters were always trying to garner the largest possible audience and some argued that market forces did not necessarily translate into programming for particular ethnic groups.

As FCC staff debated how best to fulfill the FCC's 1994 congressional mandate, they decided to focus their efforts around economic diversity and they framed programs and policies around what they believed to be well-established discrimination against women, racial and ethnic minorities, and small businesses in accessing capital. Access to capital, they believed, would be a critical issue for any potential new entrant into the telecommunications industry—not just for those groups traditionally protected by affirmative action policies. Referring to the FCC's evolving economic diversity model, Robert Pepper, the FCC's chief of the Office of Plans

37. Editorial, "A Genuinely Affirmative Action," *The New York Times,* July 2, 1990.

38. Hoogland.

39. Jeremy Gerard, "Minority Role in Broadcasting Yields Far Bigger Effect on Radio Than TV," *The New York Times,* August 1, 1990.

40. Gerard.

41. Unattributed, "High Court Hears FCC," *Television Digest,* April 2, 1990.

and Policy, said "Is this affirmative action? Absolutely not."

Others were not as confident. On September 26, 1994, the Supreme Court agreed to hear a racial preference policies case. The announcement "was a surprise," according to *The Washington Post,* which noted that the court had announced its docket a week earlier than was traditional.[42] According to Kennard, "Many people took this early announcement as a signal that the Court must have something new to say on the issue." The 1990 FCC preference cases had been the last affirmative action decisions handed down by the Court, and four of the five justices who wrote the majority decision had since retired from the bench.

FCC lawyers were looking particularly at how the case, *Adarand Constructors, Inc.* v. *Pena,* would be decided. The case evolved when Adarand Constructors, a majority-owned firm, submitted the low bid for erecting a guardrail in Colorado's San Juan National Forest. Hispanic-owned Gonzales Construction Company received the contract however, and the prime contractor received a $10,000 bonus for subcontracting to a minority group. Adarand argued that a U.S. Department of Transportation policy based on the Small Business Act of 1953 and aimed at assisting disadvantaged businesses imposed a race-based quota not warranted by actual discrimination. The policy offered up to a one and one-half percent bonus to prime contractors who subcontracted at least 10 percent of a contract to socially or economically disadvantaged enterprises. The Court would hear arguments in January 1995.

Comparative Hearings, Lotteries, and Auctions

Until the 1993 Budget Act authorized auctions as a method of assigning spectrum licenses, the FCC had allocated licenses through compara-

tive hearings on the merits of each applicant, and through lotteries (since 1982). According to critics inside and outside the FCC, both of these methods of allocation were problematic.

Illustrative of the problems with lotteries was April 29, 1991, the day when the FCC announced that it would accept license applications for a group of newly allocated radio frequencies two days later. At 7 AM on May 1 the FCC had 20,000 applications in hand; by the end of the day, the agency was faced with sorting through 46,000. The narrow filing window, an attempt by the FCC to reduce its administrative burden, was not working. There was no cost to enter lotteries and there were nominal entry criterion having to do with technical knowledge, financing, or business intentions. Many individuals and partnerships saw lotteries as an opportunity to become millionaires. Eighty-seven percent of winners, in fact, sold their licenses soon after winning them, earning themselves the name "cellionaires."[43] According to one writer, "Most analysts agree the lotteries have become a speculators' market that brings windfall profits to dentists, lawyers, and other investors who have no intention of using the airwaves."[44] According to Pepper, "the brokers' fees alone on the cellular secondary market transactions totaled over a billion dollars."

For example, in June 1990 a partnership called the Rural Area Development Group of Los Gatos, California, won a cellular license for Cape Cod, Massachusetts. Within a few months, the partnership had sold its license to Southwestern Bell Mobile Systems for a reported $30.5 million. According to a trade press commentary on the lottery process by Jeff Baumann, the executive vice president of the National As-

---

42. Joan Biskupic, "Justices Take Minority Business, Kansas City Desegregation Cases," *The Washington Post,* September 27, 1994.

43. Lygeia Ricciardi prepared this case under the supervision of Professor Richard S. Tedlow, "The Federal Communications Commission in 1994," The President and Fellows of Harvard College, Harvard Business School case study no. 795-056, December 5, 1994.

44. Eliza Newlin, "An FCC Lottery with Too Few Winners?" *The National Journal,* October 26, 1991.

sociation of Broadcasters: "In all, tens of billions of dollars worth of cellular frequencies
have been given away through lotteries. Of this,
the taxpayer has received nothing. Moreover,
the lotteries [for cellular licenses] attracted so
many applications—almost 400,000 in all—that
the assignment process has taken close to a decade and is not finished yet."[45]

The same commentary argued that the FCC's
other allocation method, comparative hearings,
were "even worse . . . It is often nearly impossible for the FCC to determine which applicant
would provide the best service . . . Moreover,
such determinations typically take years to
make, depriving the public of service in the interim. And even if a 'correct' decision is made,
licensees often transfer their licenses to someone
else in a fairly short time."

The FCC believed that auctions would address some of the most troubling problems with
lotteries and comparative hearings. According
to a 1985 working paper put out by the FCC
Office of Plans and Policy, auctions were as

> Likely to result in the same ultimate assignment
> as present mechanisms. But because they require
> winning bidders to make substantial payments in
> return for being licensed, auctions are an efficient
> way of reducing the number of applicants. . . . auc-
> tions would reduce the delays and transactions
> costs involved in initial assignments and avoid the
> need for resale . . . comparative hearings have
> proven to be a costly and generally ineffective
> means of selection . . . there is substantial disagree-
> ment about what the comparative criteria should
> be and how they should be weighted . . . There is
> considerable doubt, therefore, as to how effective
> comparative hearings are in furthering social
> goals . . . It is not uncommon for litigation to
> drag on for years, with participants incurring
> huge legal bills . . . The new licensee loses an in-
> come stream; the public is without additional ser-
> vice. But because delay favors existing licensees,
> they have strong incentives to file petitions to

deny or otherwise utilize the administrative process as a means of retarding competitors' entry.[46]

According to Peter Tenhula, an attorney in
the FCC's Office of the General Counsel, auctions prescreened bidders so that those most determined to succeed in the marketplace were
also those most likely to win licenses. According
to Tenhula,

> The theory is that in an auction, if you're not able
> to construct and operate a system, then you're not
> going to be the highest bidder. You're not going
> to value [the license], so why pay for something
> that you're not ultimately going to obtain? . . . In
> auctions, if you're the highest bidder in an open
> market, that means you're not going to try to sell
> your license once you obtain it—you'd get exactly
> what you paid for assuming the option outright.

Making Auctions Work: PCS and IVDS Auction Rules

FCC staff members were clear that auction rules
would likely vary from auction to auction. As
they considered various methods for promoting
designated-entity ownership of spectrum licenses, they also needed to address more basic
issues such as: How would the FCC define designated entity? How would the FCC screen out
"fronts"—minority or women bidders who were
controlled by nonminority investors? How
would the FCC prevent minorities and women
from themselves becoming a secondary market
which quickly sold licenses awarded through
preference programs?

Installment Payments

The Commission considered requiring full,
lump-sum payments for all winning bidders except designated entities. FCC decision makers
believed that "allowing installment payments is
equivalent to the government's extending credit

45. Jeff Baumann, "Auctions: A Saner Way . . . or Just a Quick Fix?" *Electronics,* June 1991.

46. Evan Kwerel and Alex D. Felker, "Using Auctions to Select FCC Licenses," Federal Communications Commis-sion, Office of Plans and Policy Working Paper Series, Work-ing Paper #16, May 1985.

. . . reduc[ing] the amount of private financing needed by a prospective licensee."[47] The proposal raised secondary questions regarding how to judge creditworthiness, how to set interest rates, what the size of an initial up-front payment might be, what the length of the payment period might be, whether a grace period would be allowed, and what would happen in the case of default. According to the FCC, "Most commentators agree that installment payments are an effective means of addressing the inability of designated entities to obtain financing and will enable them to compete more effectively for auctioned spectrum. They claim that installment payments will minimize the effect of lack of access to capital by small businesses and female and minority-owned businesses."[48] Some commentators felt installment payments should be available to all designated entities, some only to small-business designated entities.[49]

Bidding Credits

The Commission also considered allowing bidding credits for eligible designated entities that would require such winning bidders to pay only a certain percentage of their actual bids. According to the FCC, "Many commentators support bidding preferences instead of, or in addition to, set-asides. They claim that bidding credits address the inability of designated entities to obtain capital and would encourage non-designated entities to enter into joint ventures with designated entities."[50] FCC staff needed to determine what the size of bidding credits might be, and whether they would be allowed for every auction and every type of designated entity.

Spectrum Set-Asides

According to the FCC, "Many parties support set-asides as a general matter and some argue that only by using set-asides can the Commission carry out [its mandate] 'to ensure' that designated entities are given the 'opportunity to participate in the provision of spectrum-based services.' Others, such as Bell South and Sprint contend that to set aside spectrum blocks for bidding by women- or minority-owned applicants would be unconstitutional and inconsistent with legislative intent and the public interest."[51]

Tax Certificates

FCC managers considered enabling owners and investors in minority-owned and -controlled licenses purchased through competitive bidding to get tax certificates, entitling them to reduced tax payments, when they sold their stock interests, provided that the entities remain minority-owned and controlled. They also considered enabling licensees that assigned or transferred control of their license to designated entities to obtain tax certificates. According to the FCC, most commentators "advocate the use of tax certificates when an auction winner sells a license to a designated entity and when a designated entity sells a minority interest to a non-controlling investor . . . One commentator opposed the use of tax certificates generally because it believes that tax certificates would not sufficiently assist designated entities. Others argue that tax certificates should be used to assist designated entities in acquiring, not disposing of, licenses."[52]

Royalty Payments

Some at the FCC suggested that designated entities pay for their licenses through a combination of initial payment and royalties. Others argued that "royalties are based on the output or revenues of the winning firm and will act as a tax

---

47. Federal Communications Commission, "Second Report and Order in the Matter of Implementation of Section 309(j) of the Communications Act—Competitive Bidding," April 20, 1994, p. 91.

48. FCC, April 20, 1994, p. 92.

49. The FCC invited comment on proposed auction rules before promulgating final guidelines. Commentators were typically majority-owned and designated entity businesses, industry associations, legal and lobbying organizations, and individuals.

50. FCC, April 20, 1994, p. 96.

51. FCC, April 20, 1994, p. 98.

52. FCC, April 20, 1994, pp. 99–100.

and tend to reduce output."[53] They also argued that they would be costly to administer.

Decisions

The Congress, courts, consumers, and industry, including designated entities, each demanded that the FCC respond to its particular understanding of how the reallocation and auctioning of spectrum ought to proceed. According to Kennard, the Commission was

> Faced with the challenge early on in the auction process either to undertake token efforts and be absolutely certain that we could sustain constitutional challenges and prevail—or to do something truly meaningful and engage the legal risk. We opted for the latter route. It was the right thing to do. We wanted to make certain that what we'd done would create real opportunity. This was not like any other minority enterprise program in history . . . we were essentially designing a regulatory framework that would encourage minority- and women-controlled companies to compete with the largest companies in the world.

The financial costs to enter the competition for PCS and IVDS licenses were high, and the costs of winning licenses were higher yet. Even telecommunications giants like NYNEX and Bell Atlantic were teaming up to put together the money necessary for bids and infrastructure for the most significant licenses to be auctioned—those for broadband PCS covering entire metropolitan areas. One analyst estimated that building such a PCS network would cost upwards of $2 billion and per subscriber marketing costs would be $300 to $500.[54] Analysts predicted four categories of bidders: (1) telecommunications "incumbents" such as AT&T and NYNEX which already held cellular licenses, but wished to use the auctions to build national PCS networks, (2) noncellular telecommunications businesses, such as Sprint and Comcast, which hoped to be "newly licensed" entities which could develop national networks to chal-

lenge the incumbents, (3) "local-loop" players which sought smaller, regional licenses in order to offer services to compete with established conventional, wire-based telephone services, and (4) "niche players" which wished to offer specialized services such as limited data transmissions in small markets.[55]

As they worked out the details of the auction policy, FCC staff considered whether or not to engineer the distribution of spectrum licenses so that designated entities were more likely—or even certain—to receive them. They also considered what regulatory role the FCC should play in assuring that designated entities—typically smaller and less highly capitalized than firms like AT&T, MCI, and the regional Bell operating companies (RBOCs)—actually succeeded in the marketplace. Once the FCC awarded licenses, some consolidation was likely—even necessary, given the magnitude of telecommunications ventures—but it was unclear how the FCC should respond to consolidations which affected designated entities.

According to Kennard, some of the telecommunication giants "were saying 'this is not a game for new entrants.'" One headline questioned whether auctions, in fact, would be "A Feast for Small Fry—Or Dessert for the Big Guys?"[56] Some observers wondered whether the RBOCs and other big players would wait for designated entities to go bankrupt and pick up their licenses in the after-market.

Still, although big telecommunications companies with deep pockets could potentially reap benefits from competitive-bid auctions, Chairman Hundt had argued that the FCC was trying to turn the smaller designated entities into "magnets" that would attract financing from Wall Street investors and the more established industry players, allowing them access to these emerging industries without losing control of their companies.

53. FCC, April 20, 1994, p. 101.
54. Zitner.

55. Zitner.
56. Mark Lewyn, "A Feast for Small Fry—Or Dessert for the Big Guys?" *Business Week,* October 10, 1994.

On the other hand, J. Gregory Sidak, a former FCC employee and, in 1994, an analyst at the American Enterprise Institute, argued that FCC preference policies were an income transfer program rather than a legitimate communications policy. And, according to him, "the net effect of this policy will be to slow the development of the Personal Communications Services industry by several years."[57]

---

57. Vartabedian.

PEAK ELECTRONICS: VENDOR RELATIONSHIP WITH THE FORD MOTOR COMPANY (A)

On July 2, 1991, Earl J. Yancy was pacing restlessly in his elegantly furnished office in Woodbridge, Connecticut. As he gazed about the flowers, plants, and fine photographs, he fixed on a picture entitled *The Honeymoon*. Yancy, the owner of Peak Electronics, believed that his "marriage" to Ford Motor Company, not two years old, was in trouble already. As he noted to his plant manager, Bill Neale, "I can't believe it, but the honeymoon is over. They [Ford Electronics Division management] are not positively disposed to our loan request, and this will automatically shut down our business. We have to give them a response by 5:00 P.M. today, and get out of this mess."

Peak Electronics, Inc., a printed circuit board operation wholly owned by Earl Yancy, was in deep financial trouble. If Peak's single biggest customer, the Ford Motor Company, did not come to its rescue with some form of financial assistance, not only would it go under, but it could also take Yancy's other company, Yancy Minerals, Inc., along with it. In July, Peak Electronics had not yet reached profitability, re-

porting a loss of $911,500 on sales of $2,735,991 (see Exhibit 1 for a statement of operations for the first six months of 1991). In addition, Peak was unable to make $150,000 in loan payments currently due to Ford and $300,000 in trade payables, interest, and principal loan repayments due to creditors. Though the holiday weekend was around the corner, relaxation, much less celebration, was hardly on Yancy's mind.

Earl Yancy

Earl J. Yancy was born into a modest-income, working-class African-American family in Lafayette, Louisiana.[1] The son of a Creole construction foreman, Yancy was among the first males in his family to attend college. But he dropped out after his sophomore year to take a series of dead-end jobs where according to Yancy, "I spent most of my time moving from one minimum-wage dead-end job to the next." Viewing the military as the only way out of this situation, Yancy joined the Marines and decided that if he could survive boot camp he could do anything.

After his stint with the U.S. Marines, Yancy

---

1. Portions of this section have been drawn from "The Renaissance Man as Entrepreneur," *New England Business,* October 1989, pp. 34–36, 77; and "The Success of Earl Yancy," *Connecticut,* April 1985.

EXHIBIT 1 Peak Electronics Financial Statements for First Six Months of 1991

	January	February	March	April	May	June	6-Month Total
Sales:							
Ford	$215,947	$330,747	$391,240	$324,527	$422,029	$393,720	$2,078,210
Premiums	205,333	327,461	53,392	0	0	0	586,186
Other customers	4,598	15,098	11,985	6,855	24,501	8,558	71,595
	$425,878	$673,306	$456,617	$331,382	$446,530	$402,278	$2,735,991
Cost of Sales:							
Inventory—beginning of period	333,683	305,303	261,143	306,619	350,745	369,020	333,683
Labor	106,002	122,185	142,391	126,005	169,334	121,857	787,774
Other purchases	120,597	99,373	221,448	151,275	215,306	215,724	1,023,723
Manufacturing indirect	175,654	212,270	226,261	217,421	237,626	176,763	1,245,995
Subtotal	$735,936	$739,131	$851,243	$801,320	$973,011	$883,364	$3,391,175
Inventory—end of period	305,303	261,143	306,619	350,745	369,020	389,669	389,669
	430,633	477,988	544,624	450,575	603,991	493,695	$3,001,506
Gross Profit (Loss)	(4,755)	195,318	(88,007)	(119,193)	(157,461)	(91,417)	(265,515)
Expenses:							
Selling	6,161	11,192	12,915	6,081	11,756	11,230	59,295
Administrative	81,871	68,413	79,891	88,875	74,651	29,906	423,607
Financial	24,143	31,431	27,840	23,873	28,784	27,012	163,083
Subtotal	$112,175	$111,036	$120,646	$118,829	$115,151	$ 68,148	$ 645,985
Earnings (Loss) Before Income Taxes	(116,930)	84,282	(208,653)	(238,022)	(272,612)	(159,565)	
Provision for income taxes	0	0	0	0	0	0	
Net Earnings (Loss)	(116,930)	84,282	(208,653)	(238,022)	(272,612)	(159,565)	(911,500)
Gross Profit (%)	−95.26	−38.21	−35.07	−35.97	−35.26	−22.72	
Production Days	17	18	20	18	24	20	
Revenue/Panel	$89.15*	$74.81*	$45.66*	$36.82	$40.40	$39.79	
Panels/Month	4,777	9,000	10,000	9,000	11,052	10,109	
Panels/Day†	281	500	500	500	461	505	
Direct Labor/Panel	$22.19	$13.58	$14.24	$14.00	$15.32	$12.05	
Material Cost/Panel	$31.19	$15.95	$17.60	$11.91	$17.83	$19.30	

*Includes premiums.

†According to Peak's auditors, Ernst and Young, Peak had a maximum capacity of 1,200 panels/day.

completed his college degree and obtained an advanced degree from the School for Building Art & Architecture in Berlin, followed by a master's degree from Yale University. As a Loeb fellow at Harvard, he worked on a dissertation in educational-behavior research and, following his studies, taught architecture at both Harvard and Yale.

At the age of 31, he became restless with his academic career. The practically flat pay scales, despite the level of one's individual contributions and achievement, were particularly annoying to Yancy. He sought both higher compensation and fulfillment by applying his solid education in the business world.

He founded Yancy Minerals, Inc., in 1977 to market commodities. He chose the mineral commodities business because it did not require much money to get started. He steadily built the business to $40 million in revenues and $1.2 million in profits by 1989. Yancy Minerals purchased commodities such as bituminous coal, metals, and chemicals from major producers and then maintained or subcontracted warehousing, distribution, and fabricating facilities for reselling to customers. Due to market cyclicality, both revenues and profits at Yancy Minerals were somewhat lower in 1990.

Yancy's friends described him as tenacious and as someone who rarely took "no" for an answer. During his first year in business, Yancy set out to win a coal contract with Pittston Company. For a few months he unsuccessfully deluged Pittston's CEO, Nicolas Camicia, with phone calls and letters. He practically camped out in the corporate lobby for a week trying to get an appointment with Camicia. Nothing worked. Finally, he heard that Camicia was an early riser, so Yancy waited in the parking lot at 5:30 A.M. for Camicia to arrive at work. At 6:30 A.M. when Camicia arrived, Yancy introduced himself, was invited in, and by 10:30 A.M. left Pittston with a contract in hand.

During the 1960s, Yancy had grown interested in the martial arts, which he eventually taught while in Cambridge. The discipline and focus imparted by this martial arts training and teaching were incorporated into his business philosophy as he sought to hire employees who were secure, unintimidated by criticism, and would extend themselves. He exhorted his staff to follow his lead, take calculated risks, and be willing to be "perceived as a tenacious competitor." He aimed for a firm that would "outwork and outsmart" rather than "outmuscle" the competition.

Peak Electronics

Peak Electronics was founded in 1989 when Yancy purchased a plant to supply printed circuit boards to the Ford Motor Company. Peak's products formed the interconnection in electronic circuits that went into making the antilock brakes on rear wheels of selected Ford cars. Peak was 100%-owned by E. J. Yancy, who had invested a total of $705,000. This included equity as well as closing costs. In addition, $1.3 million in loans were provided by various sources to complete the initial financing of the business. Of this $1.3 million, Ford Motor Company's lending arm, Dearborn Capital, had provided $400,000, and Printed Boards (the seller of the plant to Peak Electronics) had agreed to accept $352,000 in deferred payments. Yancy Minerals had about $350,000 tied up at Peak Electronics—about half in direct loans and the other half indirectly through loans to Yancy.

Yancy had no experience in printed circuit board manufacturing. His main asset, in addition to his business acumen (according to a close friend and adviser) was "his stodgy tenacity and an ability to cultivate and exploit the rich relationships he establishes. That is what Yancy is good at, be it Yancy Minerals or Peak Electronics."

According to Yancy, "One of the main reasons we got into the business was to offset the cyclicality of the minerals business. We needed something more steady; and I was also keen to get us into the major leagues. This seemed like a challenging higher-technology opportunity."

"Moreover," added Yancy, "I had a keen interest in a business that relied on strict adherence to utilizing the manufacturing discipline."

Ford's Minority Supplier Development Program

Ford Motor Company, one of the largest automobile manufacturers in the world with 1989 sales revenue of $82.8 billion and profits of $3.8 billion,[2] was widely hailed as the American answer to the Japanese automotive challenge. According to *Incentive* magazine,[3] Ford was winning awards by recognizing that 60 percent–75 percent of automobile customers' satisfaction depended on quality. Ford's quality focus was reinforced with a variety of programs, including dealer incentive plans, employee involvement teams, supplier ratings and awards, and customer suggestion programs. These efforts resulted in

- Ford showing the biggest gains in domestic loyalty among buyers—from 35 percent in 1980 to 47 percent in 1988.
- Ford achieving significant market share gains—from 16.9 percent in 1982 to 21.3 percent in 1988.

The company manufactured nearly 55 percent of its components in-house and sourced about 45 percent from outside. Nearly 85 percent of the outside purchase dollars was for parts and components that went into the automobile. Called "production" parts because they went directly into the manufacturing line, Ford preferred to structure strategic partnerships with vendors of such items. Ray Jensen, Ford's minority supplier manager, explained:

We take anywhere from 30 months to 36 months to bring a car from concept to market. So we have a pretty good idea of the design features of the various components well before the model

comes up for production ramp-up. We use this lead time to structure long-term contracts with suppliers to get their technical expertise and production capabilities ready for model launch. We see them all as strategic alliances.

In contrast, "supply" items constituted only 15 percent of Ford's outside purchases and were not usually used directly in the automobile itself. For example, Yancy Minerals had a "supply" contract to provide coal to Ford's steel production plant, Rouge Steel, in Dearborn, Michigan.

Broadly speaking, Ford's purchasing operations were organized into three distinct areas. Within each area, division managers were responsible for organizing and executing the purchasing effort (see Exhibit 2). Norman Ehlers, formerly the purchasing executive director of NAAO (North American Automobile Operations) had recently taken over as vice president, purchasing and supplies staff (with responsibility for nonproduction purchasing) from Clinton Lauer who had retired after 25 years of service with Ford. Though Norman Ehlers and his staff had line responsibility for only the raw materials, supplies, and service portion of Ford's overall purchases, he and his staff had dotted-line responsibility for ensuring consistency and coordination of purchasing policies across the three purchasing organizations. Ray Jensen, an African-American and the minority supplier development program manager, reported dotted-line to Norman Ehlers, VP purchasing.

Tracing the genesis of the Peak Electronics partnership, Ray Jensen stated:

We had a healthy business relationship with nearly 350 minority suppliers. But most of them were small, and only about 80 to 90 of them supplied "production" parts. While our top 200 vendors accounted for nearly $14 billion in purchases, all our minority vendors put together supplied us only about $750 million annually. We had to break this trend. Our goal is to build each and every one of our "production" parts minority suppliers to at least $20 million to $30 million businesses within three years. At that level, efficiencies start kicking in, and our vendors are able

2. *1991 Moody's Industrial Manual* (New York: Dun and Bradstreet, 1991), p. 2968.

3. Todd Englander, "Ford: Quality Driven," *Incentive*, 163, no. 1 (January 1989), p. 23–34.

EXHIBIT 2   Ford Motor Company Purchasing Organization

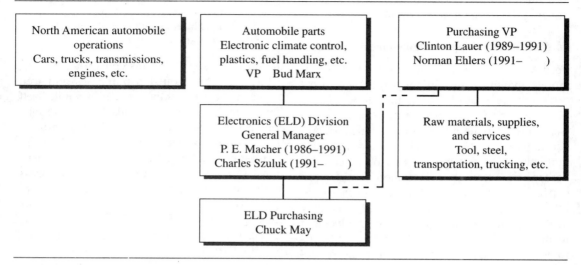

to make profits. We end up benefiting too. We get a steady and reliable supply of high-quality parts.

According to Norman Ehlers, there were three important reasons for Ford's efforts to increase minority-vendor participation:

- Business sense.
- Government guidelines.
- Social responsibilities.

Henry Ford II himself had stated in the early 1980s the need for business to aid in the task of building a well-balanced American society. The government had specific incentives and regulations in place to promote minority hiring and reduce discrimination within American businesses. Ray Jensen had added, "About 25 percent of the U.S. consumers are minorities. A one point share increase in Ford's market share is a healthy $20 million in profits for an auto manufacturer. Our minority-vendor program is important to us morally as well as financially."

In order to aid the minority business development effort, the Ford Motor Company began a Sponsorship Program with a select group of minority-owned businesses. Rather than continuing to actively manage and monitor relations with many small, often struggling minority suppliers, the Ford Motor Company decided to select about 50 minority-owned companies upon which to focus. These core companies were targeted for growth within Ford's buying patterns if they consistently delivered high-quality products. This growth was intended to help provide them with stability. Ideally, these suppliers would qualify for a sole-source contract with the Ford Motor Company, depending upon their capabilities. Corporate management paid particular attention to the success of this program.

1987: The Courtship Is Initiated

E. J. Yancy had developed relationships with many influential managers at Ford through Yancy Minerals, a long-time supplier to the Raw Materials, Supplies, and Services Purchasing Group at Ford Motor Company. Yancy maintained friendly professional and social relations with many managers at Ford with whom he negotiated coal contracts. He made it a point to cultivate these relationships as these managers progressed up the Ford ranks. In 1987, E. J. Yancy, as a minority business owner and well-regarded Ford supplier, was asked to join Ford's Minority Supplier Development Program. This program was revitalized by Ford in the mid-1980s to further enhance Ford's efforts to purchase more supplies from minority-owned companies.

According to Chuck May, supply office manager for the Electronics Division at the Ford Motor Company, in 1988 his division sought to aggressively increase its purchases from minority-owned businesses. The Electronics Division was currently dealing with 15 small minority suppliers, who were all competing in less-technical, smaller-value components. May selected printed circuit boards as a potential product area in which to create a minority-owned supplier for his division because this product was relatively easier to manufacture and at the lower end of the high-technology spectrum. (See Exhibit 3 for information on the manufacturing process for printed circuit boards.)

Chuck May felt that a minority operation could be successful in this business, given the initially relatively low-technology requirements. In addition, he knew of printed circuit board manufacturing plant geographically close to Yancy Minerals that was for sale, which could, after modifications, produce two-sided printed circuit boards. This plant was owned by Printed Boards, a major supplier of printed circuit boards to his division at Ford.

Sponsored suppliers were typically existing Ford suppliers or a new company (to Ford) with a fairly well developed non-Ford customer base. Judged by these standards, Peak was atypical. It neither supplied electronic components to Ford nor to other customers. However, May assumed that a potential minority-owned printed circuit board manufacturer like Peak Electronics, with a high-quality rating (Q1) within Ford's well-known quality system, would have little trouble expanding its revenue base to other corporate accounts. May felt, however, that a broad range of other corporate accounts would be crucial to the survival of this newly created Ford supplier given the inevitable volatility which usually accompanied Ford's purchases.

The Electronics Division devised a detailed plan which considered the effects upon and possible involvement of their current suppliers in this effort. Because the Electronics Division expected aggressive growth in Ford's new car sales, it estimated that the purchases of printed circuit boards would increase annually at a rate of 8 percent for the next several years. The division expected to bring the new supplier up to speed without any net reductions in its purchases from existing suppliers given this anticipated growth.

E. J. Yancy had built his business through his drive and ability to provide needed products at market prices without defects or delay. He had also quickly established relationships with key business decision makers. Through Yancy's early involvement in the Ford Minority Supplier Development Program at Yancy Materials, he was introduced to Chuck May. May selected Yancy because of his strong reputation at Ford as an effective businessperson. In addition, Yancy indicated a strong interest in expanding to meet Ford's needs by confirming his interest in entering the printed circuit board business. Yancy later stated that prior to this meeting he had never even seen a printed circuit board manufactured but "it doesn't matter what you are making as long as you have a Quality Improvement Plan." May and other managers at Ford's Electronics Division encouraged Yancy to select and prequalify a site in anticipation of becoming a sponsored minority supplier to the Electronics Division. However, Yancy said he would not move forward with Printed Boards without a demonstrated commitment from Ford.

September 1988—The Marriage Is Proposed

On September 15, 1988, Ray Jensen, Ford's Minority Supplier Development Manager, con-

---

EXHIBIT 3   An Overview of the Basic Process for Building Printed Circuit Boards at Peak Electronics

---

A printed circuit board is a single or multilayer card made of nonconducting fiberglass laminate which forms the basic foundation for electronic subassemblies. The bare printed circuit board provides the functional structure which will hold electronic components as well as the required circuitry pattern which will connect the components electrically. There are several steps involved in manufacturing the printed circuit board from raw board stock (laminate):

1. First raw copper-clad fiberglass laminate is precut to panel sizes
2. Drilling—Holes are drilled in specified locations where electronic component leads (ends) will be inserted and soldered in place.
3. Copper deposition—To provide a surface to allow electric current to flow from one side of the board to the other, a layer of copper is applied over the surface of the board and through the holes.
4. Surface preparation—A mechanical brush scrub is performed to provide a surface which will allow for adhesion of a photo-resistant chemical.
5. Laminate, print and develop—The board is coated with the photoresist and an image of the required final circuitry generated via CAD/CAM is laid over the board. It is then exposed to light through the circuitry image so that areas that are not to be circuitry will retain the photoresist chemical and become polymerized. The areas that are to be actual circuitry (nonpolymerized because no light penetrated through the film over these areas) then are chemically removed.
6. Electrolytic plating—The board now has polymerized photoresist (now acting as a plating resist) in areas where final circuitry will not be required. A layer of copper is plated over the circuitry (the plating-resist areas will not bind copper). Once this step is complete, the circuitry has been laid down where needed (particularly in the holes).
7. Tin lead plating—A layer of tin lead plating is then plated over the circuitry. This works as an etch resist.
8. Resist strip—The board now looks like an all-copper board with circuitry in grey tin lead. Next, the photoresist polymerized film is removed from the "noncircuit" areas.
9. Copper etch—Next all remaining copper is removed, "etched off," except for where the tin "etch resist" has been applied over the circuitry. The board now has only circuitry on it and no other copper.
10. Tin strip—Sometimes the tin that covered the copper circuitry is taken off, leaving only copper traces on the circuitry.
11. Soldermask—To prevent any circuits from bridging with solder and to protect the copper circuitry, a layer of rugged, nonconducting epoxy is applied over the surface of the board except where components will be attached.
12. Legend—As a means for technicians to identify component locations, a legend is silk-screened over the board to provide component numbers and other information.
13. Blank/Rout—The parts are then trimmed to their finished size so that they will fit in the designated location. Often at this step, the panel is punched into 8 or 12 smaller circuit boards.
14. Electrical test—To ensure that the circuit board functions electrically the way the design intended, an electrical/continuity test is performed.
15. Final inspection—A final check is performed to verify that all operations in production were performed properly.

Printed Circuit Board Applications

Starting with bare printed circuit boards, electronics manufacturers insert specific electronic components such as resistors, transistors, and computer chips into preestablished locations on the board according to the design requirements. Once the printed circuit board has been populated with all of its components (either

(continues)

EXHIBIT 3   *(concluded)*

manually or via automatic insertion machinery), these components are soldered into place by hand or with automatic wave-soldering machinery. Once the components have been secured into their respective positions with solder, the overall assembly is tested to ensure that all of the proper connections have been made to achieve the designed electronic function of the assembly. Applications of printed circuit boards are as numerous and varied as electronic applications themselves. Some of the more common uses include computer cards in PCs and larger systems, controllers for machinery and vehicles, electronic stereo components and processing equipment for sensors. Peak Electronics manufactured only the bare printed circuit board.

firmed Ford's intentions for the Minority Sponsorship of Yancy as a printed circuit board supplier. This was the first agreement entered into by the Electronics Division with a new supplier, 100 percent-sourced on specific production parts, who had no previous manufacturing experience with an automotive company. In the letter reproduced below, Jensen essentially "conveyed corporate management's support to the Electronics Division on their decision to select Yancy as the Electronics Division's sponsored supplier for printed circuit boards and the need for the sponsored supplier and sponsoring division to work together in order for the program to be successful."

Ford Motor Company
The American Road
P.O. Box 1899
Dearborn, Michigan 48121-1899

September 15, 1988

E. J. Yancy, President
Yancy Minerals, Inc.
1768 Litchfield Turnpike
Woodbridge, CT 06525

Dear Yancy:

I am writing to emphasize the commitment we, at Ford Motor, have made to the minority business community in the form of our Minority Supplier Development program. As you are aware, the central and most effective feature of this program is our sponsorship activity. Under sponsorship, Ford Motor attempts to extend long-term contracts to those selected minority suppliers who have a demonstrated capacity for producing and delivering quality products and services.

To date, this program has been very successful and is one that we at Ford intend to continue.

As this program relates to Yancy Minerals, this office has conveyed to Bill Graning of the Electrical and Electronics Division (EED) its support of EED's decision to select Yancy as EED's sponsored supplier for Electrical and Electronic components—primarily, printed circuit boards. As you will recall in our meeting with yourself, Graning, and several members of his staff and supply base, I emphasized the importance of the sponsoring division and the sponsored supplier mutually working toward reaching the long-term goals of competitive pricing and consistent quality that is monitored by stringent Statistical Process Control format.

At this writing, it is my understanding that Yancy and its technical advisers, Printed Boards, have identified, and are in negotiations to purchase, one of several manufacturing plant locations. It is further my understanding that based on product samples, specification drawings, prices, and the projected purchase volumes Yancy has received from EED, that Yancy has formalized agreements with key technical personnel and financing sourcing to support its efforts to make this sponsorship agreement with EED a success within the 7-year term of your sponsorship agreement.

Please keep us informed of your progress.

Sincerely,

R. M. Jensen, Manager
Minority Supplier Development
Purchasing and Supply Staff

November 1989: The Union Takes Place

Despite the general framework for Ford's sponsorship program, the details of a specific contract between Peak Electronics and the Electronics Division of the Ford Motor Company needed to be agreed upon. E. J. Yancy represented Peak Electronics as the sole owner. With many years in the coal supply business, Yancy was an experienced deal maker with a very aggressive "can-do" attitude. Although they were given direction by Clinton Lauer, then VP purchasing and supplies staff, the principal negotiators for Ford were Charlie Szuluk and Chuck May. The Ford representatives expected a quick, relatively simple negotiation. They thought that the standard terms of a minority supplier sponsorship were very clear and fairly generous. In addition, the Electronics Division was facilitating Yancy's purchase of the printed circuit board plant from Printed Boards with the anticipation of significant volumes to be ordered from him. Finally, this entire sponsorship effort was a part of Ford's supplier partnership program. In the experience of Ford managers, partnership meant less detail in written agreements through long negotiations but more trusting, handshake-type agreements between business partners.

E. J. Yancy entered the negotiations with a clear focus on the expected competitive position that his new company would face. All of the surviving Ford suppliers of printed circuit boards seemed to be large, entrenched companies with significant experience and well-established relationships with the managers at Ford's Electronics Division. Furthermore, raw materials and direct labor were over 60 percent of the production cost for printed circuit boards. This could potentially give the larger competitors a significant advantage over Peak Electronics through volume discounts on these raw materials. In addition, the Printed Boards facility was a multilayered board operation which had to be converted to a two-sided board facility, and this would involve retraining labor and reorienting shop flow practices.

The negotiations, which began in November 1988, were finally concluded in November 1989. During this interim period, Yancy agreed to cover Printed Boards' operating costs of running the plant. Yancy reasoned that a plant shutdown would have involved tremendous start-up costs. One difficult aspect of the negotiation revolved around financial assistance in the form of outright, nonrepayable, price premiums based on actual volume delivered, which Ford would give Peak "for purposes of assisting and sustaining Peak Electronics during its initial launching period." One Ford manager commented, "The basic contract was agreed early in 1989. Delay was due to Yancy not agreeing with Ford's premium offer and method of disbursement." Yancy believed that he needed $3.5 million over three years to achieve stand-alone profitability in three years. During the final negotiations with senior corporate executives, Ford said it would not pay more than $3 million in premiums, so Yancy agreed to $2.9 million. Selected excerpts from the November agreement between Ford and Yancy are presented below:

Audio Systems: Electronics Division
Ford Motor Company
17000 Rotunda Drive
Dearborn, Michigan 48121

November 7, 1989

Earl J. Yancy, President
Peak Electronics, Inc.
51 Carlson Road
Orange, CT 06525

Dear Yancy:

Ford Motor Company, acting through its Electronics Division, is willing to enter into a multiyear contract with Peak Electronics, Inc. Orange, CT, with regard to the supply of printed wiring boards to Ford Motor Company. This contract is for the "printed wiring board" types described in this contract for which Ford has delegated the authority to the Electronics Division to purchase on their behalf. . . .

Purchase/Supply commitment   Ford's obligation to purchase printed wiring boards is contingent upon successful completion of both process and product approvals as measured by Ford Motor Company's Q101 System Survey Engineering Sample Evaluation Report (form 2913,), and Initial Sample Report (form 292a). Ford will purchase and Peak Electronics will manufacture and supply 100 percent of Ford's original equipment requirements per the attached Estimate of Annual Usage of printed wiring boards identified in the table below (and replacements) . . . during the term of this five-year contract, commencing during Ford's 1990 model year and extending through model year 1994. These obligations apply to goods of the current design level and to those goods modified by normal engineering changes.

Ford estimates that its purchases for such goods will have an annualized value of $6,400,000 in Model Year 1991 and $8,500,000 in Model Year 1992.[4] These estimates are preliminary and will change as Ford acquires more information about the marketplace for its vehicles and these goods.

---

4. Model Years for Ford generally ran from mid-August of one year to the next. That is, Model Year 1991 cars were shipped in August 1990. Parts procurement and manufacturing would therefore typically start in March 1990. To help Peak Electronics get started, according to Yancy, Ford had promised a $3.6 million revenue base for Model Year 1990 cars. But an Electronics Division manager disagreed: "Ford Motor issues purchase orders for specific part numbers at a unit price and a percent of part requirements. Volume is a result of the vehicle sales using the individual part. Ford does not commit or promise dollar amounts."

The parts numbers from which Ford will attempt to qualify Peak Electronics and the base prices to be paid by Ford to Peak Electronics therefore, are as follows:

Part Numbers[5]	Model Year				
	1990	*1991*	*1992*	*1993*	*1994*
101	$11.11	$11.11	$11.11	*	*
102	14.16	14.16	14.16	*	*
103	8.04	8.04	8.04	*	*
104	7.11	7.11	7.11	*	*
105	11.19	11.19	11.19	*	*
106	6.77	6.77	6.66	*	*
107	7.23	7.23	7.23	*	*
108	19.60	19.60	19.60	*	*
109	17.20	17.20	17.20	*	*
110	2.79	2.79	2.79	*	*
111	10.18	10.18	10.18	*	*

*Part numbers and pricing were not yet identified for model years 1993 and 1994, and would be the same as for prior years unless other part numbers were substituted by Ford. Peak Electronics agreed to develop a program wherein Peak's prices would be fully competitive by Model Year 1993. Provided that Peak remained a qualified Ford supplier, after 1992 Ford would permit Peak Electronics to compete for additional products, in an estimated range of 15 percent per year to be purchased by Ford.

Should Ford's requirements for such parts decline substantially, Ford will attempt to identify and substitute replacement business to achieve the level of purchases contemplated by this contract.

Premiums and ongoing productivity   As Peak supplies printed wiring boards, starting during the model year 1990, Ford will pay Peak maximum premiums of $1,800,000 on a schedule of one dollar for each dollar on the first $1,800,000 of the purchase price paid to Peak for goods sold hereunder. Premium payments for model year 1991 of $900,000 will be prorated over the 1991 model year or over the remaining portion of the 1991 model year after completion of payment of the $1,800,000. In no event shall the premium in model year 1991 exceed 25 percent of the purchase price nor shall the payment period be less than 10 months (which could extend payments into the 1992 model year). A premium of $200,000 will be paid on a prorated basis for model year 1992. It is agreed duplicate premiums will not be paid.

It is agreed by both parties, that payment of premiums by Ford is for the purpose of assisting and sustaining Peak Electronics during its initial launching period. When Peak Electronics becomes profitable and does not require said premiums then it is agreed that negotiations would be initiated to determine an appropriate accelerated premium reduction schedule.

Further, in pursuit of never-ending improvement, Ford and Peak agree to negotiate, beginning in the 1992 model year, an ongoing commitment for annual price reductions based on the projected ability of Peak to achieve annual productivity improvements.

---

5. Part numbers represented the actual board placed in a vehicle, but often several boards were made in a batch on a large panel and shipped as panel. A panel could represent anywhere from 4 to 24 final boards. A price realization of about $45 per panel was usually a reasonable assumption.

Term and extension of term   This contract will provide for a continuing Supplier/Customer relationship between Peak Electronics and Ford. Accordingly, Ford and Peak Electronics will meet in June of each year to discuss and consider an extension of this contract beyond its initial expiration date at the end of Ford's model year 1994 or any extended expiration date. . . .

Economics for supplier's labor and purchased goods   Prices are based on Peak Electronics' cost for labor, purchased material, and parts as of July 15, 1989. From time to time, but no more frequently than annually, Ford or Peak Electronics may initiate negotiations to adjust prices to recognize changes in Peak Electronics' cost. To facilitate orderly negotiations, Peak Electronics will provide such data as may be reasonably requested by Ford to substantiate any requested adjustment. Any proposed price adjustments will be submitted at least 45 days prior to the requested effective date. Price adjustments during the first three years to the contract will be based upon an average of competitive adjustments granted to Ford's other suppliers of printed wiring boards for labor, purchase materials, and parts and will be effective 30 days after Peak Electronics' accrual date. For purposes of this section, labor will be deemed to be 20 percent and purchase materials and parts will be deemed to be 40 percent of the price of supplies (exclusive of premiums) of this purchase agreement.

Delivery   The delivery of printed wiring boards will be F.O.B. Carrier Seller's plant (Peak Electronics').

Changes   In pursuit of never-ending improvement, Ford and Peak Electronics both agree that design improvements to reduce the above prices are desirable and should be aggressively pursued. If Ford initiates design or other changes which result in decreased production cost, prices will be decreased to reflect the entire effect of the decreased production costs. If Peak initiates design or other changes which result in decreased production costs, prices will be decreased after recovery of nonrecurring expenses (for tooling, amortization, etc.) for the first year to reflect equal sharing of the decreased production costs and thereafter to reflect the entire effect.

QOS/Q1   Peak Electronics will develop a Quality Operating System Plan (QOS) for printed wiring boards and review it with the appropriate Ford SQA (Supplier Quality Assurance) engineer within 120 days after the date of execution of this agreement. Ford SQA is available to provide direction and consultation to Peak Electronics on the plan. Also, Peak Electronics must establish a plan for achieving the Q1 Quality rating within one year of beginning production and must submit the plan to Ford within 120 days after the date of execution of this agreement. Peak Electronics will provide timely progress on the quality plan and will review such progress with the SQA engineer at appropriate intervals. . . .

Ford technical assistance   Upon request, Ford will provide Peak Electronics with technical advice regarding SPC (Statistical Process Control) and other matters mutually agreed upon by Ford and Peak Electronics. However, Peak Electronics bears the ultimate responsibility for achieving and maintaining Ford quality requirements. Such assistance could consist of on-site personnel to help implement statistical systems for production control, process assistance, or other areas as appropriate. It is understood by Ford that Peak Electronics will also retain the services of Printed Boards to assist in these areas. One particular area for immediate assistance will be the joint Ford/Peak

Electronics development of a plan with milestones for the development and implementation, over an 18-month period, of an SPC program which Ford agrees to monitor over this period. . . .

Termination   . . . If during this agreement, (a) Peak Electronics does not meet Ford's quality standards; (b) Peak Electronics does not remain competitive in quality and delivery with other responsible suppliers or potential suppliers; or (c) Ford can substitute supplies of significantly advanced design or processing, Ford may terminate its purchase obligations in whole or in part without further liability. Ford shall provide written notice to Peak Electronics which outlines its causes for termination and specify a termination date of at least six months after the date of the notice. If Peak Electronics demonstrates to Ford, prior to the specified date of termination, that Peak Electronics will correct the causes by the termination date or a subsequent date acceptable to Ford, termination will be suspended and this agreement will continue.

If you are willing to accept the terms and conditions noted above, please indicate your concurrence below.

Respectfully submitted,

Richard J. Vitale
Purchasing Specialist
Electronics Division

Pursuant to this contract, both Ford and Yancy agreed upon an initial business plan for Peak Electronics, which projected $5.0 million in revenues with a loss of $0.9 million in 1990 and $10.9 million in revenues with profits of $1.0 million in 1991. These projections included the portion of Ford premiums allocated to each year. According to Yancy, much of Peak's initial business plan was put together by Printed Boards for Peak. Below are the profitability projections submitted in Peak's initial business plan:

Peak Electronics Initial Business Plan

	1990			1991		
	1st 6 Months (000)	2nd 6 Months (000)	Full Year (000)	1st 6 Months (000)	2nd 6 Months (000)	Full Year (000)
Revenue (including premiums)	$1,999	$3,005	$5,004	$4,995	$5,862	$10,857
Direct costs	1,053	1,445	2,498	2,462	3,316	5,778
Gross profit	946	1,560	2,506	2,533	2,546	5,079
Total overhead	1,614	1,805	3,419	2,055	2,041	4,096
Net income	$ (668)	$ (245)	$ (913)	$ 478	$ 505	$ 983

January 1990—Peak Electronics Begins Operations

Peak Electronics began operations in January 1990. E. J. Yancy carefully built Peak's management team primarily from existing Printed Boards managers but assigned a new chief financial officer who was recommended by Printed Boards as having strong analytical skills and solid experience in financial management. Finally, Bob Holloway, a retired Ford employee and an expert on Ford's Q1 quality systems, was hired by Ford as a consultant to assist Peak in setting up its quality control systems.

Yancy and his new management team recognized at the outset that a likely key to Peak's success would be its ability to install and adhere to manufacturing disciplines. As a start the team laid special emphasis on improving communication and relations between management and labor. Yancy had toured the facility with Ford personnel during Printed Boards's ownership and had concluded that the plant was being treated as a "stepchild" in the Printed Boards family and that a better human resource policy would greatly improve the operation. Daily shift meetings were instituted for all employees to facilitate better communication. Campaigns to encourage all employees to generate and share ideas on improving the operation and/or the product's quality were also instituted. A plantwide incentive program was begun to pay employees based upon actual results. Finally, training was enhanced with each employee receiving 10 hours of training per month.

The new management practices paid off for Peak Electronics. The team at Peak became one of its most valuable assets. Every Ford manager praised Yancy for his ability to build a cohesive and effective team at Peak Electronics. Chuck May stated that Peak Electronics was "amazingly effective at managing teams and people." He acknowledged that Yancy built a surprisingly solid team with very low turnover in a shorter-than-expected time frame.

The facility was converted from multisided to double-sided board production by June 1990. According to Chuck May, this conversion required upgrading the facility from a job shop to an assembly operation. The first significant order was received from the Electronics Division of the Ford Motor Company in late February 1990. Peak Electronics' processes and equipment had to be inspected and approved and the engineering department of Ford's Electronics Division had to qualify the plant's pilot output before large production run orders could be placed. As Peak began production in February 1990, its output underwent the following engineering qualifications:

- A sample lot of a minimum of 325 pieces had to be manufactured and analyzed and trial-run samples forwarded to project engineers at the manufacturing plant that would use the boards.
- Analysis would take place at Peak, at an outside laboratory, at Ford's Product Engineering Offices, and also at the user manufacturing plant. Some of the outside laboratory tests required life- and environmental-testing up to 45 days.
- After the above tests were completed and the results accepted, a production validation quantity of 2,000–2,500 boards had to be shipped to the user plant for further validation of quality.

Although prior to the plant being acquired from Printed Boards, it had achieved a minimum acceptable Ford quality rating of 140 points out of 200, Peak Electronics, under the November agreement, had to begin the important effort to achieve Q1 qualification within Ford's supplier system. The Q1 designation was the top quality status for a Ford supplier. (See Exhibit 4 for more details of the Q1 qualification process at Ford.) According to Chuck May, the typical time required for Q1 designation was 12 months. Peak Electronics achieved the required Q1 score of 165 in June of 1990, only six months into the

EXHIBIT 4

Ford's Q1 Quality Qualification Process

As part of a reformulation of its quality improvement methods, in the early 1980s Ford shifted its approach to quality from defect detection to one of detect prevention and continuous improvement with particular emphasis on the use of Statistical Process Controls. It established the Ford Q1 Preferred Quality Award for outstanding suppliers. Below is a description of the evaluation process Peak Electronics completed in order to achieve a Q1 rating in six months, the minimum time period possible.

Award Criteria

To quality for a Q1 award, a supplier must meet or exceed all of the following threshold criteria:

• Have had all initial samples approved during first-time presentation.
• Maintain an 85 Excellent overall supplier rating for over six months based on the Supplier Quality Rating System which weighs three areas of performance as follows:

Criteria	Points	Elements of Criteria
I. Adequacy of Supplier Quality System (Q101)	30	Twenty Questions (Quality System Survey)
II. Supplier Management Awareness and Commitment	20	Continuous Improvement • Understanding/Commitment • Training • Management Controls Response to Quality Concerns
III. Ongoing Quality Performance	50	Quality of Products and Services
Total	100	

Category I

30 Points: The adequacy of the supplier quality system   (As measured by 20 questions on a Quality System Survey). A supplier must earn a total score of 160 points or above with a score of 7 or greater (on a scale of 0-10) for all questions on the Quality System Survey, and earn 40 out of 50 points for the 5 questions pertaining to Statistical Methods. Ford provided its quality assessors detailed guidelines and clear directives on the evaluation criteria to make ratings as objective as possible. An example of a typical question is:

Is Statistical Process Control (SPC) utilized for significant product characteristics and process parameters?

• How are the significant characteristics chosen?
• Describe the SPC methods used. Are they appropriate to the factors being controlled?
• Evaluate the supplier's reaction to out-of-control conditions.
• Evaluate the supplier's application of SPC.

(continued)

EXHIBIT 4   *(concluded)*

Category II

20 Points: The supplier management awareness and commitment to continuous improvement and response to quality concerns   Four major question groups were rated on a 0 to 5 scale. An example of a typical question is:

Does a training plan exist to provide statistical methodology training to employees including a timing chart for implementation?

- Is a qualified specialist available as a resource?
- Have training manuals in statistical techniques been developed, and are they available to all affected personnel?
- Is training in advanced statistical techniques planned/implemented?

Similar to the other categories, Ford provided its quality assessors a detailed evaluation guideline.

Category III

50 Points: Ongoing quality performance in products and services   (Must earn 45 out of 50 points). Specific points are deducted from 50 based on past six months product and service performance including factors such as rejection rates, deficient deliveries, and field service requirements.

process, which was the minimum qualification time possible. May indicated that this achievement was particularly notable given the condition of Peak Electronics' equipment, which was "adequate but older than most." Peak Electronics' quality was consistently praised by all of the Ford managers, including Chuck May. According to Yancy, as of November 1990, Peak was making major strides in achieving its business plan objectives:

Yancy's Goals	*Achievement*
Peak be nominated for Q1 Rating by 12/1/90:	Nominated by 10/90
• Peak achieve at least 85E on monthly rating	Achieved 94E
• Peak earn a quality survey score greater than 165	Achieved 165
Peak institute manufacturing disciplines:	
• Peak achieve 95% true yield by 12/90	Achieved 76% by 9/90
• Peak achieve 10-day cycle time by 12/90	Achieved 12 days as of 9/90
• Peak be in control and capable of 75% of significant characteristics by 1/91	Achieved 62% as of 9/90

True yield percentage is roughly defined as total first-pass-conforming output quantity divided by input quantity. Ship yield is roughly defined as total conforming quantity shipped to customer (including product which has been reworked) divided by input quantity. Although Peak had difficulties achieving the 95 percent true yield goal, when panels were defective its production management was able to identify the problem areas and rework a large percentage of problem boards to achieve higher ship yields (see Exhibit 5).

EXHIBIT 5   Peak Electronics Shipment Performance

Year	Boards Shipped	Cumulative Shipped	Panels Returned
1990			
February	38,176	38,176	0
March	30,982	69,158	0
April	58,325	127,483	0
May	60,081	187,564	20
June	64,931	252,495	1
July	19,680	272,175	0
August	62,979	335,154	1
September	120,867	456,021	3
October	111,549	567,570	0
November	88,192	655,762	1
December	89,604	745,366	7
1991			
January	52,470	797,836	0
February	92,660	890,496	0
March	106,230	996,726	12
April	87,480	1,084,206	3
May	93,069	1,177,275	17
June	115,109	1,292,384	0

First Quarter 1991: Financial Difficulties Challenge the Relationship

Despite Peak Electronics' solid start in improving quality and reducing costs, Peak experienced serious financial difficulties during its first year of operation. First of all, Peak had to pay $800,000 to Printed Boards toward operating costs for the November 1988 to November 1989 timeframe when Peak was negotiating a vendor agreement with Ford. This figure was almost twice what Yancy had expected. Second, due to a nationwide recession, Ford experienced a major sales downturn which prevented it from ordering the anticipated number of circuit boards from Peak during 1990. Actual purchases from Peak for Model Year 1990 were $700,000 versus the projected $1,800,000. May indicated that the car models, to which Peak Electronics contributed, were particularly hard hit. (See Exhibit 6

for Ford overall sales in 1989, 1990, and 1991.) At a November 1990 review meeting with Dearborn Capital, one of its financiers, Peak raised the issue of liquidity and the possible need for refinancing. Peak also needed to identify and obtain non-Ford customers to grow its sales base to ensure profitability, and Ford's help would be enlisted to make introductions to other firms.

In order to meet his initial cash needs, Yancy was able to convince Ford corporate management to accelerate its premium payments to Peak Electronics. The initial agreement involved only $1.8 million in premium payments during model year 1990 out of a total of $2.9 million in premium payments over three years. However, Peak Electronics was actually paid all $2.9 million in premium payments in the 1990 model year. Yancy convinced senior Ford corporate management to accelerate this premium despite the initial objections of the operating managers in the Electronics Division. Subsequently, however, Electronic Division management concurred, based on their assumption that Ford volume would return shortly. According to Yancy:

These negotiations were difficult and strenuous because of the unique nature of the purchasing organization of large corporations like Ford. I sensed a serious conflict between mandates sent from Ford corporate to divisions regarding their purchasing practices and the corporation's expectations of how the divisions would relate with sponsored suppliers. One is a long-term vision and the other is a short-term performance orientation.

In March and April of 1991, Peak's financial forecasts understated expenses by $300,000. An additional $400,000 accounting error was also uncovered in 1990. The shortfall placed additional cash strains on Peak Electronics. To overcome this setback, Ford provided an additional $300,000 in premiums and $500,000 in price increases in April. Ford paid an advance of $100,000 against these price increases in May.

EXHIBIT 6   Ford Overall Automobile Sales in Units and Dollars for 1989, 1990, and 1991

Operating Highlights	Ford Motor Company and Subsidiaries		
	1991	*1990*	*1989*
Worldwide factory sales of cars, trucks, and tractors (in thousands)			
United States	2,869	3,284	3,721
Outside United States	2,490	2,588	2,687
Total	5,359	5,872	6,408
Sales and revenues (in millions)			
Automotive	$72,050.9	$81,844.0	$82,879.4
Financial services	16,235.4	15,806.0	13,266.5
Total	$88,286.3	$97,650.0	$96,145.9
Net (loss)/income (in millions)			
Automotive	$(3,185.5)	$ 98.7	$ 3,174.7*
Financial services	927.5	761.4	660.3
Total	$(2,258.0)	$ 860.1	$ 3,835.0*

*Includes an aftertax loss of $42.4 million from the sale of Rouge Steel Company.

Source: Ford Motor Company, 1991, Annual Report.

Ford continued to provide revolving financing for raw material, and on two occasions provided cash advances against inventories.

July 1991: Ford's Electronics Division Seeks to Discontinue Its Relationship with Peak Electronics

In July 1991, Peak Electronics was continuing to experience financial difficulties. Unfortunately, revenues from other corporate accounts had not yet materialized. Ford managers had made personal phone calls to CEOs of major companies and had written letters of introduction to corporate buyers in different industries on behalf of Peak Electronics (see Exhibits 7 and 8). Chuck May was particularly perplexed by Peak Electronics' difficulty in securing other business, given Peak's Q1 quality rating from Ford. "It is not that simple to go out and get outside business," countered Yancy. "It is a long lead-time sales process. Moreover, there is a minority bias

which is not helpful, especially when it comes to technology components."

Peak was experiencing a severe cash shortfall and again sought $150,000 assistance from the Ford Motor Company. On hearing of Yancy's requests for additional support, the Electronic Division's purchasing management recommended to Corporate Purchasing that it be denied because at that time, the Ford Motor Company itself was struggling with profit and cash flow difficulties. Chuck May of the Electronics Division described the very careful evaluation made of suppliers requesting loans: "Ford must evaluate the request like a bank would, by specifically assessing the likelihood that the loan will be repaid. Any previous investments or loans have to be considered sunk costs for Ford to prevent them from pouring good money after bad money." Chuck May added that the specific assessment of Peak Electronics involved asking the central question: Given its history of financial problems, overhead costs, and complete

---

EXHIBIT 7   Ford Introductory Letter to Hewlett-Packard

P. E. Macher
General Manager

Electronics Division
Ford Motor Company
16900 Executive Plaza Drive
Dearborn, Michigan 48126-8200

John Young, CEO
Hewlett-Packard Company
3000 Hanover Street
Palo Alto, CA 94304

Dear John:

I would like to solicit your personal support in assisting a new minority company. This new company, Peak Electronics, manufactures printed circuit boards. The company was started in January 1990 and is an Electronic Division sponsored minority supplier.

We have been receiving products from Peak Electronics since last April and have just recently nominated Peak for Ford's Q1 Award. I am sure you can appreciate that finding qualified minority suppliers in the electronics component area is very difficult. We believe Peak represents a unique opportunity for purchasing quality products at competitive prices. (Reference attached brochure.)

In order to pursue a business relationship with Peak Electronics, please have your people contact C.L. May at Ford Electronics (390-8454) or Earl Yancy, President Peak Electronics (203-795-0241). I am confident that with your personal support, your people will find that Peak is a high-quality, competitive cost supplier.

Sincerely,

P.E. Macher
General Manager

cc: E. Yancy
     C.L. May—ELD

Source: Peak Electronics.

reliance on Ford for business, is Peak Electronics a viable business? Although direct financial assistance was ultimately granted by Ford's corporate management, the actual cost was transferred to the division doing business with that supplier.

A Ford supply office manager noted:

Ford had profiled Peak as a $10 million business with 60 percent Ford and 40 percent outside sales. Yancy had developed a philosophy for Peak of full employment of a well-trained staff. Also, if quality was maintained business would come to him. When outside sales failed to materialize and Ford business did not ramp up as originally pro-

---

EXHIBIT 8   Ford Introductory Letter to Digital Equipment Corporation

---

P. E. Macher   **Electronics Division**
General Manager   **Ford Motor Company**
                                                                   16900 Executive Plaza Drive
                                                                Dearborn, Michigan 48126-8200

Ken Olsen, President
Digital Equipment Corporation
146 Main Street
Maynard, MA 01754-2571

Dear Ken:

I would like to solicit your personal support in assisting a new minority company. This new company, Peak Electronics, manufacturers printed circuit boards. The company was started in January 1990 and is an Electronics Division sponsored minority supplier.

We have been receiving products from Peak Electronics since last April and have just recently nominated Peak for Ford's Q1 Award. I am sure you can appreciate that finding qualified minority suppliers in the electronics component area is very difficult. We believe Peak represents a unique opportunity for purchasing quality products at competitive prices. (Reference attached brochure.)

In order to pursue a business relationship with Peak Electronics, please have your people contact C. L. May at Ford Electronics (390-8454) or Earl Yancy, President Peak Electronics (203-795-0241). I am confident that with your personal support, you people will find that Peak is a high-quality, competitive cost supplier.

Sincerely,

P.E. Macher
General Manager

cc: E. Yancy
    C.L. May—ELD

Source: Peak Electronics.

---

jected, Peak failed to reduce direct labor and overhead compatible with the reduced level of business.

Earl Yancy summarized the situation:

There has always been a huge gulf in the Ford people's understanding of the issues and problems facing a small business. What is called a variable cost [direct labor] has a fixed component when you get well below capacity. Differences in Business Scale and Stage of Development are at the core of the difficulties in our relationship. As well-intentioned as some people at Ford have been in extending their support, the fact remains that we at Peak Electronics are on the verge of going out of business.

PART IV

Redefining Leadership

Redefining Leadership through Diversity

In a rapidly changing business environment where both the labor force and the consumer base are increasingly diverse, where mere survival—not to mention the ability to thrive and prosper—requires the ability to recognize new challenges and opportunities and adapt to them effectively; there is a critical need for individuals who can anticipate change, hold contradictory perspectives in tension and learn from each of them, listen and respond not only to different views but also different ways of expressing them, and do all this without losing sight of their own values and perspective. In other words, there is a need for individuals who not only can and will take a leadership position in moving organizations and employees to "manage diversity" among and around themselves, but also to actually lead organizations and employees *through* diversity—who will use diversity as a lever and a tool for recognizing and optimizing the learning triggered by differences.

By "leaders," we mean any individuals who actively work to define and refine for themselves fair and effective and respectful models of interaction across identity differences, and who attempt to put those models into practice. We do not have to be the chief executive officer of an organization to lead in this way. And unlike many popular conceptions of leadership, we are not merely talking about individuals who influence others to do things *their* way. We are talking, rather, about individuals who can see many ways to accomplish the same or equivalent ends, or who may even be willing to reconsider the wisdom of the ends they pursue.

As we consider the kinds of diversity issues we have already encountered in our own workplaces, it is useful to ask ourselves what we felt; what we did, or would have liked to do; what our objectives were if we acted; and similarly what were the fears or concerns that blocked us from taking actions we might have liked to take. How were our reactions and our impulses different when we were *witnessing* the behavior or perspectives of others, or of the organization itself through policies and practices, as opposed to when we were more *personally* involved in a situation.

Given the definition of leadership provided above, we can understand our answers to the questions that were posed by taking a look at three areas of inquiry:

1. What motivates individuals to take a leadership role with regard to diversity?
2. What blocks individuals from taking such a role?
3. What skills/competencies can enhance this leadership ability?

Individual motives for leadership in diversity questions can vary widely. Three commonly seen motivations[1] or catalysts, are:

•   **A vision of interdependence:** individuals who take a broad and long-term view of their own and their organization's place in society, and who have an almost visceral sense of the interlocking destinies of individuals and organizations. These individuals are drawn to intersections: the intersection of our work lives and the rest of our lives, the intersection of the workplace and the economic/social viability of the community in which it is located, the intersection of our national identities and our global citizenships. These individuals see attention to diversity as a matter of survival.

•   **A commitment to learning:** individuals who are energized by and drawn to new points of view, opportunities to enrich their view of their work, their world, and themselves. These individuals are excited by the potential for innovation represented by different perspectives and styles of action.

•   **A commitment to fairness:** individuals who feel inequity palpably and who draw personal satisfaction from promoting behaviors and environments that foster fairness.

Reviewing these three catalysts, it is instructive to consider which, if any, of them are most compelling to us. For example, are we concerned about diversity issues because we ourselves have felt excluded from deserved opportunities because of our gender, race, age, and so forth? Have we seen this type of exclusion affect someone close to us? Or are we managers of individuals who believe that they are experiencing exclusion? If so, our motivation, whether self-generated or imposed upon us, may come from a concern about fairness.

On the other hand, are we concerned about diversity because we fear we will not be able to find qualified employees, given the socioeconomic and educational obstacles facing a large part of our potential labor pool? Are we struggling to appeal to new and growing customer groups? Or more broadly, are we worried about the problems of crime, drugs, and poverty in our cities, and the impact these realities have upon the social and economic viability of the communities where we do business? Are we questioning the emotional and psychological effects on parents and children when our jobs require grueling work schedules and frequent relocations? These concerns spring from a vision of interdependence that requires us to feel the reciprocal relationship between our own businesses and the society which they serve and from which they profit.

Or finally, are we intrigued and attracted by the methods and priorities of a co-worker who seems bright and motivated, but who sees his or her work in an entirely

---

1. These motivations are introduced and described in *Managerial Effectiveness and Diversity: Organizational Choices,* also in this volume.

different way than we do? Do we wonder why some employees never speak in team meetings—and what they would have to offer if we could connect? Do we feel sometimes as if our organization is suffering from "groupthink"[2] and that we are stuck, approaching every new challenge as if it is the same kind of thing we have seen before—even when it's not. If so, we are motivated by a commitment to learning, aware that we learn only by bumping up against differences—different ways of seeing, thinking, behaving, and communicating.

We may each be motivated in any or all of these ways at different times and in different situations, but recognizing our own tendencies can help us to see issues and rationales and opportunities that might otherwise escape us. For example, if we typically think of diversity as an issue of fairness, we may focus excessively on the negative aspects of a diverse workplace without recognizing the opportunities for learning that also exist. Or if we tend to think of differences primarily as an opportunity for our personal learning, we may miss the interdependencies that create potential innovation and increased productivity for our peers and the entire organization.

Useful as it is to expand our set of motives for attending to diversity, it is just as critical to consider what actually *blocks* us from taking leadership in this arena. If we are honest with ourselves, there are a number of such barriers. Some of the most common are:

- **Fear of exclusion or of reprisal:** We may fear that by speaking out for ourselves we risk calling even greater attention to our differences, or if we speak out for others, we may be isolated and/or ridiculed by our own peer group.

- **Feelings of inadequacy:** We may often avoid speaking up or taking action around questions of diversity because we are painfully aware of the limits of our own knowledge of those different from ourselves. We fear that we may unintentionally offend someone or reveal our own limited understanding.

- **Feelings of protectiveness for our own privileges or power:** Although it may be difficult to admit, we may fear that attention to diversity in the workplace may limit our existing privileges and power. Members of majority groups within an organization may worry that attention to diversity means dividing a limited pie into more—and smaller—pieces. Even members of under-represented groups sometimes fear that diversity initiatives may lead to conflicts between different "minorities" for scarce resources.

- **Discomfort at recognizing the limits of our knowledge, control, or merit:** Really opening our minds to the experiences and insights of those who are different from us can lead us to confront the limits of our own ways of seeing, understanding, and managing the world. We may also have to confront the self-serving notion that we have earned each of our opportunities through our own merit, or that we have been kept from each denied opportunity through the bias of others, although both of these may at times be true.

---

2. Irving L. Janis, "Groupthink," *Psychology Today,* November 1971, pp. 43, 44, 46, 74–76.

Many of these barriers are results of the limited reasoning discussed in *Ways of Thinking About and Across Difference* in this volume. As suggested there, a willingness to think in terms of multiple perspectives on any question, and an orientation toward learning in all our dealings with difference, can help us to move beyond these blocks. What is required of us is the desire and the ability to reframe what feels like a confrontation—or controversy or risk—as an opportunity for learning.

Recognizing and naming the barriers that prevent us from taking leadership on questions of diversity is the first step toward dismantling them. For example, once we recognize that our discomfort with our own ignorance prevents us from new learning, the contradiction begins to unravel. Or, for example, once we begin to name and admit our fears and discomfort, they begin to seem less shocking and more manageable—even commonplace.

Note that there is nothing in either the motivations listed earlier or the barriers listed above that determines what *type* of action we may decide to take around diversity. Rather, by triggering these motivations and dismantling these barriers we simply open ourselves up to clear-eyed, unbiased, and frank analysis of the challenges and the opportunities diversity presents.

Our third question concerned the skills and competencies that can enhance our ability to take a leadership position with regard to diversity. In his book *Leadership Without Easy Answers,* Ronald A. Heifetz identifies a number of recommendations for those who would take leadership positions in a changing and often conflicted world. His strategies prove extremely useful for those who would take such a role with regard to diversity. They are: "(1) get on the balcony, (2) distinguish self from role, (3) externalize the conflict, (4) use partners, (5) listen, using oneself as data, (6) find a sanctuary, and (7) preserve a sense of purpose."[3] Many of these are fairly self-evident and require little explanation.

"Getting on the balcony" refers to the ability, from time to time, to look at the large pattern and meaning of what is occurring, to try to understand the motives and the concerns of particular individuals and the broader impact of specific actions in terms of their effect and role in the whole situation.

The ability to "distinguish self from role" means being able to recognize when people's reactions to us are actually, for example, responses to the role we play in the organization, rather than responses to us personally.

"Externalizing the conflict" is similar to the preceding strategy. It allows us to remain engaged and perhaps, more importantly, to engage others in handling a conflict without taking the burden so personally that we become overwhelmed or too defensive to function effectively.

In his discussion of "partners," Heifetz talks about the need for support, as well as insight, from other individuals. We need to test our hypotheses, as well as mourn our losses, with our partners.

"Listening, using oneself as data" refers to the importance of self-reflection and

---

3. Ronald A. Heifetz, *Leadership without Easy Answers* (Cambridge, MA: The Belknap Press of Harvard University Press, 1994), p. 252.

self-insight. Examining our reasoning patterns around issues of diversity as was discussed in the essay cited earlier, *Ways of Thinking About and Across Difference,* is one example of using ourselves as data. This reflection sheds light not only on our own thinking but often also on the types of reasoning others may be using.

"Finding a sanctuary" means just that—maintaining space and time for ourselves to do the self-reflection mentioned above, and to simply refuel and recharge mentally and emotionally. Facing differences, which always entails facing our own limits, is exhausting as well as exhilarating.

Finally, "preserving a sense of purpose," for Heifetz, means continually asking ourselves what that purpose should be with regard to diversity questions, given the new conditions and new participants. It means preserving an openness to new directions, given the input of others, without sacrificing a sense that the direction we choose to pursue does matter.

In his book, Heifetz has provided us with a useful set of competencies to measure our own activities against. Taken together, what he is talking about and what this text has been about is the ability and the desire to learn and grow, right out there in the open.

Taking a leadership position around diversity means being willing and able to reconsider our position, to change our minds in real time; and to see this reconsideration and change not as a sign of personal failure but as a measure of mutual accomplishment. As difficult as it is to be this open, and even vulnerable, we can learn to embrace differences, to welcome the discomforting data that others may share, as opportunities for learning and growth—both personal and organizational—and ultimately prove ourselves to be far more valuable functioning in the plural than we could ever be as a singular success.

MONITOR COMPANY: PERSONAL LEADERSHIP ON DIVERSITY

In 1983, brothers Mark and Joe Fuller, and several other colleagues, founded Monitor Company, a Cambridge, Massachusetts-based management consulting firm. From the outset, they

This case was prepared by Sarah B. Grant under the supervision of Mary C. Gentile.

Copyright © 1994 by the President and Fellows of Harvard College.

Harvard Business School case 395-049 (Rev. March 15, 1995).

wanted their firm to be different from any other in the industry. According to Joe Fuller,

> Most professional service firms on a whole are pretty badly run in terms of people. They are coercive environments based on peer pressure and the economic honey trap . . . we have the audacity to say that we want to be something quite different and that a firm that allows individuals to choose their own career paths, and that values the creation of client learning and action, can prosper. We think we are changing this industry a little bit.

Monitor quickly developed a reputation for its commitment to intellectual rigor and personal reflection. Mark Fuller was on the faculty of Harvard Business School (HBS), and Joe Fuller was a post-MBA research associate at HBS when they established the firm together. Mike Porter and Chris Argyris, HBS faculty members, also had a significant impact on shaping some of Monitor's products.

The firm's distinctive academic bent meant that consultants understood their role in client companies to be that of "teachers" or "guides." Monitor consultants, as well as clients, often participated in internal "group thinking" exercises based on action science research and theories about defensive reasoning patterns in personal and organizational learning—patterns which were observed to inhibit confrontation, communication, and intellectual honesty (see Exhibit 1). Such reflective exercises were a Monitor hallmark. And, according to Monitor directors and consultants, the firm's emphasis on personal leadership was a key component of the firm's noncoercive environment. Unlike other management consulting firms, Monitor expected its consultants to find their own career paths, set their own work paces, and to confront actively any problems which should arise—including internal ones—and initiate creative responses to them.

Monitor's human resource policies and internal systems reflected the distinctive values of the firm. Compensation was based entirely on merit—the firm distributed its profits based on the skills demonstrated by consultants and on the individual's contribution to the firm's success. The firm also valued nonclient allocations—immediate revenue generation was not a primary determinant of pay. Professional development arose from open, honest feedback from those with whom a consultant worked. Consultants were encouraged to demand such feedback to maximize their individual learning. One measure of the success of the feedback process was whether an individual considered their end-of-year bonus to be consistent with the feedback

they had received. In 1994, only 4 consultants out of 350 believed the firm paid them unfairly.

Monitor avoided, where possible, titles and formal hierarchy. Monitor believed that individuals should be placed in roles that were best suited to the immediate situation and the individual's evolving skills. Titles and hierarchy, directors of the firm believed, got in the way of doing this effectively. Consistent with the lack of formal hierarchy, Monitor, in contrast with many firms in its industry, had a "no up or out" policy. If individuals were learning and adding value to the firm, they were encouraged to stay and were paid for the value they added. Individuals were not expected to make director, or any other level, within a certain period of time.

By its tenth anniversary in 1993, Monitor had offices in Amsterdam, Johannesburg, London, Los Angeles, Madrid, Milan, Frankfurt, New York, Paris, Seoul, Tokyo, and Toronto. As part of its tenth anniversary celebration, all Monitor employees participated in a "group thinking" exercise, the "Definition of Purpose," designed to define Monitor's vision of itself as it grew into its second decade.

To no one's surprise, Definition of Purpose discussions focused on the firm's corporate commitment to academic rigor, personal reflection, confrontation, and honesty. To many people's surprise, however, issues related to diversity kept recurring on surveys and in discussions. Employees at Monitor were uncomfortable with how homogeneous the firm was. After concluding the Definition of Purpose, employees wanted to think further about why this was the case, how Monitor might be different if the workforce were more diverse, and what barriers might exist to the success of nonwhite and female consultants at the firm. The firm commissioned a "Diversity Network," led by two directors, to bring together those concerned and to lead efforts to enhance diversity.

By the beginning of 1994, as the firm began to examine ways to promote a diverse workforce, deeper issues began to emerge. Consultants began to wrestle with what diversity meant, both

---

EXHIBIT 1   Excerpts from "Teaching Smart People How to Learn," by Chris Argyris (*Harvard Business Review,* May–June 1991, pp. 99–109).

Any company that aspires to succeed in the tougher business environment of the 1990s must first resolve a basic dilemma: success in the marketplace increasingly depends on learning, yet most people don't know how to learn. What's more, those members of the organization that many assume to be the best at learning are, in fact, not very good at it. I am talking about well-educated, high-powered, high-commitment professionals who occupy key leadership positions in the modern corporation.

Most companies not only have tremendous difficulty addressing this learning dilemma; they aren't even aware that it exists. The reason: they misunderstand what learning is and how to bring it about. As a result, they tend to make . . . mistakes in their efforts to become a learning organization.

. . . most people define learning too narrowly as mere "problem solving," so they focus on identifying and correcting errors in the external environment. Solving problems is important. But if learning is to persist, managers and employees must also look inward. They need to reflect critically on their own behavior, identify the ways they often inadvertently contribute to the organization's problems, and then change how they act. In particular, they must learn how the very way they go about defining and solving problems can be a source of problems in their own right.

* * * * *

. . . because many professionals are almost always successful at what they do, they rarely experience failure. And because they have rarely failed, they have never learned how to learn from failure. So whenever their single-loop learning strategies go wrong, they become defensive, screen out criticism, and put the "blame" on anyone and everyone but themselves. In short, their ability to learn shuts down precisely at the moment they need it most.

* * * * *

There seems to be a universal human tendency to design one's actions consistently according to four basic values:

1. To remain in unilateral control.
2. To maximize "winning" and minimize "losing.".
3. To suppress negative feelings.
4. To be as "rational" as possible—by which people mean defining clear objectives and evaluating their behavior in terms of whether or not they have achieved them.

The purpose in all of these values is to avoid embarrassment or threat, feeling vulnerable or incompetent. In this respect, the master program that most people use is profoundly defensive. Defensive reasoning encourages individuals to keep private the premises, inferences, and conclusions that shape their behavior and to avoid testing them in a truly independent, objective fashion.

Because the attributes that go into defensive reasoning are never really tested, it is a closed loop, remarkably impervious to conflicting points of view.

---

corporately and personally. Would demographic diversity bring with it pressures to reexamine the learning and achievement styles representative of Monitor's culture? Monitor's culture supported individualistic responses to challenges, yet a certain homogeneity of leadership style existed. As the following examples demonstrate, several individual consultants defined the challenges around diversity differently. Both organizational experiences and personal histories played a significant role in choices around the design and implementation of diversity strategies.

* * * * *

Consultants

At breakfast on the last day of Monitor's 10th anniversary celebration in Newport [Rhode Island] I bumped into Nick Basden. Nick was wearing a t-shirt with a slogan about racism. I said, "Nick, I think it's pretty great that you're raising people's awareness around these issues. What's it like being black at Monitor?" Nick said, "Take a look around the room." Nick was the only black person there. It was very discouraging to him. He said when black people came to Monitor they became discouraged quickly—turnover was high, no one ever stayed long enough to be senior, there were never any role models.

Our conversation turned to other industries where there were a number of blacks—Nick pointed to public finance in New York. And I said, "But Nick, do you think public finance was always like that, a highly integrated industry? Don't you think it was once just as bad as consulting, but that someone did something to change it? Maybe you could be the someone who changes consulting." He said something like, "Be realistic," and changed the subject. But later that day he said that he would be interested in continuing our conversation about how to change the situation at Monitor. He was still extremely skeptical, but he told me about the Diversity Network that was just getting going at the firm.

Jonathan Rotenberg, *consultant*

I feel "black" [at Monitor]. I feel different, and I feel different because I am black. Something's wrong, I can't put my finger on it, but it's uncomfortable. It wasn't as if it were the only time that I had been the first black someplace because that's always been the case. That's the reality check: "Is this the first time I've been the only black in a business setting or a school setting? No, that's not it." It's something about this situation which is strange.

Nick Basden, *consultant*

I value people like myself—and when I say like myself I mean people who have different backgrounds, different cultural heritages—I think it's valuable. I think it adds a lot to this firm. The milieu that I am used to, I want to recreate it here at Monitor because I truly believe it is a better and richer environment for

everyone. It is difficult for me to say whether or not there is something inherently better about a diverse group. When there is less diversity I do believe that the work that comes out is not as good . . . not if you look at it in terms of the ideas on the page at the end of the day. They may be the same, but other issues surrounding those ideas might be more effectively thought out by a diverse group of people.

Rajeev Singh-Molares, *consultant*

Jonathan Rotenberg

Jonathan Rotenberg worked for Monitor in the summer of 1991, and joined the company as a consultant after graduating from HBS the following year. Rotenberg's business career began long before, however, when he founded The Boston Computer Society (BCS) in 1977 at the age of 13.

Rotenberg created BCS because he thought personal computers ought to be accessible consumer products rather than techno-toys for a highly educated electronics subculture. He saw an informational void to fill, and in filling it he grew the BCS membership to over 31,000, created educational publications, a vast volunteer network of accessible explicators, and a reputation as an industry insider who got hardware and software giants to democratize their products. By the time he entered Harvard, he was a $3,000-a-day consultant to the industry.

Rotenberg traced his acceptance and commitment to diversity to three sources: his Quaker grammar school where faculty and staff engaged in debate on racism and sexism; his summer camp on Cape Cod where counselors were active in the civil rights movement; and his having been born into a Jewish family where the experience of the Holocaust remained immediate to his grandparents and, to a lesser extent, to his parents.

Rotenberg considered acceptance of diversity as the unchallenged background environment of his childhood and youth. It was not until he entered college, however, that he wrestled with diversity and his commitment to it on a deeper and more personal level. In a course at Brown University about religious perspectives on the black, gay, and women's movements, he found himself—one of the few white males in the class—labeled as conservative and unable to stand with minorities by virtue of the privileges of his race and gender. Rotenberg said the criticism "threw me off balance because I always thought that I was very perceptive and understanding of these issues and it really made me wonder, 'Am I not as understanding as I think, or are these people unreasonable?'"

For several years following college, Rotenberg was increasingly drawn to consider whether or not he was gay. Answering the question of his sexuality, he noted, involved an "extraordinary amount of suffering." For several reasons, he considered "being gay to be the worst possible thing that could happen" to him. Rotenberg considered himself to be "basically introverted," but his public life as a whiz-kid entrepreneur— followed by *The Wall Street Journal, Business Week,* and *Fortune*—allowed him little anonymity in which to examine his sexuality. He was too well known. When Rotenberg "came out" as gay while at HBS he "began to really understand what it is like to be part of a group that can be victimized by virtue of its being in the minority." He believed he had gained a "base of experience . . . what [he] had been missing," in the class at Brown.

After spending several years not able to "conceive of being gay, and even less able to conceive of being an advocate for gays and lesbians," Rotenberg began to realize that he held an educationally strategic position bridging the gulf between the often misunderstood gay world and the corporate world. He saw a role for himself in educating people about homosexuality and lessening the prevalence of the homophobia that he experienced in U.S. culture. He believed that the educational techniques that he had developed at BCS were applicable to education around a social issue such as homophobia. And, since journalists still followed his career and were eager for

him to be a spokesperson for gays and lesbians in corporate culture, he could use the public nature of his life to reduce the fear and stigma often attached to homosexuality.

In 1991, after he was invited to join Monitor but before he began work at the firm full-time, Rotenberg was featured in and photographed for a controversial *Fortune* cover story, "Gay in Corporate America." In fact, Rotenberg came out in the article. Friends and family had cautioned Rotenberg to rethink how public he wanted to be about his sexuality. According to Rotenberg,

I was very methodical . . . I said, O.K. I am actually very interested in understanding what the risks are [to being publicly "out" as a gay man], what could go wrong, what are the ramifications of those things going wrong, and is there anything that I can do to manage those risks. It's a lot of what you learn in business school; its a lot of what business is all about: managing risk. It's not about running from risk or getting "freaked out" about risk, it's about being very methodical about identifying it and thinking through ways of dealing with it.

I needed to learn what exactly were the risks that I was taking and were there any aspects of them that were unacceptable to me. In the end the benefits were so incredibly compelling. I felt like I had built up a tremendous amount of capital in terms of my recognition, the things that I had done in the computer industry, and the idea that I could spend it on something that I think, in a lot of ways, is the most important issue in my life, of wanting to make life better for the next generation of people going through this [coming to terms with being gay]. It was hard to think of any downside that could be so bad, that would make it not worth while.

After the article appeared, Rotenberg spoke to a Monitor director about it and whether his sexuality would be viewed as detrimental to his career within the firm or among clients served by the firm. According to Rotenberg, the positive support he received "was fantastic." Rotenberg believed

The most powerful weapon for eradicating homophobia and many other problems in our society is conversation . . . is learning how to have conversations with people that help them to reflect on their own beliefs and assumptions and really think through where they come from, why they believe them, and whether they actually think that they are right. Fundamentally the core of the gay rights movement, to me, is education: replacing ignorance with knowledge.

Once at Monitor, Rotenberg continued to think about ways to further that "educational conversation" and soon opportunities began to present themselves. For example, a brand new Monitor consultant called after learning coincidentally from his office mate that Rotenberg was gay. The employee, who was also gay, had become concerned at the firm's recent global orientation. He wanted to be honest and open about his lifestyle, but had felt uncomfortable at the event, as if such information might not be welcome, and he was now concerned that he would have to keep his personal life in "total secrecy." Rotenberg was able to allay the employee's fears and was grateful that he had an opportunity to talk to him. He wondered, however, if others in the firm shared this man's concerns and whether they would be able to find someone to talk to about them. Rotenberg thought that "somehow a general memo or voicemail address didn't seem appropriate," but how could such a network be facilitated?

Not long after this incident, Rotenberg's office mate, an Asian woman, began to confide in him about perceived attitudes—what she call a "red neck" atmosphere around the firm—that she feared might impede her success.

By the time Rotenberg spoke with Nick Basden at Monitor's 10th anniversary celebration about his experience of being black at the firm, he saw that each of these professionals shared a "common sense of being outside the mainstream" at Monitor—and he wondered if the firm was perhaps losing valuable employees as a result. Recalling readings from the "Power and Influence" course that he had taken at HBS, Rotenberg understood that "minorities" often experienced difficulty finding suitable mentors. Perhaps, he thought, Monitor should sponsor a "Diversity Mentor's Program."

Nick Basden

Nick Basden, a 1989 graduate of Harvard College, who worked at J. P. Morgan for three years before joining Monitor, observed there was "a lack of minorities, blacks in particular, at the firm." Although subsequently several other African-Americans joined the firm, when Monitor began its Definition of Purpose exercise, Basden, then 27 years old and with just two years experience at Monitor, was the only African-American male consultant; there was also one 25-year-old African-American female consultant, facts that Basden called "crazy." Basden felt diversity was "a genuine concern for Monitor," but was less optimistic than Rotenberg that significant understanding on the part of the directors—or change—was possible. According to Basden,

> You will not find a person [at Monitor] who thinks diversity is a bad thing, that recruiting the best and brightest people even if they have three heads is a bad thing. We still want them. Yet I don't think in the course of a day [diversity issues] cross people's minds . . . If you're busy, if you don't hit the office much, who knows what's going on. From a director's perspective . . . they probably don't see the problem, physically don't see the problem, mentally don't see the problem.

Rajeev Singh-Molares

Rajeev Singh-Molares joined Monitor in 1990. Previous to that he worked for Chemical Bank's Latin American division in New York City for three and a half years. He had a B.S. in foreign affairs from Georgetown and an M.A. in international affairs and management from Yale. Singh-Molares's mother was Spanish and his father was Indian. He was born in Europe, but spent most of his life in Manhattan where he attended the United Nations's International School. According to Singh-Molares,

> Diversity was not something that I was aware of until I got to college where I began to feel slightly different. What I thought of as normal was not the reality that most people dealt with . . . Do I feel different at Monitor Company? Sometimes. Most of the time I don't, I feel very comfortable here.
>
> Frankly, when I walk down the hallways I'd like to see more diversity. I'd like to recreate the U.N. here if it's possible. It's just appalling that we don't have more African-Americans on our staff. The reality of the community that we live and work in is that African-Americans are not given opportunities, for whatever reason, and there aren't too many in the professional ranks. This is a very demanding job that requires a very specialized set of skills and a very specialized set of personal characteristics to do well. We're not going to go out and hire people and set them up for failure. That's the last thing that we want to do. It doesn't help [minorities] and it doesn't help us.

Singh-Molares, described by one director of the firm as "a rising star," was somewhat more senior than Rotenberg or Basden. When he had first come to Monitor, he encouraged the firm's efforts to recruit, hire, and develop minority consultants. But, as the demands of his client work increased, he found increasingly less time for the firm's diversity efforts. He saw the existing lack of diversity as a stumbling block to hiring minority candidates; if minorities felt isolated, they might not stay and work to their highest potential. He felt the stumbling blocks were not insurmountable, however.

The "Advisor Network"

Soon after the conclusion of the Definition of Purpose exercise in 1993, Rotenberg, Basden, and Singh-Molares, considered Monitor's existing mechanisms for addressing personnel issues and began to talk about the need for a "Diversity Mentor Program." After floating the idea, however, they encountered resistance.

Some consultants feared that such a program might be perceived as unfair or inaccessible to the legitimate issues of straight, white men; there might be a backlash. Thus, the program was reframed as a more inclusive "Advisor Network." As such, Rotenberg, Basden, and Singh-Molares presented it to the directors involved in the firm's Diversity Network; they were quickly empowered to proceed with the project. (See Exhibit 2).

Every consultant at Monitor was already assigned a "Professional Development Advisor" (PDA) for career mentoring. But, after several conversations about the PDA system and conducting a survey, Rotenberg, Basden, and Singh-Molares found some widespread dissatisfaction with it. Individuals who, in Rotenberg's words, "fac[ed] unique career challenges as a result of being a minority at Monitor" felt they could not discuss certain types of issues with their PDAs. The challenges peculiar to minority status were seen as too personal to present to a PDA. PDAs played an informal role in performance evaluation (and therefore remuneration), and PDAs were not seen as necessarily having enough expertise and empathy with the challenges specific to minorities to give good advice.

Rotenberg, Basden, and Singh-Molares argued that an Advisor Network of African-American, Hispanic, gay and lesbian, Asian, female, and other minority persons at Monitor, trained in giving advice, armed with appropriate resources and places of referral, and practiced in keeping confidences, might be established to complement the PDA system.

Although there was broad support for the Network, less than half of those surveyed believed that they would ever use its services. Rotenberg believed that Monitor's "macho, stoic" culture might be a barrier to people's asking for advice or assistance. The Network's designers argued that a better measure of success for the Network was not whether a majority of the firm's employees used it, but whether it had a significant impact on the individuals who did. In fact, by mid-1994 there were several cases of individuals who came to the Network almost ready to leave the firm. These cases, including harassment cases, would not have come forward without the Network. Once brought forward, they were swiftly resolved. According to Rotenberg, that the persons seeking advice eventually decided to stay was attributed to the usefulness of the Network and its trained advisors.

Rotenberg asked for a time allocation to further the Advisor Network but was encouraged to take on the work in addition to his full client caseload. According to Rotenberg, "At my level as a case team leader, I was encouraged to do the work but told that it did not make much economic sense to be taken off client work. I should also say, however, that [one of the directors] was very helpful pointing to people who could help me with Advisor Network activities so that I would be less burdened by them."

The first Network training workshops for volunteer advisors had begun by spring 1994. Monitor established an anonymous tracking system to assess which advisors and which types of issues received the most attention. There was some discussion about whether the existing PDA system and Advisor Network might eventually join together at some future date. Many people, however, felt that the two advisory systems, one formal and institutional, the other informal and personal, would be necessary for some years to come—until Monitor was, in fact, more diverse.

Director/Senior Managers

We have a lot of young mothers here who feel very comfortable pulling back, defining a different role for themselves. We don't pressure them with "up or out, you've got to keep marching." We've got some very talented women who we have been able to retain, and who are very happy and have gotten their balance right. We have done a great job of keeping people like that valuable, keeping them happy, keeping our firm productive, and frankly avoiding, so far, any backlash against it because men do it too. Everybody recognizes that we pay for the value you add, and if you go half-time you probably won't add as much value and so you will be paid less. Here's where the drawback

is: Women feel no pressure to get back into the rat race, and a lot of them don't. How can I persuade some of these very happy women who are very talented to come back on full tilt?

Liz Martineau, *director*

Lately, I've been paying more attention to issues of diversity. How do we make consulting a more feasible career choice for women . . . Consulting is a very demanding career and a lot of women just don't feel the need to give that much out of their life to their careers. There's not the pressure, there's not the competition [as there is among men] with your peers. A lot of women just don't need that. They feel like they can consider themselves successful with a much lower level of exertion . . . I talk to women about their potential. It's a question of untapped potential. Women benchmark themselves against other women and feel satisfied . . . but you look at some of these women and you say, "You could really make a difference and feel really good about yourself. You could realize a much higher level of experience and capability." For some people that's exciting, it really depends on what you want.

But even I find myself, as my children grow, having to re-evaluate my own balance. It can change as you go along. At different stages of life you value things differently. I feel like I have two jobs and every once in a while I have to say, "Wait a minute, am I giving enough to the job of raising my children, am I making a bad decision?"

Caroline Firstbrook, *global account manager*

I am concerned about [gender issues] personally. In my own life my wife and I have had to make choices about who's going to work, who's going to be around home more to raise the kids. We made choices 15 years ago based on what options were available. They were the right decisions at that time, but they've been crummy decisions for her. She's filled up her life . . . but she basically gave up a career . . . because there weren't support mechanisms then that we could afford. I haven't seen things change that much really . . . I wish there were more choices. I am very proud that this is a company that can see that and allow people to have choice, that allows people to select their career paths.

David Kaplan, *chief financial officer*

Liz Martineau

Liz Martineau began to work at Monitor in 1983, the second employee that the founding partners hired. She left the firm for two academic years to get her M.B.A., but returned after graduation. She was pregnant with the second of her three children when she was named a director in 1991—the only woman in Monitor's 14-person governing body. That was the year that Martineau became "radicalized" to diversity issues. At a 1991 directors' meeting she

> . . . felt very comfortable saying, "By the way guys, [harassing behavior] ain't something that happens to other people. I have rarely been, with two or three exceptions, with a client where I wasn't harassed." They were stunned. And Caroline Firstbrook said, "There has never been a client where I haven't been harassed." And we're very senior. No one would think of us as vulnerable. We don't dress or act in any way that you could think of as suggestive. We have a strong ability to punch someone in the nose if we need to. And we were getting harassed. That was real.

According to Martineau, she "was always one of the boys" and initially resisted seeing herself as a role model

> . . . because I never realized I was supposed to be one. I always resisted being typecast because it's just self-defeating. If you are everyday proving to clients that you're competent even though you may look like their daughter, you don't want to suddenly admit that maybe there are special hurdles . . . Now I realize I'm a role model and people are looking up to me . . . I never had any [female] role models, but I did have lots of role models because they don't have to look just like you. I think a lot of people feel like if there's not someone who looks just exactly like you, then there's no path to follow. One of the things that we pride ourselves on at Monitor is that there is no path to follow, you create your own path. I think that's very healthy, but it makes people nervous too.

To the extent there was an epiphany, according to Martineau,

> . . . the big thing was when I had kids. [When you are pregnant] you become disabled in many peoples' minds, even though you are not. They don't think you should strain yourself. They feel uncomfortable and embarrassed and they can't look at your stomach, and they don't want to comment, and they don't even ask you if you are pregnant until you are eight and a half months along. It's like you are not serious anymore and they assume you are going away now. You can see some peoples' biases come out.
>
> All these incredible things happen. My first child was a girl. Nurses in the hospital came up and said maybe next time you will have a boy. When I had my third, people came up and said you finally had a boy, you did it! I saw my daughters were less valued than my son, which really pissed me off. My son is a great kid, but why should there be more rejoicing in the heavens when he was born than when my daughters were born.
>
> I was always the one who didn't worry about these things and poo-pooed people who did. Now I'm really worried about it. There are things that I can do about it, and I'm going to do them.

In Martineau's view, gender-based hurdles to effective work were not internal to Monitor, so much as external:

> The women at the firm were worried about gender issues. It was not, however, "Is Monitor going to treat me unfairly?" but, "I can't take the internal/external pressure. I want to have kids. I don't have any friends anymore because my friends are all stay-at-home Moms now. My husband and I don't have a social life because I'm not planning it." That's where the women tended to feel the pressure. It's not that Monitor's not treating them fairly, but that society was just not set up for [women and mothers to be in the workforce]. They felt very alone.

Monitor, according to Martineau, "recognized how much life is a seamless thing," and strove to address gender-based concerns even if they were not specifically related to Monitor's internal climate. It was important, according to Martineau, to

. . . listen to what people were worried about. How do you peel back from what somebody says they're worried about to what they're really worried about? How do you give advice that gets the person to find the solution themselves? When I heard some of the things that some of the junior women in the firm were concerned about, on the one hand you want to say, "That's ridiculous. Why are you worried about that?" On the other hand, if they didn't have a way to test their concerns, they'd never get past them. For example, they might be offended or deflated by client comments that seemed inocuous to me, or they would assume that they couldn't choose a different balance between work and home—despite all the evidence to the contrary.

Caroline Firstbrook

Caroline Firstbrook, a dual citizen of the United States and Canada, graduated from McGill University with a degree in electrical engineering in 1983. Ninety percent of her engineering class was male. Later that year she began work as a hardware designer for BBN, a technology firm in Cambridge, Massachusetts. The first woman hardware designer BBN had ever hired, she worked with a 40-man team. She also spent a year working for BBN on a U.S. military base in Germany. She called the base a "male-dominated environment where if you convinced one person that you were as capable as a man and that a woman should be judged based on her performance, not her sex, a million jumped up in their place to say, 'no, no, no.'"

Firstbrook joined Monitor in 1987 and worked almost entirely in Europe. In 1994 she was a global account manager, only the second woman to hold that position. Firstbrook had been

. . . aware of being a minority, but after a while you just stop noticing. I was really just one of the guys. . . . But my views on diversity have come quite a long way from a sort of "blissful ignorance" . . . from "it was easy for me, it must be easy for everyone to be a woman in a man's world," to a realization that I've had some advantages that other people didn't. Even when I was a

child I always played with the boys and all that stuff, so a lot of the attitudes that I come to naturally don't come easily to some of my female colleagues. I feel a real responsibility because I am a senior woman [at Monitor]. I feel a responsibility to extend a hand [to other women].

I used to think, "What's the problem with consulting, so people make dumb jokes once in a while. This is easy, you should try working on a military base." I started off thinking women were real wimps who couldn't hack it. More recently, I've come to a more reasonable position. For some people [the "dumb jokes"] are quite intimidating. How do we separate the provocative from the truly offensive? . . . How do you deal with a client's own uncertainty about how to deal with a woman? When I turn up to see a 55-year-old manager in an industry where the only women are secretaries, he is genuinely perplexed to have me tell him how to run his business. He thinks, "Oh, my God, a woman is going to tell me how to run my company, I can't relate to that. What's going to happen next, my dog is going to come in to give me advice?"

We don't want to reinforce any notion on the part of women that they are badly done by. Yet, we want to say to them, "Look, there's not going to be equality in your lifetime so you can't blame that on anyone. There's nobody to point to and say change everything for me. . . . Certain things require patience, certain things are getting better all the time, but it's not going to be perfect." We don't want people getting defensive about things, feeling like Monitor owes them something just because they are women.

David Kaplan

David Kaplan, an attorney and the firm's chief financial officer, took a strong personal interest in how information and Monitor's cultural values were communicated throughout company offices. He understood that the firm's demographics presented some special problems.[1] Se-

---

1. Twenty-five percent of any entering "class" left the firm, and of those who left, 75 percent left in the first two to three years. The average age of consultants was 25, and more than half had come directly from undergraduate degree programs.

nior people at the firm never questioned the intellectual credentials of junior consultants, but their youth and lack of work experience was sometimes made evident in what Kaplan called "sophomoric behavior" such as inappropriate jokes.

Over a period of years Kaplan had became increasingly interested in sexual harassment issues; case law on the subject was developing. No egregious instances of harassment had ever come to his attention, but he felt that casual remarks made within the firm and comments made in poor judgment by clients were often a source of consternation for female consultants. Kaplan believed that the firm need not make a "big deal" about harassment, but should have a formal policy on it and educate its employees about what breeches of policy were and how they would be dealt with.

Kaplan took a very broad view of harassment. Sexual harassment was a good legal starting place for an officewide discussion, he felt, but what he really wanted to address was something more fundamental, something more like professional courtesy. Consultants, he felt, needed to think about how they interacted with people who they perceived to be somewhat different from themselves—intellectually, economically, socially, or because of age, gender, race, or ethnicity.

Training on Sexual Harassment

Kaplan introduced his concerns to a 1991 directors' meeting. A law firm helped him to present the issue. He felt the legal framework provided an opening for directors to examine personal issues related to sexual harassment, and to consider harassment and its impact on the firm more generally.

During the directors' meeting Martineau and Firstbrook came forward with their own experiences of company- and client-based gender-related insensitivity. Their comments made the issues of harassment real to the directors; these were senior women whom they knew and trusted, yet harassment was clearly a part of their professional lives. According to Kaplan, the two women

> . . . expressed some things that I don't think they had ever expressed before. I think it was very hard for Liz. It was a very brave thing to be as open and as vulnerable as she was. It was also good for people to see how much emotional strain it put on a person. [The male directors] have the attitude about Liz that she's one of us, she's one of the guys and to see how upsetting this was to her and to see how much she has had to hold in was very powerful.

What the directors came away from the meeting with, according to Kaplan, was an understanding of "how pervasive [harassment] was." The 14 directors quickly agreed that sexual harassment and sensitivity training would be a worthwhile corporate exercise, and at the close of the meeting they signed off on a seminar program for all Monitor's North American offices. While the legal issues of sexual harassment remained the framework of the seminars, their goal was to get Monitor employees to think very broadly about harassment. They were designed to get employees to talk about race as well as gender issues, and to think of harassment as encompassing everything from uninvited physical contact and sexual innuendo to being abrupt with secretarial staff.

Women-at-Monitor Seminars

Two events encouraged Martineau and Firstbrook to think more proactively about the special needs of female consultants. First, there was the 1991 directors' meeting where they first spoke openly about the particular challenges that they faced as women. They began to understand that, whether they wanted it or not, junior female consultants in the firm looked to them for models of both professional and personal behavior.

Second, soon thereafter, Martineau and Firstbrook—both 1987 graduates of HBS—were approached by another female classmate to provide survey information about women in consulting. In responding to the survey, they began to think about the institutional challenges inherent to women in their chosen career. They became concerned that women see consulting as a viable career choice, and were increasingly disturbed when able women chose to leave Monitor for other industries. They began to think about what institutional barriers existed for women in consulting, and began to consider ways that Monitor could mitigate those barriers.

In early 1994 Martineau and Firstbrook organized a women's seminar to look into three areas of concern: balancing a career in consulting with social and maternal expectations, interacting with (primarily male) clients, and fitting into Monitor culture.

* * * * *

Founding Director

There is not a lot of dissent in our management ranks about whether we ought to be doing [something about diversity]. There is only anxiety around: Are we doing enough? Are we doing it fast enough? How is this going to be perceived? . . . We can do what we want, and [promoting diversity] is what we want to do. We're not happy to see talent go, and there are fabulously talented women, and Hispanics, and African-Americans.

Joe Fuller, *director*

Joe Fuller

Joe Fuller received an MBA from Harvard Business School in 1981, and had graduated from Harvard College in 1979. His general management responsibilities at Monitor included sales, management of large client relationships, and mentoring "a limited number of people who we thought were high-potential people."

Fuller was interested in the diversity mix of his firm, and took an active interest in recruiting, as his time allowed. He felt some dissatisfaction with the distance his position placed between himself and more active management of Monitor's commitment to create a more diverse work environment. But, he felt he could serve the ongoing effort by developing an external network to seek out and recruit new minority and women consultants. Fuller believed that by virtue of being a well-educated, affluent, white male,

> . . . a lot of what we need to do in this company [around diversity] I'm only marginally qualified to do. My life's experience has not equipped me to be a very good diversity mentor I suspect, but I am, I think, a reasonably empathetic person. So, I am disqualified [by virtue of my background] from executing some of the tactical aspects of managing diversity. What I can do is act as a sounding board and I can act as something of a sponsor.

Fuller's commitment to diversity arose, in part, from his and his parents' experiences at Harvard University and in the corporate world. Both of Fuller's parents were Harvard faculty members; indeed, Fuller's mother was among the first female members of the Business School faculty. Although she enjoyed significant academic success, gender issues ultimately raised some barriers for her, according to Fuller.

Fuller's father, also an HBS faculty member, left the school to work at General Motors where he became an early champion of the emerging field of human resources. Fuller can remember being extraordinarily moved at retirement parties for his father when minority executives came up to him to thank him for his father's work, and to say that without the elder Fuller's belief in their abilities they never would have been given the opportunities that led to their management successes. Joe Fuller hoped Monitor could play a similarly constructive role through its diversity efforts.

Promoting a diverse workplace, both internal to Monitor and in client companies, was consistent with Monitor's emphasis on leadership, according to Fuller:

> Integral to what we do is the role of acting as a guide, and if that guide happens to be African-American, or Asian, or female it helps to under-

mine, however, modestly, some people's belief that when they see people of diversity in their workplace they are there only for legal [Affirmative Action] reasons.

Why should I care? If companies like ours don't try, [diverse workplaces] are not going to happen. It's not going to happen in big companies. It's going to happen painfully slowly in small companies . . . I feel we have an obligation to try and to encourage [minority] people in business . . . Now your cynical HBS guy is going to say, "Why does Monitor have to carry life's burdens?" Well, I'm not trying to create an all African-American office here, but it's our obligation to try [to diversify our workforce] and I believe that we, and our clients, benefit.

If issues of diversity are going to be genuinely addressed in the workplace it's got to happen as a function of efforts of a company like ours. I know a lot about big companies, and I know some, which by any stretch of the imagination, have made heroic efforts to try to make diversity work. The hidden costs of that in terms of the backlash effect are only really becoming known now. Those programs were efforts to graft entirely new directions onto existing organisms . . . but [Monitor] is an organization that values the notion of diversity. There is nothing about this company that would make it predisposed to reject a transplant of this type. This is still a company where the organism is still evolving.

The Diversity Network

By the very end of 1993 Fuller, together with Martineau, was designing a "Diversity Network" to oversee the firm's institutional responses to diversity issues, such as how the firm recruited minorities and helped them to fit into Monitor culture, and whether a demographic audit of the firm would be useful. Monitor's directors released Basden from client cases halftime to oversee the efforts of the Diversity Network. Basden took on the assignment understanding that it would be for a limited number of months. He saw "no difference" between taking on an internal assignment and being fully committed to client cases. According to Basden, "there is no negative value judgment associated with internal assignments. This is very important work that needs to be done. It is respected within the firm."

The Diversity Network began to assess demographic information for each Monitor office, and was developing a recruiting plan that was especially attentive to seeking minority applicants. No goals had been set regarding hiring or development of minorities, but both Martineau and Fuller felt that the overt attention paid to recruiting a diverse workforce would have a significant impact within a year or two.

* * * * *

Discussion

Little time passed before the proponents of the Advisor Network, the women's seminar group, and Diversity Network found each other to coordinate efforts, work out conflicts of detail, and find resources to succeed. In many ways, the various initiatives complemented each other; they shared the goal of making Monitor a more diverse workplace but approached it from different directions—one direction focused on institutional development, the other direction focused on personal development.

Nevertheless, the sources of individual motivation and consequently the vision of what diversity might mean at Monitor often differed among emergent leaders. Without a single vision for diversity, could any real progress be achieved? Or was such a singular vision antithetical to the task?

EXHIBIT 2 The Monitor Advisor Network Brochure

The Advisor Network:
Informal Advice on
Life at Monitor

The Advisors

THE
MONITOR
ADVISOR
NETWORK

Throughout Monitor's history, consultants and administrative staff have turned to one another for informal advice. Whether looking for a quick tip on how to manage a difficult client situation or working through a personal crisis, fellow employees can be a rich source of support and guidance to each other.

Unfortunately, it sometimes doesn't occur to consultants and staff that they could ask their colleagues for help. They may not be aware that there are individuals in the firm with the knowledge and experience to help them. Or, they may not realize that colleagues who appear to be busy and unavailable are, in fact, pleased to provide assistance.

The Monitor Advisor Network was created to help facilitate the process of finding support within the firm. The Network is made up of administrative staff and consultants who have volunteered to help colleagues work through the personal and professional challenges they may face at Monitor. They are available to listen to your concerns and provide a sounding board for testing alternative solutions. They are not professional counselors, and would never substitute for professional help where it is needed.

The Advisor Network provides another tool to help you with your professional and personal development. It should not be viewed as a substitute for formal training or your Professional Development Advisor. Rather, it is a way to put you in touch with individuals who have found ways to manage personal and professional challenges and are committed to helping you as you do the same.

Individuals are invited to join the Advisor Network who have demonstrated the following characteristics:

Personal experience. Experience inside and outside of Monitor with the issues on which they provide advice.

Perspective. Have sufficient tenure at Monitor and knowledge of the firm's operations to provide knowledgeable, informed advice.

Empathic. Demonstrate excellent listening skills; recognize every concern as legitimate until proven otherwise.

Problem solving. Can help others to identify problems and find workable solutions.

Approachable. Perceived as individuals who are approachable and supportive.

Once selected, each advisor participates in a training program on giving informal advice.

If you would like to find out about becoming a member of the Advisor Network, please contact the Network coordinator [name].

Confidentiality

For many of us, asking for advice can be very difficult. It may require discussion of sensitive, personal information. To make it easier to discuss sensitive matters, the Advisor Network has a strict confidentiality policy, which every Network member is required to sign. Except for two special cases (described below), all communication that you have with a member of the Advisor Network will be kept in strict confidence. The advisor may not reveal your identity or disclose any issues you've discussed to any third party unless you give him or her specific permission to do so. In some situations, an advisor may recommend that a third party be notified; however, the final decision on whether to discuss the matter with anyone else will be yours.

There are two special and, we believe, rare exceptions to this strict rule of confidence.

If an advisor learns that a crime has been committed, or is about to be committed, the advisor must report this information. Such crimes (or threats of crimes) include: theft, actual or threatened physical harm to any individual, violation of SEC insider training regulations, and the like. Disclosure of a substance abuse problem to an advisor is not, by itself, considered a crime that must be reported.

If an advisor learns of facts or circumstances that pose a significant risk of liability to Monitor or its clients, the advisor must also report this information. Such facts and circumstances include: actual or threatened failure of Monitor personnel to carry out their professional obligations, serious risk of liability to a client discovered during a client engagement, significant violations of Monitor's policies, and the like.

If you decide to speak with a Network member about concerns related to a crime or a serious Monitor or client liability, keep in mind that he or she may need to share this information with others.

Continuous Improvement

The Advisor Network is committed to a process of continuous improvement. In order to keep making the network better, we need your feedback. Please let us know if you find the Network useful and responsive, and how you rate the quality of advice and support you receive. Please feel free to share any feedback you have with a Network member, with your RCM [Resource Center manager], or with [the Network coordinator].

(continued)

EXHIBIT 2   *(concluded)*

ADVISOR NETWORK ISSUES

The following issues were identified in the Definition of Purpose process and a 1993 AMP [All Monitor Personnel] survey as challenges faced by Monitor administrative staff and consultants. Network members are listed under issues which they are particularly interested in helping others sort through.

If you are facing an issue that is not mentioned on this list, feel free to contact any advisor you feel could be helpful. Advisors will try to be responsive to any issue you want to discuss, whether it be a major challenge or a minor concern. If you're not sure who to contact, ask your RCM [Resource Center Manager] or [name], the Network coordinator.

Issue	*Sample Concerns*	*Advisors*	**ADVISORS AS OF 9/94**
			To contact an advisor, simply call them, stop by, or send a private voicemail. If you're not sure which advisor to contact, your RCM or [the Network Coordinator] can assist you.
Lifestyle management	• Balancing work and the rest of life • Managing trade-offs between significant others, work, and self • Managing stress	name, name name, name name, name name, name name, name name, name name, name name	name, title — Milan, tel. no. name, title — Johannesburg, tel. no. name, title — Cambridge, tel. no. name, title — Tokyo, tel. no.
Administrative staff/consultant	• Breakdowns in communication • Dealing with perceived lack of respect • Lack of helpful feedback	name, name name, name name, name name	name, title — London, tel. no. name, title — Cambridge, tel. no. name, title — Cambridge, tel. no. name, title — Toronto, tel. no.
Succeeding as a woman at Monitor	• Overcoming client preconceptions • Handling unwanted intrusions or offensive comments • Developing a successful persona • Starting a family • Balancing family and work	name, name name, name name, name name, name name, name name, name name, name name	name, title — Cambridge, tel. no. name, title — Cambridge, tel. no. name, title — New York, tel. no. name, title — Cambridge, tel. no. name, title — Seoul, tel. no. name, title — New York, tel. no.

Topic	Issue	Contact	Advisor	Advisor
Succeeding as a person of color at Monitor	• Finding helpful role models	name	name, title, Cambridge, tel. no.	name, title, New York, tel. no.
	• Fitting into Monitor's culture	name	name, title, London, tel. no.	name, title, Tokyo, tel. no.
	• Handling overt and subtle discrimination	name	name, title, Cambridge, tel. no.	name, title, Madrid, tel. no.
	• Dealing with offensive comments	name	name, title	name, title
Being gay or lesbian at Monitor	• Deciding whether to come out to colleagues or clients	name	name, title, Cambridge, tel. no.	name, title, Cambridge, tel. no.
	• Dealing with homophobia or harassment	name	name, title	name, title
	• Information on Monitor's domestic partner benefits coverage		name, title, Cambridge, tel. no.	name, title, Cambridge, tel. no.
Starting a family	• Finding out how have others approached this	name, name	name, title	name, title
	• Options and choices	name, name	name, title, Cambridge, tel. no.	name, title, Cambridge, tel. no.
Sexual harassment	• Understanding what constitutes harassment	name	name, title	name, title
	• Getting support	name	name, title, Cambridge, tel. no.	name, title, Amsterdam, tel. no.
	• Deciding what actions to take	name	name, title, Los Angeles, tel. no.	name, title
Managing within the Monitor company	• Managing managers	name	name, title, Cambridge, tel. no.	name, title, Cambridge, tel. no.
	• Managing others	name	name, title, Cambridge, tel. no.	name, title, Toronto, tel. no.
		name	name, title, Amsterdam, tel. no.	name, title, Cambridge, tel. no.

If you would like to suggest a new issue topic to be added to the Advisor Network, contact the Network coordinator. Generally, new issues are considered for the Network if they: affect the quality of life at Monitor; are not addressed by other Monitor programs; and have a qualified issue champion who will take responsibility for coordinating advice through the Network.

Selected Bibliography

Nancy J. Adler, *International Dimensions of Organizational Behavior.* Boston: PWS-Kent Publishing Company, 1991.

Helen Axel, ed. *Employing Older Americans: Opportunities and Constraints.* New York: The Conference Board, 1988.

Taylor Cox, Jr., *Cultural Diversity in Organizations: Theory, Research & Practice.* San Francisco: Berrett-Koehler, 1993.

John P. Fernandez, *Managing a Diverse Workforce: Regaining the Competitive Edge.* Lexington, MA: Lexington Books, 1991.

John P. Fernandez, *The Diversity Advantage: How American Business Can Outperform Japanese and European Companies in the Global Marketplace.* Lexington, MA: Lexington Books, 1993.

Mary C. Gentile, ed. *Differences That Work: Organizational Excellence through Diversity.* Boston: Harvard Business Review, 1994.

William B. Gudykunst, *Bridging Differences: Effective Intergroup Communication.* Newbury Park, CA: Sage, 1991.

Andrew Hacker, *Two Nations: Black and White, Separate, Hostile, Unequal.* New York: Ballantine Books, 1993.

Ronald A. Heifetz, *Leadership Without Easy Answers.* Cambridge, MA: Harvard University Press, 1994.

Susan E. Jackson, and Associates. *Diversity in the Workplace: Human Resource Initiatives.* New York: The Guilford Press, 1992.

David Jamieson, and Julie O'Mara. *Managing Workforce 2000: Gaining the Diversity Advantage.* San Francisco: Jossey-Bass Publishers, 1991.

W. B. Johnston, and A. H. Pacher. *Opportunity 2000: Creative Affirmative Action Strategies for a Changing Workforce.* Washington, D.C.: U.S. Department of Labor, 1988.

Rosabeth Moss Kanter, *Men and Women of the Corporation.* New York: Basic Books, 1977.

Marilyn Loden, and Judy B. Rosener. *Workforce America!: Managing Employee Diversity as a Vital Resource.* Homewood, IL: Business One Irwin, 1991.

Nancy Dodd McCann, and Thomas A. McGinn. *Harassed: 100 Women Define Inappropriate Behavior in the Workplace.* Homewood, IL: Business One Irwin, 1992.

Brian McNaught, *Gay Issues in the Workplace.* New York: St. Martin's Press, 1993.

Ann M. Morrison, *The New Leaders: Guidelines on Leadership Diversity in America.* San Francisco: Jossey-Bass Publishers, 1992.

Ann M. Morrison, Randall P. White, and Ellen Van Velsor. *Breaking the Glass Ceiling—Can Women Reach the Top of America's Largest Corporations?* Reading, MA: Addison-Wesley, 1987.

Nancy J. Sedmak, and Chrissie Vidas. *Primer on Equal Employment Opportunity,* sixth ed. Washington, D.C.: Bureau of National Affairs, 1994.

Deborah Tannen, *You Just Don't Understand: Women and Men in Conversation.* New York: Ballantine Books, 1990.

Sondra Thiederman, *Bridging Cultural Barriers for Corporate Success: How to Manage the Multicultural Work Force.* Lexington, MA: Lexington Books, 1992.

R. Roosevelt Thomas, *Beyond Race and Gender: Unleashing the Power of Your Total Work Force by Managing Diversity.* New York: American Management Association, 1991.

Donna E. Thompson, and Nancy DiTomaso, eds. *Ensuring Minority Success in Corporate Management.* New York: Plenum Press, 1988.

Index of Cases